U.S. DESTROYERS

U.S. DESTROYERS

AN ILLUSTRATED DESIGN HISTORY

By Norman Friedman

Profile Drawings by A.D. Baker III

Distributed by:
Airlife Publishing Ltd.
101 Longden Road, Shrewsbury SY3 9EB, England

Copyright © 1982
by the United States Naval Institute
Annapolis, Maryland

Third printing, 1989

Library of Congress Cataloging in Publication Data

Friedman, Norman, 1946–
  The U.S. destroyer
  Bibliography: p.
  Includes index.
    1. Destroyers (Warships)—United States—
History. I. Title. II. Title: United States
destroyer. III. Title: US destroyer.
V825.3.F74   623.8′254′0973   81–85444
ISBN 0–87021–733–X   AACR2

Printed in the United States of America

Contents

Foreword

Decade by decade in the last couple of centuries this control of the sea business has become ever more complicated and of more consequence. When engines took the place of sails, the sizes and types of ships became nearly as numerous as the sizes and types of weapons developed to use on them. It did not take long to determine the need for many small, fast, heavily armed men-of-war, ships that were not only capable of inflicting heavy damage on any type of enemy but also of protecting our own ships (including merchantmen) from any type of attack.

Thus evolved the destroyer.

The effectiveness, and the life, of such a ship vitally depended upon both the quality and reliability of the ship herself and the courage and skill of the men who manned her.

Dr. Friedman has chosen to write a history of the less colorful portion of that mutual dependency. Much has been written about the exploits of destroyers in war, and too little has been written about the struggle to design and build these powerful greyhounds of the sea so that they could perform as they have in unforeseen situations.

Dr. Friedman discovered that the records are far from complete. That is not surprising. Neither naval officers nor engineers are noted for keeping records of "why" things were done. Their records are usually limited to the decisions made and to the engineering aspects resulting from those decisions. Those records can be boring and are sometimes discarded as being obsolete and no longer worth the space they occupy. Distressing to an historian.

Many men of many nations have deplored the lack of clear-cut, long-range national policy and national strategy, and none more so than professional military people. No nation has yet developed a method or an organization to determine either with success. There are too many variables, quite a few unknown. Future technical and social developments can only be estimated roughly. The intentions and capabilities of other nations can change radically and unexpectedly. Primarily, though, the difficulty in determining a national long-range policy is due to the strong differences of opinion on how to achieve the nation's ultimate goals.

Naval policy must necessarily be an integral part of national policy.

So naval planners, naval designers, naval builders, and naval operators must do the best they can with only the most general and ever-changing guidance on future strategy and operations, and they must base their programs on their own assumptions as to what challenges the Navy will have to meet in the distant future. So far, the United States has been most fortunate in that its ships have proved capable of doing the jobs they were designed to do with great effectiveness, and could even be quickly modified to do unanticipated tasks equally well. True, there have been some conspicuous mistakes made, but such poorly designed ships were built and tested quickly enough to be found wanting before the nation had to depend upon them.

Dr. Friedman's interesting book stresses the struggle between planners, designers, and operators in the production of a new destroyer and the changes in the composition and organization of each of these necessary functional elements throughout our history. As great technological advances were made, the complexity of destroyers increased, and the conflicts between armament, propulsion plants, electronics, sensors, and control devices—all in competition for space, weight, and noninterference—became more difficult and more intense.

Only experts in each field of technology can determine the effect of changes in their equipment on their particular systems, and each technical element impinges on many of the other technical elements. It is quite natural, and very necessary, that there be controversy over resolving these problems. Compromises must be made so that the final design will function properly and reliably in every department. Most of the mistakes in destroyer design have been made when the advice of an expert was overridden or arbitrarily ignored. That has seldom happened when all the participants have kept in mind that the function of a destroyer is combat capability.

There are two important determinants of any weapons system—time and money. There is never unlimited time and never unlimited money. Ships must be designed to be operational within a reasonable time and at a reasonable cost. The Navy, as with all other services, must be ready for combat at the time the enemy chooses, and at that time must have enough of each type of ship and other weapons system to destroy the enemy's combat capability. These two factors figure prominently in the design of weapons systems.

In recent years two additional participants in the struggle over destroyer design and procurement have emerged—the massive Department of Defense and civilian shipbuilders. The Navy recommends but the DOD decides. The actual design of destroyers and other weapons systems is now largely done by civilian shipbuilders. This has probably become necessary. These two developments have inevitably added both to the cost and the time of acquiring a ship.

Modern destroyers are complicated. Our methods of acquiring them are even more complicated.

Arleigh Burke

Arleigh Burke

Acknowledgments

This work was written originally at the suggestion of Capt. J.W. Kehoe, USN, of the U.S. Naval Ship Engineering Center (NAVSEC). Captain Kehoe was engaged in a study of Soviet warships and hoped that an account of the correspondence between national strategy and naval doctrine and design in U.S. destroyers might prove suggestive of similar links in Soviet practice. Several present and former U.S. warship designers were kind enough to discuss destroyers with me, most notably Reuven Leopold (who also helped provide much of the postwar data), Peter Gale, George Kerr, Harvey Kloehn, Wolfgang Reuter, Philip Sims, and Tom Wickert. Herb Meier was instrumental in permitting me access to much of the data. I am also very grateful to several actors in the destroyer story, who shared their memories with me: David Kassing, now President of the Center For Naval Analysis, and retired Admirals John C. Daniel, Sheldon Kinney, and Elmo Zumwalt, Jr. I hope I have done justice to all of them.

Mildred Grissom and Charles Wiseman very kindly assisted me in obtaining access to many BuShips and NAVSEC records still under Navy control at Suitland, Maryland, including many Preliminary Design files. Mrs. Lorna Anderson of the Office of the Chief of Naval Operations very kindly located for me many of the files of the old Ship Characteristics Board, which Lieutenant Commander R.W. McKay screened for classified material. I appreciate assistance with and access to the facilities of the Navy and Army Branch of the National Archives (with particular thanks to Harry Schwartz and Elaine Everly); of the wartime Bureau of Ships files at the Federal Record Center, Suitland; and of Navy-controlled files at the Federal Record Center. In each case the staffs were more than kind. For assistance at the Naval Historical Center (General Board files) I am particularly grateful to Dr. Dean Allard and to his staff, most notably Cal Cavalcante, Gerri Judkins, and Kathy Lloyd. John Reilley of the Ships Histories Division provided much valuable data, particularly on the passage of ships into and out of service. I am grateful, too, to John Vajda and to Barbara Lynch of the Navy Department Library. Mrs. Susan Weidner of the NAVSEA public relations division provided invaluable assistance. Anna Urban shepherded the nuclear destroyer chapter through its clearance procedure.

Arthur D. Baker III acted not only as illustrator but as critic; his files supplied many of the photographs, particularly of the wartime period. For their generous sacrifice of his time (not to mention his eyesight) I am grateful to his wife, Anne-Marie, and to his daughter, Alexandra.

Other good friends also deserve thanks for generous assistance: Charles Haberlein, David Lyon, Norman Polmar, Alan Raven, and Christopher C. Wright. They all provided me with very considerable material from their collections, as well as invaluable comments and corrections. I thank them for many errors caught; those not caught are my own responsibility.

My wife Rhea deserves special thanks for her patience, encouragement, and very material assistance. This book could not have been written without her help.

This work would have been entirely impossible to accomplish without the extreme patience and kindness of several secretaries, most notably Helen Iadanza, Anne Marsek, Ellen O'Neill, and Rose Marie Martin of Hudson Institute.

Key to Line Drawings

A	Auxiliary room
AC	Airconditioning machinery room
BP	Base plant
BR	Boiler room
C	Computer room
CC	Communications center
CH	Chart house
CIC	Combat Information Center
CM	Crew's mess
CMC	CPO mess
CS	Gun-crew shelter
DC	Division commander's cabin
DG	Diesel generator
EC	Emergency cabin
ECM	Electronic countermeasures
ER	Engine room
ES	Emergency steering
FC	Flotilla commander's office
FO	Fuel oil
FP	Flag plot
FW	Feed water
G	Galley
GA	Gasoline
GT	Gas turbine
H	Hangar
HR	Handling room
IC	Interior communications and plotting room
M	Magazine
MA	Missile assembly room
MC	Missile check-out room
MG	Motor/gear room
NTDS	NTDS computer room
P	Potato locker
PH	Pilot house
Q	Crew quarters
QC	CPO quarters
R	Radar room
RFW	Reserve feed water
S	Sound room (sonar)
SG	Steering gear
TG	Generator turbine
TQ	Troop quarters
TR	Torpedo room
TS	Troop stores
VDS	Variable depth sonar storage
W	Wardroom

Introduction

As this is written in 1980 the destroyer remains the oldest ship-type to have seen continuous service in the U.S. Navy, and it will retain that title well into the next century, if not beyond. Conceived as a specialized and rather fragile auxiliary to the battle line, the destroyer grew into an invaluable general-purpose warship, known in both world wars for its combination of compactness, hitting power, and toughness. This is a design, not an operational, history and so cannot do justice to destroyer men past and present, to their ships, and to their battles.

This is an account of the evolution of the destroyer concept in the U.S. Navy, of the translation of that concept into ship steel, and of the relative success or failure of the result. Organization charts show a neat downward progression from characteristics or top level requirements to detail designer, but that is never the case, and probably the greatest value of a history such as this is to show how the proponents of widely varying views of the destroyer managed to reach a common ground, reflecting to some degree U.S. naval and national policy—which generally envisaged a war very different from the one the destroyer force fought in 1917-18, in 1941-45, in Korea, and in Vietnam. Fortunately, the ships were adaptable, but far more importantly, their men were. It was a great tribute to the men of the destroyer force as well as to the designers of its ships that at Leyte in October 1944 sister ships could fight, almost simultaneously, the kind of battle for which they had been designed—a surface gun and torpedo action such as the heroic defense of the escort carriers off Samar—and a battle entirely characteristic of the new era—radar picket protection of the fast carriers. Antisubmarine screening, again by the same ships and men, came somewhere in between.

The destroyer force has always been a subject of considerable controversy within the Navy, and it is refreshing to see the extent to which particular themes and even tactical concepts survived massive changes in the Navy since the beginning of the present century. To a considerable extent, past experience in the resolution of conflicts in destroyer mission and design priority should have a bearing on current issues, as most of the past conflicts have modern parallels.

This book began as an investigation of the correlation between U.S. naval policy and the design of the ships, as a test of a similar correlation assumed for Soviet practice. From an intelligence point of view, the lesson, well worth learning, is that many factors other than national or naval policy and strategy determined the shape of the destroyer force; similar factors almost certainly applied in the Soviet case. The destroyer (and, for that matter, almost any other weapon) emerges as the product of a continuing tripartite struggle, the parties to which can best be described as the planners (General Board, OpNav, OSD), the destroyer operators, and the destroyer designers (including weapon and sensor designers). The planners always looked at the destroyer as the supporting element in a fleet dominated by capital ships—first battleships and then carriers. They also looked more to the need for numbers than to the destroyer force's desire for unit quality and offensive firepower. To a considerable extent, the controversies over the *Spruance* and *Perry* classes were struggles between planners and operators. Admiral Zumwalt's "high-low mix" was the epitome of the planner's view that the overriding need for numbers had to be balanced against budgetary limits. Both operators and planners were opposed to the ship designers, who almost never seemed capable of squeezing quite as much as was wanted into a limited hull. Probably the clearest case of such violent disagreement was the evolution of the austere missile destroyer of FY 61 into the *Belknap*; the papers that survive reveal

Five *Gearing*-class destroyers of DesRon Six steaming through the Caribbean in June 1956 symbolize the U.S. destroyer force of the time: war-designed-and-built ships modified to meet a very different threat, in this case the fast submarine. All six ships of this squadron were refitted in the late forties with a trainable Hedgehog antisubmarine projector in place of No. 2 gunhouse, with new sonar, and with HF/DF on a new mainmast. However, unlike some of the postwar ASW conversions, they retained their bank of conventional torpedo tubes. From the camera, they are the *Keppler* (DDE 765), *Berry* (DDE 858), *Norris* (DDE 859), *McCaffery* (DDE 860), and *Harwood* (DDE 861).

an almost uniform belief that BuShips could not possibly be telling the truth, that the combination of a new sonar and more endurance could not possibly be as expensive as was, indeed, the case.

Both the building and the planning organizations have changed considerably over the period of destroyer development; these changes are summarized here. In 1900, the Navy was organized into a series of independent bureaus whose only joint chief was the civilian Secretary of the Navy. Moreover, in the interest of full civil control over the military, only the Secretary could issue operational orders moving ships and squadrons. There was a Board on Construction, composed of the chiefs of the bureaus, that attempted to coordinate them, but the recent war with Spain had shown the unfortunate consequences of an almost total lack of a professional naval staff. At this time, hull and overall design were the responsibility of the Bureau of Construction and Repair (C&R), while engines and electrical equipment (and, therefore, radio and, later, sound gear) were the responsibility of the Bureau of Steam Engineering (later Engineering, BuEng). Weapons were the province of yet a third independent organization, the Bureau of Ordnance (BuOrd). Although the seagoing Navy was represented on the board by the Bureau of Navigation (BuNav), the latter was largely concerned with personnel and appears not to have brought an operational outlook to the board. Finally, there was the Admiral of the Navy, the Secretary's principal professional (line) advisor. In the latter part of the nineteenth century David Dixon Porter held this post, and used it to help bring the "New Navy" into existence.

Given the need for war planning during the Spanish-American War, it was logical for the Secretary of the Navy to formalize the process by establishing a General Board headed by Admiral of the Navy George Dewey, the hero of Manila Bay.

The General Board was initially concerned with long-range policy, including war planning, but the obvious link between planning and building programs soon made it a partial competitor to the Board on Construction. By 1907, Navy reformers, among them W.S. Sims, believed that the bureaus were far too stodgy, that they would continue to produce obsolescent and unsatisfactory ships unless some level of professional control was interposed between them and the Secretary of the Navy. Thus, the General Board came to be responsible for the over-all "characteristics" of U.S. warships from 1908 onwards, the Board on Construction passing out of existence in 1909. It should perhaps be emphasized that the board was always advisory and thus that its proposed characteristics were not always accepted by the Secretary of the Navy. This was particularly the case in battleship design.

The General Board operated until 1951, combining Navy long-range planning and responsibility for characteristics. It held hearings at which both line officers and representatives of the bureaus could debate characteristics and the merits of the designs produced to meet them. Indeed, much of the account of U.S. naval policy in 1920-42 contained in this book was drawn from these hearings. Gradually, however, the General Board lost power to a new organization, the Office of the Chief of Naval Operations (OpNav).

OpNav began as an attempt to provide the civilian Secretary of the Navy with what amounted to a professional staff, consisting of an Aide for Materiel and an Aide for Operations. The former soon proved superfluous and was abandoned, but the latter became the head of the operational Navy, the Chief of Naval Operations (CNO). OpNav soon took over the war planning task; between wars its principal subordinate divisions were War Planning and Fleet Training. Although the General Board continued theoretically supreme in the determination of characteristics, by the late 1930s the CNO was extremely influential, in some cases gaining sufficient support to override board decisions. At that time, the principal afloat command was the U.S. (Pacific) Fleet, consisting of a battle force and scouting force, and these organizations had a strong influence on the characteristics process.

Strong pressure for reform of the bureau system came in 1938-39 with the disclosure that poor coordination between C&R and BuEng had resulted in the new destroyers being overweight and top heavy, thus requiring considerable ballasting. Many within the Navy blamed Rear Admiral H.G. Bowen of BuEng, who had introduced the new high pressure/high temperature steam plants; the subsequent amalgamation of the two bureaus into a new Bureau of Ships (BuShips, 1940) effectively marked the victory of C&R over its old rival. It seems remarkable in retrospect that similar sins on the part of BuOrd (most notably in the *Iowa* design of this period) generated no effective pressure for the amalgamation of that powerful organization into a full ship design team; that only happened with the formation of NAVSEA in 1974. Some observers present at the time considered the continuing independence of BuOrd testimony to the power of the "Gun Club."

When he became CNO in 1942, Admiral King combined in his person the offices of Chief of Naval Operations and Commander In Chief, U.S. Fleet (COMINCH, rather than the CinCUS of earlier practice). His office thus took over many of the detailed planning tasks formerly the purview of the General Board, including the approval of the myriad of major and detailed changes made to warships during wartime, and even the characteristics of many of the merchant ships converted to naval use. There was, moreover, considerable dissatisfaction within the Navy as to the performance of the General Board in permitting what was perceived as a disaster in the form of the *Sumner* class. That these ships performed very effectively once they entered service does not appear to have saved the board; in 1945 OpNav created a Ship Characteristics Board (SCB) within its organization. At first the SCB was charged only with coordinating alterations to existing ships, while the General Board continued to develop characteristics for new construction. However, in 1946 the SCB began to take over the new-characteristics role, assigning each project an SCB number. For a time there was some confusion as to the relative roles of the SCB and the General Board, and the influence of the latter waned. In 1948, it tried to move to a long-range planning role with an elaborate study of the Navy of the next decade, headed by then Captain Arleigh Burke, but in 1951 the General Board was abolished.

The SCB had nowhere near the same stature as its predecessor, since in effect it was separated from the policy- and strategy-planning process. It was far more concerned with the details of design, and included representatives of all the bureaus, who had equal votes. Participants in SCB meetings recall cases in which the Bureau of Medicine and Surgery cast the decisive vote on weapon system choices. From the surviving records it is not entirely clear who within OpNav worked up the lists of projects on which the SCB worked, at least at first. For a time that was not very important, given the poverty of the shipbuilding program and the lack of any integrated U.S. concept of future warfare. Within the Navy, the ASW mission tended to dominate, and ASW coordination became an important issue. It is not clear whether fleet air defense, nominally the responsibility of DCNO (Air), received the same sort of concentrated attention, although its importance was reflected in its level of funding.

In particular, there was an absence of any type of long-range planning during the early postwar years. One historian, David Rosenberg, has referred to a "technological enemy"; the services, including the Navy, tended to develop the advanced technology resulting from World War II without too much immediate concern for tactical requirements. Such a policy was reasonable in view of the general uncertainty as to development abroad and, indeed, as to the consequences of the range of technology in view. After Korea, however, with a massive naval program (including a heavy investment in missiles) under way, it became increasingly evident that without careful long-term planning the shape of the Navy might be determined almost by chance. In 1954, an ad hoc committee was formed to study future naval operations as a guide to the long-term naval program. It was chaired by Vice Admiral R.A. Ofstie, who com-

mented that 1955 decisions would shape the 1965 fleet, and that the weapons familiar in 1955 would probably not resemble those clearly essential a decade later. The Schindler Committee on the Long-Range Shipbuilding Program was formed at the same time. Essentially, the Ofstie Committee was to give thought to basic requirements, the Schindler Committee to the means by which they might be met. Both interacted strongly with each other and with the SCB, which had to write the characteristics for the types proposed.

In February 1955, the CNO, Admiral R.B. Carney, created a Long-Range Objectives Group (LRO, Op-93) to succeed the Ofstie Committee; it was to produce an annual report looking ahead ten to fifteen years. The next year, CNO Arleigh Burke placed the LRO within his immediate office and made its first report, LRO-56, a basic Navy planning document. The precise effect of LRO studies on the overall naval planning process is difficult to gauge, as it is not clear which Op-93 initiatives resulted in new warships or weapons. LRO did press for such types as Seahawk, and it did plan in detail for the introduction of new generations of guided weapons after the "3-Ts" (Terrier, Talos, and Tartar). Parallel to the LRO was a standing committee on the Long-Range Shipbuilding and Conversion Program, and both were involved in setting the five-year programs that appeared from about 1955 onward. To some considerable extent, the entire long-range effort was badly damaged by the escalation of costs, which crippled ship procurement from 1957 on.

Although the Navy fell under a formally unified Department of Defense in 1948, the DoD structure had little impact until the advent of Robert S. McNamara. He was the first Secretary of Defense to form an independent analytical staff large enough to question the judgments of the services, and indeed to impose alternative solutions to their problems. The hand of the Office of the Secretary of Defense (OSD) is seen in this book in the battle over nuclear power and also in the decision to build the *Spruance* class. Because Secretary McNamara worked in terms of a five-year budget cycle, the very long-range theories of LRO became less and less significant; LRO became MRO (Medium Range Objective) in 1964, with an eleven-year horizon, and was abolished entirely in September 1970. Well before that it had slipped out of its initially extremely influential position close to the CNO. Since 1970, Navy long-range broad-gauge planning has been the responsibility of ad hoc groups with little or no institutional continuity; as a consequence, the long-range concepts they have produced have had relatively little impact within the Navy. It is possible that the 1980 establishment of a new Long-Range Planning office (Op-OOX) within OpNav may reverse this trend.

The ASW cruiser *Norfolk* symbolized the postwar significance of the destroyer in the U.S. Navy. Here she shows two enclosed twin 3-in./70s forward, with Weapon A superfiring above them. One of the twins carries Gunar, the postwar on-mount fire-control system. For most of her career, the *Norfolk* was an experimental ship; here she shows an SPS-12 air-search radar aft and SPS-4 and SPS-6B forward.

Meanwhile, the SCB has gone through a number of changes of name but not really of function, but with the growth of such specialist organizations as Op-03 (DCNO for Surface Warfare) its power over ship characteristics has waned considerably. For example, the development of the *Perry*-class frigates was the responsibility of Op-03 (Vice Admiral Price), not of what was then termed the Ship Acquisition and Improvement Panel (SAIP).

As for the shipbuilders, BuShips remained independent until 1966, when a general reorganization resulted in its redesignation as the Naval Ship Systems Command under OpNav control. In 1974 what was then known as NavShips merged with NavOrd, the successor to BuOrd (which for a time had been combined with BuAer as the Bureau of Naval Weapons). However, this integration into the Naval Sea Systems Command (NAVSEA) had little real effect until 1979, when much closer coordination began.

These organizational notes merely name the players in a complex game, and in some cases players not nominally significant more than pulled their weight. The key modern example is Admiral H.G. Rickover, who again and again was able to use congressional influence to override OSD and even Navy objections to the construction of nuclear surface combatants. In recent times there have also been such influential congressmen as Mendel Rivers and Carl Vinson, and growing congressional staffs (and the increasingly powerful General Accounting Office) are having a pronounced effect.

Because this book depends primarily on a combination of BuShip/C&R and General Board/OpNav papers, it is biased in favor of the planners and ship and system designers and may not entirely fairly represent the views of the men who actually manned and fought the destroyers. Moreover, it cannot adequately describe the wars they fought, or the life they lived in what, until very recently, could best be described as cramped, uncomfortable ships, the purest of purely warlike warships. The writer can only hope that the proper flavor has not been totally lost, especially in chapter 8.

Design and planning documents sometimes seem to have an air of unreality that deserves comment, as so many of them are quoted in the pages that follow. In particular, they tend to be optimistic about the performance of future systems and indeed of current ones; paper performance is rarely actual performance. In addition, the writers of those documents tend to have to look into the future, and their concept of the present is of ships just ordered or just laid down, if indeed not of systems just funded. Thus, the horizon for the planner of 1955 was 1960 or 1965, and often he was overoptimistic as to what developments, domestic and foreign, would actually be in service at that future date. Therefore, it is somewhat startling for a current reader to see a system such as Tartar dismissed as obsolete in 1956, well before it had flown, or to see the "1965 threat" comprising, among other things, an antiship equivalent of SUB-ROC, a weapon certainly not embodied in the Soviet planning of the time. It is very important to keep in mind that the increasing gap in time between conception and delivery means that systems are designed against threats that are, at most, in a very early (and undetectable) stage in the laboratories of a potential enemy. Thus, to a far greater degree than is often imagined, the development of ships and of their equipment rests on a combination of an overall assessment of enemy tactical trends and on mirror-imaging of our own laboratory developments. For example, the air defense studies of the late fifties envisaged as standard threats not some Soviet systems known, if at all, only deep in the intelligence community, but rather the B-47 and B-58 bombers familiar to U.S. analysts. Some of these points should carry important implications for those who analyze the development of foreign navies, such as that of Admiral Gorshkov.

1

Prologue: Torpedo Boats into Destroyers, 1886–1898

The U.S. destroyers are directly descended from the torpedo boats built at the end of the last century. These boats provided the technology necessary for destroyer construction. This transition from torpedo boat to destroyer, more marked in the U.S. than in many other navies, was symbolic of the transition of the Navy itself from a coastal defense-cum-cruiser warfare force to a force capable of contesting the command of the sea through the operations of a battle fleet. That is, the torpedo boats were always considered an arm of an integrated coastal defense organization, midway between the Army's forts and controlled minefields and the Navy's larger coastal defense ships and monitors. Seagoing capability was valuable largely in that it increased the flexibility of a force never numerically sufficient to cover the entire U.S. coast in detail. The largest of the torpedo boats approached the performance required of destroyers that would have to accompany the fleet, although their armament was ill-suited to the primary destroyer tasks.

U.S. interest in torpedo craft dates back to the Civil War, when both sides used spar torpedoes in combat; the steam launch commanded by Lieutenant W. B. Cushing, which sank the Confederate ironclad *Albemarle* in October 1864, was in effect the first torpedo boat. Later the first U.S. torpedo boat to be built for the purpose would be named after Cushing. Torpedoes and torpedo craft were attractive as inexpensive defensive weapons and were intensively studied during the long period of naval neglect after 1865; the Torpedo Station at Newport, Rhode Island, was founded as early as 1869, and in 1875 the Her-

reshoffs, yacht builders of Bristol, Rhode Island, built one of the world's first specialized torpedo craft, the 56-foot spar torpedo boat *Lightning*. Two of the few ships built for the Navy during the 1870s, the *Alarm* and *Intrepid*, were experimental torpedo craft. Moreover, the one naval professional who consistently shaped naval policy during the 1870s and early 1880s, Admiral of the Navy David Dixon Porter, was a strong advocate of torpedo craft; indeed, he had approved Cushing's mission in 1864. In effect he supplied the continuity formally denied the Department of the Navy by the failure of successive attempts to create a naval advisory board to interpose between the civilian Secretary of the Navy and the professional bureaus. Admiral Porter was responsible for the appointment of a naval advisory board, which began the renovation of the Navy in 1881.

The 1881 board recommended not only a considerable program of new construction, but also a resuscitation of the U.S. industrial base; for example, new ships were to be built of steel rather than of iron because "for the reputation and the material advantage of the United States it is of prime necessity that in this country, where every other industry is developing with gigantic strides, a bold and decided step should be taken to win back from Europe our former prestige as the best shipbuilders of the world." In this spirit, successive authorizing acts demanded that all American naval materiel be manufactured within the United States, even though this entailed, at times, a cost in military efficiency. However, it also entailed the development of the domestic industrial base required to support a large fleet.

A whale among the minnows, the USS *Bainbridge* (DD 1) leads a flotilla of torpedo boats. The first U.S. destroyers were indeed much larger than their torpedo boat predecessors.

The board's goal of full U.S. naval self-sufficiency was unusual in a world whose warship and naval weapon market was dominated by a few European, largely British, firms. This was particularly the case with torpedo craft, which required so much expertise for their construction that a yard practically had to design its own if they were to be successful. Moreover, they were very nearly experimental in character: their success depended upon the yard's ability to pare away unnecessary weights while retaining sufficient hull strength and engine durability. Well aware that it lacked the necessary expertise, the Navy Department through the nineties preferred to allow its torpedo-boat contractors the greatest possible latitude, adopting for its own designs many of their features. The acts authorizing these boats were sufficiently vague that it was often difficult to compare the products of different bidders; regardless of the proven expertise of some of those bidding, the department was constrained to accept the lowest bid.

This procedure was quite as dangerous for the bidder as for the department: torpedo boats were deceptively small and simple, and it was quite easy to underbid. Thus, experienced firms submitting realistic bids often lost out to newcomers, and the very small size of the market represented by the U.S. Navy of the 1880s and 1890s cannot have encouraged the formation of specialized firms. Two tried: Herreshoff, already famous for yachts and fast steam launches, and Bath Iron Works—whose founder, General Thomas W. Hyde, imported French (Normand) technology, going so far as to buy the plans of a Normand torpedo boat and translate metric measurements into English units to build the *Dahlgren* and *Craven*. He also hired Charles P. Wetherbee, an American graduate of the French École d'Applications du Génie Maritime, who had spent his summers at the Normand yard. Wetherbee continued as the Bath destroyer design specialist until the end of World War I, by which time the Navy had quite given up permitting its builders much leeway. By then, however, the argument that private firms were best at exploiting advanced technology had led the Navy to rely on the Electric Boat Company for submarine designs.

One important element in the Navy Department's perhaps militarily unwise policy of spreading around torpedo craft construction bids was political: the wider the naval construction funds were spread, the more popular would be the expansion of the fleet. For example, in 1892 the Iowa Iron Works of Dubuque won the contract for the torpedo boat *Ericsson* (the construction of which was apparently quite disastrous), and that year the Secretary of the Navy characterized this award as the beginning of a contribution by the midwestern states to the new Navy. The representatives of these states had traditionally opposed naval construction on the ground that it favored firms on the seacoasts. Another consideration was geography: boats for service on the West Coast had to be built there, even though at higher cost.

From 1881 onward successive advisory boards and Secretaries of the Navy recommended large programs for torpedo-boat construction. For example, in 1885 the Secretary claimed that 50 could be built for the price of a single ironclad; he contrasted a German program for 150, one for each 10 miles of coast ("a distance which can be traversed by the boat in half an hour in any weather in which an ironclad would venture to approach") with the nonexistent U.S. program. That year an Army-Navy board on coastal defense recommended construction of 175 torpedo boats, as well as 18 rams, to be distributed among ten operating areas: Eastport, Maine, to Cape Ann (30 boats); Cape Ann to Cape Cod (10); Long Island Sound (20); New York (20); Delaware Bay (10); Chesapeake Bay (15); Charleston (20); the Gulf Coast (10); New Orleans (10); the Pacific Coast (30). This particular board was more successful in its advocacy of the first U.S. armored warships, the *Maine* and the *Texas*.

The next year Herreshoff completed an experimental torpedo boat, the *Stiletto*, which proved so successful that she was bought the following year. In August 1886, Congress finally authorized the construction of a single boat, which became the USS *Cushing*. The Admiral of the Navy protested that numbers, not just a single experimental unit, were needed: he wanted 20, each not less than 150 feet in length and having a speed (then quite unobtainable) of about 26 knots; "these vessels, of course, should be designed by the Messrs. Herreshoff who, with their quadruple expansion engines, would have no difficulty in obtaining the necessary speed." What the Herreshoffs produced was somewhat more modest: their *Cushing*, Torpedo Boat No. 1, was not launched until January 1890 and was designed for only 23 knots.

A second boat was not authorized until 1890, although successive Secretaries kept asking for more torpedo craft; for example, in his 1889 report, Secretary Benjamin F. Tracy observed that "apart from the want of battleships, the most marked defect of the present fleet is in torpedo boats." He wanted at least five built, and the next year praised the new *Cushing* as among the best in the world:

> If this country had twenty like her, and had them equipped with effective torpedoes, they would be a material addition to its means of defense. As long as it has but two, they will be little service otherwise than to show what native skill and ingenuity can do in this direction.

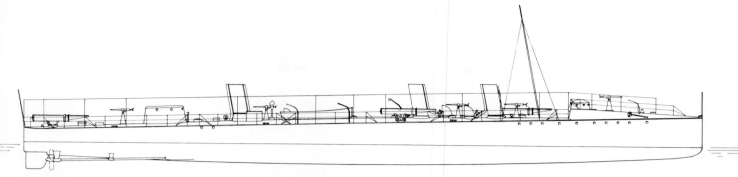

Porter TB 6   1896   175′6″ o.a.   Sister: *Dupont* TB 7

Up to this point the Navy thought of torpedo craft as a means of coastal defense, but Tracy appointed a new policy board, which added another concept: adopting Mahan's new ideas, it called for a combination of coastal and oceangoing fleets, the latter to carry a war to the enemy. In enemy waters the battle fleet would be subject to torpedo-boat attack. The board called for 15 torpedo cruisers of about 900 tons each to accompany its "ten battleships of great coal endurance" and their cruiser consorts; for operations overseas there would also be three torpedo depot ships to support short-range torpedo craft, which would be carried overseas aboard the battleships, cruisers, and the depot ships themselves.

Although the report of the board, delivered in January 1890, was greeted with derision, it did have a lasting effect, in that it led to the battleship program of the nineties, as well as to the authorization of the second torpedo boat (the *Ericsson*, a modified *Cushing* built to department plans) and a prototype torpedo cruiser. The fate of the latter is indicative of the technological problems of all small, fast craft of the time. She was to displace 750 tons and was required to make 23 knots; this called for a total of 6,000 horsepower. Congress appropriated $350,000 exclusive of armament, but it was soon realized that the engines alone would cost $325,000, and no builder was willing to bid. Tracy realized that the success of the torpedo cruiser was essential to the success of a U.S. high-seas battle fleet strategy:

The usefulness of this class of vessels has been shown very clearly in the late Chilean revolutionary war, when the ironclad *Blanco Encalada* was torpedoed and sunk by the torpedo gunboats *Almirante Condell* and *Almirante Lynch*; owing to their size, and consequent less fatigue of crew, together with an ample coal supply, they were enabled to operate a long distance from their base of supplies. If they had not possessed these features, especially the ability to keep the sea, the attempt would doubtless have been unsuccessful, if indeed attempted at all.

The particular functions of this class of vessels are to chase and destroy torpedo boats, to act as torpedo boats themselves when opportunity presents itself, and as lookout and dispatch vessels in fleet operations.

Tracy therefore pleaded for an amendment, in 1891 and again in 1892, to the 1890 Act, which would have raised the appropriation for the torpedo cruiser. He failed, but on the other hand it finally became possible to purchase rights to the Whitehead torpedo. No more torpedo boats were authorized even though Tracy asked for 30 in his last year in office, 1892.

Although the next administration felt constrained to suspend capital shipbuilding in view of the poor state of the economy, the torpedo-boat program so long awaited finally began to materialize, with three torpedo boats authorized in 1894 and three more in 1895. The former were essentially duplicates of the *Ericsson* built to Navy plans. For the next series, however, two (No. 6 and 7) were built by Herreshoff to his own plans, while another was built in Seattle to Navy plans. The department designs improved gradually, from 23 knots in the *Ericsson* to 24.5 in the *Winslow* class (No. 5) and 26 (the level proposed by Porter in 1886) in the *Rowan* (No. 8); Herreshoff pushed the state of the art, guaranteeing 27.5. These were all large oceangoing boats, as much as 175 feet long. The fleet of torpedo craft had now grown to the point at which a Secretary of the Navy observed in 1896 that it was time to make arrangements to lay up the bulk of the torpedo flotillas in peacetime, as a war reserve: it would be uneconomical to keep all manned continuously.

In 1896 there was a change in policy: three more oceangoing boats (No. 9–11) were authorized, as well as up to ten smaller and far slower ones, their number limited by total cost (No. 12–18 were built). The large boats were to be able to make the unprecedented speed of 30 knots.

In inviting proposals for the 30-knot boats, it was deemed advisable, in view of the very high speed to be obtained, to leave contractors as much latitude as possible, and for this reason, the Department did not prepare designs, exacting only the most general requirements. . . .

Bath received its first torpedo-boat contracts under this authorization, as did the Union Iron Works on the Pacific Coast, selected over Herreshoff because of its location.

The department did prepare designs for the smaller (20- and 22.5-knot) boats, although it was prepared to accept alternatives, and in fact Herreshoff, the Columbian Iron Works (who had built Nos. 3–5), and Wolff & Zwicker (who had no previous torpedo-boat experience) were awarded contracts to build their own designs. This was presumably a safe course in view of the advance to higher speeds in large torpedo boats.

For 1897 the department again sought large oceangoing 30-knot torpedo boats to bidders' designs, two not less than 230 tons and one not less than 260. In fact one of them, the *Stringham*, displaced 340 tons and so was larger than many British destroyers. Nevertheless, although she was referred to as a destroyer in contemporary naval annuals, that was at best misleading. She was, rather, a seagoing torpedo boat, a coastal defense unit armed primarily with the torpedo and only secondarily with the gun (two 18-inch torpedo tubes with one reload each versus four 6-pounders). Thus, in February 1898, the Bureau of Construction and Repair favored:

"two sizes of torpedo craft, one of about 175 tons, seagoing torpedo boats, the other of about double this size, of the torpedo boat destroyer type. If the Department were given ample funds for the construction of torpedo boats, the Bureau is inclined to think that the most satisfactory investment would be in the direction of 100-foot boats intended for operation in, and near, harbors, in other words to look upon torpedo boats as adjuncts to coast defense proper. As however there is no prospect of any large number of torpedo boats being constructed in the near future the Bureau is constrained to consider that the few boats built should be of sufficient size to enable them to make their way with speed and safety along the coast—outside—which will require a size not less than 175 tons. . . .

Assistant Secretary of the Navy Theodore Roosevelt championed the construction of additional torpedo boats, turning aside what must have been a very common argument as to their fragility. For example, on 18 February 1898 he sent the Secretary a photograph of a division of German torpedo boats in heavy weather ("It sets forth in graphic form the unsuitability of torpedo boats to do duty in rough weather, an unsuitability which must always be taken into account, even on the occasions when it is necessary to disregard it") and a report on the multitude of casualties among the torpedo boats of the French Mediterranean Fleet (of 37 boats in commission, only 9 were available for immediate service).

The experiences thus set forth . . . are curiously paralleled by our own at the present time. During the last six months we have had for the first time a torpedo boat flotilla, and we have for the first time thoroughly tested the boats by long voyages and individual and squadron drills, under all conditions of weather, off every kind of coast. The two things brought out most clearly by these tests are, first, the very great benefit accruing from the actual handling of the boats; and second the extreme fragility of the boats . . . the margin of safety is exceedingly small. In the effort to attain the maximum of speed at the sacrifice of everything else, the structure has been made so delicate that accidents continually occur if the boats are driven hard or if they get into a heavy seaway; while the scantling is so light that to scrape a dock or touch a shoal may mean rather serious temporary injury. I would suggest that the Department very seriously consider whether in building boats hereafter it would not be well to sacrifice two or three knots . . . for the sake of getting heavier scantling, and machinery less apt to get out of order . . .

The reduction of speed would of course be a disadvantage; but every warship, big or small, is nothing but a compromise. . . . A torpedo boat must be fast, for it must be able under favorable conditions to deal its blow and then escape, if escape be possible. Only about a minute will elapse between the time when a torpedo boat becomes visible under the searchlight, and the time when it discharges its torpedoes; for of course a torpedo boat can work only by surprise. Even a comparatively slow torpedo boat, one of 22 or 23 knots, could escape from a fast cruiser if it happened to be caught out in smooth water; and no torpedo boat, under such circumstances, would have its speed knocked down immediately. In cruising about looking for a hostile squadron a torpedo boat would rarely go at full speed; therefore the speed need only be considered as of vital consequence during the minute or thereabouts that it would be exposed to fire before dealing its blow . . . a sacrifice of three knots' speed in a 30-knot boat would probably not mean more than about six seconds additional exposure. In my opinion it is not worthwhile trying to economize on these six seconds at the cost of immensely increasing the fragility of the boat. I agree . . . that we should have substantially two types of torpedo boats, one of about 200 tons and the other a so-called destroyer of about 400. . . .

Experience with the torpedo boats in foreign navies no less than in our own shows that while under favorable circumstances it is undoubtedly a most terrible engine of war, yet that these favorable circumstances may very rarely occur. At present our Navy is particularly short in torpedo boats, and we need to have this arm of the service developed relatively to the others; but nothing could be more foolish than the talk of substituting torpedo boats for battleships and cruisers. Except when working at night, or under conditions which favor a surprise, the torpedo boat is absolutely helpless against any seagoing ship, armed with rapid-fire guns, whether the ship be large or small; and under no conditions is it fit to do rough work at sea. . . .

We should have in our Navy at least one hundred torpedo boats. Some of these should be destroyers of large size, probably on the lines of the one now building at Wilmington (the large torpedo boat *Stringham*, 340 tons, at Harlan & Hollingsworth). Such destroyers will of course be seaworthy, as smaller boats cannot be; though the accidents to some of the English destroyers must not be forgotten, for apparently at least half of them are constantly under repairs. The remaining boats would be the torpedo boats proper. . . .

It is possible that we may be able to reduce the extreme fragility of torpedo boats; nevertheless they will always remain as fragile as they are formidable. Every war vessel of the highest efficiency, from a battleship down, is itself a huge bit of delicate mechanism, and its efficiency is largely conditioned upon features of its structure which are liable at any time to suffer serious accident. . . .A great nation must have a great navy; and this means that it must accept without undue hysterical excitement the fact that accidents will from time to time befall the ships of its navy. If because of these accidents it stops work, whether on dry docks, battleships, or torpedo boats, it will prove that it is not a great nation and that it is not entitled to rank as such in the world.

In Roosevelt's parlance a destroyer was merely a large, oceangoing torpedo boat not, as in the Royal Navy, a fast warship designed specifically to protect a battle fleet from surface torpedo attack. Indeed, had not the Spanish War emergency intervened, it seems likely that the U.S torpedo flotilla would have come to resemble that of the contemporary German Navy, with only a secondary destroyer role.

In all navies, the torpedo boat of the 1890s was preeminently a coastal defense weapon, relying on its high speed for tactical advantage. High speed in turn depended on a good ratio of horsepower to total displacement; given the engine technology of the time, it depended on extreme weight reductions in both engine and hull, and thus on tight limits on coal and even on armament: torpedo boats carried their torpedoes, and little more in the way of guns. Limited hull weight in turn meant limited seaworthiness, and limited coal weight meant very limited steaming endurance. Tactically, then, torpedo boats could be expected to fight only near their bases. For example, the Royal Navy could expect to encounter French torpedo boats in the Channel, but not in a fleet-on-fleet battle in mid-Atlantic.

When the United States began to build up a battle fleet in the 1890s, one important justification was the Monroe Doctrine: no foreign power should be permitted to establish a new foothold in the New World. It followed that the U.S. fleet might have to meet a European fleet in the Caribbean, and indeed for some years the favorite scenario of U.S. naval strategists involved a German attempt to seize a base in the Western Hemisphere preparatory to seizing other territory. The short range of torpedo craft, inherent in the naval technology of their day, seemed to guarantee the nascent U.S. battle fleet against their attentions. Thus, although the U.S. Navy was well informed on the development of destroyers in the Royal Navy and in other European navies, it made no attempt to buy destroyers of its own until 1898.

The Spanish provided an unpleasant surprise in their success in bringing three new destroyers, the *Furor*, *Pluton*, and *Terror*, across the Atlantic. A U.S. Navy already required not merely to repel but rather to blockade its enemy in an existing base, Santiago de Cuba, would now have to face the threat of concentrated torpedo attack.

Assistant Secretary of the Navy Theodore Roosevelt headed a special war plans board; on 16 March 1898 it reported:

. . . we respectfully, but most urgently, point out that the Spanish torpedo-boat destroyers, now at the Canaries or preparing to come to Cuba, should not be allowed to come. They offer the only real menace to us, although, as I shall mention further, the Spaniards are rapidly accumulating a sufficient number of battleships to give us cause for some concern. If these torpedo-boat destroyers are allowed to come into Cuban waters they render the problem we have to solve one of great danger. Without them the problem is comparatively easy, and its ultimate solution in our favor is certain. We can, without difficulty, blockade Havana if there are no torpedo boats inside. If there are torpedo boats inside the blockade becomes one of very great hazard. Any European country would treat the mobilizing of an army corps on its borders as a cause for action, and it is much to be wished that these torpedo-boat destroyers, which of course can only be designed for use against the American Navy, shall be kept where they are or met upon the high seas. . . .

What we are most deficient in is torpedo boats. We especially need torpedo-boat destroyers, and every effort should be made to procure them. The board has communicated with Messrs. Harlan and Hollingsworth to find out how soon they could build us any torpedo-boat destroyers. If possible they should be purchased, but of this the board does not speak as it is aware you have been straining every effort to so purchase. If they cannot be purchased, then all the fine yachts and tugs available should be improvised into torpedo-boat destroyers, and those that are not used with the fleet should be concentrated at places like the eastern pass of Long Island, or the entrance of Boston Harbor, as an improvised means of defense. Also we believe that a dozen small torpedo boats of the *Gwin* type should be ordered. These ought

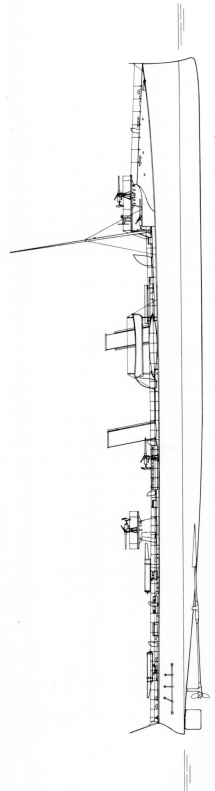

Farragut TB 11   1898   214' o.a.   Single ship. Often referred to as a destroyer in contemporary references, due to heavy gun armament of six 6-pdr (57-mm.) quick-firing guns and only two 18-in. torpedo tubes. Only U.S. TB or DD with a "ram" bow profile.

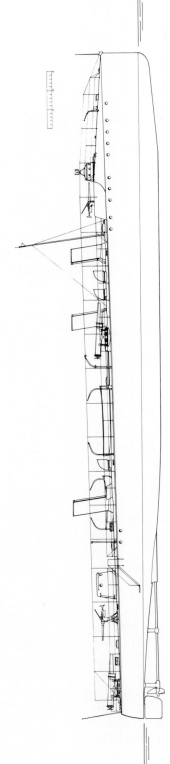

Blakeley TB 27   Dec. 1900   175' o.a.   *Blakeley* class

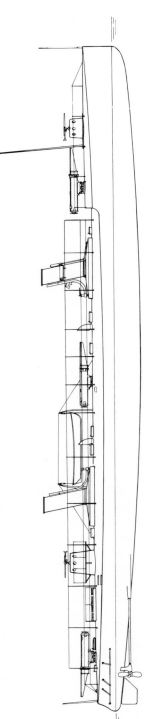

Fox TB 13   1898   148' o.a.   *Davis* class

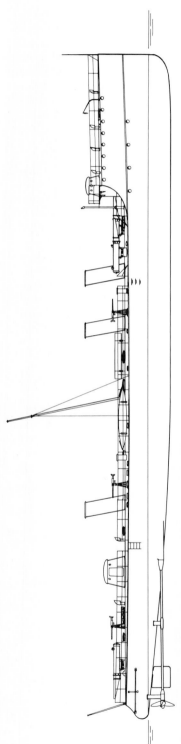

Rowan TB 8 1898 170' o.a. Pointed object on deck at base of mast is a folding canvas boat; cylinder abaft second stack was a reload torpedo locker. The *Rowan* had no sisters.

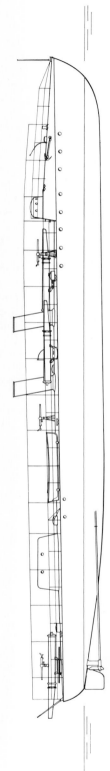

Morris TB 14 1898 139'6" o.a.

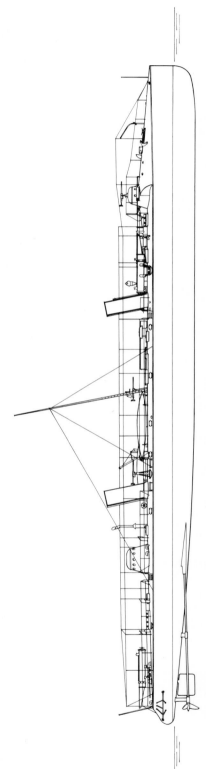

Foote TB 3 1896 160' o.a. Sisters: *Rodgers*, TB 4, *Winslow*, TB 5. Cigar-shaped objects abaft mast were folding boats. Spare torpedo carried in cylinder abaft fwd. stack. Drawing shows all awning stanchions rigged.

to be constructed in ninety days. Mr. Herreshoff says it would take about four months, but under pressure we think he could be made to guarantee that they would be done in ninety days. . . .

In fact there was no time for new construction, and the improvised yachts had to serve: at Santiago the ex-yacht *Corsair* (renamed *Gloucester*) sank two Spanish destroyers. However, the program initiated in response to the board's letter and authorized by Congress on 4 May 1898 did include the first 16 U.S. destroyers. At that time they were the largest in the world. There were also to be 12 torpedo boats, and the Navy scrambled to buy existing European units—of which only two were available, one from Schichau and the other from Yarrow. As for new construction, the iron law of mobilization is that in emergencies there is very little hope of innovation: one builds what one is already building. All 12 new boats were developments of the now-standard seagoing types (and not, incidentally, of the four large units built under the 1896 and 1897 programs). Thus the department drew up a design based on that of the *Winslow* (No. 5), and Bath built a modified version of its French-designed boat.

There was, however, no prototype destroyer, and it is notable that the *Stringham* design was not adapted. Instead, the department took its time to develop its own design, emphasizing seaworthiness and strength—though rather optimistically expecting high speed. Bidders had the option of providing their own designs, and it is not clear that all of them quite understood the department's priorities: after all, acceptance depended on trial speed, not on some subjective test of seakeeping. For example, the alternative designs dispensed with the department's full forecastle in favor of a torpedo-boat style turtleback.

Congress limited the number of boats to be built by any one contractor to four, in the interest of spreading the work and also because of the industrial expertise involved. In addition, although the Board on Construction recommended that Herreshoff be awarded two torpedo boats, the department awarded none to that experienced firm. At the time of contract award none of the earlier 30-knot boats had been completed, so there was no real experience on which to build; two officers reviewing the situation in November 1901

. . . were impressed by the evident sincerity of statements made by the contractors, which were practically universal, that the actual cost of labor and material expended by them on these vessels, not including general expenses, was in excess of the actual contract prices for them. With the exception of the Bath Iron Works, which bid on its own designs, and the Columbian Iron Works, which subsequently went

into the hands of a receiver, none of the contractors had previously completed torpedo vessels . . . the Gas Engine and Power Company had the torpedo boat *Bailey* under construction but were not far enough advanced with her to have gained valuable experience . . . the torpedo boats previously built had been generally of much smaller size and much lower requirements as to speed, and it is believed that those who built them (except perhaps the Herreshoff Mfg. Co.) had had considerable difficulty in their completion. The building of successful torpedo vessels having the "highest practicable speed" is an occupation that requires designing talents of a high order and prolonged experience in construction. There are comparatively few successful builders of torpedo vessels in the world, but the attempt was made in this country to rival the best results obtained abroad with designs which were not based on the known results of a large number of previous vessels and by builders whose knowledge and experience were of a limited character.

At the same time these contracts were taken these contractors evidently thought that the Department's designs of their own would be entirely adequate to fulfill the program laid down without difficulty, and they apparently went into the contracts with a light heart. . . . As a number of these contractors have comparatively small plans and capital, it is our opinion that if harshly dealt with they will undoubtedly be forced to the wall, and two concerns, the Columbian Iron Works and Wolff & Zwicker, have already reached that position.

The situation is further complicated by the probability that a number of these vessels will fail to obtain their contract speed or even that lower speed which, deducting penalties, allows them to be accepted at all . . . the contractors universally seem very much depressed . . . they were led to believe that the plans and specifications furnished by the Government were adequate. . . . That that is not the case is now evident and is due to a variety of causes. All the vessels built on the Department's designs that have been tried are greatly overweight, and they all appear subject to excessive vibrations, causing breakdowns when the machinery is running at high speed. The weights allowed in the designs required the most careful study of details and the omission of everything non-essential . . . it is doubtful, even with the most careful supervision, whether some excess would not have occurred. . . .

The contractors feel, with some reason, that as they bid on Department designs, or, in some cases, on bidders' designs closely akin to the Department's designs, they are not responsible for the failure to achieve results aimed at, and they all insist upon their good faith in endeavoring to carry out the Department's wishes . . . large advances took place in the price of materials shortly after the contracts were awarded, amounting to 60 percent in some cases. Another ground is that the expense of the repeated trials, resulting in repeated failures, has enormously enhanced the cost. . . .

The destroyer *Paul Jones*, in the Pacific about 1905, followed the original Bureau of Construction and Repair design with a high forecastle for sea-keeping. Two groups of funnels indicate two sets of boilers, separated by her engines, for survivability. The indentation in her forecastle, a common design feature in early U.S. destroyers, permitted two 6-pounders just abaft the break of the forecastle to train forward. The two 3-inch guns are also visible, one atop her armored conning tower forward (and largely hidden by canvas), the other right aft. Also apparent are the engine-room hatches amidships.

These laments will be familiar to anyone involved in the high-technology projects of the last three decades, and particularly to historians of the very ambitious U.S. military aircraft projects of the early fifties. In the case of the 1898 boats, not even the experienced yards were immune: Bath was thought to have made money, but very little, even though "it is believed that at the present time the employee [Wetherbee] who has charge of this character of work in their establishment is among those in this country best fitted for the designing and constructing of torpedo vessels." In the end, disaster was avoided only when the Navy reduced its speed requirements for both torpedo boats and destroyers from 30 and 28 knots to 28 and 26; vibration problems were so severe that the duration of the full-power trial had to be reduced from two hours to one.

The C&R design called for a raised flat-decked forecastle, a seakeeping feature; another was the provision for bilge keels, which, according to Chief Constructor Hichborn, were "decided upon as the result of experience at sea with even the largest of our torpedo boats, which have been found to wear out the crews in a very few days, principally by excessive and lively rolling. These are the boats that will be expected to keep the seas . . . and the fitting of bilge keels was thought to be important. Bidders were inclined to shirk them, because they were considered an uncertain factor in the high speed required. They were retained in all contract specifications, however. . . ." Seakeeping and seagoing endurance re-

quired great structural strength in a lightweight hull; the Navy design included nickel steel stringer plates and sheer strakes. In effect, then, the department design reflected a conscious choice for seagoing, rather than trial, performance. This first group of U.S. destroyers tended toward relatively heavy construction and thus toward low speed. A similar choice was made by the Royal Navy in its "River" and later classes.

In effect the high forecastle required the expenditure of structural weight to purchase the ability to sustain speed in a seaway, an exchange that in itself suggests the fleet support role of the new destroyers. In calm water hydrodynamic performance would depend completely on the underwater form of the hull, and thus would be unaffected by the presence or absence of a forecastle. Private builders appear to have taken the natural view that the one overriding requirement (and, indeed, the one requirement explicitly stated in their contracts) was smooth-water trial speed; they eschewed the heavy forecastle in favor of the usual European turtle-back, a curved deck sloping up from the bows to meet the conning tower.

In the department design, a conning tower with half-inch armor was mounted atop the forecastle, surmounted by a 3-inch gun on a platform that could also serve as a navigating bridge. The forecastle sides were cut away to permit two 6-pounders just abaft the break of the forecastle to train forward. Of two long 18-inch torpedo tubes, one was mounted amid-

A Bureau-designed destroyer, unidentified, shows her arrangement: both 3-inch guns are visible, as are two 6-pounders (one at the break of the forecastle, one abaft the fourth funnel) and both torpedo tubes (one between second and third funnels, one right aft), with their "spoons" folded back on top. Both fore and aft conning towers were emergency armored control positions; generally the ship was conned from the 3-inch gun (and searchlight) platform forward.

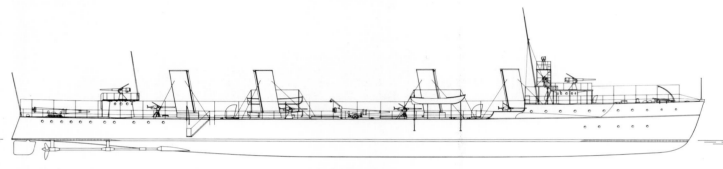

Bainbridge DD 1   1901   250' o.a./245 w.l.   *Bainbridge* class

ships between the two pairs of funnels, the other on the fantail just abaft a small structure supporting the other 3-inch gun. The remaining 6-pounders were mounted on the main deck.

The four water-tube boilers were paired fore and aft, which accounted for the distinctive funnel configuration: between the two boiler rooms was an engine room containing a pair of vertical inverted triple-expansion engines. This dispersal of the boilers suggests the much later en-echelon configuration, and, like it, was presumably a survivability feature. More direct protection was afforded the machinery by coal and by 12½-lb. nickel steel over part of the deck and the sheer strake; the description of such thin (5/16 inch) plate as "protection" suggests the very light construction of these craft.

Maneuverability was an important consideration in the design, which featured a flat spoon-shaped stern. Although it did promote good turning qualities (tactical diameters as small as 250 yards at 22 knots were claimed for the *Bainbridge*, and 225 yards at 26 knots for the *Chauncey*), it was severely criticized; according to the commanding officer of the USS *Bainbridge*:

. . . the present form of stern I consider an element of weakness in the structure of the ship in that the stresses caused by a sea striking the practically hor-

izontal overhang are too great to be long withstood, especially as the overhang itself is not a strong form of construction . . . there is danger that the shock of suddenly bringing up may start the fastenings of the propeller struts. I am well aware of the results aimed at in fitting torpedo vessels with this form of stern—decreased resistance in smooth water—in other words smooth water speed, but I am of the opinion that too much can be sacrificed to speed and that the racing machine idea as the governing one should be abandoned in torpedo boat construction.

The flotilla commander, Lieutenant L. H. Chandler, wrote that: "the stern is excellent from a handling and speed point of view but it is structurally weak . . . I am not ready to recommend replacing it by a conventional stern, but I do feel that a complete machinery disablement in a heavy sea would bring on a serious risk of machinery damage from pounding . . . ." Lieutenant Chandler's views were particularly significant because his report was made upon completion of sea duty as commander of the Destroyer Flotilla (April 1904); according to a later C&R memorandum on stern form, his report "was freely consulted in the design of Destroyers Nos. 17 to 21." The issue is important because it led the U.S. Navy to a V-form stern, which made for strength but also for very large tactical diameters, a point apparently not much appreciated until it was emphasized by

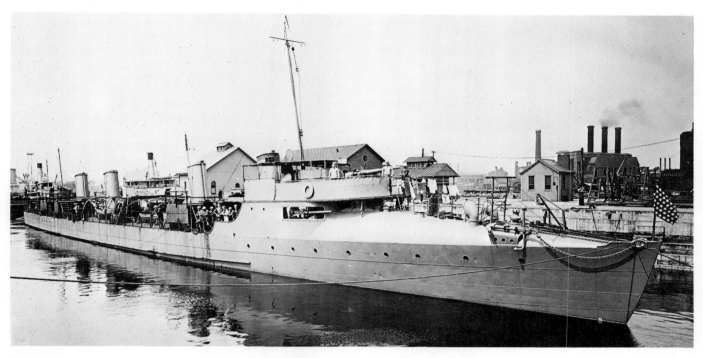

The destroyer *Worden* (DD 16) was built to a private (*Truxtun*-class) design by Maryland Steel; she shows the turtleback forecastle common in the world's torpedo craft at the turn of the century, the two 6-pounders peering out through ports. These units were considered so successful that they formed the basis for characteristics proposed by the General Board for new destroyers in 1904.

The two *Hull*s were designed by Harlan & Hollingsworth, following the bureau design except for the abandonment of a full forecastle; this is the *Hull* in May 1907.

U.S. contact with the Royal Navy during World War I. Maneuverability became a major issue in U.S. destroyer design from the late thirties onward.

Nine boats (*Bainbridge* class, DD 1-5, 10-13) were built to the department's plans. The privately designed boats could be distinguished by their funnel arrangements. Two by Fore River Engine Company (*Lawrence* class, DD 8 and 9) had theirs closely spaced (all boilers forward of the engine room); two by Harlan & Hollingsworth (*Hull* class, DD 6 and 7) had high funnels; and three by Maryland Steel Company (*Truxtun* class, DD 14-16) had shorter ones; all had turtle-backs. The two *Lawrence*s were considered the

least successful of the lot, and were unable to carry their 3-inch guns (6-pounders were substituted); the remaining five private boats more or less followed the bureau's arrangement, except that the two forward 6-pounders fired through ports in the turtle-deck under the 3-inch gun platform. The *Truxtun*s mounted an additional 6-pounder.

All took much longer to build than had been anticipated, and all came out heavy and therefore slow. A typical unit, the USS *Stewart* (*Bainbridge*, or department, class) made 29.3 knots on trial (8,000 ihp, 330 rpm) at an unrealistically light displacement of 444 tons. Fuel consumption on trial was equivalent

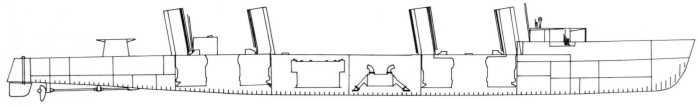

Stewart inboard

The two *Lawrence*s, built by Fore River, were considered the least successful of the first batch of U.S. destroyers. They were, for example, unable to mount 3-inch guns, and 6-pounders had to be substituted. Note, too, the funnel arrangement; all boilers were grouped together. The *Lawrence* served in the Atlantic until 1907, entering San Diego with the "Great White Fleet" and then becoming part of the 3rd Torpedo Flotilla (whence, presumably, the "3" on her hull and funnel), 1908–12. The *Macdonough* is shown below.

to a radius of action of 2,160 nm. at 12 knots (180 tons of fuel), although the figure of 2,700 nm. at 8 knots cited by *Jane's* was probably more realistic.

In 1903 the new destroyers were organized in flotillas. That December, the First Flotilla (the *Bainbridge*, *Barry*, *Chauncey*, *Dale*, and *Decatur*) was ordered to the Philippines, 18,000 miles away. Convoyed by the tender *Buffalo*, they steamed east by way of Gibraltar and Suez, arriving in April without serious incident. Several, however, ran out of fuel in mid-Atlantic and had to coal at sea.

Meanwhile the *Preble* and *Paul Jones* were sent to Panama as dispatch vessels. In 1920 Commander S. M. Robinson, later chief of the Bureau of Engineering, observed that these two operations, more than any others,

> proved conclusively that the destroyer was a reliable seagoing vessel and had a cruising radius that compared favorably with other types of ships. The fuel economy at low speed was the greatest surprise of all. At that time so little was known regarding the fuel consumption at cruising speeds that when the cruise from San Francisco to Panama was first projected arrangements were made for coaling at San Diego and every few hundred miles from there to Panama. Great was the surprise when it was found the trip could easily be made with only one stop, and without any stop by taking a small deck-load of coal.

In effect the "420-ton" destroyers became the basis for the characteristics to which the next series of destroyers, the "700-tonners" or "flivvers," were designed; the great apparent jump in displacement was just that, given the overweight of the first 16 destroyers. They set the U.S. pattern, which emphasized seakeeping and endurance at the expense of very high speed.

2

A Decade of
Developments, 1906–1916

From 1900 onward destroyer development was tied in with U.S. war planning, in that the new permanent General Board of senior admirals, presided over by Admiral of the Navy George Dewey, was concerned both with war plans and, increasingly, with building programs. Thus, in October the board recommended the inclusion of two destroyers in a 1901 program. In February 1903, it drew up a long-term program for the U.S. fleet, in which for every four battleships there were to be four "large, quick-turning destroyers." That fall the General Board drew up suggested characteristics for the ships in its program, for presentation to both the Secretary of the Navy and the Board on Construction, which included among its members the Chief Constructor. The fast destroyers were to be capable of a sea speed of 20 knots, to be sustained for 48 hours.

No new destroyers were authorized until 1906, despite the General Board's pleas. For example, in October 1904 it called for the construction of six, to make up for the failure to authorize any the previous year. New destroyers were to have "trial displacements of 400 to 450 tons [similar to those of the flotilla that went to join the Asiatic Fleet in the summer of 1904, and the later *Truxtun*], with the coal capacity and battery of the *Truxtun*, of staunch construction for safety and efficiency in rough weather, and the highest speed found attainable in association with those features and durable machinery . . . the great value of a powerful battery has been emphasized in the Russo-Japanese War." By January 1905 the board considered destroyers second in value only to battleships.

The Board on Construction, i.e., the Bureaus of Construction and Repair, Ordnance, and Steam Engineering, agreed that the *Truxtun* was highly desirable as a destroyer prototype, but pointed out that she was badly overweight: her class averaged 496 tons on trial,

and even then they were tried under special conditions which have been customary with these high-speed boats, viz., as light as possible. The deep load displacement of the *Truxtun* class is nearly 700 tons, and in the opinion of the Board on Construction, the time has come to try these vessels under conditions more nearly approximating service conditions. . . . The *Truxtun* has been given a progressive trial in service, at about 620 tons displacement, when she attained a speed of over 26 knots when handled by her naval crew. In the opinion of this Board it would be advisable to have the trials of these boats under conditions which compel the carrying of at least one-half of their full coal supply and about two-thirds of their ammunition and consumable stores. This would make the trial displacement of the new destroyer about 620 tons, and this is considered the displacement which should be provided for. . . . The Board also notes that the General Board considers the new destroyer should be a boat of very strong construction, for safety and efficiency in rough weather. It should be pointed out that there seems to be some misapprehension as regards the strength and seaworthiness of our destroyers. It can hardly be said of any vessel that it is immune from disaster under any conceivable conditions or stress of weather; but there does not appear to be any reasonable doubt as to the safety of existing torpedo boat destroyers when

An unidentified "thousand tonner" lying alongside in the destroyer tender *Melville* at Queenstown, Ireland, during World War I displays her torpedo tube arrangement, with both sets close together on the starboard side but relatively far apart on the port side. Engine-room skylights and life-raft stowage are also visible; one of the two 4-inch guns carried at the break of the forecastle can be made out forward. Of the three sets of tubes visible, note that only in one (to starboard) are the "spoons" folded back; the others are all in firing configuration. Tube-trainers sat atop each pair of tubes, their handwheels visible here.

properly handled . . . the *Truxtun*, *Whipple*, and *Worden* are of somewhat heavier construction than other vessels built upon the contractor's designs, notably the *Lawrence* and *Macdonough*. The main hull structure of the *Truxtun* . . . weighs about 195 tons, as against 123 tons for the *Lawrence* and *Macdonough* vessels of nearly identical dimensions. There was some question raised by the Trial Board as to the strength of the *Lawrence* and *Macdonough*, but since then one of them, the *Lawrence*, has successfully passed through exceedingly heavy weather which drove some large coasting vessels into port, and was reported by her Commanding Officer as having behaved in a most satisfactory manner. In order to enable vessels of this type to be pushed in a seaway more than the present destroyers, it would be necessary to provide more hull weight, and there are certain features of the *Truxtun* class which are susceptible of improvement . . . .

Opinion within the Navy does not appear to have been quite as sanguine. In 1904 Theodore Roosevelt, who had begun the Navy's destroyer force six years earlier, was President, and he continued his intense interest in the Navy. One of his many friends within the service, Commander C. M. Winslow, described to him the unsatisfactory character of the torpedo flotilla. President Roosevelt requested a fuller report, which was submitted to him on 19 August 1904:

The history of nearly all our torpedo boats and torpedo boat destroyers has been that immediately after being delivered they have gone to a navy yard for extensive repairs and alterations. They have rarely been run at any speed approximating the contract speed, and are almost continually under repairs.

A flotilla of torpedo boat destroyers recently made the voyage from the United States to the Philippines . . . [while en route, its] Commanding Officer stated that the flotilla had proceeded that far on its voyage without repairs of any consequence to the engines of any vessel of the flotilla, and cite[d] this fact in proof that the statements in regard to the unreliability and inefficiency of the engines of the destroyers were without foundation in fact. Up to the time of making the report the flotilla had cruised for the greater part of the distance at approximately its economical speed, and at no time at a high rate of speed. There was, therefore, little or no stress placed on the engines: An engine designed to develop seven to ten thousand horsepower could not be accepted as reliable though it had propelled a vessel thousands of miles at a rate requiring but a few hundred horsepower of the engines, any more than a race horse could be considered fit to win a race because he had cantered five miles on the track. . . . There is nothing more important than reliability. Extreme speed should be, if necessary, sacrificed. . . . The sacrifice of extreme speed does not, however, necessarily secure reliability. Our fastest boats, the Porter and Dupont, and others built

by the Herreshoffs, have proven themselves to be the most reliable. Many of the other boats are not reliable even at low speeds. One of the recently built destroyers was subjected to such excessive engine vibration when running at low speed under convoy to Colon that one of the main engines shook the engine framing loose from the engine foundation. The Bureau of Steam Engineering afterwards recommended that the vessel should not be run at any speed below about fourteen knots. . . .

The war in the East indicates that in future a battleship fleet in time of war must be accompanied, particularly at night and in foggy weather, by a fleet of torpedo vessels. Otherwise the Commander-in-Chief would be reluctant to take the sea except in broad daylight when the approach of an enemy's torpedo vessels could be easily detected. To limit a Commander-in-Chief to operating with his fleet of battleships during daylight alone would be out of the question. If it is admitted that a battleship fleet cannot remain at sea without protection of numerous torpedo vessels, then it becomes of great importance to determine correctly the number of such torpedo vessels to be built, as well as the type and their tactical qualities. . . . [The latter] should be determined by a board of officers who had had experience in torpedo boats, not in the boats that have been constantly under repairs at the navy yards, but more particularly those officers who have served in boats which have run at high speeds without difficulty, and have been able to keep the sea and do the work which would be required of a vessel of this class during time of war. . . .

The President took these remarks seriously enough to order the Navy to convene a board, under Rear Admiral G. A. Converse, "to consider the types and qualities of torpedo vessels and their machinery"; Winslow was made a member. A measure of the urgency of this study is that the board was first ordered convened on 19 October 1904, yet it reported to the Secretary of the Navy on 7 January 1905.

This report can be read as the first full expression of what later became the standard U.S. Navy view of the function of destroyers:

Some type of vessel should be supplied that can protect the heavy fleet from attack by hostile torpedo vessels under all circumstances, and which shall at the same time be capable of attacking offensively with torpedoes as desired. . . . [She] would still be known as a "torpedo boat destroyer," although the Board is convinced that she must differ in certain essentials from the vessels now classed under that head . . . it is a *sine qua non* that she *must be able to accompany the armored fleet under all conditions*, and that in so doing she must constitute the least possible drawback on the mobility of that fleet. . . . A small vessel cannot hold high speed in an increasing sea as long as a large one, but the Board is of the opinion that in the past the destroyer type has had its power of accompanying the fleet and its general seakeeping power unduly sacrificed in an effort to attain a very high smooth water speed. The effort to make destroyers of a speed sufficient to overtake torpedo boats possessing the maximum speed of 30 knots or over in smooth water, in order that by their destruction the armored fleet may rest secure from their attacks, has, in the opinion of the Board, defeated itself in its major object by creating a type of destroyer in which the factor of safety in materiel has been so reduced as to seriously hamper the destroyers in their efforts to accompany the fleet on the open sea, and to greatly reduce the fleet's mobility by causing it to reduce its rate of progress to enable the destroyers to cruise in company. This either hampers the action of the armored fleet unduly, or causes the abandonment of the destroyers as accompanying auxiliaries, and thus deprives the armored ships of the very protection that the high speed of the destroyers was supposed to give . . . a proper destroyer should *first of all be capable of accompanying the armored fleet without distracting from its mobility in any except the worst weather . . . sea speed* and *seakeeping ability* should be the great considerations. Destroyers that can keep with the fleet and drive off torpedo boats by use of their superior batteries are evidently a better protection to the fleet, even though they cannot overtake 30 knot boats in smooth water, than are 32 knot smooth water destroyers that have to be dropped behind the fleet when it goes to sea. . . . The destroyer recommended by the Board would undoubtedly accomplish *under adverse sea conditions* (such as obtain even in the offing of a port) the overhauling and destruction of a torpedo boat, a duty which the present 30 to 32 knot destroyer would more likely fail to accomplish owing to her lesser power to present herself in serviceable condition at the time and place where such service must be rendered. . . .

. . . a reduction in maximum speed [is required. It] is composed of two parts, one apparent and really non-existent in service, and the other real. The conditions under which acceptance trial trips of these vessels have been conducted in the past are . . . misleading in the extreme. Such trials have been run in very light condition (for our destroyers from 450 to 500 tons total displacement), and after the vessels have been fitted out for service their displacement has been so largely increased as to make all trial trip reports utterly worthless . . . [since] our destroyers in service displace from 550 to 800 tons. Past trial trips have also been for short spurt runs (one to two hours) at the maximum speed, into which it is possible to introduce all sorts of jockeying methods looking to the attainment of a high nominal maximum speed, probably never again to be attained in service, and which gives no indication whatever of probable endurance in service of hull and machinery. . . . we cannot too soon substitute longer runs at less maximum speed, but of greater duration and made under

full service load. [Under such conditions] our present vessels would . . . fall far below the results attained on the original trials, and yet such results would be the maximum actually attainable in service. . . . Any further loss of speed resulting from the adoption of the principles enunciated in this report . . . would constitute a real sacrifice of speed to gain other valuable qualities, but the Board is of the opinion that such necessary real loss would be a very small proportion indeed of the total apparent loss as shown by trial under the new conditions laid down. . . .

The Board recommends that every torpedo boat destroyer shall possess the following qualities:

On her trial trip she should start under conditions of full service load for a sea trip of maximum endurance, and should run for a long run (suggested as not less than 48 hours) at such speed as would enable her to keep company with the battleship fleet in service . . . she should show her ability at the given speed to make, on her bunker capacity alone, such a prolonged trans-Atlantic or other sea voyage as she might be called upon to do in actual war service (3,000 miles at 15 knots is suggested). . . .

A second sea trial should then be made with the vessel full loaded for service and with sufficient coal in her bunkers to enable her to steam the required distance as determined in the preceding trial, and she should then steam for a long sea trial at what may be called her maximum high power long distance speed (24 hours at not less than 20 knots for any hour is suggested). . . .

A third sea trial should then be run at maximum speed under the full load conditions prescribed in the preceding paragraph (2 hours at not less than 23 knots is suggested). . . .

The vessel should have as small a tactical diameter as possible while maintaining good seagoing qualities; should steer easily when going astern; should have artificial ventilation of engine rooms to enable her to run with all hatches shut; her hull should be strong enough to steam as fast as a battleship in anything short of a real gale; she should be strong enough to be safe in any weather when not forced in a gale; should comfortably house her personnel; should be high enough forward to keep her from being swept too heavily in a head sea; and should be high enough all around to allow ventilation in a seaway. . . .

Her boilers should be four in number, in pairs, forward and abaft the engine rooms. Her engines should be in separate compartments. The forward boilers and forward engines should be capable of separation from the rest of the plant in every particular when running four boilers, thus giving two independent steam plants, the integrity of neither one of which is dependent upon the other. . . .

Her armament should consist of 3-inch rapid firing guns and 21-inch torpedoes and tubes, as many as possible of each to be carried (suggested as not less than four 3-inch guns and four torpedoes in two twin central pivot tubes). . . . Her battery should be so arranged as to give a maximum ahead and astern fire. . . .

Her displacement should be the minimum possible . . . but certainly not over 800 tons when in full load condition. . . .

Just how rapidly the contents of the Converse report were accepted by the Navy Department is unclear; as late as October 1905 the General Board was still proposing repeat *Truxtun*s or *Bainbridge*s, but at the time that body was only loosely concerned with the detailed characteristics of individual classes. It does appear that the Converse report was the subject of prolonged debate. Thus, although Congress authorized three destroyers in June 1906 (the first since 1898: the *Smith* class, DD 17–19), no circular for bidders was issued that fall. Only in October 1906, in its annual study of the proposed program for the next year (i.e., for 1907) did the General Board alter its destroyer description to "destroyers of the type recommended by the Torpedo Board of which Rear Admiral Converse was Senior Member." The four units recommended for 1907 were expected to cost $850,000 each, compared to $750,000 for a repeat *Truxtun* (1905 or 1906 program proposals).

The Board on Construction, which was responsible for warship design policy, reviewed the General Board's proposed program in November. It commented that in view of the state of engine development, there was little point in holding to a 23-knot trial speed at deep load. Twenty-six knots should be easy for a 28-knot destroyer, which is what C&R was then in the first stages of designing.

Congress authorized two more destroyers (DD 20–21) on 7 March 1907. The next day the design of all five new destroyers (DD 17–21) was approved at a Board on Construction meeting. It provided for either reciprocating (10,000 ihp) or turbine (Curtis: 9,000 shp) engines, which were expected to give 28 knots at normal load, 26 at deep load—over two knots beyond the Converse requirements. Bidders would be permitted to propose changes in machinery; the minutes of the meeting observe that "if builders can put in the same space machinery that will send the vessels 2 knots faster, that matter can be discussed at a later date."

In arrangement the new destroyer was a greatly enlarged *Bainbridge*. In accordance with the Converse Board, C&R made all the guns 3-inch: one on the forecastle, one on the fantail, two at the break of the forecastle, and one on the centerline just before the after deckhouse. In contrast to the gun battery, the torpedo armament was little improved over that of the earlier type: three single 18-inch tubes, two at the sides of the ship between the funnels and No. 4 gun, one aft between the deckhouse and No. 5 gun. The torpedo broadside was unaltered; in effect the tube on the unengaged side of the ship could be thought of as a reserve. It is possible that the major motive for mounting tubes this way was to avoid a centerline tube at a point at which the hull was beamy enough for an ejected torpedo to strike the deck. The after tube was located at a point at which the hull so narrowed that the tube projected over the side when trained abeam. This fear later proved a major factor in the reluctance to adopt centerline tubes. If in fact it was the reason for the configuration chosen, the primacy of the gun is even more evident; the torpedo battery had been held, in effect, to that of the *Bainbridge*.

An unusual feature was an enclosed stowage for one reload on deck near each tube. This relatively cumbersome system was soon replaced by twin tubes; by 1916 all five boats had their single tubes (and stowage) replaced by twin tubes, as in the later *Paulding* class.

Work on a new stern form to replace that of the *Bainbridge*s began at the Navy's model basin, then located at the Washington Navy Yard, in the fall of 1906. A French (Normand) form was tried, as well as some characteristic of the U.S. torpedo boat *Bailey* (TB 21) and of the destroyer *Truxtun* (DD 14); ultimately a new "V" form, developed at the Navy Yard, was adopted for this class as well as for all later ones through the "flush deckers." Its principal effect was

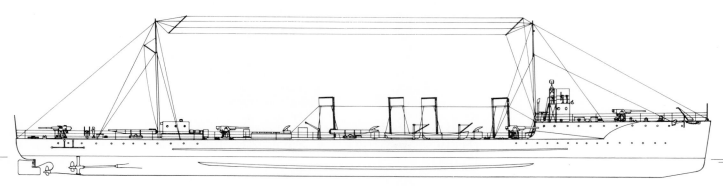

Smith DD 17   1910   293'10"   Funnels as heightened after initial trials

greatly to reduce handiness. For example, the USS *Drayton* (DD 23) turned in about 7.7 lengths (tactical diameter 860 yards) at 25 knots, compared to figures as low as 225 yards (2.75 lengths) for the 420-ton *Chauncey* at 26 knots. The poor turning abilities of modern U.S. destroyers were particularly evident when they operated with British types during World War I, and in 1920 the General Board demanded explanations. Preliminary Design concluded that "the largest factor in this inferiority is the shape of the transverse sections aft. . . . this shape not only interposes added resistance to the vessel's stern in sliding over the water, but also facilitates the water's piling over the top of the rudder, to such an extent as to decrease its efficiency. . . ."At that time it was estimated that modern U.S. destroyers had tactical diameters 40 to 50 percent larger than those of their British counterparts.

Bids were opened in September 1907. It turned out that although the *lowest* reciprocating engine bid had been for $710,000, the *highest* turbine bid was only $685,000.

> In view of the well-recognized fact that turbine machinery is specially adapted to the necessarily high speeds of revolution of propellers required for torpedo boats and torpedo boat destroyers the Board [on Construction] has no hesitancy in setting aside, without further consideration, all bids which involve the installation of reciprocating machinery. . . .

Some of the bidders proposed private designs, but the board "prefers adherence to its designs unless great benefit is proven otherwise." Thus, a very low bid by Bath Iron Works was rejected because of its hull form: it was expected to have poor seagoing qualities, experience showing the undesirability of a broad overhanging stern. Bath did get to build two C&R design destroyers, even though its bid was high, in view of its claim of a particularly light machinery installation. These were the *Flusser* (DD 20, the first to complete) and *Reid* (DD 21).

As in the case of the *Bainbridge*s and their half-sisters, the five ships varied in detail and could be distinguished by their funnel arrangement (i.e., the arrangement of their boilers). Therefore, two Cramp boats (DD 17–18) had their two amidships funnels closely paired; the *Preston* (New York Shipbuilding, DD 19) had hers equally spaced; and the two Bath boats had theirs paired fore and aft. All, however, had triple screws driven by Parsons turbines, the high-pressure unit on the center shaft, the two low-pressure turbines (and the cruising turbines) on the wing shafts. The *Smith* made 28.35 knots (9,946 shp) on trial at a displacement of 716 tons. The *Flusser*, the first to be completed, did even better: 11,541 shp, for 30.41 knots at 686 tons. Robinson commented that because of the ease with which turbines could be maintained at very high speed, "as soon as turbines were adopted, the trial requirements were immediately raised to four hours."

Turbines were thus a very natural improvement, but they brought with them two serious problems. Turbines were most efficient at high speeds, but propellers were far more efficient at low. A turbine directly connected to a propeller could not operate at optimum speed, and was particularly inefficient at (low) cruising speed—which was a point of partic-

The *Smith* was the first of the "flivvers," distinguishable by her two closely paired amidships funnels. In these ships the forward gun was mounted on the forecastle, and there was a full navigating bridge, including a protected chart table (visible projecting from the bridge proper). Skylights aft indicate the engine room.

The *Paulding*, shown here in dazzle camouflage at Queenstown in 1918, was an improved *Smith*; she and her sisters were the earliest U.S. destroyers to survive the mass scrappings of the early twenties, and she herself saw Coast Guard service against rum-runners, 1924–30.

The *Sterett*, built by Fore River, had three funnels rather than the four of her prototype, the two amidships ones being trunked together. She also had two, rather than three, shafts.

ular consequence to the U.S. Navy—thus the search for efficient means of powering destroyers at low speed, which in some cases (see below) led to the introduction of auxiliary reciprocating engines. Robinson credited the *Smith* with a cruising radius of 2,800 miles at 16 knots, almost certainly a figure derived from her trials performance. This required 304 tons of coal. The problem at high speed was absorption of very great power; the *Smith* ran her trials at 724 rpm, about twice the figure for modern types.

By this time the General Board's agitation for more destroyers was beginning to have some effect in Congress. On 4 May 1908 ten destroyers (*Paulding* class, DD 22–31) were authorized. They were improved versions of the *Smith* group, the most obvious change

being the replacement of single by twin tubes. A less obvious change was a great rise in power, to a nominal 12,000 shp: the *Paulding* made 32.8 knots (903 rpm) on 17,393 shp on her trials (711 tons). The nominal normal displacement rose to 742 tons.

A more suitable improvement, introduced while the ships were under construction, was oil fuel. Besides its well-known advantage of facilitating fueling at sea, oil eliminated the need to clear out ashes from boilers for higher power and also for greater fuel economy. Thus, Robinson credited the *Paulding* with a radius of 3,000 miles at 16 knots on less fuel (241 tons) than was used by the *Smith*.

The machinery arrangement followed that of the previous class, except that in four ships (two by Fore River, DD 26/27, and two by Cramp, DD 30/31) there

The *Jenkins* was the last of the flivvers, shown here in World War I camouflage, with splinter mattresses protecting her bridge. Note, too, the splinter shield on her forward 3-inch gun, a war modification. The most important wartime improvement, a heavy load of depth charges, is not visible. However, she does show the characteristic wartime assortment of life rafts.

were two, rather than three, turbines (Curtis in the Fore River boats, Zoelly in the Cramp boats). In these vessels, cruising stages were incorporated in the main turbine casings. Boiler installations, as in earlier classes, varied; in Cramp (DD 30/31), Fore River (DD 26/27), and Newport News (DD 24/25) boats the two amidships funnels were trunked together; the two by New York Shipbuilding (DD 28/29) had four funnels.

Twin tubes were adopted during the detail design period. They actually *saved* weight: a single torpedo tube weighed 7,460 pounds; a twin, 5,000—and the weight of the single did not include torpedo stowage.

Repeat ships were authorized in March 1909 (DD 32–36) and in June 1910 (DD 37–42). All but the *Walke* (DD 34) had triple screws; two Cramp (DD 36, 40), two Fore River (DD 34,39), and two Newport News (DD 32, 37) ships had three funnels. The remaining vessels (Bath and New York Shipbuilding) were four-pipers.

These twenty-six 700- and 742-ton destroyers were, ironically, called "flivvers," lightweights. They had been designed as especially robust protectors of the battle line in which torpedo power was deliberately limited, yet the next generation of destroyers went so much further in both directions that the "flivvers" came to be the ideal of the torpedo-attack men.

The General Board was responsible for that next step. Its practical and strategic games had convinced

it that the primary arm of the fleet was the heavy gun of its battle line, and that the most valid role of the destroyer was to protect that line, chiefly by gun-fire. The number of destroyers was to be determined mainly by the number of battleships to be guarded and by the state of torpedo technology, which latter would indicate the range at which guarding would have to be done. Thus, the 1903 long-range plan provided for one destroyer per battleship, but a 1907 revision provided for four: by that time torpedoes could already run 4,000 yards, and the end was not in sight.

This was still a very general kind of requirement. In 1909, however, the General Board was made responsible for the detailed characteristics of future warships, the Board on Construction being abolished. At first, faced with the necessity of laying out a large construction program and receiving a C&R request for guidance (12 January 1909), the General Board could only suggest repetition of the previous year's (*Paulding*) class.

This did not mean that the General Board had no new ideas. Rather, it took time for the board to produce entirely new characteristics. In answer to a C&R request for design guidance the next year (May 1910), the board once more suggested duplication of the *Paulding* type, especially "in view of the success attained by the *Flusser* class." That would cover the

FY 11 program; but for FY 12, "the General Board has under consideration . . . a destroyer of greater displacement, heavier armament, and greater steaming radius."

A memorandum of 22 June 1910 describes the General Board's views. Destroyers exist to protect the armored fleet from attack; hence

> they must be able to keep up with the fleet under all probable conditions of weather and distant cruising. That is to say, the steaming radius of the destroyers should be as nearly as possible that of the battleships. The necessary seaworthiness and habitability can be obtained only by the sacrifice of the excessive high speeds that of late years have characterized some foreign destroyers. . . . We can afford this sacrifice as the geographical position of our ports is far outside the steaming radius of destroyers of any other powers. . . .

More detailed characteristics followed. In view of the recent annual reports of Destroyers, Atlantic and Pacific, it should certainly be possible to achieve a radius of 4,000 miles at 15 knots (the *Flusser* attained 3,600); this requirement might well be met by the adoption of oil fuel. The new design should be able to make 30 knots for one hour, 25 for 24 hours. Proposed seakeeping features were to include a high bow for dryness, preferably a flaring type that would allow for more deck and berthing space; the hull would have a slight tumble home, and the propellers and rudder would be completely protected by the rounded stern. Bilge keels were to be as deep as possible. Another heavy-weather feature was a provision for towing disabled destroyers.

The board's preoccupation shows in the proposed armament: the same three twin tubes as in the flivvers, but one 4-inch or (preferably) 5-inch (long-recoil) gun to replace one of the 3-inch weapons. The 5-inch gun turned out to be impractical (in September, Ordnance claimed that a sufficiently rigid gun foundation was not possible), but the 4-inch proved more than practical. In the design C&R actually produced, 4-inch guns replaced *all* of the 3-inch guns of the flivvers.

C&R received the General Board characteristics of 22 June only on 13 September, after they had passed through the other bureaus. At that time the destroyer design was the fifth (later seventh) priority on the list; it attained overriding priority only the next February, when it was clear that destroyers would be part of the next naval bill. Between then and 7 March the preliminary design section of C&R prepared eight sketch schemes, the smallest of which they submitted to the General Board. This was essentially an enlarged (900-ton) flivver in which 4-inch guns replaced the former 3-inch but the torpedo battery remained the same. In presenting its design C&R

commented that several of the General Board features merely followed current practice, e.g, the hull form.

Congress authorized eight new destroyers on 4 March 1911 (the *Cassin* class, DD 43–50) and on 18 March the General Board approved the C&R design with the caveat that trials should be run at a realistic load: full ammunition, two-thirds fuel and reserve feed water. This was reminiscent of the strictures of the Converse Board; C&R assured the General Board that no change would be needed to enable the new destroyer to make its 29 knots with the newly specified load.

It is necessary to keep in mind that all of this development occurred before very many flivvers had entered service; the *Flusser* was commissioned only on 28 October 1909, and the last of her class only on 10 February 1910. Defects in the general arrangement of the flivvers thus came to light only after all of them had been authorized, and all but the last few laid down. In particular, the stern tube turned out to be a mistake. An 8 May 1911 C&R memo noted that "recent developments in the firing of torpedoes from vessels of the *Flusser* class have demonstrated the fact that torpedoes fired from the present after tubes at the standard speeds of torpedo boats of much above twenty knots are unreliable in direction and depth, owing to the action of the stern wave [on them]." Not much could be done with the *Flusser*s, but the Chief Constructor suggested that the after tubes be interchanged with the No. 4 gun in the new (and longer) *Cassin*s. This change was deemed satisfactory by Ordnance and was adopted in May 1911.

The General Board was sufficiently satisfied with this design to make it the basis for Destroyer 1913 (characteristics issued 6 June 1911). However, many in the fleet considered the move to nearly a thousand tons, which had brought only an increase in gun power, ill-advised. They could cite a War College study (1912) that indicated the torpedo as virtually the *only* useful destroyer weapon; indeed, the War College suggested the extraordinary battery of three triple tubes on the broadside as well as reloads. The fleet tended to agree: of 47 senior officers polled, 26 agreed outright, 8 were in general agreement, 7 had no view, and only 6 disagreed. It was no great surprise that the torpedo squadron felt very strongly: 15 of 17 officers polled agreed with the War College, and the other 2 presented no opinion.

The General Board regarded those views as quite beside the point. There was no question but that the torpedo squadron wanted to think of its boats as offensive weapons, but the board had to think of the *fleet* as the offensive weapon—and it considered the battleship gun considerably more effective than the destroyer torpedo. It was willing to allow for some

The *Downes* was one of the first "thousand tonners"; she is shown about 1919, newly returned to peacetime status, but retaining the wartime angled bridge front with its windows above (for North Atlantic operations) and the life raft support framework aft.

increase in torpedo power, but not at any great expense in gun power or in seakeeping qualities.

Ordnance was responsible for the compromise adopted. On 16 May 1912 its chief suggested that extra torpedo power come from the addition of two tubes and the adoption of the new 21-inch torpedo; he advised against any provision for reloads. This would add about 5 tons of top weight, which could be balanced by the elimination of one of the two after guns, for a reduction to four. That, in turn, would be acceptable, given the batteries of existing foreign (particularly Japanese) destroyers. A pair of twin tubes at each side in place of the originally contemplated centerline mount would also answer the objections of the destroyer operators to the latter. The General Board proposed these changes for the forthcoming DD 51 class (authorized 20 August: the *O'Brien* class, DD 51–56, was authorized 4 March 1913).

The "thousand tonners" differed from the original C&R plan in machinery as well as in battery. As early as September 1911 Cramps proposed twin- rather than triple-screw machinery, with reciprocating engines for cruising. This required a new stern form, and in fact the first of the Cramps ships, the *Aylwin*, did not make her design speed on trial. The USS *Wadsworth* (DD 60) was the first American destroyer to have her main turbines geared to the propeller

shafts. On trial she made only 30.7 knots at 16,100 shp (1,050 tons), but 326 tons of oil sufficed to drive her 5,640 nm. at 16 knots. The effect of single reduction gearing was a propeller speed of only 460 rpm, which approached the low (and efficient) value realized in the *Bainbridge*. The *Wadsworth* was a test bed and as such had little effect on destroyer design until after she ran trials in July 1915. Similar test beds were provided by the flivvers *Mayrant* and *Henley*, which were re-engined in 1915 with 13,000 shp Westinghouse geared turbines.

The *Wadsworth* did not have separate cruising engines, but all of the remaining "thousand tonners" through DD 68 did. Four units (DD 43, 44, 54, 56) each had a reciprocating engine that could be clutched to one shaft for cruising below 15 knots; eight others (DD 57, 58, 59, 61, 62, 66–68) incorporated a single cruising turbine geared to one shaft. The remaining ships were more symmetrical, with a pair of reciprocating engines in the *Aylwin*s (DD 45–53) and a pair of cruising turbines in the USS *Cushing* (DD 55).

The thousand tonners were by no means the end of the General Board's quest for more powerful (and more scout-like) destroyers. The board began to consider the FY 14 program (i.e., the authorization Act of March 1913, which ultimately produced the *Tuckers* in the early fall of 1912. In September it asked

Smoke was always a problem in destroyer design, as the short-funneled *McDougal* shows. Her near-sister *Nicholson* shows taller funnels, as well as the later, less drafty, bridge; she also carries her boats high aft, as in later U.S. destroyers. The *McDougal* served in the Coast Guard rum-runner patrol, 1924–33, as *CG 6*.

C&R to sketch a very powerful type with six twin 21-inch torpedo tubes, four 4-inch guns, and 20 floating mines, to be carried at 35 knots. The steaming radius was to be 2,500 nm. at 20 knots. The result was a striking demonstration of the advances naval technology would make in the next five years. (In 1917 destroyers quite fulfilling this specification, yet displacing only 1,100 tons, would be laid down.) In 1912 C&R proposed a 385-foot, 2,160-ton super-destroyer requiring 40,000 shp (3 shafts) to make her designed speed. A drawing of 15 October 1912 shows an enlarged thousand tonner with an extra funnel (on the lengthened forecastle) and the extra pair of torpedo tubes on the fantail. A comparison sheet showed a cost of $1.9 million for hull and machinery alone ($760,000 for DD 51–56). Even the British *Swift*, then the largest torpedo craft in the world (1,800 tons, 36 knots) would be dwarfed. In a covering letter, the Chief Constructor drew attention to

> the enormous increase in size and cost of a vessel of the suggested type over the destroyers heretofore built for the U.S. Navy, which have proved so satisfactory. . . . Attention is also invited to the general similarity of the result to HMS *Swift*. The U.S. destroyer indicated in the sketch is bigger than the *Swift*, because of her greater radius and greater battery. The British have not repeated the *Swift* . . . if such destroyers are deemed necessary in the near future, before undertaking the general construction of a considerable number of such vessels, one or two should be constructed and tried, and in the meantime, destroyers generally similar to the type of Nos. 51 to 56 should be adhered to. . . . In the bureau's opinion such a vessel . . . should properly be classed otherwise than as a destroyer. . . .

The board, however, persisted. Knowing that a variety of alternative characteristics were in preparation, the Chief Constructor wrote (6 November) that

> in view of the inclusion of destroyers in the Department's program of construction, it is important that this matter be settled at once . . . some information as to the actual performance of the eight 1,000-ton destroyers Nos. 43 to 50 should be had before going into the subject of larger vessels. A destroyer that gets too large loses many of the desirable features of the type. . . .

The board tried to reduce the size of the new destroyer by asking (8 November) for a DD 51 with only the armament changed: (a) four 4-inch, six twin tubes; (b) four 4-inch, four twin tubes; (c) three 4-inch *on the centerline*, six twin tubes; or (d) three 4-inch on the centerline, four twin tubes. C&R's reply convinced the board that only (b) was practical on the dimensions that it had in mind. The board therefore proposed that C & R (27 November) plan for a 29.5-knot (four-hour trial with two-thirds fuel, stores,

feed water) destroyer with a steaming radius of 2,500 miles at 20 knots. The battery was to include for the first time, "two aeroplane guns, if they can be developed and installed." Another new armament feature was a provision to lay 36 floating mines. It would be poor policy to waste destroyers as minelayers, "but in the absence of specially constructed vessels of high speed, the Board believes they should be fitted therefore." The bow was to be strengthened for ramming enemy *destroyers*.

The Secretary of the Navy approved these characteristics, which became the *Tucker* class, on 2 December 1912, and C&R very quickly produced a sketch plan to match. In endorsing the result (29 January 1913) the board noted the importance of steaming radius and invited attention to the wide disparity among nominally comparable ships. The report of the Commander, Torpedo Flotilla, Atlantic Fleet, showed for the DD 22–36 group a radius at economical speed varying from 2,424 nm. (the *Perkins*) to 3,919 nm. (the *Patterson*), and at 20 knots from 1,470 to 2,668 nm. in the same two ships.

> In view of this great variation in endurance of the destroyers already built, and of the military necessity of the destroyers being able to attain the requirements laid down by the Board in the matter of steaming radius, it is recommended that in the circular [for bidders] there be a clause inserted requiring guarantees.

Meanwhile BuOrd developed a triple torpedo tube comparable in weight (8,600 vs. 6,400 lbs. empty) to the twin type. In effect, 50 percent more 2,800-lb. torpedoes could be had on 40 percent more weight. The new tubes were first incorporated in characteristics for Destroyer 1916 (prepared December 1913), but they were mounted for the first time in Destroyer 1915 (FY 15), the class authorized 30 June 1914 (*Sampson* class, DD 63–68, essentially repeat *Tucker*s). These ships were completed with two 1-pounder pompoms, the first examples of the antiaircraft guns specified for Destroyer 1914.

The thousand tonners were extremely large by contemporary European standards, but on the other hand they were expected to operate under more rigorous conditions. For example, in May 1914 then Lieutenant H. R. Stark, later Chief of BuOrd and Chief of Naval Operations, interviewed officers of the cruiser HMS *Suffolk* in Mexican waters:

> Except for their grand maneuvers, covering a period of about three weeks a year, their destroyers consider fifteen knots the very outside speed for cruising performances, and normally cruise at ten or twelve knots. The entire wardroom looked aghast when I told them we normally cruised at twenty knots, and they stated that any destroyer captain in the British service who made any cruise at twenty knots would probably

The *Davis*, shown here soon after completion at Hampton Roads in December 1916, was an example of the *Sampson* class, the culmination of "thousand tonner" design, with the first antiaircraft gun (a 1-pounder just forward of the bridge) in any American destroyer class. Also visible are her triple torpedo tubes, another innovation.

immediately lose his command, or in any case would have to explain such unwarranted conduct very fully and carefully. The reason they gave for their slow cruising speed was their inability to get oil, as well as the high speed in cruising, for their destroyers. Moreover, they informed me they never made a full power run; 90 percent full power being as high as they are ever permitted to drive their destroyers . . . their new thousand-ton destroyers carry only two hundred tons of oil. . . . Except for their three weeks maneuvers, they run on about 70 percent of their complement, and only during their extensive maneuvers are they given a full complement. One officer who had been in the destroyer service for some time stated that the two longest cruises he had ever taken or that he knew about, or that were normally made in the British Service, were between England and Gibraltar and Gibraltar and Malta. . . .

The Bureau of Steam Engineering observed

. . . the marked difference in method of operation of these frail craft in the British Navy and in ours. The British method seems to be based on the belief that

material should be kept in the best condition possible, and that in order to assure this the vessels should be run only at moderate speed. . . . Our method goes to the other extreme of running everything to destruction, with the result that our Destroyers are habitually undergoing repairs. . . .

In fact the U.S. Navy ran its destroyers hard because they had to carry out such nondestroyer functions as long-range scouting; the Commander of Torpedo Flotilla, Atlantic Fleet commented that

. . . The value of destroyers depends largely upon the reliable speed they are capable of maintaining upon demand . . . to ensure the highest degree of efficient maintenance, upkeep and operation, it is essential that high speed work be frequent. . . .

The game board maneuvers and chart maneuvers of the Naval War College and the Flotilla, and the actual maneuvers with the battle fleet, demonstrate that in order to be effective in war the personnel of destroyers must be trained to maintain relatively high speed [about 20 knots] continuously during extended

The *Allen* was the sole "thousand tonner" to survive long enough to see World War II service. Operating out of Pearl Harbor, she had two of her four triple torpedo tubes removed, replaced by depth-charge projectors and 20-mm. guns, a total of six such weapons being carried. An open bridge was built atop her pilothouse, and she received considerable splinter shielding. The *Allen* is shown after the end of World War II, awaiting disposal. She retains her torpedo tubes, and the shield and mount of her forward 4-inch gun; the gun proper has been removed.

scouting and searching operation. . . . This important training cannot be obtained if a low cruising speed (which Steam Engineering advocated to preserve machinery) is established. . . .

From a design point of view, such operations translated into a need for considerable size, since high sustained sea speed required a large hull with considerable freeboard.

The General Board regarded the thousand tonners as a reasonable balance between offense and defense; the destroyer operators felt otherwise. In connection with the proposed 1915 program, they wanted a reversion to the flivvers. This was in large part a reflection of their own assessment of defensive vs. offensive values in destroyers; evidently they strongly favored the latter. This attitude shows in the poor state of their gunnery. On this basis, the smaller the boat, the less target it presented—the flivver, modified to take a bigger torpedo, was a distinctly better proposition. The operators seem to have felt that they

would have just one shot at an enemy battle line. The payoff would be in the maximum salvo, i.e., in centerline tubes. As for seaworthiness, by 1914 experience seemed to show that the 750-tonners were better off than their successors; and as for range, the boats could always be towed. After all, one need not find towing alarming if the only use of the boats was to be offensive, and at one's own discretion.

The argument in favor of smaller destroyers was sufficiently pervasive for C&R to work out (November 1914) a sketch plan for a 775-ton destroyer armed with three 3-inch guns (two abreast on the forecastle, one on a deckhouse aft) and three triple torpedo tubes on the centerline. It was expected to achieve a speed of 29.5 knots and a radius of action of 2,250 miles at 20 knots, figures comparable with those for the thousand tonners (29.5 knots, 2,500 nm. at 20 knots). However, it would be impossible to mount the 4-inch gun. Within the fleet, the small-destroyer argument received the support even of the Commander in Chief Atlantic Fleet. It was taken seriously enough for Bath

Iron Works to write the Chief Constructor (14 September 1914) that "in view of the probable reversion to 700-ton destroyers in next year's program" it would like to propose a new and lighter machinery installation.

Only the General Board disagreed with this offensively oriented change. It absolutely disagreed with any reduction in the caliber of destroyer guns—and with any reduction in the total number of torpedoes carried, which would reduce to zero the offensive value of the destroyer after a single salvo. The possibility of carrying reloads was touched on only briefly, but in later development it was constantly raised in connection with centerline vs. wing torpedo-tube arrangements.

An incidental point worth noting is that the destroyer operators seem on the whole to have been unaware of the very serious *technical* problems associated with centerline tubes, which would almost certainly have doomed their proposed design. Apparently BuOrd experiments conducted in 1914-15 were supposed to have closed this question; but it is not clear why *all* other navies were perfectly happy with their centerline tubes.

It appears that the flivver operators, for all their aggressiveness, did not expect their boats to survive the first attack on an enemy line. Best to get off all their torpedoes before they sank or were stopped dead in the water. Where a destroyer man might see a flimsy boat, however, the General Board saw a substantial warship of a thousand tons or more. It also saw the failure of 10 or 15 years of desperate effort to produce a workable torpedo defense for its own line, a failure so marked that the Bureau of Ordnance proposed the elimination of all battleship torpedo defense guns in favor of passive protection. Hence the destroyers would quite probably survive to strike again. Moreover, the General Board often pointed out, there was no gain to be had in doubling the torpedo salvo if the original salvo would quite do the job.

A major factor that the destroyer operators did not want to admit was that their ships required features that had little to do with the stated destroyer mission. Congress had consistently failed to provide the fleet with modern cruisers, so that in 1914 the United States was in the unusual position of possessing an extremely powerful battle line supported primarily by a mass of large destroyers. Some kind of scouting arm was required if the battle line were ever to succeed in engaging enemy forces; by default, the scouts had to be the big destroyers. In that case seakeeping and range, not battery, would be the most vital quality of all; and both meant size.

In fact, even a realistic use of destroyers had to mean considerable size. Thus Captain W.S. Sims,

then Commander, Atlantic Torpedo Flotilla (October 1915):

When the flotilla made its first report recommending a reversion to smaller boats the importance of radius of action was not as completely realized as it now is . . . we based our conclusions upon the radius of action that would be necessary for destroyers if used only as they should be used; and we did not fully consider that in warfare there may be many occasions upon which it will be imperative to use a flotilla as it should not be used, if it is not possible to avoid it.

Since early 1914 the flotilla has carried out a number of operations with and against the battleship fleet. In many, if not all, the restrictions in the radius of action of the small boats, as compared with that of the thousand-tonners, has been very apparent.

To consider but a single example in the department's Strategical Problem No. 2, all of the 750-ton boats were nearly at the end of their oil supply when the problem was called off, whereas the thousand-ton boats finished with about 40 percent of their oil remaining. The *Wadsworth* had 50 percent. In this problem the destroyers scouted at speeds varying between 15 and 30 knots, and covered about 2,000 miles. The conditions of the problem did not require as much steaming as would almost inevitably be required in actual warfare, where the position of the enemy (from which the problem started) would probably not be ascertained as conveniently near our coast as in the problem in question.

It should be noted that the larger boats carry very much longer masts that are placed at a greater distance from each other than in the smaller boats. The result . . . is that they have a reliable radio radius of about 300 miles, which is double that of the smaller boats. . . .

. . . it is apparent to me that a certain sum of money expended for [the DD 69 type, 1,125 tons] will provide a much greater destructive force (against an enemy's *fleet*) than the same sum of money expended for boats of less displacement.

It may be that when our navy is built up and provided with the proper number of scouts, destroyers will not be called upon to do scouting duty, and therefore will not require as great a radius of action as the 1,125 ton boats. Even in that unlikely case destroyers may be called upon . . . to steam very considerable distances at the highest practicable speed in order to reach, search for and attack an enemy whose position has been reported by the scouts. Instances of this kind have been of frequent occurrence in chart maneuvers where the Atlantic Fleet had been assigned the task of preventing an enemy from establishing an advance base in the Caribbean area. . . .

This was the General Board view—and the General Board had, after all, been in the war-game business for a long time. It had a realistic idea of fleet operations; the destroyers were only beginning to form one when the Fleet Problems were instituted.

It may seem strange that the fleet took until 1914 to become incensed with a class the first units of which had been authorized as early as 1911. However, these ships did not enter service until the summer of 1913, when the General Board was already at work on the characteristics for Destroyer 1916. Only after some experience had been accumulated could the destroyer commanders conclude that the thousand tonner was a distinct dud, and by that time they could have little effect on the design of 32 of that type (DD 37–68).

As of December 1913, the characteristics for Destroyer 1916 duplicated those of previous classes except for the provision of triple torpedo tubes and "aeroplane guns if they can be developed." However, the Bureau of Construction and Repair (C&R) suggested that a better ship could be had by the adoption of a flush deck. The two waist guns were moved onto platforms amidships, with the galley beneath them, and a bulwark fitted between galley and bridge structure. Another habitability feature was the substitution of a chart house for the searchlight platform formerly provided. This was the origin of the famous "flush decker." An interesting feature of this (May 1915) design was a ram bow "primarily for ramming submarines"; there were AA guns, but as yet depth charges did not exist. This was a fleet destroyer de-

signed primarily for surface torpedo warfare. In performance it duplicated the previous class except that Congress specified a rise in speed by half a knot, to 30 knots.*

The destroyer operators wanted more speed for their final attack, and for escape from enemy battle cruisers. Otherwise they found the design generally acceptable, since they had been denied their preferred small attack-oriented type: "the flotilla wishes to renew its recommendations that it is best to have a large number of destroyers, and is willing to make a reasonable sacrifice of battery and other qualities except speed. . . ."

The hull form of the new type was intended specifically to reduce rolling and pitching; indeed, the design history suggests that this consideration was the basis of the design. The mechanism chosen was a hull of slightly greater beam and increased midship coefficient. This form in turn required a shallower draft than in previous classes, if high speed were to be maintained without undue increase in power. Had C&R retained a conventional forecastle hull, the shallower draft would have translated as a shallow hull girder and thus an unacceptably weak hull. Hence the need for a stronger, flush-decked hull—

*The change from 29.5 knots does not appear to have been intentional, but rather a casual error in the drafting of the authorization.

The *Stockton* was one of six FY 16 destroyers, in effect the prototypes of the massive "flush-decker" program of World War I. She, the *Gwin*, and the *Connor* were unique in adhering to the original sketch design, which showed three rather than four funnels (and three rather than two screws). Note, too, the open lattice work under her waist 4-inch guns, which in later ships was filled in.

The six prototypes differed from their near-sister "flush deckers" in power, speed (30 rather than 35 knots), and in hull form aft; they had the cutaway sterns of the earlier American destroyers, rather than the raked sterns of the later ships. Here the prototype *Manley*, the first flush decker to be completed, and the mass-production *Fairfax* are compared, some time between wars.

The *Sampson*, shown soon after completion, was a "thousand tonner." Note her short funnels, later lengthened, and the very tall masts adopted to achieve long radio range, a prerequisite for the scout role such ships often had to fill. The horizontal bars strung between her masts are spreaders for the "flat top" radio antenna.

which was heavier than the previous type, although hull scantlings were the same as in previous classes. The deck sloped, its height being set forward and aft by the previously accepted fore-and-aft freeboards. However, the lack of a forecastle made the new type quite wet in a seaway. Shallow draft had another consequence: inadequate submergence of the propellers. It was necessary, then, to provide a drag, i.e., a sloping keel. In the end the ship was somewhat heavier than the last of the thousand tonners, but it was expected to be far steadier.

At first a twin-screw plant similar to that of the thousand tonners was contemplated, but in June 1915 Steam Engineering suggested that three screws would be more economical. The center shaft was to be driven by the high-pressure main turbine, clutched to a geared cruising turbine. Above decks there were to be three funnels, the two inner smokepipes being merged.

According to the design history, "difficulties arose in interferences due to the smoke stacks, which involved the movement of the torpedo tubes and deck structures considerably aft, thereby making the after deck house less in extent than we had hoped to have it. This restriction . . . resulted in entirely squeezing out the radio room and after consultation with various officers it was decided that it would be both practicable and desirable to have the radio room forward, instead of aft, as is the custom. . . ."

Six ships authorized 3 March 1915 became the *Caldwell* class (DD 69–74). They differed considerably in machinery arrangement, only the Cramp-built *Conner* and *Stockton* (DD 72 and 73) following the original C&R plans. The other four had twin screws; the *Caldwell* (DD 69) had GE-built Curtis geared turbines with separate cruising turbines linked to them by "elecric speed reducing gear," whereas her three half-sisters had Parsons geared turbines.

Appearances also differed. The two Cramp units and the Seattle-built *Gwin* (DD 71) had the three funnels of the C&R design, but the other three units had the four separate funnels of the later vast class of mass-produced "flush deckers," and indeed in arrangement were the prototypes of that series. All six ships, however, had cutaway sterns, rather than the raked cruiser sterns of the mass-production run.

The characteristics called for two (1-pounder) AA guns, one between the bridge and No. 1 4-inch gun, the other atop the deckhouse aft. During World War I the 1-pounders were replaced by 3-in./23 guns. A typical war modification replaced both the AA gun and the searchlight aft with a Y-gun (depth-charge mortar). DD 70 and 71 were completed with this weapon.

3

The Mass-Production Destroyer, 1917–1922

World War I introduced an entirely new feature to American destroyer design, a sudden need for very large numbers of ships. The problem is a recurrent one, and the dilemma is always the same: should the Navy continue to build the sophisticated prewar designs, or should it choose instead a specialized (and necessarily austere) mass-production ("mobilization") type? The solutions adopted in two world wars were quite different. In 1917 an existing design, intended for fleet work rather than for the ASW war (which had actually prompted the expansion in construction) was kept in production, for fear that any radical change would cause considerable disruption. In 1941, on the other hand, production of conventional destroyers was combined with a large program of specialized destroyer escorts. In both cases one of the major bottlenecks was turbine reduction gearing. In both cases, too, the flood of ships produced (in many cases, too late) for one war dominated the postwar period, to the extent that few new ships would be authorized to reflect the lessons of the war or, for that matter, the very different conditions it had created for the postwar fleet. Indeed, mass production was possible only because of a conscious decision to freeze the design process at a prewar stage. Such practice contrasts with the British example, in which there was enough independent design expertise in the large private firms to permit considerable evolution even in wartime without drastic loss of production. British practice progressed from types smaller and probably inferior to the U.S. thousand tonner of 1912 to the "V & W" of 1916, which set the international pattern for destroy-

ers in the postwar period, and which was clearly superior to the "flush deckers" that U.S. yards continued to turn out even after the U.S. Navy was well aware of the character of the British design.

The mass-production flush decker was a modified version of Destroyer 1916, the *Caldwell* class. The first units were authorized as part of the same massive FY 17 program that included 35-knot battle cruisers (two of which were completed as the carriers *Lexington* and *Saratoga*) and scout cruisers (*Omaha* class). Thus, the destroyers of this program, which would combine tactically with the new ships, had the same design speed. Higher speed had been sought by the destroyer operators for some time. It was estimated that the last five knots would cost nearly 50 percent more power, which would be bought in part by 90 to 100 tons more machinery and in part by the introduction of reduction gearing. The hull form was modified for greater efficiency: it combined a level keel (no drag) with more nearly horizontal shafting. The freeboard amidships was determined by the requirement that the midships modulus (for strength) remain the same. In view of the considerable hull strength of the *Caldwell* class, no increase in scantlings was required to balance the heavier machinery.

The 1916 act authorized 50 destroyers (DD 75–124) of which 20 were to be built at once, i.e., under the FY 17 program (DD 75–94). Four of the 20 were to be built on the Pacific coast, provided that did not involve excessive expense. Another 15 (DD 95–109) were provided explicitly under the Act of 3 March 1917, which also created a Naval Emergency Fund

The flush decker *Broome* displays a typical World War II escort configuration, six 3-inch/50 dual-purpose guns replacing her quartet of 4-inch surface-only weapons and her two after torpedo tubes. Note, too, the addition of splinter shields, and the fore-and-aft openings in the shield of No. 1 gun: the cigar-shaped radar on her foremast is an SE, a microwave set specially designed for flush deckers.

The newly completed flush-deck destroyer *Fairfax* is shown off Mare Island in camouflage, May 1918. At this time she had no Y-gun, her depth-charge battery being limited to stern tracks; nor does she show a second antiaircraft gun right aft.

for "such additional Torpedo Boat Destroyers . . . as the President may direct." By late May, contracts through DD 135 had been issued, for a total of 61 units.

That was only the beginning. The General Board urgently recommended massive increases in destroyer production, since "the Destroyer is, so far as now can be seen the best form of Submarine Chaser. It is not known what the future development of the Submarine may be, but there is no doubt that it will be greatly increased in size and power. Submarines of 2,400-tons displacement and carrying a battery of three 5.9-inch guns are reliably reported as built and building abroad. . . . The General Board further recommends that high speed Destroyer construction with full torpedo armament be continued, to provide Destroyers for and with the fleet where the higher speed is desirable."

The implicit reference to a slower destroyer more suited to mass production was to some extent a reaction to a Newport News proposal to build hulls identical to the fleet boats, but with half the power. A special Board on the Submarine Menace proposed a program of 200 austere destroyers. The compromise solution was a program for 200 new ships, 50 of which were to duplicate the previous units: DD 136–335. The final run of 12 units (DD 336–347) was ordered in 1918, part of an additional program that included DD 348–359, ships ultimately built to very different designs in the 1930s. Of the 273 destroyers in the wartime programs, only 6 (DD 200–205) were canceled; the rest survived to dominate the U.S. destroyer force for almost two decades.

There were two basic detail designs, one by Bath (who built the lead ship, the USS *Wickes*), and one

by Bethlehem Steel for the two Bethlehem yards, Quincy (Fore River, Massachusetts) and San Francisco (formerly the Union Iron Works, the name changing during the war). The Bath design incorporated Parsons or, in a few cases, Westinghouse turbines and Normand, Thornycroft, or White-Foster boilers. Bethlehem chose Curtis turbines and, in many cases, Yarrow boilers. The latter deteriorated in service, so that in 1929 it was announced that rather than accept the expense of reboilering them, the Navy would strike and scrap all 60 Yarrow-boilered destroyers, which had been in continuous service since their completion. At that time there were only 103 flush deckers in commission, the Yarrow units reflecting the proportion of the program undertaken by Bethlehem. All non-Bethlehem yards, including the Navy Yards (Charleston, Mare Island, and Norfolk), worked to the Bath design for what was known unofficially as the "Liberty" type.

The program was a considerable industrial achievement. In April 1917 the Secretary of the Navy queried the six private destroyer builders (Bath, Cramps, New York Shipbuilding at Camden, Newport News, and the two Bethlehem yards) as to their capacity for additional work beyond DD 109. Bath, with four under construction, felt that it could build no more until 1919. Union Iron Works was unsure of its capacity and could not guarantee deliveries until that time. The other four considered six ships each the maximum practicable order, given normal pricing practice and priorities. All felt constrained by limited gear-cutting capacity, to the extent that the next January the Bureau of Steam Engineering seriously considered ordering new gear-cutting machinery in Britain, or else ordering finished gearing there. Existing merchant ship orders were a major bottleneck. In addition, New York shipbuilding had contracts for three battleships and one battle cruiser. Newport News had three battleships and two battle cruisers. Quincy had one battle cruiser and two scout cruisers, and Cramp had five scout cruisers under contract. All were suspended in favor of destroyer construction. This does not include two battleships, which although authorized and contracted for, were not laid down until after the war.

The initial programs for DD 75–109 were concentrated in Bath (DD 75–78) and Bethlehem Steel (Quincy and San Francisco: DD 79–92, 95–109), with two awarded to the Mare Island Navy Yard, which had previously built two destroyers (DD 68 and 69, the latter the first flush decker). For the next increment, six each were awarded to the three yards that had not yet entered the program (Cramp, Newport News, and New York Shipbuilding) and repeat orders went to Bethlehem San Francisco (DD 110–112) and Bath (DD 131–134). A single ship was ordered from the Charleston Navy Yard (DD 135), which built no more. Then, in July 1917 the bureaus sent a joint telegram to the six destroyer firms: "Department has decided to place orders for about fifty additional destroyers, duplicates of those now building, for completion within 18 months."

By this time Bath, a small yard, had no excess capacity left. Instead, six were ordered from Mare Island (DD 136–141), the others going to the five private builders. Meanwhile the department pondered plans for a mass-production design, which would become DD 186–335. As part of the latter program, Bethlehem built a Naval Destroyer Plant at Squantum, Massachusetts, with ten slips for simultaneous construction. It is difficult, however, to escape the conclusion that with the suspension of capital ship and cruiser construction the established firms did not have much greater capacity. Squantum ultimately built 35 ships (DD 261–295), which compares to totals of 66 at San Francisco, 46 at Cramps, and 36 at Quincy. Bath returned to the program for the final burst of 12, together with Mare Island and a newcomer, Norfolk Navy Yard. Newport News built a total of 25 units, 6 more being canceled. Early Newport News units (DD 119–124, 181–185) were unique in being propelled by paired Curtis direct-drive (i.e., nongeared) turbines.

Like other U.S. armaments programs of World War I, this one accelerated relatively slowly; only 39 ships were commissioned as of the Armistice, and many keels were not even laid until much later. The last three ships (DD 339–341 at Mare Island) were not completed until 1922, having been laid down in 1920. Yards differed considerably in their performance. For example, Mare Island was able to commission the

USS *Ward* only 70 days after she was laid down, 15 May 1918. Wartime building times of eight to ten months were more common; probably the longest was Charleston's *Tillman* (DD 135), laid down 29 July 1918 and not completed until 30 April 1920. Bethlehem built the greatest number, including the bulk of the second (*Clemson*) series—the first of which was the USS *Delphy* (DD 261, commissioned 30 November 1918, built at Squantum). The builders' gloomy forecasts of 1917 proved correct in that very little of the program beyond about DD 145 was completed during 1918. For example, Bath did not complete the first of its second series (DD 131–134) until 20 January 1919—as had been forecast.

Workmanship, and thus performance, varied considerably from yard to yard. This was evident in their trial speeds, but was particularly noticeable in the matter of steaming endurance, which was crucial in wartime convoy operations. The General Board demanded 35 knots on trial at about 1,150 tons, and a steaming endurance of 2,500 nm. at 20 knots; the contracts actually called for about 3,600 at 15. A Navy Department (Materiel Division) memorandum of September 1918 observed that on trials the *Wickes* showed fuel consumption equivalent to about 5,000 nm. at 15 knots, or 3,400 at 20; "in fact she exceeded contract requirements at all speeds on trial. After commissioning at a displacement of 1,300 tons on one trial when running at 20 knots, the results showed 3,178 miles. The Cramp boats built under the same requirements, with the same machinery design, showed excellent results on their trials, considerably exceeding their contract requirements, although not to such an extent as the Bath boats." Typical results showed 3,990 nm. at 15 knots, 3,148 at 20. Results at Quincy were more depressing; although the USS *Bell* on trial showed a radius of about 4,000 nm. at 15 knots, her commanding officer indicated that in service she would be good for no more than 3,400 at an economical speed of between 13 and 15 knots; her sisters were worse, so that the *Stribling* reported 2,300 nm., and the *Gregory*, 2,400. "So far the Mare Island destroyers are very disappointing in radius. Their design is the same as the Cramp and Bath, yet their radius is little more than half that of the Bath boats."

Indeed, the Bath design was so effective that, of the original *Wickes* class, the 107 units built to it were styled "Long Radius Boats," although in many cases poor workmanship appears to have ruined this performance. New York Shipbuilding, for example, could not match Cramp. Newport News used geared cruising turbines to try for 3,500 nm. at 15 knots. However, a shortage of gearing made this impossible in the first units built. In the fall of 1918, before any had been delivered with the cruising turbines, it appeared that "as far as radius is concerned, they now appear more promising than some of the geared boats we are now operating." The ultimate solution to the radius problem was more fuel, 35 percent more in the *Clemson* (DD 186) class, so that even the worst of that class would equal the best of the *Wickes* group.

Aside from fuel capacity, the *Clemsons* were nearly duplicates of the *Wickes* class. That was hardly the original intention. In July 1917, the special ASW Board called for construction of 200 destroyers armed as in the fleet type but fitted to use mines and depth charges, and to be good for 4,000 nm. at 15 knots, i.e., for an Atlantic crossing. Special emphasis was placed on seaworthiness and reliability, and on suitability for mass production. A speed of 28 knots was asked, but the "Department will accept reduction in full speed to 26 knots" so as to improve seaworthiness. This "Special 1918 Type" might well be called a 1918 destroyer escort.

Table 3–1. Special ASW Destroyer of August 1917

LWL	275
Beam	26.5
Draft	8.5
SHP	13,500
Speed	26–27.5
Endurance	4,000/15
5-in./51	4
3-in./23 AA	1
21-in. TT	2 × 3
Hull	260
Fittings	41
Machinery	255
Armament	53
Equipment & outfit	36
Margin	11
Light ship	656
Ammunition	29
Stores	20
Standard	705
RFW	5
Fuel	140
Normal	850
GM	2.5

The special type was intended to meet an emergency situation, and it was the subject of unconventional procedures. For example, the characteristics were issued by the Office of Operations (i.e., by OpNav), rather than by the General Board; indeed, the General Board was later to abort it. In the interest of rapid design, the two technical bureaus queried Vice Admiral Sims, commanding U.S. forces in European waters, as to what simplifications he would consider acceptable, even as alternative sketch designs were prepared. In addition, both Bath and Newport News proposed their own simplified destroyers. Newport News suggested a standard fleet destroyer with half the power of the 35-knot type, to make 28 knots. These ships could be fitted for 5-inch guns (which were under consideration to counter the 5.9-inch guns of the German cruiser submarines) and additional oil tankage. Bath suggested a 750-tonner of 28 to 30 knots, but its design was rejected because its two boilers shared a single boiler room and a single condenser.

Preliminary Design had to work in an atmosphere of considerable uncertainty. For example, it was not clear whether the 5-inch gun would be required. Not only were the Germans mounting 5.9s aboard submarines, but many foreign destroyers were mounting guns far more powerful than the existing U.S. 4-inch type. The Royal Navy was going to a 4.7-inch weapon, and some Italian and German types were armed with 5.9- or 6-inch guns. A U.S. twin 4-inch gun had been developed before the war, and even prepared for a test aboard the destroyer *Benham*, but the war had intervened; ultimately the flush decker *Semmes* was selected in her place. Tests aboard the USS *Manley* showed that the two waist 4-inch guns could not be fired within 30 degrees of the bow, so that bow fire would be limited to a single gun. BuOrd suggested, therefore, that twin 4-inch guns be substituted for the fore-and-aft single weapons; a destroyer with a broadside of six 4-in./50s would have much the same fighting capability as one with a broadside of three 5-in./51s; "taking into consideration the high speed of the destroyer, which allows her to choose her own range, and also the difficulties encountered in the loading of the 5-in./51 guns, due to the method by which the charge is provided, a battery of six 4-inch guns is considered the logical one." The twin 4-inch mount weighed almost precisely twice as much as a single mount and, at 21,086 lbs., about 3,000 lbs. less than a 5-in./51; moreover, the deck stresses of two 4-inch firing together would be less than that of the 5-inch. On the other hand, the twin 4-inch would require almost twice the weight of ammunition of the 5-inch, for the same number of rounds per gun.

Preliminary Design envisaged several alternative batteries. The base case was the same as the fleet destroyer, with four 4-inch guns, two 1-pounder antiaircraft guns, and four triple torpedo tubes. As a maximum, the 4-inch could be replaced by 5-inch weapons, of a type previously mounted only aboard battleships and cruisers. On the other hand, two of the torpedo tubes might be eliminated, either to save weight or to simplify production.

The drastic reduction in required speed made possible a considerable reduction in the size of the new ship. The machinery would match that of the last class of thousand tonners, with the incidental benefit of eliminating the reduction-gear bottleneck; indeed, Steam Engineering began the design of a wholly new direct-design turbine for 13,500 shp. The reduction from the usual 14,000 was to save weight; 28 knots was expected at 1,100 tons. In building the *Wickes* class, Steam Engineering had introduced boilers far more powerful than those of earlier destroyers, so that the new type would need only two rather than four. That, in turn, would so reduce the length of deck consumed by boilers that the remaining super-structure and battery might be compressed into a shorter length—280 rather 310 feet on the waterline. Displacement might be cut to 970 tons. However, mass production would preclude the type of weight-saving techniques so important in high-performance destroyer hulls and engines. Allowance for less-advanced workmanship brought the prospective displacement of the new type to 1,000 tons, still 185 tons less than the (frequently exceeded) design displacement of the 35-knot *Wickes* class. Another alternative was a minimum-battery destroyer with reduced scantlings; length could be reduced another 5 feet and displacement would fall to 825 tons. In fact, length could be reduced even further. Two boilers and two banks of torpedo tubes together amounted to about 40 feet of length, and the standard 310-foot hull might be reduced to 270 feet by their omission. This hull was beamier than the specially designed ones, and so relatively little weight could be saved: the first such scheme showed a displacement of 1,060 tons. Variations included the provision of wing bunkers in the boiler rooms, as a means of adding cruising radius. This expedient was criticized as militarily unwise, but it was the key to the *Clemson* design, as it was the only means of adding fuel capacity without so radical a change in design as to interrupt production.

The great advantage of the short, beamy hull was that it provided sufficient stability to accommodate both the maximum battery and sufficient fuel. For example, the 1,080-ton Scheme 7 could make 5,200 nm. at 15 knots, with a maximum speed of 25.6 knots and a fuel capacity of 411 tons (*Wickes*: 275). However, it was argued that it would be even simpler to continue to build full-length *Wickes* hulls with half power. Such a ship, strengthened to take the 5-inch gun, would come to 1,150 tons and, thanks to its greater length, would make 27.2 knots; 370 tons of oil would drive it 4,900 nm. at 15 knots.

In August 1917, the two technical bureaus jointly recommended that Scheme 6, the full hull with half power, be adopted for five new destroyers to be built by Newport News, DD 181–185. This scheme had nearly a 2-knot advantage over Scheme 7, with al-

most no loss in endurance—and with no wing oil tanks. The Secretary of the Navy approved a plan to fit the new ships with 4-inch guns but to provide hull and deck strength for a later substitution of the preferred 5-inch weapons. Given a 310-foot hull, Preliminary Design could abandon the somewhat unsatisfactory deck arrangements of the short hulls, and ultimately (in Scheme 11) returned to the arrangement of the *Wickes* class, the only difference being in the number of funnels. Thus far the only major complaints against that arrangement had concerned the positions of the two antiaircraft guns, one of which was mounted between the bridge and the forward 4-inch gun. Preliminary Design commented that in all probability the new ships would have to be built without all of their torpedo tubes, and that guns might replace the two aftermost banks of tubes. This foreshadowed the escort conversions of over 20 years later.

Quite soon this program began to unravel. On 9 August the Secretary of the Navy ordered Newport News to duplicate its previous boats rather than await a new design. Meanwhile Admiral Sims, commanding U.S. forces in European waters, presented a report listing the simplifications he was prepared to accept; in fact, they amounted to additions to the existing design. For example, he emphasized the need for bows strengthened for ramming as well as extra-strong collision bulkheads, where the *Wickes* class had none. He was willing to accept a reduction in triple torpedo tubes actually mounted to two, but wanted provision for the usual four, and regarded the twin 4-inch gun as useful. As for the speed reductions inherent in all of the austerity designs, he regarded 30 knots as a minimum. Main-battery guns were to be mounted to permit depressed fire, so that U-boats might be engaged at close range. Thus, Schemes 6 and 11 had their bows cut down three feet at the fore end, gradually tapering to a point directly under the muzzle of the forward gun to obtain more depression for it. The main-battery guns would also be fitted with spray shields, perhaps of British pattern. Admiral Sims wanted a depth-charge release on the bridge, although existing ships had no such fire control.

On 7 August 1917, the bureaus submitted their sketch designs, including the 270-footers and Scheme 6, and such was the urgency of the situation that three days later the Secretary of the Navy approved the latter, directing further that provision be made for 5-inch guns. Steam Engineering went so far as to develop detailed plans for a new direct-drive turbine. However, quite soon the major builders began to report that any drastic change in the existing design would lead only to additional, and considerable, delays while new detail plans were produced.

The General Board was also unenthusiastic, preferring a speed of about 35 knots, which would fit all of the new destroyers for fleet service. Preliminary Design now prepared yet another alternative scheme, which it numbered 12: it was a *Wickes*-class destroyer strengthened to take the 5-inch gun. Additional bunkerage abeam the boilers increased its designed cruising radius to 4,900 nm. at 15 knots. Increased rudder area was provided and the mainmast was reduced to a stub demountable mast. The last measure was a means of providing a forward arc for the after antiaircraft gun without giving up the radio range provided by the mainmast. All of these changes reduced designed speed from 35 to about 34.5; the Secretary approved Scheme 12 on 12 September 1917 and it became the basis for 156 *Clemson*-class destroyers, DD 186–347 (of which DD 200–205 were canceled on 3 February 1919). The great inherent girder strength of the flush-deck hull took the extra loads, including about 100 tons of fuel oil (for 1,200 nm. more at 15 knots) easily; indeed, extra range was considered so important that the additional vulnerability of above-water tanks was accepted. Sims was still not completely satisfied; in October he asked for three changes, to be made only if they would not slow production: a flat stern for greater maneuverability; a steering engine in the engine room; and the bridge and forward gun to be moved aft about 8 feet. The first reflected the unhandiness of U.S. as compared to British destroyers; the last, the wetness of the flush-deck design. C&R pointed to its increase in rudder area, and proposed

a reduction in deadwood aft, which with little effect on production, would materially reduce the turning circle. However, even that minor change appears to have been foregone on production grounds.

Plans for the actual mounting of 5-inch/51 guns were made only in July 1918. At that time New York Shipbuilding at Camden (DD 231–250) was the only shipbuilder that had tried to design 5-inch magazine spaces. The nearby Cramp yard (DD 206–230) would be able to benefit from this effort, and it appeared that the last five Newport News boats (DD 201-205)—which would be canceled the next year) were so little advanced that they, too, might be modified. No effort would be made to alter Bethlehem boats (DD 251–335), as they were all designed by a common office, and the confusion of piecemeal changes would greatly delay them. In fact, of this large program, only five ships were altered (DD 231–235); in addition, two ships (DD 208 and 209, the *Hovey* and *Long*) each had eight 4-inch guns in four twin mounts.

The original flush-deck design called for two 1-pounder automatic antiaircraft guns, one between bridge and forward 4-inch gun, and the other on the port side between the bridge and the galley, on the main deck. In practice BuOrd was unable to supply sufficient 1-pounder guns, and in many ships a pair of short 3-inch guns (3-inch/23) were substituted. The location of the second gun was unsatisfactory, and it was moved to the after deckhouse in the *Clemson* class, a short mainmast being stepped forward of that structure to carry the main radio antennae. Still later, most ships mounted their after 4-inch guns

Two "flush deckers" each had four twin 4-inch mounts; the *Long* is shown alongside the destroyer tender *Dixie* in 1940. Both had very long careers.

atop the after deckhouse, exchanging them for the 3-inch/23 or, by the mid-1920s, dispensing with the latter entirely. The modification for the *Wickes* class was approved in April 1919.

Depth charges were another major modification to the original flush-decker concept. To the original depth-charge tracks were soon added Y-guns requiring centerline space. At first a single Y-gun was authorized, but by July 1918 destroyer commanders were asking for Y-guns to be fitted in threes, to substitute two single throwers for the double one, and to replace a 4-inch gun with a British-type 8-inch ASW howitzer, in effect a depth-charge projector of greater range. Later that year the department approved the installation of an additional (second) Y-gun and two single depth-charge projectors on destroyers still under construction. C&R proposed that all of the projectors be mounted, as originally envisaged, atop the after deckhouse; space would be provided by omitting the searchlight there. The latter was the subject of some controversy, since it was a special remote-controlled type designed for use in conjunction with the main battery. In effect, a choice of depth charges over searchlight was a choice of ASW over the conventional destroyer role as an arm of the battle fleet. In any event, the end of the war mooted the issue.

Given the immense size of the flush-decker fleet, alternate roles became very attractive. Mine-laying conversions were considered during wartime, pre-sumably inspired by British experience with specialized cruiser and destroyer conversions. At one point it was believed that 80 mines could be accommodated by the removal of two banks of torpedo tubes. However, the 14 postwar conversions (DD 96–102, 110–112, 171–174 became DM 1–14 in July 1920) dispensed entirely with their torpedo tubes.

As for the destroyer men's opinion of these ships, the commanding officer of the USS *Wickes* wrote in September 1918 that

> At maximum displacement, and with average condition of sea in the Atlantic, when force of wind does not exceed 6, Beaufort scale, the vessel rides nicely and compares favorably with the behavior of the 740-ton and the 1,000-ton classes . . . the behavior sometimes seems even better than that of the other classes.
>
> When the vessel is light (most of the fuel used) and the sea is of force 4 to 7, Beaufort scale, on the beam or quarter, the ship rolls excessively, buries herself deeply to leeward, and is generally uncomfortable. . . .
>
> The general behavior of the vessel in a seaway has established . . . that she is limber athwartships and that the stern is flexible, and limber in a vertical plane. The longitudinal girder strength, except as indicated, seems sufficient. . . .
>
> The steering gear has performed satisfactory to date. The *Wickes* steers a course better than any destroyer the Commanding Officer has seen or heard of. . . . The turning circle is as large as that of the earlier 1,000-ton destroyers or larger. The vessel turns

During World War I, Germany built a series of "cruiser" submarines armed with 5.9-inch guns; in response, U.S. *Clemson*-class destroyers had gun foundations strengthened to take a 5-inch/51 gun, although only five were so equipped. The *Brooks* was an example, her heavier guns distinguishable by their length. None ever had No. 4 gun mounted atop the after deckhouse, as did all the 4-inch ships. The *Brooks* became a fast transport in 1942.

more slowly against the wind than those of previous types and the turning circle appears to be greater. . . .When the vessel is loaded to full load displacement and is nearly on an even keel, if the wind does not exceed force 3, Beaufort scale, she handles well and turns acceptably with the screen. However, the indications are that when she is light and up by the head she turns badly, for her bow will blow off as she pivots around the deeper after body. . . .

There is a considerable retardation in the advance of the vessel over the ground and a considerable increase in fuel consumption when steaming into a head wind and sea. The mean retardation for a head wind of force 4, Beaufort scale, at 15 knots, is one knot per hour. The increase in fuel consumption with a head sea varies with the character and length of the sea; it is about 15 percent for the usual sea made by a breeze of force 5 or 6, Beaufort scale. With a long, heavy swell, and with the sea made by a moderate gale that has been blowing for four hours or more, the increase is 30 percent.

The relative effect of a head wind on the *Wickes* type is greater than the effect on the earlier raised forecastle type.

Suggestions for future construction included more fuel oil and a requirement that builders make fuel economy runs at full load rather than at some unrealistically light design figure: ". . . it is only when the *Wickes* has used practically all of her fuel that she is down to the displacement (contract displacement) of the preliminary acceptance trials." Turning was much discussed, and the captain hoped that the measures then in hand (larger rudder, reduced deadwood) would prove effective.

More generally, his convoy experience led him to recommend that the Navy

> Make the length of the destroyer 300 feet, or less.
> Make the bridge, ventilators, deck houses, and other weather deck fittings . . . as rugged as in the previous types, or more rugged.
> Establish as a criterion for deciding on the character, number, and location of fittings on the weather deck the assumption that the normal condition of the destroyer in the Atlantic, or at least around the British Isles, from the first of October to the first of April, is practically that of a submersible.

There has been a great deal of discussion among destroyer officers and officers in general, Allied and American, as to the relative seaworthiness of American and other destroyers, and of the relative merits of the several types of the American boat. The statement is generally made that vessels of the 740-ton class are better sea boats than the 1,000-ton type. . . .As to the flush deck type, experience has not been varied enough to warrant a conclusion.

The experience of the Commanding Officer, based on duty in all three types, with a rather full experience as regards rough weather in the 740-ton type, and a somewhat extended observation of British destroyers is:

(1) That the ability of the vessel to stand up against rough weather depends primarily upon the displacement of the vessel, *her length relative to the* length of the sea, and to the *heaviness of the sea*.

(2) That the American 740-ton vessels generally make better weather in the short, heavy seas, common in the winter off the Irish coast, than do the 1,000-ton vessels.

(3) That the question of behavior is ultimately a question of length and force of the sea, and that there are frequent occasions when the greater strength and ruggedness of the 1,000-ton vessels subjects them to less injury than is sustained by the lighter 740-ton vessels.

(4) That the American destroyers ride better than the British destroyers of the pre-Flotilla Leader Type over a greater range of sea lengths.

(5) That the hulls of the American vessels suffer more in storms than do those of the British vessels, and that the weather deck fittings of the American vessels, on the other hand, on account of their greater ruggedness, suffer less.

Other commanders appear to have been in favor of the flush deckers. They were regarded as better convoy escorts than were their British consorts: they had much better endurance and were perhaps better sea boats as well. However, their unhandiness came in for constant criticism, and one writer considered it unfortunate that their sterns had been cut away to save a few tons of weight just when the introduction of depth charges had made deck space there so much more valuable. They were also much sturdier than earlier types. Very possibly they benefited in this respect from the speed with which they had to be designed under war pressure: no careful strength analysis aimed at paring away hull scantlings could be made.

The defects of wetness and short range were remarked in wartime, but they became prominent only after the war. After 1918 the more stringent requirements of American strategy were once more what counted. There were no inferior British boats to see, only wet gun crews and long runs to dry tanks in the Pacific.

The immense fleet of flush deckers dominated U.S. destroyer thinking for some time, and the ships of the 1930s were to a considerable extent a reaction to their defects; indeed, in moving to larger dimensions C&R had to refer constantly to the earlier classes by way of comparison. The fleet constructed during the war presented a massive bloc obsolescence problem, aggravated by a shortage of funds that precluded any pre–Pearl Harbor equivalent of FRAM.* At the same time the existence of so many more or

---

* The Fleet Rehabilitation and Modernization Program, which extended the life of many World War II-built destroyers into the 1970s.

less modern destroyers inhibited any new construction: all destroyer design within C&R from 1917 on was devoted to the flotilla leaders the war program so obviously lacked. Unlike the Royal Navy and the Japanese Navy, the U.S. Navy had no reserve of fast light cruisers to stiffen its destroyer squadrons. It had only three rather slow scouts of 1908 and ten fast but fairly large light cruisers of the 1916 Program, hence the perceived urgency of heavy destroyer construction—although in fact no leaders were built. In the end the leader studies led to the first new destroyers, in 1932.

The United States did not suspend its wartime naval programs with the Armistice, and there was no wave of cancellations comparable to that which followed the end of the Second World War. Remarkably, too, relatively few of the prewar ships were stricken: only the worn-out 400-tonners and the coal-burning *Smith*s were sold out. That left the United States with the largest destroyer force in the world, a position it retained until the disposal of the large World War II fleet in the late 1960s and early 1970s.

The sheer size of this fleet inspired plans for its modernization; for, despite its newness, it represented an elaboration of a prewar design and had several outstanding defects. On the other hand, any program extending across the entire class might well be prohibitively expensive. This was the case, for example, with the issue of cruising radius.

Of the *Wickes* class, the Bath-designed ships generally exceeded their designed cruising radius and so were satisfactory, but the Bethlehem units, which had been completed in greater numbers, were far too short-legged, with a designed radius of 2,250 nm. at 20 knots (3,000 if the emergency oil supply of 50 tons were counted). Although in practice destroyers operated only out of Irish ports, and then only for five days at a time (1,500 to 2,000 nm.), full transatlantic convoy would be far more effective; the solution adopted had proven effective only because of the operating limitations of the U-boats. The advent of the U-cruisers, with their 5.9-inch guns, might also be the advent of U-boats freed of exactly those restrictions. Thus, in October 1918 the two technical bureaus suggested a variety of measures to increase destroyer endurance. It would not be possible to fit the wing tanks of the *Clemson*s, although small cylindrical tanks in the fire rooms might add as much as 15 tons of oil. Major improvements required more drastic action. The forward magazine might be converted to fuel tankage, and the cofferdam abaft it as well (54 tons, 20 percent increase). Alternatively, the forward boiler might be replaced by large cylindrical tanks (75 tons, 27 percent, with a 2-knot speed penalty due to the loss of boiler power). The most radical choice would be removal of the forward boiler and

extension of the platform deck aft. The space below the platform deck, as well as the cofferdam forward of the former boiler room, would be converted into 114 tons of tankage, for an increase of 41 percent at a cost of 2 knots.

Unfortunately, this last change was far too drastic to be acceptable in a war emergency program, although, as the department ruled on 2 November 1918, "the material increase of 41 percent fuel capacity is of greater strategic value than the 2 knots at top speed. The utilization of the forward magazines . . . is not advisable as ¾ of the gun power of the vessel is in the fore part. . . ." Plans were to be drawn up, but they would not be implemented in wartime, particularly as "more Bethlehem destroyers have been delivered than of the other types, and their progress as regards the hull structure is distinctly ahead of the others, so that if it is undertaken to increase the oil capacity, not only will more radical changes be necessary . . . but greater delay will be encountered thereby." After the Armistice, the cost of completing and manning the force of new destroyers precluded any such radical alteration, and the endurance problem remained an issue at the outbreak of World War II.

In July 1919, BuOrd asked that 50 of the new flush deckers still under construction be completed as convoy (i.e., long-range) escorts. One boiler would be removed, at a cost of 5 knots, to be replaced by 100 tons of oil (an increase in radius of 1,000 miles) and a gyrostabilizer ("for the purpose of increasing the value of these convoy vessels by rendering them good gun platforms"). At the time, it was estimated that most of the new destroyers would experience difficulty in making an Atlantic crossing.

This problem was emphasized by the experience of the fleet in its South American cruise of 1921. Only by hard work was it possible for the ships to make their runs from San Diego to Balboa and thence to Valparaiso without refueling en route. Matters would be far worse in the event of a war in the Far East.

One solution, which was to have a great effect on operations in World War II, was fueling at sea. For example, "during the recent (1928) fleet concentration, six destroyers were fueled at sea en route to Panama. Three oilers were employed, and fueling was done on only one at a time. . . .During the return voyage, the *Neches* was directed to simultaneously fuel the *Ludlow* and *Burns*. . . .Fueling at sea may develop into a vital factor of an overseas expedition on advanced base operation. . . ." (Report of CinC U.S. Fleet for FY 29.) Both astern and broadside deployment of fuel hoses was tried at this time.

With the disposal of the surviving obsolete destroyers, the Navy was left in the early 1920s with a total of 319 ships, including the 14 minelayers. There was no question of keeping all in service, particularly after the budget cuts associated with the Washington Treaty (1922). Thus, in May 1922, the General Board adopted as an *ideal* policy that 152 destroyers be maintained in active service. The reality fell far short of this. In February 1926, for example, there were 161 flush deckers out of service, 85 at Philadelphia, 76 at San Diego. Efforts were being made to maintain these ships in condition for rapid recommissioning, but it had to be admitted that the Philadelphia units would require six weeks before the first could recommission, 85 days before the first ten. Others were lost by misadventure: three in 1921 (two by collision, one by grounding) and then seven, the bulk of DesRon 11, in a famous grounding incident off Honda, California, 8 September 1923.

A few destroyers served in the Coast Guard on anti-"Rum Runner" patrol. Twenty flivvers and thousand-tonners became CG 1-20 in 1924, and five *Tucker*-class thousand-tonners were added as CG 21-25 in 1926. In 1930 six *Clemson*s replaced flivvers as CG 15-20 (DD 189, 193-196, 198, not in that order). Unlike the earlier boats, they were not scrapped after completion of this duty and remained to serve in World War II.

For the rest, 102 destroyers, including several minelayers, remained in service. Except for the Coast Guard units, all of the earlier types were in reserve, and indeed only one of them, DD 66 (the USS *Allen*) would ever be recalled to active duty. At this time the U.S. battle fleet proper included in its organization four destroyer squadrons, each comprising three six-boat divisions, a total of 72 ships; and there were four minelayers in two mine squadrons.

Plans called for running down the active destroyers and then replacing them with some in reserve; destroyers were, after all, delicate beasts and could not last so very long. Thus came the 1929 decision to dispose of the Yarrow boats, which were to be replaced out of reserve stocks. Each destroyer about to be decommissioned was assigned a successor, her crew to recommission the idle ship. This immense task, the replacement of three destroyer squadrons, was accomplished in the first five months of 1930.

In fact, a total of 58 ships were disposed of in 1930–31. The *Preston* and *Bruce* (DD 327 and 329) were expended in hull strength experiments at Norfolk Navy Yard; the others were broken up. Two more Yarrow boats, the *Sinclair* and *Stoddert*, were chosen for conversion to radio-controlled targets, to form a

The *Charles Ausburne* carried a small seaplane experimentally in August 1923 and may have served as the inspiration for a Bureau of Aeronautics proposal to fit future destroyers with a combined sextuple torpedo tube and catapult (1927). The Curtiss TS-1 did operate successfully, except that the ship's officers recommended that in future aircraft be carried aft. No similar proposal bore fruit until 1939, when the *Noa* was fitted to carry a seaplane, leading to the *Fletcher*-class catapult destroyers.

Fourteen "flush deckers" were converted to light seaplane tenders, the *Childs* (shown on 14 November 1944) being the first. All reverted to destroyer status when the new *Barnegat*-class tenders joined the fleet. Note the elimination of the two forward boiler rooms in favor of gasoline for seaplanes, the bridgework being extended to provide extra electronics spaces. The *Childs* carries a YG aircraft homing beacon on her short mainmast and two extra boats aft to service aircraft.

division of three with the *Hazelwood*. The *Stoddert* became the prototype conversion, but her sister's boilers were in so poor a state as to require her replacement by the *Kilty* and then by the *Radford* (Thornycroft boilers), which last was not, in the end, converted. The *Stoddert* herself was replaced in 1932 by the *Lamberton* (DD 119, Thornycroft boilers). The *Hazelwood* was canceled in favor of the *Boggs* (DD 136, with Normand boilers). In addition, the *Dorsey* (DD 117) and the *Elliot* (DD 146) operated as control ships, for a five-ship Mobile Target Division, which included also the battleship *Utah*.

The London Treaty of 1930 for the first time limited destroyer forces; under its provisions 35 destroyers, including the two Yarrow-boilered mobile targets, were stricken in 1935-37. Three (DD 94, 163, 259) survived as hulks in Navy hands; they saw World War II service, although not as destroyers. Finally the *Smith Thompson* (DD 212) was so badly damaged when she was rammed by the *Whipple* (DD 217) in the Philippines that she had to be scuttled, 25 July 1936.

By 1936, then, there were 169 flush deckers left,

including 4 *Caldwell*s. Of the earlier classes, all had been scrapped under the London Treaty, the sole exception being the *Allen*, DD 66. Four were converted to destroyer minelayers to replace six such units scrapped in 1930; when the remaining eight were disposed of in 1936-37, four new conversions were authorized. The *Semmes* (DD 189) became a sonar test ship (AG 24) upon completion of her Coast Guard service in 1935.

Other conversions of this period were light seaplane tenders and light transports. During the twenties, destroyers served from time to time with the Naval Air Force, their torpedo tubes temporarily removed as weight compensation for gasoline tanks. No special designation was applied. However, the *Childs* (DD 241) and the *Williamson* (DD 244) were converted to small seaplane tenders (AVP 14 and 15, then AVD 1 and 2 in 1940) in 1938. They were intended to support squadrons (12 aircraft) of patrol bombers (such as PBYs); they supplemented the first of the new destroyer-size *Barnegat* class. Conversion entailed replacement of the two forward boilers by tankage for 30,000 gallons of avgas; the torpedo tubes,

The seaplane tender (ex-destroyer) *Ballard*, originally converted in 1940, is shown following a refit at Mare Island, 18 December 1944. White circles indicate changes. Forward (opposite), she has a new SF surface-search radar in a small radome below her SC air-search radar; the mast abaft the radar mast carries a YG homing beacon. Below the SF is the crossed-wire antenna of the ubiquitous wartime TBS tactical radio. The view aft (above) shows the unusual funnel cap and the pair of airplane-servicing boats, served by a boom stepped on the short mast aft. Finally, note the loudspeaker on the foremast, just above searchlight level.

the two waist guns, and the 3-inch/23 AA gun were also removed, and the bridge superstructure was extended to provide living and office space for the squadron. A crane was stepped amidships and aircraft-servicing boats were carried in davits. Unlike a *Barnegat*, an AVD could not hoist a seaplane aboard for maintenance. The first two conversions were completed in time for the 1939 Fleet Problem, and were sufficiently successful for the CNO to order 7 more in May 1940, out of the remaining 35 decommissioned flush deckers. The conversion of 5 active destroyers brought the total to 14.

Another major conversion was the *Manley* (DD 74), which became the first of the fast light transports (APD). She was first converted (as AG 28) in 1938-39 to provide troop accommodation for 120 Marines; their boats in effect replaced her torpedo tubes. In this form her performance justified a fuller conversion at the New York Navy Yard, in which the two

forward boilers, the torpedo tubes, and one of the two waist guns were removed; the other gun was moved to the centerline, where it benefited from the clear field of fire left by the removal of the two forward funnels. She was intended to be able to carry a Marine rifle company for up to 48 hours, and could accommodate four 36-foot assault boats (LCPL or LCPR) in davits. Unlike the later DE conversions, a converted flush decker carried no Army vehicles and, therefore, no gasoline; she did, however, carry some deck cargo, including a 75-mm. pack howitzer and its ammunition. The May 1940 conversion program included five more APDs, and others would be produced in wartime in response to the urgent needs of the Southwest Pacific.

The CNO also ordered the four ships of DesDiv 52 converted to fast minesweepers, as DMS 1–4; four recommissioned ships became DMS 5–8. All tubes were removed and a squared-off false stern added to

support minesweeping davits. This sufficed only for use against moored mines; later two 60-kw turbo-generators replaced the usual three 25-kw units of a flush decker, and the capability to sweep magnetic and acoustic mines was added. As in the case of most flush deckers, Number 4 boiler was removed, but this does not appear to have been connected to mine-sweeping features. Ten more units, DMS 9–18, followed the first eight during 1941. They included the two destroyers that had originally been fitted with twin 4-inch guns, but which by then had four single mounts (DD 208 and 209, which became DMS 11 and 12).

The *Dahlgren*, although not classified as an auxiliary, was refitted as an engineering experimental ship at the New York Navy Yard in 1937. She received two Steamotive ultra-high-pressure (1,300 psi, 910 degrees F.) boilers in place of her original after boilers, the uptakes being trunked together; she also

received new geared turbines. All of her torpedo tubes were removed, but half were restored when she returned to conventional destroyer duty in wartime. The *Hamilton* had her forward boiler replaced by stabilization tanks at the New York Navy Yard late in 1939; in addition, a portable deckhouse was fitted to carry stabilizing gyroscopes. In 1941 she was converted to a high-speed minesweeper. Finally, the *Noa* was fitted with a seaplane (which replaced her after torpedo tubes) in 1940; in some sense she was the forerunner of six *Fletcher*s designed to carry catapults.

The major deletion from the ranks of the flush deckers was the transfer of 50 to Britain in September 1940. As of the fall of 1941, then, there remained in service *as destroyers* a total of 71 flush deckers; 48 others served in subsidiary roles. Of the destroyers, 13 served as the destroyer arm of the Asiatic Fleet; the remaining 58 were considered second-line ships

The seaplane tender *McFarland* has a destroyer-like appearance in this 17 August 1943 photograph: she has no aircraft homing beacon and no servicing boats aft; instead, she has an unusually heavy 20-mm. battery, with 14 guns in evidence. The external pipe on her side, running aft from the aviation gasoline tank area amidships, was an attempt to reduce the fire hazard. Her mast carries both the SA air-search antenna, common aboard destroyers and destroyer escorts, and the unusual radome of SE, a microwave surface-search radar originally developed for flush-deck destroyers but rarely used because of its inadequacies.

The destroyer *Dahlgren* was modified as an engineering experimental ship at the New York Navy Yard in 1937, her original after boilers being replaced by ultra-high-pressure units, their uptakes trunked together; she also received new geared turbines. She returned to ordinary destroyer duty in wartime, however, and indeed was unusual in not losing one funnel for additional fuel tankage. For most of that time she served the Fleet Sonar School at Key West. In this late wartime photograph she has standard flush-deck escort equipment, including Hedgehog forward.

The destroyer minesweeper conversion required a special squared-off false stern to support sweeping davits, as shown in this 23 July 1942 view of the USS *Perry*; note the sweeping winch, paravanes, and kites, and the depth-charge tracks angled to clear them. Circles show changes, including the installation of new 20-mm. guns: and depth-charge throwers.

suitable mainly for escort work, and 27 of them were subjected to extensive conversion.

The flush deckers had always been considered an important mobilization reserve against subsidiary requirements; indeed, the conversion of 18 units as fast minesweepers, which avoided reductions in modern destroyers earmarked for the battle fleet, was just such an application. ASW and AAW escort were others. In May 1940, the CNO asked the General Board to investigate improvements in the AA battery of the old destroyers. The board had in mind removal of at least the No. 1 boiler and a reduction in fuel load to provide additional ammunition and fixed ballast to balance additional top weight; this was exactly opposite to contemporary British work aimed at extending the endurance of their convoy escorts. Number 3 and 4 torpedo tubes and the antiquated 3-inch/23 AA gun would also go. The remaining 4-inch guns might be replaced by modern 5-inch/25 AA, or by 3-inch/50, or even by pairs of 3-inch/50, which with their newer construction weighed only about half as much as the older weapons. Quadruple

or twin 1.1-inch cannon on platforms would replace the torpedo tubes.

By June 1940, weight considerations seemed to require the removal of the entire former battery just to have one 5-inch/25 in No. 1 position, and two aft with 275 rounds each in place of Number 3 and 4 torpedo tubes; in addition the now-standard quadruple 1.1-inch machine cannon would be mounted on the centerline over the galley and in No. 4 gun position. A Mk 14 director for the 5-inch guns would occupy the pilothouse roof; all of this would cost a 10 percent reduction in fuel capacity, and a quarter-foot reduction in metacentric height.

Now C&R became enthusiastic. The new quadruple 1.1 seemed by far the best available AA weapon: why bother with anything else? On 17 June the bureau proposed to remove everything but the depth charges, mounting instead six of the new quadruple machine cannon, so arranged that all could fire broadside and four could fire ahead or astern; a capacity of 2,400 rounds per barrel doubled the provision suggested earlier by the General Board. There

The destroyer minesweeper *Boggs* (above and facing), reclassified as AG 19 in June 1945, shows her configuration clearly in these 30 June 1945 photographs. With only one depth-charge projector left on each side, and one funnel (and boiler) removed, her main deck is almost empty. Her battery was reduced to three 3-inch/50s forward, a twin Bofors aft, and two 20-mm.; of her former minesweeping equipment, only the large winch remained. She served as a target-towing vessel with the Operational Training Command out of San Diego between April 1944 and March 1945 before being stripped as a high-speed target tower for service in the Western Pacific, arriving at Eniwetok just at the end of the war, 15 August 1945.

would also be six .50-caliber machine guns. C&R wanted to use the forward boiler room for berthing and messing the large crew required to man all of these guns; it would merge Number 3 and 4 funnels to clear sky arcs for some of them. Even so, normal displacement would rise 25 tons. This rather gutted AA escort would have been redesignated Patrol Vessel (PA).

The General Board would have none of it. The flush deckers might be old, but they were still solid enough to be worth preserving for more general serv-

ice. This attitude was most fortunate in view of the failure of the 1.1-inch gun; the Bofors that replaced it was far too heavy for the flush decker. In any case, neither the 1.1 nor the 5-inch/25 was readily available in any numbers. The General Board saw a relatively straightforward solution in mounting 3-inch/50 AA guns in place of Number 1 and 4 torpedo tubes and Number 4 gun. On 24 July 1940 this alteration was ordered at Philadelphia Navy Yard on the destroyers *Conner*, *Stockton*, *Conway*, and *Allen*, the latter the last of the thousand-tonners. In fact, only she

was done, the others going to the Royal Navy in September 1940. On 9 August the CNO ordered guns and other equipment for eight more conversions.

Ultimately a more complete conversion was adopted; after all, the United States had on hand or under construction enough modern destroyers to ensure that the older ones would be restricted to such second-line duties as convoy escort, where they would meet aircraft and submarines, not enemy surface forces. Hence on 6 December 1940, a large refit was ordered for all the surviving old destroyers. Number 3 and 4 torpedo tubes and all 4-inch guns would be replaced by a total of six 3-inch/50s; a Y-gun (with ten depth charges in arbors) would replace the old 3-inch/23 AA gun; and extensions would bring the capacity of the stern depth-charge tracks to twenty-four 300-pound charges. The addition of two .50-caliber machine guns would bring that battery to four guns.

Of 71 active flush-deck destroyers, thirteen in the Asiatic Fleet could not be converted to escort duty in the absence of any more modern units in that fleet. Priority went to the Atlantic Fleet; two of its three DesRons (30 and 31) were finished by February 1941. They were followed by nine more ships of DesDivs 53 and 82 and finally the *Decatur*, DesDiv 66, and the four-ship DesRon 54 were scheduled for the fall. The last batch, which would have brought the total to 37 and would also have exhausted supplies of 3-inch/50 guns, was stopped by the outbreak of war, leaving a total of 27 conversions (DD 118, 126, 128, 130, 142, 144, 145, 147, 152–155, 157–160, 199, 210, 220, 221, 223, 229, 239, 240, 245, 246, 341).

Ships not scheduled for refit were: the *Dahlgren*, *Litchfield* (DD 336, assigned to Submarines, Pacific, and employed in convoying submarines through the Pearl Harbor defensive zone) and 20 units assigned to naval districts—DesDivs 70 (4 ships: 11th district), 83 (4 ships: 12th), and 80 (3 ships, plus the *Allen*, 14th), and DesRon 33 (9 ships, 15th). In September, in view of the lack of further 3-inch guns, the CNO ordered two sets of torpedo tubes removed as weight reservation for quadruple 1.1-inch guns. For the 15th Naval District he suggested the 3-inch conversion, should any guns become available. The following January the ultimate battery of these ships was set at four 4-inch guns, six 20-mm. antiaircraft machine cannon, and two triple tubes, plus (in common with the all-3-inch ships) six single depth-charge throwers (four 300-pound charges each), plus two depth-charge tracks (seven 300-pound charges each) and twenty-four 300-pound charges stowed in the torpedo warhead locker. By this time the outbreak of war had ended what amounted to a flush-decker FRAM program.

All of this effort did not attack perhaps the single greatest problem of the flush decker, its inadequate steaming endurance. Winter escort service in the North Atlantic made a solution urgent, and on 15 November 1941 CinCLant proposed the replacement of Number 1 boiler by fuel. This would increase the radius of the short-legged *Wickes* group by about 1,100 nm. (650 for the *Clemson*s which already carried some fuel in way of the boiler rooms, hence could not carry as much in addition). BuShips preferred to remove Number 4 boiler for reasons of trim.

The General Board approved; clearly these old destroyers were no longer fleet types. CinCLant had observed that

current operations in the Atlantic indicate the need for escort vessels whose speed requirements are not over 25 knots; it is also believed that possible operations in the Pacific may require numerous escort vessels in escort of train vessels; in any case, cruising radius is of paramount importance. . . . It is understood that escort vessels under consideration at various times by the Department would not have over 25 knots speed. . . . It has already been necessary to send support to one such [old] destroyer, and Escort Commanders find it necessary to favor them at the expense of newer destroyers.

The Secretary of the Navy approved this modification on 3 December 1941 for the Atlantic Fleet (DesRons 27, 30, 31); it was soon extended to the Pacific Fleet as well, and ultimately included the DM and DMS conversions. By February 1942 only the Asiatic Fleet destroyers (DesRon 29) were not scheduled for modification. The extra fuel made a considerable difference. According to an Atlantic Fleet data sheet of May 1943, a *Wickes*-class ship with three boilers could make 28 or 30 knots fully loaded, compared to 30 to 32 for a four-boiler ship; her cruising radius at economical speed (11 to 12 knots) would be 4,300 to 4,500 nm., compared to 3,200 to 3,500 for the unconverted ship, or 3,000 to 3,200 vs. 2,000 to 2,200 at 75 percent power. These figures were based on a fuel capacity of 108,000 gallons (385.7 tons) for a converted ship, 81,080 (289.6 tons) unconverted. The improvements in a *Clemson*, which began with greater endurance, were less spectacular—4,400 to 4,600 vs. 3,900 to 4,100 nm. at economical speed, 3,600 to 3,900 vs. 2,800 to 3,100 nm. at 75 percent power, on 128,000 (457.1 tons) vs. 111,000 (396.4 tons) gallons.

Thus, the surviving *Wickes*-class ships were much more urgent subjects for refit than were their longer-legged sisters. In addition, by June 1942 the Pacific Fleet was urging the refit of the surviving Asiatic Fleet units (DD 211, 213, 216–218, 222, 226, 228, 230) in view of the great distances in the Pacific. Unfortunately, conversion required as much as five weeks

The *Parrott*, one of the surviving Asiatic Fleet flush deckers, shows the effects of early war modifications in these 29 August 1942 detail views taken at Mare Island. Both after banks of torpedo tubes were removed, each being replaced by two depth-charge throwers (each with a roller loader) and a single 20-mm. gun in a splinter shield; two more depth-charge throwers were mounted aft, just forward of the depth-charge tracks that many flush deckers had carried between wars. Note, too, the new platform for two single 20-mm. guns just abaft the remaining pair of tubes and the boats, which have been moved forward. One boiler and its funnel have been removed. Note the open engine-room skylights between the two banks of triple torpedo tubes.

The *Paul Jones* was typical of flush deckers that retained their 4-inch guns. Note the removal of the fourth funnel and the addition of a total of six 20-mm. guns (two on the main deck aft, two in the 20-mm. gun platform just abaft the torpedo tubes) and the addition of six depth-charge throwers, visible beside their roller racks aft. Note, too, the unusual smoke deflector on her fore funnel. She has an SL destroyer-escort-type microwave surface-search radar forward, with the TBS antenna above it.

The *Overton* (DD 239) shows the results of the prewar escort conversion, with six 3-inch/50s replacing her former four 4-inch/50s and two of her four banks of torpedo tubes. She mounted five 20-mm. as well: two abreast her funnels, one in the small platform replacing her former searchlight platform, two on the 3-inch gun platform aft. She became a fast transport (APD) before her after boiler could be removed in favor of increased fuel tankage. Note the plated-in bridge, a splinter protection measure, and the open conning position built atop the enclosed pilothouse, a wartime change common to many classes of American warships, and partly inspired by British practice. Ironically, her bridge had originally been open, and had been enclosed between wars; the *Allen* (DD 66, see page 33), shows a similar structure. Many World War I destroyers were completed with open bridges, later enclosed. The radars on her foremast are SC for air search and the relatively rare SE for surface search.

in a yard, and escorts were scarce. Therefore, in July CinCLant suggested the indefinite postponement of *Clemson* refits. The program did resume, but in November 1943 CinCLant ended it by deferring indefinitely the conversion of the last five (DD 210, 221, 246, 248, 341—of which the *Barry*, DD 248, was soon converted into an APD with the loss of two boilers). In addition, the *Semmes*, classed as an auxiliary (AG 24) but armed almost as a destroyer, never lost any of her boilers.

The flush deckers generally served on convoy routes, where dual-purpose guns were less important than ASW ordnance. All lost two torpedo tubes in compensation for depth charges and six 20-mm. guns (five in 3-inch/50 ships). Several also had Hedgehog, the ahead-throwing weapon developed by the Royal Navy. As early as March 1942 the CNO suggested its widespread installation, in the flush deckers as well, where it appeared that Hedgehog would replace Number 1 gun forward. DesLant requested a test

The USS *McCormick*, photographed in January 1944, shows the typical result of flush-decker escort modifications, with one boiler removed and HF/DF installed aft as a long-range submarine sensor. She also has Hedgehog just abaft her forward 3-inch/50 gun, all but one of her 20-mm. guns were removed as weight compensation for the two devices. Half the torpedo tubes were retained, presumably against the threat of surface raiders; the U.S. Navy, unlike the Royal Navy, did not have one-ton depth charges that it could fire from destroyer torpedo tubes against very deep U-boats. The small radome accommodated an SF microwave radar, with a tactical radio (TBS) antenna on the yardarm just above. The aerial view shows that the cost of new ASW weapons included removal of two of the six depth-charge throwers previously mounted in such ships. In this form flush deckers combined tactically with the later destroyer escorts, having just twice their gun and torpedo armament but only half their depth-charge throwing capability.

installation in a flush decker, but did not want more than four converted until the efficacy of the new weapon had been demonstrated. DesPac, reflecting the ASW tactics of the day, considered Hedgehog useful enough against a submerged submarine during the daytime, but wondered whether at night the remaining broadside of two 4-inch guns would suffice. Generally a destroyer would head towards the submarine, in which case *no* guns would bear and the submarine might well elect to remain on the surface and penetrate the screen using both her gun and her torpedo tubes. On the other hand, the Royal Navy had been able to retain its Number 1 guns *and* Hedgehog in flush deckers.

In fact, in U.S. service, compensation was limited to one 20-mm. gun with its platform, and two depth-charge throwers; typically, two Hedgehog salvos would be held in ready service lockers, and another five in a magazine. In May 1943 the VCNO ordered installations in ten flush deckers: DD 109, 118, 128,

The *Roper* was one of 36 flush deckers assigned for conversion to fast transports; she is shown newly converted, standing out of Charleston Navy Yard, 21 November 1943. Note the elimination of the wind baffle on her bridge, as the former open structure has been largely plated in, and the elimination of both forward funnels. Her landing craft were LCPLs, for personnel only, as she had no great cargo capacity—unlike the later destroyer escort conversions.

142, 144, 145, 152, 220, 223, and 341, of the Atlantic Fleet. In addition, the two destroyers serving Sound Schools, DD 113 (*Rathburne*) and 187 (*Dahlgren*) were fitted. In May 1944 the *Rathburne* was converted to a fast transport and replaced at the West Coast Sound School by the *Crane*; the *Bainbridge*, DD 246, which had been scheduled for APD conversion, received Hedgehog. The Hedgehog-equipped destroyer force was reduced to nine operational units when the *Dupont* (DD 152) was reduced to auxiliary status in September 1944.

The flush deckers were too delicate to receive very heavy antiaircraft batteries. The sole major exceptions were two ships assigned to the Mediterranean, the *MacLeish* (220) and the *McCormick* (223). Like the more modern units operating there in June 1944, they exchanged their remaining torpedo tubes for Army-type single 40-mm. machine cannon.

The auxiliaries were more extensively modernized. Although the minelayers (DM) retained their original single-purpose (SP) batteries, the minesweepers (DMS) were scheduled to receive 3-inch/50s in place of their SP guns as early as 1942: as assault ships they were likely to be subjected to air attack. At that time the standard APD battery was three 4-inch guns, as in the *Manley*, but all the AVD were to have their 4-inch guns replaced by a pair of

3-inch/50s. It would appear that the 4-inch were retained in the light transports for their fire-support capability.

By 1943 the APD, too, had 3-inch dual-purpose guns, four in all, in place of their SP weapons. From 1944 onward their assigned ultimate battery was three 3-inch/50s, two single Army-type Bofors in place of the Number 4 gun, five Oerlikons, four depth-charge projectors, and a single depth-charge track. By then the DMSs were down to two or three 3-inch/50s and a twin (power-operated) Bofors. In many cases the production of conventional 3-inch/50 DP guns was augmented by "wet" guns taken from submarines rearmed with more powerful weapons. The DMs were also converted to the 3-inch DP gun; in 1944 their "ultimate approved" battery was identical to that of the DMS.

Many of these auxiliaries were used as escorts in wartime. In particular, new-construction AVPs of the *Barnegat* class soon replaced the AVDs, nine of which reverted to destroyer status late in 1943. They were not, however, rearmed for destroyer service, and differed from their near-sisters in having only two boilers and two 3-inch guns.

On the other hand, the APDs proved extremely useful in the confused fighting of the South Pacific, and further conversions were urgently requested. In

The fast transport *Kane*, photographed off San Pedro in April 1945, shows the deck arrangement of such ships, their four landing craft filling the space formerly taken up by torpedo tubes. At this stage of the war, fast transports were prime Kamikaze targets, and they were relatively well armed: the *Kane* shows a pair of single (Army-type) 40-mm. guns aft in place of the former Number 4 3-inch/50 gun, as well as five 20-mm., one of them before her bridge. There were also four depth-charge projectors (two forward of the after deckhouse, two abaft it) and a single stern depth-charge track. As a destroyer, the *Kane* had been armed with 5-inch/51 guns.

The destroyer *MacLeish* shows the standard modification applied to flush deckers after World War I, with the after 4-inch gun moved to atop the deckhouse, exchanged with a 3-inch/23 antiaircraft weapon. The horizontal bars are spreaders for two "flat-top" antennas strung between her masts. Alongside the after deckhouse can be seen ready-service ammunition racks, presumably for the 3-inch gun. Note the total absence of depth charges.

all, 26 ships were converted in wartime: APD 7–12 in October 1942; APD 13 in December; APD 14–18 in January 1943; APD 19 in July; APD 21, 23, 24 in August; APD 20 in October; and APD 22 in December 1943. APD 29 followed in January 1944, and APD 25 in May. Six ex-AVD became APD 31–36 in March, April, and June 1944, but the conversion of AVD 1 and AVD 7 and DD 210, 221, 246, and 341 was canceled in May 1944; in addition, the assignment of DD 237, 244, and 342 as APD 26–28 was canceled. It appears that no ship was ever chosen for conversion to APD 30. By June 1944, destroyer escort conversions were beginning to appear; at the end of the war some of the APDs, including even the *Manley*, the first, reverted to destroyer status before they were stricken.

Of the three surviving destroyers reduced to non-combatant status under the London Treaty, DD 163 and 259 became the unpowered water barges YW 57 and 56. The former became a Damage Control Hulk, DCH 1, for training at Pearl Harbor, but was scuttled en route there in December 1941. YW 56 was reactivated as the USS *Moosehead* (IX 98), and ultimately was returned to near-destroyer status by the San Diego destroyer base; she was used extensively for operational development, particularly CIC work. The USS *Taylor*, DD 94, was not used; her bow replaced that of the USS *Blakeley* (DD 150) in 1942.

From September 1944 onward, the destroyers and auxiliaries began to pass into the miscellaneous auxiliary (AG) category: AG 80–83 in September, 84–85 in October, 86 in December, 87 in January 1945, 91 and 95 in March 1945, 96–97 in May 1945, 99–102 and 106–120 in June 1945, a total of 31 (plus AG 19 and 21, which had been converted to DMS 2 and 3, and which had returned to their earlier status). AG 80–85, 104, 105, and 108–110 served as target ships for air attack training; AG 86 and 87 were converted to submarine training torpedo targets for the Atlantic Fleet; AG 98 and 99 served as plane guards and escorts for escort carriers working up; AG 100, 101, and 106 helped train submarines. The *Dahlgren*, AG 91, left the Key West Sound School for the Mine Warfare Test Station; the *Babbitt*, AG 102, served the Underwater Sound Laboratory at New London; the *Hamilton*, AG 110, carried out experimental mine-sweeping off the California coast.

Finally, in April 1945 DesLant proposed limiting all repairs to 1,200-ton destroyers "to those necessary to provide essential hull integrity and a maximum speed of 25 knots provided that the subject vessels are designated to be scrapped upon the cessation of ASW in the Atlantic." Admiral King agreed on 9 May, but asked that the 12 best be retained for refresher and shakedown training. They became AG 96, 97, 103, and 112–120. In July it was decided that ex-flush-decker APDs would either be retained as rear-area escorts (re-rated destroyers) or scrapped. By VJ-Day, apart from ex-APDs, there remained only four of the original destroyers in DD status.

The large force of flush deckers that survived hard war service was soon sold out of the service for scrap; by 1947 all were gone. An ironic footnote to the history of this type is that the last survivor was a ship converted to a "banana boat" after she had been sold out of service—in the big *pre*-war scrapping program.

4

Destroyer ASW: World War I and After

The restriction of the destroyer's mission to torpedo attack/antidestroyer defense did not last very long. While the first U.S. destroyers were being built, the Royal Navy experimented with destroyer-borne antisubmarine measures in HMS *Starfish* (1901). The first in a long line of pronouncements that the submarine menace was ended was the result. Public accounts of these trials suggest that detection of the submarine was no problem, and that its destruction could easily be assured by means of an explosive on a spar. The subject then went into eclipse, to be called back into great prominence in 1914.

The ASW problem can be broken into three parts. First, the ASW forces must be able to sense that there is a submarine in some area. They can then try to *localize* the submarine by a detailed hunt within that area; and finally they must try to sink the submarine. The last part of the problem is the most visible in terms of the ordnance aboard a destroyer, but the other two are the most intractable. In particular, the first part has never really been solved; indeed, our present reliance on Polaris is a statement of faith in that direction. The reason is, of course, that a submarine, even a primitive one, has only the weakest sort of signature.

The submarine of 1914 remained a relatively primitive warship, essentially a surface ship with the ability to hide underwater, where it would suffer serious loss of mobility. Thus, standard operational procedure for submarines was to operate on the surface, submerging only at the approach of enemy forces or for concealment preparatory to or following a torpedo attack. In fact, a major effect of the growth of

ASW forces during World War I was to force submarines to operate submerged a greater and greater proportion of the time, and so to lose much of their mobility.

As late as 1918, for example, U-boats could operate submerged at 10 knots for only 3 hours, at 8 knots for 12, at 4 knots for 36, and at a minimum speed of 1 knot for 72 hours. From an ASW point of view, these figures meant that a U-boat could stay down long enough to exhaust hunters; but on the other hand, she could not get very far in the process, and hence lost much of her own effectiveness.

For the ASW forces, the most useful signature produced by the submarine was *visual*: the "feather of a periscope, the track of a torpedo, even (in clear water) a shallowly submerged submarine"; and it was to reduce *visual* detections, after all, that the submarine submerged in the first place. All of these signatures were useful only at short range, and all required the active cooperation of the submarine.

One other type of signature was considered useful: the sound produced by a submarine's machinery and screws. As early as 1915, the Royal Navy began to experiment with passive sound gear, or hydrophones. In theory, ranges as great as one to five miles were possible against a submarine going 4–5 knots; but like any passive device, this one was subject to the self-noise of its platform and to the skill of its operator in recognizing the sound of a submarine—which could protect itself by silent running. The requirement for platform silence could be translated into a requirement that the platform stop every time it listened. In modern terms this would be a "sprint

Depth charges continued to be the standard destroyer ASW weapons through World War II, when ahead-thrown types began to supersede them. The USS *Mayo*, photographed in August 1944, clearly shows her stern tracks as well as two roller racks (to port) for K-guns. The 83-foot Coast Guard boat alongside is equipped with the new generation of weapon: Mousetrap, a rocket-propelled bomb. Its racks are visible, folded down on her foredeck. The *Mayo* has four 20-mm. guns on "portable" platforms replacing her after torpedo tubes.

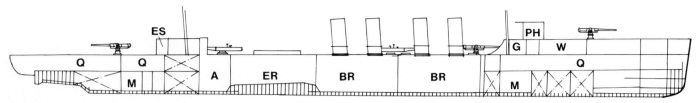

DD 56 inboard (contract plan)

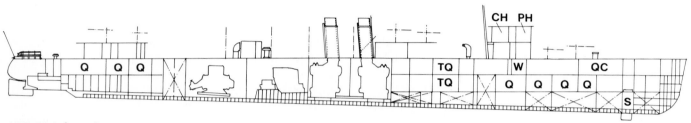

APD 20 inboard

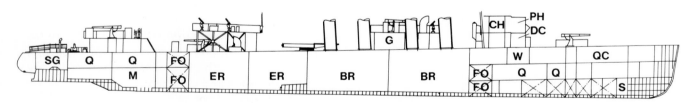

Decatur (DD 341)–in escort configuration, 1941

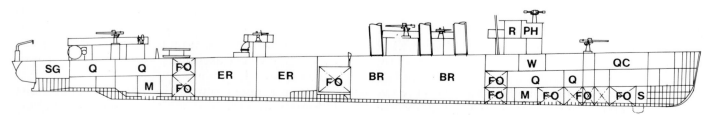

DMS 14 inboard

and drift" mode of operations; it would make sense only if the submarine could be located approximately by other means.

Efforts were made to install hydrophones in American destroyers. The Special Board on Anti-Submarine Devices designed a series of hydrophones, and in November 1917 tested a "K" (drifter) tube aboard the destroyer *Aylwin* off the *Boston* lightship "in a fairly rough sea with the ship rolling from 20 to 25 degrees each side." The destroyer could detect the submarine *G–2* at a range of 400 yards above the noise of auxiliaries, but beyond 800 to 1,000 yards she was drowned out. However, with the auxiliaries secured the submarine was immediately picked up and heard for about three miles. The test was encouraging, but on the other hand destroyers could hardly lie-to with all of their auxiliary machinery shut down. Further development led to the MV, a pair of line arrays each consisting of 12 air tubes, mounted on the bottom of a ship and steered by means of an acoustic compensator. This was sufficiently promising for the board to suggest MV installations for all destroyers; the Chief of Naval Operations concurred on 10 June 1918. Almost simultaneously, Admiral Sims reported a new "K" tube installation, which he recommended for mass fitting in destroyers. C&R immediately authorized the MV-tube installations in new destroyers under construction, with assistance to be provided by the Navy Yards, and many ships were so fitted. Generally, the MV tubes were fitted in blisters designed to reduce the loss of speed incurred.

These were not experimental installations. For example, in January 1919 Steam Engineering opposed omission of the MV-tube system in destroyers on the ground that an improved form:

> . . . will constitute a part of the standard equipment for all future destroyers. It is probable that the development of the next year along these lines will result in an electrical MV apparatus. The efficient operation of the present acoustical MV apparatus requires that the listening booth be located immediately adjacent to, and between the outboard lines. An electrical MV apparatus will permit the location of a listening booth in any part of the destroyer.

This issue will be familiar to those concerned with cable signal losses between current high-powered sonars, such as the SQS-26 and -53, and their signal processors; the signal processor of 1918–19 was, of course, the human ear, aided only very slightly (if at all) by electrical amplification. In any case, by January 1919 the listening tubes associated with the MV system were no longer being installed in new destroyers, although they were continuing to receive the blisters and hydrophones proper. Only in February was an experimental MV16B installation authorized for the *Blakeley*, then building at Cramps.

After the war, MV installations continued at a slow pace. For example, in May 1922 the installation of MV receivers on six Atlantic and six Pacific destroyers (Divisions 40 and 36) was authorized. A decade later they were gone, replaced by the new technology of magnetostrictive crystals and ultrasonic echo detection—sonar.

During World War I wide-area detection was attempted by analyzing intercepted U-boat radio traffic and by assessing standard U-boat operating procedures, e.g., their routes to and from operational areas. This led to very few kills, however, because of the inefficiency of such detectors as hydrophones for search *within* a small area. Nevertheless, radio traffic and analysis of U-boat operations made for an effective use of ASW minefields, which in the end accounted for more U-boats than any other weapon. It must be emphasized, however, that total U-boat kills were not nearly high enough by themselves, at least until the very end, to save the Allies from strangulation. It was a tactical device, the convoy, that more effectively discouraged U-boat attacks on shipping.

In effect the convoy system was an attempt to turn the problem on its head. Since the mission of the Allied navies was to protect their sea lines of communication rather than merely to sink U-boats, there was little point in dispersing ASW forces over wide areas—indeed, in many cases, over any areas *except* those that had to be defended. By concentrating the U-boats' targets in a convoy, they shrank those areas that had to be guarded. Any U-boats attacking convoys automatically localized themselves: lookouts on escorts could locate the U-boat by sighting the periscope it had to raise to make its attack, or by following back the wake of its torpedo. The sustained underwater speed of the U-boat was sufficiently low that a fast ship such as a destroyer could be relatively certain of finding a U-boat near the spot where her periscope vanished or the track of her torpedo began. Although the destroyer had no sure means of following any underwater maneuvers by the U-boat, the good chance of killing or at least severely damaging a U-boat that *had* been found discouraged U-boat commanders from exposing themselves by attacking convoys. An incidental effect of the convoy system was to reduce drastically the density of shipping over much of the ocean, so that, in the absence of intelligence as to convoy routing, the U-boats found, on average, relatively few targets. Radio traffic analysis was of course very useful in routing convoys clear of known U-boat locations.

Indeed, a major thrust of Allied ASW operations in their mature phase towards the end of World War I was the large-scale use of aircraft specifically to

Until well into World War II, depth charges were the only available ASW weapons, and they were employed by all destroyers, even quite small ones. Four destroyers, laid up at the Philadelphia Navy Yard awaiting disposal, still show theirs in this 5 March 1919 photograph: the *Lamson*, *Flusser*, *Paul Jones*, and farthest from the camera, the *Decatur*. Such small ships had to carry very heavy loads because the probability that any single depth charge would sink a submarine was quite small. Note, too, the double emergency steering wheels visible on the nearest pair of ships, with twin centerline 18-inch torpedo tubes forward. The *Decatur* shows a special depth-charge track extension to clear her raked stern.

force U-boats to remain submerged, i.e., immobile. It might be added that hydrophones would have a similar effect, since the only way of nullifying them was for the U-boat to go dead in the water, or at best to creep at very low speed. Nor were these two measures purely ones of *mobility* reduction. The knowledge that a sighting of the wake of his periscope might well lead to an attack acted as a deterrent to observation *by* U-boat commanders, and hence further reduced their effectiveness.

The earliest ASW weapon was the ram; indeed, many submarines have been lost in peacetime to inadvertent ramming. Other devices tried by the Allies included towed explosives, detonated by the ship when they appeared to foul a submarine, and nonricochet shells. All were overshadowed by the depth charge, fused to explode at a fixed depth. Its tactical theory was simple. A destroyer would pass over the suspected position of the submarine, laying charges each of which would in theory damage the submarine *if*

it exploded close enough. The suspected position, on the other hand, was subject to uncertainty due to the movement of the submarine between the time of sighting and the arrival of the destroyer; in effect, what was wanted was a *pattern* of depth charges to cover the area available to the submarine. These considerations governed all subsequent depth-charge installations.

The Royal Navy introduced depth charges in 1916. At first they were so scarce that destroyers could carry no more than one or two, hardly enough to lay any sort of pattern. As production expanded, numbers available increased to the point where the very probabilistic character of the depth charge could be appreciated. In particular, the line of charges that could be dropped from depth-charge tracks aft had only a low probability of encompassing U-boat maneuvers; the Royal Navy's solution was a depth-charge mortar.

The U.S. Navy was aware of these developments even before the American entry into World War I. It began manufacturing a 50-pound depth charge (Mk I) in February 1917. This was far too little explosive; by this time the British were using 300 pounds. A British-type depth charge with a U.S.-designed hydrostatic exploder, Mk II, was ready by the fall of 1917. These charges could be set as deep as 200 feet; as the U-boats were improved, a maximum depth of 300 feet was introduced (Mk III). The final war development was a much heavier depth charge (Mk IV): 745 pounds, 600 of which were high explosive (HE). The first were sent overseas in September 1918.

The first U.S. destroyer installations consisted of two charges in stern slings. Depth-charge tracks (Mk I) were designed in the spring of 1918: deliveries began that April. They carried eight charges each; later a five-charge extension was designed. Depth-charge loads were very large. For example, as early as August 1917, C&R was calculating the stability effects of no fewer than *68* depth charges to be carried by the *Bainbridge*; and 80 or more in the flivvers and thousand-tonners.

The lessons of wartime ASW operations are reflected in a paper submitted to the General Board in November 1920, by Lieutenant F. G. Percival, later a leading writer on tactics. Better ASW efficiency might be bought by

—Better lookouts (organization, supervision, location)
—Improved communication between lookout to officer of the deck
—Better depth-charge patterns, to cover a wider area more rapidly
—Changes in ship organization and tactics.

The emphasis on the *visual* is striking; the point of the wider area of barrage was simply that the submarine might have considerable time to maneuver effectively unobserved between sighting and attack; there is no hope here of an effective sonar, although one was under development. The depth-charge pattern was based on the probability that a submarine had a speed of 4 knots when its periscope vanished, accelerated to 5 in the first minute, 7 in the next, and finally to 8 knots; it also allowed for a loss of a quarter of speed with rudder hard over (tactical diameter, 300 yards). The pattern proposed was extremely heavy: a line of stern charges backed by two lines (at 120 and 240 yards to each side of the ship) fired by fast-reloading Y-guns and yet another line (400 yards) carried by short-range torpedoes.

Percival wanted to modify the thousand-tonners and flivvers as special ASW units, with two quick-loading Y-guns and triple tubes for the very short range torpedoes. His suggestion was rejected, but on 5 March 1921 the Secretary of the Navy did authorize some depth-charge equipment as standard for all

destroyers except the minelayers, to be exercised as part of gunnery practice.

The low estate of ASW after World War I was shown by the general relocation of the Y-guns mounted on the after deckhouse to the much wetter fantail, a 4-inch gun being interchanged with them: the anti-destroyer mission took precedence over ASW. This emphasis also showed in training: in 1935, in connection with proposed special ASW conversions of some of the older destroyers, CinC U.S. Fleet would comment that, although he did not like to lose destroyers to specialized tasks, ASW "does not progress under our present method of training, where anti-submarine work is a side issue of many ships having as a major objective the development of fleet tactics and skill in the use of guns and torpedoes."

There remained the major problem of reliable detection and tracking of a submerged submarine. By 1918 both British and U.S. scientists had begun to work with echo-ranging gear at "supersonic" frequencies. The earliest set, designated QA, was tested at sea in 1927. This operated at high frequency (20 to 40 kc) and hence at short range; in addition it was useless above about 4 knots. An improved QC began to appear in service in 1934, at which time nine QA were fitted to destroyers, and two more (DD 141 and 248) had XQC. Twenty-four more were proposed for echo-ranging gear. Many had passive listening gear.

QC was the prototype for the primary U.S. destroyer sonar of World War II; by September 1939, 60 destroyers had it, and sets were appearing at the rate of 14 a year. It was a "searchlight" type in which the operator chose a bearing, sent out his (14-degree wide) beam, and waited for a "ping" to return before trying another bearing. Such a procedure still gave a low probability of initial contact. Hence, any event giving away the submarine's position, e.g., a torpedo launch, would increase very sharply the probability of contact. A deficiency of the "searchlight" system was that a maneuvering submarine could evade attack by moving out of the relatively narrow beam—which, moreover, was so wide vertically that it could give only range and bearing, not depth of target.

Typical results were those obtained by the developmental Destroyer Division 19 (QC 1A, 24 kc sonar) off San Diego, in the fall of 1936:

Destroyer Speed	Submarine Depth	Average Maximum Range, Yards
5 knots	Periscope	3,120
10	Periscope	2,620
15	Periscope	1,750
5	90 feet	3,635
10	90 feet	3,300
15	90 feet	1,760

The theory of depth-charge attack was to cover an area of uncertainty within which the submarine was located, so that however the submarine turned to evade, she would still suffer considerable damage. The necessary pattern had to extend both horizontally and vertically. In this 1943 photograph, a destroyer in the Aleutians has just dropped a four-charge pattern; the differing circles of foam indicate different time lapses since charges exploded at different depths; the destroyer is turning to make a second attack should the first fail. A major drawback of such tactics was the effect of the explosions on sonar reception while the ship sought to reacquire the target for a new attack.

Until after World War II, the destroyer torpedo was primarily a weapon against surface ships, its ASW value limited to attacks on surfaced submarines in a very few instances. Even so, most U.S. destroyers and destroyer escorts assigned to ASW operations during World War II carried heavy torpedo batteries, and the weapons were not discarded until the need arose for much increased antiaircraft batteries in 1945. Here a *Mahan*-class destroyer fires one of her quadruple waist torpedo tubes during World War II; the torpedo is a Mk 15 Mod 3, and the occasion must be training, since helmets are not in evidence. By the time these ships had seen extensive service, there were many complaints that the waist tubes, on the main deck, were too wet and thus suffered too much from corrosion.

The flush-deck destroyer *Semmes* was a major U.S. sonar test ship from 1935 onward. She tested sonar equipment through World War II, operating also with the Key West Sound School, until the capitulation of Germany. In common with most such ships, she was provided with Hedgehog, visible forward of her bridge in this 12 April 1945 photograph taken at Charleston Navy Yard. She was almost unique in retaining all four funnels, two of which appear to carry vertical Yagi antennas, and nearly all of her normal destroyer armament (with the exception of a single 3-inch gun aft) had been removed. Note, too, the absence of any air-search radar, although she did retain a surface-search set, the new SU; she also retained four depth-charge throwers and two depth-charge tracks aft.

These figures were to prove grossly optimistic under North Atlantic conditions; the rubber dome enclosing the sonar head severely limited effective operating speed. One of the major advances achieved by the Royal Navy between wars was a thin steel dome permitting sonar operation at higher speeds.

Domes were first ordered in the fall of 1941. A 6 November 1941 report on the state of ASW weapons and devices claimed that without a dome sonar was worthless above 15 knots; and that passive detection, e.g., of a surfaced submarine, was impossible for a *submarine* speed below 3 knots. A contact made at 15 knots could be held to 20. With the dome, *search* speeds of 20 to 24 were expected. These latter figures also turned out to be overoptimistic.

An installation policy adopted in 1938 called for two sonars per destroyer, perhaps to achieve a better search rate at high ship speed. It was abandoned only in 1942, when the demand for more ASW ships quite overcame the production rate of the sonars. As the destroyer escort program expanded, the decision was made to cut the destroyer quota to one each, transferring the now-surplus sets to the escorts. Single

sonars had been specified for the surviving old destroyers in the original 1938 General Board letter, so that they suffered no reduction in capability.

It must be kept in mind that these sonars were envisaged as attack aids, *not* search devices. Thus, the commander of DesDiv 60, experimenting with sonars off San Diego: "no dependence whatever can be placed upon defense sound screening . . . a cleverly handled submarine has two chances out of three to get through. On the other hand, once the submarine's presence and location are known, time permitting, her ultimate destruction can be made fairly simple." The submarine *that gave any hint of her presence* could be tracked continuously; crash dives were no longer a certain means of escape. Effective *search* sonar would not become a reality until 1946.

Postwar weapon developments included improvements in depth charges and in their projectors. In 1936 the question of 300- vs. 600-pound charges was raised by a Special Board on Naval Ordnance. A careful mathematical analysis showed that, for a given depth-charge track, the heavier charge would always

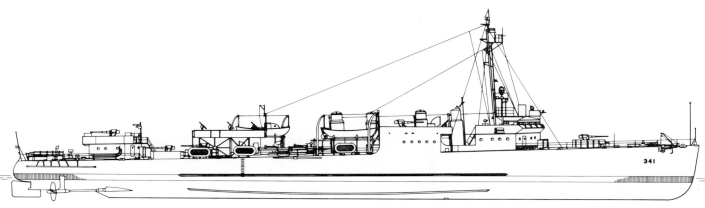

Decatur DD 341   early 1942   314'5" o.a.   One of the first "four pipers" to receive armament modernization, DD 341 retained all four stacks. Six 3"/50 DP replaced the four 4" guns and two of the four triple 21" torpedo-tube mounts. At the time of this drawing, ASW armament was one "Y" gun and two depth-charge racks. AA armament consisted of five .50-cal. water-cooled machine guns. While an "SA" radar for air search was fitted, there was no surface search, and the "crow's nest" was retained at the masthead.

Under refit at Mare Island on 21 August 1945, the destroyer *Lang* (DD 399) shows a standard late-war underwater battery, with teardrop-shaped (fast-sinking) charges stacked on her fantail and loaded in the two roller-loaders circled. The object on her main deck forward of the two twin 40-mm. guns is a 5-inch loading machine for crew practice, with two Mk 51 directors for 40-mm. control forward of it. Twin 20-mm. guns have just been fitted; note the pair on the *Fletcher*-class destroyer alongside.

be more effective, even when the lower number of such charges (six rather than eight 300-pounders in a standard track) was taken into account. On the other hand, it was impractical to design a projector for the heavy charges.

Another factor in depth-charge effectiveness was speed of sinking. Improved Mk 3 and 4 depth charges (Mk 6 and 7) were designed in 1937 for sink rates of 8 and 9 ft./sec., compared to 6 for the older types.

Within the fleet the Y-gun was disliked as a space-consuming, awkward piece of apparatus. Its existence was clearly understood to be a consequence of the probabilistic character of depth-charge barrages, i.e., of the difficulty of following a submerged U-boat. Sonar was at first seen as a solution to the latter problem, but that was not to be the case. Sonar could not see a submarine close to it, due to the shape of its beam; therefore, there existed a blind time between the firing order and the arrival of charges near the suspected location of the submarine. The best that BuOrd could do was to reduce the space demanded by the depth-charge projector. About 1936 it designed a new type of projector, the K-gun—in effect, half a Y-gun. This could be mounted in numbers along the side of the ship; it was first specified in the *Sims* class (DD 409). However, its production had low priority, and K-guns did not appear until June 1941. A major factor in the effectiveness of the projector was a simple roller rack designed to permit rapid reloading.

5

Leaders and the Interwar Period: 1917–1940

The very great number of U.S. destroyers and the total absence of light cruisers to lead them (or to scout for the fleet) made the development of large destroyers or "destroyer leaders" a major concern of late-war and postwar designers. Ultimately, as in Britain (V&W Class), the big leader would turn into the next generation of (bigger) destroyers. C&R began to consider such designs as early as 1917. One influence was a series of letters by Captain H.P. Huse advocating the merger of the light cruiser and destroyer types—a step often suggested in this period. For example, before World War I Admiral Fisher of the Royal Navy had ordered a very large destroyer, HMS *Swift*, which was ultimately used as a flotilla leader and was armed with a 6-inch gun. Certainly the Navy was aware of wartime efforts in Britain to use enlarged destroyers (leaders) as flagships of destroyer flotillas. In Germany, the merger was actually carried out, but the resulting *S113* class, armed with four 5.9-inch guns and a new 23.6-inch torpedo, was too heavily armed for its light construction; moreover, the precise role of these craft is not clear.

The first U.S. sketches were flush deckers armed either with six 5-inch guns and two triple TT, or with four 5-inch and four tubes. The latter was unexciting in view of the results being achieved with quite conventional destroyers; surely one could gain more by adding 500 or 1,000 tons. The ultimate design (February 1919) was a 2,200-ton boat with five 5-inch on the centerline and 12 TT in wing mounts. A slightly raised forecastle was provided to improve seakeeping. The extra 1,000 tons, then, in the end bought two more broadside guns, two knots, and a greater steaming radius. Surviving accounts do not show

clearly why these characteristics were chosen. An important feature, however, was a double bottom, which was a kind of implicit admission that this was no longer to be considered a cheap expendable type.

A torpedo armament of two quadruple centerline tubes was considered but rejected. This would have increased the broadside by a third, but was rejected by Ordnance:

> . . . it is desirable, under many circumstances, to hold several torpedoes in reserve. This was demonstrated in the Battle of Jutland where the British destroyers, during the initial phases . . . fired all of their torpedoes and later had numerous chances for successful torpedo attack, but did not have any torpedoes. The reservation of a number of torpedoes can best be accomplished by arrangement of tubes . . . .

This was a common argument in favor of TT that could not be trained on either side of the ship.

It was no great surprise that some in the Navy were disappointed at how little a thousand tons had bought. The outstanding critic of U.S. destroyer design at this time was Lieutenant Commander F.S. Craven, who had operational experience with the destroyer force. He therefore reflected the operator's preference for centerline torpedo tubes (indeed, for tubes mounted on the fantail). In July 1920, he submitted a sketch design to the General Board over the objections of what he considered a stodgy BuOrd. He called for a turtle-back forecastle, twin 5-inch single-purpose (SP) guns in Nos. 1, 2, and 3 positions, and a triple tube in No. 4; two more (centerline) triple tubes were to be mounted between the second funnel

Destroyers of DesRon 20 steam in line abreast for a Movietone News camera, September 1936: the *Monaghan*, *Dale*, and *Worden*. Their large Mk 33 dual-purpose directors, making them effective antiaircraft ships, were unique among the world's navies at this time.

Table 5–1. Large Destroyer and Leader Projects, 1912 and 1917–19

	Large Destroyer	Scheme 1	Scheme 2 10 September 1917	Scheme 3	Leader 26 February 1919
LWL	385	390	355	330	360
Beam	35	37.5	35.5	32	36.4
Draft	12.25	11.5	11.25	10.75	12.1
SHP	40,000	57,600	43,200	28,800	55,000
Speed	35	35	35	35	37
Endurance	2,500/20	—	—	—	2,500/20
5-in./51	4 (4-in./50)	6	6	4	5
3-in. AA	—	2	2	2	2
21-in. TT	6 × 2	2 × 3	2 × 3	4 × 3	4 × 3
Hull	593	745	608	490	775
Fittings	65	130	107	80	110
Machinery	940	875	650	445	750
Armament	60	75	75	65	70
Equipment & Outfit	95	158	132	110	125
Margin	—	25	16	14	50
Ammunition	24	77	77	57	60
Standard	1,777	2,085	1,665	1,261	1,940
RFW	33	30	20	14	25
Fuel	350	450	415	400	235
Normal	2,160	2,565	2,100	1,675	2,200
GM	—	2.8	2.5	2.02	2.5

Note: Machinery weights include machinery liquids. Equipment and Outfit weight includes 2/3 stores. Standard displacement is computed for comparison with later designs. The "large destroyer" project dates from October 1912.

and the after deckhouse. A single 5-in./25 AA gun would be mounted between the funnels.

Craven considered the fantail tubes so valuable that he expected to provide six reloads for them. Six more (for the remaining six tubes) would be stored under the searchlights between the two banks of tubes. The theory of the stern tube seems to have been that a destroyer armed with it could fire a full broadside, then unmask it once more as it turned away.

This proposal excited considerable interest; on 30 July the planning division of the Office of the CNO generally approved its provisions. A General Board proposal to set endurance at 2,500 nm. at 20 knots *and* at least 8,000 nm. at economical speed was set aside in favor of a single requirement for 6,000 nm. at 15 knots, which exceeded the later standard.

The Director of Gunnery Exercises and Engineering Performance commented that he would much prefer two or three AA guns of 3-inch or greater caliber to the single gun specified: AA made sense only in terms of zone barrage with shrapnel. This kind of improvement would be worth the loss of a 5-inch gun.

C&R reported that it would accommodate *four* sets of tubes to give a nine-tube broadside, replacing

the amidships bank with two banks, port and starboard. The fourth tube, on the fantail, would encounter seas breaking over the fantail, as well as the blast effects of the after guns—no one seems to have remembered the cautionary experience of the early flivvers, and indeed the idea of the fantail tube resurfaced in the destroyer proposals of 1930.

On the other hand, the matter of reloads remained moot, and Craven's twin 5-inch did not materialize.

An unusual feature of the characteristics adopted by the General Board was the inclusion of a small scout airplane for observation. This distant ancestor of LAMPS was at first regarded as useful but impractical. In August 1923, the USS *Charles Ausburn* (DD 294) actually operated a small seaplane (TS1) from a platform forward of her bridge, an arrangement reminiscent of that in many contemporary British and Japanese light cruisers. In 1927 the Bureau of Aeronautics proposed a flush decker equipped with a catapult atop a single *sextuple* torpedo tube abaft the funnels (the other six TT were suppressed). Among other things, however, Ordnance observed that these mounts would be heavier and hence less handy than a single cruiser 6-in./53 gun. Even quadruple tubes would present some problems in torpedo

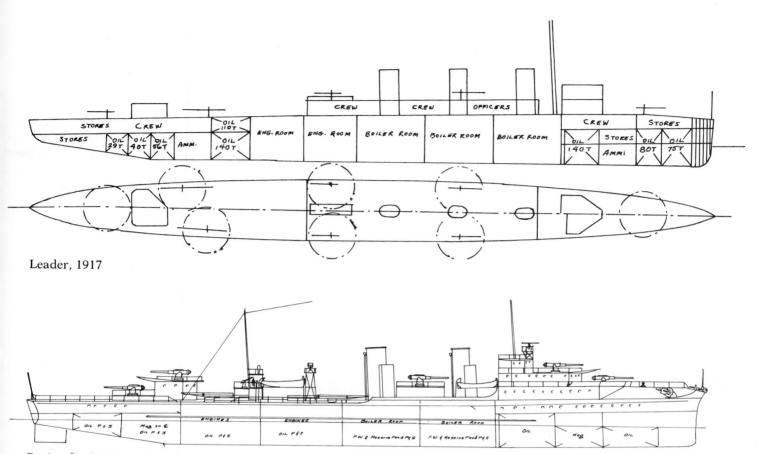

Leader, 1917

Design for 2,200-ton leader, 1919

strength at the ejection velocities required to clear the side of the ship. Several Dutch destroyers of this period actually carried aircraft, their primary function being to scout in the vast spaces of the East Indies. U.S. airplane experiments were revived in 1940.

The General Board suggested the construction of five flotilla leaders in FY 1921, but they were not authorized—perhaps Congress felt that the mass of wartime construction was quite enough. In succeeding years the 1919 design was used within the Navy Department as a basis for making cost estimates for new heavy destroyers, should such vessels be desired. However, scarce funds were put instead into the main fleet: capital ship construction (carriers) and modernization (battleships), and the construction of cruisers for very long range operations. Certainly the advent of fast carriers such as the *Lexington* decreased the prospective value of new destroyers: it was assumed that only big cruisers could escort them on long, high-speed runs.

In April 1927, C&R reopened the destroyer design question, "for the purpose primarily of incorporating a high-pressure steam plant, and secondarily, of consolidating the experience and developments since the war on existing destroyers." The new steam plant was particularly important. Indeed, with its improved fuel economy, it would be absolutely necessary if very long range was to be achieved on a moderate displacement—and range would be a key factor in Pacific warfare. No construction was planned; indeed, there existed no General Board requirement. The constructors were still impressed by the virtues of centerline tubes, and using the device suggested by Aeronautics, they could cram in all 12 tubes in two sextuple mounts. There were to be four 5-inch guns on the centerline. It turned out that many in the fleet favored the new handy 5-in./25 dual purpose (DP) over the more powerful 5-in./51 mounted in some older units. This was the beginning of proposals for DP guns on U.S. destroyers. There seems to have been little concrete consideration at the time as to just how useful such weapons would be in a lively ship with limited fire control capability.

A *normal* displacement of about 1,600 tons was contemplated; standard displacement would have been less than 1,400 tons.

The destroyer leader question remained. In the fall of 1927 C&R began studies to provide a guide for General Board characteristics. One study was an ex-

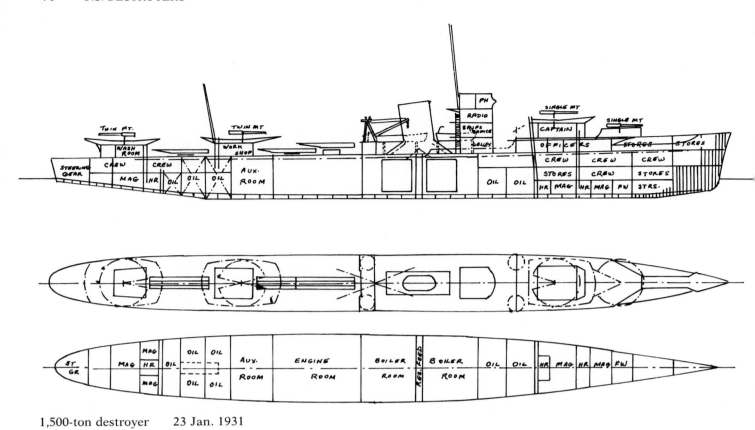

1,500-ton destroyer   23 Jan. 1931

pansion of the destroyer to 1,600 or 1,700 tons; one a 2,000-ton type; and one a larger unit comparable to the new French and Italian heavy destroyers or even the Japanese ultra-light cruiser *Yubari*. The French units were intended to operate as independent strike squadrons, a function that would have been a new one for U.S. units; the *Yubari*, on the other hand, might be seen as a prototype for heavy destroyers to screen the Japanese Fleet. This choice of studies seems to have come entirely from within the preliminary design section of C&R and so did not reflect any naval policy decisions. In the end, eight sketch schemes, ranging from a slightly enlarged destroyer of 1,421 tons to a mini-cruiser of 2,900, were presented. Mixed batteries of 6-in./53 and 5-in./25 AA guns were suggested: on 2,900 tons four 6-inch and four 5-inch as well as the usual four triple 21 in TT could be carried at a trial speed of 36.25 knots. C&R commented that "the suggestion has been made that a uniform battery of 5-in./25 AA guns might prove more serviceable than a mixed battery."

The General Board opted for a slightly enlarged destroyer, suitable for mass production and capable of maneuvering with standard destroyers. It may have been influenced by the Geneva Disarmament Con-

ference, which had proposed an 1,850-ton limit (1,500 for destroyers); In April 1928 C&R suggested

the displacement of 1,500 tons for consideration . . . in view of the possible advantage of building one or two vessels of this size that would be suitable for service as Leaders with the present destroyers and the general behavior of which would give valuable information for use in connection with future destroyer designs when the replacement of the present destroyers is undertaken.

The characteristics actually adopted (1928) called for a maximum displacement of 1,850 tons, four of the longer range 5-in./51s, 12 TT, and an endurance of not less than 6,000 miles at 12 knots. A speed of 35 knots was specified. This was in effect a destroyer with some squadron facilities, and the considerable excess tonnage seemed wasted. Both destroyer and leader remained dormant through 1929, but in January 1930 the General Board once more began to construct characteristics.

A new factor was treaty regulation, which was finally extended to destroyers. The London Treaty (signed April 1930) embodied the earlier Geneva proposals on destroyer and leader unit tonnage. Other

Table 5–2. Destroyer Leader Projects, 1927–28

	21 Nov 27	Scheme 1	Scheme 3	Scheme 5	Scheme 6	Scheme 7	Scheme 8
LWL	435	325	340	390	380	435	390
Beam	42.5	34	34.5	38.5	37.5	42.5	39
Draft (full)	13.5	10.4	11	10.8	10.8	13	11.25
Standard	2,900	1,421	1,623	2,020	1,925	2,900	2,150
Normal	3,300	1,640	1,860	2,310	2,200	3,300	2,450
SHP	56,000	34,000	42,500	54,000	54,000	62,500	62,500
Speed	35.1	34.5	35.5	37.4	38	36.25	36.25
Endurance	2,500/20	3,950/20	4,200/20	4,600/20	4,380/20	4,800/20	5,400/20
6-in./53	4	—	—	—	—	4	3
5-in./25	2	4	4	5	4	4	4
21-in. TT	4 × 4	4 × 3	4 × 3	4 × 3	4 × 3	4 × 3	4 × 3

Note: Schemes 1 through 8 are dated February, 1928. Scheme 1 incorporated a catapult. Schemes 1 and 3 were 4-boiler arrangements; 5 through 8 had 6 boilers each. All had two shafts.

clauses set national total tonnage limits. Guns of 5.1 inches and over were prohibited. France refused to sign and continued her program of super-destroyer construction (2,500 tons, 5.5-inch guns). It must be kept in mind that all of these displacements are *standard*, i.e., without fuel or reserve feed water. They are thus somewhat unrepresentative of realistic operating conditions.

This time ships actually resulted. The process began with a General Board hearing in January 1930; it was noted that C&R studies the previous year had produced a 1,440 ton, 27,000 shp boat satisfying the board's armament criteria. Presumably the extra 410 tons of the leader might go towards more modern equipment or seakeeping.

One alternative view was that the Navy should build two types: one to screen the battle line, 28 to 30 knots, 2,400 tons, many 5-in./51s; the other purely for attack, 1,100 tons, 37 to 40 knots. This was the old destroyer flotilla idea, and it did not go well with the important chief of war plans, whose reponsibility it was to get new construction into the primary war plan—which for this period we can take as the Orange plan. This was the famous plan for the fleet to fight its way across the Pacific to relieve or recapture the Philippines; island assaults seem to have been contemplated at an early date. The attack boat would not have sufficient range, and would lose its speed in heavy weather. However, there was little to be gained in the larger vessel—far better to concentrate on a single utility type. There may have been a feeling, unspoken, that Congress would never buy enough specialized types to equip a balanced fleet.

As for the gun, there was strong feeling against the 4-inch because it was too light, and because foreign types had 5-inch guns or better. The lower-velocity 5-in./25 was favored largely because it had a lighter round more easily handled in a lively ship; it was claimed that in any case the ships could not control their fire even out to its maximum range. A discussion of gun positions brought out the excessive wetness of bow guns—practically a guarantee that a major factor in new destroyers would be dryness forward, by means of a high forecastle.

In November, C&R returned with some designs: 1,375- and 1,500-ton destroyers and an 1,850-ton leader. All had the forecastle, which lowered the center of gravity (CG) of the hull in order to get good stability without great beam, hence would permit greater draft.

"With the increased freeboard forward and broader stern there is ample reserve buoyancy and the after-deck will be roomier." All three types were armed with four 5-in./25s. The leader was to have two quadruple TT on the centerline; the 1,375 tonner, four wing (triple) mounts; the 1,500 tonner, 3 triple on the centerline. The leader had half a knot more speed (35.5 knots) and an endurance (at 12 knots) of 8,100 nm. against the destroyer's 6,500. It also was unique in being armored: there was .5-inch STS (Special Treatment Steel) around the engines, gun-crew shelters, and bridge. Some weight also went into heavier construction. A discussion brought out the fact that the 35-ton margin in the leader design was sufficient to put in eight 4- or 5-inch twin mounts or five single 5-inch (25 or 51 cal.). It would seem that this should stand as a useful cautionary example of how easy it is in some cases to increase grossly the armament of an apparently tight design. Meanwhile Ordnance turned the 5-in./25 into a 5-in./38 DP gun, which they quite definitely favored over the older high-velocity 5-in./51.

In January 1931, C&R submitted a draft design as a basis for discussion. Craven's influence shows in its turtle-back forecastle, which broke before the bridge, as in some Japanese destroyers of the immediate post–World War I period. The fantail torpedo tubes, however, were abandoned: No. 3 TT was mounted between two deckhouses aft, on each of which was a twin 5-inch. Two more TT between the forward of these deckhouses and the single funnel were so cramped that, stowed, the tubes of No. 1 mount projected over those of No. 2. Of the two single guns on the forecastle, No. 2 was mounted directly atop the captain's cabin. But the whole thing would cost only 1,725 tons in normal (trial) condition, and by cramming in machinery C&R could reach 35 knots (38,000 shp) at light displacement, 200 tons of oil on board. Only No. 1 and 2 guns were dual purpose, as the twin mounts were "expected to be too heavy to be successfully used in AA fire except under the best of conditions." Weight was very tight; there was no hope of providing any kind of splinter protection for the guns.

The sacrifices seemed excessive. In March, the General Board enumerated alternative batteries; beside the one C&R had proposed, it could have (i) the three triple centerline TT with four single, protected, DP guns; (ii) two quadruple centerline TT with five guns (open mounts); (iii) two quadruple TT, one triple TT, and four open DP guns, all on the centerline; (iv) the six-gun arrangement, covered, the weight of shields absorbed by the deletion of one set of tubes; (v) two triple TT on the centerline and five shielded DP guns. Of these arrangements, (iii) was rated as overbalanced toward torpedoes and against guns; (iv) and (v) were considered overgunned; (ii) gave horizontal gunfire only slightly inferior to that of the C&R design, but sacrificed one torpedo tube. The General Board therefore recommended (i). On 5 March 1931 the Secretary of the Navy approved, subject to misgivings as to the gun armament; he preferred (ii), especially if the two forward guns could be shielded. It seems likely that he was influenced by comments made by officers attending a 27 February General Board hearing.

On 27 March, C&R submitted a new proposal in accordance with the Secretary's suggestion. Now the forecastle extended farther aft, as in more standard practice; some reduction in freeboard was necessary, but at the stem it was still nearly 5 feet higher than in the flush deckers. Five 5-inch guns in light shields were contemplated; "there is no possibility, with five gun positions, of installing three quadruple tubes; but in time of war it might be possible to install a tube aft in place of No. 5 gun, although this location is not considered desirable for such a purpose." The turtle-back forecastle had to be abandoned in view

of the shifting forward of No. 1 and 2 guns; a flat deck was required to provide sufficient working room. Virtually no margin of weight remained, and the desired 35 knots could be made only at relatively light load.

On 2 April 1931, the Secretary of the Navy approved this design with the proviso that strength be built "into the afterdeck . . . to carry the weight of depth charges and racks." This was a ship very finely balanced between torpedo attack and defense against torpedo attack by destroyers. ASW was very nearly ignored; the provision of enough strength for depth charges must be balanced against the Chief Constructor's comment that No. 5 gun might, in a wartime pinch, be replaced by a bank of torpedo tubes. On the other hand, as built, the new destroyer was provided with a sonar (QC) and a listening device (JL). In the interests of weight, the ships would be built with shields over No. 1 and 2 guns only—i.e., the shields were primarily considered as weather protection.

Much of the shipbuilding industry that had built the huge destroyer force no longer existed. Bath had gone bankrupt in 1925, and with its collapse its fund of design data was lost. Cramp went in 1927; its plant would be revived for the World War II program, but it would build no more destroyers. Bath reopened in 1927, using some machinery bought at the liquidation of the Cramp yard, but it was no longer a source of destroyer designs. That was particularly significant for destroyer machinery. Although C&R provided detailed contract plans from which builder's plans could be prepared, Steam Engineering traditionally provided almost no detail beyond steam conditions, power, weight, and a general arrangement of machinery spaces. The major yards designed and usually built their own machinery. In the early thirties that meant turbines designed by Parsons in Britain and built under license.

In 1931, then, the only remaining independent destroyer design organizations were Bethlehem Steel, New York Shipbuilding, and Newport News. There were also the central drafting offices of the major Navy Yards. For the new destroyers of the series authorized but not funded during World War I (DD 348–359), a Bethlehem design of 1,500 tons was selected for the eight *Farragut*s (DD 348–355); New York Shipbuilding designed the *Porter*s (1,850 tons: DD 356–359 plus DD 360–363). Construction was apportioned among the private and Navy yards, so that the *Farragut*s were built by Bethlehem (Quincy) and Bath, as well as by four Navy Yards (two by New York, two by Boston, one each by Puget Sound and Philadelphia). The larger *Porter*s were divided among New York Shipbuilding and Bethlehem (Quincy). At this time Bethlehem operated the Union yard at San

Radically different from their flush-deck predecessors, the *Farragut*s were the prototypes for U.S. pre–World War II destroyer development. This aerial view shows clearly their heavy gun armament and their total lack of any ASW battery, although they were all fitted with sonar as completed. Note, too, the narrow fore funnel, carrying one rather than two uptakes, to reduce smoke interference with the bridge. A 5-inch loading machine is visible between the funnels.

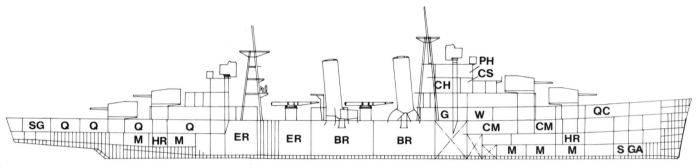

DD 356 series from contract plans

Francisco, but the large Squantum destroyer plant was gone.

These eight *Farragut*-class destroyers, DD 348–355, were the ancestors of 167 "1,500-ton" and "1,620-ton" destroyers. Some feeling for the values realized in this design can be obtained from the testimony of Admiral Land, the chief of C&R, before the General Board in January 1933. He stated the advantages of the *Farragut* over the flush decker as:

(a) Speed increased 3.3 knots
(b) Twice the GM
(c) Armament weight increased 35 percent
(d) Smaller turning circle (due to better stern design)
(e) Centerline armament
(f) Power ammunition hoists
(g) Habitability
(h) Seakeeping
(i) Direction control
(j) Greater radius

All on only 22 percent greater displacement. Land then noted some possible tradeoffs. The fifth (amidships) gun could be traded for an extra set of centerline tubes or for the "flush-decker" arrangement.

Acceptance of lighter single-purpose guns would permit a five-gun, twelve-tube (flush-decker arrangement) type. This would even save five tons. However, retention of the 5-in./38 DP would push the displacement up 12 tons "into the red," i.e., into the leader category. This quibbling over very small weights in the earliest design stage is typical of U.S. treaty-era design practice. Ironically, the 348s came out quite light, but all of our other treaty destroyers were well overweight.

Meanwhile, new characteristics were worked up for the leader. Informal discussions (January 1932) with members of the General Board indicated a requirement for at least 35 knots (Preliminary Design thought 36.5 would be a reasonable alternative) and destroyer armament (five 5-in./38s, eight tubes). Unlike a conventional destroyer, the leader would have

light protection over the bridge against machine-gun fire and, if possible, bullet-proof shields over each of the guns. In the case of the 35-knot ship it is proposed to devote the weight available to protective material over boilers and machinery . . . as to the advantages to be secured from increased displacement. . . . It was

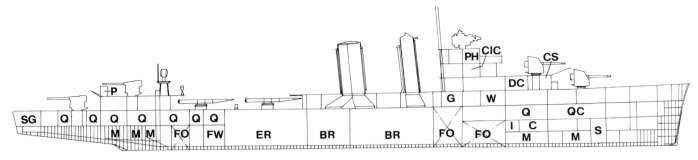

DD 349, 1944—inboard

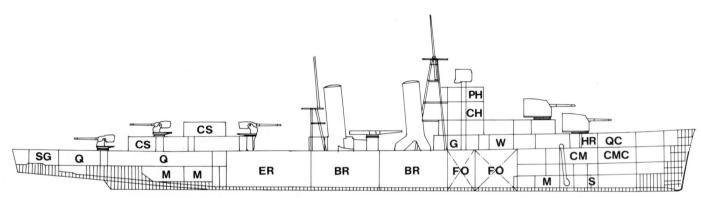

DD 384/5 inboard (contract plans)

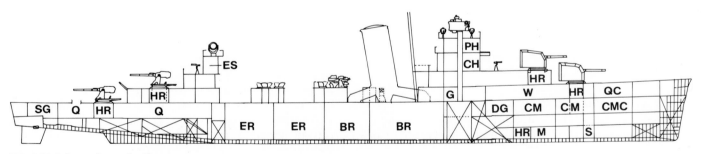

DD 398 inboard—as built

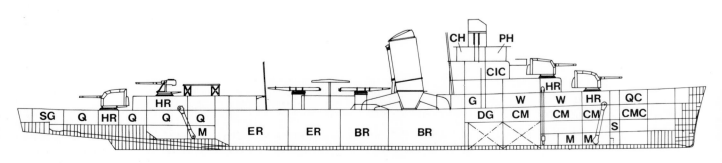

DD 410 inboard

suggested that improved seagoing characteristics, improved stability, and protection against attack from the air (i.e., strafing), constitute real advantages.

A C&R memorandum of 1 February added that

The General Board is apparently satisfied with the same gun and torpedo armament as has been provided on the destroyers now building. However, it is understood that in case weight is available after other requirements have been met an additional gun is believed desirable. . . . There is sufficient opinion favorable to four triple tubes located in the vessel's wings so that if the other features of the arrangement so required, this system could be adapted rather than a centerline mounting.

The first round of sketch designs included the large destroyer (Scheme 5) with five guns, three of them mounted forward: it was possible to sink No. 1 gun slightly below the level of the forecastle deck, with No. 2 no more than four or five feet above it, and No. 3 in a similar position relative to No. 2. An alternative Scheme 3 contemplated a single gun on the forecastle, with two more at the break of the forecastle. It evoked little enthusiasm, but both designs suggested to the General Board the interesting possibility of a six-gun design. The sixth gun might, of course, preclude leader capability, and convert the 1,850-tonner into no more than a large destroyer.

In March, C&R reported three sketch designs: the classical leader (Scheme 5, with five guns), Scheme 10 (Scheme 5 with a sixth gun added aft for a symmetrical arrangement of three at each end), and Scheme 11 (six guns, with twin mounts in No. 2 and No. 3 positions fore and aft). In each case, the two quadruple tubes of the standard destroyer were re-

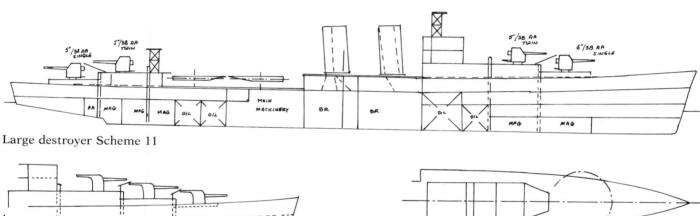

Large destroyer Scheme 11

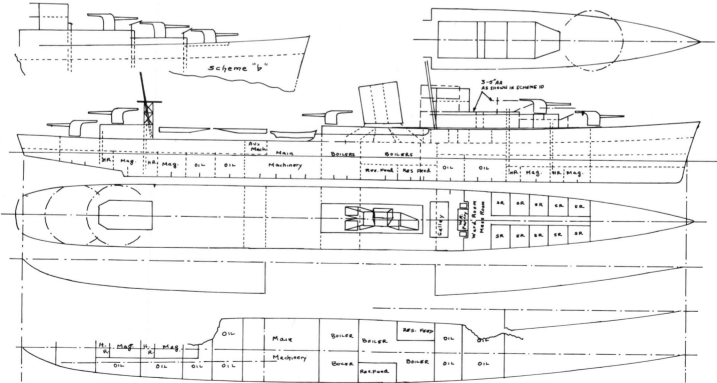

Large destroyer Scheme 5   Feb. 1932

Table 5–3. Design Projects

	Destroyer 31 Jan 1927	Scheme 5	Scheme 10 13 March 1932	Scheme 11
LWL	325	365	372	365
Beam	33	36	35.9	36
Draft	10.6	11.9	11.7	11.9
SHP	35,000	47,500	47,500	47,500
Speed	36	35	35.5	35
Endurance		6,500/12	6,500/12	6,500/12
5-in./38	4*	5(120)	6(120)	6(2 × 2, 2 × 1)(120)
3-in. AA	1	—	—	—
.50 MG	—	6	6	6
21-in. TT	2 × 6	2 × 4	2 × 4	2 × 4
Hull	508	757	776	759
Fittings	82	125	125	125
Machinery	581	655	655	655
Armament	76	100	117	117
Equipment & Outfit	44	53	53	53
Margin	25	49	13	30
Light Ship	1,316	1,739	1,739	1,739
Ammunition	45	46	52	52
Stores	25	64	59	59
Standard	1,391	1,850	1,850	1,850
RFW	19	40	40	40
Fuel	200	240	240	240
Normal	1,610	2,130	2,130	2,130
GM	2.28	3.07	2.88	2.89

* 5-in./25 or 5-in./51 single purpose.

Note: Four boilers in all of these designs. The 1927 destroyer design was more an attempt to incorporate new (post–World War I) technology than to reach a decision for construction, but the 1932 leaders were the direct predecessors of the *Porter* class.

tained. In the two six-gun designs there was no special protection (in fact the quarter-inch gun shields were not even bulletproof), but the main-deck stringers (¾-inch) in way of the boilers were thick enough to protect the main steam lines. In Scheme 5, on the other hand, the guns and perhaps even the machinery spaces could be protected. All three sketch designs had the same machinery as the new destroyers, gaining some speed because of their greater length and hence reduced wave-making resistance.

The General Board saw little point in investing in 350 tons without so much as an extra gun to show for it. Scheme 10 was somewhat wasteful of center-line space, and there was some skepticism concerning the dryness of the end mounts. On the other hand, it was widely accepted that no twin mount could fire as rapidly as could two single mounts, and Scheme 11 seemed unduly complex. The board thus chose Scheme 10 in May 1932. However, in the course of detail design it proved possible to substitute eight 5-in./38 *single-purpose* guns in enclosed gunhouses, the

resulting *Porter* class resembling a miniature cruiser. They carried only the two quadruple tubes of their destroyer counterparts, but a hidden feature was eight reload torpedoes stowed amidships. In addition, the power plants actually installed were more powerful than those of the destroyers, at 50,000 rather than 42,800 shp, for a rated speed of 37 rather than 36.5 knots. The General Board thus achieved rather more than had been expected; a final irony was that although the ships had been designed as heavy destroyers rather than leaders, they were employed as squadron flagships in the prewar fleet. The eight *Porter*s presented a particularly handsome appearance with their cruiser-like tripod masts and twin funnels.

These eight *Porter*s (DD 356–363) were built under the FY 33 program to a New York Shipbuilding Corporation design; the four built at that yard were the last destroyers built there until well after World War II. Two ships of the FY 34 program (*Somers* class, DD 381 and 383) were to have been duplicates, but

The large prewar "leaders" were almost cruiser-like, as the *Winslow* shows, with her tripod masts and twin enclosed 5-inch guns. The canvas-covered shape forward of the bridge is a quadruple 1.1-inch antiaircraft machine cannon, with another just forward of her after guns; Mk 35 single-purpose directors surmount both forward and after superstructures. Eight reload torpedoes were stowed around the second funnel, between the torpedo tubes. At the end of the war the *Winslow* was converted into an experimental radar picket of the Operational Development Force, serving through 1950 and surviving (in reserve) as late as 1956.

The *Jouett* was the last of the 1,850-ton "leaders"; she and her *Somers*-class sisters (DD 381, 383, 394–396) were quite badly overweight. She shows canvas-shrouded 1.1-inch machine cannon fore and aft, but no after director and a light pole foremast. When ships of this type were rebuilt with dual-purpose guns during World War II, their Mk 35 directors were refurbished, two being installed in the heavy cruiser *Pensacola* (main battery control). The Mk 35 visible above the *Jouett*'s bridge makes a boxy contrast with the contemporary Mk 33 dual-purpose type in 1,500-ton destroyers.

The newly completed 1,850-ton "leader" *Davis* shows her simplified after superstructure in this 18 October 1938 photograph. The two short kingposts support boat cranes, and there was a T-shaped torpedo crane to starboard. By this time U.S. destroyers were all being completed with depth-charge tracks aft, but no depth-charge throwers (Y-guns) were fitted prewar. Note the raised 1.1-inch gun platform just forward of No. 3 gun mount.

instead were built to a new Gibbs & Cox design by Federal Shipbuilding, as part of the transformation of American destroyer machinery design to be described in connection with the *Mahan* class. The new machinery added another 2,000 shp, for a design speed of 37.5 knots. Externally, it showed in a single funnel. A third quadruple torpedo tube was mounted in place of the reloads, weight being saved by replacement of the heavy tripod masts by poles, and elimination of the after director. These *Somers*-class units and DD 394–396 of FY 35 rather stretched the 1,850-ton treaty limit and had little reserve of weight and stability for later additions.

There was a disinclination to waste money and tonnage on a big destroyer presenting only limited advantages; in fact, there was so little difference between "leader" and "led" that no special "destroyer leader" designation was ever used. Effort was concentrated on the orderly evolution of the 1,500-ton type. One of the major forces operating within the Navy was a widespread belief that torpedoes were the primary destroyer weapons—that guns were secondary and should be pared away if necessary to improve the torpedo armament. As for ASW, it was usual to strengthen the bows for ramming submarines and to adapt the sterns for depth-charge tracks.

However, depth charges were not included in the normal equipment. Almost certainly this was a matter of shaving to fit within treaty limits, not doctrine. It was quite common for U.S. designers to adopt artificially low armament and equipment allowances so that their ships might remain just within

the specified limits. The same thing had been done when Congress specified the maximum displacement of battleships (1905). These designs were, however, adapted to take the realistic load in wartime.

The General Board began to consider new destroyer characteristics in January 1933. Although the 8-tube broadside of the *Farragut*s was equal or superior to that of any destroyer in the world (save only the Japanese 1,700-ton *Fubuki*, 9 tubes), there was strong sentiment in favor of increasing the armament to 12 tubes, even at the cost of one gun. It must be kept in mind that the officers did not require that all tubes be on the centerline—indeed, many of the senior officers of the fleet favored the "flush-decker arrangement." The extra tubes were, in effect, reloads. On the other hand, sentiment was most strongly *against* abandoning the DP gun to save weight. Indeed, there was no existing 5-in./38 SP prototype, and it was feared that any switch would slow down destroyer production. On 31 January 1933 the General Board requested a new design with "the maximum possible number of 5-in./38 guns, preferably of the dual-purpose type" and 12 tubes, "space to be reserved for the stowage of reload torpedoes as an emergency measure."

This began a General Board requirement that *space* be reserved for reloads. From DD 409 through the *Fletcher* class, racks for four torpedoes—the equivalent of one quadruple nest—were always set aside. However, weight for these torpedoes was not included in the standard displacements. It is possible that the prominent torpedo derricks often mounted near the forward bank of tubes (through the *Fletcher* class) are associated with this feature. They might represent a slow reload capability at sea away from an engagement. On the other hand, the Japanese made major efforts to provide a reload apparatus for their larger torpedoes, so that in effect they had 12 or 16 TT in nominal 8-tube destroyers.

C&R claimed that it could keep all five guns *and* provide four triple TT—provided the dual-purpose feature was abandoned. This the General Board approved:

> Due to its small size and great maneuverability, a destroyer is not a likely target for high-altitude bombers, and direct gunfire defense for it against these bombers would not be necessary. Against dive bombers the machine gun is a better defense. The AA fire of the 5-inch guns would however be useful in breaking up passing flights of enemy bombers or torpedo planes, in giving warning of and designating enemy aircraft, and in assisting in the defense of larger vessels against air attack . . . the DP feature . . . is desirable, but its value is not sufficiently great to warrant its installation at the cost of reduction in number of either tubes or guns.

This view of destroyer function emphasized a Jutland-style fleet action. The CNO regarded it as narrow:

> The most probable campaign of war which will confront this nation will include an overseas operation, conducted at a distance from home waters . . . in all probability many operations of such a campaign will be conducted before the fleet battle, if it ever eventualizes, takes place . . . the enemy fleet would normally be secure in well-defended home bases from which it would emerge only at will, while our own fleet would be more constantly at sea, exposed to torpedo attack, and at a greater distance from adequate docking and repair facilities. Under these circumstances the enemy might assign relatively greater weight to the torpedo armament of its destroyers, but we cannot afford to minimize the gun armament of our own, upon which largely depend its chances of survival, its power to defend our own major ships, and its ability to drive in a torpedo attack upon the enemy . . . the CNO cannot recommend any design of destroyer which subordinates the gun to the torpedo. . . . He wants our destroyers to have an even better chance of sinking enemy destroyers than they have of destroying our own craft.

Moreover, the campaign prior to a main fleet engagement might well demand covering action against aircraft.

On 27 March Preliminary Design began to sketch a new destroyer that might be a compromise between the desires of the General Board and the fleet's desire for a DP armament. The new features were to be a new battery arrangement and a new engineering plant, which later permitted the adoption of a slacker bilge permitting a saving of about 3 percent ehp at 35 to 36 knots and—more importantly—an increase in GM of 0.5 to 0.75 feet.

In the resulting design, a third quadruple TT replaced No. 3 gun; the two TT in the waist were moved

The *Mahan*s (the *Flusser* is shown) introduced high-pressure boilers and a variety of detail improvements over the *Farragut*s: note the high breakwater protecting No. 1 gun mount, the tripod foremast (to free antiaircraft fire of interference by mast stays), and the gun-crew shelter abaft No. 2 5-inch gun mount, atop which .50-calibre machine guns were mounted. Note, too, how close the waist torpedo tubes were to the ship's side. Newly completed, the *Flusser* flies the Bath Iron Works house flag at her foremast while running builder's trials.

to the sides of the ship in order to release centerline space for an extension of the after deckhouse to accommodate No. 3 gun just ahead of No. 4. Although the characteristics specified that "at least two of the five guns shall be dual purpose," all five were. Only No. 1 and 2 were shielded. Space was to be reserved for reload torpedoes. An unusual feature of the design was a tripod foremast adopted to improve AA field of fire by eliminating stays. A net increase from 1,365 to about 1,500 tons (std) was divided into 79 tons to increase shp to 50,000; 18 to buy an extra TT; and 32 for a more robust structure and fittings; it had been fortunate indeed that the *Farragut* had come out so light.

Ultimately, the new class incorporated prototypes of a new generation of destroyer machinery, which combined increases in pressure and steam temperature with a new type of lightweight, fast-running turbine. In the eyes of Steam Engineering, this was a move away from the very conservative characteristics of Parsons (and, therefore, of the major shipyards) towards new developments in land-based machinery by such firms as GE, Westinghouse, and Allis-Chalmers. Indeed, Rear Admiral H.G. Bowen, chief engineer at the height of the controversy over "high-temperature, high-pressure," described the change as one from shipyard as ship and engine builder to shipyard as assembly plant, with machinery built elsewhere and then installed aboard ship.

The new generation of machinery was both simpler and far more efficient than the old. For example, a typical GE Curtis turbine carried 1,750 blades, compared to 17,500 in a typical lower-speed Parsons. The rotor of the high-speed turbine was generally 25 percent shorter than that of the older one, and was machined from a forging rather than built up; all of these features made for a combination of lighter weight and greater ruggedness. In a typical installation, three turbines were used: cruising and high-pressure turbines were coupled through reduction gearing, and the high- and low-pressure units were coupled to the propellers through double reduction gearing. By way of contrast, the earlier installations often incorporated no cruising turbine, an indication of their greater size and weight. Typically, too, the low-pressure turbines had also been low speed (2,320 rpm vs. 3,460 rpm in a *Farragut*, compared to 4,926 vs. 5,850 rpm in the new ships). Earlier installations incorporated single reduction gears. Boiler improvements included an advance in steam conditions for greater thermodynamic efficiency (pressure rose to 600 pounds in the *Somers* class, temperature from 650 to 700 degrees F. in the *Mahan*s, although the latter were initially designed for 850 degrees), the addition of economizers (which preheated boiler feed water) and later with air-encasement, which in effect

separated combustion air from air in the fire room and ended the need for sealed fire rooms. From the *Farragut*s onward the boilers had been superheated as well.

The major builders were unwilling to abandon their traditional practices, and Steam Engineering looked elsewhere for the design of its new plants. The firm of Gibbs & Cox had made a considerable impression with the design of a class of liners for the Grace Line; these ships, built by the Federal Shipbuilding and Drydock Corporation of Kearny, New Jersey (a subsidiary of U.S. Steel), operated at 375 pounds and 743 degrees F. and employed double reduction gears. By contracting with small builders who did not build their own turbines, the Navy was able to encourage the incorporation of the new marine engineering technology; Gibbs & Cox proved to be the instrument of change. Among the weapons used was a ruling by Steam Engineering in 1935 that henceforth the espionage laws were to be enforced against firms that, under their licenses with Parsons, transmitted details of U.S. warships abroad.

Gibbs & Cox thus became the design agent for most U.S. destroyers from the new *Mahan*s onward. Contracts for the first six of the new ships went to the three small yards: United Shipyards of Staten Island, Bath Iron Works, and Federal of Kearny. Ten more were built in pairs by the major Navy Yards (Boston, Philadelphia, Norfolk, Puget Sound, and Mare Island), and United built two ships of a somewhat modified design (DD 384 and 385). All were engined by GE.

In all, 26 destroyers were built with essentially identical machinery: 16 *Mahan*s (DD 364–379), 2 *Dunlap*s (DD 384–385, with prototype 5-inch enclosed mounts in No. 1 and 2 positions), and 8 *Bagley*s (DD 386–393, with different batteries). In the course of design, major improvements were made in boilers, so that 50,000 shp could be attained in the space formerly required for 42,800, a change that shows in better trial performances, with speed rising from 35 to 38 knots. Increased fuel economy shows in greatly improved effective steaming range, from 7,400 nm. in the *Farragut*s to 8,730 nm. in such late 1,500-tonners as the *Benham* (DD 397). On the other hand, the *Mahan*s were much criticized for their cramped machinery spaces.

The *Mahan*s had the first emergency diesel generators. A 25-kw diesel replaced the storage batteries of earlier classes; in later ones 80-kw generators were fitted, to take the load of auxiliary steering.

One major innovation in the *Mahan* class was the provision of gun-crew shelters for the superimposed guns fore and aft, one shelter before the bridge (omitted in the two *Dunlap*s with their enclosed guns) and one atop the shelter deck aft. Atop each was

The USS *Fanning* was a near-sister to the *Mahan*s, the difference being that both of her forward 5-inch guns were housed in the new fully enclosed base-ring mounts; consequently, she had no forward gun-crew shelter. She shows the effects of mid-war modifications in this 22 November 1943 post-refit photograph off the Mare Island Navy Yard: two twin Bofors guns replace No. 3 5-inch gun, with two 20-mm. abreast her second funnel, and three more forward of her bridge; depth-charge throwers are visible alongside the after deckhouse, just below No. 3 (former No. 4) 5-inch gun. Note, too, the solid bulwarks extended aft almost to the waist torpedo tubes, common in late prewar and wartime destroyer practice. Her radar suit is that standard in mid-war: Mk 4 atop her director, with SG for surface search and SC-2 for air search atop her pole mast. A smoke generator is visible on her fantail.

The newly rebuilt *Cassin* stands out of Mare Island, 26 February 1944. She and her sister *Downes* were nearly destroyed at Pearl Harbor; their engines and main batteries were installed in new hulls built by the Navy Yard, and they emerged to the modified design shown. Note the British-style bridge, used at this time in reconstructed "leaders," *Sumner*s, and destroyer escorts. They were unique among *Mahan*s in having Mk 37 directors and centerline tubes raised above the main deck. Their relative modernity did not save either from scrapping after the war, even though neither saw very much wartime service.

mounted a pair of .50-caliber water-cooled machine guns, the standard antiaircraft weapon of the prewar fleet destroyers. In some later classes the after crew shelter ultimately served as a base for a twin 40-mm. cannon, as ships were rearmed for greater antiaircraft firepower.

Three *Mahan*s were severely damaged at Pearl Harbor: the *Shaw*, which lost her bow, and the *Cassin* and *Downes*, virtually destroyed in a graving dock. The *Shaw* was rebuilt along conventional lines, but gained about 60 tons, which was to prove unfortunate when she underwent an emergency AA refit in 1945. She was probably unique among her class in mounting, as an interim automatic battery, one quadruple 1.1-inch machine cannon and four Oerlikons.

The *Cassin* and *Downes* were a very different matter. Their machinery and main batteries were salvaged from their wrecks and shipped to Mare Island, where entirely new hulls were built, but they retained their original names. They were unique among the *Mahan*s in having Mk 37 directors and also in having two banks of torpedo tubes on their centerlines, like the *Sims* and later classes. The bridge was the British type that was fitted to the reconstructed 1,850-tonners and also to the 5-inch-gun destroyer escorts. The automatic battery amounted to two twin Bofors and six Oerlikons. Given the numbers of new destroyers in service by 1943, the effort that went into these two was something of a waste and perhaps more an expression of the spirit of the Mare Island Navy Yard than of anything else. Even though both

Four *Gridley*-class destroyers (DD 380, 382, 400, 401) were designed by Bethlehem Steel for the FY 34 and FY 35 programs. They were the first of twenty-two 16-tube destroyers of three distinct classes, and were unique among modern U.S. destroyers of World War II in *not* being refitted with 40-mm. guns. They could be distinguished from the *Bagley* class by their much less prominent uptakes. The *Craven* (DD 382) is shown on trial, flying the Bethlehem house flag from the fore.

ships were essentially new at the end of the war, they, like their sisters, were broken up.

Even as the *Mahan*s were being built, advocates of the torpedo became more and more vocal. It turned out that one of the guns could be exchanged for an additional quadruple TT, and developments in torpedo design suggested that in action a destroyer could fire all of her wing tubes at once, using "curved ahead fire," i.e., gyros to correct the course of the torpedo once it had been fired. In effect, then, a destroyer with four quadruple TT disposed two on each beam could fire all of them as a single massive salvo.

It was also hoped that by restoring all the TT to the main deck the designers could avoid the disadvantages of failure of torpedoes to clear the ship's side on ejection, as well as inconvenience in torpedo handling. The General Board issued these comments in March 1935, before any *Mahan* entered service. The 1935 characteristics called for the four-tube, four-gun arrangement. At the same time a single-funnel arrangement was adopted, possibly to clear the bridge of smoke and possibly to clear deck space amidships. The General Board also wanted to retreat from the 1,500-ton limit so as to gain a speed of 38 knots without increasing power; in the end it asked formally for 37 (or about 44,000 shp).

Twenty-two 16-tube destroyers were built in three classes. The original series of ten consisted of two Bethlehem units (the *Gridley* class, DD 380 and 382)

and eight of Navy design that duplicated the *Mahan* hull and machinery (the *Bagley* class, DD 386–393). The latter were built by the Navy Yards. Finally, the *Benham*s (DD 397–399, 402–408) were a Gibbs & Cox design built by Federal and by the Navy Yards. They differed visually from the earlier types in that they had less prominent boiler uptakes, the result of a reduction from four to three boilers. They also had all four guns in "base-ring" rather than pedestal mounts—No. 1 and 2 in gunhouses, No. 3 and 4 in open mounts. The new mount, which appeared in all subsequent classes, incorporated a rotating platform on which the entire crew stood, as well as the shell hoist proper. Out of the FY 35 series of 12 destroyers, 2 (the *McCall* and *Maury*, DD 400 and 401) were built by Bethlehem San Francisco to the same plans as DD 380 and 382, and formed a sub-class with them. Of these three classes, which ended the original 1,500-ton series, the *Benham*s came out quite heavy, approaching or even exceeding 1,500 tons in the light (unloaded) condition.

At the same time, sentiment grew within C&R for a reexamination of the rationale for the 1,500-ton type. In particular, it seemed that a great deal was being spent on rather large yet flimsy ships. According to a C&R memo of 18 February 1935, summarizing studies of armored destroyers in 1934/35, "it is evident that for two such ships as we now have to engage each other would mean only mutual suicide.

Eight *Bagley*s (DD 386–393) were built by the Navy Yards; this is the *Patterson* after a mid-war refit at Mare Island, 6 March 1944. Her 40-mm. gun tub is just visible forward of the two after 5-inch guns; she retains her prewar gun and torpedo battery, plus depth charges and light antiaircraft weapons. These ships duplicated the *Mahan* hull and machinery. They had much more prominent uptakes than did the four *Craven*s, as well as a large deckhouse between their torpedo tubes, carrying a searchlight; in the *Craven*s, the analogous deckhouse was much smaller and the searchlight was mounted atop the gun crew shelter aft.

The *Benham*s (DD 397–408), the last of the 16-tube destroyers, had three rather than four boilers and, therefore, less prominent uptakes. The newly completed *Rhind* is shown off Philadelphia Navy Yard, 5 June 1940.

It appears debatable, to say the least, whether or not the great loss of destroyers which would result from an attack on capital ships is not in itself sufficient reason for endeavoring to give them more of a chance to carry out a successful torpedo attack. . . ." Tests on two ex-destroyers, the *Marcus* and *Sloat*, showed that very considerable damage was to be expected from the fragments of bombs as small as 100 pounds exploding as much as 40 feet away; and the .50-caliber bullets of strafing aircraft would quite suffice to disable destroyers whose only protection was the quarter-inch shields of some of their guns.

Accordingly, studies were carried out on protection against 5-inch gunfire. It was estimated that

about 227 tons would be required merely to cover machinery, magazines, steering gear, and a conning tower. We can see C&R's idea of priorities in the cuts proposed to obtain this kind of weight. The basic idea was that, since the destroyers already overperformed, weight could be saved by pruning them back to the minimum General Board characteristics. For example, the hull could be shrunk from 334 to 300 feet to reduce the scantlings required, and a reduction in fuel supply would further reduce stresses. However, even rather drastic measures would leave personnel and armament vulnerable. Hence, C&R produced a second proposal in which splinter protection and subdivision were emphasized. This generally meant ½-inch to ⅝-inch STS with heavier plate (2.5 inches) over the turret face. The total weight of protection was unchanged. Some economy in space was achieved by the use of twin gunhouses—which, however, would have been less acceptable from the point of view of survivability against penetrating shellfire. A major problem in these designs was the paradox that in order to gain ruggedness in battle (i.e., protection) they had to adopt flimsier construction. Although these studies were considered a failure, they raised within the Navy the questions of just how high destroyer performance should be, and of how large warships should be allowed to grow before serious measures were taken to ensure their survivability.

Another survivability measure, the adoption of a unit or en-echelon arrangement of machinery, was as yet impracticable; the boilers could not yet be squeezed down sufficiently.

At the end of 1935, the CNO initiated a general review of destroyer policy, which meant that C&R and the various operational commands had a chance to formulate their policies. At this time only the eight *Farraguts*, which had been designed in 1931, were in service; the succeeding large classes had been designed almost without modern operational experience. This situation was unique among the major sea powers, the rest of which had started new construction programs in the mid-twenties.

C&R at once proposed that weight be added to hulls to achieve greater stiffness. The fleet felt that the new destroyers were too flimsy; claims were made that hulls were unduly flexible. Great weight-saving efforts had in fact been made, including the introduction of longitudinal framing. Stresses were to be reduced by paring away excess radius (i.e., fuel weight) and speed. C&R itself described the new structural design as radical, but resisted allegations of insufficient strength. A large weight and moment saving was to be expected, too, if the superimposed guns were brought down to deck level by the introduction of twin mounts. Such a change would have the added advantage of decreasing air resistance. This consideration was most important at cruising speed, i.e., most crucial to *steaming radius*. For example, at 15 knots the *Mahan* required about 1,800 shp. But a 40-knot head wind would involve a resistance of 565 hp. Consequently, driving the ship into a 25-knot wind at 15 knots would require 2,335 shp. It was estimated that streamlining could save about 10 percent of the shp. The model used had single guns forward and a high bridge, and larger reductions were expected with the twin mount and low bridge. However, to concentrate the guns would increase the consequences of a single hit.

Meanwhile a new naval treaty was signed, eliminating the former destroyer subcategories and sub-stituting limits of 3,000 tons and 6.1-inch guns. However, the limit on *total* tonnage in this category remained, so that any desire for numbers would keep unit displacement in the 1,500-ton range. In any case, any serious attempt to go to the tonnage limit so as to match foreign construction would involve a long pause while an entirely new design was evolved. In this way the suddenness of the treaty process and the retention of an overall limit tended to dissuade American constructors from anything but an evolutionary design. Hence, the reply to the relaxation of the limits was only a suggestion for an increase to about 1,570 tons, basically to gain a more robust hull.

In framing the new characteristics, the General Board polled the commanders of the main fleet, its scouting and destroyer forces, and the captains of the first four 1,500-ton boats, 48 of which were already in various stages of construction. They showed heavy sentiment in favor of the lighter gun armament. The question of torpedo reloads was raised, and the destroyer officers wanted the actual reloads included in the standard outfit. The CinCUS Fleet wanted depth charges deleted. Officers seemed impressed with the dryness of the new boats and with the effectiveness of their AA armament.

These were tactical and operational views that seem in many cases to have been based mainly on a very limited vision of future naval warfare. They were balanced against the detailed strategic vision of War Plans. In March 1936, that division forwarded to the CNO a study of the employment of destroyers in the event of a war with Orange (Japan). A deciding factor was the superiority of the Blue (American) battle line, consisting of 15 ships to Orange's nine. This superiority, even not counting the individual superiority of Blue ships, was so great as practically to predetermine the outcome of a classical naval engagement. Orange's main hope would have to be to erode Blue strength on the long voyage across the Pacific. An evaluation via the N-square combat law showed how valuable to Orange any Blue losses would be. A ratio of 15 to 9 in equivalent ships would be a force ratio of 225 to 81 or 2.77 to 1. However, the loss of three Blue ships would reduce this ratio to 1.77, i.e., would cut effective Blue strength by over a third.

The effect of the naval treaties was to make it very difficult for Orange to redress the balance by building new battleships. Hence, the best Orange strategy would be to keep his battle fleet in protected ports while lighter forces eroded Blue strength by bomb, torpedo, and mine. These latter weapons had the great advantage over heavy naval guns of promising disproportionate damage for relatively low initial investment. In particular, aircraft and auxiliary minelayers were impossible to regulate by treaty, since it was not even theoretically possible to check on their numbers. The main torpedo carriers, destroyers and submarines, could be built up very rapidly in any case.

This was exactly the Japanese view. Their way of implementing it was to spend great effort on a super torpedo, the 24-inch "Long Lance" extreme-range, oxygen-fueled weapon. Normal tactics called for launch and then withdrawal without announcement of the appearance of their forces by gunfire. The torpedo itself would not be observed, and could be relied upon to work at ranges as great as 40,000 yards.

Another important point was that Orange enjoyed a considerable superiority in cruiser strength. This superiority was held to give Orange control of the destroyer approach paths, at least in daylight. Hence War Plans assumed that the U.S. destroyers could not profitably be used in good visibility; in any case, the outcomes of many war games were taken to imply that torpedo craft were most useful to the *weaker* battle line.

Therefore, the primary function of the destroyer force must be to protect the battle line from the kind of unconventional attack likely to be mounted by Orange. This meant a demand for

(a) Maximum dual-purpose firepower. Orange torpedo planes would be a particular menace. Another point in favor of DP guns was that many assaults on islands were expected. Destroyers could provide AA cover if they had DP guns, and then the heavier ships would not have to be held near such fixed positions, vulnerable to air and underwater attack. In particular, War Plans opposed a recent decision to save weight by adopting an all-single-purpose 5-inch battery. This would in any case have saved no more than about 15 tons, 1 percent of the displacement.

(b) Torpedoes for favorable conditions, i.e., short-range attacks under poor visibility. This implied a desire for wide salvo dispersion.

(c) ASW gear, i.e., depth-charge tracks.

(d) War Plans was not explicit, but implied a desire for suitability for high-speed mine sweeps.

This was the view adopted for the next (*Sims*, DD 409) class. The five-gun DP battery was reinstated as the maximum practical on 1,500 tons, and as providing a fair chance against the Orange 1,700-ton, six-gun type, especially as the latter mounted its guns in twin gunhouses, which should reduce their effective volume of fire. The 12-tube (centerline and two wing mounts) arrangement was revived, but proponents of more torpedoes were given provision for four reloads.

The new destroyers introduced a new fire control system, the Mk 37, which would appear in U.S. warships through 1945. It introduced a below-decks computer, for which internal space had to be found; in addition, destroyers now had more powerful emergency diesel generators to keep their heavy, enclosed 5-inch guns in operation even after main machinery damage. One problem of design was the isolation of the generator from the delicate fire control computer. The Mk 37 itself was not ready for the first of the *Sims* class and several ships were commissioned without it in place.

The base-ring mounts were repeated in the new ships. The No. 5 gun was enclosed for the first time. A new armament feature was the actual installation of depth-charge racks. Protective plating was also specified for the first time: half-inch STS around the front, sides, and top of the pilot house, and—if it could be done without so great an increase of weight as to cause excessive vibration—on the director. The

The *Sims* class returned to the *Mahan* main-battery arrangement, with a more robust hull and a new fire control system. The Mk 37 system took longer than expected to develop, many ships being commissioned without it; the *Anderson* is shown at Kearny, 18 May 1939. All suffered from overweight, which at the time was blamed on poor estimates of the weight of their new high-pressure power plants; as a result of this scandal, the Bureaus of Engineering and Construction and Repair were merged in 1940.

gun shields, on the other hand, were to be ⅛ inch thick. According to a C&R internal memorandum, 8 May 1936, reporting the General Board's preliminary characteristics:

> Special emphasis is to be placed upon ruggedness and dependability. It is for these characteristics that the Board is accepting the weight in excess of 1,500 tons standard. The Board contemplates an increase of approximately 8 feet in the length of the machinery and corresponding increase . . . to retain the same or more space for accommodations, stores, etc. Maximum fuel of about 457 tons is acceptable on the assurance that this will give the radius specified [6,500 nm. at 12 knots].

Of the 70 tons added, about 10 tons went for engineering weights, 18 for ordnance, about 5 for protection of pilothouse and director, and about 30 for hull and structure strengthening.

As for C&R's proposals, there was no willingness to surrender high speed. A typical comment was that high speeds in trials were not indicative of performance in more realistically loaded conditions. For example, at 47,500 shp the *Benham* could make 40 knots at 1,765 tons; but a more representative displacement would be 2,170, in which case a similar ship (the USS *Bagley*) made only 35.6. In fact, most of the more spectacular performances had been turned in under relatively light loads. As another indicator of realities, the *Craven* made 41.53 knots on 46,351 shp at 1,761 tons (standard displacement about 1,570 tons) but only 37.40 on 52,885 at 2,117 tons. In a 1939 discussion of those questions, it was noted that the best speed of the 1,500-ton destroyers in a West Coast smooth sea was about 40 knots. However, the speed of attack would be about 7 knots less. For example, the *Worden*, 40.38 knots on trial (at the very light displacement of 1,580 tons), could be counted on *in formation* for only 32 knots. Part of this might be due to a loss of about ¹⁄₁₀ rpm per day out of dock, due to fouling. The endurance (not speed) required was based on a condition four months out of dock. Finally, a great value was placed on *acceleration*. For example, consider two destroyers, maximum speeds 36 and 40 knots, steaming at 32. The faster one could accelerate to 36 twice as fast as the slower. For the new characteristics, the speed requirement was changed from the former 36.5 to 38 knots at designed displacement (about 1,725 tons) to a more realistic 35 at full load less ⅓ fuel and feed water, i.e., about 2,050 tons.

However, C&R did go ahead with streamlining, and the 1937 destroyers (the *Sims* class, DD 409–420) show careful attention to the curvature of the bridge front and even to a radius worked into the deck edge forward. No evaluation of the efficiency of this device has been found, but some measure of streamlining was applied to subsequent U.S. types, until the exigencies of the war program forced its abandonment.

Even though a considerable growth had been allowed for in their design, the new *Sims* class turned out to be decidedly overweight—and top-heavy. In August 1939, a C&R report noted that at light displacement the first ships of the class were nearly 120 tons overweight; a table of over- and under-weights shows 132.75 tons underweight for the *Farragut* and 30.29 for the *Mahan*; every other type had been over: 29.22 for the *Gridley*, 23 for the *Dunlap* (a repeat *Mahan*), 89.21 for the *Benham*—and now 117.05 for the *Anderson*, lead ship for the *Sims* class. This top weight (GM at light load was 1.68 rather than the designed 2.69 feet) was cut back by the removal of ordnance. One of the two quadruple TT in the waist was eliminated, and the other moved to the centerline atop a new deckhouse; the broadside remained the same, but (in effect) a set of reloads was sacrificed. An advantage of the new arrangement was that the after TT could now be used in more severe weather than before. Additional features were 60 tons of fixed ballast and the elimination of splinter protection around the director, director tube, and the pilot house. Displacement (trials) rose from 1,933 to 1,946 tons, the center of gravity falling 0.09 feet and the metacentric height increasing from 2.36 to 2.43 feet.

This C&R proposal was approved by the Secretary of the Navy on 25 September 1939, in time for many of the *Sims* class to be completed to the new standard. A total of 12 of these FY 37 destroyers (DD 409–420) were built, all to a Gibbs & Cox design, all engined by Westinghouse. They were built by Bath, Federal, Newport News, and by the Navy Yards. By this time United was no longer an independent yard, having been absorbed by Bethlehem as the latter's Staten Island facility; it would not return to destroyer production until the advent of the war program.

The *Sims* class was completed just as the U.S. Navy began to emphasize antisubmarine operations in the North Atlantic. The last ship of the class, the USS *Buck*, ran her trials in December 1940 and experienced severe icing on the two exposed after mounts (No. 3 and 4). BuOrd designed a half shield whose top could be closed with a canvas cover, so that it resembled the heavier full shield, providing shelter with reduced top weight. These half shields were applied retroactively to the *Benham*s and later to the early *Benson*s.

Above all, Atlantic ASW required heavy depth-charge batteries, for which weight compensation was necessary. The standard prewar fleet destroyer battery of two five-charge tracks (i.e., ten 600-lb. charges) was supplemented by a Y-gun on the fantail with ten 300-lb. charges in two racks, and the standard tracks

The *Sims* class was altered to reduce top weight, one bank of torpedo tubes being eliminated and another moved to the centerline, as shown in this 9 May 1940 view of the *Sims* herself; she also shows the new Mk 37 fire control system atop her bridge. Later both raised guns aft were semi-enclosed to protect them from water damage in the North Atlantic winter. Quadruple tubes released by this program were mounted in the *Atlanta*-class light cruisers in place of the triple mounts originally planned.

were extended to take twelve 600-lb. charges each. As modified in mid-1941, *Sims*-class destroyers in the Atlantic were also fitted for four additional .50-caliber machine guns, two on the main deck and two on the deckhouse aft, and with extensive splinter protection. Weight compensation included the removal of No. 3 5-inch gun, the smoke generators, one of the torpedo directors, the bridge rangefinder (whose place was taken by the other torpedo director), and both 24-inch searchlights.

Benham-class destroyers in the Atlantic were similarly modified for increased depth-charge batteries, but they had no fifth 5-inch gun to surrender. Instead, No. 3 and 4 torpedo tubes were removed, and three rather than four .50-caliber machine guns were added. Splinter protection included half shields for both of the exposed 5-inch guns aft.

The lack of protection in the *Sims* class did not mean that there was any great complacency at the prospect of such large ships being entirely without power to survive. Early in 1937 Steam Engineering was able to report that new boilers would finally make a unit machinery arrangement possible. A delay of six weeks in contracting and up to six months in delivery was considered entirely acceptable for the next (FY 38, DD 421 series) batch. The new type was envisaged as a slightly enlarged version of the DD 409, 1,620 instead of 1,570 tons. The new weight went into the less-compact machinery and into a stronger hull. Visually, this was reflected by a switch from one funnel back to two. The only other change was to have been a longer bulwark shielding the waist torpedo tubes from the sea. It was expected that the 1939 series would be virtually identical.

The combination of enlarged machinery spaces and the internal plotting room associated with the Mk 37 director made for some congestion. BuOrd com-

plained that the vibration of the emergency diesel generator would upset the computer, but it was argued that the former would be turned on only after battle damage; it would of course be a useful standby in cruising, with only one main turbogenerator operating, but in battle it would be turned off, as both steam plants would be on line. In reviewing the design in July 1937, Commander Destroyers Battle Force was particularly pleased with the installation of the 100-kw emergency diesel on the main deck, well clear of any underwater damage. He was concerned with the possibility of smoke interference to the bridge, and asked that special attention be paid to the elimination of any areas of reduced pressure there. On the other hand, he liked the improved protected access to the bridge structure in the new design.

The FY 38 destroyers were yet another round in the battle of destroyer machinery designs. Both Bethlehem and Gibbs & Cox proposed alternative designs. Bethlehem Quincy designed and built the *Benson* and *Mayo*, DD 421 and 422; Gibbs & Cox designed, and Bath built, the *Gleaves* and *Niblack*, DD 423 and 424. Initially, all ships were to have incorporated the new type of machinery first introduced in the *Mahan*s. However, after contract award Bethlehem asked to modify its contract, returning to a two-turbine arrangement (high-speed high-pressure driving through single reduction gears, with no cruising turbine). Steam Engineering accepted the Bethlehem proposal, partly because that yard had no previous experience with the new machinery, and partly because Bethlehem claimed that its machinery would equal the new type in efficiency; the *Benson* would, then, provide comparative data. In the spring of 1938, Steam Engineering decided to increase the superheat in the FY 39 class, DD 429–436; no further Beth-

The *Benson* and *Gleaves* classes were the culmination of pre–World War II "1,500-ton" destroyer development. The *Gleaves* and *Niblack* (DD 423 and 424) were both designed by Gibbs & Cox, by way of contrast with the Bethlehem-designed *Benson* and *Mayo*. Both are shown newly delivered, the *Niblack* flying the Bath house flag, 16 July 1940. The *Gleaves* is running the measured trial mile off Rockland, Maine, at 25 knots, 28 May 1940; neither yet mounts her 50-calibre antiaircraft guns, and each retains the prewar luxury of boat cranes aft.

lehem-design ships would be built. These decisions were based in part on the very satisfactory performance of the *Mahan*s and their immediate successors. Moreover, it proved possible to extend the machinery change (which gave 850° F.) to the two Bath boats of FY 38. The remainder of the FY 38 program (DD 421–422, 425–428) were built to Bethlehem designs. Bethlehem tendered a bid for the FY 39 program, offering repeat versions of its FY 38 design, but was rejected in favor of the Gibbs & Cox design, to be built by Bath and Federal (as well as the Navy Yards) with engines by Westinghouse.

In the fall of 1937 the General Board once more polled the fleet, and summarized service opinion as in favor of

(a) Ruggedness
(b) Splinter protection for machinery spaces
(c) Retaining 5-inch DP but increasing light AA
(d) Centerline TT
(e) Depth-charge projectors to be included
(f) No reduction in speed

The third (c) and fifth (e) represented the triumph of the War Plans view. The popularity of centerline torpedo mounts grew as crews began to experience trouble with the heavy quadruple wing mounts, too close to the corrosive effects of the sea. Much of the weight increase from 1931 on had gone into ruggedness, but as we have already seen, any serious splinter protection would have an unacceptable cost—a minimum of 2,000 tons and 2 knots. At least the en-echelon machinery arrangement would go some way toward reducing vulnerability. Indeed, this arrangement may have saved the *Kearny*, torpedoed in the fall of 1941 by a German U-boat; her survival was considered a striking proof of the viability of the new destroyers.

As for machine guns, the FY 39 characteristics showed six rather than four .50-cal. guns. This was quite clearly very little, but weight precluded the installation of the new 1.1-inch quadruple AA. Finally, the General Board expressed itself as perfectly happy to return to an all-centerline torpedo tube arrangement even at a cost in total torpedo battery, in view of the existence of 22 boats with 16 TT each.

However, even this problem was soon eliminated by the success of a new quintuple mount. This actually *increased* the broadside by a quarter while saving 6 to 7 tons (some of which was then lost in the higher mountings).

The 1938 and 1939 classes and their production successors were very similar: the Bath/Gibbs & Cox *Gleaves* or *Livermore* type (DD 423–424, 429–444, 453–458, 461–464, 483–490, 493–497, 618–628, 632–641, 645–648) and the Bethlehem *Benson* class (DD 421–422, 425–428, 459, 460, 491, 492, 598–617). Navy willingness to accept what Admiral Bowen called a "bastard" machinery arrangement in the *Benson*s was a matter of the exigencies of mobilization: after DD 428, the *Benson*s were the products of Bethlehem yards: San Francisco (459, 460, 605–611), Staten Island (491, 492, 602–604), Quincy (598–601, 616, 617), and a new yard at San Pedro (612–615). The other destroyer builders completed *Gleaves*-class ships, using Westinghouse, GE, and Allis-Chalmers turbines; the *Benson*s generally used Bethlehem turbines. Externally, the two classes could be distinguished by the shape of their funnels: flat in *Benson*s, round in *Gleaves* (which were also called *Livermore*s, because the design was standardized with the *Livermore*, DD 429). The *Benson*s were often referred to as the 1,620-ton class, the *Gleaves/Livermore*s as 1,630-tonners, although in fact all ships came out very overweight, so that their light displacements generally exceeded these design standard figures.

The *Benson*s were built at a time of radical change in destroyer mission and weaponry, with depth charges and automatic guns increasingly edging out conventional heavy dual-purpose guns and torpedo tubes. As the basic design was being modified for "repeat" ships, the first units were completed as planned with five 5-inch guns and ten tubes and assigned to an Atlantic Fleet increasingly concerned with convoy ASW and with the potential problems of air attack. In addition, the configurations of many ships were determined at least in part by the availability of the new standard antiaircraft weapons, the

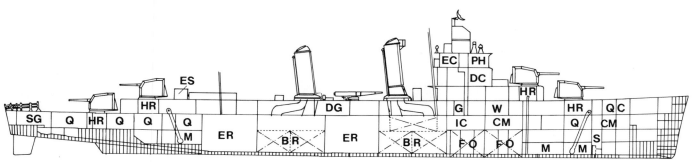

DD 488 inboard

The "repeat" *Benson*-class destroyer *Stevenson*, newly delivered, shows the results of prewar and wartime changes: a flat-faced bridge with a low director, a single set of torpedo tubes, and an unusual arrangement of her gun tubs, with 20-mm. tubs opposite (empty) 40-mm. ones, aft and abreast the second funnel. She shows the round funnels of the Gibbs & Cox design.

The *Plunkett*, in New York harbor, 5 August 1942, shows the effects of the first wave of modifications, with both No. 3 gun and No. 2 bank of torpedo tubes removed in favor of 20-mm. guns. She has the early type of depth-charge thrower reload stowage, in which charges with arbors attached stood on deck, loaded by means of large davits; three are visible. Note, too, the half-housing on No. 3 gun mount, with a canvas top, a type devised after the winter of 1940.

twin 40-mm. Bofors and the single 20-mm. Oerlikon machine cannon. Thus, the evolution of the *Benson* battery combined lengthy paper studies with the extemporized refits of Atlantic Fleet units in 1941.

In December 1940, the CNO authorized for "repeat" units (DD 598–628, 632–641, 645–648) an improved antiaircraft battery in which No. 3 5-in./38 gun would be surrendered in favor of a quadruple 1.1-inch machine cannon; an alternative proposal by the coordinator of shipbuilding to remove, instead, one bank of torpedo tubes was rejected, as that would halve the torpedo battery whereas the elimination of one 5-in./38 would reduce the gun battery by only 20 percent. In any case, the General Board considered the Bofors much superior to the 1.1, and in January 1941 it was decided that No. 3 gun, the four reload torpedoes, and the six .50s should be sacrificed in favor of two twin Bofors with their directors and four Oerlikons. At first it was hoped that one Bofors mount could be placed forward and one aft, but that proved impossible, and the closest BuShips could come to all-round fire was to sponson the two twin Bofors well outboard, to give them considerable arcs ahead. The 36-inch searchlight originally to have been mounted on the elevated structure on the after deckhouse was to be relocated, together with the emergency steering position. The CNO approved this modification on 11 January 1941, and in March it was extended to DD 453–464 and 483–497, provided that no delays would be incurred. In fact, Federal (DD 453–456, 483–490) proposed merely to omit No. 3 gun, retaining the high structure on the after deckhouse as originally designed. Thus, the *Bristol* (DD 453) was completed in this form, with four 5-inch guns and ten tubes.*

Meanwhile, those units completed for the Atlantic Fleet were being modified to suit the conditions of North Atlantic warfare, which required not merely better antiaircraft batteries and better splinter protection, but also more depth charges. The original design called for two five-charge (600-lb) stern tracks and six .50-caliber machine guns. The Atlantic Fleet modifications included the addition of extensions for seven more charges to each stern track (for a total of twenty-four 600-lb. charges on deck) and a Y-gun on the fantail with ten 300-lb. depth charges. Splinter protection in the form of a half shield was to be applied to the 01-level 5-in./38 guns aft, and splinter protection bulwarks were to be provided for bridge personnel and for the crews of the machine guns.

Two alternative schemes for weight compensation were promulgated in April 1941. DesRon 7(DD 421–428, 431) surrendered the after bank of torpedo tubes, a 36-inch searchlight being mounted on the former torpedo tube foundation. Four machine guns were added, two in place of the former pair of 24-inch searchlights, and two atop the after deckhouse on sponsons; the pair formerly mounted atop the after superstructure were brought down to 01 level and that superstructure eliminated, the after (emergency) steering position built abeam them. The remaining ships, DesRons 11 (DD 429, 430, 432–436, 440) and 13 (DD 437–439, 441–444, and 453) were all either modified or completed to an alternative design, in which all ten tubes were retained but No. 3 5-in./38 gun was surrendered as weight compensation. Six .50s were added, for a total of twelve.

The Atlantic Fleet effort and the general effort at revision of the *Benson* design came together when depth-charge and antiaircraft requirements were combined. By August 1941 the basic design had been modified in both directions, and the General Board was calling for a distinction to be made between fleet destroyers and ships intended for sea control, i.e., for operations against submarines, aircraft, and surface raiders. The General Board wanted to use the *Benson*s in this role, reserving the new *Fletcher*s for fleet operations. It followed that both antiaircraft and antisubmarine batteries would have to be emphasized, and the only item available for weight compensation was the second bank of torpedo tubes. That would buy thirty 600-lb. depth charges (two tracks plus warhead magazine stowage) and thirty-two 300-lb. depth charges (eight Mk 6 "K-guns"). Additional weight compensation would be obtained by eliminating two of the 20-mm. cannon bought by elimination of the 5-in./38s (which were in fact restored before this program was carried out), and even more could be obtained if No. 4 5-in./38 were temporarily removed; in that case up to eighty 300-lb. depth charges might be carried. The General Board recommended that repeat ships not yet well advanced have their beams increased by about 1 foot 4 inches to make up for the increases in top weight thus contemplated. In fact, however, only DD 634 and 635 were beamier, and they were increased only from 36 feet 1 inch to 37 feet.

The *Bristol* and all later ships were soon modified to a five-tube standard (as ordered by the CNO, October 1941), although the Bofors guns specified early in 1941 were not to be available until well into 1942. In addition, in December 1941 the CNO reduced the depth-charge battery to six projectors (with twenty-four charges and twenty-four more stowed, and fourteen depth charges in the tracks aft, with another ten 600-lb. charges stowed). The three 5-inch alternative battery was not implemented, but it was carried on the books as late as January 1943. In practice,

---

* She was unusual in that she was completed without gun shields. The *Aaron Ward* (DD 483) and *Lardner* (DD 487) had enclosed centerline shelters (supporting 20-mm. guns) forward of their bridges.

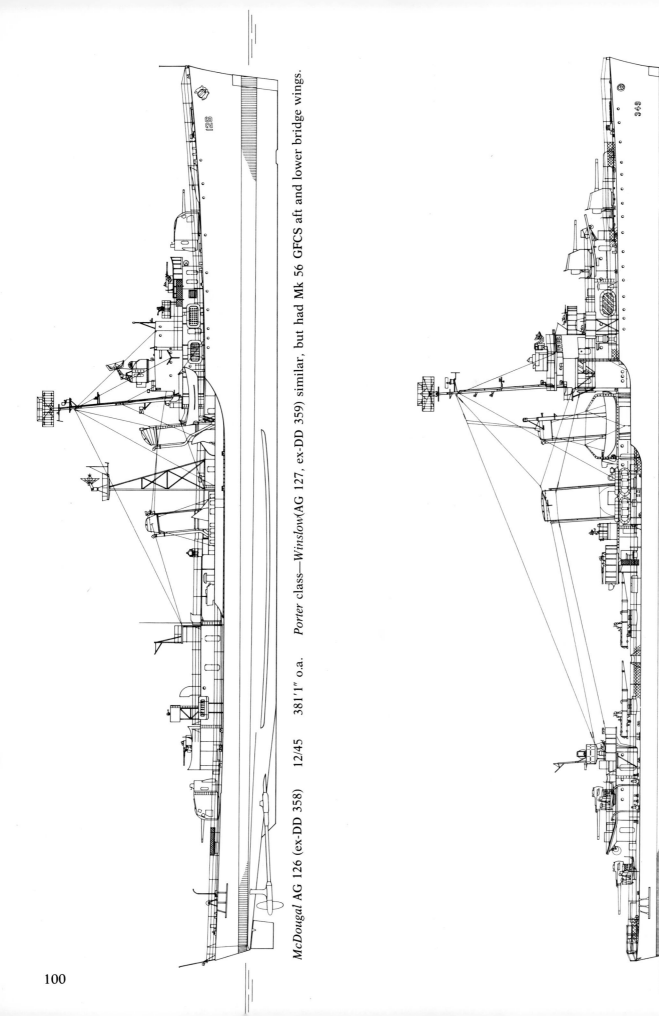

McDougal AG 126 (ex-DD 358)　　12/45　　381'1" o.a.　　*Porter* class—*Winslow*(AG 127, ex-DD 359) similar, but had Mk 56 GFCS aft and lower bridge wings.

Dewey DD 349　　Sept. 1944　　341'3" o.a.　　*Farragut* class, late-war appearance. Still later, the pilothouse windows were replaced by portholes.

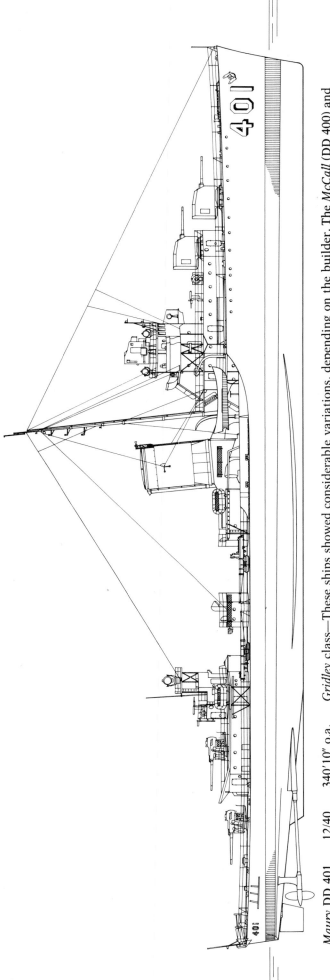

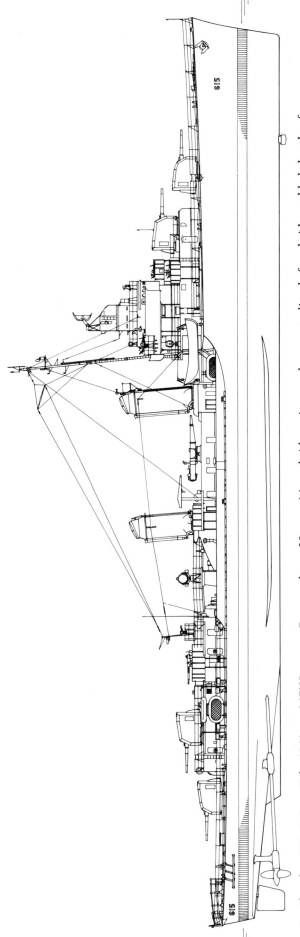

Maury DD 401   12/40   340'10" o.a.   *Gridley* class—These ships showed considerable variations, depending on the builder. The *McCall* (DD 400) and *Maury* were similar. Higher-numbered units had lower stack bases similar to those on the *Sims* class. As completed, they carried a third boat abreast the stack to starboard, had portholes fore and aft at the first platform deck, and had no bulwarks amidships.

McClanahan DD 615   Feb. 1943   347'9" o.a.   *Benson* class—20-mm. AA on bridge wings and on centerline before bridge added shortly after commissioning. The *Livermore* class basically similar, but had round stacks.

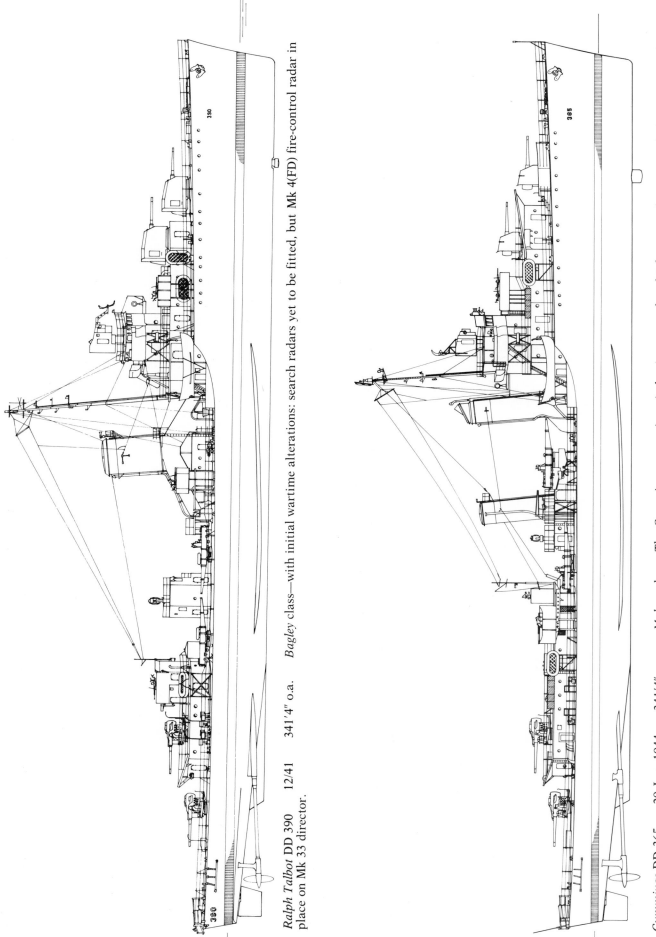

Ralph Talbot DD 390   12/41   341'4" o.a.   *Bagley* class—with initial wartime alterations: search radars yet to be fitted, but Mk 4(FD) fire-control radar in place on Mk 33 director.

Cummings DD 365   29 Jan. 1944   341'4" o.a.   *Mahan* class—The *Cummings* was unique in having an enclosed Mk 33 gun director, with the Mk 4 radar's antenna atop, rather than projecting from the forward face. Also unique to this ship was the location of the three forward 20-mm. AA in one "tub" at the same level before the bridge; DD 365 also lacked most of the normal length of bulwarks on the main deck abaft the forecastle "break."

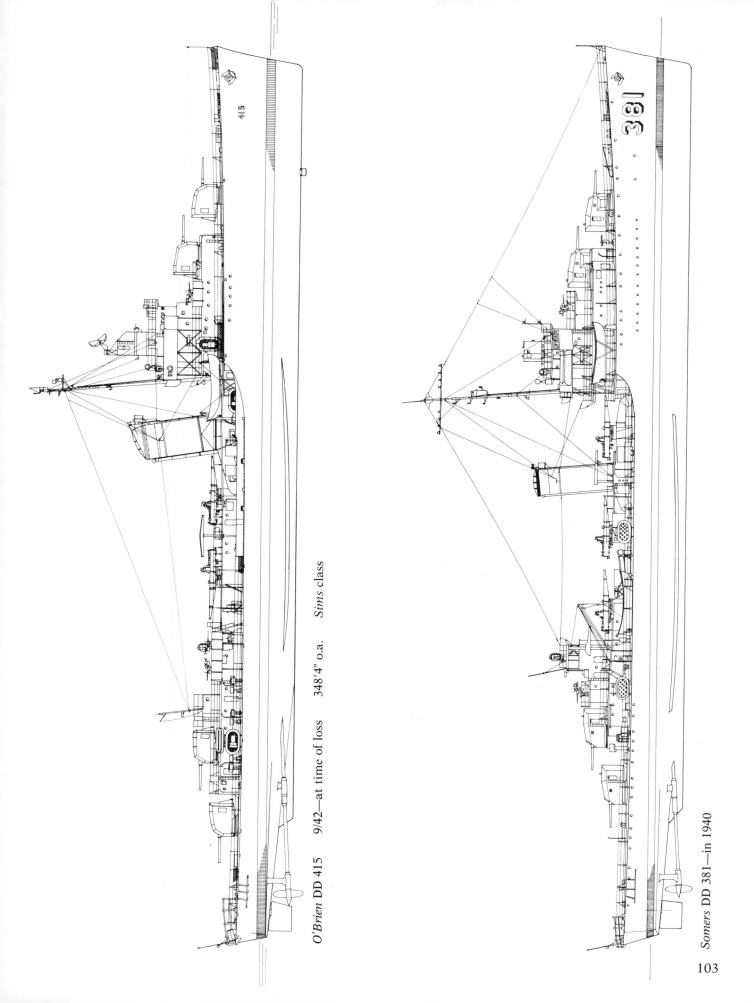

O'Brien DD 415   9/42—at time of loss   *Sims* class   348'4" o.a.

Somers DD 381—in 1940

in January 1942 many Atlantic *Benson*s had a pair of 12-charge stern tracks, with stowage for 16 more 600-lb. charges, plus the Y-gun. A few Atlantic ships actually carried the eight K-gun battery; Pacific *Benson*s were limited to four. Generally, the latter had twenty 300-lb. charges in their throwers and 22 more stowed, with five-charge stern tracks. By late in the war the usual Atlantic allowance was a pair of seven-charge stern tracks (with eight 600-lb. charges in reserve, for a total of 22).

Automatic batteries did not correspond to expectations, because Bofors guns were in short supply until well into the war. Thus, the five-gun *Benson*s soon surrendered their .50s in favor of six Oerlikons: two on the deckhouse aft, two abeam the second funnel, and two before the bridge. Later, the ultimate battery of all of these ships (DD 421–444) was altered to four guns and ten tubes, although the nine originally armed with five guns and five tubes had an alternative: one bank of tubes and four extra Oerlikons on a "portable" platform. A few operated in this configuration, but by 1944 all surviving units of the DD 421–444 series had ten tubes and four guns.

For repeat ships (DD 453 and above) the temporary approved battery was one quadruple 1.1-inch machine cannon sponsored out to starboard, with an Oerlikon opposite and four more Oerlikons forward. A few were completed with the ultimate battery of two twin Bofors aft, the *Coghlan* (DD 606) being the first U.S. warship to mount the twin Bofors gun. However, not all ships had these weapons before 1944. Meanwhile, the Oerlikon battery was increased. In November 1942, three were added to the planned ("ultimate") battery of the repeat *Benson*s: one on a raised platform forward of the bridge, and two more on the bridge wings.

As war approached in 1941, the Navy tried to simplify the *Benson* design by eliminating curves in its superstructure. In fact, this improvement applied only to the ten ships built by Seattle-Tacoma (DD 493–497 and 624–628) and to the last ten built by Federal (DD 618–623, 645–648), all of which had square-faced bridges and directors lowered to their pilot house roofs. In addition DDs 645–648 had their 40-mm. tubes staggered and had no 20-mm. guns at the forward ends of their pilot houses as completed.*

In August 1941, the Bureau of Ships and the General Board recommended further production of an improved *Benson* as a means of increasing the number of new destroyers; they would form the middle of a destroyer spectrum whose high end would be the *Fletcher*s and their successors (which turned out to be the *Sumner/Gearing*s). The board wanted the usual minimal improvements: a streamlined retract-

able sonar dome, splinter protection amidships against the effects of near misses, and a diesel emergency generator, relocated below decks near the plotting room in the interest of stability and greater separation from the main machinery plant. Meanwhile, in at least some ships, the emergency diesel generator was being removed, in silent testimony to the overcrowding resulting from the modifications already made.

BuShips redesigned the 1,630-ton destroyer as Scheme A, Scheme B being what became the *Sumner* (see chapter 6). The results suggest the extent to which a ship designed only in 1939 was already badly overloaded. The intent was, first, to avoid entirely the use of fixed ballast. Preliminary Design commented that, although it had retained the configuration of the *Benson*s, "the after quintuple tube, the two Bofors guns, and the two after 5-inch guns are grouped so closely together that one hit, even from a small bomb or projectile, would put a large part of this armament out of action. The close grouping of these units is such as to make mutual interbattery interference probable in normal operations and almost inevitable in case casualties or action damage occur." Preliminary Design also looked at a ship in which the after bank of torpedo tubes was eliminated and two single Oerlikons added (Scheme A–1); this would permit the after 5-inch guns to be separated and the two twin Bofors further separated to achieve a considerable arc of noninterfering fire, i.e., a series of arcs on which both mounts might bear.

The bureau observed that the *Benson*s had originally been designed on the basis of a trial condition in which only 100 rounds per gun were carried, i.e., 2,080 tons, but that actual ammunition loads had brought this figure up to about 2,260, including 40 tons of fixed ballast. On the same basis Scheme A–1 would come to 2,295, including 15 tons of structural weight for increased beam.

These efforts were carried along in parallel to the studies that became the *Sumner*s. Thus, characteristics for a "medium destroyer" were promulgated by the General Board in April 1942; "the General Board, having in mind the need for numbers and for economy where possible has reviewed the characteristics of the 1,630-ton class of destroyers, has taken cognizance of the experiences abroad during this war and of the probable demands of our current war effort, and of the desirability of building and having in service general-purpose destroyers which will compose the bulk of the replacement program." It appeared that standard displacement would rise to about 1,740 tons, with a battery of four 5-in./38s, two twin Bofors and four Oerlikons, one quintuple torpedo tube, two depth-charge tracks aft, and six throwers. Stowage would be provided for forty-six

* They later carried three 20-mm. forward.

Ultimately, all of the early units were restored to a 10-tube configuration: this is the *Gwin* off Mare Island, 23 February 1943, with twin Bofors aft. The unusual-looking machine-gun directors aft are the unsuccessful Mk 49, soon replaced by the much simpler Mk 51.

The *Aaron Ward* comes alongside in the South Pacific, August 1942. Her port anchor has been removed, presumably to save weight. She has an early SC air-search radar but no IFF and no surface-search set.

The *Emmons* (1 November 1943) illustrates a typical mid-war configuration, with a pair of twin 40-mm. guns aft, six depth-charge projectors with roller racks alongside her after superstructure, and seven 20-mm. guns, the two in her bridge wings showing prominent pipe guards.

Off New York on 14 August 1943, the *Tillman* shows the 20-mm. battery adopted as "ultimate" in November 1942: three 20-mm. forward of her bridge, with two more in the bridge wings and two more abeam her after funnel. Her air-search radar is the early SC, and the "stovepipe" on her yardarm is an IFF antenna, with the long dipole of a tactical radio (TBS) projecting down from the opposite one. Fighting lights are visible farther down her mast.

The *Beatty*, 23 January 1943, shows both after 5-inch mounts fully enclosed, the earlier half-shield having been abandoned. A smoke generator is visible between the depth-charge tracks aft.

300-lb. and twenty-two 600-lb. charges. There would be no emergency generator, but that might be justified on the basis of the redundant power plant, consisting of two independent units, each including a ship service turbogenerator capable of carrying the battle load.

Admiral King rejected the General Board's proposal: he found the 1,740-ton destroyer "deficient in torpedo battery. ... There are now building Destroyer Escorts of 1,200 tons and Destroyers of 2,050–2,100 tons. The General Board has recommended Destroyers of 2,500 tons and here recommends Destroyers of 1,740 tons. In all four, destroyer-escort types would be under construction in the near future, which is unacceptable from both the material and the production standpoint."

That ended the production of the *Benson*s, and left them either the most modern of the prewar types or the least modern of the wartime destroyers; they were destined to be retained postwar as a mobilization reserve. Once they had reached the batteries decided upon in 1942, they were little modified in wartime, except for the large anti-Kamikaze program of the spring of 1945. All torpedo tubes were to be eliminated, a quadruple replacing the former pair of twin 40-mm. AA aft, and twins mounted between the fun-

nels, for a total of twelve 40-mm. In addition, the Oerlikon battery would ultimately be reduced to twins forward of the bridge, but two singles were retained amidships until blind-fire directors became available. Of the 19 surviving 10-tube ships, 12 (DD 423, 424, 429–432, 435, 437–440, and 443) were refitted. Of the later type, 16 out of 37 were refitted: DD 497, 600, 601, 603, 604, 608, 610, 612–617, 623, 624, 628, of which the *McLanahan* (DD 615) had four twin Bofors, as quadruple mounts were not available when she was refitted.

Postwar, the *Benson*s were laid up and only the *Nicholson* and *Woodworth* remained active, as Naval Reserve training ships. They were subject to a Class Improvement Plan (CIP) drawn up by the Ship Characteristic Board (SCB) for mobilization planning. In March 1951, this called for removal of the Oerlikons and of one depth-charge track, and for the fitting of dual Hedgehog, as in contemporary active destroyers. More radical improvements were also considered. For example, on 9 March 1950 the senior member of the SCB queried BuShips as to the feasibility of installing Weapon A, the two Hedgehogs, and the two twin 3-in./50s with a Mk 56 director on the centerline in place of the Bofors guns. One depth-charge track would have been removed, and the single rudder en-

One of the last active destroyer minesweepers, the USS *Thompson* is shown after an overhaul at San Francisco, 11 February 1954. Conversion entailed removal of No. 4 gun and the addition of a new turbogenerator. She was, moreover, one of the series of ships converted in 1945 to reflect the anti-Kamikaze rearmament program, with quadruple Bofors guns aft. By 1954 all ASW weapons and all 20-mm. guns had been landed, and she had been modestly refitted with new electronics, consisting of an SU-2 surface-search radar and a Mk X IFF for her wartime SC-series air-search radar. The ECM radomes on her second funnel were wartime DBM radar direction-finders, but the small radome atop her topmast appears to be a postwar URD-4 UHF/DF. The small dipoles on her foremast served UHF tactical radios, the successors to TBS.

larged as in the *Fletcher*s. Other planned improvements were scanning sonar and modern radar. This was close to the DDC conversion planned four years later (see chapter 12).

In fact, the only modernizations of these ships were accomplished prior to their transfer to foreign navies, and by the mid-1950s the *Benson* CIPs were little more than a formality.

The only ships that continued on active service postwar were those converted to destroyer minesweepers. They were successors to 18 flush deckers converted in 1940–41. Even before that, the conversion of modern ships had been considered and the

DD 364–408 series rejected, as they would hog under the strain of towing sweep gear. The *Benson*s would be suitable, but at the time they were considered far too valuable for such employment.

By August 1944, the value of destroyer minesweepers had been thoroughly demonstrated, and destroyers were quite plentiful. A BuShips sketch design for a *Bristol* conversion showed the removal of both the torpedo tubes and No. 4 gun, as well as the reduction of the stern depth-charge racks to a capacity of seven 300-lb. charges each. The destroyer sweeper had to cope with magnetic as well as moored mines and required extra magnetic and acoustic sweeps, powered by a new 540-kw turbogenerator. Admiral King ordered 24 ships converted on 7 October, and more detailed studies showed that four depth-charge projectors and two 24-inch searchlights would have to be landed, and below-deck stowage reduced from sixteen 300-lb. and eight 600-lb. to fourteen 300-lb. charges. Only 12 Atlantic Fleet ships were converted during 1944 (DD 454–458, 461, 462, 464, 621, 625, 636, and 637 became DMS 19–30), with another dozen following in 1945 (DD 489, 490, 493–496, 618, 627, and 632–635 became DMS 31–42). The latter incorporated the anti-Kamikaze antiaircraft modifications and were armed with two quadruple Bofors aft, plus twin Oerlikons forward and two singles aft. Of the earlier ships, only the *Hobson* was so refitted.

Twelve DMS survived into the postwar fleet, maintained in three MineDivs, two in the Atlantic and one in the Pacific. They proved totally ineffective in Korea and were sent home because their personnel could be more efficiently spread among smaller units. Thus, the active units were reduced to reserve in 1954–55, with the exception of the *Hobson*, lost by collision in 1952. All DMS reverted to destroyer status at this time, but were not modified to reflect that change. The last unit, the USS *Fitch* (DMS 26), was decommissioned in February 1956 after duty with the Operational Development Force.

There remains one major footnote to the story of the interwar destroyer projects, the last of the leaders. In a sense, the *Atlanta* class reflected the need for destroyer support duties. Moreover, in November 1939 the General Board called for a new destroyer leader design based on the last 1,850-ton class, with either (i) armament reduced to that of a 1,620-tonner; or (ii) dual-purpose rather than single-purpose guns, the beam to be increased to retain stability. BuShips estimated that (i) would cost 1,970 tons (DD 394, the *Sampson*, had come out to 1,988 despite a design limit of 1,850); with dual-purpose guns, (ii) would cost 2,024 tons. Both projects were mooted by the advent of the *Fletcher* class, but they show the continuing interest in leader design.

Yet another leader project was a very small cruiser. On 24 August 1939, the Chief Constructor asked Preliminary Design to study a 3,000- to 3,500-ton cruiser of 28 knots or more, to carry eight to ten 6-inch single-purpose guns and two or three aircraft. "The above vessel is intended to be used as a destroyer leader. It was characterized in conversation with the CNO as a 'glorified flotilla leader.'" However, the project

did not quite die. On 5 March 1940, the President requested a 3,400-ton cruiser-destroyer to mount 6-inch guns, or perhaps the new 5-in./54 then under consideration. A month later he was rewarded with a sketch design for a 4,050-ton (4,920 full load), 460-foot ship to carry eight 6-in./47 (now DP: those guns would later arm the big *Worcester*-class cruisers), eight .50-caliber machine guns, and 12 torpedo tubes (in triple mounts), as well as two aircraft, all at 35 knots (75,000 shp). Protection would have to be restricted to ¾-inch STS over boilers, engines, pilot house, and directors. This seemed very little protection for a unit price of $16.25 million; the General Board characterized the project as a satisfactory (if overpriced) destroyer but by no means a cruiser; its chairman commented that "I do not know for what purpose this vessel is proposed." The result seemed a terribly expensive way to carry a very poorly protected battery at the moderate speed of 31 knots. Subsequent correspondence revealed that a major motive for the project had been its aircraft; the aircraft-carrying *Fletcher*-class destroyer was built instead.

Table 5–4. Flotilla Leader, 12 September 1939

LWL	425
Beam	46
Draft	14.4
SHP	50,000
Speed	31
Endurance	7,000/12
6-in./47	4 × 2
QUAD 1.1	2
Hull	1,509
Fittings	268
Machinery	800
Armament	334
Equipment & Outfit	170
Margin	80
Light ship	3,161
Ammunition	215
Stores	125
Standard	3,501
RFW	40
Fuel	400
Normal	3,941
GM	3.77

Note: Armament includes 27 tons for aeronautics; this ship had a catapult.

6

To the Big Destroyers, 1941–1945

In retrospect the *Fletcher*s are often described as the most successful of all American destroyers: fast, roomy, capable of absorbing enormous punishment, and yet fighting on. They fought in the classic destroyer action of World War II, the unequal battle off Samar, in which a few *Fletcher*s and destroyer escorts faced the Japanese battle line; a few hours later *Fletcher*s delivered the last U.S. destroyer surface torpedo attack in the Battle of Surigao Strait. The *Fletcher*s fought through most of the Pacific war, from the night battle of Guadalcanal (November 1942) onward. So successful were they, and so fondly were they remembered, that the first postwar mass-production destroyer, the *Forrest Sherman*, began as a project for an updated *Fletcher*.

In fact, the *Fletcher*s were the first of a generation of U.S. warship designs finally freed of treaty restrictions. Although the *Sims* and *Benson* classes were formally unlimited, the need to continue production at a high tempo forced their designers to adapt existing (treaty-limited) designs rather than start afresh. The same considerations applied in other classes; thus the *Cleveland*s, for example, suffered throughout their careers from limitations inherited from earlier treaty-limited light cruisers, and even though the *Essex*-class carriers were about 15 percent above the displacement of the previous (treaty-limited) *Yorktown* class, they were considered cramped. The *Fletcher* class was representative of a new generation of U.S. warship designs, typified in other categories by the *Midway*-class carriers, the *Montana*-class battleships, and the *Alaska*-class large cruisers.

In effect, the *Fletcher* enjoyed an increase in size just *before* that larger size was loaded down to a condition of crowding commensurate with that of earlier (or later) types. One consequence was the astounding increase in light armament the ship could accommodate without serious degradation in performance or visible loss in main battery. For example, of the long series of destroyers designed to carry five 5-inch guns, only the *Fletcher*s retained that battery through the war, and until the mass rearmament of 1945, only the *Fletcher*s combined that gun battery with a full ten torpedo tubes. It seems likely in restrospect that part of their popularity was due to a perception that the next class, the *Sumner*s, was overloaded, particularly forward, and therefore was unduly subject to sea damage. However, like the "flush deckers" of two decades earlier, the flush-deck *Fletcher*s suffered in seagoing performance compared to previous forecastle types; they are remembered favorably partly because they spent their wartime careers almost exclusively in the Pacific.

Finally, the *Fletcher*s dominated the war in the Pacific largely because of their numbers: 175 were built, far more than any other class. The "iron law" of mobilization is that only equipment already in production can pass into mass production, and the design of the *Fletcher* coincided with the great acceleration of U.S. naval shipbuilding just prior to and early in World War II. Although there was some consideration to continue the *Benson* production line, the virtues of standardization were such that only one class of fleet destroyer could be built in large numbers. That was the *Fletcher* and its production successor, the *Sumner/Gearing*. Once production began, output was swift indeed: by August 1942, a total of 10 were in commission, with 19 more added by the end of that year. By the time these units were in service, the production program had gained so much

After 1945 the *Fletcher*s were considered a mobilization reserve, the oldest truly satisfactory U.S. destroyers. For a time all were scheduled for conversion to escorts, as in the case of the *Nicholas*, shown here at Mare Island, 17 March 1951. The ASW projector in No. 2 position was a Mk 15 Hedgehog.

Larger than the prewar "leaders," the *Fletcher*s were the first U.S. fleet destroyers designed to accommodate a multiple machine cannon. The newly completed *La Vallette*, shown off New York on 8 October 1942, displays nearly the original configuration, with a twin Bofors in place of the 1.1-inch machine cannon aft, and with 20-mm. guns in place of the .50-calibre machine guns of the original design. She has, however, an additional twin 40-mm. gun aft, near her depth-charge tracks. Note the early-type depth-charge stowage near her six depth-charge projectors aft and the splinter shielding around all light weapons, the latter not a feature of the original design.

momentum that there could be no question of revising the design; indeed, by that time the next design, the *Sumner*, was already on order.

The evolution of the *Fletcher* class, Destroyer 1941, actually began in the fall of 1939, with the General Board most concerned with what was considered the excessive size of existing ships. For example, in October it circulated a questionnaire to the divisions of the Office of the Chief of Naval Operations and to the bureaus:

Since destroyers are primarily torpedo vessels—for use chiefly against enemy battle line—do not the latest type destroyers carry *too few torpedoes?*

Since destroyers, primarily torpedo vessels, are unarmored and extremely vulnerable, have they not grown so large as to present targets *unfavorable for survival* in torpedo attack?

Since the use of destroyers as anti-submarine vessels fits in with their usual employment with the battle line—and with their likely use as convoy escorts—have they sufficient capacity *as to depth charges* both as to numbers and "throwers"?

To what degree has the premise of meeting opposing destroyers with gunfire resulted in destroyers becoming unduly large targets?

Since destroyers require high speed—to offset their vulnerability and to maneuver adequately in battle— what should be their designed speed—36 knots?

DDs 409 et seq. are of some 1,625 tons *standard* displacement—rising to 2,300 tons *full* load displacement. *If minimum target is essential*, in what particular area must reductions be made to reduce the *standard* displacement to 1,500 tons?

Against these fears of the consequences of large unit size, there could be placed the general desire for a more effective antiaircraft battery (i.e., a director-controlled 1.1-inch machine cannon) and for splinter

protection against bomb attack, particularly over the machinery spaces. Neither would be inexpensive. Nor would the kind of drastic reductions needed if destroyers were indeed to be cut back to 1,500 tons be forthcoming.

At a 16 October General Board hearing, Captain Crenshaw of War Plans described the current torpedo battery of two quintuple tubes on the centerline as sufficient: "to add more would necessitate undesirable sacrifice of other armament." However, Admiral Furlong (BuOrd) considered 12 torpedoes a minimum; the 10-tube ship could, of course, accommodate four reloads and so satisfy both points of view. The General Board's hope of cutting down the size of the destroyer was generally dismissed. As for depth charges, Captain Crenshaw noted that current tactics called for a 7-charge pattern, so that the proposed allowance of 28 charges allowed for four patterns. Such a pattern in turn required the use of two Y-guns on the centerline, which would compete with guns and torpedo tubes for that valuable space. Indeed, at that time there was considerable interest in a second Y-gun to be provided aboard existing destroyers of the *Sims* and later classes. The sole dissenter was Admiral Leary (Fleet Training), who called for twice the standard depth-charge allowance. Admiral King, later CNO but then on the General Board, saw intense competition for space between torpedoes, guns, and depth charges; Captain Crenshaw replied that War Plans "would like to have five 5-in. double-purpose guns but we think it is necessary to get two Y-guns . . . we can accept four guns but five would be better." Admiral King concluded that the desirable battery was 5 guns, 12 torpedoes, and 28 depth charges.

It seems odd in retrospect that Ordnance did not mention the new "K-gun," then in development, as a solution to the centerline problem: four K-guns would, in effect, replace the pair of Y-guns at no sacrifice at all in that precious dimension. In fact, all U.S. destroyers built during World War II were completed with from four to eight K-guns, providing them with thrower batteries beyond the number possible with the earlier projectors.

As for speed, Captain Crenshaw called for 38 knots, i.e., about 5 knots faster than the fastest heavy units then in prospect, the *Iowa* and the *Yorktown*-class carriers. Admirals Leary and Furlong were willing to settle for not less than 36, which Captain J. M. Irish (Engineering) felt could easily be obtained with existing machinery plants. However, to pass to 38 knots would probably require 20 percent more power and, therefore, 10 percent more weight, not to mention increased space. Commander Cochrane of Preliminary Design, who would be responsible for the preliminary design of the new ship, commented that "changing from 'not less than 35' to 'not less than 36' would not affect the present design. . . . To change the requirement to bring it up to 38 will seriously affect the design; will increase the length to provide more room in the machinery compartments; increase displacement, and there would be quite a considerable modification of design involved. . . ."

Finally, there was the issue of overweight and stability: as the board met, the new *Sims*-class destroyers were requiring lead in their bottoms to overcome excessive top weight. Cochrane believed that the easiest corrective measure would be an 18-inch increase in beam, with a corresponding growth of 15 to 20 tons and a loss of about .2 knots in speed.

The next day the General Board issued its first tentative characteristics. It hoped that a new destroyer would not exceed 1,600 tons and would accommodate at least four 5-in./38 guns, two quintuple torpedo tubes on the centerline (with four reloads), and 28 depth charges (with two racks and not fewer than two throwers). The overweight problem was reflected in a provision for "inherent transverse stability in all conditions of loading," and the ships were to be "of such rugged construction as to enable high speed to be maintained in heavy weather." The antiaircraft battery was to consist of four (preferably six) .50-caliber machine guns, and trial speed was to be 36 knots. Endurance was to be that distance at 15 knots corresponding to the usual 6,500 nm. at 12 knots, four months out of dock.

Three design alternatives were suggested: (i) a *Benson-Livermore* modified to accommodate the increased depth-charge stowage; (ii) a ship with four 5-in./38s in single mounts, with the weight made available by the omission of No. 3 gun invested in depth charges and torpedo stowage, with some depth charges below decks; and (iii) a ship with four dual-purpose guns in a combination of single and twin mounts (twin fore and aft, or twin forward, two single aft, or two singles forward, twin aft). The latter arrangements had a considerable potential for reducing the profile of the destroyer, and thus its vulnerability to shellfire. On the other hand, a single hit on a twin mount would disable it and half the destroyer's firepower at one blow, and it was widely suspected that the twin mount could not fire nearly as quickly as two singles. Moreover, the single mount could be trained by hand in the event a ship was disabled, albeit not very easily in the case of the enclosed base-ring types. Emergency diesel power was provided, in general, for only half the battery.

By November, C&R had produced six alternative designs. All were based on the current hull design, introduced in the *Sims* (DD 409) class, except that the beam was increased a foot for stability in four cases (Schemes 1, 2, 5, and 6, with, respectively, five and four single mounts, two singles and one twin aft, and one twin forward and three singles aft). Schemes 3 and 4 had one twin mount forward and, respectively, one twin and two singles aft. The twin-mount designs showed the reduction in silhouette possible, as they omitted one level of the forward deckhouse. In all six designs deck heights in the deckhouses were reduced as much as possible, and aluminum was used extensively to reduce top weight. All incorporated the latest 50,000 shp power plant, and were expected to achieve 36.5 to 37 knots, with an endurance of 6,500 nm. at the new cruising speed of 15 knots, thereby exceeding the General Board's desires: fuel tankage cost very little. However, none mounted the desired six .50-caliber antiaircraft battery, as top weight was at a premium.

Scheme 1 was essentially a demonstration that the existing destroyer design, only slightly modified, could meet the General Board's requirements on a standard displacement estimated at 1,720 tons; with one gun removed, that would fall to 1,690. Indeed, C&R felt that "although (Scheme 2) carries only four guns it has greater volume of fire and flexibility in use of the battery than any of the other four-gun schemes. It appears to represent a well-balanced compromise among the various requirements for destroyer design, and from this point of view appears to be the best design in the series." The two single-mount designs and the schemes with single guns aft (4 and 6) were provided with pairs of K-guns alongside their after deckhouses;

> . . . as compared with Y-guns aft, the single throwers on the sides have the advantage of not interfering with any arcs of fire, but have the disadvantage of obstructing the sides of the deck for handling lines, etc. The single throwers on the sides would also be farther than the Y-guns from the depth charge stow-

age below decks; but to offset this, ready service lockers are provided for one reload, and for the stowage of arbors. . . . On the assumption that depth charges will be laid in patterns of seven (three from the racks and four from the throwers) racks at the stern have been provided to carry three charges each. The throwers will carry four charges for one pattern. The remaining 18 . . . will be carried in the warhead locker (assuming warheads on the torpedoes). . . .

In wartime, it would be standard practice to carry three reloads in a roller-loader next to each K-gun, and depth-charge tracks aft would normally carry five or more charges each.

At a General Board hearing on 22 November, Admiral Watson of the General Board began by asking Commander Cochrane once again why destroyers had grown about 200 tons above 1,500 with no obvious gain in military characteristics. Commander Cochrane cited increased hull scantlings for ruggedness, 7 feet more length, and heavier hull fittings, chiefly steering gear, anchor gear, and ventilation. Commander Mills of Engineering added that by alternating the engine and fire rooms and adopting air-encased boilers considerable weight had been added, and that diesel (emergency) generators had grown considerably, from none at all in the *Farragut*s to 25 kw in the *Mahan*s and now 80 kw; moreover, depth charges had been added. Of those present, Admiral Furlong (Chief of BuOrd) favored the single-mount schemes, and preferred Scheme 1 for its extra gun. Moreover, "he considered it very important to settle on some standard design rather than to change the basic destroyer design each year as we have done in the past." Captain Crenshaw also favored Scheme 1 "unless, on Scheme 2, 30 tons of weight could be put into protection over the boiler and engine rooms. He stated that he would prefer this protection to protection for the ship and fire control stations." Cochrane noted that the 30-ton difference between Schemes 1 and 2 would provide about ¼ inch more plating than now existed over the machinery spaces.

Meanwhile, Cochrane had evolved yet another scheme, a flush decker based on Scheme 2. At the time of the November hearing this was as yet little advanced, but "it appeared to offer considerable promise for improvement in range of stability and for the dryness of the main deck—two factors that are very important in destroyer design." It would, moreover, be best adapted to the new longitudinal system of framing, in that it would eliminate the break in the hull strength girder at the break of the forecastle. "The principal objection to this proposal seemed to be the objection raised by Admiral Leary that this would introduce another variant in the destroyer program." The flush decker became Scheme 7, at about 1,685 tons.

At this time, there was still room for considerable debate concerning the arrangement and number of torpedo tubes. For example, there were advocates of quadruple tubes, and Commander Mills "stated that he had had considerable experience in the fleet in connection with repairing damage to torpedo tubes. The quadruple tubes mounted on deck had frequently suffered damage due to the wash from the ship ahead when making high speed turns. Some of these tubes had also been damaged when destroyers were nested close together in port . . . opinion in the fleet was unanimous in favor of centerline tubes." Thus, advocates of 12 rather than 10 tubes had to ask for three quadruple mounts, all on that precious centerline space.

Admiral King asked for further study of Scheme 2 on the basis of three centerline torpedo tubes (each at least quadruple): depth-charge stowage moved to the vicinity of the throwers (which would be K-guns alongside the after deckhouse); lengthened depth-charge racks moved aft. Some weight and space compensation might be obtained by a reduction in 5-inch ammunition to that required for four guns. A discussion brought out the fact that BuOrd considered the new quintuple tube satisfactory, although it had to admit that the quadruple mount was the largest in service. Four antiaircraft machine guns would suffice, and there was a general preference for K- vice Y-guns.

On 24 November, the General Board asked for four more designs. One would mount the standard battery of five guns and eight or ten tubes, but with protection against .50-caliber machine-gun fire, i.e., 20 lbs. (half-inch) special treatment steel (STS) over engine and fire rooms. This was the true progenitor of the *Fletcher*. An alternative was to have a similar battery, but 20-lb. protection over fire and ship controls—a third, to have combined protection. Alternatively, Scheme 2 was to be modified to incorporate three quadruple tubes, increased machinery space length (one frame space, 21 inches, in each engine room), depth-charge stowage abreast the throwers, and STS protection for director, pilot house, and director tube.

Now displacement began to rise. In Scheme 2-A, three quadruple tubes and the less-cramped machinery spaces were provided, as well as six-charge racks and protection over the controls; the cost was a rise in standard displacement to 1,720 tons; beam increased 6 inches to maintain stability. Preliminary Design observed that this was a crowded design at best, with little or no margin over 36.5 knots. The addition of protection would require an entirely new design:

These weight additions would reduce the stability of Scheme 1 to a point where little margin would remain for development, or in the worst cases, to a point where stability would be initially unsatisfactory. Further increase in beam . . . would add weight, still further reduce speed, and does not assure the stability characteristics that are desirable for a destroyer. . . . in order to accommodate the weight increases with properly proportioned dimensions two new designs have been studied. Since complete redesign would be required in either case, it was decided to base both studies on the flush-deck type of hull, which offers important advantages. . . .

Both half-inch (20-lb.) and three-quarter-inch (30-lb.) STS protection was evaluated. Applied to a conventional destroyer hull (i.e., to Scheme 1), 20-lb. STS over fire and engine rooms would cost 17 tons; over controls, an additional 13. Alternatively, 30-lb. STS would cost, respectively, 48 and 17 tons, for a total of 65. Moreover, it should be noted that the effect on total displacement would be a multiple of the actual weight added for armor, since the ship herself would have to grow to allow for such heavy weights high up. More powerful machinery might well be needed if speed were to be maintained. Thus, the 20-lb. scheme, numbered 8, grew to about 1,825 tons with a length of 355 feet, to accommodate a total of 30 tons of protection. It was estimated that the corresponding 30-lb. design (Scheme 9) would come to 1,900 tons, with a length of 369 feet—i.e., would approximate the *Sampson*-class leaders. Preliminary Design commented that "if the (present) armament were placed on a *Sampson* hull in lieu of the present *Sampson* armament, the margin of stability would be insufficient to permit protecting the director and pilot house with STS, or increasing the protection over boiler and machinery spaces. . . ."

Schemes 8 and 9 were so much larger than earlier destroyers that it seemed worthwhile to try for the 38 knots that Captain Crenshaw had wanted. Thus, late in December, C&R proposed yet another design, Scheme 10, lengthened to 362 feet (2,000 tons) to suit a 60,000 shp power plant, with 20-lb. protection. It appeared that further lengthening to 369 feet would increase standard displacement to 2,025 tons, and speed to 38.5 knots. Apart from a moderate level of protection, the 2,000-tonner showed almost no obvious improvement over the *Benson* class; at the least it showed no increase in gun battery. There were, to be sure, some subtle improvements. For example, Scheme 2 showed only 480 rounds of 5-in. ammunition in standard condition, whereas Scheme 1, 8, 9, and 10 showed 600. Total stowage, however, remained constant at 2,100 rounds. Ultimately, a slightly modified Scheme 10-B was submitted to the General Board, at 2,017 tons, 365 feet long, with 20-lb. deck and sides over machinery, but 30-lb. protection over bridges.

By this time the General Board was sufficiently interested in protection to abandon any hope for a small fleet destroyer: if the ship had to be large, it might as well be protected against bomb fragments and strafers. On 6 January 1940, it asked for two more alternatives, one with 30-lb. STS over the sides of the machinery spaces (Scheme 10-C), and one with 30-lb. deck and sides (10-D); in addition, the bureau looked at Scheme 10-D lengthened four feet to recover the speed lost through increased displacement (to 2,068 tons, 365 feet, rising to 2,082 tons, 369 feet), which became Scheme 10-E.

Some of the concern with protection may have been due to British war experience. In a 3 March 1940 description of the *Fletcher* design, BuShips noted that

recent reports indicate that HMS *Mohawk* was seriously damaged by fragments of a heavy bomb which exploded as it struck the water about 50 yards from the vessel. The side above water was riddled and many of the main transverse bulkheads were penetrated, the main battery director and several of the guns were put out of action. Many essential leads were cut, and serious loss of life occurred.

For some reason, the *Marcus* and *Sloat* experiment (see chapter 5) was not cited.

These latter schemes were so large that increases in armament were possible. Thus, the characteristics adopted by the General Board on 9 January 1940 (and approved by the Secretary of the Navy on 27 January) included provision for a quadruple 1.1-inch machine cannon (director-controlled) as well as four .50-caliber machine guns (two before the bridge and abaft No. 2 gun, two on the main deck in the waist), four reload torpedoes, and 28 depth charges (with an additional mobilization allowance of 14). Protection was to follow that of Scheme 10-C, i.e., with a 30-lb. side and 20-lb. deck as well as 30-lb. top, front, and side of pilot house and a 5-inch director and tube. Of the 5-inch guns, the two forward mounts were to be enclosed in weather shields, the three after ones open. In a departure from the concepts advanced at the General Board hearings, the entire normal depth-charge supply would be carried topside: 12 in the stern racks (for 3 charges/pattern) and 4 at each thrower. Upon mobilization, the torpedo warheads would be fixed to the torpedoes, and their locker would become available for 14 additional charges. The four reload torpedoes were to be stowed alongside the after deckhouse.

By this time, C&R and Engineering had merged into the new Bureau of Ships. In its brief description of the preliminary design, BuShips noted that the new ship would actually show no improvement in internal space compared to the earlier classes, due to the loss of the forecastle. In fact, the wardroom country would have to be moved from the main deck to the first platform, with crew messes moved to the second platform, restricting deck area availability in the forward part of the ship. Even on so long a hull, it appeared that there was no natural location for a 1.1-inch director on the centerline; one would have to be provided on either side of the after funnel.*

This was the *Fletcher* class, Destroyer 1941. The *Fletcher* production program required the addition of new yards, some of them originally either financed or expanded by the Maritime Administration. Thus, Bethlehem San Pedro, formerly a repair facility, was upgraded to merchant and then to naval status. The Gulf Shipbuilding Company yard at Chickasaw, Alabama, was expanded by the Maritime Administration and then further by the Navy funds to build destroyers. The Consolidated Steel Corp. of Long Beach, California, built an entirely new destroyer yard at Orange, Texas, reminiscent of the World War I Squantum Plant. Seattle-Tacoma added new facilities for the same purpose, building some repeat *Bensons* before moving on to *Fletchers*. Detail design was carried out by Gibbs & Cox, and orders began even before the official beginning of FY 41: DD 445–448 at Federal, 449–451 at Bath, 465–466 at Federal, 467–469 at Bath, 470–471 at Bethlehem Staten Island (formerly United), 472–476 at Boston Navy Yard, 477–479 at Charleston Navy Yard, and 480–481 at Puget Sound, all in June/July 1940. They continued through the year: 498–502 at Federal; 507–517 at Bath; 518–522 at Bethlehem Staten Island; 523–524 at Bethlehem San Francisco; 525 at Bethlehem San Pedro; 526–541 at Bethlehem San Francisco; 544–547 at Bethlehem San Pedro; 550–553 at Gulf; 554–568 at Seattle-Tacoma (Seattle plant; it had built some *Bensons*); 569–580 at Consolidated Steel, Orange, Texas; 581–586 at Boston Navy Yard; 587–591 at Charleston Navy Yard; and 592–597 at Puget Sound Navy Yard; as well as the apparently unassigned 542–543 and 548–549. All were ordered on 9 September. Finally, seven ships (DD 523–525, 542–543, 548–549) were all

*In fact, a much smaller AA machine-gun on director was adopted, and it was mounted on the centerline just forward of the 1.1-inch or 40-mm. mount.

canceled on 16 December, and at the same time six more *Fletchers* were ordered from Bath (DD 629–631, 642–644). Work at Puget Sound was delayed by the DE program and by ship repair work, so that two ships were not completed until February 1945, but the great bulk of the class was in commission by late 1943. Thus, out of over 200 ships ordered in a remarkable burst of activity in the second half of 1940 (DD 445–648), fully 119 were *Fletchers*. Two more, DD 452 and 482, were specialized engineering prototypes intended to employ *Fletcher* hulls. The others were repeat 1,620/1,630-tonners, as well as four experimental light destroyers, DD 503–506 (see chapter 7).

With the outbreak of war, the Navy formulated a "maximum effort" program based on shipbuilding capacity. BuShips was already at work on a follow-on destroyer design that would become the *Sumner*, but with the *Fletcher* in production 56 "repeat *Fletchers*" were ordered, for a class total of 175: DD 649 at Charleston, 650–653 at Bath, 654–656 at Gulf, 657–658 at Bethlehem Staten Island, 659–661 at Federal, 662–664 at Boston, 665 at Charleston, 666–680 at Federal, 681–682 at Bethlehem San Pedro, 683–684 at Bethlehem San Francisco, 685–687 at Bethlehem Staten Island, 688–691 at Bath, 792–795 at Bethlehem San Pedro, 796–798 at Bethlehem San Francisco, and 799–804 at Todd Seattle (formerly Seattle-Tacoma Seattle Yard).

Such large ships were amenable to considerable improvement in wartime. As in other ships originally designed to mount the quadruple 1.1, the *Fletcher* was assigned a twin Bofors in its place; the four .50s were to be replaced by single 20-mm. cannon. The three after 5-in./38s were ordered enclosed following the *Buck* trials (early 1941). Only the first few units were completed with the 1.1-inch weapon, as twin Bofors became available about when the *Fletchers* were almost completed.

The CNO began to formulate a new antiaircraft battery for the *Fletchers* late in December 1941. By this time, two more depth-charge throwers had been added, for a total of six. In line with studies for a new destroyer, the CNO proposed a new battery: two

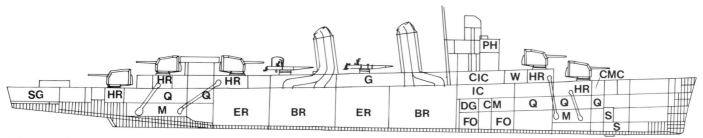

DD 513 inboard

twin 40-mm. guns, and two rather than four 20-mm. The after quintuple torpedo tube was to be surrendered as weight compensation. By late January, it appeared that both banks of tubes might be retained if only one twin 40-mm. were mounted, and that in addition six rather than four 20-mm. might be mounted. The CNO preferred this scheme as "it is considered that, for a fleet destroyer, the retention of two quintuple torpedo tubes is more desirable than the installation of one additional 40-mm. machine gun, particularly if such an installation causes the loss of two 20-mm. machine guns." Moreover, it appeared that on later ships of the class changes to the superstructure and particularly the lowering of the director about six feet and the reduction of its protection to 10 lb. (¼ inch) would make possible the addition of a second twin Bofors, with four rather than six 20 mm.

These proposals were taken up by the General Board in April. Weight compensation would include reductions in the height of the after deckhouse, generally by one deck. In the case of the *Fletcher*s, the General Board chose the elimination of protection over the ship and fire controls, while retaining the full 5-inch and torpedo batteries:

These changes are premised on the use of this destroyer as a fleet and task force destroyer normally in company with heavier combatant units rather than upon use for general utility or for submarine hunting. The modifications proposed are expedients; no thoroughly acceptable solution is possible on this tonnage. The result desired is a responsive ship, up to speed, within draft, well trimmed, with excellent and unimpaired damage control, and within stability and weight standards without ballast if possible.

Thus, within two years the immense and oversized destroyer of 1940 had become marginal at best; the General Board was looking to a much larger ship, which would not actually emerge until well after the war.

The board's proposals, formulated in April and approved in June by the Secretary of the Navy, called for the elimination of the reload torpedoes and all depth charges in excess of those sufficient for five patterns; if need be, two projectors would be removed. One level of the after deckhouse and six feet of the 5-in./38 director tube would also be removed, as well as the 2½-meter range finder, one of the heavy 1.1-inch directors, and as much 30-lb. plate as possible from pilot house and director, which would instead be protected by 10-lb. plate; ultimately, 20-lb. was applied to the 5-in. director. The fantail was to be used for guns with one twin 40-mm. there and another replacing the 1.1 between No. 3 and 4 5-in./38. The warhead locker was turned over to automatic weapon ammunition, and thus depth-charge stowage had to be limited to deck carriage, i.e., to five 300-lb. per thrower and two eight-charge tracks for 600-lb. charges aft, with a pair of five-charge stowage racks between them. This solution more than provided for the required five patterns.

In practice, the General Board's changes produced two very similar *Fletcher* classes. Ships already nearly

The *Thatcher* illustrates the maximum 20-mm. battery of a high-director *Fletcher* early in World War II: four guns around the bridge, with another four in the waist, and two twin Bofors, one in the stern (later replaced by three 20-mm.). She had the improved air-search antenna of SC-2, but as yet without its characteristic IFF "billboard" above the main antenna; note the "stovepipe" IFF antenna on her starboard yardarm. The 40-mm. director aft is the early Mk 49.

complete retained the high bridge and high director of prewar design practice, although ultimately their batteries nearly matched the later ships. Ships not yet well under way received low squared-off bridges with substantial open areas for better visibility in antiaircraft action. The open bridge appeared in late production ships, at least in DD 518–522, 526–541, 544–547, 554–568, 581–591, 594–597, 629–644, and in all of the "maximum effort" ships ordered under the FY 42 program (DD 649–691 and 792–804).

The assigned antiaircraft battery grew very rapidly. Closed-bridge ships generally received an additional 20-mm. gun atop the pilot house as well as one on a platform before it, together with the two mounted atop forward either side of the deckhouse, and four (rather than the original two) in the waist, for a total of eight guns. Early in 1943, the fantail Bofors mounting was eliminated in favor of three 20-mm. guns; two more Bofors (for a total of three twins) would be mounted abeam the second funnel. Open-bridge ships would have a total of ten 20-mm. (none atop the open bridge); closed-bridge units, eleven. Restoration of the fantail twin Bofors was briefly considered, but in June 1943 an ultimate battery of five twin Bofors and seven Oerlikons was announced, the fourth and fifth guns replacing the three or four Oerlikons forward of the bridge. At the same time a CIC was fitted. Many Fletchers were completed to this five-mount standard, which remained through early 1945. It was a remarkable achievement: five twin Bofors alone weighed 29 tons without their ammunition, and seven Oerlikons added another 5.5, not counting splinter shields. By way of contrast, the original quadruple 1.1 weighed about 4.7 tons; the effects of change in AA battery considerably exceed the 18 or 19 tons of a single enclosed 5-in. gun.

The great late-war armament change was the replacement of the forward topedo tubes and the two twin Bofors in the waist by two quadruple Bofors with Mk 63 blind-fire directors; the seven single Oerlikons would be replaced by six twin mounts. This was part of the anti-Kamikaze program promulgated in April 1945 (see chapter 10), and was not applied so extensively to the Fletchers as to their six-gun cousins; only 53 had been modified by November 1945 (ships denoted thus * were under refit at the end of the war): DD 445–448, 473, 478, 481*, 499, 502, 520, 521, 528, 530, 531,534–539, 541, 550, 554, 556, 563, 577, 578, 580, 583, 586*, 589, 590, 592, 643, 657, 661, 665, 668–676, 681, 682, 685, 686, 800, 802, and 804.

The Fletchers were undoubtedly very successful, but they did not quite meet their designers' requirements. They were wet forward, though not so much so as their successors. They were also hampered by the very considerable extra weight added in wartime. Not merely was there extra armament, but full magazine capacity, rather than the very limited standard supply, came to be the standard for trial performance. Thus, the original trial displacement of 2,550 tons soon rose to 2,700; in many units extra weight was added because the original aluminum-alloy deckhouses were replaced by steel in view of the shortage of aluminum. It was estimated in 1942 that an all-steel ship, DD 666 (the Black) would gain about 54 tons, due to increases in miscellaneous fittings and furniture as much as in the deckhouse structures proper. On trial, the Nicholas made 37.1 knots at 2,589 tons, but the Stembel made only 35.1 at a more realistic 2,800 tons; 36.1 had been expected at 2,700. Thus, the original estimate of 38 made for a realistic 35, the speed actually required of earlier classes. This reduction fueled sentiment in favor of a much larger destroyer, which would restore the appropriate speed margin and which ultimately became the Mitscher class.

There were also steering problems. In common with previous destroyers, the Fletchers had only a single rudder. Due to their great length, they had a very large turning radius, so much so that only the introduction of twin rudders in the subsequent Sumner class appeared to offer a solution. Thus, in wartime, Fletchers were notorious for turning outside Iowa-class battleships. After the war, an enlarged single rudder was developed to cure this problem, and all Fletchers reactivated for Korea were fitted with it.

The surviving Fletchers were laid up in 1946–47; by 1950 only five, which had been assigned to Naval Reserve training since the summer of 1946, remained active. Twelve others were in the process of conversion to DDE, with seven more scheduled for conversion. The remaining ships were a mobilization reserve, the only really effective destroyers available. Seventy-six were activated for Korean War duty (1950–52) and the reserve units brought to full commission. Nineteen of these 81 active units were returned to reserve following the cease-fire.

Forty of the reactivated units were modernized under the FY 52 program (SCB 74A): DD 519, 520, 527, 528, 530, 532, 535, 537, 544, 547, 556, 561, 564, 566, 629, 630, 642, 644, 650–652, 655, 659, 666, 669, 670, 674, 677, 678, 679, 681, 685, 687, 689, 793–796, 799, and 804. Two more scheduled for conversion (DD 538 and 541) were not done, nor were 40 more proposed (but not funded) for FY 53. The prototype, USS Picking (DD 685), was taken in hand at Boston Navy Yard, 4 June 1951. Conversion entailed replacement of the two quadruple Bofors abeam the second funnel and the twin Bofors between No. 3 and 4 guns with twin 3-in./50, a 3-inch director displacing No. 3 gunhouse. Fixed Hedgehogs replaced the two

The *Ringgold* illustrates the fantail Bofors position particularly clearly, with a director nestled between the depth-charge tracks, and another just forward of her other twin Bofors. Relatively few ships were completed with the very high after deckhouse originally contemplated, and illustrated by *La Vallette*.

The *Hutchins* illustrates the arrangement of all *Fletcher*s late in World War II, with twin 40-mm. guns replacing the 20-mm. before the bridge; their Mk 51 directors occupied the small tubs atop the pilothouse. Two more twin Bofors were paired in the waist, and the small mainmast carried ECM gear. Her Mk 37 director carries the late-war suit of Mk 12 and the Mk 22 "orange-peel," and her yardarm carries a "ski-pole" IFF antenna (to starboard, replacing the earlier "stove pipe"). This photograph was probably taken late in 1944, as the ECM masts were not installed until 1944, and most carried different antennas by the end of the war.

"GQ Johnny" *Johnston* was perhaps the most famous *Fletcher*; she lasted less than a year in service, sinking in the heroic action off Samar. This completion view (taken in Seattle harbor, 27 October 1943) shows a typical low-bridge unit, with five twin 40-mm. guns.

*Fletcher*s brought back into service for the Korean War were refitted in accordance with the anti-Kamikaze program of 1945. This is the *Cogswell*, 4 February 1952, with the characteristic pair of quadruple Bofors guns in her waist. The small radar dishes atop them show control by Mk 63 directors, the directors standing atop the small deckhouse between the two gun tubs. However, the two twin 40-mm. normally carried forward of the bridge were replaced by fixed Hedgehogs, ready-service ammunition boxes for which can be seen to each side of the unit visible on the 01 level forward. There were also some postwar electronic improvements: the earlier Mk 12/22 radar was replaced by the dish of Mk 25, atop her Mk 37 director, and her wartime SG was replaced by a postwar SU for surface search. She retained her earlier SC-2 air-search radar, but its characteristic IFF array was removed because the United States changed IFF systems in the early fifties. Note the retention of 20-mm. guns in the waist and right aft. Ships refitted at this time were also given enlarged rudders for much improved maneuverability.

Under refit at Mare Island in July 1943, the *Schroeder* displays most of her antiaircraft battery, including both waist and after twin Bofors and the fantail triplet of Oerlikons. Note the life-raft stowage between the depth-charge tracks, and the roller-racks for the three port K-guns abreast the after superstructure. She is being fitted with a new Mk 51 director for her 40-mm. guns; the destroyer beside her appears still to have the earlier Mk 49. A Mk 51 controlling one of the waist Bofors is visible on its sponson on the after funnel, and the after superstructure carries the floater nets fitted at this time. Their racks are being fitted to the destroyer in the background, and two floater nets are visible on her 01 level aft. The *Schroeder*'s T-shaped torpedo crane can be seen just forward of her Number 3 5-inch gun mount; the circular structure atop her torpedo tube protected its trainer from the blast of that gun. Note, too, the ready-service racks for assembled clips of 40-mm. ammunition arranged around the inside of the waist 40-mm. splinter shield.

01-level twin Bofors before the bridge. Short-range ASW torpedoes (Mk 32), launched by dropping gear, were also specified.

This new armament required an improved sensor suit: new radars, which in turn required a new tripod foremast for support; ECM equipment; a new CIC in what had been the unit commander's cabin; and a new sonar (QHB) with an associated ASW fire control system.

Thirteen more *Fletcher*s were converted for foreign navies to which they were transferred: six to West Germany, four to Greece, two (in Japan) to Japan, and one (ex-DD 509) to Spain.

Five-gun units reactivated for Korean War service received a less ambitious conversion in which Hedgehog (MK 10 or Mk 11) replaced the twin Bofors before the bridge; scanning sonar and the enlarged rudder were fitted as well. Those ships that had not already received two quadruple Bofors in place of No. 1 bank of TT received them; and, in many cases, new radars (and a tripod foremast) were fitted. They remained active until quite late: in 1958, of 61 active ships, 23 had the original battery. By 1965, only 16 were left in the active service, of which 2 (DD 682 and 684) had five guns.

By the late sixties, the few remaining units had had their 3-inch guns and torpedo tubes removed, two triple tubes for MK 43/44 lightweight ASW torpedoes being fitted. In a few five-gun units the latter replaced the Bofors normally mounted abeam the second funnel. In at least some cases, the other Bofors were removed as well.

All the active units had gone out of commission by 1971, leaving only two ships used for reserve

Thirty-nine *Fletcher*s were modernized under the FY 52 program; the *Mullany* is shown a decade later, on 19 February 1963, off the coast of Oahu. Her bridge has been partially enclosed and her 21-inch torpedo tubes replaced by the usual pair of lightweight Mk 32s; her depth-charge throwers are gone, and she is down to a single track aft. However, she retains all of her 3-inch guns, two twin mounts in the waist controlled by Mk 63 directors (located atop a deckhouse just abaft the fore funnel) and one aft, with a Mk 56 director, which could also control 5-inch fire. Her tripod mast carries the standard postwar destroyer air-search radar, SPS-6B, as well as the much smaller antenna of SPS-10, with UHF tactical radio antennas above. The two randomes on the second funnel are radar direction-finders. The small breakwater on her fantail protects the winch of a towed torpedo countermeasure, Fanfare.

Six *Fletcher*s were scheduled for completion with four guns and a catapult, although only three were so fitted. The *Halford* illustrates this configuration off Point Jefferson, Washington, on 24 April 1943. Her only 40-mm. gun was the twin mount right aft, between her depth-charge tracks, and her 20-mm. battery was also quite limited, to four mounts in the waist and four forward (one atop her pilothouse). After the failure of the experiment, when these ships were converted back into standard configuration, at first they lacked the raised deckhouse between the two 5-inch guns on the 01 level aft. In this photograph the *Halford* has not yet received any depth charges, and her tracks and roller racks are empty.

training. The last of these, the USS *Shields* (DD 596), a five-gun *Fletcher*, had been in continuous commission either as a Reserve Training ship or as a regular fleet unit, from 1945•through her striking in 1972, after which she was transferred to Brazil, where she remains active in 1980.

A variation on the basic type was the aircraft-carrying destroyer. The failure of the 3,500-ton "flotilla leader" (see chapter 5) led to a series of alternate proposals for bringing aircraft into the scouting forces, including a catapult on a *Fletcher*-class destroyer. On 18 April 1940, C&R passed two sketch studies to the General Board: a catapult could be mounted on the fantail in place of No. 5 5-inch gun, or else abaft the after stack in place of No. 3 gun. In the latter case the quadruple 1.1-inch machine cannon would also have to be removed; in both cases tanks for 2,000 gallons of gasoline and 150 gallons of lubricating oil were to be added. The second scheme was accepted. On 20 May, a small airplane was successfully flown from the old flush decker *Noa* (DD 343) and a week later the Secretary of the Navy approved six *Fletcher*-class conversions (DD 476–481), with the proviso that the guns deleted in favor of the catapult be retained in reserve. This proved wise. Only three of the six were actually fitted with the catapult, and operations proved disappointing; the equipment was landed in October 1943, and the remaining conversions canceled.

Two *Fletcher* hulls, DD 452 (*Percival*) and DD 482 (*Watson*) were ordered as test-beds for experimental machinery, the former for very high pressure boilers and the latter for an all-diesel plant. On 15 June 1940, the Secretary of the Navy approved a C&R/Bureau of Engineering suggestion that one of the new destroyers be used as a prototype diesel warship, a new lightweight diesel having been produced. It was expected that a diesel electric plant would be fitted, which would facilitate subdivision. Other supposed advantages included clearer decks and the elimination of much piping. Surprisingly, they did *not* include improved endurance. Very little work seems to have been done on this project, and the ship was never built.

Very high pressure steam was close to the mainstream of Navy machinery evolution. Although DD 452 was not laid down, work on her machinery continued through the war. By the end of the war, the machinery was nearly ready but *Fletcher* hulls were no longer being built. Fortunately, the *Sumner*s and *Gearing*s had virtually the same plant and hence the same machinery spaces; a new *Gearing* hull, DD 828 (*Timmerman*) was selected to receive the machinery intended for DD 452.

She was fitted with two advanced propulsion systems, one of 875 psi/1,050 degrees F., and one of 2,000 psi/1,050 degrees F., which were to be used to evaluate alternative steam conditions. Other advanced features included 400-cycle generators and lightweight pumps; on less weight than a *Gearing*'s 60,000-shp plant the *Timmerman* could, in theory, produce 100,000. A variety of measures were taken to reduce her top weight, and she was given increased freeboard, to keep her dry at extreme speeds. Otherwise she was a conventional destroyer, albeit without torpedo tubes or ASW ordnance. For some years *Jane's* listed her as *rated* at 40 knots, although a list of trials for her to run suggests that 43 was anticipated. For some years, too, she functioned more as a floating laboratory than as a warship, with several times her normal complement assigned to her. At least as late as March 1954, the *Timmerman* had not gone over half power due to deficiencies in her electrical equipment. Full power trials were expected in the summer of 1954, but no results have ever come to light, and it is not clear that such trials were ever run.

It appears in retrospect that the *Timmerman*'s greatest value lay in demonstrating to engine builders that her steam conditions were not impossible ones, so that the transition from 600 psi/850 degrees to 1,200 psi/950 degrees was smooth. The ship herself was reclassed as an auxiliary (AG 152) in 1954 and by 1957 had been reduced to reserve, largely gutted. She was soon broken up.

Almost from the completion of the *Fletcher* design there was agitation for a radically new destroyer, which became, by the usual indirect path, the *Sumner*. At first the issue was the high silhouette of the existing type, which it appeared could be reduced only by means of a twin mount. In June 1940, the Board of Inspection and Survey reported on the trials of the new *Gleaves* (DD 423) and

> was particularly impressed with the high deck structure and top weights forward on this class. . . . The Board questions the stability of this vessel under adverse sea and loading conditions. . . . For new construction being authorized or designed, the Board is strongly of the opinion that top weights forward should be reduced as much as practicable. It is believed that this could best be brought about by substituting a twin 5-inch mount on the forecastle in lieu of the two forward single 5-inch mounts, and reduction of the height of the structure by one deck height and of the main director of about 13 feet. . . .

The General Board, having just fought out precisely these issues, was still willing to reconsider, and asked for studies of the new 2,100-ton destroyer with (i) replacement of the two forward mounts by one twin, (ii) reduction of the forward superstructure by one deck height, and (iii) installation of one quadruple 1.1 inch forward to overcome the blind arc there. BuOrd cautioned that the twin mount in production could not be hand-trained, and moreover that all mounts already on order were assigned to large ships on order. "It is the opinion of this Bureau that . . . a twin mount should never be placed on an unprotected ship."

In July, BuShips added its opposition to the proposal. The desired visibility from the pilot house could not be maintained; indeed, the height of the twin 5-inch gun would limit any decrease in the height of the pilot house to 19 inches. Moreover, eliminating one gun mount would not necessarily eliminate the need for a deck level, as the superstructure deck level of the bridge contained activities (radio and coding rooms, .50-caliber belting and crew shelter, and ventilation machinery) that would be difficult to relocate. These objections contrast with BuShips' support for the twin-mount schemes advocated about eight months earlier. The bureau was willing to accept a twin mount forward with a quadruple 1.1-inch gun replacing the former No. 2 mount, and elimination of the former four .50-caliber machine guns, at a cost of about 25 tons, as long as the twin mount had only a weather shield.

There the matter lay until the following September (1941), when the General Board, looking to improved antiaircraft firepower, asked for studies of the 2,100-ton destroyer. The series of sketch designs was entitled "B," Series A having been assigned to improved versions of the 1,620-ton destroyer (see chapter 5). In submitting six alternative schemes, BuShips noted that:

When the characteristics of the DD 445 class were established in January 1940 the importance of air attack was recognized and some features were incorporated in the design to provide both active and passive defense. . . . Since that date, however, the seriousness of air attacks has been emphasized increasingly by experiences of ships in the present war. Some degree of protection against splinters and bomb-case fragments is now generally considered essential for exposed personnel on the topside including those at gun stations. Active defense with heavy machine guns against dive bombing attack to the maximum degree practicable is a necessity—with the so-called "four-cornered" arrangement of heavy machine guns being considered very desirable. It is now generally accepted that some sacrifices in other characteristics are warranted even in destroyers to attain these features, whereas this was not the case in January 1940.

Torpedo attack has been considered to be the primary function of destroyers, with speed and a 5-inch gun battery provided to permit driving through destroyer opposition to push the attack home. The essence of torpedo-boat design since its inception has been to sacrifice durability and any form of protection for speed. . . .

The large destroyers of the 2,100-ton type unquestionably fall in the class which should have armaments suitable to assist in "gaining control of the seas." Technical developments indicate that even in this respect however the role of the destroyer in itself executing an attack against heavy ships is becoming increasingly difficult. Enemy air scouting, increased speed of major units, and radar are the present factors. Others may appear. British Fourth Destroyer Flotilla had extreme difficulty in executing attacks against the Bismarck in low visibility during the night of 26 May, firing at ranges of 3,000 to 9,000 yards. This was due apparently to radar although Bismarck was unscreened and steaming at a maximum speed of not over 10 knots. Bismarck apparently was actually stopped for at least part of the night.

It appears desirable to reassess the weight which should be given to the various elements of total displacement of destroyers and particularly in the distribution of the total weight of the armament, as between torpedoes, 5-inch guns, depth charges, and close-in AA defense. . . . The arrangement of the battery to disperse the risks of damage and minimize the ill effects of any single hit and gain maximum sectors of effective fire for each gun or tube must also be considered. . . .

Thus, BuShips proposed to reopen the question of the twin mount, which would permit better dispersal of the battery and therefore less vulnerability to single hits. Of six schemes proposed, only two (B and B-I) incorporated single mounts. Scheme B was a Fletcher, with a twin 40 mm. replacing the 1.1-inch mount of the original design and another offset to port abeam the second funnel. In B-I, one of the two quintuple torpedo tubes was omitted in an attempt to relieve congestion. In B-II the five single mounts were replaced by three twins, and the two twin 40 mm. aft (with one bank of torpedo tubes) retained; the effect was a markedly less congested arrangement. The Office of the Chief of Naval Operations suggested that two twin 5-inch mounts might well suffice, and that it would be advantageous to disperse the torpedo battery in two triple rather than one quintuple mount. In Scheme B-III, the twin mounts were at the ends; in B-IV they were superimposed forward. In each case the weight of one twin mount was replaced by a single 5-inch, to provide stern fire, and the four twin 40 mm. concentrated aft; the torpedo battery was to consist of two triple tubes. In the last three schemes the great advantage of four twin 40 mm. was the "four-cornered fire" advocated by BuShips and by the Office of the Chief of Naval Operations. BuShips saw B-V as a demonstration of how excessive armament could congest a design, although it was far from the level of congestion routinely reached in practice a few years later.

The Bureau recommended B-II, the six-gun design:

The advantage of having a strong 5-inch battery located forward appears to be of great importance for destroyers which, of necessity, depend upon high speed and volume of their own fire for security during an attack. Also, in studying destroyer batteries it is not looking too far into the future to consider the improvement of antiaircraft fire which the introduction of radar promises. If air targets can be brought under effective fire by 5-inch guns early, the provision of four such guns on the forecastle becomes increasingly attractive. . . .

The General Board was somewhat hesitant, and asked for two more schemes: a modified B-II in which No. 2 5-inch gun was removed farther from the director, and one in which one twin 5-inch/38 was mounted forward, three singles aft, as well as two twin 40 mm. and four single 20 mm. and two quintuple tubes (B-VI, 2,175 tons vs. 2,200 for B-II). B-VI was in fact reminiscent of one of the early *Fletcher* sketch designs, and presumably responded to the requirement for a low silhouette. The bureau noted that "it is understood that the principal reason for proposing the battery arrangement of Scheme B-VI . . . is to improve the separation between the 5-inch director and the nearest 5-inch gun . . ." to reduce blast. In fact the bureau suspected that even in the original B-II there would be little difficulty, as compared, for example, to the *Porter*s. Thus, BuShips again preferred Scheme B-II, which indeed was the progenitor of the *Sumner* class.

The General Board was less easily convinced, and on 3 December again proposed a modified *Fletcher* with two twin 40-mm. guns; this design, indeed, corresponded to the battery that would soon be proposed for existing ships. The only important change requested was, again, increased separation between the director and the superfiring 5-inch gun.

For its part, the Bureau of Ordnance strongly favored Scheme B-II "unless two twin mounts on the forecastle should render (it) excessively wet forward. . . ." However, the sacrifice of one quintuple torpedo tube seemed excessive, so that B-VI with ten tubes might be favored. "Unless particularly heavily opposed by other light craft, B-VI with ten torpedoes would be better in torpedo attack, while B-II would be better in screening and when gunpower is at a premium. . . ." Twenty experienced officers were polled; all agreed that, at least until very recently in the Mediterranean, destroyer torpedoes had been far less important than expected. Moreover, "there was a majority opinion that, as carriers of torpedoes, destroyers now were secondary to submarines and torpedo planes. . . . About a quarter of the officers . . . did not think double-purpose guns more important than torpedoes. Another quarter were undecided. But about half thought that the importance of screening now had made double-purpose armaments on destroyers more important than their torpedo armaments."

By early 1942 Admiral King, who had participated in the General Board hearings on the *Fletcher* design, was both CNO and Commander-in-Chief U.S. Fleet. BuShips made models of Schemes B-I and B-II, and held several informal conferences with his representatives, at which it developed that the powerful forward firepower of Scheme B-II was "by all means the most desirable main battery for a destroyer of this size, aside from the question of hand operation. . . ." In particular, properly arranged, B-II could fire not four but six mounts forward, No. 3 mount firing over the mast and bridge. However, there were only five tubes, and in its 3 December letter the General Board had noted its preference for ten. Thus, the bureau produced yet another sketch design, B-VII, in which the gun battery of B-II was combined with a second bank of tubes and two more 20-mm. guns, for a total of two twin 40 mm. and four single 20 mm. The net cost was expected to be about 180 tons and 1 knot, as compared to that of a *Fletcher*. The result did show far more congestion than the bureau wanted, but length was not increased in hopes of avoiding any decrease in maneuverability. Indeed, the bureau preferred B-II, but suspected that only B-VII would prove acceptable. One new feature was a covered passageway aft at main-deck level, with sheltered access to the machinery spaces, an important feature in what would turn out to be a relatively wet ship.

Ultimately, B-VII was approved as the basis for the next mass-production destroyer, the *Sumner* (DD 692) class. However, the choice was uncertain almost to the end. For example, at the General Board hearing on this type (April 1942), a proposal was made to replace the after gun with a torpedo tube, retaining one other between the stacks, to produce something like the British "1942 Destroyer" (*Battle* class). This received some support on the theory that (i) astern fire was not too important, and (ii) torpedoes could always be fired to discourage pursuers. No studies were made, however, and characteristics reflecting the B-VII design were approved by the Secretary of the Navy in May, to be built in numbers as the *Sumner* class.

Important design features included slower-turning propellers (to reduce cavitation) and twin rudders, which substantially reduced turning radius. There was also a considerable increase in the electric power plant, due in part to the requirements of the heavy twin 5-in./38 mount. Thus, where a *Fletcher* had two 250-kw ship-service turbogenerators supplemented by one 100-kw diesel emergency unit, a *Sumner* had a pair of 400-kw ship-service units, and two rather than one 100-kw emergency generators, the second having been added in September 1942. Located aft, it was available for steering and for the after battery. This survivability feature was paralleled by the installation of a second evaporator in the second engine room, making the two power units truly independent.

Berthing spaces for both officers and men were designed to accommodate half the personnel forward, half aft. This, too, was a survivability feature; the Design History commented that "the loss of every experienced officer aboard *USS Turner* (DD 648) with the first explosion forward in that ship underlines the wisdom of this separation." There was, to be sure, the crowding experienced by all wartime destroyers, indeed by the entire fleet; for example, junior officers beyond those required were ordered aboard "for indoctrination and training" but became permanent additions to ships' companies. An enclosed main-deck passageway extending the length of the topside structures was an important safety feature in heavy seas, which would wash down the ships' decks due to the low freeboard. The fire fighting system included special risers and manifolds fore and aft to supply eight hoses to another vessel.

The *Sumner*s must have been the first new class of destroyers to incorporate a Combat Information Center when completed. The provision of a CIC in destroyers was the subject of a preliminary conference in the COMINCH office in April 1943, but no decisions were taken; in June, BuShips proposed a CIC comparable to that developed at about the same time for the *Fletcher*s by the Forces Afloat and by Pearl Harbor Navy Yard. This was considered adequate, and had the considerable advantage of not requiring much rearranging of ships already well along in construction, since BuShips faced a critical shortage of draftsmen. However, when the bridges of the *Sumner*s were totally rearranged it proved possible to provide a new, larger CIC that could better accommodate the mass of electronic equipment already envisaged. It was located on the 01 level in the bridge structure, i.e., just below the pilot house and the open bridge.

In 1942, the General Board considered the *Fletcher* already overloaded and slow; B-VII was no more than an interim choice, and indeed would even be about 1.5 knots slower than a *Fletcher*. Thus, it considered the B-VII no more than an "interim" destroyer that would remain in production briefly until the "ultimate" 2,500-ton type was ready, perhaps 9 or 12 months later. The latter would restore the speed margin lost with the *Fletcher*s and their even slower successor; in fact it was not ready until 1948. Nor did it displace only 300 tons more than a *Sumner*. At the April hearing, BuShips argued that it would be 12 to 14 months before any entirely new destroyer design could be laid down, whereas completions of *Fletcher*s would free building ways for new keels by January or February 1943. Thus, B-VII was attractive because its hull dimensions very nearly duplicated those of a *Fletcher* (i.e., it required no enlargement of building facilities) and its machinery was already

in mass production. The General Board and OpNav reluctantly agreed, and the "interim" mass-production destroyer appeared in great numbers, both in its original form and in a later (stretched) version that became the *Gearing*. Out of a series of 117 destroyers (DD 692–808) ordered 7 August 1942, 69 were completed to the *Sumner* design, 13 were completed as *Fletcher*s, and 35 were reordered as *Gearing*s. In addition, DD 857, one of a series ordered 14 June 1943, was completed to the original design. These series broke according to the ease with which yards could switch production; destroyers were a mass-production item by 1942–43.

By this time, too, the number of yards building destroyers had been drastically reduced and the series assigned each yard considerably increased. Thus, DD 692–721 were assigned to Federal; 722–743 to Bath; 744–756 to Bethlehem Staten Island; 757–769 to Bethlehem San Francisco; 770–776 to Bethlehem San Pedro; 777–791 to Todd Seattle; 792–795 to Bethlehem San Pedro (*Fletcher*s); 796–798 to Bethlehem Staten Island (*Fletcher*s); 799–804 Todd Seattle (*Fletcher*s); 805–812 to Bath; 813–814 to Bethlehem Staten Island; 815–825 to Consolidated at Orange; 826–849 to Bath; 850–853 to Bethlehem Quincy; 854–856 to Bethlehem Staten Island; 857–861 to Bethlehem San Pedro; 862–872 to Bethlehem Staten Island; 873–890 to Consolidated, Orange; 891–893 to Federal; 894–895 to Consolidated; 896–904 to Bath; 905–908 to Boston Navy Yard; 909–916 to Bethlehem Staten Island; 917–924 to Consolidated, Orange; and 925–926 to Charleston Navy Yard. Ships beyond DD 890 were part of a large program proposed in 1945 but disapproved by the President that March; their yards indicate the direction the program was to have taken and suggest the extent to which the original mass-production yards were overtaken by congestion. The four built at Quincy were originally to have been built on the West Coast but had to be moved east, again due to the congestion of the primary destroyer-building yards. Each of the main yards switched to *Gearing*s during these series: Federal with DD 710, the prototype; Bath with the *Frank Knox*, DD 742; Bethlehem San Francisco with the *William C. Lawe*, DD 763; Todd Seattle with DD 782, the *Rowan*; Consolidated with the *Corry*, DD 817; Bethlehem Quincy with the *J.P. Kennedy, Jr.*, DD 850; Bethlehem San Pedro with DD 858, the *Fred T. Berry* (*Bristol*, DD 857, being the last *Sumner*); and Bethlehem Staten Island with DD 862, the *Vogelgesang*.

Probably the most remarkable feature of these ships was the achievement, on almost the same displacement and dimensions, of a 20 percent increase in main battery *and* a considerable advance in light battery over the original *Fletcher*. It would later be

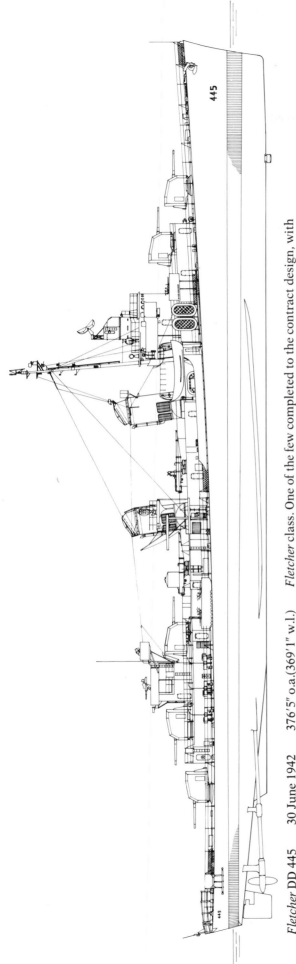

Fletcher DD 445   30 June 1942   376′5″ o.a.(369′1″ w.l.)   *Fletcher* class. One of the few completed to the contract design, with but one quadruple 1.1″ AA mount. Several others had this initial appearance, then some got two twin 40-mm.AA, with one mount on the fantail.

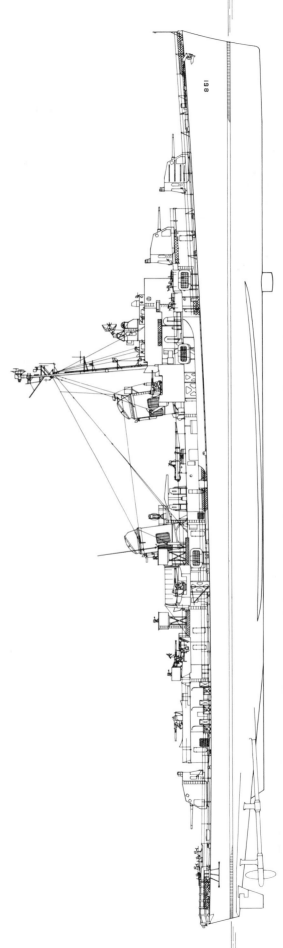

Harwood DD 861   Oct. 1945   390′6″ o.a.   *Gearing* class (later had Mk 15 Hedgehog in "B" position)

claimed that in no previous destroyer had the light armament received such intense attention; and indeed the light battery finally installed was the heaviest to date. The battery originally specified was a pair of twin Bofors offset to port (forward) and starboard (aft) abaft the second funnel; opposite each was an Oerlikon gun tub. This left plenty of deck space on the long deckhouse for the two banks of torpedo tubes; and it was a very impressive battery—for 1942.

In the course of detail design the Bofors guns were interchanged with the Oerlikons opposite for improved ammunition supply, and in April 1943 an additional pair of twin Bofors was ordered mounted on box-like structures abaft the bridge. These latter would be a most characteristic feature of the class. At the same time it proved possible to add another Oerlikon.

This was still insufficient. ComDesPac wanted *six* twin Bofors at the expense, if need be, of all the Oerlikons; CincPac agreed. The VCNO's response was to replace the two twin Bofors abaft the second stack with *quadruple* Bofors guns, so that in the end *Sumner*s were completed with very nearly the AA battery applied to the *Fletcher*s in 1945 as a desperation measure, *and* with a full torpedo battery. There were eleven 20 nm. as well.

Even more was asked. For example, in January 1944, Boston Navy Yard suggested that two more twin Bofors replace the 01-level Oerlikons forward of the bridge, as in the late *Fletcher*s. The proposal was rejected in view of blast interference and masking of No. 2 gunhouse—which suggests the limited value of these guns in the *Fletcher*s. Instead, the "temporary" alteration adopted as an AAW measure in the summer of 1945 was replacement of No. 2 bank of torpedo tubes by a third quadruple Bofors, for a total of *sixteen* 40 mm. There remained enough weight margin to permit the 20-mm. battery to be very nearly doubled (to ten *twin* mounts).

A controversial feature of the design was the bridge structure, which incorporated a British-style closed pilot house separated physically from the open bridge by a sonar room. The original bridge wings, each of which had incorporated a single 20 mm., were cut back to clear arcs of fire for the two twin Bofors between bridge and fore funnels. The result was considered so unsatisfactory by the destroyer officers that the first few ships had to be rebuilt with open bridges, which were fitted to the remainder of the class. A key compromise in the redesign turned out to be the decision that the sonar room would be as useful contiguous to the CIC as to the pilot house. Similar problems were encountered in many DEs with similar bridges, but the DEs were not considered worth altering (see chapter 7).

A trial displacement of 2,880 tons was expected, and model tests showed that this excess weight would cost about 1.5 knots—which in late 1941 seemed to imply a speed of 36.5 knots. However, this prediction turned out to be unjustified. At 2,880 tons the *Barton* made only 34.2 knots; the *Moale* made only 33.6 at 2,865. On the other hand, at a more realistic displacement of 3,068 tons, the *Moale* made 32.8 knots on designed power. By overloading the engines by 10 percent, these ships could be pressed to 35.0 and 34.6 knots; such an overload could be maintained indefinitely: it seems to have been standard practice to assume that a rated 60,000 shp plant could be considered in fact a 66,000 shp plant. In principle, a 10 percent increase in power should have covered roughly a 15 percent rise in displacement. A November 1945 BuShips memo noted that the 10 percent margin

... was not specified by the Bureau or the Design Agent but resulted from vendors' margins ... since it is nearly as important in a Naval ship to not over-design as it is to not under-design, definitive requirements should form a part of contract specifications to insure that no "up the sleeve" factors are included

The *Sumner*s were originally completed with a British-style bridge, as in these 1944 views of the *Sumner* (DD 692). The bridge was badly crowded by the barbette of the Mk 37 director; as rebuilt, more of the forebridge was open, but a new pilothouse surrounded the director base.

by the Design agent or manufacturers . . . inclusion of contract penalties in failure to make specified power would not be equitable . . . required speeds for destroyers should be specified as the speed corresponding to Full Load displacement and the Design Power specified as 1.35 of the power required for this ("fleet") speed. . . .

Such a change in criteria for full speed may be one reason why U.S. destroyers appeared to be slower than foreign postwar construction.

These serious speed losses occurred at the same time that the fleet experienced a very considerable increase in its own speed. In 1931 the battle line had a maximum speed of about 20.5 knots and probably a speed in formation of about 18. The Orange battle line was assumed to have a maximum individual-ship speed of about 23 knots, i.e., a line speed of about 20. A destroyer *operational* speed of about 34 knots would provide the 70 percent margin required for successful maneuvering.

From 1936 on, however, the United States built up a much faster main fleet. This would have been the case even had the balance not shifted from battleships to fast carriers. The adoption of very fast warships such as the *Essex* and *Iowa* classes brought fleet speed into the 30-knot region, which the old rules translated into an absurd 51-knot destroyer speed. Even so permissive a margin as 5 knots could no longer be met. In November 1945, the Bureau of Ships deduced a requirement that the "fleet speed" of any future destroyer "should not be less than 38 knots."

One effect of higher capital-ship speed was a higher cruising speed for the fleet, 20 knots rather than the previous 12 or 15. Fuel quite sufficient for 6,500 or even 8,000 miles at 15 knots would not last nearly as long at 20—only 3,300 miles, including allowances

for foul bottom and bad weather. Although not much could be done to improve the speed situation, Bu-Ships could add some tankage on an emergency basis—shades of 1918! Fourteen feet were added to the DD 692 hull, with the result that endurance at 20 knots rose to 4,500 miles—still far short of the figures previously considered essential for Pacific warfare. The extra length improved speed performance, but not to the extent BuShips hoped. The *Sarsfield* of this "long hull" type showed that she could make only 33.2 knots as against a predicted 36.8 on design power. An increase in weights of 150 tons during construction shaved off another 0.4 knots; and at full load she would be good for only 31.6. It was estimated that another knot would have to be allowed for fouling and bad weather, so that a 36.8-knot estimated speed guaranteed the fleet only 30.6 knots operationally. In service, 66,000 shp would give a speed of 31.4 knots. On this basis the *Fletcher* would be good for 33.2 knots, the *Sumner* 31.8, representing, among other things, weight growth of 187 and 180 tons, respectively.

The resulting *Gearing* (DD 710) type was the ultimate development of the *Fletcher* concept. The interweaving of *Sumner* and *Gearing* hull numbers shows to what extent the long-hull type was merely a production modification of the earlier type. Out of the Series DD 692 to DD 926—a total of 235 hulls ordered in 1942 (DD 692–808), 1943 (DD 809–890), and 1945 (891–926)—152 were ordered as *Gearing*s. The end of the war brought a wave of cancellations. Eleven 1943 ships (DD 809–816, 854–856) and all 36 of 1945 were never laid down. In addition, DD 768–769 were scrapped on the slip. Nine more were delivered incomplete (DD 719–721, 766–767, 791, 824, 825, and 827). Of these latter, four would be completed in 1949 as the prototypes of a new generation of ASW escorts,

The *Gearing*s were the ultimate development of the wartime destroyer series that began with the *Fletcher*s; they were essentially lengthened *Sumner*s, with no change in arrangement or in armament. Here the name ship, newly completed, displays her two banks of torpedo tubes, the trainer's position of the after one protected from the blast of the after twin 5-inch gun mount. In both *Gearing*s and *Sumner*s the after mount was expected to fire dead ahead at long range, for a potential six-gun concentration of fire.

The *William R. Rush* illustrates the anti-Kamikaze refit of 1945 as it applied to *Sumner*s and *Gearing*s, a third quadruple 40-mm. gun mount replacing the after bank of torpedo tubes. In addition, two of the three were provided with radar fire control (Mk 63), as shown by the radar antennas atop them. She also illustrates some late-war electronic improvements: the new SR air-search radar, distinguishable by its rounded edges, at her foretop, and a short stub mast immediately abaft her foremast carrying a TDY jammer. The small radomes on the second funnel were DBM radar direction-finders. In *Fletcher*s and in some earlier destroyers, the radomes and the TDY were concentrated on a short mainmast, e.g. between No. 3 and 4 guns.

two would be scrapped incomplete in 1955 (DD 720–721), and DD 766–767 and 791 would survive incomplete until 1958–61 as a mobilization resource. Finally, one ship, DD 828 (the *Timmerman*), was completed to a revised design as an experiment.

The 93 ships actually completed to the *Gearing* design dominated the postwar destroyer force by sheer weight of numbers. They and the *Sumner*s were the only types retained in service after 1945, although many *Fletcher*s were recommissioned for Korea. Certainly, the powerful battery of three twin 5-inch/38s seems to have been the upper limit of what could be achieved on the *Fletcher* hull; contemporary accounts describe the *Gearing*s as wet forward, with a tendency to take weather damage on No. 1 5-inch gunhouse—tendencies that contributed heavily to the *Forrest Sherman* design.

For the first time since before the war, the increase in size was not exploited for an increase in battery; this omission can perhaps be read as a comment on the crowded midships section of the *Sumner*s. As in the earlier class, the response to the AAW emergency of 1945 was replacement of the after torpedo tubes (on a "temporary" basis) by a quadruple Bofors.

The *Gearing*s and *Sumner*s (except for 17 units laid up and one scrapped due to war damage) were the only wartime destroyers maintained in full commission postwar; the laid-up *Sumner*s and most of the *Fletcher*s were activated for Korea. All three classes were notoriously wet, the *Gearing*s probably being the worst. For example, both six-gun classes required reinforcement of No. 1 gunhouse to overcome the effects of sea damage. The *Fletcher*s were considered the best of the lot, as they were the least overweight

and thus had the highest sustained speed and by far the best acceleration.

Between 1950 and 1960 all of these ships were subject to modernization, which applied to antiaircraft batteries, to antisubmarine capability, and to habitability. The basis of antiaircraft improvement was the 3-in./50 gun, originally developed in 1945 as an emergency anti-Kamikaze measure, but not in fact available until 1947. Designed to replace the quadruple Bofors on a one-for-one basis, it gained weight during development to the point where replacement had to be on a two-for-three basis. Thus, the standard *Sumner-Gearing* battery was six such weapons, two twins and two singles (which replaced the former pair of twin Bofors). The two twins were generally carried on the 01 level aft on the centerline, controlled by a single Mk 56 director that could also control the after 5-inch guns. In some ships the Mk 56 was carried between the two after 3-inch mounts, one of them sponsored out to port. The single 3-in./50s were fitted for local radar control, each carrying the dish of a Mk 34 radar, associated with a Mk 63 fire control system (the more sophisticated successor of the wartime Mk 51). In a *Fletcher*, the standard was three twin 3-in./50s, which required removal of one of the single 5-in./38s, and its replacement by the combination of a Mk 56 director and a 3-in./50 where the former twin Bofors had been. The two quadruple Bofors mounted between the funnels in ships refitted in the 1945 anti-Kamikaze program were also replaced by two twin 3-in./50s; these latter were generally controlled by two Mk 63 systems, the mounts carrying the associated dishes of Mk 34 radars.

The *Sumner*-class destroyer *John R. Pierce* illustrates the effects of typical postwar modifications in this 3 October 1959 photograph: 3-inch guns have replaced her former 40-mm. weapons, the two single mounts abaft the bridge being controlled by Mk 63s, the after twins by a Mk 56 director, which could also control the after twin 5-inch gun mount; it is not clearly shown. The port Mk 63 is visible to the left of the single 3-inch/50 abeam the fore funnel. The after funnel carries ECM gear: warning (omnidirectional) "swords" at the yardarm ends, and direction-finders in radomes inboard, their sizes corresponding to their frequency ranges. The short dipoles on her foremast yardarm were for UHF tactical radios, operating on much the same range of frequencies as her SC-series air-search radar; the triangular array of dipoles above was for ship-to-air communication. The short IFF array atop the air-search radar antenna was associated with the Mk X system, then standard in all U.S. warships. Note, too, the Hedgehog that replaced the 20-mm. guns formerly carried on the 01 level forward, and the absence of depth-charge throwers aft.

The rearmament of all of the large war-built destroyers was planned, but this program had to be cut drastically, given the rising cost of new construction. Thus, the FY 51 program called for ten rearmaments, and the FY 52 for another 109, a total of 41 *Fletcher*s (of which 39 were carried out), 40 *Sumner*s, and 38 *Gearing*s (of which 33 were carried out). Another 75 planned for FY 53 would have completed the program: 13 *Sumner*s, 11 *Gearing*s, 11 *Lloyd Thomas*-class DDEs, 40 *Fletcher*s; but nothing was done, and destroyer rearmament figured as an option in early versions of later budgets at least through FY 57. The FY 52 program also included the rearmament of the 24 existing DDRs, and the 12 new DDRs were rearmed with 3-in./50s from the first. Thus, the numbers requiring rearmament declined as the five-gun *Fletcher*s were decommissioned and the DDEs were dropped from consideration: indeed, by 1960 most of the DDEs were so weight-critical that they had landed half their Bofors guns. Of the ships not converted in the early fifties, the *Gyatt* (DD 712) was unique in that she was fitted with 3-in./50 guns as part of her conversion to a missile ship. Finally, some *Fletcher*s were rearmed for transfer abroad.

Thus, 13 *Sumner*s (DD 699–701, 730, 734, 747, 756, 759, 760, 761, 778, 781, and 857) and 13 *Gearing*s (DD 710, 712, 782, 783, 785, 787, 836, 837, 848, 851, 864, 869, and 886) retained their Bofors guns through the fifties. In addition, the *Kraus* (DD 849) was reclassified as an experimental unit (AG 151) and so was not rearmed, and the experimental *Timmerman* (DD 828) was completed as an experimental ship with Bofors guns.

Other aspects of improved air defense were the new generation of air search radars, the L-band SPS-6, for which ships were fitted with tripod foremasts; ECM, which generally involved small radomes at the forward edge of the second funnel; and improved ship-to-air communications.

Improved antisubmarine performance generally required a scanning sonar, dual Hedgehog at the 01 level forward, and launching racks for homing torpedoes. The sonar set initially specified in all three classes was the late-war QHB, later superseded by the postwar SQS-11 or -11A. By the mid-fifties the ideal was the much more powerful SQS-4, which operated with greater power at much lower frequency, and which required substantial space and weight compensation for its installation. An ASW feature peculiar to the *Fletcher*s was the requirement to install a new rudder.

All of these considerations are evident in the Class Improvement Plans (CIPs), which the SCB (Ship Characteristics Board) began to evolve for the big destroyers from 1952 onward. The goal was maximum AAW capability in the DDR (air direction and detection, *not* kill), maximum ASW capability in the DDE, and all-around efficiency in the general-purpose destroyer (DD). At this time, the best air search radar was the new SPS-6; the best fighter control radar, the SPS-8 of the radar pickets; the best sonar, SQS-11; and the best ASW kill device, Hedgehog or Weapon A. It took about a year for the SCB to work out its menu of compromises.

Improvements to general-purpose destroyers would include the installation of new UHF radios; an underwater telephone (AN/UQC-1); ECM intercept and D/F gear (ULR-1 and SLR-2); Mk X IFF; and a new towed antitorpedo countermeasure, Fanfare, to replace the wartime FXR. SPS-6 radar and SQS-11 sonar could be installed, and the depth-charge battery reduced to four side throwers and one stern depth-charge track. In addition, the ships would all be fitted with dual Hedgehogs forward and with launching and stowage facilities for three Mk 32 lightweight homing torpedoes. Improvements to the gun battery were limited to the installation of the 3-in./50 antiaircraft guns and to the replacement of the wartime combination of Mk 12 and Mk 22 radar with a single Mk 25 dish, for main-battery control. In the case of a *Fletcher*, it would also be necessary to increase the capacity of the ship-service generators.

Installation of SPS-6 radars in all destroyers would make the fleet vulnerable to ECM, in that a potential attacker would not have to cover more than one radar frequency band. Thus, in February 1953, the CIPs were changed to show only three of every four destroyers converted to the new radar, the fourth to retain the wartime SR or SC. This proved fortunate, as in practice the long-wave wartime sets were capable of much longer ranges against air targets. Their performance, in fact, led to the development of a new generation of long-wave air search sets, SPS-28, -29, -37, and -43.

As for the ASW battery, SQS-4 with Dual MCC* could be fitted only if the four side depth-charge throwers were removed as compensation. It operated at four distinct frequencies (i.e., was built in four distinct mods) and it was standard practice to fit the four ships of a division to operate at different frequencies. In a six-ship division, no more than two ships were to operate at the same frequency. In ad-

dition, the Mk 32 torpedo originally specified was superseded by a generation of small-diameter types, Mk 43, then 44, leading to the current Mk 46. They required torpedo tubes (Mk 32) rather than the earlier racks.

The other major issue addressed by the CIPs was habitability. All three classes had been built under war conditions, and represented standards of crowding unacceptable in peacetime. Thus, minimum proper standards were defined in a March 1954 SCB study as a bunk and a locker in a regular berthing space for each enlisted man, the bunks to be in tiers of not more than three; a bunk in chief petty officer (CPO) country for each CPO, with a dedicated CPO mess, no bunks located therein; two-tier bunks in three- or four-man staterooms for officers; double staterooms for department heads; and single cabins for captain, executive officer, and unit commander when embarked. The reality was rather different. The *Fletcher*s, described as cramped when they were originally designed, had been intended to accommodate a unit commander, a captain, 8 officers, 15 CPOs, 227 men in bunks, and 25 men in hammocks. The hammock hooks were rigged in the mess compartments, and were considered acceptable because they would normally be stowed between reveille and taps, so that these spaces, with a seating capacity of 136, would be clear for meals and for recreational purposes.

In fact, the original unit commander's cabin and stateroom were generally converted to a CIC. Ships specially designated as unit commander's flagships later had an additional stateroom built onto the superstructure, but one of the two ship's boats had to be sacrificed as compensation. In ships converted to the preferred 3-in./50 configuration, 15 berths were sacrificed to make way for installation of the Mk 56 fire control system, and 6 more were removed to permit installation of the main-battery fire control radar. Counting wartime increases, the total complement of a four-gun *Fletcher* was increased to 20 officers, 18 CPOs, and 277 men. All officers except a unit commander had to be accommodated in the captain's stateroom and in eight other staterooms, three of which were fitted as three-man rooms, and four as double rooms. The CPO complement exceeded by three the original estimate. As for the crew, two or three more bunks were installed in many spaces, including some passageways, and one of the two large messing compartments was given over entirely to berths. About 21 bunks were installed in the other mess, and the seating capacity reduced to about 50. Some of the tables were tilt-top to permit easy access to bunks, and others were usable only when bunks were triced up, so that the messing compartment often could not be used for recreation.

*See chapter 11.

In the *Sumner*s, there was no major increase in hull volume to balance the increase in complement due to their heavier battery: 11 officers and 325 enlisted men (plus 4 officers and 10 men in flagships) were accommodated within the same space that in a *Fletcher* had been designed for 9 officers and 264 enlisted men. Again, there were new encroachments: 15 berths eliminated in favor of Mk 56, 6 in favor of a new sonar control room. The situation in *Gearing*s was similar, as the 14-foot section added amidships contained no berthing space.

These figures only suggest the extent of the problem, as they do not include such problems as the crowding of CICs, which could not really be enlarged; or the loss of one of two ship's boats, which would sharply reduce the crew's access to the shore in many harbors; or the effect of the elimination of awnings.

Some fairly drastic measures were proposed. For example, DesRon 7 proposed that in the *Sumner*s the after diesel emergency generator and emergency fire pump be removed. Either of the two main turbogenerators could maintain the normal battle load, so that an emergency generator would be needed only on failure of both. One such generator could handle all vital auxiliaries plus one single and one twin 3-in./50 mount. The space saved would berth 18 men. The after emergency fire pump supplied only 8½ percent of total pumping capacity, and its removal would increase storeroom space considerably. Both measures were rejected, as war damage experience had shown that the existence of a generator and a pump might be essential to ship survival in some circumstances. On the other hand, the smoke generator was eliminated, and several relatively minor changes made, the destroyer *Meredith* (DD 890) acting as prototype. Particular attention was paid to reductions in the space taken up by the 3-inch and 5-inch loading machines; for example, the internal space generally used for the 5-inch machine could be converted into berth space for 23 men rather than the 6 formerly housed. Ultimately, both loading machines were moved topside to the 01 level.

It was soon clear that any real improvement in habitability would require some removal of controversial items, such as the diesel generator, which were characterized by the SCB staff as "marginal contingency items of the 'we need it just in case' category." They included additional directors such as the Mk 63s "for taking the possible third target under fire." For example, removal of the Mk 63s eliminated the need for 12 men, and the space thus freed might go into eliminating some of the bunks in the mess compartment. Relocation of the machine shop to the carpenter shop would provide 12 or 18 bunks and permit removal of the remainder of the bunks located in the mess compartment. Removal of

the two single 3-in./50 mounts would reduce manning requirements by 16 men, and might either relieve congestion or provide for recreational space.

In 1946, all of the large destroyers were marginal in their capacity for additional top weight, and a decade later matters were considerably worse, compensation being required for additions as small as 4,500 lbs. (SQS-4 improvement by means of Rotating Direction Transmission, RDT) or 1,200 lbs. (washdown system), or 500 (radar trainer). Compensations proposed at this time included replacement of the steel sea cabin by a plastic one in the *Sumner*s and *Gearing*s (4,000 lbs.), reduction in torpedo allowance from five to three (7,500 lbs.), even replacement of engine-room steel floor plates with aluminum (4,000 lbs.). Additional weapon installations were quite another matter: in January 1957, it was estimated that a RAT (Rocket Assisted Torpedo) installation in the six-gun ships would require removal of either one twin 3-in./50 or the torpedo tubes. On the other hand, the additional high top weight of a long-wave SPS-28 or -29 radar was approved in half the destroyer force, to achieve frequency diversity and consequent improved performance against enemy jamming.

For most of the large wartime destroyers, the series of CIPs ended in November 1958, as they underwent FRAM reconstruction soon afterward. Work continued on those ships not reconstructed, however, the result amounting to an austere FRAM. By 1962, ASW was paramount. Surviving *Fletcher*s would surrender their torpedo tubes and depth-charge track and would be fitted with two triple Mk 32 tubes for Mk 44 or 46 torpedoes. A VDS (SQA-10) would be fitted to *Sumner*s, as well as a pair of Mk 25 long torpedo tubes for wire-guided torpedoes.

Two years later there was considerable interest in modernization. Some *Fletcher*s had been refitted while in reserve in the late fifties, receiving scanning sonars, and almost ten years later they were still regarded as a useful mobilization resource. Schemes for full modernization of *Fletcher*- and *Sumner*-class destroyers in reserve were requested by Op-36 in April 1964, combinations of ASROC, Mk 32 and Mk 25 torpedo tubes, and SQS-23 and SQS-4 sonars being considered. Fire control was a major problem, since the existing Mk 105 system was not compatible with the new Mk 48 torpedo. Thus, where the Mk 48 was specified, the system had to be replaced by an austere "centralized control group" consisting of a Plotter (Mk 22) and two computers (Mk 134 and 143).

The alternative studies suggest the extent of the obsolescence of these ships. In a *Sumner*, the two existing 400-kw ship-service turbogenerators would be rewound for 500 kw each, and in three schemes (D, E, and F) a 500-kw gas turbine would be added to power an SQS-23 sonar plus an SQA-13/SQS-35 independent VDS. Endurance would fall from 3,489 nm. at 20 knots (2-boiler split plant) to 2,580 nm. In Scheme D, which was essentially a FRAM, the battery would be reduced to two twin 5-in./38s, and a Mk 114 underwater fire control system would control one ASROC and two Mk 32 triple tubes. Other features would include air conditioning and silencing (Prairie Masker), and the cost was estimated at $13.7 million for the lead ship, $12 million for others, with a corresponding yard time of 11 months. In Scheme E ($14.1/$12.3 million) the underwater battery would be a pair of long Mk 25 tubes (10 Mk 48 torpedoes), DASH (14 torpedoes), and the Mk 32s (12 torpedoes, as in D, with 16 ASROCs in that version). Finally, in F ($13.3/$11.6 million) all three twin mounts would be retained, and the underwater battery limited to torpedo tubes. Schemes G and H were far more austere, with SQS-4 sonars but no VDS at all. Scheme G amounted to a slightly modernized ship, with dual Hedgehog and a pair of Mk 32 torpedo tubes (18 torpedoes), at a cost of $6.4/$5.5 million, with endurance reduced to 2,800 nm. at 20 knots. Air conditioning would amount to 50 tons rather than the 120 of the more sophisticated ships. In H, the existing Mk 105 underwater fire control system was to be modified to control the Mk 37 Mod 1 torpedo, fired from two Mk 25 tubes, and only two twin mounts were to be retained. The cost would rise to $7.9/6.6 million, and both of the austere schemes were expected to cost only 6 months of yard time, compared to 11 for the more complex ones.

The corresponding study for the *Fletcher*s has not survived, but it must have been similar. In any event, nothing beyond Scheme G was ever attempted, and it appears that the non-FRAM *Sumner*s were modified to about their standard. They did not survive for very long beyond 1964, and the remaining story of the big war-built destroyers is the story of the FRAMs, as recounted in chapter 11.

The big hulls were used, even during World War II, for purposes other than standard destroyer functions. Thus, two dozen *Gearing*s were converted to radar pickets (see chapter 10). A dozen *Sumner*s became destroyer minelayers, successors to the flush deckers. Even in 1940 the force of eight elderly ships was considered inadequate, and mine commanders sought more modern ships. In March 1940 for example, Commander Battle Force Minecraft suggested the conversion of *Farragut*s, but C&R replied that they could not take the top weight involved. Compensation for 85 mines would amount to the removal of the torpedo tubes, and of both No. 3 and No. 5 guns, as well as the addition of 20 tons of fixed ballast. Matters rested there until early 1943, when Commander Service Squadron Six (Pacific Fleet) asked for four more conversions. He was rejected on grounds of the scarcity of destroyers, but Admiral King did authorize BuShips to design kits for quick temporary conversion of general-purpose destroyers. The maximum gun battery was to be retained.

To some extent it would appear that this request reflected the beginning of offensive mine operations in the Solomons, and the success of those operations later in 1943 undoubtedly encouraged the conversion program. Ideally, minelayers were to operate in units of three or four, but in the spring of 1943 two were occupied as escorts in the Hawaiian area and three more were in Alaskan waters supporting the Aleutians operation. All suffered from low speed and age. Admiral Nimitz, commanding the Pacific Fleet, saw the presence of only two in the South Pacific as evidence not of scarcity but rather of uselessness, and his skepticism would slow the program.

Studies were made of both *Bristol* (DD 453) and *Fletcher* conversions, only the latter showing much promise. Removal of the main-deck machine guns, the depth-charge projectors, the No. 2 bank of torpedo tubes, and No. 5 gun would buy a capacity of 90 old-pattern or 84 new-pattern mines. Moreover, a suitable destroyer tender could accomplish this conversion in a week. In September 1943, Admiral King ordered four kits fabricated at Mare Island; they were ready in December. They were never used, however, as the *Fletcher*s were considered too valuable. DesPac suggested that the 1,850-ton "leaders" be used instead, and late in January Admiral King asked for conversion studies. Three units (the *Sampson*, *Warrington*, and *Phelps*) were scheduled for overhaul, including conversion to a 5-inch dual-purpose battery, but in April all were ordered to the Atlantic for use as convoy flagships.

The project did not quite die, as by now Admiral Nimitz was more convinced of the value of destroyer minelayers, given combat experience in the Solomons. On 24 June 1944 he recommended the conversion of 12 *Sumner*s then under construction. Admiral King countered with a proposal to convert four new ships and eight *Fletcher*s, but Nimitz preferred all new ships. He wanted them ready for combat by 1 February 1945, which would require them to be completed by 1 November 1944. Ships from Bath (DD 735 to 740 became DM 23–28), Bethlehem Staten Island (DD 749–751 became DM 29–31), and Bethlehem San Pedro (DD 771–773 became DM 32–34) were selected, the prototype, the *R. H. Smith*, commissioning as a minelayer on 4 August 1944.

Weight compensation amounted to both sets of torpedo tubes, three Oerlikons at the stern, and two of the six depth-charge projectors, and maximum mine capacity was set at 120, although that rather exceeded the stability limits preferred by BuShips. Kamikaze antiaircraft improvements were limited

The *Aaron Ward* was a typical *Sumner*-class minelayer, her torpedo tubes landed as weight compensation for mines, carried on tracks visible running down her starboard side in this 9 February 1945 view. Otherwise, except for depth-charge projectors, she duplicated a 10-tube *Sumner*. She was severely damaged by Kamikaze attack off Okinawa, repair work being suspended on 24 August 1945.

The last of the *Gearing*s, the *Timmerman* was completed to a modified design as a high-temperature, high-pressure steam test platform, her 100,000 shp taking up no more space than the 60,000 of a standard destroyer. In theory she could make 40 knots, but it does not appear that she ever ran at much more than half power. In that expectation, however, her bow was higher than that of a standard *Gearing*. She had a standard 40-mm. antiaircraft outfit, but no torpedo tubes, depth charges, or Hedgehogs, and her bridge resembled that of the DDEs completed as such postwar. Here she runs at speed in Massachusetts Bay, 22 April 1953.

to the addition of a third quadruple Bofors in place of the depth-charge throwers atop the after superstructure, and the replacement of the single Oerlikons (8) by five twins. About 25 mines had to be landed as compensation.

Most of the minelayers, which saw no service as such in wartime, were laid up after the war, and in 1950 only four, all in the Atlantic, remained active. Even after the great Korean War reactivation there were only two in the service, the *Gwin* and *Shea*, one on each coast. Wartime destroyer minelayers had sometimes been employed as sweepers, and interest was expressed in a similar capacity for the newer ships—the *Gwin* actually being converted at a cost of nearly 20 tons of top weight. The Mine Force protested that this was a very expensive way to buy a secondary capacity. In any case, the minelayers remained in service beyond their sweeper counterparts (see chapter 5), and were laid up only in April 1958.

7

The Destroyer Escorts, 1941–1945

The large destroyer program of the thirties was intended primarily to screen the fleet, be it battleships or fast carriers, in a trans-Pacific offensive. As war approached, it became evident that destroyers or destroyer-like ships would also be needed—and in large numbers—for many lesser tasks, such as ocean ASW escort. As in 1917, the issue was whether to design a new austere or second-rate destroyer for mass production; as in 1917, the design bureau (C&R and then its successor, Ships) argued that much time would be lost in the production of any specialized type. Several times a new type was proposed, and several times it was abandoned, but ultimately it emerged as the Destroyer Escort, or DE. The program was gigantic, and, as predicted, somewhat late. Thus, much of the DE story is a series of attempts to make use of a flood of robust if specialized hulls as the production machine was turned on, sharply accelerated, and then drastically braked to make way for alternative naval projects, particularly landing craft. It is a great tribute to the soundness of the emergency DE design that so many survive in foreign service, well over three decades after their completion.

American interest in specialized escort craft declined after World War I and did not revive until 1937, when efforts were made to design a successor to the World War I Eagle Boat. The new craft, which became the 173-foot PC, was intended to serve the Naval Reserve in peacetime and to release elderly destroyers for ocean escort duty in war by filling the local ASW role. Thus, the vast fleet of four-pipers was considered the principal war reserve for long-range ASW work, and no new destroyer-size escort was contemplated. Indeed, the only small destroyer proposed at this time was a very fast aluminum-hulled "torpedo boat," an unsolicited Alcoa proposal

that the General Board rejected as it "has no place in our Fleet organization which cannot be better filled by the current type of 1,630-ton destroyer."

By 1939 considerable efforts were being made to facilitate mobilization in the event of war. That June, Commander Robert B. Carney, who was involved in the mobilization effort through his post in the Shore Establishments Division, suggested the design of "an intermediate or second-line torpedo craft or patrol craft falling somewhere between the subchaser and the modern large destroyer." Very large numbers would be needed in wartime, and in many cases full destroyer characteristics would not be required. Moreover, Carney suspected that the industrial base for mass production of the sophisticated mobilization-prototype destroyers, the 1,850-ton and the 1,630-ton classes, did not exist. He asked whether they could be produced nearly as fast as the flush deckers had been in World War I, and whether a simpler design might not be delivered in numbers more quickly:

industrially there is little doubt that a simplified type can be produced quicker and in greater volume, and it is not at all improbable that in time of war this country would have urgent and immediate need of a number of reasonably fast and effective torpedo craft or patrol craft which could be obtained more quickly, more cheaply, and in greater quantity than we could turn out our most modern types. From a strategic and tactical viewpoint there is one advantage in numbers; whatever else a destroyer may be called upon to do in war-time, it is certain that some sort of screening duty will be a major requirement—screening against surface craft, air craft, or submarines—offensive screening or defensive screening. In many types of screening, two boats, covering more ground than one, can be of more use than one, even if they are inferior in fighting strength. . . .

DE 240, USS *Moore*, an FMR-type destroyer escort, comes alongside in the Atlantic. Aft she shows the characteristic HF/DF mast of Atlantic destroyer escorts, and her British-style open bridge betrays Admiralty influence in her design.

The General Board called for proposals for prototype characteristics. Therefore, in September the War Plans Division suggested a mobilization prototype designed to assist in the "exercise of control of the sea," i.e., in escort duty. Speed and striking power but not cruising radius might be sacrificed:

at the present time it is thought that such tasks would fall to the 1,200-ton destroyers now available, either in commission or to be recommissioned in emergency, but these vessels are not entirely suitable and with their elimination, due to age and service, a special type . . . could relieve our new destroyers of these duties . . . .

War Plans envisaged a simple, robust vessel;

since the . . . tasks are all war missions and require no training not now afforded by existing types, actual production, except for two or three vessels to prove the design and develop the reliability of the propulsion and other installations, is not believed desirable . . . the characteristics of the vessel visualized. . . involve research in the industrial field and special technical information which is not available to the Division. However, maximum offensive power against submarines and effective anti-aircraft armament are considered as minimum requirements which must be met to justify the development of the type at all. . . .

War Plans suspected that, like a flush decker, the new class would displace about 1,200 tons. It would be armed with stern racks and depth-charge throwers or Y-guns "sufficient to produce an effective pattern laterally as well as longitudinally, controlled from bridge" as well as "an effective double purpose battery with necessary fire control. The size and number of guns of this battery is believed to be the determining factor as to the practicability of the ship. It is thought that at least four guns are necessary, but whether these should be 3-in./50, 5-in./38, or whether a new gun and control system should be developed is a technical question for the Bureau of Ordnance. Unless, however, an effective battery can be produced in less time than would be required for the present type destroyer, the ship should not be built." There would be at least 24 depth charges in ready service stowage above decks, with another 24 below, and speed would be not less than 25 knots fully loaded; the latter figure was chosen "to permit the vessel to perform its functions, which will require escort for comparatively high-speed vessels used as transports. Twenty-five knots is also required to permit quick acceleration if the full tactical possibilities of listening devices are to be realized." Machinery was to be twin screw, "simple and rugged, with the view to operation by comparatively inexperienced personnel. Diesel engines are suggested as a possibility offering mass production capabilities and long cruising radius." The goal for the latter was set at

6,000 nm. at 12 knots, and the ship was to be designed specifically for sea-keeping qualities. "It will be noted that no torpedoes are included in the above characteristics. It is evident that considerable sacrifice of present characteristics must be accepted or we come back to our present destroyer. For the duties visualized, it is thought that torpedoes are least necessary."

For all practical purposes, this was the DE as designed almost a year later, but the General Board balked at a truly second-rate ship. It seemed more reasonable to the board to resurrect the smallest successful modern destroyer, the *Farragut*; surely advances since 1931 would make it easy to squeeze into this hull—which, after all, was not so very small—a sufficient AA and ASW battery. In particular it seemed to the board that the very existence of the *Farragut* proved that on less than 1,400 tons one could have four guns, eight torpedo tubes, three twin 1.1-inch AA, and four depth-charge throwers and two tracks. The pitfall in this theory was that what seemed on paper to be minor updates of a ten-year-old well-understood design were in fact radical improvements requiring something entirely new. For example, the *Farragut* did not incorporate the echelon machinery arrangement standard in 1939–40. The General Board was willing to accept a reduction in trial speed to 33 knots, but the standard destroyer plant in production was too powerful. Moreover, a new machinery plant would be about 60 tons heavier and 14 feet longer than the original. This and other changes would ruin the stability of the original design. The longer engine room space, for example, squeezed out crew space even as new weapons would have required a growth in complement of about 10 percent. Finally, there would be a loss in freeboard.

There was no question but that a new design would be feasible, but then it would carry a high cost in lead time. Thus C&R could argue persuasively in January 1940 that it was far better to duplicate the existing 1,630-ton class. The same argument very nearly won out in 1941, and the "economical" 1,630-ton type was once again offered as a mass-production type in 1942, when it was seen primarily as a second-rate AA/ASW escort that would consume less material than would the more expensive *Fletcher/Sumner*. By that time, however, there was already an austere escort in production: the DE.

The austere destroyer was revived in the summer of 1940, as both Gibbs & Cox and BuShips tried to design mass-production types. The precise origins of the Gibbs & Cox project are obscure; the record shows only a request by the Coordinator of Shipbuilding on 3 August 1940, but the two design sketches were submitted to the President, which suggests the latter's direct intervention, perhaps in response to some

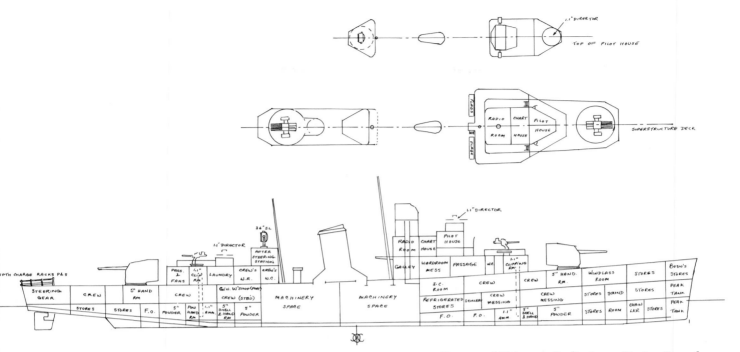

Escort destroyer—general arrangement   Scheme 4   Navy Department, Bureau of Ships   Preliminary Design Branch,
Washington, D.C.   October 5, 1940

earlier proposal by Francis Gibbs. Certainly Gibbs had a close personal relationship with President Roosevelt. He was not interested in austere, slow escorts; rather, he proposed conventional fast lightweight destroyers: a 1,050-ton type with two 5-inch DP, 2 quadruple 1.1-inch AA, four .5-inch machine guns, and two quadruple torpedo tubes, all to be carried at 35 knots; or, alternatively, a 750-tonner with two 3- or 4-inch guns, one quadruple 1.1 inch, and triple torpedo tubes.

President Roosevelt was sufficiently enthusiastic to order the Navy to buy four such ships, two of each type; they were actually ordered from Federal Shipbuilding in September 1940, even though they clearly had little to do with Navy requirements. Indeed, most likely they achieved their respectable armaments at considerable cost in seakeeping and habitability, not to mention the lack of any margin for future improvement. These sordid truths gradually made themselves felt, and in November 1940 the Federal order was changed to four 1,175-ton units of BuShips design, which were the forerunners of the DE.

In effect, the President's interest in light destroyers revived the proposals of the previous fall. On 16 August Admiral Stark, the CNO, asked Preliminary Design for proposals: he wanted a ship of 750 to 900 tons, armed with three or four 5-inch/25 antiaircraft guns, capable of 25 to 30 knots. The very heavy AA battery was intended to provide cover for both the escort and her convoy: in the summer of 1940 it was by no means clear that aircraft would not be the

primary threat to any convoy in mid-Atlantic. High speed was a prerequisite for any ship intended to escort a fast (15-knot) convoy.

In September 1939 War Plans had suspected that 1,200 tons would barely suffice for rather less than what Admiral Stark wanted, and the Preliminary Design studies showed that he was over-optimistic as to what 900 tons would buy. Scheme 1 of 24 August showed three 5-inch/25s, as well as one quadruple 1.1-inch machine cannon, two depth-charge tracks (each with five 600-lb. charges) and four throwers (each with two 300 lb.), a speed of 30 knots (28 when four months out of dock), and an endurance of 6,000 nm. at 15 knots. The admiral felt this was relatively little when on only 400 tons more a *Farragut* could provide more speed, torpedo tubes, and five more powerful guns. However, even one more gun cost 25 tons, as well as a reduction of power by a third, to 12,000 shp (and a loss of 3.5 knots); the crew had to be increased by 25 merely to operate this weapon. The General Board rejected both tentative schemes and asked for a third, which was to mount four 5-inch/38s and two quad 1.1-inch guns, would be capable of 24.5 knots, and would emphasize seakeeping. It emerged on 19 September, lengthened from 294 to 300 feet, and with displacement increased to 1,175 tons (standard; 1,525 fully loaded), to accommodate four of the then-standard base-ring 5 inch/38s. The power plant was the 12,000-shp unit of the earlier studies; endurance fell by a thousand miles. It was estimated that such a ship would cost $6.8

Table 7–1. Small Destroyers and Destroyer Escorts

	Gibbs & Cox Studies 8 August 1940		Scheme 1 24 Aug 1940	Scheme 3 19 Sept 1940	Scheme 5 15 Oct 1940	Scheme B February, 1941	BDE Design July, 1941
LWL	292	264	294	300	260	280	280
Beam	31	28	31	34.5	32	34	34
Draft	10' 4"	9' 3"	9	9' 9"	8.8	9.75	9.5
SHP	35,000	25,000	18,000	12,000	6,000	12,000	12,000
Speed	35	35	30	24.5	21.5	24	24
Endurance	8,900/15	6,100/15	6,000/15	5,000/15	5,000/15	6,000/12	6,000/12
	1,100/35	1,000/35					
5-in/38	2	—	3*	4	2	2	—
4-in/50	—	2	—	—	—	—	—
3-in/50	—	2	—	—	—	—	3
Quad 1.1	2	1	1	2	2	1†	—
.50 MG	4	4	—	—	—	2‡	5‡
21-in TT	2 × 3	2 × 3					
DC proj.	—	—	—	—	—	1 × 3	1 × 3
Hull			365	469.5	364.5		465
Fittings			71	83.5	60.1		89
Machinery			297	370.0	205.0		335
Armament	86	47	53	109.7	71.3		27
Equipment & Outfit			34	43.5	32.3		44
Margin			20	25.0	20.0		30
Light ship			840	1,101.2	753.2		990
Ammunition	50	33	65	101.1	39.1		55
Stores			83	94.8	77.5		74
Machinery Liquid			13				25
Standard	1,050	750	940	1,175	875	1,125	1,144
RFW			14	21	1.0		14
Fuel			200	240	112		132
Trial	1,365	980	1,225	1,525	1,050	1,350	1,290
GM				3.5	3.24		3.8

* 5-in/25
† Quadruple 40 mm vice 1.1 in
‡ 20 mm vice .50 caliber

million; Admiral Stark noted unhappily that the British *Hunt*-class light destroyer, which had inspired much of his effort, cost about $6.4 million.

For its part, Preliminary Design traced the growth of this Scheme 3 to the need for new guns, ammunition, fire control, and a new electrical plant. Moreover, a return to the original 18,000-shp plant would entail only a small additional increase in displacement, and would increase speed to 27.5 knots. Much more would be required, however, to restore the original 30 knots. Scheme 3 formed the basis for the ultimate DE design, but at the time it seemed so expensive that the General Board asked for an alternative series. An escort with only two 5-inch/38s, powered by two submarine diesels, came to $4.7 million and 775 tons, and could not even satisfy a two-compartment flooding requirement, given the ex-

cessive size of its engines. It was abandoned at an informal conference between General Board and BuShips representatives on 8 October, and attention returned to Scheme 3.

In effect, Scheme 3 was the ship suggested by War Plans the previous year. It resembled a short destroyer with a single funnel, and could be built only by using exactly the sophisticated construction techniques that had been implicitly rejected by the War Plans Division: indeed, one might say that the feasibility of the design only showed the extent to which the size of a conventional destroyer was driven up by the demand for high speed and for a torpedo battery. In effect, Scheme 3 traded heavy destroyer machinery for fire power.

For a short time both Scheme 3 and an advanced smaller design were pursued. Thus, the addition of

100 tons to the 775-ton Scheme 4 bought 2,000 bhp and one knot of speed (21.5 knots); in each case the battery was two 5-inch/38s and two quad 1.1 inch as well as the standard outfit of depth charges. However, there were hidden costs to the reduction in displacement; for example, the small escorts were to have only 300 rounds per 5-inch gun, as compared to 400 for the larger unit. Even so, on 22 October the General Board approved characteristics for both schemes, preferring the larger of the two. Then, in mid-November Admiral Stark killed the 875-ton ship on grounds of inadequate antiaircraft fire, and proposed that all four light destroyers be built to the 1,175-ton design. Secretary of the Navy Knox approved this plan on 15 November, but none of these ships were built.

The problem was that the escort really saved very little money at a great cost in capability. Indeed, even before the November order, Admiral Stark had suggested cancellation of the entire project. Admiral Robinson, Chief of BuShips, preferred a standard 1,500-ton destroyer with quad 1.1s in place of torpedo tubes. In September 1940 it was estimated that a new 1,620-ton destroyer cost $8.1 million, compared to $6.8 for Scheme 3. This savings was too small to be worthwhile, and the Federal order was converted to one for 1,620-tonners in January 1941. The estimate of 50 to 60 percent of the cost of a destroyer was probably optimistic; in 1943 the rather simpler DE cost $5.3 to $6.1 million, 51 to 59 percent of the cost of a $10.4 million 1,620-ton destroyer.

The escort concept was not quite dead, however. On 31 January 1941 Admiral Stark asked an informal board to recommend types of small craft to be procured under the fourth supplemental estimate for 1941; it recommended the construction of "fifty escort vessels for the sole purpose of protecting convoys against submarines and for use in the western part of the North Atlantic." A week later (7 February) the Secretary of the Navy authorized construction "as soon as definite military Characteristics are determined." On 28 February the General Board asked for studies of "an escort vessel designed to protect convoys against submarines in the western part of the North Atlantic where extensive opposition from the air is not expected." Simplified design for mass production was required, and the ships were to be capable of at least 17 knots. The emphasis on the Western Atlantic reflects the U.S. decision to take over convoy escort in those waters to relieve the Royal Navy of some pressure, while remaining officially out of the war. The low speed suggests the influence of the British corvette. However, in fact this requirement was the true beginning of the DE, since the escort program became known to the British and then formed the basis for a request by them for Lend-Lease units.

Captain E.L. Cochrane was now head of Preliminary Design. He had been detached from BuShips in the fall of 1940 to study British practices as Assistant Naval Attaché, and he had become impressed with the *Hunt* class, although he found them wet in a seaway due to their narrow beam. In addition, he appears to have become impressed with the British open bridge, which he considered ideal for convoy watch-keeping, given its unobstructed view from one beam to the other.

The General Board issued tentative characteristics in late February, calling for a 22-knot escort armed with single-purpose guns (5-in./51 or 4-in./50). Cochrane chose to develop Scheme 3, reducing its length to 280 feet and its speed to 24 knots; he commented that an alternative 6,000-shp plant would save only 25 to 35 tons, and would reduce speed to 21 knots, below the specified figure, and would leave "no margin for the service speed of 20 knots which appears to be essential for satisfactory escort duty." Endurance would be 6,000 nm. at 12 knots, precisely the standard War Plans had aimed for over a year earlier. As for armament, Cochrane was heavily influenced by his British experience; although the General Board had specified two single-purpose guns and two 20 mm., he provided an alternative scheme (B) with two 5-in./38 dual-purpose weapons:

> the Bureau considers that the provision of these guns has the important advantage of offering opposition to air attack not only against the escort vessel itself, but also against the convoy. The direct weight increase for this change . . . is about 10 tons. The double-purpose battery is considered to be worth this weight increase in order to provide anti-aircraft fire even though that may be considered of improbable need for these ships. The theater of employment of such ships and the nature of attacks against which they are to provide defense appear difficult to predict. It may well be that the services of these ships will be required in areas where opposition from the air is of high probability. . . .

As for the 5-in./51, it was a powder-bag gun and Cochrane questioned its viability in so lively a ship. He had to admit that in a simplified ship he would be unable to provide the kind of remote power control that made a destroyer so effective as an AA platform, but he still felt that the high-angle mounts would be well worthwhile. In addition, he proposed a quadruple Bofors aft as well as two 20 mm. near the stack; BuOrd, trying to simplify the design, suggested two 20 mm. in place of the 40 mm. His British experience also showed in Cochrane's proposal for triple torpedo tubes amidships, which might be taken from older destroyers:

> The experience of the British in the present war has shown the importance of providing in escort vessels

some threat against large surface raiders. Accordingly in their latest escort vessels, the modified *Hunt* class, they are providing one twin 21 in. tube on the centerline. . . .

The cost of the triple tube and its torpedoes would be only 12 tons.

This was the DE, designed from the outset with enough space, strength, and weight to take the final battery of two 5-in./38s, which fewer than half actually carried. It is not surprising that its size daunted the General Board, one member of which asked for a revived version of the smaller escort, capable of 10 knots in rough water (sea state 5 or 6), 18 to 20 maximum, and armed with one 4-in./50, two twin 20 mm., two twin Bofors, 50 depth charges, and capable of 4,000 nm. at 12 knots. Scheme B, with two 5-in./38s, came to 1,125 tons (1,350 full load); this Scheme C came to only 825 (950), with a length of 215 rather than 280 feet—it was the size of a fleet minesweeper.

The General Board was clearly unhappy with the proposed ships. On the one hand, it wanted an escort capable of effective AA fire; on the other, even though Cochrane could provide dual-purpose guns, he could not provide a modern fire control system, which would require considerable below-decks volume or else considerable weight high in the ship. On 17 April it submitted characteristics based on Scheme B but armed with two 4-in./50s, two twin Bofors, and one or two 20 mm. to cover any arcs left blind by the Bofors. There were to be the usual two depth-charge tracks aft and four depth-charge throwers, as well as at least 75 depth charges. Cochrane's torpedo tubes were not included; indeed the board commented that it saw no reason to modify its original characteristics. However, it also saw no reason to build the escort that had, in effect, been forced upon it; in its letter of submission to the Secretary of the Navy it observed that it

> does not believe that the resulting vessel, because of its weakness against air attack, is a proper vessel to escort convoys or that its military value is commensurate with the expenditure involved.

Once more, the conventional destroyer seemed far the better bargain; on 16 May the CNO proposed that no escort destroyers be built, and the 50 ships were canceled three days later. Two months later the Secretary of the Navy approved a further suggestion by the CNO and the General Board that no escorts be built, in view of the two-year time lag expected before any might enter service and the large number of destroyers that were either under construction or might be produced in the two years.

Cochrane was apparently convinced of the need for such ships, and he persisted with the design despite the cancellation of the 50-ship order. The pre-liminary design completed early in June 1941 called for two 4-in./50s and five 20-mm. guns but could accommodate up to two 5-in./38s, two twin Bofors, and two single 20 mm.; there was also provision for a triple 21-in. torpedo tube and for 75 depth charges. Displacement was 1,085 tons (1,300 fully loaded) with the 4-in. battery. He noted that

> if the situation develops so that escort vessels, similar to the present design, are needed to supplement and relieve some of the more valuable destroyer types, this Bureau believes that the general characteristics of the present design are such as to make this type of considerable value for the purpose. . . .If at any time in the future it is decided to include some vessels of this type in the program, the Bureau believes that their value would increase almost in direct ratio to the rapidity of their construction. Every effort would be made during the development of the design to obtain simplicity in both hull and machinery so that construction in comparison with that of destroyers could be expedited. Several important steps of this nature have already been taken in the early stages of the design. . . .

Indeed, interest was by no means completely dead. For example, on 17 June Admiral Stark asked for data comparing current U.S. and British (*Hunt* and *River*) escort designs. Accompanying notes suggested that the increased weight of the 1941 as compared to the 1940 design might be traced to an attempt to gain simplicity in hull and machinery construction; there was also a question of the availability of the guns and directors incorporated in the AA-oriented 1940 design. Indeed, BuShips believed that its 1941 escort would cost about 55 percent of the cost of a destroyer, compared with 75 percent for the 1940 escort and 20 percent for a 173-foot PC.

The DE project was saved by the desperate need of the Royal Navy for escorts; on 23 June 1941 the British Supply Council in North America asked the Secretary of the Navy to release some escort destroyers; 100 in all were wanted. The changes requested were a dual-purpose armament (three 3-in./50s were adopted, in view of the shortage of 5-in./38s) and torpedo tubes. A strikingly British feature introduced later was the tall open-topped bridge, in which the conning officer stood on the level above the pilot house, rather than on the same level as in U.S. practice. An enclosed "Asdic Hut" was built into its forward side, stepped down from the open bridge. The British requested this bridge in February 1942, and the Admiralty comment of that date seems ironic in view of later U.S. complaints:

> The design of the bridge shown in the general arrangement (i.e., a U.S. type) does not meet requirements, as it is too cramped and does not provide adequate facilities for an all round look out. A mod-

ified design of bridge, in which the Asdic cabinet is sited on the upper bridge, and A.R.L. plot, look out positions, and Type 271 (Radar Lantern) R.D.F. are provided, would better meet the requirements. . . .

Detail development of the design included one major improvement, the substitution of twin for single rudders. Advocated by Gibbs, Cochrane, and also by the doyen of American naval architects, William Hovgaard, the new configuration was adopted in November 1941. Model tests showed a reduction in turning circle of about 25 percent, and in a sense they were confirmed by DE, as compared to frigate (PF), performance. Both were of about the same size, and had similar rudder areas. In tank tests, a model of the long-hull DE showed a tactical diameter of 350 yards with rudders hard over at 15 knots; for the PF model the equivalent figure was 480 yards. At the same time, twin rudders were adopted for the *Sumner*-class destroyer, which showed a similar level of superiority over its *Fletcher*-class predecessor.

Production problems plagued the new program. President Roosevelt approved the production of 50 British DEs (BDE) on 15 August 1941, despite arguments the previous month by BuShips that yards already building destroyers could almost certainly deliver "repeat" destroyers more readily than they could shift to escorts. In fact, most DEs were built by yards that had never built destroyers, although the lead DEs were laid down by a Navy Yard, Mare Island. Thus, to some considerable extent the Navy was able to receive both its general-purpose destroyers *and* its specialized escorts, because its expansion program included both increases in numbers of ships and increases in the naval production base. In fact the DE program competed with destroyers, if at all, only in the issue of the supply of 5-inch guns. The principal bottleneck turned out to be machinery production. The flood of new destroyers and other steam-turbine combatants required geared turbines, which in turn strained the national capacity for gear-cutting. The production of a new plant depended upon the delivery of complex machine tools, some of which took as much as a year to build.

The scramble for power plants shaped the DE program. If the full geared turbine installation could not be provided, one alternative was diesels. There was already a proven submarine diesel plant in production: four 1,500-bhp units driving propellers through DC generators and motors. The full 12,000 horsepower required by the DE could be made up by adding to this plant another four diesels driving through gears "of a smaller size which was then not critical." The price of the less-compact power plant was 3.5 feet of length and 130 tons, but it had the crucial advantage of availability within what seemed a reasonable time. However, in an expanding war economy diesels were in short supply, and quite soon the number of DEs on order was increased very sharply. The solution was to halve the DE diesel power plant: although the DE hull was redesigned and lengthened to take all eight engines, in practice diesel-powered DEs received only the four driving through generators and motors, for a total of 6,000 bhp and the loss of 4.5 knots.

The USS *Engstrom*, seen here newly completed, off Philadelphia Navy Yard on 2 July 1943, was typical of the diesel-powered short-hull (*Evarts*, or GMT class) destroyer escorts. Her after quadruple 1.1-inch machine canon, elevated to about 90 degrees, is barely visible forward of the after 3-inch gun.

This was not particularly satisfactory, and turboelectric drive was adopted as an alternative. Turbines themselves had not presented great production difficulties, but drive through generators and motors were considerably less compact than gearing. The DE hull had to be lengthened to 300 feet and displacement had to rise 200 tons. In fact, the reduction in wave-making resistance due to the greater length balanced off the increase in frictional resistance due to the greater wetted surface, and speed was held to the original design figure of about 24 knots. The 300-foot hull was standardized for ease of production, although some ships employed the diesel-electric plant in it. Late production DEs, benefiting from the ex-

pansion in gear-cutting plant, were powered by diesels and steam turbines through smaller, more easily produced gears.

Combined with a variation in main battery, the variations in hull and propulsion converted a homogeneous class of destroyer escorts into six distinct classes. The principal original classes were the *Evarts*, or GMT (GM Tandem Diesel, the original half-powered short-hull class); the *Buckley*, or TE (Turbo-Electric, the long-hull turbine type); the *Cannon*, or DET (Diesel-Electric Tandem drive, in a long hull); and the *Edsall*, or FMR (Fairbanks-Morse Reduction-geared, in a long hull). Substitution of 5-inch for 3-inch guns in a fast DE produced the *Rudderow* (TEV,

The *Lake* (DE 301, above) and *Crowley* (DE 303, facing, whose quarterdeck is shown) were GMT-class destroyer escorts completed in 1944; these photographs were taken at Mare Island that April. The arrangement of exhaust pipes in the *Lake*'s funnel clearly indicates her diesel powerplant. Note, too, the passage from her open bridge to the sonar room built into the forward end of the bridge structure, and the waveguide emerging from the rear of the bridge structure before passing up the foremast to the radars located there. The range-finder atop her bridge was used in 3-inch fire control. Forward, she shows a Hedgehog with its spigots bare of projectiles, tilted to form an extended pattern. Her radars are the usual combination of SA for air search and SL for surface search, the latter in a small radome. Aft, the *Crowley* shows the unusually heavy battery of eight depth-charge throwers, the four aftermost ones angled aft, and two 12-charge tracks, with smoke generators between them. The six curved objects stowed just above the deck to the right of the large crate on the fantail are spare arbors for her K-guns. Note, too, that although she has a medium-frequency direction-finder (the loop on the platform facing aft from her mast, which is covered in the close-up), she has no HF/DF; this lack may have been due to her assignment to the Pacific Fleet.

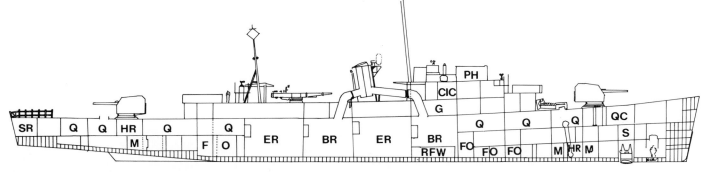

TEV inboard

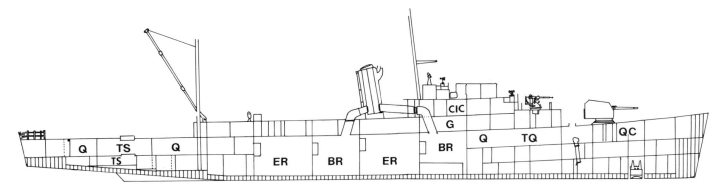

APD 100 class

Turbo-Electric drive) and *John C. Butler* (WGT, West-inghouse Geared Turbine) classes, both of which had a new low bridge.

The DE gun battery was also set by production and other considerations; for example, the Bofors of Cochrane's design were eliminated in favor of five 20 mm. because the smaller Oerlikon was far easier to produce. In February 1942, the U.S. Navy replaced the two 20 mm. superfiring over No. 3 mount with a quadruple 1.1-inch machine cannon. This latter was already in some disrepute, but on the other hand the DE was primarily an ASW ship, and the limited number of Bofors guns available was more urgently required by first-line combatants. Provision was made for its replacement by a twin Bofors when production permitted. The Admiralty had similar ideas: on 11 February it instructed its agents in the United States to ask that the torpedo tubes be deleted in favor of more antiaircraft weapons, for a total battery of one twin Bofors aft, four Oerlikons abaft the funnel, and one more forward of the bridge. This battery was soon made standard for all of the short-hull DEs under construction.

Ships with long hulls had sufficient deck space for both torpedo tubes and the heavier AA battery, although DEs for the Royal Navy received no tubes. Thus, the first long-hull ship, the *Buckley*, had two Oerlikons on the 02 level before the bridge, and two more on the 01 level between funnel and torpedo

tubes. It proved easy to add more; the DE was sufficiently stable that weight was no problem, and the long hull provided considerable deck space. In later units, two more were added abeam the funnel, and two more on the 01 level just abaft No. 2 gun, for a total of eight. Later, two more were usually mounted right aft near the depth-charge racks. The shorter hull could accommodate nine Oerlikons (but no torpedo tubes): one on the 02 level superfiring over No. 2 gun, two more on the 02 level (port and starboard), four around the funnel, and two more abaft it; later units often mounted two on the fantail.

As for the main battery, the original 3-in./50 was no more than a compromise between British desires for a dual-purpose weapon available in the United States, and the original U.S. decision for a 4-inch single-purpose weapon that would be available in large numbers. However, there had always been the potential for a 5-inch battery, which Cochrane had provided from the first. By the fall of 1942, concern was being expressed about the weakness of the main battery of the DE, particularly in the face of the strong air opposition to be met in offensive operations near enemy bases. Therefore, in December a shift to 5-inch batteries was undertaken on a "not to delay" basis, with the result that 340 of the existing program of 800 were to get such batteries, together with all 205 of the additional program then being prepared. The number to be converted was limited only by the

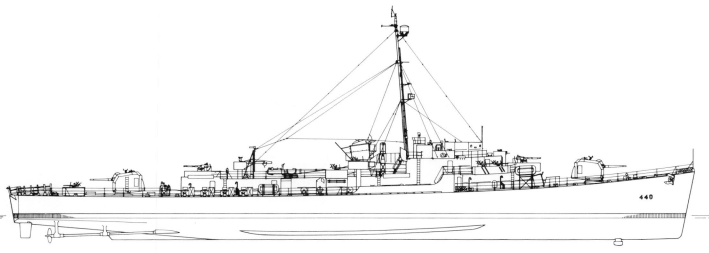

McCoy Reynolds DE 440   July 1944   306′0″ o.a.   *John C. Butler* class(WGT design)—The *Rudderow*-class ships were externally very similar.

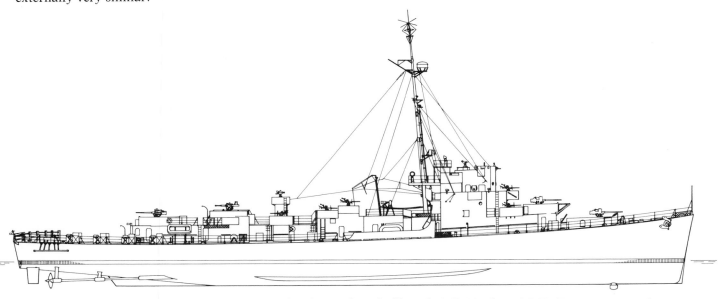

Bebas DE 10   5/44   289′5″ o.a.   *Evarts* class(GMT short hull) with 1.1″ AA aft and HFD/F array at masthead vice air-search radar antenna.

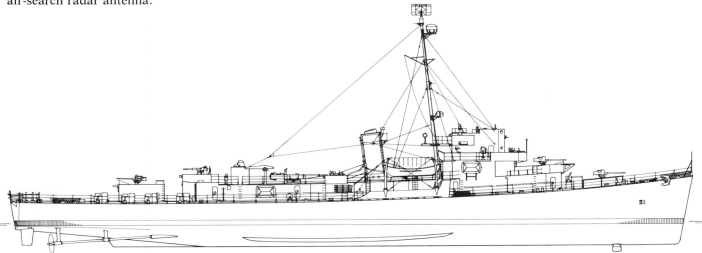

Buckley DE 51   15 May 1943   306′0″ o.a.   *Buckley* class—As initially commissioned. *All* other units of this numerous class received additional 20-mm AA on 01 level abreast centerline 20-mm AA and abreast stack, as well as on the fantail. Most had a quadruple 1.1″ AA mount where the *Buckley* had a twin 40-mm AA. Note the hooded director for the 40-mm mount.

The *Koiner*, a long-hulled diesel destroyer escort (FMR), shows the effects of antiaircraft rearmament in this 24 May 1945 photograph: her original quadruple 1.1-inch gun has been replaced by a quadruple Bofors gun, and two power-operated twin Bofors with Mk 51 directors have replaced her torpedo tubes. The stub mainmast was generally fitted to carry HF/DF, but that does not appear to have been the case for her.

The *Moore*, a long-hulled diesel destroyer escort (FMR), shows the standard late wartime arrangement, in which a separate HF/DF mast was stepped aft (14 May 1944 off New York); earlier, many ships had mounted the HF/DF antenna in place of their air-search radars. She probably still has her triple torpedo tube abaft her four 01-level 20-mm. guns amidships, since no heavier automatic antiaircraft weapons are in evidence there.

requirement that 260 escorts be completed during 1943, and about 720 by the end of 1944, to meet the submarine situation.

Given the obvious superiority of the steam-turbine 24-knot ships, the 5-inch redesign applied only to these types, the TE and the new WGT. In both, the opportunity was taken to revise the bridge design; they received a low bridge similar to that of contemporary *Sumner*-class destroyers. The British-style Asdic hut was eliminated and the open bridge dropped from the 03 to the 02½ level; but captain and helmsman were still separated, as in British practice. A sonar room occupied an after corner of the pilot house. The second twin Bofors planned for the original design was restored, superfiring over No. 1 gun. All four of the forward Oerlikons were mounted at the 01 level, and many ships were completed with the two fantail guns, for a total of ten.

The DE was above all a specialized ASW ship. Although the early design studies called for no more than four depth-charge throwers and two stern tracks (for a 9-charge pattern and a total of 75 charges), the Admiralty wanted twice as many throwers and at least 100 charges; later some British DEs would actually carry twice as many. The detailed Admiralty letter of February 1942 envisaged a 14-charge pattern, a total of 112 charges (8 attacks). Contemporary fleet destroyers, such as the *Fletchers*, carried two fewer throwers and many fewer charges.

Unlike a fleet destroyer, the DE carried a Hedgehog, an ahead-throwing ASW mortar. The Admiralty considered it so important that in requesting the new weapon it was willing to dispense with No. 1 3-inch gun, i.e., with a third of the AAW battery. This proved unnecessary, given the enormous reserve of stability designed into the DE. The Hedgehog was generally mounted just abaft No. 1 gun; in 5-inch DEs the forward gunhouse was cut away to clear it. Standardization required that the after gunhouse be cut away as well. Ammunition for six 24-bomb attacks was provided.

Compared to a fleet destroyer, there was no great difference in underwater sensors between the DE and its larger sister. Indeed, the prewar destroyer allowance of two "searchlight" sonars had to be reduced to one in order to provide enough sonars for the DEs. On the other hand, in 1944 50 British Type 147 depth-finding sonars were allocated to DEs, presumably to improve the accuracy of Hedgehog attacks; no comparable installation was required for the fleet destroyers. Moreover, most DEs were fitted with HF/DF, a vital ASW sensor, which in some cases displaced their air search radars.

With or without 5-inch guns, the DE had little antiship armament apart from her torpedo tubes. By June 1942, surface attack seemed a remote possibility. The British ordered tubes deleted even from long-hull DEs assigned them, even though they retained tubes in their own fleet destroyers converted to ASW. These tubes were intended to launch not torpedoes but one-ton depth charges (Mk X); in British DEs such charges were launched over the stern from spe-

In this 26 June 1944 photograph, the *Runels* (DE 793), a turboelectric destroyer escort (TE), shows an unusual mixture of single Army-type Bofors guns (in place of her torpedo tubes) and a quadruple 1.1-inch machine cannon (her original weapon). The two long trunks to her single combined uptake are also visible; the steam destroyer escorts had separated fire rooms. Pipe guards were necessary for the Bofors guns because they were neither power-operated nor director-controlled, and so had no stops to prevent them from damaging the ship while following an air target. The *Runels* ended the war as a fast transport.

The *Rudderow* was the prototype 5-inch-armed destroyer escort; she is shown newly completed, in July 1944, bearing her torpedo tubes and twin Bofors fore and aft. The cutaway on her after 5-inch gunhouse is clearly visible.

cial rails welded to the deck. The U.S. Navy did retain tubes on its long-hull units, and in the action off Samar, 25 October 1944, U.S. DEs fired their torpedoes to protect escort carriers under attack by the Japanese battle line. In addition, at least one Atlantic DE fired her torpedoes at a surfaced U-boat.

DE production began quite slowly; the first orders were only placed on 1 November 1941 and the first keel not laid until the following February, at Mare Island. By 28 February 1943 only four units had appeared; by way of comparison, in July 1941 the estimate of potential *destroyer* production was 60 in the 18 months ending 31 December 1942, 97 in 1943, and 8 or 9 per month thereafter.

The first 50, ordered for the Admiralty, were followed the next January by an order for 250 U.S. units. All 300 were to be identical, pooled for issue to either Navy. By September another 420 had been ordered, for a total of 720 in the program. That October, President Roosevelt directed BuShips to com-

plete 260 DEs in 1943, and the Maritime Commission another 50 (which ended up as the PF). BuShips found that additional building ways would have to be brought into the program to assure completions at the required level, and therefore ordered 80 more units. On 25 May 1943 VCNO directed that another 205 DEs be built, for a total of 1,005, although all of this last batch as well as many earlier units were subsequently canceled, only 563 being completed.

By 1941 production resources were becoming overloaded, given the very large destroyer orders already issued during 1940. The only remaining labor reserves for shipbuilding were inland on the Great Lakes and in the South, and yards in both areas built a large fraction of the destroyer escort fleet. The first 50 units were assigned to three Navy Yards: Boston (DE 1–12), Mare Island (DE 13–36), and Puget Sound (DE 37–50) but that was decided upon before the outbreak of war and in particular before West Coast yards were flooded with ship repair work.

Aside from armament proper, the most noticeable modification applied to many destroyer escorts in wartime was the enlargement of the sonar room built into the forward part of the upper bridge, as shown here on the short-hull *Deede*, photographed at Mare Island, 21 May 1945. Visible atop her bridge is the Mk 52 3-inch director with its Mk 26 range-only radar behind the range finder.

For mass production, the government built three entirely new yards: one for Bethlehem at Hingham, Massachusetts; one for Brown Shipbuilding at Houston, Texas; and one for Federal at Port Newark, New Jersey. In each case, landing craft orders (LCI(L)) followed and competed with DE construction, some reassignments being necessary. A fourth government-built yard, Consolidated Shipbuilding at Orange, Texas, also built large numbers of DEs. The other private yards brought into the program were Dravo at Wilmington and later at Pittsburgh; Defoe at Bay City, Michigan; Western Pipe and Steel at San Pedro; and Tampa Shipbuilding at Tampa, Florida. There was considerable switching between the yards and between private yards and the DE-building Navy Yards, which ultimately included Charleston, Philadelphia, and Norfolk. On the other hand, ships originally assigned to Newport News (James River) were all transferred to Norfolk.

Although some of these yards had originally built only merchant ships, the DE was designed to naval standards and thus was almost as difficult to build as was a full destroyer. When the Maritime Commission undertook to build escorts, it sought a simplified design more suited to its own mass-production yards. Gibbs & Cox modified the British *River*-class frigate to suit American practice, and detailed specifications were prepared by Kaiser on the West Coast. Production was to be spread between the Great Lakes and two yards on the West Coast, Consolidated at San Pedro, California, and Kaiser at Richmond, California. Later Walsh-Kaiser (Providence, Rhode Island) was added to the program. One production problem was that whereas the new West Coast yards were accustomed to lifting prefabricated sections weighing 40 or 50 tons, the smaller Great Lakes yards (Walter Butler, Globe, Leatham Smith, American Shipbuilding, Froemming) could lift only about 10. Thus, the original West Coast planning had to be redone for the Lakes. In addition, the frigates were unable to pass through the Sault Ste. Marie locks between 15 November and 15 April due to ice; those built on the Great Lakes therefore had to go down the Mississippi, with pontoons to reduce their draft from 13 to just over 8 feet.

Modifications to the original design included a foot more beam for added stability, and length added amidships to relieve congestion in the machinery spaces. The battery was equivalent to that of a DE without torpedo tubes, and the propelling plant was reciprocating steam, which proved to be in relatively short supply. Orders were increased from 50 to 70 and then to 100. However, although in December 1942 69 units had been scheduled for completion during 1943, deliveries did not reach this figure until June 1944. Nevertheless, the program of 96 (4 were canceled) was completed by October 1944. Once momentum was attained, matters went swiftly indeed.*

The same might be said of the DE program itself. Relatively few ships appeared until well into 1943. After that, completions accelerated rapidly; but by May 1943 a great deal had already been done to resolve the ASW crisis that had inspired the crash DE program in the first place. It must be admitted, too, that the program suffered heavily from diversions to other craft, particularly landing craft. For example, in March 1942 the DEs were placed after major surface combatants in priority; by July they were near the top except for landing craft. By October 1943 the DEs of the first series were eighth in priority, and by June 1944 they had dropped to last (thirteenth) place.

Cancellations became necessary just as the DE program reached full speed, with 378 launchings in 1943. The entire final program of 205 ships, all with 5-inch guns, was canceled on 15 September 1943, and further cuts were soon made. The irony was that the ships most subject to cancellation, i.e., the ones least advanced, were also the most satisfactory types, the 24-knot, 5-inch classes. It was necessary to balance off the industrial disruption implicit in canceling ships already well along against the cost to the fleet of operating the unsatisfactory and lightly armed diesel types, particularly in the Pacific. At the end of September, the VCNO wrote Admiral King that

> . . . there is a prospective demand for small attack transports, small bombardment vessels, and AA vessels to relieve destroyers and other more important combatant ships of those duties. For all of these purposes the 5-inch, 24-knot vessel is considered necessary, not only to have adequate gun power, but also to have the mobility and speed essential for the projected operations. It is not possible at this time to stop or convert 3-inch vessels into 5-inch vessels during the building period.

However, ships with 3-inch guns already well advanced would have to be launched merely to clear their slips. Moreover, a mass cancellation of diesel DEs would have a catastrophic effect on manufacturers essential to the augmented landing craft program—which, ironically, had been a major cause of DE cancellations in the first place. Thus, Secretary of the Navy Forrestal feared that the waves of DE

---

*In service, the U.S. frigates were manned by the Coast Guard (as were some destroyer escorts). The Royal Navy received 21 as the *Colony* class. Twenty-eight were transferred to the Soviet Union in 1945. Returned late in 1949, 13 were reacquired and recommissioned for local escort service during the Korean War. Opinion differed as to their success. Morison described them as unbearably hot in the tropics, but one officer recalls them as the most comfortable-riding of any U.S. escorts, thanks, perhaps, to their British (rather than U.S.) stability and seakeeping design standards.

cancellations would arrest the momentum of the program as a whole and lessen the sense of urgency among shop workers and managers.

Attempts were made, therefore, to reduce diesel DE production as much as possible without undue disruption, so that the second wave of 100 cuts (2 October 1943) affected 38 DETs as well as 32 TEVs and 30 WGTs. Another program of 100 cancellations (March 1944) began to affect ships on the slip: 4 GMTs and 4 DETs, but also another 51 TEVs and 41 WGTs. Only the TE and FMR classes were unaffected, and further cuts through September 1944 reduced these classes, finally, to 62 TEVs and 85 WGTs, as against original orders for, respectively, 252 and 293. Finally, two WGTs (DE 541 and 542) were canceled on 7 January 1946.

Thus, it was the least effective DEs that survived the wave of cancellations. Although slow diesel units could not be fitted with more powerful engines, they could be rearmed. In October 1943 the Chief of BuOrd noted that

> Although . . . the urgency of the need for this type of ship for A/S work in the Atlantic is so great that delays in their construction are unacceptable at this time . . . it (is) inevitable that as these ships are released from such operations in the Atlantic, and their employment in the Pacific theaters is taken under consideration, the low gun power of those armed with 3-inch guns will be found to be a severe limitation in such employment—too severe, probably, to permit the use of these ships for operations in which they will be most needed.

However, Cochrane, now a rear admiral and Chief of BuShips, objected that the volume of work involved in conversion of all 3-inch ships would be far too great to permit quick execution.

Admiral King's solution was to defer actual conversion while altering the "ultimate battery" of all DEs to include two 5-inch/38s, so that weapons ordered for the canceled units might be retained for later use in a mass conversion program. The ultimate battery also included a quad Bofors superfiring over No. 2 mount. There would be very little space over No. 1, as the Hedgehog would have to be moved up to clear the new 5-inch/38 there. By December 1944, refit plans had been altered to include two twin Bofors in place of the torpedo tubes. Two single-Army-type Bofors, which took up very little space, were to be mounted just abaft the Hedgehog. Eight 20 mm. were specified.

In the fall of 1944 the expected lead time of the program was 4 months, with a total of 18 months to two years required for completion. In November, Admiral King reduced the total number of units to be converted by eliminating the two least satisfactory classes, the diesel-electric GMT and DET, from the program. They would receive instead improved close-range batteries: quad vice twin Bofors in the GMT, two twin Bofors in place of the torpedo tubes in the DET. Of the other 3-inch DEs, the TE and the FMR, all but those destined for foreign navies and the 20 reserved for special shore-bombardment conversion would be refitted.

In fact, this program was sharply curtailed. Only one FMR, the USS *Camp*, was refitted, following an April 1945 collision. By mid-1945 the TE program had been scaled down to 40 units, which were to be retained in service postwar. However, only 11 (DE 217–219, 678–680, 696–698, 700–701) were done. All of these conversions could be distinguished from their TEV and WGT cousins by their high bridges, Hedgehogs on the 01 level, and prominent funnels.

The *Camp* was the only FMR-class long-hull diesel escort to be rearmed with 5-inch guns in wartime, following collision damage. She is shown off Boston on 25 April 1945, her Hedgehog transplanted to her 01 level forward, replacing the 3-inch gun formerly located there. The *Camp* later became a radar picket, was transferred to the South Vietnamese Navy, and escaped to the Philippines when South Vietnam fell in 1975, surviving as the Philippine Navy *Rajah Lakandula*.

In many cases the 5-inch ships adopted, on refit, the quad Bofors aft.

Routine wartime armament changes to the basic DE design were relatively minor. In common with other escorts operating in the Mediterranean, two FMRs, the *Frederick C. Davis* (DE 136) and *Herbert C. Jones* (DE 137), were rearmed early in 1944 with two single Army-type Bofors in place of their torpedo tubes. At least in the case of the *Davis*, this modification was intended to improve her antiaircraft firepower in defense of such ports as Anzio; she also had missile-jamming equipment. By May she had four Bofors guns amidships, and the modification spread to many other ships. Thus, in June the "temporary approved" battery of all "long-hull" DEs—other than those scheduled for conversion to fast transports or those transferred to the British, French, and Brazilian navies—was altered to include four single 40 mm. and no torpedo tubes. In October, this was further amended: when available, two twin (power-operated) Bofors would replace the four single mounts. The change was more important than it may have appeared, in that the twin mounts were director-controlled.

The last units to be completed incorporated the new battery. Thus, six 5-inch (WGT) units (DE 448–450, 510, 537–538, the last of their class, completed in 1945) had a quadruple Bofors aft, three twin Bofors, and ten single 20 mm. Four TEs completed in 1944 (DE 575–578) had the four single 40 mm. Finally, two WGTs completed late in 1944 had no tubes but also no additional light armament (DE 371–372). Ironically, the only major combat use of DE torpedoes came in the epic battle off Samar, well *after* the decision to abandon these weapons.

Quite early in the DE program it became evident that there would be more DEs than were necessary to meet ASW requirements. Therefore, in July 1943 the VCNO asked BuShips for suggestions, perhaps in collaboration with the Admiralty, for alternative roles for these robust, stable hulls. Entirely abortive studies concerned a conversion as an amphibious command ship (AGC) or as a mine-layer, the latter as an alternative to a *Fletcher* or 1,850-tonner conversion. In each case the DE had grossly insufficient stability or internal space: it was just too small. However, other ideas proceeded to or beyond the point of conversion.

One was a long-hull DE rearmed with three 5-inch guns for landing fire support or for shore bombardment. This AA/bombardment ship would also mount one quad and twin 40 mm. and eight 20 mm., and would have a Mk 33 fire control system, comparable to that of early treaty destroyers. Its ASW battery would be reduced essentially to that of a destroyer: four throwers and two depth-charge tracks, but no Hedgehog. Alternative schemes restricted to low-angle fire (five submarine-type 5-inch/25 or 105-mm. Army howitzers, two twin Bofors, two twin 20 mm.) were rejected because of the increasingly evident value of plunging fire in shore bombardment.

By October 1943, the DP variant was being considered within OpNav, and in November it was approved by Admiral King, who required the retention of some ASW capability (sound gear and at least two depth-charge tracks); he directed the bureaus to proceed with development and planning on the basis of a conversion run of 20 units. A year later he ordered preparations made for conversion at East Coast yards, not to begin before 1 February 1945, with DEs to be

The *Bassett*, a TE converted to a fast transport, is shown in June 1951. These ships could be distinguished from the TEV conversions by their lattice kingposts aft and their high bridges. Both types retained only a minimal ASW capability in their depth-charge tracks aft and their sonars.

released to the program upon the defeat of Germany. However, the entire program was canceled on 14 May 1945, just as the ships were released; by then other roles, such as the radar picket, were far more important for the Pacific.

A fast transport conversion (APD) proved far more successful. In his September 1943 letter the VCNO had suggested the conversion on the slip of 100 DEs to APDs and bombardment ships, to avoid the cancellation of a further 100 units (from 700 to 600); he was overruled, but studies of an APD conversion proceeded. Thus, in October sketch plans were drawn for alternative conversions of DEs and frigates (PF) as troop carriers, on the basis that nine ships should be able to transport a reinforced battalion lightly equipped. Each would, then, carry 10 officers and 150 men, four LCVPs, six quarter-ton trucks, two 1-ton trucks, four ammunition carts, four pack howitzers, and 6,000 cubic feet of ammunition, 3,500 of general cargo—and 1,000 of gasoline. The mission envisaged was the seizure of a small island or a beachhead with a maximum depth of three miles, to be held in each case for up to two weeks. Both classes appeared suitable, the PF requiring two additional deck houses to accommodate the troops. There the matter stood until the next March (1944), when Admiral King asked for detailed conversion plans incorporating a more powerful battery; the PF was rejected due to excessive trim by the stern and poor stability.

However, the DE project proceeded, almost 100 ships being converted. Plans for TEs and WGTs were drawn, a TEV conversion also being feasible. Both showed a much enlarged deckhouse, provision for four LCVPs in davits, and removal of all 3-inch guns

as well as the Hedgehog and the depth-charge throwers. The APDs would be armed with a single 5-inch/38 forward, as well as with three twin Bofors and six 20 mm. The fantail would be cleared for cargo stowage, served by a pair of 5-ton booms, and gasoline would be stowed between the remaining pair of depth-charge tracks.

Admiral King approved 50 TE conversions (APD 37–86) on 17 May 1944, including 6 ships (DE 668–673) still under construction. The others were to be provided at New York (1 ship per month) and Philadelphia (four per month) beginning 1 July. Meanwhile, BuShips considered the conversion of 50 TEVs or WGTs as part of an additional reduction in the DE program; the TEV plan involved laying fewer entirely new keels and was therefore adopted for APD 87–136. In the event, five TE conversions were canceled (DE 214, 665, 666, 790, 791 were selected for radar picket conversion and so did not become APD 64, 67, 68, 82, and 83). Four additional conversions (3 TEVs DE 684, 685, 709, and one TE, DE 637) were ordered in 1945 in partial replacement for units scheduled for radar picket duty rather than APD conversion; however, two were never done (DE 684, 685 as APD 137 and 138); DE 709 became APD 139 to end the series. DE 637 became APD 40.

Of the 95 units converted, one (APD 47) was sunk off Okinawa, where two more (APD 54 and 58) were so badly damaged that they were scrapped in 1946. The last three active units in U.S. service were not decommissioned until 1969, although as early as 1945 the Comstock Board evaluated the APD as very limited in capability. Were it not for the great number of APDs that had survived the war, the absence of any postwar construction might be taken as confir-

The *Kleinsmith* was a typical TEV conversion. This basic design, with internal volume added amidships, was later adapted for destroyer escorts converted to radar pickets.

At Mare Island on 7 March 1946, the converted TEV-class destroyer escort *Gosselin* (above and facing) makes a nice contrast with a partly stripped (and unidentified) TEV-class destroyer escort alongside, the latter showing both her HF/DF mast and her torpedo tubes. Changes in the *Gosselin* are circled: fore to aft, they include a range finder forward of her bridge and a Mk 52 director atop it. The difference in bridge arrangement between the two ships is evident, the TEV having an extended wheelhouse with, presumably, an enlarged sonar room. In contrast to the converted flush deckers, these former destroyer escorts carried LCVP landing craft, capable of carrying vehicles, which could be loaded from the empty fantail by means of twin booms. The tall radome atop *Gosselin*'s foremast carries an SU surface-search radar, with the usual SA for air search above that.

mation of this view. However, postwar plans show that the APD was considered essential as a means of moving advance parties into the area scheduled for amphibious assault; the later amphibious assault submarine (LPSS) did not have nearly the capacity of an APD. The APD could also act as an AAW and ASW escort for a fast amphibious convoy. Even so, it is possible to view the entire APD program as little more than an attempt to make use of a robust, stable, high-powered hull whose primary function was rapidly receding. It may, then, be significant that of the APDs presently in foreign service many serve as escorts rather than as fast transports, having been reconverted to their original role.

Seven served as flagships: two for UDT teams in 1945 (APD 55 and 86); APD 63 was permanent flagship of an APD division at this time. Four more conversions of 1953–54 (APD 101, 128, 130, and 132) were intended for landing-ship flotilla commanders and transport squadron commanders. Troop and cargo

capacity were reduced; in all but the *Knudson* (APD 101) a twin (APD 55) or quad Bofors replaced the crane on the fantail. A planned conversion of the *Wantuck* (APD 125) appears not to have been carried out.

Although they had only depth-charge tracks, the APDs did retain their sonars, and hence a residual value for general ASW mobilization. Two of them were fitted with a pair of short (Mk 32) torpedo tubes during the sixties. More effective ASW batteries had been proposed but rejected in the early fifties: this CIP alteration would have involved scanning sonar, an attack director, and a launching system for lightweight torpedoes.

Four TEs were refitted with large cable reels amidships as emergency power plants, largely to support Pacific amphibious operations. They were carried on Navy lists as TEGs, although their type symbol was not changed from DE. As late as 1960 three (DE 634, *Whitehurst*, 667, *Wiseman*, and 699,

Four TE-class escorts were converted to serve as floating powerplants, with large cable reels amidships, to support Pacific amphibious operations: this is the *Marsh*, still active on 25 August 1959, with an extended bridge, depth-charge throwers aft, and no 20-mm. guns.

Marsh) were still in use as Naval Reserve ships; the fourth, DE 59, the *Foss*, was in reserve.

The postwar disposition of the DE classes gives some idea of their relative perceived value. Almost immediately after the end of hostilities, all of the short-hull GMTs were sold out of the service, two being transferred to Nationalist China. Most of the other unsatisfactory class, the DETs, were placed on the sale list. Badly damaged units of other classes (3 TEs, 1 TEV, 1 WGT) were scrapped. In 1946 the active postwar fleet included 31 TEs and six TE radar picket conversions (see chapter 10); in addition, two DETs and two TEs were in semireserve as Naval Reserve training ships. All of the 5-inch ships completed in that form were laid up, as well as all of the FMRs. The many units (32 GMTs, 46 TEs) lent to the Royal Navy under Lend-Lease were returned for scrapping, and the ranks of the TE and TEV classes had been depleted further by APD conversions. Thus, there remained a total of 50 TEs, 20 TEVs, 79 WGTs, 81 FMRs, and 57 DETs.

In 1950, after several transfers, only 9 DETs remained on the Navy list; another 44 were up for disposal. As late as 1957 they were the only type the U.S. Navy was willing to transfer to foreign fleets. In 1944, eight were transferred to Brazil and another six to France (plus eight more in 1950). Four went to China (1949), four to Greece (1951), six to the Neth-

erlands (1950–51), three to Italy (1951), three to Peru (1952), two to Uruguay (1951), two to Japan (1955), two to South Korea (1956), one to Thailand (1959), and one to the Philippines (1968). In 1952 only 18 that were still on the disposal list were restored to the reserve fleet. By way of contrast, the only WGT transfers were two units that went to Portugal in 1957; the only TEV transfers were one to South Korea (1963) and one to Taiwan (1968). One FMR went to Mexico (1973).

Their relatively low ratio of firepower to personnel doomed most of the DEs to the reserve fleet; they were carried in naval calculations as a mobilization resource. On the other hand, the simplicity of DE machinery as compared to that of the DD made the former preferable for Naval Reserve duty. Thus, by 1950 the force had been reduced to 10 active TEs, plus 17 NRT ships (2 TEs, 3 TEVs, 6 each of WGT and DET). These numbers were scheduled for further reductions in FY 51, but the Korean War intervened and many (32 WGTs, 4 FMRs, 7 TEs, 3 TEVs, 2 TEGs, 4 ASW mobilization prototypes, and the NRT ships) were recommissioned. In addition 12 FMRs were loaned to the Coast Guard (1950–54), 6 as weather ships and 6 for search and rescue in the Pacific in support of Korean War operations. Several were later converted to DERs. In 1960 only one TE and two FMRs served with fleet units; another 28 DEs trained reservists (8 TEs, 4 TEVs, 11 WGTs, 2 DETs, 3 FMRs). Mass scrappings of ships remaining in reserve began five years later; the last World War II-built DEs were stricken in 1973, leaving only DERs on the Navy list.

An evaluation of the World War II DE as a ship and as an ASW escort is difficult at best. The destroyer escorts were known as heavy rollers, but also as good sea boats, at least in U.S. service. In November 1945, a board chaired by Commodore Merrill Comstock was convened by the CinC Pacific to report on lessons of the Pacific War as they applied to ship and aircraft types. It found the DEs, particularly the diesel types, too slow to combat the newest types of submarine, i.e., the German Type 21/26; a margin of 5 knots over both surfaced and submerged speeds was required. Other points included the great value of open bridges (TE, FMR, DET) as opposed to closed (WGT, TEV), which is why the TEs were the ones to be retained in the postwar active fleet; the need for 5-inch guns in power-driven mounts; the need for a new sonar; "the feasibility of using gas turbines for the main propulsion should be further considered." The board's reasoning in the last case is not clear, but it may be that it found the high power density of a gas turbine attractive for a small ship. Finally, the Comstock Board recommended as basic characteristics for a postwar DE two twin 5-inch DPs (fore and aft), six quadruple Bofors, the latest sonar, 28 knots fully loaded, and an endurance of 3,000 miles at 18 knots. The emphasis on AA fire, and the lack of specific guidance as to ASW weapons, suggest both the conditions of the Pacific (as opposed to the Atlantic) war and the state of flux of ASW in 1945.

Postwar, both high and low bridges came in for intense criticism. The high bridge:

a) Gave a poor vantage for conning the ship in restricted situations (in part because of the absence of bridge wings).

b) Required reliance on voice tubes for engine and helm orders.

c) Had peloruses poorly located relative to the open bridge.

d) Prevented free access between pilot house and open bridge.

e) Made it impossible for personnel on the bridge to see the extreme bow of the ship.

f) Made for many falls because of the three distinct levels of grating.

g) Had no satisfactory plot for piloting in bad weather.

h) Was over-crowded; present sonar space was awkward.

The low bridge was considered only marginally better.

British experience of DE operations is interesting because British commanders were able to compare the U.S. type with contemporary corvettes and frigates. Initial impressions were favorable. Thus, a member of the British Director of Naval Construction (DNC) Department visiting HMS *Bayntun*, the first DE to arrive in Britain, commented that

> The ship is generally excellently designed and fitted out, though naturally the American practice in many respects differs considerably from our own. For example, for convoy escort work the gun armament appears light for attacking U-boats, being essentially AA in character. Except for A gun on the forecastle, the guns are very well situated and could be fought in any weather. Ammunition supply arrangements from the magazine are generally poor, but this is overcome by a good R.U. [Ready Use] supply near the guns. A Hedgehog is situated immediately behind A gun, but an unexpected difficulty arises through the ejected cartridge cases from A gun when firing on a forward bearing fouling the spigots or ammunition of the Hedgehog. The quarter deck is very well arranged for astern depth charge attacks.
>
> The most striking feature in the hull design is the large beam to draught ratio for the relatively light armament. This has resulted in a comparatively large initial GM for the size of vessel and a resulting tendency for excessive rolling . . . [which] may prove an unpopular feature of this class. . . .
>
> The bridge was well designed but was stated to be very draughty. . . .

However, according to the captain of HMS *Duckworth*, a TE,

> They are agreeably dry in most weather and after riding out a sharp North Atlantic gale I can report that there seems to be small risk of weather damage. . . . In fact the ships behave like corks.
>
> On the other hand they cannot be driven anywhere within 4 points of the sea at above 10 knots in the prevailing short steep seas of the North Atlantic. In a large swell they ride very well but a special reduction such as above in ships operating as a support group seems a big handicap.
>
> Rolling—since this report is written at sea it is difficult to describe with reticence the nauseating movement of these vessels in the open sea. . . .
>
> The violent "lurching" is the principal controlling factor in efficiency. As gun platforms these ships are satisfactory only under the most favorable weather. . . .
>
> Depth charge reloading is possible in a moderately heavy sea pounding the ship. . . . Under average conditions however it must be an even bet whether the throwers lob their charges vertically upwards and on to the quarter deck or immediately alongside propellers. . . .
>
> Limitations on speed and course to windward impose a severe limitation on depth charge attacks whilst the Hedgehog is inaccurate in a short head swell on account of the unpredictable roll and the resultant tilt.

Built presumably in the principle of "Never repair, sink or replace," these ships present no problem at all as to damage control. There is none.

All main electric power cables run along the ship's side, as do all store-rooms. Shoring would be impossible in most spaces and this drawback may be particularly exasperating if a near bomb miss or shell splinter penetrates the hull. There is no proper pumping line. Incidentally there is no lifeboat either but American life jackets are better than ours.

There is no emergency power supply.

Everyone knows a 3-inch projectile will not put a dent in a pat of butter and after my regrettable battle with U.S.S.S. *Bluejacket* I heartily endorse the views on this subject expressed by sub officers in the Mediterranean.

Pending change of armament proposals . . . the following is urgently required:
—Some form of splinter shield as protection for gun's crews against effect of own blast and enemy's Oerlikon fire.
—Some simple Eversheds director for night action to prevent trainer being blinded by gun flash. . . .
—Flashless ammunition. . . .

It is unenviable to serve on a ship on which all hands are hoping for a draft note.

It is influenced by excessive and uncontrollable rolling which is a factor which obscures every virtue these ships may possess. It cannot be urged too strongly before the "market is flooded," that all the most strenuous measures be taken to mitigate this overwhelming defect in all vessels of this class.

Similarly, Captain (D) at Belfast wrote in October 1943 that

Commanding Officers of both types of Captain Class Frigates are unanimous in their complaints about the rapid rolling of these ships. The quickness of the recovery not only causes physical exhaustion but makes the efficient operating of weapons and instruments most difficult. It has contributed largely to the defects experienced with the gyro compass. . . . the rapidity of the roll appears to be due to the lack of topweight. . . . It is estimated that those Captain Class Frigates could carry an additional 40 tons at superstructure deck levels, which would greatly improve their performance. It is submitted that topweight should be added in the form of additional armament and gun control units, such as a Gun Director and range finder on the bridge, which were included in the original plans, and Unicorns and additional AA guns on the superstructure deck. . . .

The motion of Captain Class Frigates in a seaway, though not excessive in extent, is so violent in character as to be a menace to life and limb, to equipment and property, to seasoned stomachs, and to normally equable nerves and tempers. Morale cannot fail to be affected. Fighting efficiency will certainly suffer. . . .

The (British) Director of Naval Construction suspected that "the trouble is due to the rapid recovery from large angles of roll," i.e., the large GM due to a substantial reduction in top weight relative to the original design. "In Atlantic Winter, the most prevalent sea has a length of 200–300 feet. According to reliable measurements, this sea will occur in about 32 percent of the gales. A sea of 200–300 feet length has a period of 6½ to 7½ seconds, which is the period of roll of the BDE and DE's. In order to minimize the probability of synchronism, therefore, it is essential to lengthen the period to over 8 seconds. . . ." by reducing the GM or by increasing the radius of gyration "by winging all weights possible." Reductions in GM were unattractive, given the usual loss of stability with age.

The DNC concluded that

the principal cause of this violent motion is the inadequacy of the bilge keels and action is being taken in vessels already delivered to lengthen the existing bilge keels by extending them aft to 120 frame and increase depth to 24 inches. . . . In view of the severely taxed repair facilities in this country, it is hoped that the American authorities will agree to carrying out this work in America in ships not yet handed over.

Other elements of a short-term policy were to increase the number of depth charges carried on deck to 160, and even to fit upper deck ballast, both of which would reduce metacentric height. In addition, all ammunition would be removed from the after magazine and stowed forward. This was primarily an anti-GNAT (homing torpedo) measure, but did serve to reduce GM. A 4-inch twin mount aft was suggested, as a further addition of top weight, but only 140 rounds could be carried.

This suggestion was possibly part of a long-term plan that would cure the armament deficiencies of the DE as perceived by the Royal Navy. Proposals included the replacement of the 3-in./50 DP guns by 4.7-inch weapons and the installation of torpedo tubes eliminated at Admiralty behest, to enable the DE to fire the one-ton Mk X depth charge. Ultimately the DNC proposed as his long-term policy to fit twin 4-inch guns in lieu of the 3-inch DP already mounted; to fit Squid in place of No. 2 gun, and land the Hedgehog; and to fit six twin and four single Oerlikons. Some of the 16 ten-charge patterns might be landed in view of the effectiveness of the Squid.

In December 1943, the Royal Navy seriously considered re-equipping its DEs as specialized ASW and AAW escorts. The ASW version would be armed with a double Squid with ammunition for 24 salvos (in place of No. 2 gun), and would have a pair of 4-inch guns in place of the remaining pair of 3-inch. British search (144) and depth-determining sonar (Asdic 147B) would be fitted. Quite soon the alterations were cut to sonar refit, addition of 2-inch rocket flare launchers, replacement of SL by SU radar, and CIC (AIO in

British parlance) modernization. The AA version was to have had three 5-inch DP guns (Mk 50 director), three twin Bofors, four single Oerlikons, and an Asdic 128D for self-defense. In compensation, depth-charge armament would be reduced to 12 charges plus two throwers and one rail, i.e., three S-charge patterns.

All of these radical proposals fell afoul the problem of congestion in the yards and the pressing need for North Atlantic escorts. Moreover, the British DEs were far too advanced in U.S. yards for them to receive the deeper bilge keels in the United States: that project further congested the British yards. It was, however, quite successful.

For example, HMS *Goodall* was fitted with the new keels at Harland & Wolff in February 1944:

the violence of roll has been most noticeably reduced, now ship rolls comparatively slowly and from observations appears to be much steadier than a CASTLE Class Corvette. . . . How much of this improvement is due to the upper deck stowage of Depth Charges is not known.

Similarly, the captain of HMS *Grindall* reported upon conversion to "British standards" that

the excessive rolling formerly experienced has been completely eliminated and provides a much steadier gun platform. There is no vibration. The turning circle has been increased with much more heel than before but this has had no effect on steering capabilities. Pounding reduced fore and aft. Care must be taken in a moderate head sea at speeds above 16 knots as the bow does not rise to the sea as it did before. I was extremely pleased . . . and consider the conversion of great benefit to both sea going and fighting efficiency.

The U.S. Navy, responsible for these ships, was not entirely in sympathy with the British. Thus, a Captain Burris of BuShips visited England in January 1944 to discuss defects in the DEs of the Royal Navy. He felt that the Admiralty's insistence on removing the torpedo tubes was the problem, stating that the U.S. Navy had received no complaints of excessive motion; however, British constructors calculated that fitting the tubes would add only 0.16 seconds to the period of roll; moreover, Admiral Cochrane had stated that the problem was the decision not to mount 5-inch guns. For his part, presumably based on U.S. experience, Captain Burris "stated that the diesel-electric ships would be a constant source of worry and maintenance, but that the turbo-electric ships would be all right."

As the congestion in their yards cleared in 1944/45 the British were finally able to convert some of their DEs for special duties as light craft headquarters, as fighter-director ships (where the lack of 5-inch guns was sorely felt), and as mobile generator ships. The details of these conversions are beyond the scope of this book.

Late in World War II, 50 sets of British Type 147B depth-determining sonar were obtained for installation in DEs, applying at least to TE and TEV classes. In addition, some high-bridge ships were fitted with enlarged sonar rooms, visible as extensions at the front of the bridge structure. No similar expansion was possible in a low-bridge DE, in which the sound room was built into the side of the pilot house.

In 1947 four 5-inch TEs (DE 217, 218, 697, 700) were modified for improved ASW efficiency (Ship Improvement Guide project 232), with a new open bridge on the 02 level surrounding the former pilot house, incorporating a 4-foot bulkhead, a windshield, and a canvas canopy. A trainable Hedgehog replaced the former fixed type. Similar bridge modifications were made in the low-bridge DE 414 (SIG 232), 532 (SCB 63 ASW reconstruction), and 535 (SCB 63A).

Those DEs that survived the postwar scrapping were retained largely as a mobilization reserve. From 1952 on, the SCB prepared Class Improvement Plans (CIPs) for them on the assumption that

(a) They would provide the bulk of transoceanic escorts on the outbreak of war.

(b) It would be infeasible to convert these old units of limited speed to modern ASW units.

(c) ASW would take priority over AAW improvements.

(d) Since the CIPs would not take effect except in the event of extensive mobilization, the CIPs could include weapons and sensors that might not as yet be beyond the early development stage.

In general, the CIPs called for power-operated 3-in./50 guns (Mk 26) in place of the 3-in./50 Mk 22 fitted to the 3-inch DEs; for two fixed Hedgehogs in place of the original one (e.g., on the 01 level as in contemporary destroyer refits); for Fanfare in place of the wartime Foxer; for a launcher for three light-weight ASW torpedoes; for an Attack Director and Computer for ASW attacks; for an emergency generator; and for better sensors: new air search (SPS-16) and surface search radars (SPS-5), and a new attack sonar (SQG-11 or -11A) and a depth scanner (SQR-4). The existing battery of two depth-charge tracks and eight projectors was to be adapted for automatic laying of a 19-charge pattern. In effect this would be an austere SCB 63A, in which all or most of the Bofors guns would be retained.

Classes differed in detail. For example, SQS-4 or SQS-5 with DMCC was specified for the TEs. By 1954 it was expected that the 5-inch DE would be fitted with a trainable Hedgehog (Mk 15) in the superfiring position forward; thus the ultimate automatic battery of the 5-inch TE, for example, was set at one quadruple and two twin Bofors. Weight and moment compensation was a constant problem. One solution, in the 3-inch DEs, was cancellation of the ultimate 5-inch battery, for which weight and moment had been reserved.

Few were so modified. In 1960, for example, only three TEGs, four FMRs, one DET, and two TEs had the dual Hedgehogs. The analogous (and more effective) installation of a Mk 15 trainable Hedgehog in a 5-inch ship extended, beyond the special conversions, to 12 WGTs, 3 TEVs, and 4 more 5-inch TEs (DE 219, 679, 680, 696).

By 1960 Class Improvement Plans called for SQS-4 and the Mk 105 fire control system in all DEs, to control two triple Mk 32 torpedo tubes, a single depth-charge track aft, and the improved Hedgehog battery. Light automatic weapons were to be cut to one twin Bofors or, in a few cases (ASW conversions, ex-DER, TEG), entirely eliminated.

By 1956 the air search radar had become a serious problem. SPS-16 had failed its evaluation, and there existed no current or prospective radar comparable in weight to the old SA—which would soon have to be replaced as worn out. SPS-6, the standard destroyer radar, was twice its weight, and in any case stocks were exhausted. Were it to be fitted, weight compensation would probably require removal of a depth-charge track and perhaps a twin Bofors. It seemed preferable to dispense with air search in what was, after all, primarily an ASW ship.

The large reserve fleet was subject to limited improvement. For example, under a program terminated in FY 59, 105 ASW ships, including many DEs, were modernized to the extent of receiving new scanning sonars and minimum communications (UHF) and IFF systems. Interest in the improvement of the reserve fleet revived in 1963 when Op-423 requested a study of the emergency modernization of the reserve DEs and of the conversion of 220-foot fleet minesweepers to emergency ASW escorts. DE modernization schemes were as follows:

I	II	III
Retain one 3-inch or 5-inch gun, GFCS		
SQS-4 (RDT)	SQS-23	As II but 28–29 knots
Mk 108 or Mk 10/11	ASROC	
2 Mk 32 TT	2 Mk 32 TT	
Mk 105 UBFCS	Mk 114 UBFCS	
Aspect	Aspect	

In fact, by this time the large DE force was too elderly to be attractive as a mobilization reserve, and the ambitious modernization plan was never implemented. Probably the last serious attempt to provide

the old DEs with effective ASW batteries was the plan to arm the *Calcaterra* (DER 390) with long-range homing torpedoes to match the capabilities of the SQS-20 sonar planned for her under the FRAM program.

The postwar Navy continued to see the DE hull as valuable for amphibious operations, particularly in view of the postwar policy to increase the speed of amphibious forces to 15 and then 20 knots. This meant, among other things, that the former close support ships (LSMR, a converted landing type) were no longer suitable; in 1948 the conversion of an APD to fire shore-bombardment rockets was suggested. Ultimately a special ship, the *Carronade* (IFS) was produced instead. However, it cost so much that it could not be duplicated, and subsequent fire-support projects foundered. Yet another amphibious role was filled by three DECs, Destroyer Escorts (Control), two TEs (DE 704, *Cronin*, and 705, *Frybarger*) and one 5-inch TE (DE 698, *Raby*) employed with amphibious forces. This role turned out to be short-lived: commissioned from reserve in 1950–51 with added communications gear, they were returned to reserve in 1953–54. The DEC designation was itself abolished in 1957. By this time the DEC had been replaced by the APD flagships.

The destroyer escort was designed for limited wartime service and for mass production, and many of its shortcomings can be traced to the fact that it succeeded so well at its primary purposes that it was pressed into services for which it had not been intended. It was above all robust, relatively simple to operate, and serviceable. Thus, postwar, DEs proved well suited to the needs of the minor naval powers and to those of the Naval Reserve; even in 1980 there remain 15 DEs, 23 APDs (9 of them converted back into escorts by Taiwan), and 2 of the former DERs in foreign service; a third DER captured by the North Vietnamese when they overran Saigon in 1975 does not appear to have been restored to service. However, the austerity designed into the destroyer escort limited its postwar usefulness from a U.S. point of view. Even the fast DEs did not have a sufficient margin of speed to cope with the new generation of fast submarines modeled on the German Type 21, nor did they have reserves of volume sufficient to permit ASW modernization comparable to that applied to the large destroyers of the *Fletcher* and *Sumner-Gearing* types. The few modernizations actually carried out were more an attempt to provide against mobilization requirements than an approach to creating an effective standing postwar ASW force. In this sense the vast fleet of DEs remaining after 1946 were almost more an embarrassment than an asset, in that their existence discouraged Congress from providing for more effective escorts.

The DE program is probably most interesting historically as an example of an attempt to achieve large numbers by sacrificing unit quality, by deliberately building "low-end" ships. The lesson to be learned is somewhat obscured by the lengthy delays in the decision to build DEs in the first place. By the time a decision had actually been made, material and such subsystems as engines, which had been relatively plentiful at the time of design, were in very short supply, and the DE program had become a direct competitor with other defense programs. This was only an example of the general competition for scarce resources that any mobilization engenders; the DE program in particular was hindered by numerous shifts in the relative priorities accorded various naval and non-naval programs. The end result was lengthy delays, so that DEs did not enter service until the crisis of the antisubmarine war, which they had been built to fight, had passed. In consequence the program began to be curtailed at almost the same time that the first units became operational.

Curtailment was quite as complex as the initiation of the program had been. The firms building DEs were an important element of the naval industrial base, and the Navy could not afford to ruin them by sudden elimination of existing orders; much of the specialized material for those orders was already in the pipeline. There was also concern that workers who had been urged to build DEs as fast as possible would become badly demoralized as the same hulls were canceled. They had to retain their momentum, as the builders were switched to the landing craft and other programs. Thus, much effort went into finding alternative uses for the DE hull, the APD program being by far the most successful. The austerity built into the DE (in order to promote mass production) was a major problem, as there was little or no internal space available, given the relatively bulky powerplants that had been accepted. Nor was there sufficient margin of stability to accept major additions of top weight such as mines. These limitations had consequences for the war program as a whole. For example, because DEs (and PFs) were unsuited to conversion into amphibious flagships, the very successful *Campbell*-class Coast Guard cutters had to be withdrawn from duty as Atlantic convoy flagships, and 1,850-ton destroyers withdrawn from the Pacific in their place. The unsuitability of the DE for minelaying meant that new *Sumner*-class destroyers had to be converted instead, and these same hulls were not available as ASW platforms postwar.

DE production experience can also be read as an object lesson in the pointlessness of austere designs for mobilization. In World War I the Bureau of Construction and Repair successfully opposed an attempt to build a new type of austere ASW destroyer on the ground that planning and design work in itself

would so delay the new type that existing (and more complex) ships could be built far faster. In 1941 the Bureau of Ships used a similar argument but failed to convince the President, and the DEs were ordered. There were significant delays as designs were developed, and it can be argued that the bureau was correct in its preference for a slightly redesigned 1,620-tonner for "sea control." This experience was read postwar as indicating that although time and money might be saved by austerity, it was necessary to build mobilization prototypes in advance of any emergency. The *Dealey* and *Claud Jones* classes resulted. Unfortunately, their relatively unimpressive characteristics, necessitated by the mobilization requirement, made them very unpopular.

Probably the chief irony of DE production was that the last ships were by far the most satisfactory, as the general growth of U.S. war production made some of the early sacrifices unnecessary. However, it was precisely these more satisfactory units that had to be canceled in great numbers. The mass-production character of the program made major improvements in earlier ships, ships still under construction, almost impossible, and there was never enough yard capacity to modify these earlier units. Postwar, the limitations of the DE hull precluded major refits, although many units (including some in reserve) did have ASW refits, which maintained them as mobilization resources.

Comment on the seagoing characteristics of the DE is relatively sparse. In U.S. service they were known as bad rollers, although no U.S. writer has ever been nearly as negative as the British captains quoted earlier. It is conceivable that part of the difference lies in the fact that the Royal Navy escorted convoys in the North Atlantic, whereas U.S. convoy activity (particularly late in the war) was concentrated in the Central Atlantic. In addition, most U.S. DE officers had little experience of other destroyer or escort types, and so tended to accept the behavior of their ships, whereas British officers, particularly senior ones, tended to have a wide spectrum of experience that would have made them more aware of comparative seagoing behavior.

The verdict, then, if there is to be one, is that the DE was unfortunate in the timing of its program. Had it appeared in numbers a year earlier than was the case, it would have made a decisive contribution to the Battle of the Atlantic, and it would have been so superior to existing escorts that it would have received universal praise. Coming when it did, the DE was liked well enough but was sometimes more of an embarrassment than an asset; and its numbers had important—and perhaps unfortunate—consequences postwar, conferring a misplaced confidence in U.S. abilities to counter large-scale Soviet submarine operations.

8

Destroyer Warfare, 1941–1945

It is impossible to do justice to the war the destroyer force fought during World War II in a design and policy history such as the present volume, but some of the experience of that war had so strong an effect on subsequent destroyer design policy that it must be described in some detail. It should be emphasized that the examples that follow by no means constitute a balanced history of U.S. destroyer operations in World War II. Many of them are taken from the wartime series of "Battle Experience" accounts of engagements in the Pacific issued by the Headquarters, U.S. Fleet (COMINCH), incorporating commentary both by COMINCH and by the commanders of subordinate ships and units.

The destroyer force that fought World War II had three principal components: the surviving "flush deckers," most of which could best be lumped with the destroyer escorts and which were primarily ASW and rear-area escorts; the 1,500- and 1,620/1,630-ton "treaty" and post-treaty destroyers; and the *Fletcher*s and *Sumner/Gearing*s. The high-forecastle 1,500/1,630-tonners were better sea boats than the later units and thus were far better suited to Atlantic conditions; on the other hand, the large destroyers could absorb far more battle damage and had much more powerful antiaircraft batteries. Throughout the war, the demand for destroyers was so great that very little difference in employment can be discerned between the treaty and the later destroyers in the Pacific, even though only the *Sims* and later classes had fully effective antiaircraft batteries. However, the *Fletcher*s dominated the destroyer force by the sheer weight of their numbers. For example, it was the *Fletcher*s that formed the squadron of "Little Beavers" led by Arleigh ("31-knot") Burke, it was *Fletcher*s that delivered perfect torpedo attacks at Surigao Strait, and it was *Fletcher*s that drove back the Japanese battle line off Samar in probably the most famous (and surely the most heroic) of all American destroyer actions of the war. By 1945 *Fletcher*s and *Sumner*s predominated to such an extent that most of the destroyer pickets off Okinawa belonged to these two classes. Postwar, so many destroyer officers had had very satisfactory experiences in the *Fletcher* class that these ships became the model for future development. The earlier highforecastle types, except for the destroyer minesweepers, were soon reduced to reserve, and they were little referred to after the war. It seems at least possible that the much larger *Fletcher*s were so much roomier that there was no comparison; moreover, in the Pacific, which was by far the dominant theater, the effect of low freeboard in a *Fletcher* or *Sumner* was less important than in the Atlantic.

Throughout the war the destroyer force was generally organized into nine-ship squadrons (DesRons) consisting of a leader and two four-ship divisions (DesDivs); the leader (flagship) was one unit of a five-ship DesDiv. The four-ship DesDiv was the basic tactical unit, many DesRons not operating as such in combat. In 1939 all modern destroyers were concentrated in the Pacific as part of the U.S. Fleet; there were not enough modern units to absorb the full force of 1,850-ton "leaders," so seven of them formed DesRon 9, with the *Moffett* as flagship. Subsequent practice was not to build specialized leaders, and it is not clear to what extent particular ships were so employed consistently. On the other hand, DesDiv

The Mediterranean was a particularly difficult theater because ships were almost always within range of German airfields; Mediterranean destroyers were the first in the U.S. Navy (other than flush deckers) to exchange torpedo tubes for antiaircraft weapons. Short distances also made destroyers and other ships subject to motor-torpedo-boat attack. Here a destroyer lays smoke off Salerno, 30 November 1943. The ship in the foreground is a prewar cruiser, probably a *Brooklyn*.

The Destroyer Force first experienced World War II in North Atlantic convoy operations. Here the *Gleaves* steams through pack ice early in the war; her Atlantic ASW refit involved removal of the after bank of torpedo tubes but not of No. 3 5-inch gun. Note that both No. 3 and No. 4 guns are in half-shields with dark canvas tops.

membership did remain fairly stable throughout the war, although the designation of particular divisions changed from time to time.

With the outbreak of war in Europe, ships began to be transferred to the Atlantic to enforce a Neutrality Zone; at the same time interest in antisubmarine operations and in cold-weather practice increased—Atlantic destroyers being specially modified. New-construction ships went to the most active theater, the Atlantic. Thus, as of January 1941 the Atlantic Fleet included five DesRons of modern destroyers: DD 362 and 394 as leaders, plus DD 402–404, 409, 410, 414–416, and the whole of the new *Benson-Livermore* class. By June all of the *Sims* class and all but two (DD 397 and 398) of the *Benham*s had joined, and there were eight leaders (DD 358, 359, 362, 363, 381, 383, 395, 396) in two DesDivs. All of these ships were modified to increase their antisubmarine firepower.

Ships began to be transferred back to the Pacific after Pearl Harbor; many of the *Benham*s and *Sims* went back west, leaving only DD 402–405 and 418–420 in the Atlantic. However, new *Benson*s continued to be assigned to the Atlantic, only 19 units (DD 459, 460, 483–488, 598, 599, 602, 605–608, 828–831) serving exclusively in the Pacific. One Bethlehem-built DesDiv (DD 609–612) served briefly in the Atlantic after shakedown, but was released to the Pacific in the fall of 1943 as destroyer escorts became available for the Atlantic. Two more Atlantic DesDivs (DD 418, 441–443 and DD 645–647) were transferred to the Pacific in January 1944. However, other *Benson*s did not go to the Pacific except upon conversion to fast minesweepers or upon conclusion of the Battle of the Atlantic.

The large "leaders" were a special case, unique among the modern U.S. destroyers in that they mounted single-purpose 5-inch guns. Five spent the entire war in the Atlantic (DD 359, 362, 381, 395, 396); DD 358 was the last to be detached to the Pacific, in September 1942. Pacific leaders fought at Midway and Guadalcanal (where the *Porter* was sunk), but by 1943 four of them (DD 361, 368, 383, 394) had been assigned to Balboa in the Canal Zone as convoy escorts, seeing action only when they brought convoys into the combat zone. Three others (DD 357, 360, 363) fought with the fast carriers at Attu and in the Marianas. Plans for general reconstruction of the 1,850-ton destroyers were delayed by their reassignment as convoy flagships in 1944, all 11 surviving

Destroyers operated in support of amphibious operations through World War II; here two maneuver off Casablanca during Operation Torch, 8 November 1942.

Converted destroyers and destroyer escorts performed an important amphibious mission throughout the Pacific war, landing raiding parties on hostile beaches. Here the fast transport *Hopping* operates off Okinawa amid infantry landing craft (LCI) headed for the beach, with the two old battleships *New York* and *Idaho* in the background.

units operating with the Atlantic Fleet. The Coast Guard "Treasury" class cutters that formerly operated in that role were then being rebuilt as amphibious flagships for the Pacific.

The large new destroyers were assigned to the Pacific. Indeed, as early as 1941 the General Board had sought to differentiate between *Benson*s for "sea control" (i.e., for convoy operations in which they would face submarines, aircraft, and surface raiders) and *Fletcher*s for the fleet. Generally, new destroyers built on the East Coast would shake down in the Atlantic under the control of DesLant, but would see combat only in the Pacific. There were only two exceptions. The USS *Capps* (DD 550) was temporarily attached to DesDiv 20 for a raid with the British Home Fleet (and the USS *Ranger* and *Tuscaloosa*) in Norwegian waters in November 1943. In addition, DesDiv 119 (DD 722–726) fought at Normandy, in effect testing the new *Sumner* design in combat.

The prewar concept of destroyer operations, and indeed the prewar U.S. concept of fleet operations in general, emphasized the conditions of the Orange war plan, in which the battle fleet would advance west towards Japan and a decisive Jutland-style engagement in Philippine waters. Destroyers were designed to support that campaign, protecting the battleships from air and submarine attack en route to the major surface battle. In that battle, they would help protect the battle line from Japanese torpedo attack, and in strict conformity to the movements of the battleships, deliver their own offensive torpedo strikes. To some limited extent destroyers screening fast carriers were expected to protect their charges by attacking enemy heavy units, such as heavy cruisers, with their torpedoes, but such defensive attacks were secondary. "Sea control" functions, particularly convoy screening, were also of secondary import, although they were much more prominent after it became obvious that the United States might have to fight a two-ocean war.

In practice the destroyer force operated in four distinct roles during World War II, none of which quite corresponded to that for which it had been designed and built. Probably the fast task force screening role came closest; however, in that case the primary threat turned out to be air rather than surface torpedo attack. The Orange Plan had envisaged shore bombardment as the fleet seized bases in the Mandated Islands en route to Japan, but on nothing like the scale encountered in both oceans during World War II. Similarly, ASW was a standard destroyer role from 1917 on, but it was rarely emphasized before 1940 and certainly was not a major element in fleet destroyer design. The unexpected role, and the one that most caught the imagination of the destroyer force, was operating in cruiser-destroyer or all-destroyer Surface Action Groups (SAGs), hunting enemy SAGs or enemy transport formations, first in Indonesian waters, and then much more extensively in the Solomons.

SAG Operations

The destroyer man always resented his relegation to an auxiliary status within the battle fleet, and even more, his essentially defensive role within that fleet. He preferred to think of his ship as an offensive weapon; he saw the torpedo as an equalizer that gave him at least some power over the largest enemy capital ship. This view, reminiscent of the French "jeune école" of the 1890s, prevailed in some navies but was generally frowned upon in a U.S. Navy dominated by the capital ship (battleship and then carrier) community. The destroyer community's struggle for a more aggressive orientation began well before 1914 and continues today. It accounts for the very strong influence that SAG experience had on wartime destroyer thinking, typified by comments on proposed characteristics for a large destroyer (1942–44, described in chapter 11).

Even well after the war, when potential surface targets were few and very far between, torpedo tubes were retained; as one Korean War destroyer skipper, concerned about growing Soviet surface strength, said, "Please leave the destroyer an offensive weapon that all ships dread, or you will no longer have a destroyer." There was, however, as early as 1945 a widespread suspicion that in view of developments in aircraft and in shipboard radar, torpedoes were no longer effective. A special board on ship characteristics convened by CinCPac disagreed:

one school of fleet thought holds that radar has outmoded the surface-launched torpedo attack and that all tubes should be removed to gain additional space for anti-aircraft guns. This Board does not concur.

. . . The damage inflicted in this war by surface-launched torpedoes, by own and enemy forces, before and after the advent of radar, is impressive. To sacrifice, at this time, the offensive possibilities of torpedoes because of radar, which can already be jammed, does not appear justified . . . the removal of all torpedo tubes from destroyers now would be premature and unwise.

The torpedo was above all an equalizer, as the heroic action off Samar (25 October 1944) showed. It was, therefore, retained (at least at first) in the specialized fast task force escort designed in 1954 (see chapter 13), and after its demise there were demands for missile equivalents, as in Rear Admiral Daniel's call for Terrier aboard his "destroyer of the future" in 1956 or, for that matter, more recent pressure to deploy Harpoon aboard destroyers in place of some ASROC ASW missiles. In each case the antiship weapon consumes space and weight that might otherwise be devoted to the destroyer's primary function as it is understood by the Navy as a whole, i.e., AAW and ASW protection of high-value units. The intense popularity of SAG concepts suggests that the spirit of the destroyer as a small, tough ship to attack rather than defend is far from dead.

That spirit was hardly emphasized in the prewar fleet. U.S. naval doctrine emphasized coordinated fleet operations, in which destroyers functioned as essential elements of the antidestroyer screen, and in which they would be ordered to attack the enemy battle line in highly coordinated fashion, generally from under smoke screens. Although considerable effort was spent in improving torpedoes and their fire control, the prewar fleet was dominated by the "Gun Club," and long-range shell fire was considered the supreme destructive weapon. This view is reflected, for example, in the decision to remove torpedo tubes from U.S. heavy cruisers, a step almost unique among the world's navies. Tactically, in the Solomons it was reflected in the strict conformity of destroyer to cruiser movements, rapid 6-inch fire being considered a far more important and efficient offensive weapon than the torpedo; indeed, destroyers were often unable to use their torpedoes effectively. Although CinCPac commented caustically on the failure to make efficient use of destroyer torpedoes, tactics did not change until very late in the campaign. Thus, the night battle of Empress Augusta Bay (2 November 1943) was described by Admiral Pye, president of the Naval War College, as unusual in that

the destroyers were not tied in close to the main battle line, and held there within gun range. They were loose, well removed from the cruisers, with flexibility and freedom of action. They were used offensively instead of defensively, and were sent to fire their torpedoes before opening gunfire.

Prewar U.S. practice emphasized day rather than night actions, but most of the Solomons engagements occurred at night; U.S. commanders unused to night action considered radar almost a magic solution to their problems, and did not realize that the Japanese could often detect U.S. warships beyond their radar range, launching their very long range torpedoes before U.S. warships could open fire. Given the lack of confidence in U.S. torpedo tactics, senior officers did not believe in the existence of the Japanese 24-inch "Long Lance," which had such a devastating effect in the cruiser-destroyer night battles. One is said to have been recovered on Cape Esperance as early as January or February 1943, yet before the Battle of Kula Gulf (6 July 1943) the U.S. commander, Rear Admiral W.L. Ainsworth, dismissed talk of 10,000-yard Japanese torpedoes as "scuttlebutt." Ironically, the man who warned him was the captain of the cruiser *Helena*, lost that night to precisely that weapon.

Given this doctrinal problem, destroyers rarely operated in the kind of independent surface hunting group that seemed most attractive to many of their commanders. The prewar Asiatic Fleet was composed almost entirely of destroyers and submarines, so that there was in fact some limited SAG action in the then Dutch East Indies early in 1942, including the U.S. Navy's first surface battle since 1898, an attack by the four elderly flush deckers of DesDiv 59 on an anchored Japanese troop convoy. This battle off Balikpapan (24 January 1942) was a tactical victory, but it was marred by what appears to have been poor torpedo performance, itself quite possibly a consequence of that general neglect of torpedo development that had such serious consequences for U.S. submariners.

Early cruiser-destroyer engagements in the Solomons were marked by concentration on cruiser shellfire to the exclusion of torpedo tactics. For example, in the second Savo Island night battle (11–12 October 1942) the U.S. force (Task Group 64.2) consisted of four cruisers (2 heavy, 2 light) screened by five destroyers, three ahead and two astern; COMINCH commented that

> it appears that this disposition where destroyers were divided was more defensive than offensive. Could not the destroyers have been formed into striking groups to attack the enemy from the flank with torpedoes and/or make a torpedo attack on enemy ships close inshore? Or was it more desirable to keep concentrated in order not to inadvertently have own cruisers firing at own destroyers retiring from torpedo attack on approaching enemy ships?

In the ensuing battle, a faulty disposition was not the only problem. Rear Admiral Callaghan flew his flag in the USS *San Francisco*, which did not have an effective surface search (SG) radar; he therefore did not have the best information. Thus, the night battle showed not only the need for better tactics but also the value of what would soon be known as a Combat Information Center; COMINCH observed that

> it is essential that the OTC [Officer in Tactical Command] have the best and most complete information available at all times, otherwise he is at a great disadvantage and his chances of success are greatly reduced. The flagship in this battle was not equipped as well in radar as other ships in company. It might have been advisable for the Task Group commander to have shifted his flag to one of the ships which were better equipped in this respect. The TBS is a splendid communications channel but with continuous reports coming in from various ships a confused and uncertain situation is presented to the OTC. He does not have the best picture. It is doubtful that an adequate tactical plot was maintained showing own track, enemy contacts and tracks from which an OTC could obtain a clear and accurate picture of the situation. If this type of tactical plot is not maintained by all ships, immediate steps should be taken to do so. Night actions at best are confused and every effort should be made to keep the situation as clear as possible. Complete dependence should not be placed on TBS, Radar, DRT, and other mechanical conveniences. Keeping own track is not sufficient.

The development of the "plot" referred to, which became CIC, was at least as important for effective night surface action as for the antiaircraft action with which it is usually associated. As the newer destroyers fitted with CICs appeared in the South Pacific, their potential for effective night torpedo action considerably improved. However, to realize that potential it was necessary for them to be released from close coordination with heavier gun-armed ships, if only because of the vast difference in character between gun and torpedo. The latter was very much a weapon of surprise, requiring a long running time between launch and impact; if gunfire were opened first, the enemy would have warning and would probably be able to evade. The longer the range, the longer the running time and the more important the precise prediction of enemy course and speed—and hence the more important the precise plotting inherent in a CIC operation. An effective CIC also reduced somewhat one of the great dangers of night operations, the lack of good IFF. That is, as long as opposing forces were tracked consistently in CIC, it might be possible to recognize which ships were friendly. Modern NTDS practice in air control follows the same principle: interrogation. However, once identified, they can be consistently tracked and need not be reidentified. In many cases the character of their tracks alone gives a good indication of their identity. This was particularly important to battle areas off the Vietnam coast, overflown by large numbers of airliners.

This particular battle (second Savo Island) was one of the first in which U.S. warships were equipped with an effective surface search radar (SG); indeed, only those ships that had to use their searchlights to illuminate their targets were themselves hit. One CO commented that

> the outstanding event in this operation was the fact that this was a night action between light forces of apparently nearly equal strength. The target was picked up at about 28,000 yards by SG radar and completely developed as to course, speed, and probable composition. Fire was opened with what is believed to be a straddle using radar range and bearing, and the first enemy target was sunk or disappeared from sight and radar screen in about two minutes.
> . . .

Later the naval historian Samuel Eliot Morison would comment that U.S. officers were entirely too confident in their radar, and that targets often vanished from radar screens when they passed out of range or when they merged with the returns from land masses. Even so, SG was a prerequisite for what would become effective U.S. night SAG tactics. Its necessity was in turn a consequence of the neglect of nonradar night tactics before the war; the Japanese Navy functioned effectively at night without radar.

For the third night battle off Savo Island, 12–13 November 1942, Admiral Callaghan again split his destroyers, four ahead of a column of cruisers and four trailing. COMINCH disapproved:

> this battle formation did not recognize the different types of ships with their different armaments and capabilities. . . . Why types were not grouped together for mutual support and so stationed to bring the greatest fighting effect into play is not known. Destroyers are essentially an offensive weapon, particularly at night with their torpedo batteries. Destroyer gunfire at night is secondary. . . . The four destroyers in the rear could have been more effectively employed in the van concentrated with the other destroyers prepared to make a high speed torpedo attack and retirement from the immediate vicinity of the action. . . . One of the reasons for this arrangement of ships in the battle [with an antiaircraft cruiser leading two heavy and one light cruisers and then another CLAA bringing up the rear] may have been consideration of availability of SG radars and enemy threat on flank and rear of formation by torpedoes. It is not clear why the second in command was placed ahead of the OTC in column unless it was intended that the *Atlanta* support the van destroyers. [The] *Atlanta* [which was sunk] carried torpedoes. [Her] employment in the battle line does not appear sound. This type is essentially an antiaircraft cruiser. Command must recognize functions of various types of ships and employ them properly. The OTC should

> use a ship equipped with the best radar until all ships are so equipped. . . . The senior destroyer division or squadron commander should have been in the *Fletcher* [which had SG radar] so that a coordinated radar controlled torpedo attack could have been made. . . . If leading destroyer had had SG radar, she would not have been obliged to wait until sight contact had been made.

Destroyers were not the only victims of rigid battle doctrine that was ill-suited to conditions of low visibility; Admiral Callaghan held fire until targets were visible at relatively short ranges; COMINCH felt that "doctrine for night action should have provided for opening fire at targets of opportunity when ship was ready and had problem solved." Thus the light cruiser *Helena* began firing at 4,300 yards, although she was capable of inflicting severe damage by rapid 6-inch fire at much longer ranges. The combination of rigid procedure and an emphasis on the gun effectively disarmed the eight destroyers; COMINCH asked "why were not all van destroyers delivering a torpedo attack at this time [of opening fire]? Doctrine apparently had not provided for it. It is doubtful whether the OTC had a clear picture of the situation," with neither good radar nor, more importantly, a CIC with which to filter tactical information.

The destroyers tried to operate independently; at one point in the battle, DesDiv 10 turned to parallel the enemy track, but the OTC ordered it back into column formation;

> ComDesDiv 10 appears to have attempted to make an attack but was prevented by OTC. . . . The order for leading destroyer to resume column prevented *Sterett* from making a coordinated torpedo attack. . . . Destroyers were not employed properly. They should be used offensively. Their torpedoes are their primary weapons and should be used properly at every opportunity.

COMINCH felt that had the OTC been aware of the closeness of the range, he would have operated very differently:

> It appears that he blindly went into action. TBS could not have given the OTC [a] clear picture. It does not appear sound to close to point blank range at night when at best the situation is confused. It would appear better to delay closing range until a coordinated destroyer torpedo attack can be made and destroyers withdraw clear of the battle area.

Such tactics, although proposed in March 1943, were not to be realized for another eight months. The destroyers did succeed in torpedoing the Japanese battleship *Hiei*, which was later sunk by torpedo bombers; COMINCH commented dolefully that "it took a total of seven torpedoes and two 1,000-lb. bomb hits to finally sink this battleship. This does not speak well for our weapons." Moreover, "it appears that the *Sterett*, as well as the other destroyers, were obliged to steam along in the van and rear and took serious punishment with no great freedom to coordinate and attack offensively with torpedoes."

By the time of the fourth night battle of Savo, 30 November 1942, the four destroyers were concentrated on the bow of the cruiser column; they opened the battle by delivering a torpedo attack, after which the five cruisers opened fire. This time the Japanese force succeeded in launching torpedoes well before the U.S. force had begun firing, and four of the five U.S. cruisers were torpedoed within 16 minutes of the order to open fire. Once more, failure could be blamed on the close control of the destroyers (which had to await OTC orders to make their attack). Under Pacific Fleet tactical doctrine the destroyers made torpedo attacks, after which they would engage enemy cruisers or destroyers at which the U.S. cruisers were firing, illuminating them with star shells. In view of the danger of enemy torpedo fire, "insofar as practicable the range will be maintained in excess of 12,000 yards until our destroyer attack has been completed. Commencement of fire *will be ordered* at a range of between 10,000 and 12,000 yards" (Battle Orders of the OTC, Rear Admiral C.H. Wright). COMINCH felt that the hits on the cruisers were probably unavoidable, given the narrowness of the channel and the lack of prior training in night action: "speed, high speed, is a cruiser's main protection against torpedoes." The Japanese success was particularly puzzling because of U.S. ignorance of the excellence of their torpedoes, as well as of the existence of facilities for quick reloading of torpedoes aboard Japanese destroyers. Thus,

> attempts to analyze the torpedo attack which disabled the *Minneapolis* and *New Orleans* have proven particularly baffling. . .the observed positions of the enemy surface vessels before and during the gun action make it seem improbable that torpedoes with speed-distance characteristics similar to our own could have reached the cruisers at the time they did. . . .

Nonexistent submarines were blamed.

SAG tactics were revived in the Solomons because of the shortage of cruisers for tactical support. At Vella Gulf (6–7 August 1943) the six destroyers of Task Group 31.2, consisting of DesDivs 12 and 15 (minus the *Gridley* and *Wilson*) made coordinated night radar attacks that achieved the level of surprise that had brought the Japanese a torpedo victory about a year earlier at the Battle of Savo Island, sinking three out of four Japanese destroyers instantly, at about 6,300 yards. Gunfire was opened only after the torpedoes had been launched.

Tactically, the U.S. Task Group was divided into two independent divisions, each consisting of three destroyers;

since the Task Group was to operate as a destroyer attack unit it was decided that Division A-1 upon making contact would dash in to a close torpedo firing position, let go her torpedoes, haul tail to about 10,000 yards, watch the torpedoes hit, then open with gunfire or/and make further torpedo attacks depending on the effectiveness of the first attack. After the initial attack, Division A-1 was to be on the alert to intercept a possible second enemy force. It was known that on previous occasions the Japanese had operated with two well separated groups. It was therefore vital in case of an engagement that our force be so disposed as not to be taken by surprise. . . . Division A-2, when A-1 started the torpedo attack approach, was to cover A-1, taking station clear of A-1 and if possible on the disengaged bow of the enemy. . . . If A-1 was not taken under fire, A-2 was to commence firing when torpedoes hit and to take advantage of opportunities for secondary torpedo attacks. . . .

A-1 consisted of three 16-tube destroyers, A-2 of three *Benham*s which had had two of their four quadruple tubes removed.

Commander of Task Group 31.2, the U.S. destroyers, concluded

> That our destroyer doctrine is sound. . . . That surprise throws the enemy into utter confusion. . . . That our torpedo fire is equal to or better than that of the enemy. . . . That the primary battery of the destroyer is and always has been the torpedo battery. That a night torpedo attack is a deadly weapon and must be fully exploited. That a combined night operation with other types under conditions of low visibility (such as will enable a destroyer attack unit to arrive at torpedo firing point without detection) destroyers can best be used as the primary attack unit, the cruiser unit being used as a support or covering force. That the CIC is a highly important part of the destroyer organization and must be developed to the peak of efficiency. . . .

The commander of Division A-2 went further, noting that the CIC "is the most important activity on the ship"; indeed, much of the analysis of the action was directed towards improvements in CIC arrangement and organization, suggestions including the movement of the CIC to the bridge and the modification of the DRT (dead reckoning tracer), which the USS *Dunlap* felt "would be like trading a '26 Ford in on a '42 Buick."

The USS *Craven*, a unit of Division A-1, commented that

> this is the first battle where destroyers were handled tactically as they should be; as an offensive unit. Our full radar control of torpedoes and guns make us far superior to the enemy in any night action.
>
> Our destroyer doctrine is sound, and our years of hard work will pay dividends, providing we use destroyers offensively and not for the protection of

cruisers and battleships, as they have been used in the past. . . .

This action proves the value of an efficient CIC in destroyers. What might otherwise have been a confusing series of reports and orders became a coordinated flow of evaluated information because of CIC.

By this time the destroyers had efficient CICs, and all had SG surface-search radars. There was also a healthy respect for Japanese torpedoes, although the details of the Long Lance were not well known, and the existence of battle reload gear for Japanese torpedoes remained unknown. This device, for which the U.S. Navy had no equivalent (considering torpedoes still in tubes as reloads), effectively doubled the effective torpedo firepower of Japanese destroyers, as all tubes could be reloaded within about 20 minutes. Its impact on American destroyer men shows in late-war and postwar interest in reload gear and also in extremely heavy surface torpedo batteries. Tactics at Vella Gulf were based on the view that Japanese torpedoes were probably far better than those of the U.S., but that U.S. radar-controlled gunfire was superior, so that it would be best to engage at maximum range. In addition, DesDiv 12 had trained for some time in making its own radar-controlled night torpedo attacks.

For the U.S. Navy in the Pacific, the conditions that made SAG operations possible in the Solomons were unique. The Japanese Navy, otherwise quite conventional in its determination to concentrate its forces into one or two balanced fleets, was willing in the Solomons, first, to pit cruiser-destroyer forces against the U.S. beachhead area, itself defended by the detached cruisers and destroyers of a badly weakened U.S. fleet. Later, independent cruiser-destroyer forces were used to ferry troops to Japanese enclaves. Once the Japanese lost the war in the South Pacific, there was no point in independent operations, and their destroyer force reverted to its two conventional functions: screening the Combined Fleet, and fighting the growing U.S. submarine offensive. Neither role made for effective use of SAGs, and by the end of 1944 there were few if any surface targets within reach of U.S. surface ships that were unsupported by carrier aircraft. Thus, the last SAG action of the war was an inconclusive stern chase off Biak, 8–9 June 1944.

Ironically, although SAGs involved only a very small fraction of the U.S. destroyer force, and although they required conditions for their success that were unlikely to be duplicated in an aircraft-dominated postwar world, the SAG experience was a major factor in the destroyer force concept of operations and in particular in the destroyer force view of the nature of the future destroyer. To some extent, too, the role of the destroyer as an anti-surface-ship

screening vessel was also important. As the carrier became more and more the focus of naval attention, her peculiar lack of capability against surface attack became more significant. That is, as long as the carrier could strike potential surface threats long before they approached to within the gun range, she would be safe. However, failures of scouting or even overoptimistic damage assessments might well make it possible for heavy enemy units to close to within gun range. Except for battleships, only destroyers possessed weapons that could stop a heavy-gun ship— as the destroyers demonstrated very heroically in the Battle off Samar, 25 October 1944. There, a small force of three destroyers and three destroyer escorts stood off the Japanese Battle Force, primarily (though not entirely) by the threat and the use of their torpedoes. Similar defensive attacks were also partly responsible for the escape of a U.S. cruiser-destroyer force in the Battle of the Komandorski Islands in the Aleutians, 26 March 1943.

Only once did destroyers function in the coordinated night attack role for which they had been designed, i.e., as part of a combined destroyer-battleship team. Using the same loose tactics that worked so well at Empress Augusta Bay, DesRons 24, 54, and 56 delivered night torpedo attacks at Surigao Strait. Captain J.G. Coward's DesRon 54 made a coordinated radar attack that struck five ships and sank three, including the battleship *Fuso*. Other attacks by DesRons 24 and 56 damaged the other Japanese battleship, *Yamashiro*, perhaps fatally, and sank the one destroyer remaining in company with her. Surigao Strait was both the last classic gun action and the last torpedo action of the U.S. destroyer force; Samuel Eliot Morison rates the attacks in this battle as "some of the best [on either side] of the entire Pacific war, and that of Phillips's division [of DesRon 54] may well be considered the most successful."

The U.S. destroyer force experienced relatively little surface action in the Atlantic, although it did encounter large numbers of small surface craft (German S-Boote, Italian MAS, German explosive motor boats and human torpedoes) in European coastal waters. For example, S-Boote (MTBs) torpedoed two of the destroyers at Normandy. During the invasion of Southern France, U.S. destroyers sank four German corvettes, as well as lesser craft. Light surface craft were also encountered in the closing stages of the Pacific war, their threat adding to the value of the enlarged automatic batteries then being fitted (see chapter 10).

Task Force (Antiaircraft) Screening

Task force screening was perhaps the closest wartime approach to postwar destroyer operations, and the concerns it generated dominated the postwar

Destroyers were above all fleet screening ships, their powerful dual-purpose batteries making them effective in antiaircraft action. Here a *Sumner* screens an *Essex*-class fleet carrier and a *New Orleans*-class heavy cruiser in the Pacific, 24 March 1945; another *Sumner* steams behind the heavy cruiser.

destroyer force. Wartime development showed a considerable shift in the function of the destroyer within the screen. At the outbreak of war, the destroyer was a means of breaking up attacks on the capital ships, and its 5-inch gun was its primary weapon. Although the carrier had a large fighter force, there was no great confidence that those fighters alone would be able to protect her. Beginning about 1943, however, the carrier fighter aircraft became the primary element of task force air defense. The guns of the screening ships were considered a means, not of stopping the entire attack, but rather of dealing with aircraft leaking past the fighter Combat Air Patrol (CAP). Thus early radar warning and fighter control became vital functions, and they were assigned to the destroyers. These functions grew through the war, but they became dominant from Leyte Gulf onward, as the intensity of Japanese air attacks grew, and, indeed, as the Kamikazes began to inflict severe damage on the fleet.

Until that time, air opposition was relatively light or, if intense, did not have any great duration. The carrier task force could count on tactical surprise, and once it had beaten off a short series of intense raids it could stand down, remaining alert only against the occasional night attack. Pickets were an important means both of preserving surprise and of dealing with low flyers, but they were not in themselves objects of intense attack, and the Japanese did not mount what amounted to attrition campaigns against the fleet. That changed sharply as the fast carriers and the amphibious force merged in the Philippines, within easy reinforcement range of the vast reserve of aircraft on Formosa and, indeed, on Japanese soil. Although no one expected any future war to feature such intense raids, the experience off Okinawa was considered extremely instructive in view of the much greater lethality to be expected of each attacker and particularly in view of the similarity between post-

war guided missiles and the wartime suicide attacker.

In the conventional task force air defense practice the 5-inch gun was the principal screening weapon, since it alone could provide effective protection of ships other than the destroyer proper. Perhaps the clearest indication of the relative roles of 5-inch and 40-mm. guns was the use of the four *Gridley*s (which alone of the prewar treaty destroyers never mounted Bofors guns) as fast carrier escorts within one of the carrier task groups of Task Force 38/58. They were not detached from this duty until the very end of the war, when all other destroyers were refitted for much improved antiaircraft self-defense to allow them to survive experiences such as Okinawa. The very large number of destroyers generally assigned to antiaircraft screens was predicated on 5-inch range, the screen forming an interlocking circle around the capital ships, large enough to permit them to maneuver relative to it.

Limited destroyer endurance was a constant source of difficulties in task force operations. For example, in a carrier raid conducted by Task Force 17 (built around the USS *Hornet*, two heavy cruisers, two AA cruisers, and six destroyers) in October 1942, the heavy ships were able to run-in to the launch position at 28 knots, but the destroyers had to proceed independently at 19 in order to conserve fuel; COMINCH observed that "the cruising radius of destroyers should be increased rather than be decreased." Tactically, it was hoped that the carrier group would achieve surprise on its approach, and that the destroyers would rejoin by the time the air group was recovered, providing additional antiaircraft firepower "should an enemy attack follow the returning air group." COMINCH added that the organization adopted for the task force made it a "powerful, fast, and highly effective" unit, but that his ideal for a task force screen would have been 3 light cruisers, 3 AA cruisers, and

14 destroyers, i.e., 2 destroyers per heavy ship. Such large numbers were not approached even at the end of the war, but by that time the immensely increased effectiveness of the VT fuze and the increased numbers (and efficiency) of carrier fighters more than made up the difference.

A carrier task force doctrine proposed in March 1943 envisaged the ideal task force as two carriers

> tactically concentrated until an attack becomes imminent and tactically re-concentrated immediately the attack has withdrawn. When air attack becomes imminent, carriers with their designated heavy units and destroyers should separate as soon as possible to at least 25 to 30 miles and operate independently. . .carrier task force screen should consist of 10–12 destroyers and three CA per carrier or 10–12 destroyers and 1 BB (new), 2 CLAA, or combination of each. Screening ships must be permanently assigned to each carrier in a Carrier Task Force and suitably stationed in relation to the carrier. Destroyers should be stationed on the 15 or 2500 yard circle. . . .

The wide separation of the carriers under attack was intended to simplify fighter control and to avoid interference; it also greatly increased the number of destroyers required per carrier. For example, in 1944 Task Force 38 operated with 16 carriers and 57 destroyers rather than the 160 to 192 destroyers that the 1943 doctrine would have required.

By November 1943 there were enough carriers (and enough experience in close coordination of several at once) for Task Force 50, which seized Tarawa, to be split into four task groups, each containing two fleet and one light fleet carriers (TG 50.4 had only one fleet carrier). Screens varied; TG 50.1, for example, consisted of 5 heavy cruisers, 1 CLAA, and 8 destroyers, and the fast carrier force had a total of 33 destroyers attached. This was close to the type of organization standard at the end of the Pacific War. The destroyers themselves were a mixture of treaty and more modern types: all *Fletcher*s in three of the task groups as originally constituted, *Benham*s and a *Benson* in the other.

In this operation, the Japanese introduced what was to become their trademark: low-level night attacks by land-based torpedo bombers. Task force radar provided virtually no warning; the captain of the light carrier *Independence*, which was severely damaged, felt that "the stationing of picket vessels and/or low-flying airplane pickets equipped to make radar and visual contacts should do much towards preventing the repetition of this form of near surprise attack." COMINCH noted the sparse destroyer screen, in one case only five destroyers to three carriers and four cruisers; at the time of the attack one destroyer had been ordered off to investigate a submarine contact.

The strength of the task groups and of their screens grew as the fleet filled out with new ships. Thus, by October 1944 each task group of Task Force 38 consisted of two fleet and two light fleet carriers, screened by cruisers and destroyers; for example, the screen of TG 38.1 comprised three heavy and one light cruiser supported by 15 destroyers, some of which carried fighter director teams and could function as radar pickets. As Kamikazes became more prevalent, the pickets became more important, particularly when the fleet had to operate in confined waters, supporting amphibious assaults.

Off Leyte,

> the threat of the suicide bomber, which places the brunt of the anti-aircraft defense burden on the ship being attacked, has necessitated reconsideration of carrier task group AA dispositions. Disposition 5-V, which proved so successful against torpedo attacks, has been found to provide inadequate protection against dive and glide bombers, and more specifically, against suicide bombers. Against torpedo attacks, which were the enemy's chief tactic against our surface forces for more than a year, the 5-V disposition, with all ships except carriers in the screen, provided maximum firepower against enemy aircraft. Planes breaking through the screen were taken under fire by the carriers and continued to be targets of ships of the screen.

> During the Marianas operation, however, the Japanese reverted to dive and glide bombing, with planes passing over the Screen at high level and diving out of clouds on carriers at high speeds. Against such attacks ships of the screen found their high firepower capacity virtually helpless as a protection for the carriers. The inadequacy of the standard AA disposition became even more apparent in the Leyte operation when the enemy pressed his dive bombing with fanaticism, resorting to suicide dives against our ships. . . .

> As carriers will be the chief target of glide and dive bombers during attacks on carrier task groups, their firepower must be supplemented by that of ships of the screen. Bringing in heavy ships from the screen will serve that purpose, but has serious limitations. The arc of fire is limited by the presence of destroyers in the outer screen. And destroyers are so thinly dispersed that they are of little value in defending numerous important targets against torpedo attacks.

> It is likely that a plan will be developed to meet the threat. . . by tightening the entire screen to bring enemy planes within range of heavy ships' automatic weapons. This may place ships of the screen on circle 4,* with carriers on circle 2.5, or the screen on circle 5 and carriers on circle 3.5, permitting a high concentration of fire against planes diving on carriers. Against torpedo attacks the screen could expand to circle 5 with a minimum of confusion. . . .

*I.e., on a circle of radius 4,000 yards centered on formation center.

Two destroyers on the picket line shoot down a Kamikaze, 15 June 1945. The number of shell bursts testify to the intensity of the action—and to the difficulty of shooting down so difficult a target.

Dusk torpedo attacks by low fliers continued to be effective, and Task Group 38.1 commented that

> the use of picket destroyer(s) to the East and a dusk anti-snooper patrol of night fighters may prove the answer. . . . The *Woodworth* proved most valuable when stationed 10 miles to the East on the night of 14 October. It had been planned in addition to give the *Woodworth* a dusk fighter patrol, but at the last minute the weather ruled against the launching of night fighters. The liability of having to recover night fighters in extremely bad weather with bogies continuously in the vicinity cannot be overlooked. . . .

In modern parlance, then, the *Woodworth* was placed out on the threat axis to provide a combination of early warning and fighter control. In effect she was a platform for her radar and her CIC team, an extension of the task group rather than an independent unit. Her guns were valuable primarily as a means of preserving the all-important sensors.

In general, the difficulty of shooting down Kamikazes or other diving attackers focused attention on the fighters of the Task Group Combat Air Patrol—and on the means for their effective control. For example, the specialized radar picket destroyer (DDR) appears to have been proposed by Admiral Mitscher (CTF 38) after his experiences at and before Leyte.

At Okinawa 15 picket stations were established. Picket functions included early radar warning; fighter direction; the destruction of incoming enemy aircraft and the disruption of incoming raids with gunfire (pickets were instructed to fire on any unidentified aircraft within 12,000 yards "whether or not they had a good solution," i.e., whether or not they had a good chance of shooting any down); and search and rescue for friendly aircraft. This series of antiair stations was separate from an ASW screen and an antisurface screen, which were also maintained, and ships of which were assigned as radar pickets. Some destroyers functioned only as pickets and not as fighter directors, although "stations designated were occupied by fighter director vessels as far as possible."

Commander, Cruiser Division 6 commented of the Okinawa operation that

> fighter direction. . .was well-handled, particularly in view of the many new problems imposed on account of the large size and geographical location of the area in which our forces were operating. There were no surprise raids and the great majority of enemy planes which approached during daylight failed to reach the most vital targets in the transport area. . . . The many successful interceptions resulted from splendid coordination of fighter direction by the Force Flagship and efficient work of numerous other vessels—es-

pecially the destroyer types which acted as radar pickets. . . .

The need for radar pickets is fundamental. Facilities for early information of approaching enemy planes and their interception by CAP controlled by fighter direction ships from advanced positions must be provided in naval operations. This is true whether the operations involve the approach of a fast striking force toward a land objective, the pre-landing-day work of underwater demolition, minesweeping, bombardment, etc., of an amphibious support force, or a large-scale amphibious attack where massive naval forces must remain concentrated at the objective for an extended period of time. . . .

In this operation it was necessary to station pickets at considerable distances (75 miles) from the center of the area in order to cover the most probable directions of approach of aircraft from enemy bases and at the same time to prevent approaching enemy planes from taking advantage of adjacent land masses. While the picket stations were close enough to each other to permit passing control of friendly fighters from one ship to another without losing contact, the stations were not close enough to permit mutual support against either air attack or surface raiders. Steps were taken to alleviate the condition by the assignment of an additional destroyer to each of the pickets in the "more vulnerable" stations and by stationing various small craft such as LCS's and LCI's in position to support the pickets. . . .

Losses (and severe damage short of loss) were so common on the picket line that drastic measures were proposed to solve this problem. Examples included the immediate seizure of outlying islands for radar stations, and even the use of submarines; "after detecting and reporting the approach of enemy planes, the sub could dive. Limited range of present submarine radar—plus rearrangements inside hull—are problems to be solved before submarines can perform this duty."

The airborne picket was also coming close to fruition, in the form of carrier-borne Avengers and also Flying Fortresses, both with large search radars installed (Project Cadillac). Even special CAP sections to protect the early warning pickets were proposed.

The number of attacking aircraft was prodigious, and the Japanese seemed well aware of the importance of the destroyer pickets as targets in themselves. Relatively few had even the increased antiaircraft batteries proposed a short time before, and several were subjected to saturation attacks. For example, at one point ten aircraft (four on the starboard bow, four on the port bow, and two astern) attacked the *Hugh W. Hadley* (DD 774), which was leader of a force consisting of two destroyers, three LCS, and an LSM. They were supported by a 12-fighter CAP group.

On the morning of the action, 11 May 1945, radar detected a series of five incoming raids, estimated to

total 156 aircraft; the entire CAP section was ordered out to engage. They reported 40 to 50 aircraft shot down. The rest attacked the two destroyers, the *Hadley* and the *Evans*. Some tried to pass headed for Okinawa, but the destroyers took them under fire, the *Hadley* claiming four. Then the concentrated attacks on the pickets began, the *Hadley* shooting down a total (as claimed) of 23 aircraft including 3 suicide splashes. They, in turn, destroyed her as a warship; she was hit by a bomb aft, by a Baka (human) bomb, by a suicide plane aft, and by a suicide plane in her rigging. Both engine rooms and one fire room were flooded and all 5-inch guns put out of action. However, she was saved.

In his battle evaluation, COMINCH commented that "the ship's mission was gallantly completed but inadequate air support was evidenced. Proper air support was necessary and urgent. Was the system in use too inflexible? Our fighters were outnumbered over 5 to 1. A picket should be part of a system and not just an uncoordinated unit." The Task Force commander, Admiral Mitscher, commented that

experience gained in this operation indicated that with improved radar equipment the radar patrol line operating 30 to 40 miles in the direction of the enemy will be able to detect and destroy low-flying enemy planes before they sight the main force. This may very well be the answer to the suicide plane. For the present, planes approaching above 10,000 feet will be handled by the CAP over the task group. However, it is conceivable that with the introduction of SP radar, the radar patrol line will be able to handle a greater number of interceptions. If this condition materializes, a greater percentage of the CAP will be turned over to the radar picket line Fighter Direction Officer.

Throughout the battle, the cry was too many targets, too few aircraft. The destroyers on picket duty were able to detect almost all approaching enemy aircraft, and in many cases they were able to keep operating even after taking severe damage. For example, the destroyer *Stanly* reported that "just prior to the period covered by this report, additional radio equipment was installed in CIC and radio central to handle all phases of destroyer fighter direction. All equipment functioned well and remained in operating condition even after the ship had been hit by a suicide plane and shaken badly by a plane that crashed just off the port bow. SGA and SC-4 were in full operation during and after the attack. . . . The noise level in CIC became excessive when ship's tactical and fighter direction circuits were in use."

The *Bush*, which was lost, had a special fighter direction team aboard and was assigned control of aircraft on four different occasions. On the afternoon she was sunk, control of four fighters was passed to her after the raids had been picked up and had closed to 25 miles; she was able to intercept the first, "but there were too few fighters to handle all four raids. At other times when control of CAP was passed to *Bush*, it was already too late to make an interception; the enemy had in most cases passed and was headed for the transport area."

Many officers thought that the pickets needed protection, that more destroyers should have been concentrated on picket stations. The commander of the USS *Colhoun* wanted at least two destroyers per station at any one time;

> vessels of other types (should) not be assigned, as DD's must then sacrifice speed, maneuverability and possibly some fire power to help protect them or else leave them with no mutual support, which defeats the original purpose. It is further suggested that each picket vessel be assigned an individual CAP of at least 2 fighters to be controlled by them on a frequency other than primary fighter direction. It is suggested that they orbit ship at about angels 10 [10,000 feet] or at mattress, whichever is lower, at a range of around 5 to 10 miles, that they have strict orders not to chase any enemy beyond ten miles from ship, and that they attack any enemy within 10,000 yards of ship without orders. The ship will have to be thoroughly indoctrinated not to shoot down own planes, but it is thought that this can be accomplished. The presence of friendly planes is a high morale factor to anyone engaged in picket work, because it gets pretty lonesome sometimes.

The USS *Mannert L. Abele* suggested CAPs for all radar picket stations during all daylight hours;

> there can be only one certain defense against the suicide attack and that is in maintaining a large CAP in the air at all times with each picket having control of at least 8 planes, 4 of which could be directed visually. It is also the opinion of this officer that the small LSM(R)s [i.e., LCS] are literally worth their weight in gold as support vessels, but larger 40 mm. batteries should be installed and the number assigned each picket increased to a minimum of 4. Maneuvering to remain close to supports is difficult but not impossible.

The *Sterett*

recommends that radar pickets [stations] be manned by two or three destroyers when in "hot" areas. . . . While the Commanding Officer does not wish to detract from the splendid performance of the LCS's, he does not believe they can adequately support a radar picket. Their speed and the short range of their batteries result in the destroyer leaving them far behind. The only alternative is to stay with them at slow speed and hope to knock the planes down. The two LCS's were placed in column 500 yards astern of *Sterett*, for concentration of fire. However, as the raid closed and was finally sighted, the LCS's were about 3,000 yards astern, within effective range of only one (the first) of the planes attacking. . . their complete attention was taken up by the fifth plane which hit

the mast of LCS-36. They do furnish some armed support and a lot of moral support, so have a definite value if larger ships cannot be obtained. . . .

Commander of DesDiv 126 saw CAP aircraft as

the greatest protector of the Radar Picket. They don't stop all the suicides, but they whittle the numbers down to the point where a ship gets an even break with her guns. For suicide runs coming directly in at the ship, 100 percent VT fuzes are believed to give the most efficient form of defensive fire . . . the attack develops so fast that there is no time for a solution or even a range, and the time fuze is worthless or at best, if a close barrage is used, only partially effective. . .[a second destroyer] is a *must* if the Radar Picket is to stand any chance of survival. The Japs can't and don't always overlook the distinct advantages of a simultaneous attack from opposite sides. It is almost bound to succeed unless there are two destroyers in mutual support. Until the attack on 12 April the writer felt that the LCS's assigned to him were wonderful moral support, especially handy to pick up the pieces after one suicider got through. But as far as additional AA support was concerned, it was felt they were almost more trouble than they were worth. They got lost at night, wouldn't always stay where they were put and were too slow to keep within mutually supporting distance of the destroyers. After the way they took care of a group of VALs on the 12th, the writer would particularly desire to have them in any kind of an engagement.

COMINCH added that "small supporting craft have accounted for numerous enemy plane kills. Their work has been outstanding. Indoctrination of this type vessel for mutual support is recommended."

By the end of the war the radar picket function was so important that the commander of Task Force 38, Admiral Mitscher, recommended the construction of specialized ships for the purpose, provided with complete fighter direction facilities, heavy AA armament, and high speed.

The rise of the radar picket function paralleled the rise of the carrier; once fighter planes were available in numbers, they were a far more potent defense for the task force as a whole than were the guns of the individual destroyers, which latter were reduced to the role of self-defense. Picket experience left a strong impression, and as late as 1956 the Atlantic Destroyer Force staff vigorously opposed the introduction of the Tartar (rather than the Terrier) antiaircraft missile largely on the basis of its short range. To a limited extent the development of very long range antiaircraft missiles did restore to the destroyers a measure of their former role as active antiaircraft rather than sensor/fighter-control platforms, but the role forged in 1943–45 remains the central one in 1980.

Destroyers in the Mediterranean fought a very different antiaircraft war, with no carrier fighter support and sometimes almost continuously opposed by massed land-based aircraft while the fast carriers still faced large air attacks only intermittently. Moreover, in European waters the Germans deployed guided bombs and missiles from September 1943 onward; some destroyers and destroyer escorts were fitted with specialized jamming transmitters for convoy and port protection. In addition, ships assigned to the Mediterranean in 1943 in some cases exchanged their torpedo tubes for single Army-type Bofors guns on a temporary basis.

Antisubmarine Warfare

In 1941 destroyers were the only U.S. warships really suited to ocean convoy work, and some early convoys were escorted exclusively by modern destroyers. Gradually the balance shifted towards the new mass-production escorts, the British corvettes and frigates, and the U.S. frigates and destroyer escorts. However, most of these craft were relatively slow, with a speed advantage over their convoy charges but without much of an advantage over a surfaced submarine. Nor did they have the speed in hand that would permit a surface escort to investigate a distant contact (or to seek out stragglers) and then quickly rejoin its convoy. This issue was emphasized by the advent of ship-borne HF/DF, which made it possible to detect surfaced submarines broadcasting at ranges as great as 30 miles. Moreover, the submarines transmitting on the surface (and moving on the surface in daylight) were also the submarines that made the German "wolf pack" system work, since it was they that shadowed the convoys and called in the other submarines. Many postwar analyses showed the value of high speed in destroyers formed into Surface Action Units (SAUs), and in ships provided with very long range detectors in the form of convergence-zone sonars such as SQS-26. The new factor after the war was the ASW weapon that could reach out from a ship to take advantage of long-range detection without much maneuvering on the part of the destroyer proper.

Convoy operations in the North Atlantic were the first U.S. naval involvement in World War II, beginning in September 1941 and continuing into the winter. Generally destroyers operated between Newfoundland and Iceland, in very high seas and extreme conditions. Indeed, the standard operation plan is an indication of the hardships encountered: it called for a week's overhaul at Boston after dropping off a convoy, then a week or ten days at the destroyer base (Casco Bay, Maine) for training and gunnery. As in the contemporary Royal Navy, such slow turnarounds were unacceptable, and training time was eliminated. Morison suggests that 5 days

out of 45 at Boston was a great deal, and the captain of the USS *Niblack* reported in November 1941 that his ship had had no gunnery practice since May.

The winter of 1941–42 brought home once again the convoy escort lessons of the First World War, particularly the supreme importance of steaming endurance. The flush deckers had been satisfactory when U-boat operations had generally been restricted to "focal areas" close to shore, so that escort was required only for a 48-hour outbound run, followed by a meeting with an inbound convoy for a similar inbound run. However, by 1941 the U-boat command had the benefit of air reconnaissance and code-breaking, and could deploy its wolf packs anywhere in the North Atlantic: destroyers *had* to escort convoys across the ocean. Typically they operated in relays, turning over convoys at "ocean meeting points" or "omps": "Westomp" and "Momp" (mid-ocean meeting point). Thus a typical run might last ten days, from Argentia (Newfoundland) outbound to Westomp, thence to Momp to pick up a convoy for Iceland. The flush deckers had sufficient endurance for such runs in good weather, but their fuel consumption nearly doubled in heavier seas running against them, when counted in gallons per mile made good. Matters were only complicated by the slow steaming of the merchant ships, which might arrive at a rendezvous several days late, while the destroyers awaiting them burned their fuel.

The fuel problem explains the urgency of the program to refit the flush deckers for greater endurance, as well as the insistence of DesLant on longer endurance in the new destroyer proposed in wartime (see chapter 6). In practice, all that could be done was to fit merchant tankers to fuel destroyers en route, a technique first tried with the USS *Babbitt* in June 1942. With fuel available in quantity, an escorting destroyer could make sweeps ahead of her convoy without regard to fuel economy. The *Babbitt*, for example, was able to steam all the way from the United Kingdom to "Westomp," leave her convoy, and make Boston at 20 knots.

This problem had at least been anticipated before the war, but convoy operations had many features that were not at all expected. For example, there was no satisfactory means of communication within convoys, as merchant ships were not equipped with VHF radios such as the naval TBS. Such tactical systems were nearly immune to interception and thus to homing by U-boats, but the standard longer-wave sets were not. Steam whistles and loud hailers were the principal substitutes, but destroyers were sometimes used as couriers within a convoy—and were subject to the danger of collision. The USS *Ingraham* was lost in this manner, and the USS *Buck* severely damaged.

Once the United States entered the war, it began a series of troop convoys to Britain, escorted by a combination of destroyers, cruisers, and often capital ships. Some merchant convoys were also subject to U.S. escort, and at this time the only ships available were destroyers and the large "Treasury"-class Coast Guard cutters, which many considered superior to the destroyers for ASW. They were larger and more seaworthy, but not nearly as fast.

By late 1942, the North Atlantic had been divided into a Western Local Area, between the United States and Westomp, in which convoys were escorted by British and Canadian forces; a Mid-Ocean Area (U.S., British, and Canadian ships based in Newfoundland); an Eastern Local Area (Eastomp to Britain, with British escorts); and an Iceland Shuttle (U.S. destroyers based in Iceland, escorting convoys to and from a designated Momp). Generally, the United States controlled the Western Atlantic, the Admiralty the Eastern. One advantage of this system was that it did away with escorts at the Momp awaiting slow convoys; moreover, with fueling en route, destroyers could accompany their convoys all the way from one shore to the other. However, in the absence

Once they became available in numbers, destroyer escorts dominated U.S. ASW operations. Many, such as the ship illustrated, the USS *Martin H. Ray*, were manned by the Coast Guard. Note her HF/DF antenna aft, a major means of U-boat detection at long range; her foremast carries both air- and surface-search radars, as well as IFF antennas at the yardarms and a tactical radio (TBS).

of air cover in mid-Atlantic, the convoys suffered badly during the latter part of 1942.

The peculiar significance of air cover was a consequence of the German tactics, which required the U-boats to remain surfaced a large part of the time in order to gain mobility. Typically, a surfaced U-boat might shadow a convoy, calling in other boats of a wolf-pack, all of which would attack on the surface at night. The U-boat's ability to submerge was important primarily as a means of evasion after it had attacked. To force the U-boat to remain submerged was to deny it mobility and hence to prevent it from closing a target convoy. That could only be done by aircraft, since the U-boats preparing for an attack generally had sufficient speed in hand to remain out of reach of the surface escorts. Only the high speed of a destroyer made counterattack practical.

The other aspect of U-boat warfare was the boats' dependence on communications. The U-boat was managed from a shore headquarters, and the boats themselves had to report regularly. Their transmissions could be used as the basis for HF/DF (high-frequency direction-finding) "cuts" made aboard specially equipped escorts, and the submarines run down. In addition, once the command code had been broken, it was possible for U-boat positions to be predicted with fair accuracy. That, in turn, made it profitable for the Allies to employ offensive ASW groups specifically designed to hunt down submarines at the positions deduced from their intercepted orders. Many destroyers and destroyer escorts were fitted with HF/DF sets, but even those without them benefited from the network of strategic (shore-based) stations, which could often provide bearings accurate enough for tactical use, at least to the extent that concentrations of submarines might be evaded by convoys.

Convoy tactics are inherently inefficient, in that very large numbers of escorts are required, proportional not to the number of submarines, but rather to the number of merchant ship targets at sea at any one time. Offensive tactics were always more attractive, if they could be made practicable by means of some long-range means of submarine detection that could bring the offensive forces into contact with the submarines. This existed in the form of shore-based HF/DF and also in the form of Allied code-breaking organizations that could read the directives issued by the German U-boat command. In neither case did the long-range system provide precise location data; some ASW ship or airplane had to run down the datum and find the submarine in the area indicated. Successful offensive ASW therefore required a unit fast enough to close the datum before the submarine could get far from its estimated po-

sition, and yet with sufficient endurance to search long and hard. In the case of code-breaking, the task was somewhat simplified, as the attacker could arrive on the scene of the submarine's expected position. (Probably the most celebrated case of this type was the destruction of a Japanese submarine patrol line by the destroyer escort *England*.)

Beginning in 1943, the U.S. Navy was able to deploy escort carrier (Hunter-Killer, HUK) groups in support of convoys. Typically, they consisted of an ASW carrier and a screen of about four destroyers or destroyer escorts, and at first they were used primarily to provide air cover over that central Atlantic area beyond shore-based air cover. The carrier aircraft could keep U-boats down, and, in some cases, could sink them. More commonly the submarine would dive, and the surface ships would have to prosecute the contact, a process which might take several days and immense patience. The carriers (and often their consorts) were equipped with HF/DF, which gave them (in effect) an over-the-horizon means of submarine detection, whereas sonar was rarely effective beyond 1,000 yards.

Given the success of code breaking and the system of strategic HF/DF, close escort of convoys was a relatively inefficient use of the escort carrier groups, and by June 1943 they were being used independently and offensively, effectively driving the U-boats from the mid-Atlantic. Given the combination of long-range shore-based aircraft and carrier aircraft, it was no longer safe for submarines to operate on the surface, even at night, and they were reduced to immobility and, therefore, to near impotence. Actual destruction might require destroyer action, but neutralization quite sufficed from the Allied point of view.

The surface ships of the HUK group protected the carrier from submarine attack, as the carrier herself had no means of reliably detecting all submarines in her area. She could detect only those submarines that cooperated by transmitting HF signals or by operating on the surface where they could be seen by eye or radar. Until the advent of the heavy helicopter with dipping sonar it was the destroyer or destroyer escort that guaranteed the security of the carrier. It was also the destroyer that could prosecute a distant contact.

Then the Germans introduced the snorkel, which allowed their submarines to operate at a considerable speed while submerged, and the situation was reversed. The snorkel, moreover, was relatively difficult for airborne radar to detect, so that carrier and land-based aircraft experienced a great reduction in their effective search rates and efficiencies. The efficacy of surface ship HF/DF was sharply limited by another German development, Kurier, a burst transmitter. Thus, of the wide-area detection devices, only code-breaking remained at the end of the war. Aircraft were reduced to searching very limited areas with high-definition radars and then dropping patterns of sonobuoys to find their targets, whereas the destroyers could screen convoys, or could search areas known to contain submarines.

One of the final U.S. ASW operations of the Atlantic war illustrates conditions in 1945, after the advent of the snorkel and Kurier (anti-DF), but before that of the very fast U-Boat, the Type 21 that figured so prominently in postwar thinking. Six German submarines were known to be approaching U.S. waters, and there was some reason to believe that they were associated with a German project to bombard the United States with long-range rockets. Between 5 and 22 April 1945, two escort carriers, the *Croatan* and *Mission Bay*, and 12 destroyer escorts maintained a barrier patrol in the path deduced for the U-Boats, presumably on the basis of broken codes. Each escort carrier was screened by four DEs, and four others patrolled the barrier proper, prepared to pounce on contacts made by carrier aircraft flying overhead.

For example, on 9 April a pilot picked up a small object on his radar at a range of two miles. It was identified as a snorkel, and the pilot also thought he saw a puff of smoke (presumably diesel exhaust). The destroyer escort *Swasey*, on the barrier five miles away, was detached and made sound contact after a search around the datum provided by the initial contact. She attacked with magnetic-fuzed depth charges and heard four explode. Contact was never regained, and it was assumed that the submarine had been destroyed.

Due to the lack of any efficient long-range positive submarine detector, the barrier was quite porous. For example, shortly before midnight on 15 April, the destroyer escort *Stanton*, screening the *Croatan*, made a radar contact 5,000 yards from the carrier, which was steaming slowly through heavy seas. The blip soon disappeared, but the *Stanton* made sound contact and delivered a Hedgehog attack, claiming two hits. Six minutes later all ships in the area were shaken by a terrific explosion, but the submarine apparently survived, as contact was regained three minutes later and she appeared to be moving slowly. The *Frost* had joined the *Stanton* by now, and both ships attacked with their Hedgehogs, the *Stanton* claiming three hits after her third attack. Now there was a strong odor of diesel fuel, and a few minutes later both ships were so badly shaken by an underwater explosion that they thought they had been torpedoed. Even the *Croatan*, 12 miles away, was badly shaken.

Now a second submarine appeared, approaching the task group at high speed on the surface. The *Frost* detected her by radar, then fired star shells at 600 yards, and fired every gun that would bear, down to 20 mm. Her No. 1 and No. 2 3-inch guns were unable to fire due to the heavy seas breaking over her forecastle, and she was unable to ram in the heavy sea. The submarine submerged, only to be picked up on sonar an hour and a half later. There were now four destroyer escorts in pursuit, and the *Frost* coached the *Stanton* into a successful Hedgehog attack in which four hits were made.

> Four minutes later a terrific explosion, even more severe than that obtained from the first submarine, was felt by all ships. All four DE's made contact with the submarine four minutes later, the target showing no action and being located below a large oil slick. Several minor explosions were felt for about five minutes following the severe explosion . . . all four DE's lost contact [which] was not regained.

On 16 April the carrier was ordered to retire 100 miles to the westward, presumably on the basis of intelligence and some estimate of submarine speed of advance.

> At 1127 on 4 May in position 45-16N, 37-30W (about 15 miles from COMINCH's estimated position for a U-Boat that day), *Stanton* made sonar contact but could not hold it when she approached closer than 900–1000 yards. It was believed that this might be a deep submarine so the other five DE's of CortDiv 13 were sent to assist. Contact was regained again at 1830 (3 DE's of TG 22.13 being added to the searching forces at this time) . . . later . . . 3 DE's had a contact at the same time in three different places . . . in view of the continual air and surface search for 48 hours that resulted in no further contact, it is questionable if a sub was present. . . .

This was the last Atlantic ASW cruise of the *Croatan* and her consorts, and her commander took the occasion to praise CortDiv 13 and particularly the *Frost* and *Stanton*. Of seven submarines sunk by the group, six were credited to the destroyer escorts. In effect, the carrier functioned as a hunter, the ships as killers that had to reacquire the submarine and then harry it to death. Aircraft could also destroy submarines, but they had only primitive means of attacking them once they submerged, and above all could not make attack after attack. The heavy dependence on integrated externally supplied intelligence (e.g., COMINCH's U-Boat position estimates) is very striking.

ASW was above all a very lengthy process, and success often depended upon the ability of the hunter to remain in contact with her quarry until the latter had exhausted her battery power and, therefore, her ability to remain submerged. Successful chases might take several days, and the destroyer's ability to remain in contact depended upon her speed in a seaway, a consideration much emphasized in postwar

ASW escort designs. The vast bulk of wartime attacks were made on nonexistent targets: fish, wrecks, even underwater currents. Estimates of the rates of false to real contacts run as high as ten to one. Even when an attack was made on a real submarine, the chance of success was relatively small; success rewarded only the most persistent attackers. The postwar lesson was that ASW ships required sufficient weapons for numerous attacks, and this magazine capacity imposed a minimum limit on escort size.

The attacks themselves were no trivial matter, as submarines had considerable staying power. For example, on 31 October 1943, the USS *Borie* depth-charged a submarine, which elected to surface and fight. During a lengthy running battle, the submarine crew tried to man her deck gun, but the *Borie's* 20-mm. cannon prevented them from doing so; finally the gun was wiped out by the *Borie's* cannon. However, the *Borie* was unable to sink the submarine by 4-inch fire, and both ships maneuvered on the surface, the destroyer attempting to ram and the submarine to evade. When the flush decker finally did ram, she rode up over the submarine's deck, sustaining severe underwater damage along her entire port side. As the two ships rolled together, the *Borie's* crew repelled boarders from the U-Boat with small arms and even sheath knives. Even then the submarine was not finished; when the ships separated she attempted once more to escape, the destroyer firing a torpedo after her. The *Borie* then turned to ram once more, but the submarine evaded again, and, coming alongside, the destroyer fired four depth charges set at 30 feet, which straddled the conning tower and lifted the submarine bodily from the water—but which also damaged the nearby destroyer, almost dead in the water. Even now the submarine was able to move, and the *Borie* turned once more to use her two remaining port side torpedoes. However, according to her action report,

> just prior to firing, with tubes 10 degrees from bearing, the main battery fired a full salvo which knocked an engine room hatch open, catching the underside of the tube, jamming it. One torpedo was fired and seen to pass within 10 feet of the sub's bow, but did not hit. However, a main battery salvo struck the sub's starboard diesel exhaust (the second hit in this spot) and sub immediately slowed, stopped, and surrendered. . . . Within two or three minutes the sub sank stern first at steep angle and exploded, possibly from scuttling charges. . . .

The *Borie* herself was severely damaged and badly handicapped by the large turning circle built into the flush deckers. She sustained such damage that she had to be scuttled the next day. It was no wonder that all U.S. destroyers were fitted with bow reinforcements for ramming shortly afterwards. The *Borie's* ordeal also goes some way towards explaining the postwar insistence on 5-in./54s for the *Mitschers*.

The submarine was not the only problem. Although no casualties were sustained in this latter battle, "because of adverse weather conditions, three officers and twenty-four men were lost when ship was abandoned."

Survivability

Destroyers and their crews proved far tougher than had been expected before the war, from the survival of the *Kearny* in October 1941 through the successful fights against Kamikazes in the spring of 1945. In general, it took damage that had been expected to sink a destroyer to disable her, and damage that had been expected to disable destroyers in many cases failed to do so. Prewar tacticians had seen destroyers as too large and too vulnerable, not merely to shells and to underwater attack, but also to near-miss bombing. This perception accounts for the very strong pressure against the growth of destroyers both in the United States and in foreign navies. War experience, particularly with the modern longitudinally framed ships, was an impressive demonstration of the survivability of the unarmored destroyer, and undoubtedly justified the postwar program of essentially unarmored destroyers and frigates. Particular wartime experiences were used to justify such postwar practices as the adoption of a single screw in destroyer escorts, the use of twin rather than single funnels, and the continued use of splinter protection steel amidships in frigates and large destroyers.

In 1947, BuShips published a summary of war damage to destroyers, concluding that

> A modern destroyer, efficiently manned, may be expected to survive extensive damage from gunfire, bombs, or guided missiles. . . . Virtually without exception the buoyancy and stability characteristics of our destroyers have proved satisfactory up to the point that hull girder collapsed due to extreme structural damage or until the extent of flooding exceeded the floodable length which comprised at least four main compartments.
>
> The main power plant of a modern destroyer occupies over a third of the length and about half the volume of the hull of the ship. It is probable, therefore, that when major damage is sustained by this type of ship some machinery will be deranged. . . . Split plant operation offers the best assurance of retaining mobility and is therefore the basis of casualty control.
>
> One of the outstanding examples of successful casualty control through split plant operations was *Johnston* (DD 557). Her after turbines, gears, and boilers were completely disabled early in the action by heavy caliber gunfire, nevertheless the ship con-

The damaged destroyer *Nelson* steams into Boston harbor after having lost her stern to a German motor torpedo boat off the Normandy beaches, 13 June 1944; 24 of her crew were killed and another 9 wounded. Note the platform for four 20-mm. guns between her after funnel and her Bofors gun platforms, and the removal of her torpedo tubes and No. 2 gun mount to save weight. She was back in action by late November.

tinued to effectively engage the enemy at speeds of around 20 knots for two hours afterward although additional hits finally sank her. In *Hyman* (DD 732) a Kamikaze crash, bomb blast, and severe gasoline fire in way of the forward engine room caused her starboard shaft to wipe its bearings and lock, and also forced personnel to abandon the forward plant. Employing only the independent after plant, *Hyman* continued a vigorous anti-aircraft action for over an hour, maneuvering radically at 18 knots and assisting in shooting down three more attacking planes. . . .

Emergency Diesel generators have repeatedly proved themselves invaluable in damage control. Ships of the 1,630-ton class had to have their Diesel generators removed for weight compensation and were seriously handicapped thereby. Subsequent classes have retained their emergency sets and the 2,200 ton class each carry two, one forward and one aft below decks outside the main engineering spaces. The latter arrangement has largely overcome the formerly frequent casualty of losing all electric power. Two Diesel generators, each with an automatic starting feature, a separate emergency board and an independent riser for casualty power distribution, have very much simplified the problem of establishing control of fires and control of flooding after damage, because emergency power becomes immediately available and its distribution may be kept completely independent of all other installed systems. . . .

High pressure steam piping has demonstrated surprising resistance to blast and fragments although several cases could be cited where virtually intact plants have been made inaccessible by steam leaks. In *Albert W. Grant* main steam lines withstood the full impact of a 6-inch AP projectile in two instances. . . .

In any consideration of the survival powers of the modern destroyer the personnel factor must be recognized. The ship as built has proved its ruggedness, but many vessels survived unprecedented damage largely due to the high degree of training and the heroic determination of the ship's damage control organization. For the same reasons, several that were eventually lost were enabled to remain in action appreciably longer. . . .

The *Kearny* survived a torpedo hit that would have sunk most destroyers, at the break of her forecastle, a point of structural discontinuity. Her forward fire room flooded, and her No. 1 boiler was wrecked completely. The starboard (forward) engine, however, was not badly damaged, although it was slightly deflected. When she was hit, the *Kearny* was steaming with her plant split, i.e., with her forward fire room connected to her forward engine, her after fire room to her after engine. Thus, the damage forward did not affect her after plant, although power was lost for a time due to contamination of the fuel lines by salt water. It took about 15 minutes to clear them, after which the *Kearny* could operate one shaft. At first her after fire room could not supply steam to her forward engine (i.e., could not be cross-connected) because the necessary valve could not be found in the wreckage of the forward fire room, but after a time a cross-connection was effected, and both engines drove her to Iceland, where she was temporarily repaired by the repair ship *Vulcan*, operating in very primitive conditions. In its analysis, the Bureau of Ships commented that the performance of welded connections under considerable stress was most gratifying, and that the survival of the after machinery plant proved the wisdom of its practice of avoiding any access openings between machinery spaces. However, the bureau felt that a somewhat differently placed torpedo hit, near Frame 87 (bulkhead separating forward fire and engine rooms) or Frame 103 (bulkhead separating forward engine room from after fire room) might have been far worse; in the latter case all power might well have been lost, as both elements of the split plant would have been disabled.

Although her hull was noticeably weakened, the *Kearny* did not break up. Moreover, after temporary repairs, she survived a severe storm while en route to Boston for permanent repair. The Royal Navy, which had experienced numerous (and generally fatal) cases of similar damage to her own destroyers, was impressed. In particular, the survival of half of the *Kearny*'s split plant was cited as justification for the decision to adopt a split plant in the 1943 destroyer design that became the postwar *Daring*s and *Weapon*s. In his analysis of war damage to destroyers, the Soviet expert Korotkin noted that in general, although a modern destroyer could survive an underwater hit fore or aft, blowing off bow or stern, she would be sunk by one amidships. Yet, of 20 cases of severe underwater damage amidships to modern U.S. destroyers (including ground and moored mines), 11 survived. In a few cases, moreover, ships remaining afloat but dead in the water had to be scuttled due to the battle situation; late in the war such ships were generally salvaged.

There were a few striking exceptions. Both the *O'Brien* and *Benham* sank as a result of hulls weakened by severe whipping after torpedo hits forward. Such damage is the object of modern under-the-keel munitions, which attack the entire hull girder rather than the watertight integrity of the ship. During World War II fatal whipping damage was more commonly done by magnetic mines. Thus, the destroyers *Corry* and *Meredith* were broken up by German ground mines off Normandy in June 1944. However, the *Meredith*, a *Sumner*, had such residual strength in her hull that she took 29½ hours to sink. She was hit under her forward engine room, and lost all power as three machinery spaces flooded through a 65-foot hole in her port shell. Towed to an anchorage, she gradually broke in half as her unflooded bow and stern worked during the night. The *Rowan*, hit off Salerno by an MTB torpedo, sank after a mass detonation aft, probably of her depth-charge magazine. She was considered a unique instance of the explosion of a weapon instantly setting off a magazine; indeed, one of the surprises of the war was the extent to which high explosives in magazines and in torpedo warheads could endure damage and fire without "cooking off." In other cases, severe damage (leading to the loss of

the stern) resulted in progressive flooding that could not be controlled.

In a 1945 analysis of underwater damage to destroyers, BuShips observed that survival after severe damage amidships depended not only on the extent of the damage, i.e., on the extent to which the hull girder survived, but also on the sea state and the extent of flooding outside the damaged part of the ship.

Among the 1,630-ton destroyers, *Hambleton* was struck by a torpedo on the port side in way of the forward engine room. The remaining effective strength members after damage consisted essentially of about one-half of the main deck, the starboard sheer and the next two lower side strakes, with their longitudinals. Two main machinery spaces were flooded to the waterline, and a third to a depth of about 4 feet. The two ends of the ship worked noticeably relative to each other in a light sea. Calculations indicate that the minimum section modulus of remaining effective structure was reduced to approximately 15 percent of that of the intact transverse section. With the ship in the still water condition, it is estimated that the tensile stress at the lower edge of the partially intact "C" strake approached 22 tons per square inch, the yield point of high tensile steel, of which the middle one-half length was constructed. Although the warhead charge is estimated as equivalent to about 860 pounds of TNT, the vessel survived, principally because of good weather, the proximity of a safe anchorage, and excellent damage control measures. *Bristol*, another 1,630-ton destroyer, was hit in way of the same machinery space by a torpedo with a warhead charge believed to be somewhat smaller. The same three machinery spaces were involved, but all three flooded to the waterline rapidly. Although sea conditions were favorable, about 4 minutes after being hit, *Bristol* broke in two. Possibly the somewhat greater stresses induced the third machinery space flooding completely to the waterline . . . was an important factor. *Beatty*, another vessel of the same class, incurred a reduction in section modulus about the same as that of *Hambleton*. However, three main machinery spaces flooded to the waterline, and some 4 hours and 20 minutes after the detonation, in spite of only a light swell, complete structural failure, similar to that of *Bristol*, resulted.

Among the 2,100-ton destroyers, *La Vallette* was struck by a torpedo on the port side abreast the forward engine room. The torpedo had an estimated charge equivalent to about 522 pounds of TNT. . . . Two machinery spaces flooded to the waterline immediately, and a third to a depth of about 4 feet. The sea was moderate. There was no evidence of any working of the hull. *La Vallette* survived handily. . . . The detonation of the mine which damaged *Wadleigh* left only the main deck, the sheer and next lower strakes on each side, with their longitudinals, as the main effective strength members . . . the section modulus of remaining effective structure below the new neutral axis was reduced to about 14 percent of that in the intact condition. Three main machinery spaces flooded to the waterline. The bow and stern worked noticeably with respect to each other. That *Wadleigh* survived was due primarily to favorable sea conditions. *Ross* was damaged by two well-separated mines, which were much less powerful than the one in the case of *Wadleigh*. Less than a 40 percent reduction in cross sectional area occurred, and *Ross* was never in danger of breaking up. *Ross* incurred flooding not only of three main machinery spaces, but also of a considerable portion of the ship aft of the after engine room. Despite this extensive flooding and severe structural damage in two locations, *Ross* safely rode out a severe storm.

There are a number of reasons why the 2,100 and 2,200-ton destroyers have shown greater resistance to breaking up than have the earlier classes. Compared to the earlier destroyers the two later classes have greater beam and depth to hull and also much heavier scantlings with correspondingly smaller bending stresses in the intact condition. In addition, in the middle one-half length, the sheer and next lower side strakes and all main deck strakes are STS rather than HTS. This has resulted in a greater margin of strength in the ship girder to resist breaking in two after damage.

According to BuShips,

The loss of *William D. Porter* (DD 579) illustrated the danger involved in the loss of watertight integrity on the first platform deck aft. A bomb detonated under the ship in way of the after engineering spaces, flooding the after engine room and distorting some doors and hatches along the first platform deck aft. Slow flooding progressed through four compartments abaft the engine room and also filled the after fire room through the damaged bulkhead gland on the starboard shaft. For three hours ... the draft aft increased slowly until the after half of the main deck

was immersed and the fantail was 16 feet under water. The ship then rolled on its beam ends and plunged by the stern. ...

In later vessels of the DD 692 class there are no doors in the third bulkhead abaft the after engine room. Access fore and aft is obtained by going up and over via the deckhouse. An alteration sealing the doors in bulkhead 170 both in the remaining ships of the 692 class and in the 445 class has now been authorized and, when accomplished, will markedly reduce the vulnerability of these ships to progressive flooding in the after end of the ship. Owing to the narrower beam and higher freeboard forward, flooding in that area is not so serious and a similar precaution is not required. ...

In many cases, what mattered was not so much the ultimate loss of the ship as her ability to keep fighting despite fatal damage. That was particularly the case with the "small boys" covering the escort carriers off Samar. Faced by 4 Japanese battleships, 6 heavy cruisers, and 2 light cruisers leading 12 destroyers, the 3 *Fletcher*s and 4 DEs covering Taffy 3 could only hope to hold off their enemies with a mixture of torpedo attacks and gunfire that might put off Japanese fire controls. Their mere survival, with torpedo tubes intact, represented a threat that the Japanese commander had to respect.

Their torpedo tactics were the classic ones practiced prewar: attack from behind a smoke screen. The *Johnston* came first, launching her ten torpedoes from 10,000 yards at a heavy cruiser, and making one hit on the *Kumano*, flagship of one of the two Japanese cruiser divisions. She was then hit by three 14-inch shells that penetrated her main deck and passed through the after machinery spaces, detonating in her reduction gears, turbine, and No. 2 boiler. Shortly afterward she was hit by three light-cruiser shells. The after fire and engine room were

The action off Samar epitomized classic destroyer concepts and was responsible for postwar interest in antiship torpedoes for fast task force escorts. Here two ships of the screen lay smoke to protect the escort carriers from the Japanese surface attack force; the ship at the left appears to be a destroyer escort. An early postwar account of this heroic action was, appropriately, entitled "Destroyer Dust," for that is nearly what the screening force became.

lost, and speed fell to 17 knots; in addition, all power to the after three 5-inch guns was lost. However, the *Johnston* was far from finished. A rain squall provided enough cover to permit emergency repairs, so that No. 3 and 5 guns could fire in partial director control (follow-the-pointer), although No. 4 had to fire in complete local control. Steering was shifted to manual aft, the phone link with the bridge surviving. The *Johnston* remained game enough to fire on the battleship *Kongo*, using a radar ranging system that still, incredibly, continued to function. She was ultimately a victim of progressive flooding due to small-caliber shells that tore up her side amidships. However, it took about two and a half hours for this damage to kill her, and that was after she and her consorts had dissuaded the Japanese battleships attacking Taffy 3.

BuShips commented after the war that "but for the continued presence of the enemy after the ship was immobilized, it is likely that *Johnston* could have survived. No uncontrolled fires were raging, no serious list had developed, and the rate of flooding was slow enough to permit control if attention could have been given to the problem. . . . Few destroyers in their battle performance have more completely capitalized on their design features than *Johnston*. That she fought so effectively at such a critical time for over two hours after severe initial damage not only inspires deep admiration for her ship's company, but also considerable confidence in her design and construction."

The other destroyer victim was the *Hoel*, the screen flagship. She made directly for the *Kongo*, opened fire with her guns as soon as the range closed sufficiently, and delivered a half-salvo of torpedoes at 9,000 yards, after taking a hit on the bridge that destroyed all voice radios. Like the *Johnston*, she soon lost one of her two engines, as well as bridge steering control, her fire control system, and her after guns; but she forced the *Kongo* to slow down in order to evade those five torpedoes. Similarly, she launched a half-salvo at the heavy cruiser *Kumano*, at 6,000 yards, and although that ship was not hit, her evasive maneuvers bought valuable time. By this time torpedo control had been reduced to manual train and selective aim by the local torpedo officer. A modern reader has very much the sense of the value of manual backups, even when highly centralized combat system control is necessary for optimum results. According to Morison's account, "the one idea of her skipper as of Commander W.D. Thomas (ComDesDiv 93) on board, was to inflict maximum damage on the enemy while she floated, in the hope of diverting major-caliber fire from the escort carriers and giving them a few minutes' grace." The *Hoel* was hit by over 40 shells from 5- through 16-inch, riddled at her

waterline and with major-caliber detonations in her forward machinery. She was abandoned only when dead in the water with a 20-degree list to port and her main deck aft awash, and she capsized 15 minutes later. In all, she survived about 90 minutes after her first hit.

The third destroyer, the *Heermann*, was much more fortunate. She was able to dodge most of the fire directed at her, chasing salvos, and engaged three ships with partial torpedo salvos. Shell damage was limited to two medium-caliber (cruiser) hits, one below her bridge and one forward, which passed through without detonating.

Thus, except for large shells that found some solid piece of machinery against which to detonate, the destroyers proved largely immune to single major hits. They succumbed to cumulative damage, which literally tore away their waterlines, flooding them. For example, the *Johnston* was able to control the flooding from her first hits, few of which in any case penetrated her waterline. Some of the holes in her side admitted water only when she heeled over in tight turns. However, after one hit (the thirteenth) disabled her forward fire room and opened holes that flooded it, she was left dead in the water, to be riddled at 1,000 yards. Even then, she did not sink. Rather, since the enemy was closing rapidly, her captain ordered all watertight doors forward opened "to facilitate sinking" and she was abandoned. Some minutes later her bow went under, she rolled over, and plunged. That kind of steadily mounting damage could not keep them from carrying out their mission, thanks to the degree to which the usual centralized control from the bridge could be replaced by local control—and given the courage and determination of their crews.

The destroyer escorts provided a similar performance. Although equipped with torpedo tubes, they had never practiced torpedo attack tactics, either singly or in company. They could not form up with the destroyers for their torpedo attack, but were ordered to prepare for a follow-up. The *Samuel B. Roberts* actually went in with the three destroyers for their second attack, firing successfully at the Japanese heavy cruisers, which evaded her. Once that salvo of three torpedoes was gone, she had no equalizer left, and could only serve to dissipate enemy shellfire. She was too slow to evade fire for very long, and after her No. 1 fire room was knocked out, she took many hits, which literally tore up her hull structure, sinking her. About ten minutes after her first hit, there was a large explosion amidships, credited at the time to HE (rather than AP) 14-inch shells, which tore a hole 30 to 40 feet long and 7 to 10 feet high on the port side, wiping out all power with No. 2 engine room, rupturing the after fuel tanks, and

The *Fletcher*-class destroyer *Hazelwood* survived a Kamikaze that struck and demolished her bridge, killing 10 of her 19 officers, including her captain, as well as 67 enlisted men, 29 April 1945, off Okinawa.

starting a fire on the fantail. Ten minutes later she was abandoned.

Miraculously, her three companion DEs survived. Both the *Raymond* and *Dennis* succeeded in launching torpedoes, although neither made any hits; only the latter was struck, by a pair of cruiser shells. One passed through above the waterline without exploding, and the other damaged the after 40-mm. director. Considering the volume of fire that day, such an escape was most remarkable. Again, the ineffectiveness of the Japanese ammunition, almost certainly armor-piercing, against unarmored ships is notable. As for the remaining ship, the *John C. Butler*, she was too slow to be able to reach an effective firing position. Instead, she laid part of the smoke screen behind which Taffy 3 sought to escape. Morison comments that the leading Japanese heavy cruiser was making better speed than the *Butler*, and thus the latter could not close to effective torpedo range unless the enemy changed course toward the carriers. As for damage, she managed to evade the enemy shells, and after a time the Japanese shifted fire to the carriers, their main targets in any case. The intensity of the battle was such that the ship had to cease fire after about an hour, as she was about to run out of ammunition; she then shifted to the forward edge of the formation to afford it better smoke cover.

Kamikazes accounted for nearly half of all destroyers damaged (or lost) due to above-water attack, and they were of particular interest postwar because it was believed that they indicated the type of dam-

age to be expected from antiship missiles. The Kamikaze combined an impact explosion by its bomb with the threat of fire from the gasoline remaining in its tanks. It could not penetrate deep into the structure of its victim, but on the other hand, the sudden, intense, and widespread fire was evaluated by BuShips as probably the greatest single damage control problem it introduced. "One such fire, uncontrolled, led to the handling room explosion and loss of *Abner Read*, despite only minor initial structural damage. In *Hughes* (DD 410), efficient firefighting personnel brought a fire of similar proportions under control.. . ."

BuShips felt that the two most spectacular cases of survival after Kamikaze damage were the *Sumner*-class minelayers *Aaron Ward* (DM 34) and *Lindsey* (DM 32). On 3 May 1945 the *Aaron Ward* and *Little* shared a picket station off Okinawa. The first Kamikaze was splashed at a range of about 100 yards, but momentum carried the engine and propeller into the after deckhouse: in modern terms the missile lost its control surfaces but then "went ballistic." There was little damage, and a second Kamikaze was splashed at a range of 1,200 yards. However, a third was able to drop a bomb that exploded in the after engine room; it crashed just below the after 40-mm. mount, spraying gasoline over No. 3 5-inch gun mount, which lost all power and communication and which then had to operate in local control. The next few Kamikazes did not press home their attacks, and damage control parties were able to fight the fires. However, the general destruction around No. 3 gun mount appears to have cut communications leads aft, so that the ship could only be steered from the fantail. A very heavy attack followed, and the *Aaron Ward* was still capable of destroying two of the attackers. However, a third just missed her bridge, cutting the steam line to her whistle and several antennas. A fourth hit amidships, releasing its bomb just before crashing to blow in the side of the forward fire room. Now there was no main power plant left, just the forward emergency diesel generator. A fifth attacker crashed the deckhouse at the base of the forward funnel, and a sixth hit the after stack, its bomb detonating in the after uptakes. Morison (but not BuShips) also mentions yet another airplane, coming in just after the hit on the forward funnel, destroying the after starboard Bofors.

In effect, the entire superstructure from the fore funnel aft to No. 3 twin 5-in./38 gun mount was demolished, and of the spaces between Frames 72 and 170, i.e., between Mk 37 director and the after end of the superstructure, all but the forward engine room and some starboard water tanks flooded. In all, 1,650 tons of water was shipped. Fire-main pressure and power forward remained throughout, thanks to the forward emergency generator.

It was all over very quickly: the concentrated air attack lasted only from about 1859 to about 1921, and two LCS(L) came alongside to help at 1935; fires fires were under control by 2024. In all, 45 men died and 49 others were wounded, out of a total of over 300 on board. At 2106 her sister minelayer *Shannon* took the *Aaron Ward* under tow for Kerama Retto, where she was made ready for sea again in six weeks, proceeding to New York on one engine.

Her companion, the *Little*, was less fortunate. She was hit amidships in quick succession by four Kamikazes. The first hit her port side and its engine penetrated to demolish her after low-pressure turbine and condenser. Another also crashed into her after engine room, and another hit her port side amidships, bodily moving No. 3 boiler. The fourth crashed into her after torpedo tubes. In these explosions the decks, bulkheads, and shell plating were demolished in way of the three after machinery spaces. Secondary explosions may have helped: Morison reports that the air flask of the torpedoes in the tubes aft exploded and that the plane's engine or bomb continued in to destroy No. 3 and 4 boilers. In any case, enough structural strength was lost to make the ship jackknife and sink 14 minutes after the first hit. Even well before that, she was left dead in the water, without internal communications. Seven minutes after the first crash, with her main deck awash, her CO ordered Abandon Ship. She suffered 6 dead, 24 missing, and 79 wounded.

The *Lindsey* (DM 32) was hit by a Kamikaze on her starboard side below her bridge, then by another diving steeply into her port side, striking near her magazine forward. The second plane's bomb appears to have touched off a mass detonation of the forward 5-inch powder magazine, which was separated from the No. 2 mount magazine by the refrigerated stowage space. The entire bow forward of No. 2 gun mount was blown off, hinging upward. The rest of the ship remained relatively intact, however, and the *Lindsey* was refitted.

There were two major exceptions to this generally excellent record. Four destroyers were lost by foundering in storms, and two were lost by internal explosions, generally attributed to ammunition. Of the four storm losses, three were incurred in the great Pacific typhoon of December 1944, through which the fast carrier task force (Task Force 38) steamed: two *Farragut*s (the *Hull* and *Monaghan*) and one *Fletcher* (the *Spence*). Both of the older destroyers were operating with their fuel tanks about three-quarters full, which in normal circumstances would have provided sufficient stability. However, caught in huge waves and winds as high as 110 knots, they rolled heavily, and the free surfaces of the partly filled tanks proved fatal. In each case the ship was pinned on her beam ends and flooded through topside openings; there were few survivors. For example, of 18 officers and and 245 men aboard the *Hull*, 7 officers and 55 men were rescued. Only six enlisted men survived the *Monaghan*. Several of their sister ships were very nearly lost in similar circumstances. For instance, the *Dewey* found herself broadside to the wind and in the trough of gigantic waves. She jettisoned topside weights and went to the length of ballasting the tanks on her weather side to increase her righting moment. Morison comments that, had she passed the eye of the typhoon at this time and the wind whipped around, she would have been lost; and she was close to the eye of the storm. Ultimately, important factors in her survival included not only prompt weight reduction and the risky weather-side ballasting, but also continuous pumping and bailing, and the fortunate loss of No. 1 stack (with its considerable sail area). The *Aylwin* also water-ballasted her weather side and survived.

By this time it was Third Fleet doctrine for destroyers to ballast with salt water when encountering rough weather. However, destroyer commanders always had an eye to refueling, given their short legs, and once tanks had been filled with salt water they might take as long as six hours to clear. By then a ship might miss her chance at the tanker. Morison argues, too, that the wartime expansion of the fleet resulted in command by relatively junior officers, who had graduated in the Naval Academy classes of 1937 and 1938. Thus, it may be significant that the *Dewey* was flagship of DesRon 1, commanded by a relatively senior officer, Captain P.V. Mercer, formerly Admiral Nimitz's assistant chief of staff; certainly her CO credited his ship's survival to Captain Mercer's "steadying influence, sound advice and mature judgment." The *Aylwin*, the other survivor, flew the pennant of Captain J.T. Acuff, commanding the Third Fleet logistics and plane-replenishment group.

The *Farragut*s were well loaded with fuel when the typhoon struck, but the *Spence* was down to 15 percent capacity. She formed part of the screen of Task Group 38.3 but, upon failing to fuel from the battleship *New Jersey*, was sent to Captain Acuff's group in the hope of fueling there, as she was down to 24 hours' fuel at 8 knots. Again, there was a great reluctance to fill tanks with salt water, and again the ship rolled very heavily. Only 1 officer and 23 enlisted men were rescued.

The case of the 1,850-ton *Warrington* in the Atlantic may have been parallel. She departed Chesapeake Bay escorting a stores ship to Trinidad, 11 September 1944, and was caught in a severe hurricane. Both ships hove-to, and soon lost contact. She suffered a "derangement" of her main engines, and within three hours began to take on large quantities of water as she rolled on her beam ends. Now all power was lost, and the survival of the ship herself came into question. Top hamper was jettisoned, but that did not solve the problem, and the ship was finally abandoned at 1300 on 13 September, sinking about 15 minutes later. An official inquiry suggested that the cause of her loss was the complete loss of power due to flooding through hatches and uptakes; her CO was acquitted of any blame.

The destroyer escorts showed superior seaworthiness in both Atlantic and Pacific storms, riding them out like corks, although they rolled heavily and could hardly be described as comfortable. An important safety feature in their design was the covered passage fore and aft, which made it possible for men to move about without risking loss on the exposed decks. Destroyers, which were far more heavily loaded, tended to be far wetter.

The two ammunition explosions were both attributed to the sensitivity of Hedgehog/Mousetrap projectiles, which were contact-fused to explode against submarine hulls. On 3 January 1944, the destroyer *Turner* exploded and sank off Ambrose Light; she was one of 12 *Benson*s armed with Mousetrap. On 30 April 1946, the destroyer escort *Solar*, unloading ammunition at Earle, New Jersey, exploded, destroying not only herself but also much of the adjacent pier. Both cases were cited postwar in the standard BuOrd manual on ordnance safety, as cautionary examples of the sensitivity of these weapons, and they were again cited to support a proposal to delete Hedgehog from what became the DLG 6 design.

War Alterations

A variety of changes made to destroyers in wartime, beyond the widespread antiaircraft and ASW rearmament treated elsewhere, deserve special mention. These might be grouped under the heads of increased survivability and increased fighting power against aircraft and submarines. The former required, for example, the provision of portable gasoline-driven pumps that could operate even when power was lost; improvements to fire-main systems so that they became less vulnerable to single hits; improvements in watertight integrity as internal and external hull openings were sealed. Ships were fitted with degaussing cables, as the threat of the magnetic mine was dramatized by British experience in 1939–40; in addition, they were "depermed" in special fixed installations. Much of the usual peacetime outfit had to be given up to save top weight, reductions in boats being the most obvious modification. It should be kept in mind that nearly all of the destroyers built within treaty limits were considered top-heavy even in 1941, and that matters never really improved: normal margins had been shaved to achieve very heavy batteries on those restricted displacements. Another, and very visible, wartime survivability feature was the wide use of splinter protection, which shows as bulwarks around fire controls and automatic weapons. Less visible but equally essential was the effort to armor the floors of exposed sponsons, as fragments from bombs bursting alongside were apt to strike them.

In some cases a choice had to be made between some aspects of protection and the need to avoid the top weight that might itself sharply reduce a ship's powers of survival. Perhaps the most dramatic such case was the decision to give up emergency diesel generators in the *Benson* class. There were also careful attempts to pare down the weight of splinter protection, for example, from ten to three pounds of STS.

Bridge design itself was an issue of considerable controversy. In the United States Navy it was (and is) standard practice for the conning officer to stand near the helmsman. The latter was generally in an enclosed pilot house, with projecting wings by means of which the ship could be conned. Standard British practice, on the other hand, calls for a physical separation between officer and quartermaster, with the former often placed on an open platform. Early war experience, which the British freely transmitted to the Americans, suggested that the uninterrupted view from an open conning position was particularly valuable in dealing with air attacks, as the officer could follow aircraft crossing over the ship. In convoy operations, a similar uninterrupted view was valued as it permitted a complete scan of the horizon, again in a complex situation in which targets might be crossing the ship's bows. This requirement explains the unusual bridge structure of the "high bridge" destroyer escort, and also the semiopen bridge adopted for later *Fletchers* and for *Sumners* and *Gearings*. In the earlier ships the removal of the 2½-meter range finder previously mounted atop the bridge left open a space that could be used by the conning officer, and the prevalence of enclosures there suggests that this was often done. Just how standard this practice was appears to have depended upon the views of the particular CO involved. Postwar, the open bridge became less and less popular as destroyers operated more often in extreme weather, and as radar and long-range weapons came more and more to dominate antiaircraft actions. Existing open bridges were gradually enclosed, and the debate over bridge arrangement shifted to one concerning the relationship between bridge and CIC. Arguments now turned to the vulnerability of ship control, given the concentration of bridge and CIC personnel and equipment, versus the need for close coordination as time to react grew shorter and shorter.

The wide use of power-driven automatic weapons (40-mm. and 1.1-inch) and great increases in radar, radio, ECM, and sonar suits all added considerably to the normal power loads that destroyer electrical systems had to absorb. However, with two exceptions it does not appear that they were fitted in wartime with more powerful ship-service turbogenerators. The flush deckers did have their standard pair of 25-kw machines replaced by a pair of 60-kw turbogenerators, and as rebuilt, the *Cassin* and *Downes* were fitted with the standard pair of 200-kw AC/40-kw DC units then in production for the repeat *Benson* class; presumably the 132/40-kw type with which they had originally been fitted was no longer available.

Wartime additions had a dual effect on habitability. First, more men (particularly technicians) were required to maintain and operate the new weapons and sensors, and destroyer complements in general grew considerably. For example, in 1938 the USS *Mahan* was rated to accommodate 12 officers, 14 petty officers, and 178 enlisted men. In 1945, her sister ship, the *Drayton*, was rated for 16 officers and 235 enlisted men, including petty officers. At the same time, wartime improvements tended to encroach upon the space originally assigned to berths and cabins. For example, in many classes the new CICs displaced

officers' staterooms. Enlarged sonar spaces took up scarce hull volume, as did the many types of radar shipped in wartime—not to mention their stocks of spare parts. Crowded conditions were accepted in wartime, but the classes retained postwar had to be made more comfortable if the Navy were to retain its experienced men. This last point, a continuing theme in U.S. warship design since the early 1950s, first really surfaced in a study of the habitability of the wartime *Fletcher* and *Sumner* designs. Although in wartime both had easily accepted enormous additions of weapons and sensors from a weight and strength point of view, both had been designed with prewar (i.e., before radar and most automatic weapons) manning in mind, and both showed signs of severe overcrowding.

Perhaps the least-noticed wartime change was a massive increase in ammunition stowage. The tables of weights carried show doubling of ammunition weight in many cases. This was not disastrous from a stability point of view, because most of the added weight was relatively deep in the ship. It did, however, contribute to the enormous growth of destroyer displacements in wartime, which is evident from the tables. In addition, prewar design figures are somewhat misleading. That is, standard and full load displacements were computed on the basis of a standard allowance of 100 rounds per gun plus 100 rounds of illuminating shells (star shells) per ship. However, magazines were designed to accommodate in addition a "mobilization" supply, normally stowed aboard tenders, to bring the total per gun to 300 rounds, plus a total of 200 rounds of star shell per ship. The peacetime figure was important because of treaty restrictions on destroyer displacement as well as legal restrictions on total U.S. Navy destroyer tonnage, which remained in force even after the end of the treaty regime. The logic involved was tortuous. For example, in 1937 it was proposed that, as space aboard tenders was limited, 150 rounds per gun be carried aboard destroyers. The extra 50 were, however, excluded from the standard displacement calculations on the ground that they were stowage, for peacetime only, whereas standard displacement referred to a ship ready for battle.

Early war experience showed that 300 rounds per gun was far from enough, and by 1945 capacities in some classes approached the postwar standard of 600. The *Bensons* could carry 1,800 rounds (360 per gun), and the *Fletchers* were designed for 2,100 (425 per gun), although by late in the war a typical unit, the *Van Valkenburgh*, carried 2,775 (525 per gun) in her magazines and another 250 in ready-service stowage. The *Sumners* accommodated fewer rounds. For example, the *Fraser*, a minelayer, carried 2,110 rounds in her magazine (352 per gun) plus 292 rounds of star shell (47 per gun), plus 300 of ready service. She was penalized in that her hull had essentially the volume of a *Fletcher*, and so could not accommodate a 20 percent increase in magazine volume. Prewar ships could accommodate no such increases; for example, in 1944 the *Aylwin* carried about 1,000 rounds for her four guns, plus 50 per gun in ready-service stowage. The 1,850-ton "leaders" were even more constricted.

The first postwar destroyer, which became the *Mitscher*, was originally designed for 350 rounds per (slow-firing) 5-in./54, and 700 per rapid-fire 3-in./50. With the adoption of the rapid-fire single mount the capacity per mount was held steady at 700 (now 700 per gun). In later types the 5-in./54 magazine typically holds about 600 rounds, and 450 are provided for a 3-in./50 (plus 150 in ready-service stowage, and 36 on the gun mount).

This does not even count the massive increase in light weapons and in their ammunition. For example, in 1942 the standard allowance for a 40-mm. gun was set at 2,400 rounds, i.e., over two tons of ammunition; existing destroyers were generally assigned half this load. Generally, 500 more were in ready-service stowage, 150 rounds in racks on the bulwark and 350 in ready-service rooms adjoining the mount or just below it. In the *Sumner*s an attempt was made to provide sufficient stowage for the full 2,400 rounds per barrel, but the great increase in the number of guns probably made this impossible. Many were carried in ready-use racks at the weapons, where they contributed to top weight; late in the war BuShips felt constrained to limit ready-use ammunition quite sharply. In March 1945, a Gibbs & Cox employee on temporary Navy duty commented that "considerably more ammunition is stowed topside than is provided for on plans or contemplated. This is particularly true of 40 mm. and 20 mm." Again, postwar, to provide enough proper stowage for ammunition capacities of wartime size, designers had to accept considerable growth in destroyer use.

Indeed, the general lesson, if there is one, of the additions made during wartime was that all of them violated the policies of margins laid down by BuShips designers, so that properly designed ships with the same "paper" characteristics—and particularly equipment—were far larger than their wartime equivalents. This type of growth is impossible to analyze, yet one cannot but be impressed by the size of the postwar *Forrest Sherman*s, not so very different (at least at first) from the wartime *Gearing*s as they emerged from the waves of war modifications.

9

Destroyer ASW:
World War II and
After

If the convoy was the great tactical invention of World War I ASW, one might see the wolf pack as the great innovation of World War II. The Germans saw the concentration of escort power embodied in a convoy as a force that had to be matched by a similar concentration of submarines. Such a concentration would of necessity leave wide areas of ocean empty of U-boats; it would be vital to the concentration strategy for the central U-boat command to follow convoy movements in detail. Signal intelligence became a vital element of the submarine campaign.

It followed that submarine operations against any particular convoy would require very extensive communication between the centralized U-boat command and the boats at sea, and between the boats of a wolfpack itself. Signal intelligence would therefore provide the ASW forces with vital information; and the *tactical* use of radio by the individual U-boats presented the possibility of using radio direction-finding to pinpoint their location. This opportunity was realized in the form of high-frequency direction-finding (HF/DF).

As in the earlier war, the chief effect of aircraft was to keep U-boats immobile; but now aircraft could also kill submarines they found on the surface and to some extent they could detect submerged submarines via magnetic anomaly detection (MAD).

The great new fact of surface ship ASW was sonar, which permitted a destroyer to *track* a submerged submarine reliably—as long as the destroyer did not pass too close to the submarine. This limit was the result of the horizontal direction of the sonar beam; there was a "dead" space in a wide cone extending out from the ship unless, as in many British ships, a downward-looking "depth-finding" set was installed.

In effect, the standard depth-charge attack was no longer the best way to proceed, since in making it the destroyer would be giving up its sonar contact with the submarine. A simple way around this difficulty was for destroyers to attack in pairs: one to keep the submarine under observation, the other to be coached in to attack. A more basic solution was an ASW weapon that the destroyer could fire at a submarine still within sonar range. This was Hedgehog, the British-developed spigot mortar.

Hedgehog had to take into account not only the close-range fade of sonar contact, but also the absence of accurate depth determination. The solution adopted was to fuze the projectile to explode only upon contact; in effect, it made up for the lack of reliable depth data by sweeping all depths, as opposed to depth charges with their hydrostatic fuzes. The larger charge of the latter would be effective even if they did not actually strike the submarine; and the explosion of depth charges that did not actually do lethal damage was taken to have considerable incidental effect. This was an important argument in favor of a depth-charge projector such as Squid or the later Weapon Alfa. At the end of the

The development of scanning sonar made possible much larger and more powerful sonar arrays, and ultimately led to the use of very low frequencies for extreme range; where World War II sets typically operated at 15 to 25 kilocycles, the SQS-26, illustrated aboard the large destroyer *Willis A. Lee* in Boston (April 1966), operates at about 3.5. At this time the ship was being fitted with a rubber dome, which greatly improved sonar performance by reducing energy loss as sound passed through it; earlier sonars (including earlier installations of SQS-26) had used thin steel "windows." Bow installations were proposed as early as 1948, but none was made until the late fifties. That they brought drydocking problems is evident from this photograph.

war, proximity fuzes for Hedgehog were in the experimental stage, but the Hedgehog warhead was too small to derive very much benefit from them.

In 1943 the Royal Navy introduced a new depth-charge mortar, Squid, which used a special sonar to aim three mortar-fired depth charges at a contact, fuzing them to explode at the proper depth. The system was considered accurate to within 20 feet of actual depth below 100 feet, and good down to 800 feet. Results of RN operations in 1943–44 showed a kill probability of 20 percent, compared to 15 percent for Hedgehog and only 5 for a single depth-charge pattern. In theory the higher sinking rate of such a weapon would be of particular value at great depths, i.e., for the submarines coming into service in 1944–45. Such a weapon is essentially a gun, and in naval architectural terms it takes up the kind of space and weight that a gun does. Ultimately, that had to mean stabilization, director fire, and magazine capacity.

In a more general sense, wartime ASW weapon development emphasized reliable underwater trajectories, which were necessary if the sonar data were to be used effectively. Thus, considerable effort was spent on a new teardrop depth charge (Mk 9), which was both faster (14.2 ft./sec.) and straighter-sinking; to achieve these qualities the designers were willing to reduce the HE load to 200 pounds. The other major force in wartime depth-charge development was the greater crush depth of wartime-constructed U-boats. Thus, the standard maximum setting of 300 feet had to be doubled by 1942; and sink rates had to rise if the charges were to arrive anywhere near the submarine. That is, a charge sinking at 10 ft./sec. requires a full minute to reach 600 feet—during which time a submarine scuttling off at 6 knots travels about 600 feet. As a first step in this direction, 150 pounds of lead were added to depth-charge cases.

Another wartime development was a proximity depth charge with a magnetic or acoustic (doppler) fuze. The first magnetic type, Mk 8, weighed 520 pounds, which included 250 lbs. of HE and 150 of lead (sink rate, 11.5 ft./sec.). A hydrostatic fuze was provided to detonate the charge in the event it did not come close enough to a U-boat for the magnetic exploder to work. It did not work out in practice; the acoustic exploder was only developmental at the end of the war.

U.S. weapon policy at the outbreak of war was to arm all fleet destroyers with a pair of stern tracks for five 600-lb. depth charges each (authorized for the Battle Force January 1941); the older flush deckers, which could not take the new heavy charges, were to get tracks for 24 or more 300-lb. charges. K-guns were soon added. Thus in June 1942, the *Farragut*s had two five-charge tracks and were authorized for four K-guns on a temporary basis; however,

these were to be landed when the twin Bofors became available, which shows the fine balance between ASW and AAW in a fleet destroyer. K-guns were similarly excluded from the ultimate batteries of the tender leaders; but the five-gun 1,500-ton destroyers were all destined for four K-guns each. This was not the case in the four-tube ships, which were short of deck space. However, some of the *Benham*s had already had two banks of tubes removed; they were to have seven-charge tracks and four projectors. Some already had a Y-gun as well. The *Sims* class had six K-guns and the longer tracks; in a few ships a 12 (600-lb.)-charge track was a temporary feature. The "1,630 ton" and later classes are covered in chapters 5 and 6.

A striking feature of U.S. policy was that no fleet destroyers had Hedgehog. The Hedgehog spigot mortar was mounted in every DE and PF—and in many flush deckers converted to escort configuration. Hedgehog was quite heavy, partly due to its massive recoil. Early in April 1943, the commander of the Atlantic Fleet ASW Unit at Boston recommended the installation of ahead-throwing weapons in destroyers. The Commander of Destroyers, Atlantic, approved, preferring the new rocket (Mousetrap) to Hedgehog in view of the former's greater range and simplicity as well as its far lighter weight. However, the Mousetrap launcher could not compensate for the ship's roll. Ultimately, Admiral King approved 12 conversions, with three eight-rocket (Mk 22) launchers per ship. Twelve *Livermore*s were nominated: DD 493, 620, 622, 623, 635, 637–639, 645–648; in November 1943, DD 609 was substituted for DD 645. The 12 installations did make for a quick evaluation, but not for a positive one, and removal was authorized on 9 March 1944. The only survivor was the *Gillespie*, DD 609, which still had hers in the Pacific a year later. They were gone by the end of the war, and U.S. fleet destroyers did not again mount ahead-throwing weapons until after 1950.

The United States began World War II in December 1941, with QC-series searchlight sonar aboard 170 destroyers. The first basic improvement on this equipment was the new QGA sonar (in a new type of dome) fitted to the 2,200-ton destroyers in 1944. QGA incorporated the new Bearing Deviation Indicator, BDI, to permit its operator to sense changes in target bearing so as to avoid losing contact, as well as a permanent magnet, which saved space—and half a ton of weight. It used a dual-frequency system to achieve accurate bearings (which required short waves, i.e., high frequency) and long range (which required low frequency); in 1942 "high" and "low" meant 30 and 14 kc. The new dome was essential to take advantage of this new equipment. It was expected that the 100-inch-long streamlined dome

Twelve Atlantic Fleet destroyers were fitted with the Mousetrap rocket launcher, three eight-rocket rails being fitted forward. They are visible, in the raised position (they could lie flat on the deck) aboard the *Herndon*, 10 October 1943. Much lighter than a Hedgehog, they were also far less satisfactory, partly because they could not be roll-stabilized.

Hedgehog, the primary ahead-throwing weapon of U.S. destroyer escorts, produced a circular or elliptical pattern of contact-fuzed projectiles; the two patterns shown were produced by the converted destroyer *Sarsfield*, steaming past in the background. The *Epperson*, another ASW destroyer, steams through the foreground of this 15 June 1950 photograph, taken near Key West. In theory the submarine-sized pattern precluded escape; in practice, in wartime, Hedgehog was about 15 percent effective when used singly. In 1950 installations of a double Hedgehog (port and starboard) began aboard U.S. fleet destroyers.

would allow detection at up to 30 knots (assuming the destroyer to be rigged for silent operation) and attack at 18 to 20 knots. Previous figures had been 17–18 and 12–15 knots, respectively. The efficiency of the dome was reflected in its low water resistance, 200 pounds at 30 knots, versus 7,000 pounds in earlier types.

The high frequency (i.e., short range) transducer *tilted* to allow the sonar operator to maintain contact with a submarine at short range, i.e., to fill in the dead zone of a conventional sonar. The new feature was designated "Maintenance of Close Contact" (MCC). Advanced forms of MCC (not QGA) incorpo-

rated sonar beams narrow enough to allow depth determination.

QGA was first tested early in 1944. Production was slower than expected, and many *Sumner*s received (at first) the new sonar dome combined with QC-series searchlight sonars descended from those first installed in the *Farragut*s. It seems somewhat surprising that this advanced sensor went into fleet destroyers rather than into such primary ASW units as the DEs. It may be that MCC was considered less important in a ship armed with Hedgehog.

At the end of hostilities, then, the *Sumner*s and *Gearing*s with their QGA tilting searchlight sonars were the most advanced fast escorts; Hedgehog, the ahead-thrown rocket, was the most effective available weapon. Neither sonar nor weapon was entirely adequate. For example, in November 1945 a board convened by CinCPac to report on lessons of the Pacific War as they applied to radio (including sonar) observed that "The present gear . . . is ineffective against high-speed submarines such as the German Type XXI, midget submarines, Japanese one-man suicide torpedoes, or any submarine equipped with effective sonar countermeasures. Such craft have rendered the conventional single-beam echo-ranging equipment practically obsolete. The high-speed submarine can avoid standard echo-ranging search, and our listening gear is masked by our own ship noises at speeds of 15 knots and above. The man-piloted torpedo is so small that echo-ranging on it with our modern heavy equipment will not produce an echo because of the thinning out of the sound beam at the surface with a normal gradient. Any standard fleet submarine, such as our own, can effectively mask itself against listening and echo ranging by means of sonic and supersonic noisemakers and decoys and can, by means of its ordnance, shift to the offensive without coming to periscope depth. . . ." Ranges of at least 5,000 yards were considered imperative. An efficient sonar with plan-position indicator (PPI) presentation and a means of accurately determining submarine depth was required. However, wartime sonars were considered capable of picking up a submarine at 1,500 to 2,000 yards at a ship speed of 17 to 18 knots. By 1948 equipment improvement would increase the speed limit to 23 knots, but the sonar developers could promise no range improvement.

The searchlight sonars gave range and bearing. If full use were to be made of underwater weapons with reliable trajectories in the water, some means had to be found of accurately determining target *depth*. One of the earliest such devices was the British Asdic 147B, used with Squid. About 50 were supplied under reverse Lend-Lease for installation in U.S. destroyer escorts. A contemporary U.S. set was QDA, a high-frequency (50 kc) tilting searchlight sonar limited by propeller noise to the sector 60 degrees to either side of dead ahead, and limited in range by its high frequency and low power (50 vs. 300 watts for the standard searchlights). Only 44 were made, but the method of using a searchlight sonar with a narrowly diffused ("sword") beam continued after the war.

An entirely different approach to the sonar problem was the scanning sonar. The first type, QHB, entered service in 1946. In place of the 14-degree-wide searchlight beam was an omnidirectional (360-degree) transmitter coupled to an assembly of fixed receiving transducers that would automatically switch into and out of operation to cover 360 degrees; the

signals would be displayed on a radar-like PPI scope. Such a sonar increased greatly the probability of initial detection. However, since only the receiving function was scanned, for the same power radiated, its range was considerably less than that of a searchlight. The much higher probability of contact was considered a more than mitigating factor. In any case, the fixed unit of a scanning sonar could transmit more power than could a searchlight: QHB was rated at 3,300 watts (QCS of 1941, a standard searchlight: 300). Full use could not be made of all this power, however: much later, *transmission* was made directional as well (RDT, Rotationally Directed Transmission).

Scanning also made practical much larger sonars, since there was no longer any need for mechanical steering. These in turn could employ lower frequencies, i.e., achieve better acoustic performance. This equipment could also be stabilized electronically to cancel out the roll and pitch of the ship carrying it. The ultimate ASW sensor envisaged by 1948 was the "integrated" sonar, consisting of a horizontal scanning sonar for detection and bearing and a vertical scanning sonar to give target depth; the entire assembly was stabilized.

A major wartime development was an automatic range plotter (Tactical Range Recorder, TRR) to determine the optimum attack point. This was the beginning of the development of sophisticated underwater fire control, requiring internal underwater-battery fire control spaces, comparable in volume to those used for gunnery plot. Ultimately (1948) this was perceived to mean a CIC plus two centralized control stations. It was this internal space squeeze that determined that the *Fletcher* was the *minimum* destroyer suitable for ASW conversion. Only much later did the sheer size of sonar arrays become an important consideration.

The other major wartime ASW sensor was HF/DF, ship-mounted high-frequency direction-finding gear, which took advantage of the high density of communications inherent in German wolf-pack tactics; Allied code-breaking exploited the landward end of the same communication links. Aboard escorts a DF antenna often replaced the air search radar at the masthead; in other ships a mainmast was stepped specially to carry it. The German counter to HF/DF was Kurier, a burst transmitter whose signal was so short-lived that standard DF gear could not obtain a "cut" on it. Until then HF/DF was by far the longest-range shipboard ASW sensor. Although in principle it gave bearing only, in practice experienced operators were able to estimate range as well.

These developments, together with radar-equipped aircraft (to defeat surfaced submarines) defeated the U-boats. However, they were far from the ideal desired by the ASW forces. In April 1945, the Bureaus of Ordnance and Ships presented a report to the CNO. Programs for "1946" (interim) and "1948" (ultimate) were suggested. For the near term an integrated sonar combined with wartime weapons, including influence depth charges, was envisaged. In the long term improved weapons could be combined with a shift in control gear to a new ASW control center equivalent to the gunnery plotting room of a major warship. The report proposed in addition two new ahead-throwing weapons, "A" (Alfa) and "B" trainable, launchers for fast-sinking 250- and 50-pound influence or depth-fuzed rockets. Ranges of 400 to 800 yards were envisaged; Weapon B was intended for lighter ASW warships. Both were regarded as far superior to the British fixed-range, limited train Squid.

Target-seeking torpedoes were envisaged for the near future. As early as the fall of 1941 work had begun on a low-speed passive homing torpedo, which had become the Mk 24 "mine."* This aerial ASW weapon proved quite successful in combat, and inspired experiments with surface-launched torpedoes. Two systems were tried, passive and active. Active homing was expected to be simpler to implement, because the torpedo did not have to overcome

*The "mine" designation was used to camouflage the adoption of a homing *torpedo*.

its own self-noise and also because it presented no problems of homing on the noise of its launching ship. A small torpedo, Mk 32, based on the Mk 24 "mine" was developed.

The 12-knot Mk 32 appears to have been considered a self-propelled successor to the depth charge. The Official History describes it as a solution to the surface vessel conning problem:

> ... such a mine could be launched from a surface vessel and, using the attacking vessel's sonar information, could then take up the attack where the surface vessel left off ... a simple tactic would protect the launching vessel and lead to an almost certain attack ... the self-propelled body would glide downward at a fixed angle while steering tight circles and pinging as it went ... the speed of the mine body was such that the target could be intercepted before it had escaped from the vicinity of the launching point even if it were operating initially at a depth as great as 400 ft ... since it would retain its effectiveness in the face of noisemakers ... its development was undertaken on a priority basis.

The earliest launching device, a set of rails on the fantail, reinforces the image of a depth-charge replacement—a close-in weapon. Mk 32 was the direct ancestor of the later lightweight ASW torpedoes (Mk 43, 44, 46): small active acoustic homers for short ranges. Later launching systems were a Mk 4 launcher-

Lightweight ASW homing torpedoes are descended directly from World War II research programs. The early ones, such as this Mk 32, had fins larger than their bodies and so could not be launched from tubes. Instead, ships were fitted with Torpedo Launching System Mk 2, a "poor-boy." The standard outfit of three torpedoes per launcher (as evident here) was continued with the tube-launched Mks 44 and 46, which employ a triple launcher.

rack to flip torpedoes over the side, followed by the present Mk 32 tube.

Although Mk 32 had almost a full torpedo diameter (19 inches), it was only 83 inches long and weighed only about 250 pounds. These characteristics made it suitable for aircraft use; indeed, the subsequent light torpedoes have all been dual-purpose types. From Mk 43 on they have also been of small diameter (10 inches in Mk 43, 12.75 in Mk 44 and Mk 46; all are about 100 inches long). Mk 43 weighed 265 pounds, Mk 46 about 500. A technological irony, comparable to that implicit in the story of the Tartar missile, is that the extra weight of Mk 46 allows it to become a medium- to *long*-range weapon.

The passive option was also pursued in the shape of a full-size active/passive torpedo: Mk 35, 21 inches in diameter, 162 inches long (vs. 252 inches for standard antisurface ship torpedoes), 1,800 (vs. about 3,300) lbs. with a 255- to 270-pound warhead (vs. 600 to 800). It was considered the ultimate defense against fast deep-driving submarines, themselves equipped with long-range torpedoes; but ten years of work and about $90 million failed to make it operational. The changing fortunes of Mk 35 were why large-diameter fixed torpedo tubes kept appearing and then disappearing in American ASW ships; clearly it would be a boon if it did work, but there were always problems such as noise.

Passive homing had another implication as well. Unless the torpedo began to listen for its quarry some distance from its launching platform, it might tend to home on its launcher. Such a weapon, if it was not air launched, was therefore inherently long range, with a straight run to the presumed vicinity of the target before it began its spiralling search pattern. In some later torpedoes (Mk 37, Mk 39) wire guidance was used to allow the surface ship to provide the torpedo with sonar data during this otherwise "dead" period of run-out.

The failure of Mk 35 did not, of course, end the history of the long ASW torpedo. A 19-inch Mk 37 (330-pound warhead, 1,430 pounds/135-inch length or 1,690 pounds/161-inch) was deployed in numbers aboard destroyers and submarines. A measure of its success was the long torpedo tube initially mounted on many FRAM II destroyers.

Mk 48 was supposed to be the successor to Mk 37; long tubes for it were fitted or at least were provided for in the transoms of many U.S. escorts and in DLG-26-class missile frigates. It has, however, been confined to submarine service; as of 1981 it appears that the long-range surface-ship-launched torpedo is gone.

These weapons were still quite unknown within the fleet in 1945. *Operational* views on ASW can be gauged from the November 1945 report of the Board

(chaired by Capt. G. P. Kraker) on ordnance lessons of the Pacific War. It was considered essential to have a sonar good to 35,000 yards, fire control effective to 15,000, and a self-guided, self-propelled weapon to be fired 15,000 yards, then to proceed at 5 knots under its own power. In fact, there were only depth charges, the 190-yard Hedgehog, and Squid. The last was tested aboard the USS *Asheville* (PF 1) in 1944. However, all Squids were returned to the Royal Navy at the end of the war. A 1946 project called for an experimental double Squid installation in a destroyer in conjunction with the integrated sonar. Squid was installed, briefly, in the USS *Dealey* (DE 1006) ten years later.

Postwar developments of Hedgehog included Mk 14 (trainable) and Mk 15 (trainable and stabilized), which were comparable in size to a heavy AA gun. The next step was the Mk 108 or "Weapon Able"* of the April 1945 report. It was installed in a stabilized and trainable mount controlled via the new integrated A/S Fire Control System. It could fire up to 12 rounds per minute from its 22-round ready supply. The 22 rounds were considered one attack; reloading from a magazine took half an hour.

This was still far from Kraker's ideal. His ASW ranges had been set primarily by the very long range of submarine torpedoes. During the war the Germans had already introduced an acoustic homing torpedo, T5 (25 knot, 6,000 yards; homing radius over 500 yards on a 15-knot escort). In effect such a weapon would place an attacking submarine well outside sonar range without forcing it to sacrifice very much accuracy. A longer range ASW system was required.

Only the weapon part of that system was in prospect in 1945–46, the Mk 35 ASW homing torpedo. For shorter ranges Alfa (minimum range expected to be 250 yards) could be used. In addition the unguided Alfa would not be subject to countermeasures that might nullify the torpedo; Hedgehog was to be an interim installation. Finally, some depth charges might be carried to "embarrass" a submarine within the minimum range of Weapon Alfa. A longer-term prospect was the light homing torpedo in place of depth charges.

It was ironic that the primary ASW weapon, the torpedo, was also the least visible. Postwar ASW ships show prominent mountings for elaborate Hedgehogs and Alfa rocket launchers; but their main battery was conceived to be a set of fixed TT in a deckhouse. Many conventional destroyers retained their trainable TT, not because of continued belief in the efficacy of torpedoes but as a means of reserving weight

---

*Weapon Able became Weapon Alfa when the phonetic alphabet was changed.

and moment for ASW homing torpedoes and for long-range wire-guided torpedoes. Ordnance also claimed at various times that the new weapons would be compatible with existing tubes.

For longer ranges there was under development Grebe, a ship-launched, torpedo-carrying remote-piloted vehicle (RPV) similar in concept to the present Ikara. It was to carry a Mk 41 deep-diving homing torpedo up to 20 miles—i.e., far beyond sonar range. By the late forties the Grebe program had expanded to include a simple rocket-boosted torpedo with a range of about 5,000 yards, a figure far closer to then-realistic sonar ranges. The very long range initially chosen may have been intended to exploit HF/DF contacts. In any case, Grebe was canceled, but the idea of a medium-range, rocket-boosted torpedo lived on in the more austere RAT (which carried the lighter-weight Mk 43 torpedo as payload) and in ASROC. RAT itself was not viable until the widespread introduction of a new and far more powerful sonar, SQS–4, in the mid-1950s.

The sonar part of the problem was far less tractable. Quite early the problems of surface-ship sonar were ship self-noise and insufficient depth of transducer. In 1948 quiet, submerged submarines could already hear snorkeling subs at 35 nm., and destroyers at 70 to 105. The latest passive sonar system was a low-frequency array, GHG, which had been captured from the Germans, and which in 1948 was being applied to U.S. submarines and (prospectively) to surface ships. In the latter, it appeared to require a fin keel 25 feet deep and 25 feet long, to keep clear of turbulence. A typical installation would also include an active searchlight sonar in the bows. In effect, then, the only way out of the sonar muddle would be a quieter ship of greater draft—VDS had not yet been invented. This meant not only that the big destroyer could not be an ideal ASW type, but that it seemed best to go to a light cruiser, the *Norfolk*.

The bulbous bow array was still in the future; in 1948 sonar meant a dome under the keel. This location often turned out to be very nearly the worst possible one, because it was directly in the path of bubbles swept down by the bow. The remedy was to move the dome either farther aft (where it began to be affected by the propellers) or into the bows. Other solutions included "dunking" sonars (from helicopter or blimp) and even a squadron of "sonodrones," self-propelled unmanned miniature submarines, transmitting back to their control ship by radio.

Attempts were also made to defend the escorts against long-range torpedo fire. A noise-maker, Foxer, had been devised by the British during the war as a countermeasure to T5; but there was also a general

recognition that very long range torpedo fire (non-homing) was an immediate and realistic threat. Attempts were made to devise countermining systems; complaints that even damaged torpedoes still kept coming bear a certain resemblance to fears of the failure of more recent antiship missile defense (ASMD) systems. Many postwar ASW ships were temporarily fitted with two or four Mk 31 rocket launchers intended to fire NAE noise beacons as a countermeasure to homing torpedoes; however, the Mk 31 was ultimately rejected as unsafe, given its automated train and firing. Ultimately, a more sophisticated towed countermeasure, T Mk 5 Fanfare, was introduced. For a short time in the late forties, torpedo countermeasures seemed so promising that it was planned to fit most large combatants with scanning sonars for torpedo detection, but this optimism soon dissipated.

Postwar prospects were somewhat ambiguous. Against conventional (World War II) submarines, they were good: in 1948 the General Board heard an ASW presentation in which it was estimated that against modern ASW forces employing radar-equipped aircraft, World War II fleet boats would have to exchange two submarines for every merchant ship sunk. A snorkel boat of limited underwater endurance and speed (e.g., the German VII-C with snorkel) would not be too much better, at a rate of one submarine per six sinkings.

The more efficient submarines were quite another matter. A postwar OEG report described Type 21, submerged, as quite as efficient on patrol as Type VII-C fully surfaced; moreover, the submerged boat could operate nearly independently of the weather. She need not surface except for morale purposes and was far more habitable than the earlier boat, yet she presented a smaller target. As compared to Type VII-C, Type 21 had longer underwater (nonsnorkel) range (360 vs. 108 miles), and higher underwater speeds—silent (5 vs. 2 knots), burst (12 vs. 5), and maximum (16 vs. 7); and at silent speed she could detect and track a 16-knot destroyer at several times the destroyer's effective detection range. Moreover, she was designed to operate at a safe depth of 435 feet (crush depth 600 to 800 feet), and therefore could use the thermal layer to hide from sonar. And in 1947 U.S. sound gear was considered reliable only to 400 feet.

Type 26, the Walther U-boat with closed-cycle propulsion, would have an even higher underwater speed, albeit of limited endurance.

A major motive behind the first postwar submarine conversions (GUPPY program) was the requirement to provide ASW forces with experience against Type 21-like adversaries. In 1948 the General Board heard a report that the USS *Odax*, our first GUPPY

Through the fifties, U.S. destroyers retained their 21-inch torpedo tubes more as a space and weight reservation against future ASW weapons than for attacks against surface ships. The long-range antiship torpedo program was canceled in 1956, partly because the standard trainable tube could not accommodate homing torpedoes requiring heaters. Here the *Ozbourn* (DD 846) fires an antiship torpedo, August 1957. Note the characteristic fire-room air intakes on her funnel, adopted in the *Fletcher*s and later destroyers to overcome sea damage experienced in earlier ships that had their air intakes under their funnel casings.

conversion, could outrun a DE in any sea state above 3 by heading *into* the sea submerged; at about 17 knots submerged she was comparable to Type 21. A 25-knot submarine could usually expect to outrun surface units in the North Atlantic. The very fast closed-cycle submarine would use its speed primarily for postattack escape, as it would be nearly impossible to avoid pursuit once detected, in view of advances in sonar. Typical high-speed endurance was expected to be 10 hours; the submarine would have to refuel after each attack. However, as early as 1946 a nuclear power plant was envisaged. This might permit an endurance of 60 days at a constant 25 knots. A nuclear submarine could use its passive sonar to pick up targets at tens of miles, close, fire long-range torpedoes from beyond sonar range and retire undetected. The earliest characteristics for the post-war *Tang* class called for nuclear or closed-cycle propulsion to give an underwater speed of 25 knots (17 with a conventional plant should this alternative prove impractical, as, in fact, it did). In 1948 ONI reported that "present information shows Soviet emphasis on the Type 26," so these were very real concerns.

Each year after 1945 the Navy held a high-level ASW conference to coordinate its counter to what was already perceived as a powerful Soviet underwater fleet. The 1946 conference called for the establishment of special (hunter-killer) ASW groups: one in 1947 to be capable of countering Type 21, one in 1949 to be capable of defeating Type 26, the Walther boat. These entailed the special destroyer ASW conversions, as well as ASW conversions of small carriers (see chapter 12).

10

Destroyer AAW: World War II and After

Since World War II the destroyer has had two quite distinct functions in antiaircraft warfare. Its classical function is the direct destruction of aircraft (or, now, missiles) by its own weapons, guns, and missiles. This is no more than an extension of the original screening role of the destroyer, with aircraft substituted for the original enemy, the torpedo boat. However, within the carrier task force a new role evolved. The destroyer became a platform for early-warning radar and for fighter control. In effect, it came to employ a Combat Air Patrol section as its principal antiaircraft weapon. A powerful radar on a destroyer at some considerable distance from the carrier provided early warning of low-flying enemy aircraft and so allowed interceptors based on the carrier to engage them; fighter controllers on the destroyer reduced the load on the carrier's controllers and so increased the capacity of the task force as a whole. This role became, if anything, more important postwar as the consequences of enemy penetration of task force air defenses became more severe—thus, the conversion of destroyers for picket duty and the provisions for picket duty in some new designs, such as the *Mitschers*.

The weapons themselves developed considerably in wartime. In 1939 the standard antiaircraft guns of the destroyer force were the dual-purpose 5-in./38, the 1.1-inch machine cannon (mounted only in the 1,850-ton "leaders" with their single-purpose 5-inch guns), and the .50-caliber water-cooled machine gun. In theory, the 5-inch gun could counter either horizontal or torpedo bombers; it could not fire nearly fast enough to present any threat to dive bombers, which, ironically, were probably the most lethal threat to fast, maneuverable craft such as destroyers. However, it could be argued that in practice the dive bombers would go for larger and more lucrative targets, and that the machine cannon effective against them had ranges far too short to allow screening destroyers to provide protection. Finally, the .50-caliber was considered effective against strafers trying to break up the antiaircraft barrage that the destroyer screen might try to erect around the battle fleet. In an important sense the choice not to arm U.S. fleet destroyers with the 1.1-inch gun was a choice for antidestroyer over antiaircraft firepower, a choice in favor of classical battle line concepts.

War experience soon showed the immense value of the heavy automatic cannon. By 1940 both standard U.S. automatic weapons, the 1.1-inch and .50-caliber, were considered ineffective. For example, it was believed that all such weapons achieved their greatest effect by deterring an oncoming pilot. Unlike the British 2-pounder, however, the 1.1-inch round did not explode at the peak of its trajectory and so might well go unnoticed by its intended victim. By

The tripod mast of a destroyer radar picket displays a combination of fighter-control and radar jamming equipment. At its top is a YE radar beacon, essential as a point of reference for aircraft control. It rises from a platform supporting an SP pencil-beam radar, with the framework of the BO IFF antenna on its face. The yard carries two sets of omnidirectional radar intercept receivers, operating on two frequency ranges: the small (higher-frequency) "derby" at each end, and the much larger "sword" closer in. Both antennas remain in use more than three decades later. Farther down is the standard late-war jammer, a TDY with two sets of dipoles and reflectors, to operate on two alternative frequency ranges; it was cued by a radar direction-finder, DBM, in the small radome. A 5-inch loading machine stands at the extreme right, and the tall whips on the funnel were for HF (beyond line of sight) communication, with ships or shore rather than with aircraft.

this time there were U.S. naval observers with the British fleet, and the United States adopted the 20-mm. Oerlikon machine cannon that had proven so successful with the Royal Navy. Installation began late in 1941, the Oerlikon replacing the .50.

Initial responses were enthusiastic; Pacific Fleet records show that between Pearl Harbor and September 1944 the Oerlikon was responsible for 32 percent of all identifiable kills. After that date ranges increased, the Japanese shifted to night attacks, and heavier 40-mm. batteries and proximity-fuzed 5-in. guns began to increase their share of the kills. By the end of the war, the Japanese had shifted to Kamikaze attacks. Now deterrence was almost irrelevant. Like a cruise missile, the Kamikaze had to be destroyed before it could enter a ballistic path into the ship. That required a much more powerful weapon, at least a 40-mm. gun, at the most a new 3-in./50. Thus in May 1945 the commanding officer of the USS *O'Brien* reported that "when the 20 mm. opens fire, it's time to hit the deck"; according to another report "20-mm. fire was a signal to the engine room to shut down the blowers to keep the flash of the explosion from the suicide hit being drawn into the machinery spaces."

The Oerlikon's wartime partner was another foreign-developed weapon, the 40-mm. Bofors gun, generally in a twin or quadruple power-operated and director-controlled mount. Where the Oerlikon could be bolted down in almost any free area of deck, the Bofors required elaborate wiring and water-cooling arrangements, and its installation was a shipyard job. The first twin mount was installed aboard the *Benson*-class destroyer *Coghlan* on 1 July 1942. By this time there was a considerable program of installations planned for existing ships, and new destroyers were being redesigned (see chapters 6 and 7), but the rate of Bofors production precluded the completion of this program before the summer of 1944.

The Army also adopted the Bofors, but in an air-cooled single-barrel version, which weighed about a third as much as a twin mount, even with power drive. It was, therefore, well-suited to temporary installations, as in the case of the Mediterranean destroyers and destroyer escorts in 1944. Later it was used extensively in destroyer escorts in place of their torpedo tubes. These weapons were generally not director controlled and thus had no automatic cutoffs to keep them from firing into their own ship: their tubs were fitted with pipe guards.

The guns were only the most visible elements of an elaborate antiaircraft system. Prewar development of destroyer fire controls was limited to 5-inch directors, first the Mk 33 employed in the *Farragut*s, then the Mk 37, which incorporated a below-decks computer. It was clear that some type of director was required for the heavy automatic weapons, but prewar attempts to develop one for the 1.1-inch gun were not successful. However, quite early in World War II Charles Draper of MIT developed a simple but effective computing gunsight for the 20-mm. gun, the Mk 14. Mounted on a "dummy gun" it became the Mk 51 director, which controlled twin and quadruple Bofors guns through the war. Late in World War II Mk 51s were adapted for 5-inch fire control, permitting 5-inch batteries to engage multiple targets simultaneously. Destroyer escorts were ultimately provided with a Mk 52 director, which corresponded roughly to Mk 51 except that it incorporated a range-only Mk 26 radar. Both Mk 51 and 52 were useful only in daylight, since they could track targets only optically. However, war experience emphasized the need for night capability. For example, after 1943 the Japanese frequently attacked at night.

At that time only the 5-inch guns with their radar directors were capable of "blind" fire. However, several automatic-weapon directors with radar/blind-fire capability were developed late in World War II: Mk 56, for guns of up to 5-inch caliber, and the much more modest Mks 57 and 63, the latter an important component of the anti-Kamikaze program of 1945. The radar antenna of Mk 63 was mounted on the gun mounts, as in the twin 3-in./50 automatic gun mount designed in 1945. Finally, there was Gunar, a self-contained fire control system actually incorporated in the gun mount, and employed in some postwar destroyers.

Postwar gun fire-control development was limited in view of the effort that went into guided missiles. A Mk 67 was developed as a successor to the prewar Mk 37; it appeared on the *Mitschers*. Its successor, Mk 68, remains in service aboard many destroyers and frigates. The *Spruance* class is the first to incorporate a wholly new gun fire-control system, Mk 86, which also has some missile control functions, and the *Perry*s employ the Dutch-developed Mk 92.

Behind the directors lay specialized radars and the Combat Information Center (CIC) in which radar and other data were synthesized to permit commanders to make effective decisions. The earliest U.S. naval radar experiments at sea were conducted aboard the elderly destroyer *Leary* in 1937. By 1941 there were air search sets compact enough to fit destroyer foremasts, the SA and SC (and, late in the war, SR) series that were standard through the war. A series of centrimetric radars, SG in destroyers and SL and then SU in destroyer escorts, provided surface search and were also effective against low-flying aircraft.

SA, SC, and SR were all descendants of the prototype naval air search sets, and all operated at metric wavelengths. In 1945 it appeared that better ra-

SC-2 was the standard fleet destroyer radar of World War II, seen here atop the foremast of the destroyer *Coghlan* at Mare Island, 2 July 1945. The panel at the top of the antenna was an interrogator for Mk III IFF, and dipoles for the alternative Mk IV system were worked into the main radar antenna; one or the other could be energized. IFF transponders ("ski-poles") sit at the yardarms, and a TBS tactical radio antenna flanks the mast proper. At this time special efforts were being made to save weight; the *Coghlan* carries a Mk 28 radar antenna (a dish) atop her main-battery director in place of the usual combination of Mks 12 and 22. The pipe-like waveguide running up the mast fed an SG surface-search radar, no less essential for surface warfare than SC-2 was for anti-air operations. The circle around the 20-mm. gun tub forward of the bridge indicates installation of a twin mount as part of the ship's anti-Kamikaze program refit.

dar performance could be achieved by a drastic reduction in wavelength, for a more precise beam and hence more accurate determination of target bearing. The SR-6 and then the SPS-6 series of L-band radars resulted, and for a time it appeared that they would entirely replace the earlier series. Before this could be accomplished, however, the virtues of a mix of search sets in the fleet began to be appreciated. With radars of both 1.5 meter *and* 23 centimeter wavelength operating together in the same force, it was impossible for an airborne intruder to operate without duplicate warning and jamming equipment. Although SPS-6 proved less effective than the earlier sets (and their later derivatives, SPS-28 and -29), it was retained in many ships just to achieve this mix. Later air search radar development was directed largely towards maintaining a spectrum of sets that would complicate enemy countermeasures. These sets would also suffer from radar-blanking effects such as sea surface reflection, and one series would balance off the other's weaknesses. Both SPS-40 and the new SPS-49 originated in this frequency-diversity program. However, by the 1960s the virtues of diversity had to be balanced against the economies of standardization, and the latter triumphed. Although the long-wave sets continued to be developed (as SPS-37 and then SPS-43), almost all destroyers received the shorter-wave SPS-40, and it appears that SPS-49 will serve primarily as a replacement for the long-wave air search radars; it is also the air search radar of the new FFG 7 and CG 47 classes.

Wartime destroyer search radar also included the pencil-beam height-finder, SP, aboard pickets. It could determine for fighter control the altitude of an airborne target, and it could also track that target automatically. In addition, its very well defined beam was useful for detecting low-flying aircraft. Postwar SP was superseded by an SPS-8, whose fan beam was not as useful for tracking, but which was primarily a height-finder.

An antiaircraft missile was essentially an unmanned fighter, requiring radar of fighter-direction quality, with a very high data rate corresponding to the high speeds of missiles and their prospective targets. Generally, this has meant electronic (frequency) scanning in elevation, and mechanical scan in azimuth, in two series of radars: the Hughes SPS-26, -39, and -52 and the much more capable (and larger and far more expensive) ITT-Gilfillan SPS-48, which employs multiple scanning beams. These sets also solve one of the principal problems of classical destroyer (and other) air search radars, the blind spot at the zenith, directly over the ship.

Zenith search became a major concern in the fleet as early as 1943, and by 1945 there was a solution in the form of a special reflector for the standard SG surface-search radar. Generally, both reflectors were mounted together, although the switch from one to the other was manual. In postwar destroyers the combined centrimetric set was either SG-6 or SPS-4, depending upon its operating frequency. Zenith search was abandoned as jet aircraft reduced the time any air target would spend directly overhead and hence the probability that any such target would be detected. In missile ships, the upper elevation limit on the frequency-scanning ("three-dimensional," because of their ability to measure range, bearing, and altitude) radars was high enough to eliminate most of the zenith problems.

Although the radar antennas were the visible elements of the system, the CIC was quite significant for future trends. Particularly at night, an officer in CIC had a far more complete tactical picture than one on the bridge, and some captains preferred the CIC to the bridge in combat. By 1945, too, it was possible to conn a ship into port from the CIC. Destroyers designed before the advent of radar did not have sufficient space to provide a CIC adjacent to the bridge. For example, by late in the war the standard *Fletcher* CIC location was on the main deck below the bridge, in the spaces originally reserved for the unit commander cabin and stateroom. In postwar destroyers the requirement that CIC be easily accessible from bridge and pilot house was a major factor in destroyer design. In any case, the concentration of information in CIC made it a natural location for fighter directors: the combination of CIC and radars determined the efficacy of the radar picket destroyers. It should be noted that the CIC arrangement, i.e., the relative positions of plotting boards, radios, telephones, and radar scopes, largely determined the efficiency of the CIC and hence the combat efficiency of the ship. This relatively invisible factor might have almost the same impact as the addition or deletion of several weapons. In more recent practice, the number of consoles (operator positions) in CIC may determine the number of targets a ship can engage simultaneously, or the number of different types of engagement she can carry out simultaneously (e.g., AAW and ASW).

Wartime CICs were manual: that is, radar data observed by radar operators was transferred by hand onto a master plot where it could be combined with other data such as radio reports. There was no automatic means of extracting data from radar scopes, and no automated means of storing that data and updating it. This limited the number of targets on which the CIC could maintain tracks. As CIC became saturated, the accuracy of the plotting would tend to decrease, and with it the accuracy of the ship's fire. In the case of a destroyer radar picket, for example, beyond a certain point track accuracy would deteriorate until interception would no longer be possible. In effect, the system of CIC plus search radar and other sensors (and communications links) amounted to a combined track whole-scan (search) system, the tracking (CIC) aspect being necessary for fire (or fighter) control. Development since 1945 has been in the direction of automating the CIC and then of integrating the detection and tracking functions. The latter requires some automated means of extracting radar detection information from the radar itself, a requirement met by current Automatic Detection and Tracking (ADT) systems, which can feed directly into combat control systems such as the new AN/SYS-1. It cannot be sufficiently emphasized that the success of such development determines destroyer AAW performance quite as much as does the success of programs for increased nominal radar and missile range. The progression is from visible indicators of ship capability, such as guns and torpedo tubes, to hidden systems that determine the efficacy of the weapons themselves.

The evolution went through several stages. By the late forties some form of electronic data storage for CIC was clearly required to overcome saturation. The Naval Research Laboratory assembled an air defense system incorporating a British-developed Comprehensive Display System (CDS) in 1951; from it was developed the Electronic Data System (EDS), the forerunner of the current Naval Tactical Data System (NTDS). EDS was first tested at a land site in 1953 and was later installed aboard several destroyers and missile ships, serving until it was replaced by NTDS in 1968. Procurement was recommended following an evaluation of EDS in connection with Project Lamplight, a Navy study of the sea-based contribution to Continental Air Defense. The first shipboard installation was aboard the frigate *Willis A. Lee* (DL 4, 1956), followed by four radar pickets of DesDiv 262 (DDR 817, 838, 855, and 859), and then aboard missile cruisers, for a total of 20 systems procured.

EDS combined data storage in each ship with a means of data exchange among ships, so that a force could be more effectively integrated. The first demonstration of data linking, which is such an important element of NTDS operation, was a 1959 transmission among the four radar picket destroyers of DesDiv 262, at ranges of up to 400 nm. At this stage transmission was by teletype, and the displays were analog. A fully digital system would be both more efficient and would permit data security by encryption. As early as 1952 NRL had constructed a digital data link by means of which computer memory data could be exchanged among the ships of a formation. The production system was HICAPCOM, or High Capacity Communications System, and it was an es-

sential feature of NTDS-equipped ships. It required not merely extensive radio transmission and reception facilities, but also dedicated computers, and so contributed to the growth of CIC and CIC-related hardware aboard ship. The first sea trials were carried out on three destroyers of DesDiv 61 (the *Noa*, *Meredith*, and *Stribling*) in 1957, just as NTDS development began.

NTDS combines the data-handling efficiency of the former EDS system with digital data transmission. When the ships of a task force are properly coordinated in position, NTDS in effect permits all of them to share the sensors and data available to each, which makes for considerable improvement in detection ranges. In theory, the presence of digital data in the NTDS computer greatly simplifies the problem of hand-over from search radars to fire control for gun and missile fire; NTDS maintains tracks on targets, which simplifies their identification and which permits priorities to be assigned to large numbers of incoming threats. In this way it helps overcome saturation tactics. The principle of NTDS leads directly to greater CIC automation and ultimately to systems that can detect, track, and fire at incoming targets, with operator interference limited to the power to override and abort missile fire. This latter capability is extremely important in an era of fast, low-altitude pop-up weapons such as the Soviet submarine-launched SSN-7 missile.

The first NTDS systems went to sea in 1961 aboard the carrier *Oriskany* and the missile frigates *King* and *Mahan*. Trials of this group of ships in July 1962 proved the value of the system, which has continued in production, in modified form, down to the present, together with its specialized digital data link, Link 11.

Wartime radar development was not limited to fixed search and fire control sets. Indeed, perhaps the best-known wartime radar development was the VT (Variable Time, or proximity) fuze. It made the 5-inch gun the most lethal medium-range antiaircraft weapon. Previously, heavy shells had been contact and time fuzed; the smaller weapons were all contact fuzed. Time fuzing was necessary because it was unlikely that the 5-inch shell would actually hit its airborne target, whereas it might still be effective within a considerable lethal radius if it exploded nearby. Thus, time estimation and fuze setting were major functions of dual-purpose fire control systems. The VT fuze was a miniature radar set built into the shell, exploding it when it approached a target, regardless of whether that approach occurred at the predicted range.

Both fire control radar and the VT fuze were united in the final antiaircraft gun development of World War II, the automatic twin 3-in./50 intended specifically as an anti-Kamikaze measure. It was, in effect, the smallest gun that could fire a VT-fuzed shell and could be expected to destroy an oncoming airplane, and it was expected to replace the quadruple Bofors gun on a one-for-one basis. The twin mount incorporated a Mk 34 radar dish, with the radar equipment below decks. Although it was an extremely urgent program, the general fleet rearmament with 3-in./50 guns did not begin until 1947, and indeed was never completed in some classes of active-fleet destroyers. By that time, too, a longer-range wartime program, the very elaborate 3-in./70, was in advanced development. Its misfortune was a combination of excessive complexity (i.e., very slow development) and poor timing (so that it appeared just as jet aircraft and missiles were making elaborate antiaircraft guns quite obsolete).

The other major postwar antiaircraft gun was the rapid-fire 5-in./54, which appeared in the *Mitscher* and later classes and was roughly equivalent to a twin semiautomatic mount. In antiaircraft stopping power it was considered slightly inferior to the twin 3-in./70, but it was generally preferred because of its superiority against shore and surface targets. Both weapons were considered far superior to the wartime 5-in./38. Thus in 1948, the ratio of effectiveness between two single 5-in./54s and two twin 5-in./38s was given as about 1.5, and between two twin 3-in./70s and two twin 5-in./38s as 2.20, the pair of twin 5-in./38s being considered a minimum lethal combination against an airplane at medium range.

The wartime configuration of the destroyer force was largely dictated by the need to increase short-range antiaircraft firepower. This entailed both the installation of new weapons (and the consequent removal of existing 5-inch guns and torpedo tubes) and the elimination of top hamper to clear sky arcs. Studies for fleet AA improvement began with a board headed by then Rear Admiral, later CNO, E.J. King, in the spring of 1940. King was loath to sacrifice existing antidestroyer and antibattleship capabilities. Short of removing a gun or a bank of torpedo tubes, the 1.1-inch machine cannon could not be mounted, and the King board confined itself to recommending that destroyers double their .50-caliber battery to eight such guns.

However, war experience showed the severity of the dive bomber threat, and in February 1941 the General Board proposed that the interim emergency battery of all modern fleet destroyers include a quad 1.1, which would replace one 5-inch gun, 20 percent of the antisurface gun battery (which was preferable to one-half to one-third of the torpedo battery). The four-gun, 16-tube ships would not be suitable for this modification, however. For the longer term, 20-mm. and 40-mm. weapons would be available. Ultimately, the five-gun ships generally received a pair of twin Bofors at the cost of one 5-inch gun (but no tubes); the four-gun, 16-tube ships were originally assigned a pair of twin Bofors but could not accommodate them. Thus, the *Bagley*s were eventually fitted with one twin Bofors atop their after deckhouse;

The *Macdonough* illustrates the wartime antiaircraft refit applied to the *Farragut* class, two twin Bofors guns replacing the former No. 3 5-inch gun, with three 20-mm. forward of the bridge and two more aft.

the *Gridley*s, with insufficient weight margin, were unique among U.S. destroyers of modern design in receiving no Bofors guns at all. On the other hand, the *Benham*s which had two of their four banks of tubes removed as compensation for depth charges, received the usual two twin mounts. In each case Bofors fire was concentrated aft, with extra Oerlikons before the bridge to cover the forward arcs. Ships were fitted at first with all-Oerlikon antiaircraft batteries, as production of the 40-mm. gun was slower than that of the lighter weapon. In *Benson*s and in the big "leaders" there were in addition 1.1-inch machine cannon (which the latter had carried from shortly after their completion).

In each class considerable weight had to be removed to make up for the new weapons. Standard removals included the previous .50-caliber battery; 5-inch ready-service ammunition beyond 40 rounds per gun (30 in the *Benham*s); one of two smoke-screen generators; all 2½-meter range finders; and in the Atlantic Fleet, removal of one 26-foot motor whaleboat, anchor chain, one anchor, and hawse pipe. In five-gun ships one 5-in./38 was also eliminated, and there were further removals on a class-by-class basis.

In the *Farragut* class the after torpedo loading racks and davits, the crow's nest, and the stub mainmast were eliminated. On an interim basis four Oerlikons replaced No. 3 gun, and four others replaced the four .50s. This battery had only limited fire ahead, and when a pair of twin Bofors replaced the four amidships Oerlikons, one of the latter was mounted on the centerline forward, raised above the two on the 01 level forward. Thus, the final battery was four 40 mm. (two twin) and five 20 mm. In the *Mahan*s, the bridge wings were cut back; the searchlight opera-

tor's shelter, potato locker, port torpedo loading crane, torpedo tube blast shields, gun shelter on the after deckhouse, mainmast, and tripod foremast (which was replaced by a pole mast) were all eliminated. The end result was similar to a *Farragut*, with three Oerlikons before the bridge and two flanking the second funnel.

The only other prewar five-gun class was the larger *Sims*. The former light weather shields for 5-inch guns, which had been replaced by heavier ones (¼ vs. ⅛ inch, STS rather than mild steel), were returned to their original condition; the depth-charge track extensions were removed, together with both smoke-screen generators, one torpedo director, both 24-inch searchlights, and the overhang of the after deckhouse. The quarter-inch machine gun splinter shields (bulwarks) were reduced to .075-inch mild steel. This extensive list presumably reflects the top-heaviness of the class to begin with; these ships mounted only four Oerlikons (three before the bridge, one aft) and two twin Bofors. Atlantic units, even more in need of stability than their Pacific cousins, had even more removed to gain the same final battery: 45 fathoms of anchor chain, weather-deck lighting, all but one boat-handling flood light, the slop chute and garbage rack, the watertight hatch cover to the forecastle deck, the single platform above the pilothouse, the life jacket deck lockers, the torpedo director platform, and a 26-foot motor whaleboat.

Next in line were the *Benham*s. Although built as 16-tube ships, they had half their tubes removed in favor of depth charges during Atlantic service in 1941, and so could accommodate the full pair of twin Bofors. Unlike earlier ships, they had only two Oerlikons before their bridges, with two more just abaft

At first Bofors guns were quite rare; few destroyers received their "ultimate assigned" batteries until late 1943 or early 1944. The *Conyngham* of the *Mahan* class is shown off Mare Island on 10 July 1942, with a pair of 20-mm. guns in place of her third 5-inch gun, with two more abreast her second funnel and two more atop the 5-inch gun-crew shelter forward. Note, too, the bulwark atop her pilothouse, fitted to provide a makeshift open bridge.

The *Mahan*-class destroyer *Lamson* received her twin 40-mm. guns only in 1944, this photo having been taken at Mare Island in May 1944. The white circles show changes, including both the guns and their Mk 51 directors. Note the retention of all 12 torpedo tubes: the U.S. Navy preferred to trade 5-inch guns rather than tubes for its self-defense automatic weapons. The emergency steering station aft is just visible at the lower right hand corner of this photograph.

The *Mustin* was typical of *Sims*-class refits; in this 21 October 1943 photograph she shows three gun tubs aft for a pair of twin Bofors and a single 20-mm. gun, plus three 20-mm. forward of the bridge.

The *Sims*-class destroyer *Walke* illustrates early war modifications after a Mare Island refit, 24 August 1942. She received a Mk 4 main-battery fire-control radar and splinter-shielded 20-mm. guns, as well as roller-racks for the four K-guns aft. Note, too, the smoke generator displacing one of her depth-charge tracks toward her starboard side aft. Floater net stowage behind her bulwark has also been circled (port side amidships). At this time she had a total of six 20-mm. guns, four of them replacing her former No. 3 5-inch gun aft. Note, too, the half-shield on her No. 3 gun, with canvas covering its top, as indicated by the supports beneath it.

One of two *Benham*s *not* transferred to the Atlantic Fleet for the Neutrality Patrol, the name ship of the class retained all four banks of torpedo tubes; she is shown screening heavy cruisers early in 1942, apparently as yet without radar. All others in the class had two banks of tubes removed in favor of Y-guns, permitting installation of two twin Bofors guns later.

their single stacks; a third pair mounted on the deckhouse aft were ultimately replaced by a pair of twin Bofors. Removals in Pacific ships amounted to all structure above the top of the after deckhouse, both 24-inch searchlights, and much of the top of the pilothouse overhang. In the Atlantic ships these sacrifices were dwarfed: among other things 11 feet were cut from the foremast and the size of the pilothouse reduced. Otherwise, reductions generally followed those carried out in the similar *Sims* class.

The 16-tube destroyers had limited deck space, and by 1943 the assigned battery of the *Bagley* class was one twin Bofors and six Oerlikons—three before

the bridge, three surrounding the after end of the funnel. There was little scope for radical weight reduction; for example, unlike other destroyers a *Bagley* could not have her after deckhouse razed because it provided the base for the twin Bofors, which had to have the widest possible arc. In the superficially similar *Gridley* class much more extensive removals, including the crow's nest and the torpedo tube blast shields, as well as the addition of ten tons of fixed ballast, bought only eight Oerlikon and no Bofors.

The big *Porter*-class leaders were a special case, requiring very extensive reconstruction to provide them with the dual-purpose battery that was now

At Mare Island on 5 May 1944, the *Stack* shows *Benham*-class antiaircraft modifications, including installation of two twin Bofors aft (one of them shown). Note the 5-inch loading machine on the main deck between the Bofors guns and the small deckhouse supporting their Mk 51 directors.

The *Bagley*s retained all four banks of torpedo tubes, and so could be fitted with only one twin Bofors gun, in a raised position aft. This is the *Mugford* off Mare Island Navy Yard, 28 February 1945, with her tubes trained outboard. Using curved fire (i.e., gyro corrections), such ships could attack one target with all 16 torpedoes, although it appears that the tubes on the unengaged side of the ship were more often considered, in effect, reloads. The *Mugford*'s depth-charge projectors carry the wartime "teardrop" fast-sinking charges.

The big *Porter*-class leaders were little modified early in the war, except for a general reduction of top hamper and top weight: this is the *Porter* in 1942, with her after quadruple 1.1-inch machine cannon moved over to starboard to make way for 20-mm. cannon to port.

Details include new fighting lights on the *Porter*'s foremast, life-raft stowage amidships, and nonstandard roller racks for her two depth-charge throwers aft, each showing four charges. Note, too, the torpedo director visible on the bridge wing, just forward of the "flag bag" and the signaling light.

The *Moffett* (above and top right), photographed on 13 July 1944 off Hampton Roads, shows the standard mid-war *Porter*-class configuration, with all 1.1-inch cannon replaced by twin Bofors fore and aft, and a quadruple Bofors replacing No. 3 twin 5-inch gun mount. An HF/DF mainmast testifies to her primary role as a convoy flagship, and the presence of only four depth-charge projectors testifies to the top weight problems of all of these ships. The use of unshielded 20-mm. guns may have had a similar cause. Note, too, her raised forefunnel cap.

clearly required. Initial plans called for a total of six 5-in./38s, twin mounts in No. 1 and 4 positions, and singles superfiring over them. As an interim solution, a third quadruple 1.1 might be added to the two already aboard; in 1940 it was estimated that this would cost the after 5-inch director and the main-mast. Thus, late in 1941 the *Porter* and *Clark* had one quad 1.1 forward, and two aft on a cleared deck-house, with the others of the class scheduled for like modifications. By that time there was little hope of any reconstruction, yet without it the ships were con-sidered nearly helpless in the face of enemy aircraft. Wartime alterations short of reconstruction ulti-mately involved replacement of No. 3 gunhouse by a shielded quad Bofors, the automatic battery com-ing to one quadruple and three twin Bofors and six Oerlikons. This was an ideal, not attained in every case. Planned reconstruction ultimately involved a five 5-inch battery, the formerly envisaged No. 2 gun

being replaced by a quadruple Bofors, with two twins aft, and six Oerlikons. In fact the reconstruction pro-gram was delayed by the transfer of the 1,850-ton-ners to the Atlantic, where they replaced "Treasury"-class Coast Guard cutters as convoy flagships; the latter were needed as amphibious command ships in the Pacific. Thus, the *Clark* and *Balch* were never rebuilt, and the *Moffett* ended the war half-converted at Charleston. The *Somers* class was similar, but suf-fered from top weight and so could not be quite so heavily armed. For example, in their final recon-structed form they had only a twin Bofors in No. 2 position.

The modification of the later destroyers (many or all of which were completed with 20- and 40-mm. batteries) is described in chapters 5 and 6. These were also the only ships of wartime construction to receive 3-in./50 batteries as envisaged in 1945; the earlier classes were all broken up after the war.

Through World War II, reconstruction of the surviving "leaders" was planned, the *Phelps* showing the configuration selected (off Charleston Navy Yard, 28 October 1944). She received only five dual-purpose guns, as well as one quadruple and two twin Bofors, and retained her torpedo tubes. The anti-Kamikaze program of 1945 envisaged replacement of the torpedo tubes by two more quadruple Bofors, for a total of three. Note the direction-finding loop antenna on her after funnel, as well as HF/DF aft, and the British-style bridge.

At the end of the war, the *Winslow*, which had already been rebuilt, was selected for further conversion as an experimental radar picket to serve with the Operational Development Force. She is shown in Boston Harbor on 20 May 1946, with an SP fighter-control radar but without any ECM gear, and she retains all three quadruple Bofors guns, the two twins in the waist having been removed as compensation for the new radar mainmast. In this form she tested the new Mk 56 director, visible on a pedestal aft.

The *Somers* class was refitted similarly to the *Porter*s: the *Jouett* is shown following a Charleston refit, 20 April 1944, lacking her old midships bank of torpedo tubes and armed with four twin Bofors guns after the removal of No. 3 gun mount. The radar atop her director, which superficially resembled the Mk 4 of most destroyers, was a Mk 3 single-purpose set, akin to those mounted on capital ships and cruisers. The small circle at her forefoot indicates strengthening for ramming submarines, a common modification of the time.

Photographed near Charleston on 13 August 1945, the *Jouett* showed the effects of the originally planned reconstruction as well as of the anti-Kamikaze program, trading her after pair of twin Bofors for two quadruple mounts, and landing both remaining sets of torpedo tubes. Note, too, the elimination of her HF/DF mast aft: she was intended for Kamikaze, not submarine, waters when the end of the war abruptly ended her career.

The destroyer force retained this configuration through the middle of the war, receiving additional weapons only in 1945 in the face of the Kamikaze threat. Four Atlantic destroyer divisions assigned to the Mediterranean in March 1944 were the sole exceptions. In view of the very heavy level of enemy air attack to be expected, they each exchanged one bank of torpedo tubes for Army-type single Bofors, three for the *Sims*-class *Wainwright*, two for the *Bensons*, which she led. The ships involved were DesDivs 13 (DD 421–424, 431), 14 (DD 425–428, of which 426 was sunk in April 1944), 21 (DD 429, 430, 432, 440), and 25 (DD 419 as leader, and 437–439); all but the *Wainwright* (DD 419) were restored to their original batteries upon their return from European waters; the *Wainwright* was not restored until the spring of 1945. This episode is noteworthy as the sole important case of extemporized USN destroyer armament during World War II; it also suggests the reluctance of the U.S. Navy to sacrifice torpedo batteries for antiaircraft guns, even though by late 1944 there can have been few tempting torpedo targets, particularly in the Pacific.

This pro-torpedo policy makes the other major wartime destroyer rearmament program, the anti-Kamikaze program, all the more striking. In January

1945, in view of the emergence of this new threat, the *Mahans* were ordered modified: their two waist tubes would be eliminated, the weight saved used to replace their two twin Bofors with quadruple mounts. In the event, only the *Lamson* was refitted to this standard. In April, the CNO ordered wholesale antiaircraft improvements at the cost of torpedo tubes; all tubes were to be removed in the earlier classes, and one bank in the *Fletchers* and *Sumner/Gearings*. Only normal refits and major battle damage repairs were permitted, which meant that relatively few ships had been modified by the end of hostilities. By this time the emphasis was on the Bofors gun, and all of these were to be the heavy power-operated type. Plans were prepared on a class-by-class basis, and by the end of the war examples of most classes had been refitted. The exceptions were the elderly *Farraguts*, the *Gridleys* (the only class with insufficient reserve stability to take Bofors guns in the first place), and the *Bagleys*. Details of *Benson-Livermore*, *Fletcher*, and *Sumner/Gearing* refits are given in chapters 5 and 6.

As for the earlier ships, the *Mahans* were to have their remaining single bank of centerline tubes removed as compensation for a pair of twin Bofors, for a total of twelve 40-mm. barrels. Only the two twin Oerlikons between the bridge and No. 2 gun would

Massive antiaircraft improvements could add unacceptable top weight, as shown by these views of the *Shaw* (above and facing) at Mare Island on 5 August 1945. As a *Mahan*, she surrendered all of her torpedo tubes in favor of two quadruple Bofors guns, for a total of 12 40-mm., retaining only two 20-mm. mounts (converted to twins) forward. However, repairs after her old battle damage at Pearl Harbor had added enough top weight to make this change impossible; she had to land her No. 3 gun as compensation, largely negating the antiaircraft improvement sought. Note the newly installed twin Bofors around her second funnel, with their new Mk 51 directors; the quadruple mounts aft replaced twins installed earlier.

be retained, for forward fire, although two more were to be installed on the main deck forward of the twin Bofors pending the availability of blind-fire directors. In fact, only one ship, the USS *Shaw*, was refitted. She had been badly damaged at Pearl Harbor and had gained considerable weight in the course of repairs. A post-refit inclining experiment showed her dangerously top-heavy, and she had to land her No. 3 5-inch gun as weight compensation. As this removal largely negated the increase in antiaircraft armament, Commander Destroyers Pacific insisted on her reassignment to the Atlantic Fleet; her place in the Pacific was taken by the *Drayton*.

In the 16-tube *Bagley*s, the removal of all tubes would buy the addition of two quadruple and one twin mount, again for a new total of twelve 40-mm. barrels. The high deckhouse aft that had supported a single twin Bofors would be cut down to support the pair of quadruple mounts, with the two twins forward of it. As in the *Mahan*s, the Oerlikon battery would be reduced to a pair of twin mounts before the bridge. But no ships were refitted.

In the eight-tube *Sims* and *Benham* classes, removal of the tubes would buy only two twin Bofors, for a total of four mounts, eight barrels; plans also called for a total of four twin Oerlikons. Three ships

in each class were refitted: the *Lang*, *Sterett*, and *Wilson* of the *Benham* class, and the *Mustin*, *Morris*, and *Russell* of the *Sims* class. At least in the latter three, the alteration of the 20-mm. battery was not completed; the *Russell* had two twin and two single mounts, and the others retained their single weapons.

The rearmament of the ex-leaders applied only to those ships that had already been modernized with dual-purpose main batteries. In a *Porter*, elimination of the eight torpedo tubes bought replacement of the two twin Bofors aft by quadruple mounts and the addition of two more twins just abaft the second funnel, for a total of sixteen 40 mm. Weight compensation included elimination of the two forward depth-charge projectors and of one of the depth-charge tracks; the 20-mm. battery was reduced to a pair of twin mounts forward. The *Selfridge*, *Winslow*, and *Phelps* were refitted. In a *Somers* the same changes applied, except that the 40-mm. mount in No. 2 position was a twin rather than a quadruple, so that the new total was fourteen 40 mm. The *Davis* and *Jouett* were refitted.

The very heavy gun batteries of 1945 did not match the severity of the air threat, which from the previous spring onward included bomber-launched guided missiles too small and too fast to be vulnerable to gunfire. For example, the quartet of 5-in./38s mounted forward on a *Sumner* or *Gearing* was considered lethal against one airplane, but in June 1946 the OEG (Operations Evaluation Group) reported that its kill probability against a guided missile would be under 20 percent. An April 1947 study noted that

it is possible to splash a target beyond 5,000 yards, but the probability of doing so is small in comparison with the probability of splashing it within 5,000 yards. . . . No AA gun in existence or in design can be . . . effective at 10,000 yards. Nor is such a gun of conventional design likely to be developed in the near future. . . . The defense of a task group beyond 10,000 yards will be the job of the combat air patrol or of guided and/or homing missiles.

The threat of the bomber-launched guided missile was a driving force in U.S. naval thinking from 1945 onward. It was known that the Soviets had captured

The *Mustin* illustrates the anti-Kamikaze refit as applied to a *Sims*-class destroyer, except that she received twin rather than quadruple Bofors guns aft. Note the replacement of both banks of torpedo tubes by another pair of twin 40-mm. guns in her waist, with their Mk 51 directors just forward of them, and the retention of all 20-mm. guns mounted forward of her bridge. The small dish atop her Mk 37 director was also a means of saving weight, compared to the usual Mk 12/22 combination of other wartime destroyers. She is shown, newly refitted, off San Pedro on 14 August 1945, just too late to see further war service.

the German technology, and it was feared that bombers armed with stand-off weapons would be able to attack a task force in bad weather from well beyond gunfire range. In fact, the United States Navy introduced its own antiaircraft missiles in the mid-1950s at just about the time that its chief enemy, the Soviet Navy, introduced the antiship weapons derived from the earlier German work. The American program, Bumblebee, grew out of an April 1944 requirement and a December 1944 proposal by the Applied Physics Laboratory (APL) of Johns Hopkins University,

until then responsible for the U.S. VT fuze program. It was accelerated as a result of the appearance of the Kamikaze, but did not produce workable systems until the early fifties. Indeed, Terrier, the missile initially carried by cruisers and frigates, began as a supersonic test vehicle for the principal Bumblebee weapon, the much larger ramjet Talos.

A missile ship required far more than the missile launcher proper. Time delays inherent in missile operation required aircraft detection far beyond missile range. For example, in April 1956 it was estimated

For *Benson*s, the anti-Kamikaze armament conversion removed remaining torpedo tubes, replacing the twin Bofors aft with quadruple mounts, and adding a pair of twin Bofors between the funnels, as in this view of the *Nields*. Weight was critical, leading to such expedients as replacement of the usual Mk 12/22 fire-control radars by the less-effective Mk 28, and elimination of one anchor (with its hawse pipe plated over). Note, too, the installation of a single 20-mm. gun in the waist at the after end of the long bulwark.

The former *Gearing*-class destroyer *Gyatt* demonstrated that even Terrier could be accommodated aboard a small ship. In fact, however, she did not go to sea until well after the Terrier frigate program had been approved. One unusual feature of her missile installation was that her Mk 25 5-inch fire control radar doubled as a missile control set, presumably with a special drive to an appropriate radar beam motion for missile guidance. Here she proceeds to sea from Boston Navy Yard, 13 December 1956, with what must have been the least complex radar suit of any U.S. Navy missile ship. Her conversion was the most austere possible, and within a few years she reverted to destroyer status, acting as a radar test ship for the Operational Test and Evaluation Force.

that Terrier, which then had a range of about 10 miles, required target detection at 150 to 250 nm. and tracking by the equivalent of an air intercept radar at 100 nm., against a Mach 2 target that could cover about 20 nm. per minute, or 100 nm. in five minutes. The latter would permit accurate pointing of the pencil beam that Terrier rode. The CIC was the key to effective missile operation, as a long-range search radar had to be used to bring the intercept radar to bear, and the latter in turn had to direct the guidance beam set. Thus, a typical Terrier ship (and,

indeed, almost any missile ship) had three quite distinct sets of major radars, all of which required both deck space and clearance overhead. The standard destroyer Terrier installation consisted of twin rails served by an automated loader, with a pair of SPQ-5 or SPG-55 guidance radars nearby.

Although Terrier was originally designed to be launched from small platforms, it was soon realized that it was far too large for destroyer use. In January 1951, a requirement was issued for a much smaller weapon with a range of about 10 miles, suitable for surface ships from destroyer escorts up, and ultimately as the defensive armament of merchant ships. Several companies proposed weapons to meet this specification, but very little was done: the big Talos and the medium Terrier were far more urgent programs. However, the Applied Physics Laboratory found that its Terrier Improvement Program provided a natural solution for the small-ship missile problem. It was interested in semiactive (CW) homing as a solution to the low-altitude deficiencies of the Terrier beam-rider, and was also working on a more powerful series of rocket engines, as well as tail rather than wing control. In the fall of 1954 APL and Convair Pomona conducted a study of a new small missile incorporating as many improved Terrier features as possible, and it proved successful beyond expectation. The Navy approved the program, which became Tartar, early in 1955, and almost immediately work began on a missile version of the then-standard destroyer, the *Forrest Sherman* (see chapter 13).

Tartar could replace a standard 5-in./54 or twin 5-in./38 mount on a one-for-one basis. Unlike Terrier, its loader was totally automated. In the earlier missile, loading was mechanized, but wings and fins, the latter necessitated by the size of the booster, had to be attached by hand. That made not only for relatively slow operation, but also for a considerably larger loading area. In Tartar, the advent of tail control permitted a considerable reduction in wing chord, so that a winged missile could be stowed compactly. The tail itself could fold. A new boost-sustain engine made the separate booster unnecessary. Finally, semiactive guidance considerably simplified the shipboard end of the missile guidance system. The Tartar illuminator (SPG-51) was much smaller and simpler than the SPG-55 of a Terrier, and (at least in theory) even a gunfire control radar with CW injection could be used as a back-up illuminator. Tartar development was rapid partly because the new missile incorporated many Terrier components: in effect Tartar was a Terrier second stage with a new two-pulse (boost plus sustain) engine.

Physically, Terrier was stowed horizontally in revolving rings, rammed onto its launching arm after wings and booster fins were fitted by hand in a special finning space. Thus, a Terrier launcher required not only considerable external clear space, but also a long magazine and then a long handling space, all consuming valuable centerline length. Generally, fire control radars could be mounted above the loader. They had to be close to the launcher because the missile had to be "captured" by the guidance beam quite soon after launch. By way of contrast, the Mk 11 (twin arm) or Mk 13 or 22 (single arm) Tartar launcher was loaded from below, the missiles being

stowed in one or two concentric rings in a cylindrical loader immediately beneath the launcher arm. The centerline space requirement was not far from that of a 5-in./54, although, as in the Terrier, additional length was consumed by the guidance illuminator or illuminators. Automation made for rapid fire in the Tartar launcher. For example, a Mk 10 Terrier launcher is rated at two salvos per minute, 30 seconds (at least) per reload. The Mk 13 fires a Tartar every seven seconds. The increased rate of fire possible with a single-staged weapon explains the transition from Terrier to Tartar or Tartar equivalent in U.S. missile ships designed after the *Belknap* (DLG 26, later CG 26) class, and is probably particularly significant for antisaturation systems such as Aegis.

Although the Bumblebee (or "3-T") missiles were primarily useful against aircraft, they had a significant antiship capability. Terrier in particular was designed to accept a nuclear warhead, and when guns were abandoned in the 1958 missile frigates (*Leahy* class), nuclear missile fire was considered an effective substitute for antiship and antishore fire. Tartar was non-nuclear, but even so was credited with considerable antiship potential. However, it had the defect of relatively short range, and in 1956 the Atlantic Destroyer Force, led by Rear Admiral J.C. Daniel (DesLant), lobbied unsuccessfully to have the Tartar DDG program discontinued in favor of Terrier: "the rapid development of enemy capabilities raises the real possibility that Tartar, now programmed for new DDGs, may well be inadequate for air defense before it becomes available for the operating forces. The lack of a programmed anti-surface atomic capability in Tartar gives the argument for Terrier added cogency. Finally, the anticipated counter-missile requirements of the future will certainly demand the performance potential of the Terrier."

The decisive counterargument was the BuOrd long-range missile program. In May 1958 the chairman of the Standing Committee on the Long-Range Shipbuilding and Conversion program wrote that

present plans for improvement in Tartar will give (it) range and altitude at least equivalent to BT-3 Terrier. An important new element is now injected into this picture by the fact that BuOrd has submitted to the CNO a long-range missile growth and improvement study under which no major changes to the Terrier missile after the HT-3 is in production are contemplated, and Terrier will be produced only as required for the ten existing ships. On the other hand the so-called Super Tartar which may be available for the 1961 program will have performance characteristics greatly superior to those of the current Terrier missiles. I am outlining this missile situation in order that you may not inadvertently say that you want Terrier instead of Tartar without knowing what the future holds for these missiles.

Super-Tartar was soon to be redesignated Typhon (Medium Range).

Both Tartar and Terrier were developed on an emergency basis to meet a massive perceived threat. Deployment was based not on an estimate of missile requirements per task force, but rather on the availability of funds and equipment. Both weapons were vulnerable to saturation attack, since each required a dedicated missile control radar for each target, from missile launch to destruction. By 1958 APL, which was the lead organization for naval missile development, suspected that the future threat would be so massive that some entirely new system would be required to counter it. That was Typhon, which ultimately led to the current Aegis.

In its time, Typhon was a prime example of the adage that "the best is the mortal enemy of perfectly good enough," which sometimes seems to be the motto of U.S. weapon development. Its potential led to the curtailment of several missile ship programs, but its immense cost led to its own cancellation in 1963, leaving only a large gap in task force air defense formations. Attempts to revive missile ship production following its demise had only the most limited success, and indeed the first conventionally powered area-air-defense ships to follow the Tartar DDGs are the four ex-Iranian *Kidd*-class destroyers authorized in FY 79, almost two decades after the last of the DDG 2 series. Between FY 61 and FY 78, when an Aegis-armed heavy missile destroyer (later re-rated missile cruiser) was authorized, the only new missile ships approved were five nuclear missile frigates (FY 67–72 and FY 74–75). The very large force of missile destroyers programmed in the late fifties was delayed again and again in hopes of achieving truly satisfactory systems, and even the conversion program of the mid-sixties was drastically curtailed.

Several problems intersected. First, the entire Bumblebee program was conducted on a crash basis. Terrier entered service well before it achieved the requisite capability, and as late as 1962 it appeared that none of the $6 billion worth of surface-to-air missile ships then in service were capable of their assigned task. Perhaps the most graphic demonstration of this incapacity was the failure of the new missile frigate *Dewey* to shoot down a propeller-driven drone during a display for President Kennedy at about this time; the President ordered the installation of at least some guns aboard all U.S. warships as a back-up. It was not that the missile systems were fundamentally flawed or that they had been incompetently produced. Rather, they represented a number of new technologies not yet mature. For example, they suffered from unreliability, as did virtually all the advanced military electronic systems of their time. When they worked, they could indeed achieve the peak performance desired; but too often they did not work. The new technology also cost far more than had been forecast. Thus from FY 57 onward, drastic reductions in the shipbuilding program were required to balance cost overruns. Again, this was a natural consequence of the immaturity of surface-to-air missile technology, recognizable in many more recent military programs. At the time, however, it was a relatively new and extremely unsettling phenomenon.

Bumblebee was essentially a reaction to 1944–45 missile attack technology. It embodied concepts that had been laid down at that time, and it was ill-suited to counter massive raids or pop-up missiles of which there would be no real early warning. Throughout its career, events always proceeded on two parallel time scales. On one, the scale of actual fleet service, the systems conceived soon after the end of World War II did not enter service in quantity on either side for 10 to 15 years after 1945, so that the age of the concepts embodied in the system was of no great concern. However, the time-scale of system development always looked ahead the 10 or more years necessary for a system to come into existence. Thus, studies of the mid-1950s, conceived when Terrier was first being tested, looked toward a world of massive supersonic jet bomber raids and submarine-launched antiship ballistic missiles patterned on the U.S. SUB-ROC, which was then only a concept. In 1958, APL was justifying Typhon on the basis of the imminent obsolescence of Talos, Terrier, and Tartar—systems not yet in full service.

Typhon was a reaction not only to the incapacity of the Bumblebee missiles, but also to the high cost of their platforms, which already seemed to imply that the Navy would never be able to buy or convert sufficient numbers of missile ships. APL believed that through advances in aerodynamics and fuel chemistry a ramjet of Terrier size would be capable of range performance in excess of that of the enormous Talos, while a single-stage Tartar-size missile might exceed Terrier performance. The new system, in fact, began development as Super-Talos/Super-Tartar, and was renamed largely for budgetary reasons, as funds were not at first forthcoming for what seemed only a modified version of the existing missile systems. The weapons were renamed, respectively, Typhon (Long Range) and Typhon (Medium Range). Economies were to be realized by a reduction in the number of missile ships through a combination of longer individual missile ranges and a reduction in the size of the individual missile installation. On the other hand, Typhon required a far more powerful radar than did its predecessors, and each of the smaller number of ships would have to stow more missiles for each of the smaller number of launchers. Escort-ship size would also be driven up by advances in ASW sensors and weapons.

The heart of the system was a massive electronically scanned (Luneberg Lens) tracking radar, SPG-59, which was to appear in two versions: a 3,400-element type for missile destroyers, and a 10,000-element type for missile frigates (cruisers). Electronic scanning permitted, among other things, multiple-target tracking and a very high data rate, as well as the very narrow beam required to achieve high accuracy at extreme range. Like the earlier Talos, and the later Aegis, Typhon combined terminal semiactive homing with command guidance for midcourse flight. In practice, although both long- and medium-range missiles flew successfully, the big radar did not go to sea until 1964, much later than expected and indeed after the program had been canceled.

Typhon died largely because of the immense cost of its platforms, a cost imposed by the complexity of the fire control system and the size of the SPG-59 radar. The effect of its death was to waste about five years of missile-ship procurement time. That is, with Typhon ships in prospect for the FY 63 and later programs, it seemed unwise to continue the headlong pace of AAW ship acquisition; for example, the program of Talos conversions of Baltimore-class cruisers was stopped. The initial round of problems did not seem fatal, so that procurement of a Typhon DLG or DLGN scheduled initially for FY 63 was put back to FY 64, a total of seven Typhon ships being planned. Continued delays put the Typhon ship back to FY 65, but it was stricken from that program on 13 December 1963 and Typhon itself canceled shortly thereafter. For FY 66, then, the only missile system available for any new warship was Tartar or a Tartar derivative, a weapon considered obsolescent when Typhon was first ordered in 1958. There was, for example, no hope of providing Tartar with the ability to counter saturation raids, at least without the development of a new fire control system quite comparable to that of the dead Typhon system.

The failure of Typhon did not end Navy interest in the surface-to-air missile problem—quite the opposite. In his FY 66 report, Secretary of Defense Robert S. McNamara explained both the cancellation of Typhon and his decision to abandon a program of Tartar and Terrier conversions of existing destroyers and frigates, the latter "pending successful completion of the Tartar improvement program or the availability of a new, better missile system." By this time over $340 million had been programmed for the "3-T Get Well" program, which sought to bring the Bumblebee systems up to the standards originally specified, and further procurement of already unsatisfactory systems seemed unwise. Part of the general

improvement program was a new Standard Missile, intended to replace both Terrier and Tartar with a common airframe. Like Typhon, it was to be built in both Extended-Range (with booster, Terrier replacement) and Medium-Range (Tartar replacement) form; the Medium-Range Standard would incorporate Typhon engine technology, but not Typhon guidance techniques. Even at this level the improvement in the basic Tartar engine was impressive. The original Operational Requirement of 1951 called for a 10-mile range, but in 1975 Standard (MR) was officially credited with a range of 20 nm., i.e., with the range originally credited to Terrier. Standard (ER), with a Terrier booster, is credited with a range of 30 nm. In effect, then, Tartar, a much more compact and more easily handled missile, could replace Terrier. If the size and manning constraints associated with Terrier were accepted, a considerable improvement in range would be possible. On the other hand, electronic advances were limited to much-increased missile and guidance reliability. Thus, there was only a limited improvement in defense against the saturation raid threat. Nevertheless, the general transition from analog to digital computer technology and the introduction of the Naval Tactical Data System offered considerable improvements, bringing existing missile systems much closer to maximum potential performance. A new Tartar D system incorporating these advances was developed for the South Carolina-class missile frigates; it also made use of the new solid-state electronics for greatly increased reliability. Tartar D was to have been installed in a new FY 67 DDG and in several other classes.

The austere missile improvement program also included the development of an entirely new family of rapid-fire missile launchers, Mk 26. These twin-arm devices can accept a wide variety of missiles and so permit a mixture of Standard, ASROC, and new antiship weapons such as Harpoon. Like the simpler Mk 13 of Tartar DDGs and the Perry class, they load vertically and so are economical consumers of valuable centerline length. The next step may well be an even simpler vertical box launcher that is currently proposed for the follow-on DDGX, and for CG 47-class cruisers beginning with the fifth or sixth unit.

The very limited production of new missile ships during the 1960s can be explained almost entirely on the basis of the promise of new systems. As Typhon sank late in 1963, a new project, the Advanced Surface Missile System (ASMS), was begun (November 1963). For about two years it appeared that ASMS would require an entirely new missile. Consequently, Navy requests for new missile destroyers (DDG) in the FY 66 program were rejected by Secretary of Defense McNamara: there was little point in buying one more obsolescent ship class, when it appeared that a far better weapon was just over the horizon. It seemed preferable to invest in modernization of the existing missile-ship fleet.

However, quite soon it was decided that, although ASMS might ultimately require a new missile, it would be developed in an evolutionary manner, at first using the Standard Missile airframe and launcher. It followed that new DDG construction under the FY 67 program would be attractive; the new ship would be equipped with Tartar D. Now, however, the stumbling block was a proposal for an entirely new series of destroyers. The Office of the Secretary of Defense proposed a program combining the new DDGs and a new fast ASW destroyer, DX/DXG. The FY 67 missile weapon system was to be incorporated in a new DXG, large numbers of which were to be built. In fact, only the DX element of the program ever materialized, as the *Spruance* class. The DXG weapon system appeared in a nuclear equivalent, the *Virginia* class. The *Spruance* was designed with an alternative DDG option in mind, which was purchased by the Iranian government, then repurchased by the U.S. Navy as the *Kidd* class in the FY 79 program, almost a decade after its conception.

ASMS itself developed more slowly, to meet a combination of the saturation raid and a short-range pop-up threat typified by the Soviet Styx (SSN-2) missile. In each case reaction time was an important limit on effective firepower. Like Typhon, ASMS (which became Aegis) used an electronically scanned radar to search and track targets simultaneously. Command guidance is used to separate raid-handling capacity from the limit imposed by the number of illuminating radars. That is, the missile is launched into a footprint near its target, the fire control system applying mid-course correction in flight. Illumination is required only for that fraction of the missile's flight near the target, and the illuminator is slaved to the central electronically scanned (phased array) radar, SPY-1. In effect, the illuminators are time-shared among the targets.

When the ASMS system contract was finally awarded to RCA in December 1969, the existing Standard Missile was specified: Aegis incorporates a wholly new fire control system and a wholly new radar, but the SM-2 missile differs from SM-1 only in that it incorporates a programmable autopilot that can accept mid-course guidance. However, there is considerable growth potential. Moreover, even with the existing missile engine, the command guidance technique permits the missile to fly a much more energy-efficient trajectory, so that Aegis outranges previous systems by as much as 55 percent. The new SPY-1 Aegis radar first went to sea aboard the former seaplane tender *Norton Sound* (which had carried the

sole SPG-59) in May 1974. At first it was assumed that the Aegis platform would be a nuclear frigate, which became the *Virginia* class. That sized the system. However, just as development began, Admiral Zumwalt became CNO. He was determined to reverse the trend away from numerous missile-armed carrier escorts, and wanted to increase the number of combatant ships by ruthlessly cutting irrelevant costs, as in the *Perry* class (see chapter 15). This was the occasion for yet another shift, to an austere destroyer that was to be called DG or DG/Aegis. On 9 August 1971 Admiral Zumwalt requested that the Chief of Naval Materiel prepare a plan for Aegis deployment in very large numbers; in December he reoriented the program toward smaller and less costly ships. He hoped to limit them to $100 million (FY 73 dollars; the *Perry* was to cost $45 million) and 5,000 tons. The detailed evolution of the class, which grew to the current CG 47, is described in chapters 13 and 14. It suffices here to note that the series of violent shifts in ship characteristics associated with changes in CNO produced delays quite as severe as those that hopes of new missile systems had produced a decade earlier.

Tartar, Terrier, Typhon, and Standard were all large missiles designed to serve as the main battery of a destroyer. However, as the air threat to warships developed in the late 1950s, it became clear that even ships that could not accommodate such systems would require some limited missile cover for self-defense. A program of "point" (as opposed to area) defense weapons produced first a naval version of the Army Mauler and then, when the Army version was canceled, the familiar series of Sea Sparrows. In both cases the essential features were compactness and simplicity of operation. For example, there is no automatic loading system; the Sea Sparrow launcher holds eight rounds and can be reloaded (if at all) only by hand. In the original version, the semiactive missile was directed by a radar illuminator that was hand-pointed. As in other systems, development has been in the direction of greater sophistication, including a better missile, a lighter and more compact launcher, and an automated director. Point defense requires very fast reactions to rapidly closing threats: the current system employs a Target Acquisition System (Mk 23) in which a combination of ESM and a doppler radar detects and tracks an incoming object, determines that it is hostile, and opens fire.

The original Sea Sparrow was first tested aboard the destroyer escort *Bradley* (DE 1041) in 1967. It was one of several lightweight systems then under consideration, another being Chaparral, a version of the air-launched infrared-seeking Sidewinder. The latter was actually mounted aboard nine Pacific Fleet FRAM I destroyers in 1972, on their former DASH flight decks, but plans to employ it aboard destroyer escorts not equipped with Sea Sparrow did not come to fruition. The destroyer escort *Downes* (DE 1070) tested the Improved Point Defense Missile System (NATO Sea Sparrow) for which the Target Acquisition System was developed.

The point defense weapons are important because they figure prominently in the development of the dedicated ASW ships, the *Knox* and the *Spruance* classes of chapter 15. In 1980 it appears that they will soon be supplemented by the Vulcan-Phalanx Gatling gun, and, within a few years, by a new lightweight Rolling Air Frame (RAM) missile. These last developments, however, have not yet affected the shape of the destroyer force.

Destroyer AAW evolution has not been confined to improvements in weapons and their control mechanisms. Even in 1945, massive increases in the short-range batteries of screening destroyers added relatively little to the air defense of the carrier task force as a whole. Improvements had to come, rather, from increases in the range at which enemy aircraft could be intercepted, and in the probability that any given attacker would be intercepted at long range. That is, the destroyers had to improve the performance of the Combat Air Patrol fighters that constituted the principal air defense of the formation: shipboard guns were effective because they destroyed those few aircraft that leaked past CAP. Throughout the war, fighter direction was a major theme of task force development. However, destroyers at the edge of the formation were valuable advanced radar stations, and it was natural for them to carry fighter direction teams as well. The USS *Trathen* (DD 530) was the first destroyer to serve in this role, in the invasion of the Baker and Howland Islands at the end of August 1943. Her special equipment was limited to fighter-type VHF radios, and a fighter director officer was stationed in her CIC. During the fleet's approach she was stationed in its van, 30 to 65 nm. ahead of the carrier. No enemy aircraft penetrated to within sight range. The destroyer *Kimberly* operated in a similar role in the approach to the Gilberts the following November, and others were used to provide early warning during the Marianas invasion. By 1945 most four-ship destroyer divisions included one fighter direction ship.

By that time, too, much more elaborate conversions were in hand. Fighter control required the standard aircraft homing beacon (which the fighters assigned to the destroyer could use as a reference point); generally both YE and a back-up, YG, were provided. Fighter control also required target altitude as well as range and bearing; the standard destroyer air search set (SC-2 or SR) provided only the latter two data. Altitude could be estimated by means

of a "fade chart," showing the relation between blind ranges and target altitude. A specialized pencil-beam height-finder radar was a more precise alternative, but it required a mast of its own, with consequent sacrifices in other equipment. It was, indeed, symbolic that the tripod carrying the SP height-finder and radar jamming gear replaced the one remaining bank of torpedo tubes on the *Gearing*-class destroyers converted to this picket role in 1945. These ships no longer carried their main batteries on board: their main batteries were now sections of the carrier-borne Combat Air Patrol.

This might be considered a first step in the integration of the carrier task force, individual ships no longer carrying their own weapons, but rather achieving their effects only in cooperation with the entire force. Radar and radios, then, could no longer be considered mere auxiliaries to the weapons of a single ship, but rather contributions to the total information-gathering capacity of the task force, which capacity would in turn contribute to the total combat capacity of the force, directed in unison. This ideal would not be realized until almost two decades later with the advent of NTDS, but the path was laid down in 1944–45 with the conversion of the pickets.

That conversion program appears to have been a direct consequence of fleet experience in the Leyte campaign. On 31 December 1944 representatives of the Third and Fifth Fleets, Air Forces Pacific, Destroyers Pacific, and Service Squadrons Pacific staffs jointly recommended the conversion of 12 long-hull destroyers for picket duty. A tripod carrying SP radar would replace the forward bank of torpedo tubes. In January, Admiral King designated DD 742, 743, 805–808, 829, and 873–877 for conversion, which would follow shakedown cruises on all but the incomplete DD 806–808 and 829 which, with 742 and 743, would be converted at Boston Navy Yard. The others would be done at Norfolk. The program had high priority, and it was estimated that it would require six to nine weeks per ship. In May, Admiral King designated another twelve: DD 830–835, 878–883. By this time the emergency antiaircraft program had eliminated the after bank of tubes in *Gearings*, and new pickets had no torpedo tubes at all. A few ships did have one bank of torpedo tubes as initially converted, however.

In fleet operations early in 1945, destroyers were fitted out as advanced pickets or Tomcats. According to the official battle report, they were

> used on Strike Days as advanced radar pickets and guide ships for returning strikes. The use of these ships was twofold: to assist in control of returning strike aircraft and, secondly, to give advanced warning to the force of approaching enemy aircraft. . . . These same destroyers also served as orbit points for

The *Charles P. Cecil* typifies the destroyer radar picket conversions of 1945; in armament she duplicates her destroyer sisters, except for the total absence of torpedo tubes. Indeed, the radar pickets were carried on the Navy List as destroyers until well after the war. The radars on her foremast were SR, the postwar and late-war air-search set, and SG, with a DBM radar direction-finder below both in a small radome. Her tripod mainmast carried the standard mixture of fighter-control and countermeasures equipment.

returning strikes where the destroyer CAP was used to "inspect" for possible trailing bandits. The return of the strikes from the pickets also served to define a friendly "lane" for planes approaching the Force. When properly complied with by returning pilots this procedure simplified to a remarkable degree the radar and identification picture for all Fighter Director Officers. . . .

At this time special picket features were often limited to homing beacons and additional VHF radios, as the first of the specially converted *Gearing*s did not appear until Okinawa, and even then they were not available in numbers.

Picket operations foreshadowed PIRAZ (Positive Identification Radar Advisory Zone) operations off Vietnam, where a radar picket/air control ship was responsible for all friendly air activity over an enormous air space extending inland from the Gulf of Tonkin. Such ships employed their radars and their automated CICs as their primary weapons, achieving far more kills by fighter direction than by their own guns and missiles, which in many cases were no more than self-defenses. The success of the PIRAZ concept required not merely advanced search and height-finding radars, but also the ability of the picket ship

to keep track of the hundreds of aircraft, including neutral airliners, moving through the controlled air space. This, in turn, depended upon the development of the automated CIC, the Naval Tactical Data System, NTDS. Although quite far removed from the manual plots of 1945, NTDS was a direct development of such systems. Automation was essential to the PIRAZ role because of the sheer number of aircraft that had to be tracked simultaneously. From World War II onward, the picket problem was two-fold. All unfriendly aircraft (or, later, cruise missiles) had to be detected and tracked to destruction, but at the same time positive identification and location of all friendlies (and, in many cases, neutrals) was necessary. The latter both permitted the appropriate assignment of CAP fighters to targets and also prevented the waste of defense assets on nontargets, not to mention the destruction of friendly aircraft. The numerical balance between enemy and friendly aircraft could vary widely, and the problem was perhaps most severe in an environment such as Vietnam, in which very few of the detected aircraft were potential targets.

Parallel to the destroyer radar picket program was a program of destroyer escort conversions, apparently intended to provide the slow amphibious task force with fighter cover equivalent to that enjoyed by the fast carrier task force. The precise origins of the program are not clear, but it was in train by May 1945. Ten DEs (all TEs: DE 51, 57, 153, 213, 220–223, 577, 578) and 10 DEs scheduled for APD conversion (DE 204, 210, 214, 665, 666, 790, 791, 798–800) were ordered converted to pickets, the former about 15 May and the latter two weeks later. These conversions were to take precedence over the large program of APD conversions already in progress. However, "because of the operational need for additional DEs" all of the APD picket conversions and 3 of the 10 DE conversions were canceled on 4 August 1945, leaving only DE 51, 57, 153, 213, 223, 577, and 578. Conversions were carried out by New York Navy Yard (DE 51 and 223; 204, 214, 220, 800 canceled), by Philadelphia (DE 57; 211 canceled), and by Brown Shipbuilding of Houston (DE 153, 213, 577, 578, with many cancellations). It appears that the ships scheduled for APD conversion were to have been refitted as APDs and then converted, as plans were drawn up to use the extra deckhouse space in an APD, and indeed as the picket plan appears to incorporate some APD features.

Like the destroyer picket, this conversion was to have added SP radar and countermeasures gear on an amidships tripod, with additional deckhouse space below to accommodate personnel and equipment. Rearmament would result in an ultimate battery of two single 5-in./38s controlled by a Mk 52 radar director, plus three twin and one quadruple 40 mm. (with, respectively, three Mk 51 and one Mk 63 blind-fire directors), four twin 20 mm., and two depth-charge tracks (the Hedgehog and six depth-charge projectors having been eliminated as weight compensation).

With the end of the war, the specialized slow picket was abandoned. Of the seven ships converted, one, the *Buckley* (DE 51), was not included in the postwar active fleet. The others served with the Operational Development Force; five of them were decommissioned by the fall of 1947. The seventh, the *William T. Powell*, survived as a Reserve Training Ship as late as 1957. Although all were redesignated DER in 1949, none was considered suited to the new radar picket role, and all were returned to the DE category in 1954 in view of their very limited capabilities.

The destroyer pickets, or DDRs, were quite another matter. They were a vital element of the fast carrier task force, which the Navy considered one of its greatest successes. Twelve more (DDR 711–714, 784, 817, 838, 842, 863, 870, 888, 889) were authorized under the FY 52 program as SCB project 79.

The *O'Hare* was one of twelve *Gearing*s converted to radar pickets under the FY 52 program; she is shown at Norfolk Naval Shipyard, 19 September 1953. The new SPS-8 height-finder was so heavy that mounting it atop any kind of mast was out of the question; that, in turn, made the arrangement of the 3-inch antiaircraft battery more complex. The two single mounts usually carried just abaft the bridge were eliminated as weight compensation, but there were two twin mounts (port and starboard) in the waist, for a total of six guns. These ships also received two Hedgehogs on either side on the 01 level forward and, when it became available, TACAN. The small radar antenna at the foretop is a zenith-search/surface-search set, either SG-6 or the very similar SPS-4, with SPS-6B below it.

Where the original radar picket (redesignated DDR rather than DD in 1949) had been a fleet destroyer with a pencil-beam radar and a slightly improved CIC, the newer one would operate in concert with carrier-launched airborne pickets, and would control much faster interceptors. She would require the new TACAN air control beacon as well as improved communications and countermeasures. The new air control radar would be the heavy stabilized SPS-8, which was characteristic not merely of the DDR but also of the new generation of DER pickets, and of the new *Mitschers* (see chapter 11), which had an important picket function. It was far too heavy to be carried aloft in a destroyer.

That caused problems, as the armament arrangement in a *Gearing* left almost no deck space abaft the funnels, and the space between them was unacceptable in view of radar interference. On the other hand, there was great reluctance to eliminate one of the two twin 3-in./50s aft in view of the greater exposure of a DDR (as compared to a destroyer) to air attack. The solution finally adopted was to replace the twin mount abaft the second funnel with two on sponsons disposed to port and starboard. The two single 3-in. abaft the bridge were eliminated as weight compensation, and the SPS-8 cleared the two wing mounts on a small deckhouse. The other characteristic feature of the new DDR was TACAN, an air navigation beacon that replaced the earlier YE and YG. It first became available in June 1956 and was mounted on a short tripod mainmast, which also carried ECM gear.

Unfortunately, five of the earlier DDRs had already received the new 3-in./50 battery before the SCB 79 design was completed in February 1952. It was estimated that they could be rearranged at a cost of $1.16 million and five months. Alternatively, they could remain in service, cramped, with poor communications, poor ECM capability, no airborne early warning terminal capability, and no TACAN. They were far too important for such limitations to be acceptable, although in fact conversions were spread over several refits in order to remain within a budget limit.

All of the DDRs received scanning sonar; in September 1955 ComCruDesPac remarked that "usage requires DDR to perform ASW tasks identical to those of standard destroyer types." All DDRs had the standard QHBa scanning sonar and twin fixed Hedgehogs. At first the SCB rejected a suggestion that the new and far more powerful SQS-4 be included in the DDR Class Improvement Plan (CIP), in view of the AAW mission of the type, but it was overruled. By 1956 there was, in addition, the Electronic Data System (EDS), a forerunner of NTDS. Its automatic plotting feature was clearly essential to an efficient radar picket. The SCB estimated that SQS-4 *and* EDS would cost one twin 3-in./50. In fact, however, most DDRs ended the 1950s with all six 3-in./50s still in place, their CIPs unfulfilled. A few had only one twin 3-in./50.

By that time, too, new radars were in prospect: SPS-29 and -40 for air search, and SPS-30, an improved SPS-8B, for height-finding. By this time, the DDRs were not merely weight but also *power* critical, and would require an additional generator with its attendant top weight. The new radars were fitted to most of the surviving DDRs as part of the FRAM program (see chapter 12), which entailed modifications far beyond those envisaged as part of the CIP. By that time, most of the DDRs were converted back to ASW ships, since there were either in service or in prospect large numbers of new missile ships with radar and CIC facilities, not to mention sea-keeping qualities, far in advance of those available aboard elderly converted *Gearings*.

The postwar radar picket program also embraced a number of newly converted destroyer escorts. Unlike their wartime equivalents, they were intended to form part of the Continental Air Defense System, providing early warning for land-based interceptors. The continental air warning net, extended seaward by DERs, was authorized by the Joint Chiefs of Staff in 1949, and by 1950 a total of about 30 picket ships were envisaged. The seven 1945 conversions were regarded as so obsolete that the cost of updating them would be equivalent to the cost of new conversions, and they remained in reserve. The FMR type was selected for its long (diesel) endurance.

The selection of the FMRs, the best of the diesel DEs, was not entirely popular. Rear Admiral R.L. Hicks, the Chief of Fleet Maintenance, argued in May 1948 that the FMRs would be more useful as ocean escorts for convoys operating at 12 knots or less, and that, equipped with scanning sonar (QHB), they would be able to oppose modern (Guppy) submarines. The 48 DETs then laid up in Green Cove Springs, Florida (and earmarked for transfer to foreign navies) seemed preferable, as they were similar in construction and in cruising radius but about one knot slower.

Preliminary characteristics for this SCB 46 project (July 1948) envisaged an FRM conversion suitable for mass production in the event of mobilization. She was to act as a radar station, as a fighter control station, and as a collection point for information gathered by long-range patrol aircraft. It was recognized that a large radar suit would require weight and space compensation, and the SCB was willing to accept a reduction in effective cruising radius to 7,000 nm. at 12 knots, oil tanks being turned over to other uses. This would entail a reduction of 42,000 gallons in a total capacity of about 98,000. The bat-

The *Joyce*, one of the first of the continental air-defense radar pickets, is shown off Mare Island, nearly complete, on 28 February 1951. Her mission was considered so important that she was provided with two of the relatively scarce air-search sets, SPS-6B forward and SPS-6 aft, with an SPS-4 zenith-search set at her foretop and a platform for an SPS-8 height-finder atop her bridge. Before long one of the two air-search radars had to be removed to help redress shortages in the Fleet, the *Joyce* being left with what became the standard radar picket suit.

tery would be reduced to two 3-in./50s and two twin 40 mm., with four free-swinging machine guns and one fixed Hedgehog. The radar suit was to include two of the new air search sets (SPS-6B), two height-finders for fighter control (SPS-8), and a hemispheric search set, the abortive SPS-3, and the ship would be fitted with a terminal for airborne early warning data; in all, she was to be capable of directing four simultaneous intercepts. The sonar would be the QHB scanning type.

In May 1949, it was decided that the existing slow-fire 3-in./50 would be replaced by single rapid-fire weapons, and the Bofors dispensed with. There would also be four twin 20 mm. Conversion would entail complete rearrangement of the crew space and construction of an aluminum deckhouse and aluminum radar masts to assure stability. The underwater battery was revised to consist of a Mk 15 trainable Hedgehog and a single depth-charge track aft with 12 charges. The radar suit was further enlarged, to consist of two long-range air search sets with complementary antenna patterns (SPS-6 and -6B) plus two SPS-8. In the absence of the hemispheric scan set, the surface search radar (SPS-4) would be fitted for "zenith search."

The new DER was an austere design, and it was not entirely satisfactory. For example, BuShips commented that damaged stability, already poor in the FMR, would not be improved; indeed, no specific damaged stability study had been made. The removal of CIC from the 02 level provided space for the commanding officer's cabin and chart house without changes in the original pilothouse and ship controls. The need for a very large CIC (ultimately

installed on the first platform deck, forward) required expansion of the existing deckhouse, and all berthing and messing facilities had to be relocated.

> . . . the berthing and messing for the complement required is the tightest feature of the study. The unusual treatment of the wardroom was necessitated by the provision for a foul-weather passage to CPO quarters to avoid the traverse of the CIC otherwise necessary. Expanded communication requirements on the 01 level resulted in the combination of the commanding officer's sea cabin and quarters into one space at the 02 level. The crew's messing space is congested, but cafeteria and scullery arrangements are such as to require uni-directional traffic during meals.

The result seemed rather expensive in the face of the tight budgets the Navy was then encountering, and in September 1949 the SCB asked BuShips to investigate possible savings if requirements were cut to two simultaneous intercepts. This entailed the elimination of one SPS-8 and its associated IFF antenna; in addition, two of the four radar scopes in CIC could be eliminated. Ultimately, the SCB decided to remove the radar but not the displays, so that under some conditions the ship would still be able to conduct four interceptions. This reduction eliminated a requirement for an additional 100-kw generator to supplement the existing two 200-kw ship-service, one 100-kw auxiliary, and one 100-kw emergency generators. A saving of about $340,000 was realized, about 10 percent of the conversion cost.

A visit to the USS *Strickland*, refitting in Boston in August 1953, brought out some of the problems of the original SCB 46 design. There was some sluggishness in steering, particularly under eight knots, i.e., at patrol speeds. Operation on one shaft would be most economical, but in that case the ship became unmanageable.

> The trim by the head of about two feet may also be a sizable factor, i.e., by bringing the propellers and rudder out of the water, and should be corrected as fast as practicable.* Seaworthiness would be considerably improved by more freeboard forward and speed should be improved by greater propeller immersion. The forward 3-in./50 . . . is useless in a heavy sea . . . this mount must be provided with a spray shield to be fully effective. . . . The ship is always conned from the open bridge above the pilot house with orders to the helmsman by voice tube. This is not a desirable arrangement. The open bridge could be provided outside the pilot house similar to that on the late DDs by very little alteration. This would permit considerable reduction of topside weight and silhouette. The deck grating is presently raised about three feet above the 03 level in order to provide vision over the sonar control room. The sonar control room is hot and crowded and should be moved down. . . .

Crowding was pervasive. For example, the standard bunk had to be shortened to fit into the captain's cabin; "this was not objectionable to the present Captain, a rather short man, but will certainly not be satisfactory to his relief, six foot three. The wardroom is not adequate to seat officer complement so that two shifts are required. . . ."

Although the air defense mission, reflected in the powerful radars, was paramount, the new DERs retained considerable ASW capability in the form of the Mk 15, a depth-charge track aft (often with considerable depth-charge stowage) and in some cases, depth-charge throwers. They also received scanning sonar. A proposal to fit the later DERs with the SQS-1 scanning sonar was rejected in favor of the far more capable—and more costly—SQS-4; indeed, earlier units were retrofitted with this powerful sensor. A factor in favor of the retention of ASW systems may have been fear of possible Soviet missile submarines, a fear articulated as early as the late forties, when the U.S. Navy had itself successfully fired modified ex-German V-1 cruise missiles from submarines.

The AA or surface battery was restricted to a pair of rapid-firing single 3-in./50s; in most cases Mk 17 spray shields were fitted, at least to the forward mounts. This rather light battery derived from the strategic warning mission: heavy bombers flying high overhead en route to targets in the U.S. would be detected and reported long before they could attack the DER. There would be little point in wasting part

of a strategic attack force on a DER—which would provide warning by its disappearance.

The first two conversions, the *Harveson* (DER 316) and *Joyce* (DER 317), had two big tripods, each carrying on SPS-6 air search radar; the extra set was a standby mounted "in view of the special mission of this type ship." The foremast also carried a sea search radar with a special zenith search reflector (i.e., a height-finder for aircraft flying in a 20-degree cone directly overhead, which the other radars could not touch); on the mainmast was an aircraft beacon. The big SPS-8 was mounted on a short pedestal atop the bridge.

These two FY 49 FMR conversions retained their original high bridges, as did four more of FY 51 (DER 142, 244, 318, and 333). Later ships had only one SPS-6: special mission or not, the big radar was in critically short supply; one was removed from the first two ships. With the weight of a second SPS-6 eliminated aft, it became practical to mount the SPS-8 abaft the mainmast.

It was no great surprise that the high bridge proved unpopular; but at $110,000 per reconstruction (1954) the SCB was loath to order it lowered on DERs already in service. The best that could be promised was relocation of the sonar room when SQS-4 was fitted. The remaining 28 FMR conversions (SCB 46B) incorporated from the first a new, low, open bridge. They were done under the FY 54 (4), FY 55 (6), FY 56 (12), and FY 57 (6) programs. A planned run of 6 (FY 53) had been dropped in order to release funds for carrier construction. By the time these later DERs were ready, the new TACAN aircraft beacon was available; it was mounted on the top of the mainmast.

SCB 46A (FY 54) was designed specifically for the completion of the only two steam DERs, two WGTs, the *Vandivier* and *Wagner*, that had been suspended at the end of World War II. The WGT was considerably shorter legged than the FMR, and thus a much less satisfactory subject for conversion, but it was available in considerable numbers. Characteristics of January 1954 listed the detection of enemy submarines approaching the U.S. coast among the primary tasks of the picket, in a departure from the original concept of SCB 46. The designed endurance of 5,500 nm. at 12 knots could not be increased given limited internal volume; one additional 100-kw generator was required. In the spirit of a mobilization design, the ships were to retain their two original enclosed 5-in./38s, all lighter weapons being eliminated. The underwater battery would consist of a Mk 15 Hedgehog, a single stern track, and two launching racks each for three Mk 32 homing torpedoes. The radar suit would consist of a single long-range air search set (SPS-12), a height-finder (SPS-8), and a

---

*This was never corrected. DERs remained impossible to keep headed on a course below 8.7 kts (one engine/one screw minimum speed) and trimmed by the bow despite installation of about 87 tons of lead ballast aft.

The *Hissem* shows the configuration of the great majority of radar pickets in this 17 January 1957 photograph. She was armed with two rapid-fire 3-inch guns and a Mk 15 trainable Hedgehog forward of her bridge, fire control being limited to a Mk 63 director atop the bridge. The air-search radar was the new SPS-12, with an SPS-10 for surface search above it, zenith search having been abandoned by this time. The mainmast carried the TACAN aircraft beacon, essential if the ship were to control defensive aircraft, as well as passive ECM antennas, and the SPS-8 height-finder sat on the deck abaft it. Note the similarity of her general configuration to that of an ex-TEV fast transport.

The *Vandivier* (shown) and her sister *Wagner* were the only continental air-defense radar pickets to mount 5-inch guns; they were also the only steam ones, fundamentally less satisfactory than the diesel units because of their shorter range. In effect they were mobilization prototypes for the mass conversion of existing WGT-class escorts. The unusual-looking director atop her bridge is a Mk 69. This photograph was taken on 21 May 1956.

simple surface search radar (SPS-10), and the sonar would be the most powerful available scanning type, SQS-4.

The far longer-legged FMR conversions were superior for long deployments on station, and the two steam DERs were the first to decommission.

The Ocean Picket system was augmented by 16 converted Liberty ships (FY 55–58) on mid-ocean patrol. Ocean picket duty was considered important enough to warrant very great improvements to units in service. Thus the DERs were among the earliest recipients of the new SPS-28 air search radar. All had it by September 1958, although it had appeared in the first place only in January 1957. In 1959, despite the expectation that all would be out of service (worn out) within four or five years, the DERs were scheduled for the even more powerful SPS-29 and for a more effective form of SPS-8, SPS-8B, later SPS-30. The latter was expected to require compensation: in the DER 316 group it would aggravate an already unfortunate trim condition. But the DER was above all a mobile radar station: by January 1959 its CIP called for the removal of No. 2 3-inch gun to make way for the new and even heavier SPS-30 height-finder. Matters were simplified somewhat by the decision to replace SPS-29 by the ligher SPS-40; however, the newer systems were never fitted. It is interesting to observe that the CIP did *not* provide for any reduction in ASW battery, which at this time included the Mk 15, the stern track, and two triple Mk 32 tubes for light homing torpedoes.

By this time the DERs, in common with the rest of the destroyer force, were well worn. In December 1959, it was planned to retire all six of the DER 316s, four of the later DER 386 series, and both steam DERs during FY 61 due to their material condition. In fact, the ships soldiered on slightly longer; only eight had been decommissioned when the warning/barrier force was abolished in mid-1965. Their long endurance and excellent habitability made them ideal platforms for coastal surveillance of Vietnam, and the last active service of most DERs was spent in Operation Market Time, the blockade of seaborne arms traffic during the Vietnamese War. Their height-finders, TACANs, and Hedgehogs were removed. Others served for a time in support of American operations in the Antarctic (Operation Deep Freeze), for similar reasons.

Plans to extend the life of four ships by FRAM II conversion (two each in FY 62 and FY 63) were dropped. The FRAM refit was to have included replacement of the former SQS-4 series sonar with the newer SQS-20, and also fitting of SPS-30. The last ship was stricken from U.S. service in 1973; eight years later the former *Thomas J. Gary* (DER 326) remains active in the Tunisian Navy, and the former *Camp* (DER 251) in the Philippines Navy, after service in the former South Vietnamese fleet.

11

The Ultimate Destroyer, 1944–1951

When the General Board met in April 1942 to debate the characteristics of what would become the *Sumner/Gearing* design, it had in mind something very different—a fleet destroyer that would restore the appropriate speed margin to the fast task force screen, i.e., that would be capable of 38 knots on trial, given the new and much more stringent trial load requirements that were expected to reduce considerably the speed of the new *Fletcher*s. The board believed that, if all other features were held constant, the increase of 1.5 knots over the 36.5 expected for the new interim destroyers would be achievable on 300 more tons, i.e., on 2,500 tons standard displacement. In fact, by the end of the process six years later, the new destroyer would not only mount an entirely new battery, but would displace over a thousand tons more than the April 1948 estimate—and even then it would attain no more than 36 knots, using an entirely new power plant. Moreover, this new destroyer, the *Mitscher*, would be so large as to price itself out of the mass-production destroyer category entirely, leading to a new division between fast task force escorts, or large destroyers (which became the DL, or frigate, series) and the new austere fast escorts, the new destroyers of the *Forrest Sherman* and *Charles F. Adams* classes.

In 1942 these problems were as yet far in the future, and the 2,500-ton destroyer was treated as a near-term project. BuOrd, for example, complained that

38 knots is considered excessive . . . there is a constant demand for reductions in weight of all types of mounts. Several metals, necessary for strong alloy steels, are critical materials. Recently four forecastle mounts have been damaged by heavy seas in vessels of the 1,500–1,600 ton types; one at a speed of 28 knots. These mounts were designed to withstand loads of 1,000 lbs./square foot. Unless the higher bows of the proposed ships will provide a much greater freedom from impacts of solid water on the shields, it will be desirable to build greater strength into the shields. This will cause increases in weight.

Indeed, the addition of 300 tons in itself would lead to pressures for growth. BuOrd rejected suggestions that the 5-in./38 be replaced by the more powerful 5-in./54 then being developed for the *Midway*-class carriers and the *Montana*-class battleships, but did want two more depth-charge projectors, and a second emergency diesel generator. The bureau's implicit demand for a forecastle design to replace the flush decker would have added even more weight, but it was never pursued seriously.

The characteristics for 2,500-ton destroyers were approved by the board on 24 April 1942 and by the Secretary of the Navy on 11 May, and they gradually circulated through the fleet. In October 1943, Rear Admiral M.S. Tisdale, Commander Destroyers Pacific Fleet, reported his views on the proposed 2,500-ton destroyer:

. . . based upon the generally accepted concept that a destroyer's paramount duty is, and will be, *offensive* with secondary duty as a screening vessel; that it is the Navy's primary surface torpedo carrier, that anti-aircraft guns, as such, are defensive, the greatest importance of which is to fight the ship to the torpedo firing point, and secondarily to protect a convoy against attack; that the destroyer is the nearest approach to the "all purpose" vessel of any combatant type.

In 1945 the United States had a large, but obsolescent, destroyer force; 15 years later much of it required reconstruction. This is the *Allen M. Sumner* following her FRAM refit, showing her modified bridge (with bridge wings), DASH hangar, and a variable-depth sonar aft. All typified the shift towards specialization in ASW within the destroyer force.

The *Willis A. Lee* began life as the postwar destroyer that would reflect the varied lessons of World War II, but instead was commissioned into a new class of "frigates" whose DL symbol reflected an initial belief that she and her sisters would be "destroyer leaders." Her apparent emphasis on ASW (as shown by two large Weapon As, one fore and one aft) was also deceptive: above all she was a task force air-defense ship, with a combination of the latest guns (the 3-inch/50s shown were later replaced by the twin 3-inch/70s of the original design) and radars, including an SPS-8 aft for fighter control, and a zenith/surface-search radar at her fore. The Mk 67 5-inch director forward was mounted only in this class and in the command cruiser *Northampton*.

This was a view heavily influenced by experience in the torpedo and gun battles around Guadalcanal, and yet informed by the shift in emphasis in Pacific warfare towards the fast carrier task force, in which the destroyer would be very much a screening unit and very little an offensive ship. Admiral Tisdale had had considerable experience with the *Fletchers*, but none of the "interim" *Sumners* were as yet under his command. Thus, he could call for ships "much handier than the 2,100-ton class. A turning circle less than that of the newer carriers and battleships is vital." This had in fact been accomplished in the twin-rudder *Sumners*.

In line with his emphasis on torpedo warfare, Tisdale wanted "tubes adequate to fire a *minimum* of ten torpedoes in a salvo to either side. Two quintuple centerline torpedo mounts unfortunately are probably all that can be carried. Provide quick reloads if considered practicable." ASW was far less important, and the new ship was to carry only enough for "three large patterns." As for the gun battery, it would be well to replace the existing 5-in./38 with the more powerful 5-in./54; in other discussions of such a shift, it was often suggested that the 5-in./54 represented some sacrifice in antiaircraft firepower (due to its rate of fire) but that it would be a great advance for surface engagement. Admiral Tisdale advocated an antiaircraft battery of at least three quadruple 40-mm. guns, with directors fore and aft, and "20-mm. guns . . . installed wherever space is available . . . four cornered defense should be provided . . . ." He strongly favored a considerable improvement in speed and in endurance: "at trial displacement . . . the speed should be at least six knots greater than the designed

maximum speed of any larger ship with which these destroyers are expected to operate." A steaming endurance of 9,500 nm. at 15 knots (nonsplit plant) "would assure at least 7,500 miles war steaming radius at 15 knots with split plant operation. This increased radius is essential and should be provided at no reduction in maximum speed even if it is necessary to increase the size and displacement. The great defect in the 445 and 692 classes is the lack of radius required in such an otherwise marvelous, offensive ship."

The admiral's speed and endurance requirements were far beyond what would be achieved postwar, even with rather advanced power plants, but nonetheless he felt that increased reliability through increased simplicity would be desirable; "if practicable separately fired (Foster Wheeler Type) radiant superheater control boilers should not be used." That is, the new propulsion technology, which had provided the performance of existing destroyers, was to be rejected as too complex, "especially with inexperienced personnel."

As for ASW, ". . . the vessel should be equipped with echo-ranging equipment capable of providing a thorough echo search over an arc of 3,000 yards or more with a ship's speed of advance of 25 knots . . . attack equipment and armament should be based on the principle of quick, accurate attacks on submarines in disputed waters by destroyers which must soon rejoin operating task forces. Excessive reserves of depth charges should be sacrificed for the gain of gun and torpedo armament."

Destroyers, Atlantic generally concurred, although Admiral R.E. Ingersoll, commanding the Atlantic Fleet, suggested that reload torpedoes might well be unnecessary. Atlantic conditions were reflected in a suggestion that "the design should incorporate provisions to permit reloading at sea with vessel rolling moderately," and the depth-charge battery was to be increased to four 11-charge patterns "with space provided for two extra full patterns when operational employment necessitates." The speed (38–39 knots) and endurance requirements of Destroyers, Pacific were generally accepted, and Destroyers, Atlantic suggested non-superheat control boilers, generally similar to those in the Bethlehem-design destroyers of the *Benson* class. Experience in countering German submarines showed in a suggestion that "sonic" as well as "super-sonic" sound gear be fitted, i.e., that a German-type low-frequency passive system be employed.

BuShips took up the design of a new destroyer early in 1944, and in April presented Admiral King with a sketch design; it

> believe[d] that the time is now appropriate to consider construction of at least a small number—perhaps 20—destroyers of new design . . . if construction of these ships were authorized in the near future they could follow immediately after destroyers in the present program, or it might be found possible to substitute some of the new type for corresponding numbers of the DD 692 type toward the end of the present program. From the standpoint of gaining military benefits which would accompany an increase in size, plus certain improvements resulting from technical progress, this Bureau considers that it would be very desirable to introduce the new design as soon as possible without causing delay in the completion of destroyers now building.

The objective was still higher speed, with no increase in battery over the new *Gearing* class. The new ship would have a longer hull, and thus gun mounts could be spread out; for example, the two twin Bofors mounted abaft the bridge in a *Gearing* could now be forward of it. BuShips estimated that the addition of 14 feet to the new "long hull" design would buy a reduction in wave-making resistance sufficient to raise trial speed to 36 knots. The existing power plant could be modified to increase its rating by 10 percent, for a trial speed of 37. However, 38 knots would require a new power plant and, therefore, a much enlarged hull, with a displacement of 3,500 to 4,000 tons. BuShips suggested that if such a price were to be paid, the trial speed should rise to at least 40 knots.

Admiral King convened a conference to determine characteristics for the new ships; on 19 July 1944, it decided on a trial speed of 40 knots, which would guarantee a "service speed" of 38. Endurance was to rise to 6,500 nm. at 20 knots under wartime (split-

plant) conditions, and armament was to follow that of the *Gearing*s. The studies that followed were not encouraging. A 450-foot, 3,775-ton destroyer using a special lightweight power plant to achieve 80,000 shp could indeed attain 39 knots, but only with fuel stowage restricted to 400 tons, i.e., to 2,400 nm. at 20 knots. Similarly, an increase in fuel stowage to 1,100 tons would buy a radius of 5,500 nm. at 20 knots, still below that required, but would also reduce speed to 36 knots. BuShips suggested that a ship might be designed for the greater fuel capacity, but arranged so that about 700 tons of fuel might be burned without any ballasting to compensate, so that the ship would leave port with a maximim speed of 36 knots, but would fight at 39. However, "if top speed were considered more important than cruising radius . . . it would be preferable to design hull and propellers specifically for the 3,700-ton displacement condition . . . ." Any attempt to gain both speed *and* endurance would drive up displacement yet again, although 3,700 tons must have seemed excessive. Thus, a 500-foot ship with a full load displacement of 5,000 tons and a lightweight 100,000 shp power plant might exceed 39 knots fully loaded and might yet have a cruising radius of 5,400 nm. at 20 knots.

The bureau suspected that neither of the large destroyers it proposed would approach Admiral King's desires, and proposed to study in addition the minimum hull that could support the new 80,000-shp plant, which it suspected would be a 425-foot ship with a full load displacement of about 3,800 tons, a trial speed of 37 knots, and a cruising radius of only about 3,000 nm. at 20 knots.

What made all of this embarrassing was that BuShips had at hand what appeared to be a physical realization of the ideal of a very fast large destroyer. Several French superdestroyers were refitted in the United States. On standardization trials, *Le Triomphant* achieved 38.92 knots on about 98,000 shp at about 3,170 tons. She made about 37.7 on 90,000 at 3,370 tons, and it was estimated that she could make about 36.2 at a full load of 3,680. In 1934, moreover, she had exceeded 43 knots on trial, very lightly loaded (about 2,570 tons), at about 100,000 shp. Probably the most interesting thing about these figures was the wide variation with displacement: it is very hard to make a high *honest* speed at a useful displacement. *Le Triomphant* did show the inherent contradiction between speed and endurance, as she could make only 2,000 nm. at 20 knots. BuShips suspected, too, that she had been designed to make 90,000 shp, although her rating was only 74,000.

The mere existence of such a ship seemed to show that the characteristics could be met: surely BuShips could match the power produced by an obsolete plant and yet retain enough weight and volume to achieve worthwhile armament and cruising radius. By March 1945, BuShips was sketching a 425-foot, 80,000-shp ship capable of 36.9 knots and a radius of 4,500 nm. at 20 knots, on 2,975 tons standard (4,025 full load) displacement. The speed may seem low, as the endurance merely matched that of a *Gearing*; but it was to be achieved at *full load* where the lighter and more powerful French ship would make only 36.2 knots.

Speed and cruising radius are largely invisible qualities, especially where they concern paper projects. Most American destroyers of the Second World War were always advertised as capable of 36 knots or so, and only those who looked carefully could see that this was not quite the case. Indeed, rated speed and endurance were reduced considerably by the very stiff standards of loading and foul weather allowance employed. Thus, the larger jump in destroyer size suggested by the Bureau of Ships may seem excessive, on paper. Indeed, many at the time felt that some other improvement was in order.

Admiral King's reaction to the BuShips studies was to ask his commanders once again what they required in destroyer speed and endurance. BuShips felt that 35 knots and an endurance of 6,500 nm. at 15 knots would really suffice, that its studies really showed that 38 knots was excessive. Commander, Fifth Fleet (Admiral Halsey) agreed, although his colleague, Admiral Spruance (Third Fleet), suspected that 4,000 nm. at 20 knots might be more useful. Only Commanders Cruisers and Destroyers, Pacific held out for the speed margin of 5 knots over a 33-knot heavy-unit speed, for 38 knots and 4,500 nm. at 20 knots. Destroyers, Pacific looked toward the use of destroyers in independent strike forces, a concept Admiral Nimitz, commanding the Pacific Fleet, found

> . . . challenging. It is realized that such higher speed would require additional displacement, unless radius is sacrificed to some extent. However, the subject designs are really postwar. There is time for research and improvements. We must raise our sights to what we obviously need. It is therefore recommended that a destroyer design be attempted that will insure a battle speed of 38–40 knots, with a radius of 4,500–5,000 miles at 20 knots.

Thus, the commander of Pacific Fleet destroyers still looked towards torpedo warfare: "with the completion of the 2,200-ton destroyer program we shall have an adequate number of *slow* destroyers for battle line and carrier screens and that we should now develop a fast destroyer type which can be used offensively . . . as Destroyer Striking Forces into enemy waters. Such destroyers will also be valuable in expediting deployment for battle from a large approach disposition . . . ." Thus, he wanted reloads for his torpedo tubes. Moreover, he saw a steady loss in

cruising radius, from 6,430 nm. at 15 knots or 4,450 at 20 knots in the *Mahans*, to 4,150 and 3,240 nm. in the *Fletchers*, with even more disappointing performance expected in the *Sumners*. Pacific Fleet views had enormous weight in the Navy of October 1944, and the high-speed destroyer project was pressed forward.

There was, to be sure, some considerable increase in firepower in prospect. For some years BuOrd had been developing a 5-in./54, which it now proposed in twin-mount form for both the new destroyer and a new antiaircraft cruiser. With a quarter-inch shield, it would weigh 112,000 lbs. (plus a 3,800-lb. loading ring) compared to 96,300 for a 5-in./38. There was also the new twin 3-in./50, to replace the existing quadruple Bofors gun. Thus, in April 1945 BuShips submitted a 3,200-ton, 36- to 36.5-knot, 80,000-shp design, essentially an enlarged *Gearing* with the new guns. The increase of a thousand tons over the original *Sumner* had not improved endurance beyond 4,250 nm. nor speed beyond the original design figure for the earlier ship—although of course the newer figure was considered a far more realistic one.

This was a horrifying conclusion. When the new design was presented to the General Board in August, one member, Admiral Kalbfus, requested a sketch design of a lighter type. One might see it as a return to the torpedo-oriented type; the main weight (cost) saving was to be accomplished by the elimination of part of the rather powerful DP armament of the proposed class. The question of the utility of torpedoes was then raised; very few had been fired by U.S. destroyers during the closing phases of the war. On the other hand, there was some sentiment in favor of the torpedo as the only available weapon in unflyable weather, and as a useful long-range weapon for independent surface strike forces. Ultimately, a reluctant General Board had to approve the very large BuShips proposal, with the interesting caveat that one of the two banks of torpedo tubes be interchangeable with a twin 3-in./50 DP gun.

On 10 May 1945, Secretary of the Navy Forrestal ordered the preparation of plans for a new (5-in./54) antiaircraft cruiser, fleet carrier, submarine, and destroyer. Only the two latter projects were built, as the *Tang* and *Mitscher* classes. The antiaircraft cruiser project was later dropped because it was considered less effective than would be unarmored destroyers with their heavy DP guns. The carrier eventually merged with the postwar flush-deck "strategic carrier," which was canceled in 1949. One feature was a request for 24-inch torpedoes in the destroyer and the submarine, a reaction to Japanese successes with their "Long Lance." Although the destroyer was to have "substantially increased radius and maximum obtainable top speed" no special qualities were de-

Table 11–1. Evolution of the *Mitscher* Class

	Fast Destroyer April 1944	Heavy Type November 1945	Intermediate August 1945	Scheme C October 1946	Scheme L-3 April 1947
LWL	397	450	*Fletcher*	476	450
Beam	42–6	46	Hull	47–6	46
Draft	13–3	15		14–3	14
SHP	66,000	80,000	60,000	100,000	70,000
Speed	37	36		38	34.6
Endurance	3,880/20	4,250/20	2,500/20	4,500/20	5,010/20
5-in./54	3 × 2(333)‡	3 × 2(350)	2 × 2	3 × 1(700)	—
3-in./50 twin	3*	4(700)	3	4(700)	3†
20 mm.	11	—	—	—	—
21-in. TT	2 × 5	2 × 5	2 × 5(15)	—	—
ASW TT	—	—	—	2 × 2(14)	2 × 2(8)
Weapon A	—	—	—	1(20)	2
DC Projectors	6	6	6	—	—
Hull	946	1,276		1,488	
Fittings	166	195		225	
Machinery	946	1,189	783	1,280	
Armament	246	317	203	267	152.3
Equipment & Outfit	68	76		95	
Margin	35	—		—	
Light Ship	2,407	2,908	2,053	3,187	
Ammunition	192	223	178	239	188.7
Stores	177	169	129	219	
Standard	2,560	3,300	2,181	3,645	3,209
RFW	69	68	67	50	
Fuel	710	848	335	929	852
Full Load	3,556	4,400	2,803	4,600	4,304
GM		4.68	3.50	4.36	

* quad 40 mm.
† 3-in./70 rather than /50
‡ 5-in./38
Note: The Intermediate type of August 1945 was based on *Fletcher* dimensions and weights; no detailed design was produced.

manded of the submarine, a lack perhaps reflected in the absence of any new specialized ASW ship in Secretary Forrestal's program. The emphasis on carrier and AA cruiser reveals the Pacific/Carrier Task Force orientation of the Navy at this time.

The new destroyer was, then, to be the physical embodiment of wartime development; this time the Navy would not cease ship development at the Armistice, only to be saddled in a later emergency with an obsolete fleet and a depleted corps of ship designers. Such an outlook may well have encouraged both greater elaboration than would otherwise have been acceptable, and greater boldness in design practice. For example, in August 1945 Ordnance proposed to solve the torpedo reload problem by adopting a ten-barrel torpedo tube. Alternatively, this might replace the conventional pair of quintuple tubes, saving weight, crew, and "35 feet of the most highly

critical centerline space." The bureau observed that a ten-barrel mount would approximate in weight a twin 5-in./38, a *fifteen*-barrel mount a twin 5-in./54.

Meanwhile, the function of the fleet destroyers was shifting. There was a lack of torpedo targets late in the war, as the Japanese Fleet was destroyed. However, the destruction of that fleet did not end the usefulness of the U.S. battle fleet, which had come to mean the U.S. fast carriers. These units could and did project naval air power at tactical and then strategic targets in the Japanese Empire—first the occupied islands, ultimately industrial centers in Japan proper. The Japanese replied with unconventional weapons, which might be visualized as the conceptual descendants of those of the thirties. This progression represented far less change than one might see at first. The Japanese were still unable to challenge the main fleet on its own terms; and penetration of their home waters was still a disaster for them. Denial, as opposed to control, of sea areas is the province of the poorer power: it is exercised by very destructive weapons mounted on relatively flimsy—hence cheap—platforms. With the disappearance of the Japanese battle fleet, the essential asymmetry between U.S. and Japanese arsenals became obvious. It also began to be clear that what we have characterized as the General Board view of destroyer function would have to prevail. There was little point in retaining an independent antiship capability in the destroyers at the expense of their vital screening function.

What the Japanese did not have was an effective submarine arm. The fast task forces were generally immune to underwater attack, and the new heavy destroyer was limited to a standard allowance of depth charges and a sonar in a retractable dome. In retrospect, it seems remarkable that the striking success of *American* submarines against the Japanese main fleet was not taken more into account in the design of our future fleet escorts. Indeed, after VE-Day some of the ace Atlantic escort groups were handled very roughly by veteran Pacific Fleet submariners. It may be that the somewhat slower cruising speed of the Japanese Fleet, and its lack of radar, were considered decisive in this regard. Certainly, there was little incentive to use 35-knot ASW units against 10-knot fleet submarines.

However, there gradually percolated through the fleet the understanding that this pleasant circumstance could not be expected to last. In their Type 21 the Germans had actually fielded a very fast submarine capable of evading DEs in a seaway. They had very nearly completed the Type 26, a closed-cycle (Walter) submarine intended to make 24 knots underwater, and had completed a Walter prototype, Type 17. Both the Soviets and the Western Allies captured examples of Types 21 and 17. Postwar tests showed the total inefficacy of what had been perfectly adequate escort ships: it appeared that in future destroyers speeds would be required to counter modern submarines. For example, one of the earliest postwar ship design projects was a *30-knot DE*. A very extensive conversion of the existing *Fletcher*-class *destroyer* (DDE) was adopted as an *interim* DE. It was a fortunate coincidence that high sustained speed in a seaway had been the salient feature of the 1944/45 heavy destroyer studies.

Thus, the large postwar destroyer evolved as an escort for the new fast carriers, which would be menaced largely by air and underwater attack. Air attack meant effective guns, extensive radar, and, as seemed natural in so large and expensive a unit, radar picket capabilities.

A destroyer conference held in October 1946 suggests the state of mind of the postwar destroyer force. It then appeared that two fundamental types would be required, a DS, to screen naval forces, and a DE, an escort for utility duty with naval forces. No great point was seen in retaining any surface attack capability, although the DS might well be readily convertible. The conference proposed, too, to continue and to expedite two new types, the air control destroyer (DVC, ex DDR), and the ASW killer or picket (which it called DK, but which would soon be the DDK/DDE). When feasible, DVC/DK features would be incorporated in the DS, although clearly the urgent need for new fast screening ships would prohibit the incorporation of all potential improvements in that type. If practicable, however, the DS hull might be used for DVC and DK as well.

The conference wanted the 1945 destroyer to become the basis of the new DS, which is just what happened. It was to be undertaken on the basis of the 38-knot requirement generated in wartime, but the conference was well aware of the cost of such speed and wanted requirements for speeds over 35 knots and endurances beyond 4,500 nm. at 20 knots reevaluated.

Worst of all, it was quite clear in 1946 that only a few of the new DS would be available in the near term; war-built destroyers would have to substitute for them. That would limit ASW improvements to items involving no material reduction in their antiaircraft batteries: partially improved sonar; improved ASW fire control; homing torpedoes; improved air search radars. As soon as possible destroyers would have to be converted for ASW; "when they can be replaced as screens, the bulk of them must be so converted." The conference had in mind as prototype ASW conversions the new *Witek* and *Sarsfield*. Conversion would involve substitution of Weapon A "or better" for one forward and one after 5-inch mount; maximum sonar improvement; A/S plot and integrated sonar fire control; improved surface search radar; and airborne early warning terminal equipment, to receive radar data from search aircraft with the only existing efficient antisnorkel/periscope radar. Such units would be suited to utility duties, and one or more would be needed in each major combatant formation.

Major elements in the design of any fast task force escort were speed, seakeeping, and endurance, all of which militated in favor of substantial size. A traditional force *against* the growth in destroyer size had been the desire for maneuverability (largely to deliver torpedo and ASW attacks). However, in 1946 there was no further demand for surface torpedo capability. The advent of trainable long-range ASW weapons eliminated a remaining strong incentive for compactness. On the other hand, there was a new urgency to reduce the torpedo target represented by the destroyer, and to avoid submarine torpedo attack.

By early 1946 BuShips had completed plans for a conventional superdestroyer armed with a new twin 5-in./54 gun and capable of about 36.5 knots fully loaded, on a displacement of 3,200 tons—which seemed rather high for a destroyer. A less visible improvement over previous destroyers was the provision for two, rather than one, diesel (emergency) generators, at 100 kw each. Splinter protection was to be equalized, with 25-lb. STS sides and deck over the boiler and machinery spaces. By June 1946, detailed work had raised displacement to 3,450 tons, and speed had fallen to 35.5 knots. It was proposed to save tonnage by eliminating the STS hull protection, but war experience had shown that this material not only furnished vital protection from strafers, but also increased the margin of strength of the upper flange of the ship girder; in the case of major damage, it might "mean the difference between a safe return of the damaged vessel or her loss through breaking up."

Thus, the original 38-knot requirement was abandoned, as was the endurance of 6,500 nm. at 20 knots. In 1948, in explaining its characteristics for the new destroyer, the General Board noted the inadequacy of the *Gearing* class, with a maximum service speed of 31.8 knots:

> . . . some increase is necessary. However, the question of what maximum service speed is acceptable is subject to widely divergent interpretations. In general, an increase in the maximum speed will entail a corresponding increase in the size of the ship. It has been assumed in these characteristics that an increase in speed over that of the 692 class of about 2 knots would be acceptable, making the desired service speed about 33.5 knots. Since it is not possible to accurately specify a maximum service speed, some measurable trial speed must be set . . . . The Board has, in conjunction with the design personnel of the Bureau of Ships, determined that for a ship of the type under consideration a differential between service and trial speed of about 3 knots is average. The resultant trial speed will therefore be 36–37 knots.

Therefore, the wartime estimates involving the actual service speeds of the heavy ships were given up, in view of the immense cost of high speed.

A similar reduction of endurance was argued on the basis of the distances the new destroyer would have to cover in service:

> During the preliminary stages of the study of this design, opinion in general was fixed on an endurance of 5,000 nm. at 20 knots. However, after more searching study the justification of 5,000 nm. as compared with 4,500 nm. is difficult. Modern methods of refueling at sea have made excessive endurance undesirable since it results in increasing the size of the ship without a corresponding increase in the payload. It is actually necessary to include only such endurance as will permit both reasonable periods between refueling and moderately fast passage between bases. The distance from Panama to Pearl Harbor is about 4,700 nm. and from Pearl to Guam 3,500 nm. In general, these are representative of the longer distances. An endurance of 4,500 nm. at 20 knots will therefore permit an adequately high speed of advance between bases and will also permit longer periods between refueling, while in the theater of operations, than all of the previous types of DDs except the long hull 692 class.

The shift in destroyer priorities is evident in the evolution of the big destroyer design. The original 476-foot, 3,682-ton type with six 5-in./54s and four twin 3-in./50s was denoted Scheme A. It was expected to make 38 knots on 100,000 shp at 4,600 tons. This was a conventional, if somewhat spectacularly large, destroyer, with ten torpedo tubes. In July the new type was adapted to take a new automatic single 5-in./54 (the current Mk 42) in place of each former semiautomatic twin mount: Scheme B.

It had to be admitted that even fast task forces faced serious submarine opposition, and that ten torpedo tubes took up a great deal of valuable centerline space. Scheme C introduced in their place two fixed torpedo tubes to port and starboard (14 homing torpedoes); a Weapon Alfa was mounted amidships and the 3-in./50 rearranged (two twin mounts fore and aft in place of two amidships and one at each end). Unlike the Weapon Alfa that was fitted to U.S. ships later, this was a four-barrel affair similar in outline to the Swedish Bofors type. Another mark of increased ASW emphasis was a better sonar. There was no longer any great point in arranging the 5-inch guns for surface pursuit (i.e., maximum fire forward); the next step was to mount two of the three aft (Scheme D). The after twin 3-in./50 was moved amidships and the Weapon Alfa there moved forward to *No. 1* position.

The submarine menace received more and more attention. In Scheme E a second Weapon Alfa (amidships) was added at the cost of one of the two after 5-in./54s (amidships pair of twin 3-in./50s moved aft). The design was beginning to resemble its final version.

All of these 476-foot schemes were roughly the same size, about 3,600 tons (3,691 for Scheme E, the heaviest), which was quite expensive. An alternate type (Scheme F) was 450-feet long, 3,337 tons (armament as in Scheme A); on 76,000 shp it was expected to make 35 knots (4,185 tons on trial). Scheme F was armed conventionally for easy comparison with A.

By this time considerable effort was being spent on a new ASW ship, which became the *Norfolk* (see chapter 12). A natural question was whether the big new destroyer could not do as well. Scheme G (August 1946) was a first cut in this direction. In place of the mixed armament of 3- and 5-inch guns there would be three twin 3-in./70s, a new type (2 aft); two Alfas would be mounted forward, one amidships. Scheme H was a similar type based on the smaller hull of Scheme F, but slightly uprated to 80,000 shp (34.4 knots); on the greater displacement, 1,200 (rather than 844) tons of oil could be carried, for an endurance of 6,320 (vice 4,500) nm. at 20 knots.

Meanwhile, there was the radar picket function. The fleet destroyers, the most developed of which had been Scheme E, were certainly large enough to act as effective pickets. The first scheme to incorporate such a feature was E-12 (28 February 1947): by moving the amidships Weapon Alfa forward to a position beside the one already there, a big SX "intercept radar" could be mounted amidships. The size of this device can be gauged from the fact that it had previously been mounted only in aircraft carriers and aboard the special armament research ship *Mississippi*. It combined the height-finder of the later SPS-8 with a search radar, and was (probably optimistically) expected to cost 27 tons, which included a tripod. *Light* displacement rose from 3,418 to 3,426 tons. Some feeling for the balance between AAW and ASW is given by the sacrifice of half the Weapon Alfa *ammunition* in rearranging the two projectors. By this time a trial speed of 37.64 knots was expected.

Some minor revisions were incorporated in the next scheme, J (F, G, H being offshoots and K being abandoned). Now the Weapon Alfa was finally moved aft, to abaft the forward 3-inch guns; and power was reduced to a more manageable 80,000 shp. However, at 3,782 tons (standard; 4,631 on trial, with 805.5 tons of fuel) this was awfully large for a destroyer.

On 13 March 1947, DCNO (Operations) tried to have the Ship Characteristics Board (SCB) prune the new type back to essentials. He (and the General Board, CinCPac, and CinCLant) considered 3,200 tons an upper limit. On this he wanted at least two twin 3-in./70s on the centerline; 35 knots, 5,000 nm. at 20 knots; the new ASW suit; and "radar for close surface surveillance, and either radar or terminal equipment for air search, air surveillance with height-finding and air control of one attack at a time, and for surface search." Seakeeping qualities were to match those of the 692s. From the point of view of surface or air warfare, this is a very sensor-oriented design; in one generation we go from 5-in./38s down to 3-inch guns. It is not at all the balanced AAW/ASW ship capable

of striking on its own; it is much more a sensor platform designed to enhance the effectiveness of a carrier air group.

Preliminary Design tried to approach this requirement via the *Gearing*-class DDR, which it first modified to give an endurance of 5,000 nm. at 20 knots and a speed approaching 35 knots. This seemed practical on 2,478.7 tons (standard; 3,241.8 trial) and 68,000 shp (Scheme L-1).

It was, however, cramped, and L-3 (May 1947) required the 450-foot hull. It was capable of about 34.6 knots on 70,000 shp. Three twin 3-in./70s, 2 Alfas, 2 twin 21-inch fixed TT, and one depth-charge rack were mounted, with provision for ten torpedoes and 66 rockets/mount (3 attacks per Alfa). All of this could be had on about 3,200 tons.

Work proceeded in parallel on variations of Scheme J. Thus, J-5, 80,000 shp, could be expected to make 36.4 knots at 4,477 tons (3,664 standard). She was armed with two 5-in./54s, two twin 3-inch, two Alfa, two twin TT, and a depth-charge rack. This was expensive, and in J-12 the length was cut to 464 feet—which proved too little. Finally in J-13 something approximating the final *Mitscher* class was evolved—two 5-inch./54s, two twin 3-in./70s, two Weapon Alfa, two twin fixed TT. This was an expensive ship at 3,650 tons, and as such was opposed by many commanders. However, in June the CNO came out strongly in favor of the larger ship since

i) It would cost only 12.5 percent more; "arbitrary limitation of tonnage is undesirable unless there are compelling industrial or budgetary reasons therefore. . . ."

ii) The all 3-inch battery was inadequate to destroy a surfaced submarine "and for this reason alone is not acceptable. . . .The battery proposed not only gives greater effective AA range, provides for taking two separate air targets under effective gunfire simultaneously, and provides for defending itself against a combatant vessel of comparable size, but also adds to the versatility of a type which may be expected to operate under a wide variety of conditions incident to the performance of its mission to screen fast task forces against modern aircraft and submarines.

The General Board had favored the smaller type. It observed that the requirement to sink a surfaced submarine was hardly germane; "in World War II U.S. forces sank 155 enemy submarines and out of this 155 only 3 or 1.93 percent were sunk by surface gunfire. It is not clear from the records available whether or not those three had previously been forced to the surface in a seriously damaged condition by other methods of attack." By way of comparison, the Royal Navy built a series of ASW frigates (the *Blackwood* class) with a heavy ASW projector (Limbo) and only 40-mm. gun armament. One assumes that the critical factor in the U.S. designs was actually a desire to retain effective antiship and shore bombardment armament. In both of these schemes the fixed torpedo tubes represented a residual antiship capability, since surface torpedoes could be substituted for ASW types.

In effect the 3-inch-gun ship was seen as exclusively a task force AAW/ASW escort; the mixed-caliber type was still a general purpose destroyer; 12.5 percent seemed relatively little to pay for this extra utility.

The result of all this was a very large ship, and some of the features adopted were natural consequences of this size. For example, an attempt was made to increase seaworthiness:

> Our previous destroyer designs have been the subject of a large volume of adverse comment in regard to their ability to operate in adverse weather. In conjunction with BuShips design personnel, a study was made of previous specifications to determine the reasons . . . the method of prescribing characteristics has in a large respect defeated the desire to obtain a high degree of seaworthiness. In order to include armament, trial speed, and other characteristics while still remaining within a fixed tonnage, it was necessary to save weight on hull structure. . . . The result was a ship of adequate strength under normal conditions but one which was easily damaged in rough weather. For a ship of the size under consideration, approximately 100 to 150 tons more steel is required than would be put into a hull of the same size by previous standards. In addition to the increased resistance of the hull to damage, an increase in seaworthiness over that of the 692 class will be obtained as a result of the increase in size. . . .

In addition, it proved possible to incorporate a double bottom "without any material increase in weight."

The long evolution of the armament permitted the designers to go back to first principles. They sought 360-degree coverage against all air targets, without blind spots. Thus, the gun battery had to be symmetrical fore and aft; "the number of targets which the ship is to be capable of engaging simultaneously will then determine the number of effective groups of guns which must be installed." The two alternatives were one- and two-target coverage, the latter based on one target per semicircle fore and aft. "If this concept is accepted one lethal grouping of guns in the forward semicircle and a second group in the after semicircle are required, with sufficient overlapping of the arcs of fire to insure that a target cannot pass from one to the other without continuously being subjected to effective fire." During World War II, four 5-in./38 barrels had been considered effective at moderate ranges; however, they were ineffective at close range, given their low rate of fire, and had to be backed up by 40-mm. and 20-mm.

weapons. Postwar evaluation suggested strongly that the new 5-in./54 automatic single mount and the 3-in./70 twin would each be about twice as effective as a twin 5-in./38 in the existing *Sumner/Gearing* series. The General Board then looked at the other requirements to be levied on the gun.

For surface fire, the 3-in./70 was expected to perform well against light surface craft, but the 5-in/54 would outperform it against destroyers, particularly at long range. For destruction of light defenses and neutralization fire in shore bombardment, the higher rate of fire of the 3-in./70 was preferable; but the heavier gun would be required "for knocking out heavier defenses and strong pillboxes, and for long-range work." These arguments are reminiscent of the reasoning behind the current 8-in. lightweight gun. The alternatives, then, were a pair of 5-in./38 twin mounts, a pair of 5-in./54 singles or 3-in./70 twins, or a mixed battery of one single and one twin 3-in./70. If two twin 5-in./38s were considered the standard (unity) in AA firepower, then two single 5-in./54 rapid-fire would be 1.5 and two twin 3-in./70, 2.2. The mixed battery would be rated at 1.9, but on the other hand it would have superior surface and shore bombardment capabilities; it was selected.

The General Board saw no point in mounting 20- or 40-mm. guns,

> . . . however some weapon, if for nothing more than harassing effect, is desired to cover the remote possibility of complete power failure. A 1.4-in. [35 mm.] free-swinging machine gun is under development but, as a result of its low priority, will not be ready for installation in these ships. The installation of 40 mm. would necessitate an increase in weight of over 100 tons and would still require power for effective operation. For this reason, four 20-mm. twins have been specified since they are light and can be operated without power.

The same unwillingness to dedicate the gun battery entirely to antiaircraft fire shows in the fire control installation. In 1948, the best antiaircraft director was the Mk 56. However, for surface fire the new Mk 67, successor to the wartime Mk 37, was required, as it had a range finder and range keeper; "it might be possible to fit a range keeper to a Mk 56, but the radar of this director is primarily for AA and not suitable for surface or bombardment work. BuOrd states that it has no present plans for adapting the Mk 56 for dual-purpose work, and doubts if efforts along this line would be profitable." Ultimately, the Mk 67 was mounted atop the bridge, the best and indeed the only all-round position; it was supplemented by a Mk 56 aft to provide a full two-target capability. In addition, the forward twin 3-in./70 and after single 5-in./54 mounts were fitted with gunars, on-mount radar fire control systems. Again, it would

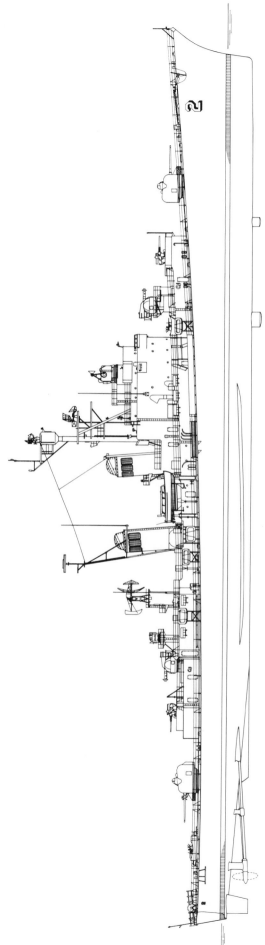

Edson DD 946   8/72   418'0" o.a.   *Hull* class (*Forrest Sherman* class with higher freeboard forward, positions of Mk 68 and Mk 56 gun directors reversed). The *Edson* is the only unit of the class remaining in the "all gun" configuration to receive the enlarged enclosed bridge added to the AAW and ASW modernized units of the class.

Mitscher DL 2 (ex-DD 927)   1953   492'3" o.a./475'7¹⁄₁₆" w.l.

be possible for the ship to handle two targets simultaneously.

Four of these rather large escorts were laid down as the *Mitscher* class, DD 927–930, two at Bath (927–928, later DL 2–3) and two at Bethlehem Quincy (929–930, later DL 4–5). While under construction they were reclassified as destroyer leaders (DL) and then as "frigates," but in fact they had been designed as fast task force escorts, the predecessors of the ships described in chapter 13. They had been designed to incorporate the fruits of wartime research, and they were largely experimental. For example, the new 3-in./70 was not mounted at first, as it did not become available until about 1956. The *Mitscher*s were the first ships fitted with the new 1,200-lb., 950-degree boilers, and indeed the light weight of this new plant made their design feasible. All suffered from machinery trouble, and the last in service, the two Bath units, were scrapped partly due to it, after they had undergone extensive missile conversion. During their service careers, all four were used to test new weapons and sensors. For example, the two Bethlehem units were the first in the fleet to have the new SQS-26 sonar, mounted in bow domes. Both were decommissioned in the fleet cutback of 1969; their sonars had never been linked to the appropriate ASW fire control systems.

What is particularly interesting about them is the difference between what we know to have been the priorities in their design and what we would guess at as priorities from a quick study of their final characteristics. We know that they were designed for

i) Speed, endurance, seakeeping;

ii) AAW—both as radar picket and as AA screen ship;

iii) Fleet escort ASW.

But that is not what we see at first. We see a rather large ship with what seems to be a rather flimsy gun armament. There are prominent Weapon Alfa mounts where on smaller, "tougher" DDs there would be big twin gunhouses or masses of AA weapons. What is not at all apparent is the weight and moment effect of adopting automatic heavy DP guns. It is particularly ironic that ships considered *primarily* AAW escorts should have been derided as sacrificing too much gun armament in the interests of ASW. One might almost say that these large units begin the trend of *apparently* underarmed U.S. destroyers.

One example of the divergence between appearance and reality was the apparent emphasis on ASW. An invisible deficiency in ASW efficiency was self-noise. In 1948 an important technique for quieting was the use of large-diameter propellers that could turn much more slowly. But they could be applied only to relatively deep-draft ships such as the *Norfolk*.

Certainly the automatic single 5-in. is a prime ex-

ample of the postwar U.S. choice in favor of fewer but more efficient launchers with more magazine capacity. Some might even say that to equate one such mount to a twin 5-in./38 is to exhibit a touching faith in the reliability of complex equipment in a trying environment; but our perception of these and later units changes drastically if we are forced to think "twin 5-in./54" every time we see a single automatic 5-in./54.

A good example of a nearly invisible cost is the decision to give the new destroyer radar picket capability. That required a big stabilized height-finding radar (SPS-8), the equivalent in total weight of a twin 3-in./50 or more. It also cost a "stable element" to allow its servos to keep it vertical, and very considerable electric power; and it makes sense *only* in the context of task force operations.

Ironically, after all kinds of invisible sacrifices had been made to enhance the *AAW* capability of DD 927, the chairman of the SCB referred to it (May 1954) as useful primarily for ASW in recommending the design of a new destroyer leader; and the DL 6 Design History (June 1956) refers to the DL 2/DD 927 design as "predominantly an ASW ship."

At the time the new destroyer was seen as a special-purpose ship; the SCB described it as

a special type ship for screening fast task forces and not to be considered as a general purpose or conventional type destroyer ... its design and armament will be in accord only with the requirements of the mission and tasks and will include in addition to the four gun mounts two trainable weapon throwers for use against submarines. The weight and space requirements of the torpedo armament for use against surface vessels has been eliminated from the General Board requirements because of the probable lack of targets for this weapon, and only four fixed tubes for ASW will be provided. In the event that the strategic situation requires, some or all of the ASW torpedoes can be replaced by long-range types.

In fact, there was some ambiguity about the balance between ASW and AAW. A design history produced about 1947 emphasizes the dangers of the deep-diving fast submarine, and notes further that "... the use of aircraft in A/S screening is not too promising at the present time and it is therefore essential that primary importance in these ships be given to the most effective ASW battery and equipment, in order that they may effectively screen the [task] force against the high submerged [speed] deep diving submarine." However,

During World War II it was demonstrated that defense of a task force against aircraft was of primary importance. Since the advent of jet propulsion and the trend towards higher air speeds, the problem of defense has been greatly increased. It is conceded that the best defense was and still is a numerous and effective combat air patrol. However, it is possible that the theater of operations of the future may be such that weather or the proximity of land-based aircraft will make it necessary for a great deal of the defense of the force to devolve upon the screen. It is therefore envisaged that the ability to screen the force against air attack is of primary importance, second only to ASW capabilities.

The new destroyer was a horribly expensive proposition, clearly impossible to produce in great numbers in wartime—Gibbs & Cox estimated in January 1951 that a mass-production version, necessarily cruder than the original, would displace no less than 4,040 tons (standard). Surely there was some way to turn back from such a light cruiser to a "real" destroyer like the *Fletcher*?

The Bureau of Ships had been working on its own mass-production prototype for some time. A comparison sheet of 8 December 1950 described a 2,800-ton, 425-foot ship of 70,000 shp (34.45 knots on trial, compared to 35.7 for the 80,000-shp DD 927), to mount three of the new twin 3-in./70s, 2 Weapon Alfas, and

2 twin ASW torpedo tubes. This was a design heavily biased in favor of ASW and AAW; a sheet of proposed characteristics worked up by the bureau (7 March 1951) described it as an "escort for fast task forces" with *primary* tasks "to detect and destroy submarines with torpedoes and thrown missiles" and "to destroy planes with gunfire"; a *secondary* task was "to oppose light surface forces with gunfire." In effect the new design was a modernized version of DDK 825 (see below).

The SCB had other ideas. When the CNO rejected DD 927 as the basis for mobilization planning (16 February 1951) he ordered the SCB to develop a new destroyer of "reasonable" size. Within the fleet the sentiment was strong that the only good destroyer in existence was the *Fletcher*, so the SCB tried for a new *Fletcher*. In April 1951, it issued preliminary characteristics for a new standard type, at the time designated SCB 85. On a maximum standard displacement of 2,500 tons, she was to mount three of the new 5-in./54 single mounts, four twin 3-in./50s,

Table 11–2. Mobilization Destroyers

	December 1950	Scheme 1 March 1951	Scheme 2
LWL	425	415	415
Beam	44	44	44
Draft	13.8	13–10.5	13–7
Hull		1,046.5	1,046.5
Fittings		202.3	202.3
Machinery (dry)		986.2	943.9
Armament		226.4	240.0
Equipment & Outfit		78.3	78.3
Margin		150.0	150.0
Light Ship		2,689.7	2,661.0
Ammunition		167.7	162.6
Stores		214.8	214.8
Machinery Liquids		93.3	85.3
Standard	2,820	3,165.5	3,123.7
RFW		72.0	71.0
Fuel	800	735.0	677.0
Normal	3,730	3,668.4	3,586.7
Full Load		3,972.5	3,871.8
GM			
SHP	70,000	70,000	64,000
Speed	34.45	34.3	33.5
Endurance/20 Kts	4,500	4,500	4,500
5-in./54 RF	—	—	2
3-in./70 Twin	3	3(1000)	3*
ASW TT	2 × 2(22)	4(22)	2
Weapon A	2(72)	2(88)	2
DC Projectors	1(12)†	1(12)†	6
20 mm.	4 × 2	4 × 2	—

* 3-in./50
† DC Track

four fixed torpedo tubes (with four reloads), two (fixed) Hedgehogs, and depth charges; and all were to be carried at a maximum speed of 32 knots "which will enable this destroyer to maintain a formation speed of 30 knots." An endurance of 4,500 miles was required.

Three single 5-in. did not look like so very much, but they were more than equivalent in weight—and in weight of fire—to three twin 5-in./38s. It had been found that twin 3-in./50s could replace the former quadruple Bofors only on a two-for-three basis; in effect, then, the SCB wanted a *Gearing* with six quadruple 40 mm. *and* Hedgehogs *and* torpedoes—on less tonnage. Once more this is an example of the difference between the *appearance* of few barrels or few launchers and the *reality* of an expected high rate of fire.

What is striking is the retreat from ASW features. In March, the Bureau of Ships had expected a requirement for *22* reloads for the torpedo tubes; and for the big Weapon A. Now Weapon A had been traded for a far heavier gun battery, on the theory that a good general-purpose escort should emphasize antiair fire. In fact, the characteristics state as a *primary task* "to deny enemy submarines *unopposed* penetration of the screen" and "to extend . . . *detection* ranges of the screened body" and "to *destroy* enemy aircraft approaching the screened force." (Emphases are added.) In any case, as we have seen, the primary ASW weapon was retained; and in 1951 there were large numbers of destroyers quite suitable for ASW conversion (see below). A further important consideration was almost certainly that destroyers would operate mainly with fast task forces not likely to be very subject to submarine attack. This attitude is apparent in the evolution of the DD 927 design, and will also appear in the case of the fast task force escort (DL 6, below).

It should have been no great surprise, then, that DD 927 could not have been duplicated on 2,500 tons, even at the sacrifice of a few knots. In May 1951, the Chief of the Bureau of Ships produced a comparison of features required in various modern destroyers:

	SCB 85	DD 710	British Daring	DD 927
Weight of Armament	305	229	208	332
Weight of Ammunition	200	155	200	206
Sustained Speed	32	30.4	30.3	33
Endurance	4,500	4,000	3,300	4,600
Standard Displacement	—	2,543	2,610	3,726

The chief constructor felt that on about 2,700 tons he could accommodate either two 5-in./54s and four 3-in./50 twin, or three twin 5-in./38s and three 3-in./50 twin. In either case there would be in addition four fixed tubes, two fixed Hedgehogs, six side depth-charge throwers, and one stern rack. The endurance requirement could be attained, but one knot of sustained speed would have to be sacrificed.

Within two weeks the SCB had decided in favor of an intermediate arrangement: three 5-in./54s, one forward and two aft; and two twin 3-in./50s. In the end that still meant 2,800 tons; but the SCB was quite willing to make sacrifices to get the mass-production design it wanted. The resulting DD 931 (*Forrest Sherman*) class showed few unusual features; it was, after all, a design "carried out to fill the need for prototype general-purpose destroyer, incorporat-

Conceived as a mobilization destroyer, the *Forrest Sherman* class eschewed elaborate ASW weapons such as Weapon A or a trainable Hedgehog, although at first it did have four, long fixed torpedo tubes (visible here) capable of launching homing weapons. By April 1958, when the *Forrest Sherman* herself was photographed in Guantanamo Bay, the original depth-charge battery had been reduced to a single stern track, the only other ASW weapons being the usual dual Hedgehog on the 01 level forward. These ships were often compared unfavorably with the *Gearing*s, as they *appeared* less heavily armed, even though (at least on paper) each of their automatic 5-inch/54 mounts was more than equal to a twin 5-inch/38. Note, too, that the Mk 68 5-inch director is mounted aft, with a Mk 56 (of lesser capability) forward, reflecting the balance of the main battery.

Later *Forrest Sherman*-class destroyers, such as the *Bigelow* (DD 942, photographed in 1958) and *Hull* (DD 945, off Bath, 15 April 1958) were completed to a modified design, with more freeboard forward for dryness, and with the positions of the two gun directors reversed, reverting to a more traditional arrangement. The *Hull* shows the new SPS-28 long-wavelength air-search radar, related to the World War II SR—*Bigelow* the earlier SPS-6C. Both show ESM antennas on a tripod mainmast, although original plans had called for such installations in some ships only. The small antennas were radar direction-finders, and in later ships were radome-enclosed. Note, too, the small 3-inch director just above the *Bigelow*'s pilothouse.

ing the latest proven technical developments and avoiding features which have proven unsatisfactory. It was evolved from the DD 692 design rather than the DD 927; the latter was considered too large and elaborate to serve as a prototype for extensive construction." (Design History, December 1952.) A feature conspicuously absent from the Design Report is the main-battery arrangement, one gunhouse forward and two aft. One suspects that "particular attention to be given to ... dryness of the weather decks" (Characteristics) was taken to mean that weight reduction forward would be helpful. The concentration of fire aft was also more acceptable for AAW and shore bombardment than for the classical destroyer surface attack mission.

Eighteen units were built: DD 931–933 (FY 53), 936–938 (FY 54), 940–944 (FY 55), 945–951 (FY 56). DD 934 was reserved for a unit of the FY 53 Program, not built. Some modifications were introduced in the course of production. For example, Captain P.W. Snyder of BuShips was present during Exercise Mariner in the North Atlantic (1953). His observations suggested that destroyers had too little freeboard forward, and from DD 936 on the sheer line of these ships was raised three feet at the bow, tapering down to the original sheer line at about the forward gun. The FY 53 units were too far along to be so modified. There was also the amalgamation of attack and search sonars. As designed, these ships were to have had separate scanning (search) and depth-determining (attack) sonars. However, it proved possible to combine both funtions in a search sonar with "dual MCC" or "dual maintenance of close contact," which is why later ships could have single more powerful sonar systems. Dual MCC was fitted to all the Forrest Shermans. Yet another change from the original design was the provision of a mainmast for ECM gear. Originally this was to have gone only into every fourth ship; but in the end tripod mainmasts were standard. Such a decision may have been occasioned by the realization that the SCB 85s would always constitute a distinct minority of the U.S. destroyer force.

The arrangement of the fire controls was somewhat unusual, in that the smaller and less capable Mk 56 director was forward, the larger Mk 37 or Mk 68 (for the 5-inch guns) aft. This arrangement did not please the SCB, and was reversed for the last seven ships, which were of modified design (SCB 85A). Another fire control feature was a fire control searchlight, reintroduced to U.S. practice as a result of Korean War lessons: it was expected to be useful in identification of objects visible on radar, and in the rescue of airmen.

That the new destroyer would retain the fixed Hedgehog of World War II surprised the commanders of both Atlantic and Pacific Fleets, who advocated

in its place a single trainable Mk 15. BuShips was able to convince the CNO to retain the more primitive battery on grounds of cost: the optimum ship including a Mk 15 would be 432 feet long, 2,937 tons—additions of 22 feet and 137 tons. Even if considerable interference between the end guns were to be accepted so as to save length, the cost would still be 10 feet and 67 tons—unacceptable in a mass-production design that had already grown considerably.

In any case, the torpedo was the primary ASW weapon. The original SCB 85 had four fixed long torpedo tubes, a dropping system for lightweight torpedoes, and two fixed Hedgehogs. SCB 85A was to have incorporated eight tubes, but in 1956 the Bureau of Ordnance became disenchanted with long torpedoes as the primary ASW weapon. There was a prospect of a much better long-range ASW weapon in the form of rocket-boosted torpedoes, and the long TT seemed a waste of weight if they were to be primarily antiship weapons. Hence, for the time being only the short (Mk 32) triple torpedo tube would be fitted, and consideration would be given to fitting the new RAT and ASROC. But the latter were resisted on the ground that they would cost part of the gun armament—which was more important in a fleet escort.

In fact only DD 931/932 were completed with four torpedo tubes, the remainder having the torpedo dropping system. However, BuOrd turned back towards the long torpedoes in 1958/59 in view of the success of the new Mk 37 ASW torpedo and the slow development of ASROC/RAT. This is why some FRAM destroyers had long torpedo tubes. Similarly, DD 931–933 had four torpedo tubes in December 1961.

On the other hand, as early as 1 January 1959, the SCB 85/85A group were all slated for an ultimate armament of two 5-in./54s (aft superfiring gun deleted), two twin 3-in./50s, 2 Hedgehogs (Mk 11, as built), ASROC, and the torpedo dropping system. Eight ships were ultimately modernized (less the 3-in./50 and the Hedgehogs) in 1967–72. Six others were dropped because of cost escalation.

The Forrest Sherman was the last U.S. all-gun destroyer until the Spruance of almost two decades later, and indeed it was very nearly the last U.S. general-purpose destroyer. By 1954 the state of destroyer development had become extremely confused, with a great variety of specialized ASW and AAW (radar picket) types as well as the new fast task force escorts typified by the Mitschers. Moreover, by this time it appeared that the Navy would be able to establish a steady program of new construction leading to a new fleet within a decade. A standing committee on the Long-Range Shipbuilding and Conversion Plan and then, in 1955, a new Long-Range Objectives Group (Op-93) were formed. The standing committee, chaired

In the late fifties all 18 *Forrest Sherman*s were scheduled for conversion to missile destroyers, a program stopped by Secretary of Defense Robert S. McNamara because of the limited value of the Tartar missile and the high cost of the conversion—a cost that escalated when the Navy decided to fit the powerful SPS-48 three-dimensional radar instead of the less effective (but much simpler) SPS-39 of earlier missile ships. As converted, these destroyers make an interesting contrast with the *C.F. Adams* class, which was originally conceived as a Tartar missile installation on a *Forrest Sherman* hull. Here the *Somers* steams away from an underway replenishment, 30 June 1971. Note that, in contrast to the *Adams* class, she has only a single-channel missile system—i.e., can engage only a single target unless the radar on her 5-inch director is used to illuminate a second target. Many SPG-53 radars have been so modified, but even so they are a poor substitute for a second SPG-51 missile target tracker-illuminator.

by Rear Admiral W. G. Schindler, began with a study of destroyer force composition.

In May 1954 the Schindler Committee reported in favor of specialization and against the mass-production general-purpose destroyer. It would be best to build specialized fast task force escorts in which AAW armament would predominate (DLs); specialized fast ASW ships, preferably conversions of existing destroyer types such as the DDC; and mass-production convoy escorts. Although for a time they would supplement the frigates, "the general-purpose destroyer as such may fade from the scene. This means that the new program will require building DL-class ships and terminate the building of destroyers such as SCB 85." The Schindler Committee's conclusions were incorporated in the standard statements of destroyer function. Perhaps most importantly, the Schindler Committee explicitly recognized the transformation of the destroyer from a mixed offensive-defensive ship to a purely defensive screening type, its speed important only in terms of the speed of the ships escorted.

In the past such a concept had always drawn fire from the destroyer operators, who much preferred to think in offensive terms. The Schindler Committee was no exception. Rear Admiral J.C. Daniel, the new Commander of Destroyers, Atlantic (DesLant) appears to have been the moving force. He must, however, have benefited from the fact that the new Chief of Naval Operations, Admiral Arleigh Burke (named

CNO in May 1955) had been his predecessor as DesLant, and had had long experience in destroyer operations. Admiral Daniel was a strong proponent of the general-purpose destroyer, which was to be armed with a full missile battery for independent offensive operations;

> high speed jet aircraft and nuclear weapons have inaugurated an era in which either one plane and one bomb, or one submarine with one torpedo, will sink a battleship or carrier as easily as a destroyer. It is generally conceded that a determined air attack ship can succeed in getting a high percentage of attacking planes to the target. A small ship can pack a "Sunday Punch" capable of sinking the largest ship with one nuclear missile . . . . This concept does not necessarily imply the scrapping of the large carriers or other large surface vessels already existing; however, in view of the attractive target they represent it is believed that their area of effective operations will be limited to the open sea. . . .

In September 1955, Admiral Daniel attended a conference in Washington with Rear Admiral W. K. Mendenhall, Jr., head of the SCB, and Admiral T.M. Stokes (Cruiser-Destroyer Force, Pacific); Mendenhall described the official concept of new destroyer development. Three types were scheduled for construction:

—A large destroyer capable of high speed in rough seas to screen carrier task forces, and carrying the best available air search radar, air defense weapons, surface offensive/defensive capability, but with limited ASW kill capability. These frigates (DL) would also serve as radar pickets.

—An austere convoy escort, suited to mass production: the destroyer escort or ocean escort, typified by SCB 131 (see chapter 12).

—An intermediate ship with the best possible AAW, ASW, and surface warfare capabilities the hull can carry, but not the best available. This would be the successor to the former general-purpose destroyer; it was clearly a response to the great cost of the frigates, which would make it impossible to provide enough of them. By this time guided missile destroyers were planned, with the Tartar missile that could replace a single 5-in./54 mount on a one-for-one basis.

Admiral Daniel concluded that

due to considerations of safety in handling and stowage and the early stage of development, guided missiles would be introduced slowly and conservatively into the destroyer-type shipbuilding programs. Present planning provides only one twin Terrier launcher

aft on DLGs beginning in FY 56, and possibly one twin Tartar launcher aft on the DDs (DGs) beginning in FY 57. No guided missile installations are now contemplated for DEs. The destroyer types . . . are all defensive in concept and planned for escort duty of one kind or another. There appears to be an open field for a future destroyer designed as an offensive instrument of war on the high seas. It is in this direction that the thoughts and purposes of experienced destroyer men are pointed in their concepts of the destroyer of the future.

He wanted the two-tier destroyer concept abandoned in favor of a single high-quality type, probably of *Mitscher* size, with the best available air, surface, ASW search-and-kill weapons. He believed that the minimum size required might shrink with advances in technology, but felt that seakeeping would set a lower limit at about the size of the *Forrest Sherman*. The hull form would be adapted for high speed (35 knots sustained speed), sonar (with a range of 20,000 yards), and seakeeping; Admiral Daniel wanted nuclear power as soon as possible. He believed that a *Forrest Sherman* hull could accommodate Terrier at the cost of two out of the three 5-in./54s and the 3-

*Forrest Sherman*s not modified for missile operation were refitted for improved ASW performance, as in the *Barry*, shown here on 17 October 1971. They combine an SQS-23 bow-mounted hull sonar (made evident by the more sharply raked bow and bow anchor, installed to clear the sonar) *and* an SQS-35 Independent VDS, on the fantail; very few U.S. warships with SQS-23 were ever fitted with a VDS. Hedgehogs and 3-inch guns were all removed, and the position of the two gun directors reversed, with the Mk 68 moved forward. Like the missile ships, these ASW units received ASROC and short torpedo tubes, ASROC replacing No. 2 5-inch gun. The need for increased internal volume, presumably for electronics and electronics technicians, is particularly striking, reflected both in the plated-in section of the superstructure aft and in the considerable additions topside.

Some units received no major refit, but did have detail improvements. The *Mullinix*, in the Mediterranean on 11 September 1970, retained her forward fixed Hedgehogs but had her 3-inch guns removed. She was fitted with an SQS-23 sonar in place of her original SQS-4, but not in a bow dome; she has neither a clipper bow nor a bow anchor. Note, too, that her gun directors are in the original order, with the Mk 56 forward.

inch battery, and much favored this weapon over the smaller Tartar. Above all, the missile battery was to be dual purpose, capable of nuclear as well as conventional bombardment, and the new ship would have the rocket-assisted torpedo then in the development stage. No future destroyer should have "second best" equipment.

Further, it was undesirable to specialize any type other than the DE to the point at which it could perform only one function with full effectiveness;

> The cost of the basic hull, machinery, and personnel necessary to achieve adequate speed and seakeeping qualities alone makes it much more efficient in materials and manpower to achieve versatility in a ship by a small expansion in size of the basic hull to take the additional equipment than it would be to construct two or three hulls almost as large, to carry specialized equipment.

He was, however, willing to concede this point should his requirements force size much beyond that of the *Mitscher*.

Admiral Daniel went on to advocate a nuclear destroyer that became the *Bainbridge* (see chapter 14) and in a sense his concepts foreshadowed those represented by the large missile frigates. Economics, however, never permitted the Navy to abandon the austere designs with more limited capabilities, and through the fifties general-purpose missile destroyers continued to be developed alongside fast frigates.

For example, in December 1955 Admiral Mendenhall sought to explain the need for what amounted to a high-low escort mix. The original estimate for the FY 57 shipbuilding and conversion (SCN) budget had been $2.8 billion. However, this was pared to about $1.8 billion within the office of the Secretary of the Navy prior to submission to the Secretary of Defense. The latter was reportedly unlikely to countenance anything much over one billion dollars. This particular pinch was typical of those the Navy faced in the late fifties, as the costs of such new technologies as missiles, nuclear propulsion, and advanced sonars led to very rapid cost escalation, and to drastic reductions in planned programs. Austere (low-end) task force escorts thus seemed far more attractive late in 1955 than they had over a year earlier, when the costs of destroyer and frigate missile batteries were not yet prominent: in May 1954 both DD and DL were all-gun. In FY 57 both were to be missile-armed. Thus, after the end of the SCB 85 program in FY 56, a new DDG (*C.F. Adams* class) series began, to continue from FY 57 through FY 61: for more than a decade, general-purpose destroyers were consistently budgeted, albeit in small numbers. Much larger numbers were both desired and required to screen the planned level of task forces and other naval formations. For example, the proposed FY 53 budget of July 1951 called for 12 destroyers, although only 3 were authorized. In any case, the Schindler Report would have had little impact before FY 56 or so.

The *Carpenter* was a very sophisticated *Gearing* conversion, in effect a test bed for the much larger *Norfolk*. Here she shows her massive twin 3-inch/70 and Weapon A superfiring above it.

12

Postwar ASW Escort

As the war in Europe ended, the Allied armies seized completed German Type 21 submarines together with masses of nearly assembled prefabricated boats and semicomplete Walter submarines. Almost immediately the OEG (Operational Evaluation Group) began a series of urgent studies of the implications of the new weapon, and then of possible countermeasures. Quite clearly the vast fleets that had won the Battle of the Atlantic were insufficient; for example, a Type 21 about to surrender in the North Sea had found no difficulty in making dummy attacks on major British units, including a heavy cruiser.

It seemed to OEG that it was best to concentrate on the problem of detecting the new submarine. A mass of escorts built around efficient sonars might suffice to keep the Type 21/26 from penetrating to torpedo range; clearly the high speed of the submarine would enable her to escape if she ever crept close enough to strike. In this concept there was little point in high speed for the escorts, which could probably be deployed around slow convoys and which would have to be built in astronomical numbers.

In the end all that survived of the OEG concept was the attention to sonar considerations. The sonar picket was transformed, within OpNav, into a specialized killer of fast submarines. Now a key consideration became speed in rough weather: enough margin to chase down a 25-knot submarine in most seas. That and a reasonable endurance had to mean great, even prohibitive, size. Size, in the form of deep draft, could also contribute to sonar efficiency and to hull silencing via large diameter, i.e., slowly turning, propellers. By August 1946, it could be stated

that the primary weapon of the "Submarine Killer Ship" would be

> 12 high speed, deep diving, homing torpedoes, with facilities and control for 4 ready torpedoes, 2 on each side, and for reloading in minimum time, not to exceed 15 minutes . . . . The ultimate secondary battery shall have a surface range not less than double the tactical diameter with such volume and accuracy of fire as will assure destroying in a single attack a submarine capable of 25 knots submerged speed and of 1,000 feet submergence. As an interim armament, it will be acceptable to provide three Type A launchers, two forward and one aft, with a surface range of 800–1,000 yards.

There were to be enough of their own weapons for at least 20 attacks. For the interim battery, there would be 108 ready rounds (36 per mount) plus 500 more in magazines.

A very elaborate sonar installation was planned. It would include low- and medium-frequency search sets, and a high-frequency (i.e., high definition) fire control system. There would also be the sonar equivalent of IFF (SRI, or Sonar Recognition and Identification); a search receiver (in effect, Sonar ESM); an underwater object locator (presumably largely to detect bottomed submarines in shallow water); "sonar countermeasures and counter-countermeasures"; and, a modern touch, "provision for towing deep sonar and handling gear for it." This was far in advance of the technology then available, and indeed is more extensive than typical modern installations. The sonar and ASW control was to be centralized in a special

The newly completed escort destroyer *Basilone* displays most of her battery in this 21 July 1949 view; note the waist-mounted trainable Hedgehog, a weapon soon abandoned as impractical. Her foremast carries the short bar-like antenna of SR-6, a postwar air-search radar that proved unsuccessful because it provided so little antenna; it was replaced by the electronically similar SPS-6 series, with very large mesh antennas. The small antenna at her foretop is a zenith/surface-search type.

ASW plot, to be located near CIC, with a captain's tactical plot between CIC and the ASW plot.

AAW considerations were clearly secondary: two twin 3-in./70s, with twin 3-in./50s acceptable as an interim battery. The ship would, after all, be covered by aircraft and by less specialized surface craft. Speed was fixed at 35 knots in order to ensure a service speed of 30 knots in heavy seas, as well as to guarantee good acceleration.

BuOrd strongly suggested that the antiaircraft battery be increased to four twin 3-in./70s, to be controlled by two dual-purpose directors (Mk 56) and two gunars; it also suggested eight free-swinging guns, which were to be the new 35-mm. type then under development as a successor to the wartime Oerlikon. Two single Weapon As and one aft could be provided, to fire 12 rounds per mount per minute; they would best be mounted on the centerline. As for the homing torpedoes, two triple tubes could be installed on the centerline: "the tubes can be installed one on each side but the fire control equipment will be simplified if [they] are on the centerline." In addition, "the installation of homing weapons and throwers for Type A Weapons will result in slowing down development of satisfactory fire control for torpedoes to be carried during the first part of the run by pilotless aircraft. This latter weapon is considered to be the only one effective for long-range attacks on the submarines and should supersede both the Mk 35 torpedo and Weapon A in ships of this type." This presumably referred to Grebe.

BuShips submitted sketch designs in December, to carry four torpedo tubes, five Weapon As (four in a lighter ship), three twin 3-in./70s (one forward, two aft) and eight single 35-mm. free-swinging mounts. All three sketch designs could accommodate a total of 20 torpedoes; each also accommodated 100 Weapon A projectiles per launcher, and each was provided with an inner bottom. Two heavy ships (with speeds of, respectively, 35 and 33 knots and standard displacements of 5,580 and 5,245 tons) were based on the successful Atlanta-class light cruiser hull; they required new power plants of 100,000 and 70,000 shp, respectively, and were expected to be able to steam 6,000 nm. at 20 knots. The Atlanta hull was attractive because the original ship had the speed and acceleration qualities considered paramount. Alternatively, the bureau proposed a lighter ship based on the new (DD 927) destroyer, which would be able to make 33 knots on 65,000 shp and would have an endurance of 5,000 nm. at 20 knots. In each case the number of Weapon A launchers was increased because BuOrd had chosen to develop a single-barrel type rather than the four-barrel model originally contemplated. At the same time the original allowance of 200 rounds per launcher was halved.

It appeared to BuShips that either light or heavy hull would be the basis for a satisfactory "killer ship," and that "these ships represent upper and lower limits of killer ship sizes . . . construction costs and building period will be in the approximate ratio of 2 to 3 for the light and heavy ships." It also appeared that the lighter ship might be built on about 75 percent of available slips, and that it could meet the speed requirement for a service speed of 30 knots, i.e., a 5-knot advantage over a 25-knot submarine even in rough weather. The SCB commented in February 1947 that "the Atlanta class has proved that this is possible in the large ship. It is doubtful that the 'light ship' would meet this paramount requirement . . . ." The heavy ship would have other advantages as well. It would be better able to keep the sea, would be a steadier platform, would have the capacity for countermeasures, more torpedoes, and prospective new ASW weapons such as Grebe. The addition of torpedoes was particularly important, as Op-34 soon asked for a total of ten tubes; the six additional required compensation in the form of removal of one Weapon A, leaving a total of four.

In February the SCB chose the heavy ship, which was now designated CLK, or sub-killer cruiser. BuShips added a fourth 3-in./70 mount since

> it was found that the dimensions, strength, and power plant of the design were such that the fourth mount could be carried with no penalty to the ship except for the direct weight effect of the mount itself. Since refinements in weight estimates indicated a reduction of more than this amount over the figures used at the time the Characteristics were formulated, it was considered that the addition of this mount would be desired . . . .

On the other hand,

> the requirement for ten fixed torpedo tubes capable of firing either homing or long-range torpedoes is somewhat of a handicap to the arrangement . . . . This would be considerably simplified if the number of tubes were reduced or if the necessity of handling the long torpedoes [i.e., antisurface types] could be eliminated.

Ultimately the torpedo battery was reduced to eight tubes (30 torpedoes), but the surface types were retained.

The elaborate underwater sound installation was to include a low-frequency passive array, presumably modeled on the German GHG; a high-power scanning sonar; a medium-frequency passive array using the GHG hydrophones and an appropriate filter system; and a high-frequency stabilized fire control system. The latter would consist of a searchlight sonar; a depth-determining sonar; a recorder resolver; a data computer; a stable element channel; and an attack director. The sonar search receiver (effective between 1 and 200 kc) and underwater IFF were also still required. In addition there were to be torpedo countermeasures. In 1947 that meant a quartet of Mk 31 rocket launchers firing NAE noise beacons, which had originally been developed as submarine decoys. There would also be an FXR-type towed decoy.

The first sketch design was based on the 33-knot heavy ship, 520 feet long, 6,646 tons in trial condition, with three twin 3-in./70s and a complement of 540. The addition of a twin 3-in./70 (Scheme B) added 99 tons in trial condition, and formed the basis for the design finally adopted. Refinement of the design (Scheme B-1) showed a reduction in trial displacement to 6,227 tons, actually less than that of the original three-mount Scheme A. However, it did not provide sufficient length and height for the 80,000-shp power plant finally adopted. Ultimately, then, a new Scheme E-2 was developed in which the beam was increased 18 inches and the hull depth about 20 inches. Hull scantlings were also increased, and trial displacement came to 6,626 tons. Trial speed was expected to be 33 knots, and endurance was to be 6,000 nm. at 20 knots. The eight torpedo tubes could fire either Mk 17 antisurface or Mk 35 antisubmarine torpedoes, and Weapon A ammunition was reduced to 88 rounds per launcher.

Because of the increased electrical power requirements of the new generation of heavy antiaircraft guns, characteristics called for two emergency diesel generators fore and aft, each capable of supplying power for half the ASW battery or one 3-in./70 twin mount, together with fire control, radar, sonar and emergency ship control, radio, lighting, and interior communication. Where 100 kw had been the standard for wartime destroyers, 500-kw diesels were proposed for the new ship. However, such large generators would have required a minimum deck height of 10 ft. 6 in.; in turn, this would have required reductions in 3-in./70 magazine spaces. Two 250-kw units were substituted in the design phase; 300-kw generators were ultimately fitted. The main ship-service generating plant consisted of four 750-kw units. The great size of the killer ship in itself permitted roomier machinery spaces than in the contemporary DD 927 design (see chapter 11), the boiler rooms being two feet longer. In addition, the forward machinery plant was separated from the after plant by 20 feet for improved survivability.

The major features of the design were invisible. A rugged hull was intended to be driven at "up to 30 knots even in heavy seas and under unfavorable conditions in order to track, overtake, and attack advanced type submarines." This meant great freeboard forward—greater indeed than in the heavier *Atlanta*,

which had had good seakeeping qualities. In view of a requirement for possible Arctic operations, a great reserve of stability had to be provided against top weight due to icing. For example, in trial condition the submarine killer ship had a designed metacentric height of 4.51 feet; by way of comparison, the figure for the larger light cruiser *Oakland* (CL 95) was 3.81 feet. The killer had 2.3 feet more freeboard amidships and 1.8 feet more beam, on a hull ten feet shorter than that of the light cruiser. Special attention was of course paid to maneuverability, an unusually large (though single) rudder being used.

Another invisible feature was silencing. Early in the development of the design, a triple screw installation had been proposed, partly on the theory that at search speed (20 knots) only the center screw would have to be driven; the hull would tend to mask the sonar from the screw's noise. However, a bubble screen (Nightshirt) between propellers and sonar was sufficiently promising to permit a more conventional twin-shaft solution. Special efforts were made in the selection of the hull form (to reduce flow noise) and in the use of large propellers—even at full power, the screws turned at only 175 rpm, compared to about 350 for a destroyer, 280 for a CL 95-class cruiser. The single rudder was adopted largely to avoid the noise associated with two rudders constantly in the propeller slip stream; even transom immersion was minimized to eliminate burbling at the stern at 20 knots.

A new factor in destroyer design was nuclear attack, which for the killer ship was assumed to be a combination of fallout and direct blast. A fairly large deck camber was adopted specifically "to make the task of washing down the deck after an atomic attack more rapid. A sharp deck edge with scuppers was adopted in preference to a rounded deck edge. This decision was made after consideration of decontamination problems, dryness of the ship in heavy weather, and stability. The rounded deck edge was considered particularly unfavorable because the radioactive products washed off the deck would flow down the sides of the ship and deposit on the sides . . . ." In the superstructure, overhangs were avoided "in order to minimize blast damage from atomic attack."

This ship was so large that she was built to light cruiser rather than destroyer standards, which meant that she had a double bottom. In fact, the inner bottom extended up to the second deck, and amidships was 30-lb. STS from that deck down to the first platform. Amidships, too, the outer shell was 25-lb. STS from the main deck to below the waterline; and the main deck itself was a *minimum* of 25-lb. STS amidships. In addition, the space between inner and outer bottoms was filled to somewhat above the waterline. The 3-inch/70 and Weapon A handling and ready

The *Norfolk* was conceived as the ideal postwar submarine killer, but she was far too expensive to duplicate, and spent most of her career as an experimental prototype. She is shown newly completed, on 6 July 1953, as yet without her enclosed 3-inch/70 antiaircraft guns, and mounting twin 20-mm. weapons. Her ASW torpedo tubes were enclosed within her after superstructure and so are not clearly visible here; note her four Weapon Able rocket launchers.

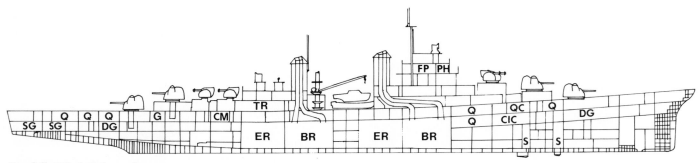

Norfolk, DL 1, inboard

rooms were also protected by 25- and 39-lb. STS. All of this was hardly cruiser armor, but it did provide rather more than destroyer protection.

Two were authorized under the FY 48 program as CLK 1 (the *Norfolk*) and CLK 2. The latter was deferred (1949) and then canceled (1951): $61.9 million ($38.1 for construction, $23.8 for ordnance) was too much to pay for an ASW unit that might be needed in considerable numbers. The CLK category was itself abolished in 1951. The *Norfolk* became DL 1, the first of a new category of "destroyer leaders" and later "frigates." Neither designation was particularly apt. The *Norfolk* spent her career as a test ship, evaluating, among other developments, ASROC and the big sonars. Proposals during the late fifties and early sixties to convert her to a missile frigate proved abortive.

The specialized submarine killer was a long-range project, but in 1946 there was an urgent need for advanced ASW ships with which to develop the tactics to counter the new generation of submarines. In September 1946, the CNO proposed the completion of four wartime destroyers, two as destroyer escorts and two as submarine killers; the latter would serve as interim substitutes for the two specialized killers. Notes to the characteristics adopted for the former

refer to the obsolescence of the large wartime fleet of destroyer escorts, due to their low speed compared to that of the new submarines.

> . . . in addition all modern destroyers have had primary emphasis placed on torpedo and anti-aircraft armament to the subordination of anti-submarine features . . . while these ships have sufficient speed for offensive action against the high-speed submarine, they are notably weak in their electronic equipment and armament . . . it is necessary that effective anti-submarine vessels be provided as soon as practicable to permit evaluation of weapons and tactics . . . . A study of the means of attaining this end has shown that the quickest and cheapest method of accomplishment is to complete, as "Escort Types," two 2200 ton destroyers now partially built.

The "killers" were conceived as capable of offensive action against submarines, i.e., of being individually capable of attacking and sinking a fast submarine. Their gun battery was to be limited to self-defense. The escort, on the other hand, would be able to detect and track a submarine, but would have to combine with other ships in order to make an effective attack. Her gun battery would protect a screened force against surface and air attackers. Thus in October 1946, the

In one of her early incarnations as a test ship (about 1958), the *Norfolk* mounted the prototype frequency-scanning three-dimensional radar, SPS-26, abaft her second funnel. One of two torpedo-tube covers is visible as a dark square on her after superstructure just to the left of the covered boat amidships, and she mounts the enclosed 3-inch/70s originally specified.

SCB proposed batteries for the DDK (Killer) and the DDE (Escort):

Interim	DDE	DDK
Hedgehog (trainable)	1	2 (or 1 plus Squid)
Twin 5-in./38	2	—
Twin 3-in./50 or 40-mm. quad		3 or 4
Single Fixed Torpedo Tubes	4 (4)	4 (20 torpedoes)
20-mm. twin mounts	6	6

Ultimate	DDE	DDK
Weapon A	1 (fwd)	2
5-in./54 rapid-fire	2	—
Twin 3-in./50		3 or 4 or
Twin 3-in./70		1 or 2
Single Fixed Torpedo Tubes	4 (4)	4 (20)
35-mm. Single Mounts	6	6

The two escorts, *Basilone* (DDE 824) and *Epperson* (DDE 719), were to have priority. Conversion involved the replacement of one twin 5-inch mount by Weapon A, and of the two twin 40-mm. mounts abaft the bridge with trainable Mk 14 Hedgehogs. The battery of five trainable tubes was replaced by four fixed ones (with six reloads), one of the depth-charge racks aft was to be removed (which was not done), and all K-guns were eliminated. The remaining 40-mm. guns were replaced by two twin 3-in./50 mounts. The bridge structure itself was altered to include a CO tactical plot on the navigation bridge, and an antisubmarine attack station adjacent to the CIC on the level below; an antisubmarine fire control station, in conjunction with the sonar space, was fitted below decks.

By this time large scale DDE conversion of the *Fletchers* was contemplated:

... the completion of the work specified in these Characteristics will form an index of what can be

The *Gearing*-class destroyers *Carpenter* (DD 825) and *Robert A. Owen* (DD 827) were completed as prototype "killer" vessels, experimental stand-ins for the *Norfolk* and her proposed sister ship. Here they are shown as newly completed, as yet with 3-inch/50 rather than 3-inch/70 main gun batteries, and with a combination of Weapon A and the trainable Hedgehog forward. ASW torpedo tubes are not in evidence, nor are depth-charge throwers. Note, however, the retention of a 20-mm. battery in the *Carpenter* as completed, the unusual forward funnel cap, and the HF/DF mast and antenna before the second funnel. The small splinter shield atop the after superstructure protects a secondary (emergency) steering position, the raised tub a fire control for the after twin 3-inch/50. The redesigned bridge, as compared to standard *Gearing*s, is also noticeable.

accomplished with the large number of 2100-ton destroyers now in the inactive fleet which are similar to the 2200-ton class and are similarly deficient in their A/S capabilities.

Although austerity was to govern, the tentative characteristics included sonar facilities comparable to those planned for the *Norfolk*. In 1947, the low-frequency array was specified as effective between 200 cycles and 5 kc, i.e., up to the level attained by the SQS-23 a decade later. Medium frequency (active and passive search) was specified as 5 to 30 kc, i.e., as between SQS-23 and QHB frequencies. The high-frequency fire control sonar was to operate at 15 to 100 kc.

The passive array was the German-developed GHG; the high-power scanning sonar the developmental QHC or QHD; the fire control set the high-frequency SQG-1; and the search receiver the QXB, which in 1948 was considered an effective means of detecting

incoming torpedoes. It does not appear that the passive array was ever fitted.

In tests the two trainable stabilized Hedgehogs on the beam proved useless; instead, a pair of fixed Mk 11 Hedgehogs were fitted alongside the Weapon A in No. 2 position forward. Due to their blind arcs forward, it was estimated that the trainable waist Hedgehogs together had no more than half the probability of hitting a fast (Guppy) submarine as did a single trainable Hedgehog mounted forward on the centerline. In addition, they needed excessively violent turns by the ASW ship to counter submarine evasion, so that in one third of a series of test runs attacks proved impractical.

The two hunter-killers, the *Carpenter* (DDK 825) and *Robert A. Owen* (DDK 827) were towed to Newport News for completion with 3 Weapon As, 4 torpedo tubes (10, with 20 reloads, were planned at first), and a single depth-charge track. Although a

The *Carpenter* steams away from the carrier *Constellation* after fueling at sea, 2 March 1963. Just about to be given a FRAM refit, she had her open 3-inch/50s replaced by the more effective (and more complex and less reliable) 3-inch/70, and her trainable Hedgehog removed.

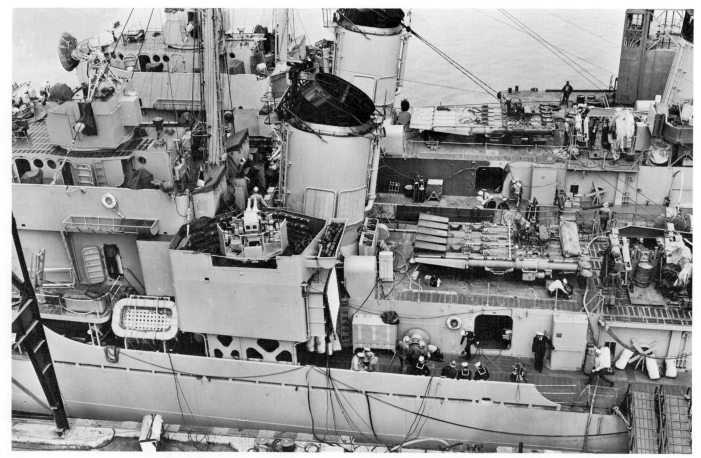

Many of the DDE conversions were extremely austere, as shown in these detail views (above and facing) of the *Fred T. Berry* (DDE 858) and her sister ship *McCaffery* at Mare Island on 28 April 1949, before the DDE designator had even been applied; they were then known as "ASW DDs." Compared to standard *Gearing*s, they show only the replacement of No. 2 gunhouse by a trainable Hedgehog and the addition of an HF/DF mast aft; note, too, that some of the 20-mm. gun barrels have been removed although the mounts remain in place (around the after funnel).

battery of two twin 3-in./70s was planned, 3-in./50s were substituted at first, and in fact DDK 825 was completed with her Weapon A launchers replaced by a Mk 15 trainable Hedgehog, on the 01 level forward. She also had a far more powerful depth-charge battery than originally envisaged, two tracks and four K-guns, with two more of the latter authorized. Bridge modifications were comparable to those carried out in the two DDEs.

Both new classes were provided with torpedo countermeasures (four Mk 31 and FXR). Both were also weight-critical, and relatively little could be done in the way of silencing. Thus, although on paper they very nearly matched the much larger *Norfolk* in ASW sensors and battery, they were much inferior in practice. However, they were far from the most austere conversions that could be carried out.

DDK and DDE categories merged (as DDE) on 4 March 1950. These specialized units were unavailable in the numbers required to fight a big fleet of Type 21s. What the Navy did have was huge numbers of war-built destroyers and destroyer escorts. In 1949,

after all prewar destroyers and all of the slow DEs had been disposed of, the Navy still had 343 DDs and 227 DEs, of which, respectively, 135 and 13 were active. There were also 66 escort carriers (7 active). These figures do not count the APDs or the minecraft, all suitable for ASW operations. The sheer size of this recently built fleet had to make Congress reluctant to agree to further new construction. A major consideration in U.S. ASW had to be attempts to modernize the war-built ships.

In 1946 the First ASW Conference recommended that two task groups be set up to work out advanced tactics. Each would consist of a specialized carrier and escorts. The first, to counter the Type 21, led to ASW conversions of DesDiv 81 (DD 818, 819, 820, 847, 871; DE 217, 679) and of the CVE *Mindoro*. The five *Gearing*-class destroyers had their superfiring 5-inch guns replaced by large trainable Hedgehogs. A stabilized sonar useful at 25 knots was also specified. This conversion was far more austere than the original DDE/DDK, in that bridge arrangements were not revised for improved ASW coordination. Revised sonars (QHB scanning sonar and QDA depth-determining sonar) were to be fitted, as well as fire control gear suited to the new Mk 14 trainable Hedgehog: a Mk 23 computer, a Mk 4 Mod 1 A/S director, a Stable Element, and an A/S Attack Plotter (ASAP). These were such minor changes that the ships were not even redesignated DDEs until well after their conversion—on 4 March 1950. For example, they retained their quintuple torpedo tubes and other destroyer gear.

The two DEs were of the 5-inch TE type. The original recommendation had been for *five* DEs and two DDs, but the numbers were reversed. The DE conversion generally followed that of the DD, a big trainable Hedgehog replacing the former fixed Hedgehog and pair of Army-type Bofors in No. 2 position. The two twin Bofors amidships were removed, presumably as weight compensation, and a new low bridge built (see chapter 7). This ASW conversion project embraced also the USS *Currier* (DE 700) and *LeRay Wilson* (DE 414, a WGT).

The second task group was expected to be able to counter even the Type 26. It was built around a fast light carrier and included a second series of six DDEs. DDE 764, 765, 858–861 were converted under SCB 53 of the FY 50 program. The conversion originally was to have matched the original DDE: replacement of the superfiring 5-inch gunhouse by Weapon A, of the two twin 40 mm. abreast No. 1 stack by a pair of trainable Hedgehogs, and replacement of the five trainable torpedo tubes by four fixed TT. In fact this ambitious program was only incompletely carried out; ultimately only a single Mk 15 Hedgehog was fitted, and the quintuple TT was retained. All retained their DC tracks and projectors. The CVL conversion was SCB 54.

The other two four-gun *Gearing*s, *Witek* and *Sarsfield*, were used for experimental purposes, and classified as EDD from time to time. The *Sarsfield* was the prototype for the SCB 53 conversion. In 1960, for example, the *Witek* had a Mk 15 in No. 2 position flanked by two fixed Hedgehogs; she retained one bank of TT. The *Sarsfield* was similar except for RAT mounted atop her after gunhouse.

An additional potential source of *Gearing* DDEs was three incomplete hulls (DD 766/767 and DD 791) held suspended since the end of World War II. SCB 88 (FY 53) contemplated their completion as standard six-gun/five-tube *Gearing*s, with the standard ASW battery of two fixed Mk 11 Hedgehogs and dropping equipment for lightweight torpedoes. In the late fifties the completion of the *Seaman* (DD 791) was again proposed (and rejected, given its high cost) as SCB project 200.

However, no other *Gearing*s were converted for ASW. The combination of heavy AA armament and good endurance were too valuable to sacrifice for ASW qualities. At the same time, 12 *Gearing*s were converted to radar pickets (DDR) to supplement the 24 already so fitted in 1945. One might see in the conservation of the all-gun *Gearing*s, both as DD and as DDR, an indication of the primacy of the AAW

The principal nightmare of the post-1945 U.S. Navy was a sudden massive submarine war in the North Atlantic. For peacetime missions, which would now be described as "crisis reaction," the carrier strike force was essential, but the cost of maintaining large numbers of ASW vessels in commission would have consumed the entire naval budget. Nor was Congress about to purchase large numbers of new ASW vessels, given the massive backlog of surviving World War II construction. One possible solution was to convert reserve ships, which might then be maintained in reserve against emergencies. Thus the *Fletcher*-class destroyer *Nicholas* underwent DDE conversion and was immediately laid up, as shown by this 16 February 1950 photograph. The program ended shortly afterwards, as it appeared that the current Soviet threat could be met by much more modest improvements, whereas the future threat was beyond the capabilities of existing ASW weapons and sensors, and required research and development rather than crash production.

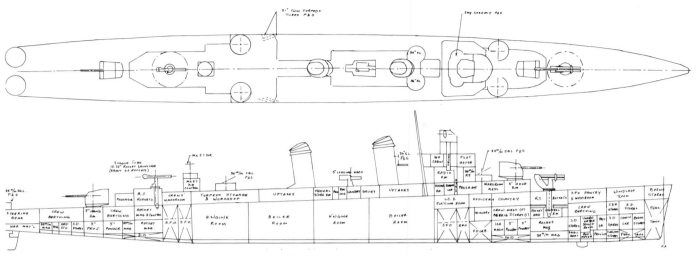

DD 445 class—Conversion to DE—arrangement plan

role for potential task force escorts. Certainly 36 fast radar pickets were a lot.

There remained the mass of "1,630-ton" *Benson*s and the *Fletcher*s. The former were considered so unsuitable that they were all laid up soon after the war; the latter should be amenable to the conversions carried out on their half-sisters.

Early in 1946 one of the SCB projects was SCB 7, a new destroyer escort with speed (30 knots) commensurate with the new submarines. The initial rough characteristics sheet asked for two twin 3-in./50s, the usual ASW weapons, silent machinery, and rapid acceleration. Three screws would guarantee good maneuverability. An endurance of 3,000 nm. at 20 knots was suggested. It would be hard to sell a program of such units to Congress in the face of a laid-up fleet of two- and three-year-old DEs; but (except for an excessive displacement) the big destroyers seemed suitable. *Fletcher* conversions would be the interim SCB 7s.

The *Fletcher*s were not quite comparable to *Gearing*s, even though their hull lines were similar. Thus, for example, a BuShips (Code 440, hull division) memorandum of December 1946 cautioned against "too close an analogy" between the two classes. "For example, the DD 445 class CIC could not begin to accommodate all of the equipment proposed for the 2,200-ton DE combined CIC and A/S Attack Station."

Thus the *Gearing* was a more satisfactory DDE. However, as the 1948 characteristics for SCB 7 note,

... the 2200-ton DD with its twin 5-inch mounts is more valuable as a destroyer than the 2100 ton DD with single 5-inch mounts; the conversion of the latter will result in withdrawing the least valuable destroyer from the fleet .... All design work shall be such as to permit the rapid conversion of these val-

uable ships to effective anti-submarine vessels in the event of hostilities.

An ASW attack station was to be fitted at the navigating bridge level, as well as an underwater battery plot (ASW fire control) and a sonar switchboard.

The first study (1946) was based on contemporary ASW ideas and specified an endurance of 4,000 nm. By August the latter had been dropped in order to provide reasonable ASW armament without jeopardizing stability. An arrangement of two Weapon As forward and two twin 3-in./50s aft would give a trim by the head, so a more symmetrical plan was adopted. Main armament would be 2 torpedo racks and 12 torpedoes, plus 200 Weapon A rockets per mount. In October the 3-in./50s were replaced by 5-in./38 DP single mounts, and four single TT were specified.

By 1948 the conversion plan envisaged removal of 5-inch mounts 2, 3, and 4, No. 2 being replaced by Weapon A, with a stabilized Hedgehog (Mk 15) on the centerline between the stacks. All depth charges would be removed, and four fixed tubes (ten torpedoes) fitted. The Hedgehog was later dropped, in view of the unsatisfactory tests of waist Hedgehogs in converted *Gearing*s, in favor of a pair of fixed Mk 11s on the 01 level forward.

However, Weapon A took time to produce and was replaced in many units by the Mk 15 Hedgehog. Similarly, many units retained their quintuple TT as weight and moment reservation against the availability of the new fixed tubes. Later, there were also the usual DC tracks (2) and projectors (6), retained against the ultimate availability of the Mk 108. The number of long TT fluctuated as this weapon went in and out of favor. For example, on 1 April 1955, DDE 445 had one tube and was authorized for two;

The *Waller* was a typical *Fletcher*-class escort destroyer, her principal weapon a trainable Hedgehog forward; many of her sister ships had Weapon A instead. Fixed torpedo tubes were installed in her deckhouse, firing through ports on the main deck below the after funnel; their ports are barely visible here. Note the absence of depth-charge projectors in this 20 July 1950 photograph.

a year later she had four but was authorized for two again. The (short) torpedo dropping system and the usual beacon launchers were also fitted.

This somewhat disappointing ASW armament was balanced by a heavier gun armament than had been specified: two twin 3-in./50s aft as well as the two 5-in./38s. It would seem that the gun armament grew as it began to be appreciated that these DDEs would have to operate against enemy ships and aircraft without benefit of air and gunnery cover.

If the *Fletcher*s could be considered inferior as destroyers to the *Sumner*s and *Gearing*s, the "1,630-ton" ships were the worst of all. As early as 1948 studies of DE conversions began. These bore little fruit until the advent of the Schindler Report of May 1954, which proposed as one of the four basic desirable types a 1,700-ton ASW unit of 27 knots, i.e., a gutted *Benson*-class destroyer. This "corvette" (DDC) "can be readily obtained by conversion of the 421 and 445 classes . . . . For example: removing one or two boilers, adding fuel tanks for greater radius, and providing excellent detection and attack sonar with latest A/S weapons. The resultant top speed of 27 knots is considered adequate." The DDC would co-operate with an ASW carrier and destroyers.

Two conversions were proposed for the FY 55 program (SCB 130). It was estimated that on three of her original four boilers, the DDC would have a sustained speed of 28 knots at a full load displacement

of 2,560 tons (endurance, 4,000 nm. at 20 knots); with two boilers, the corresponding estimates were 26 knots and 4,500 nm. The conversion was to entail elimination of No. 2 5-inch gun in favor of, at first, a trainable Mk 15 Hedgehog; there were also to be a Mk 2 launching system for Mk 32 lightweight torpedoes (with 6 rounds), as well as a single stern rack and six throwers, very nearly the World War II standard. All would be controlled by a sophisticated underwater fire control system (Mk 105) employing an SQS-4 sonar with dual MCC. The earliest proposals envisaged retention of three of the original four 5-in./38s, as well as of both twin Bofors aft. In August the SCB selected the three-boiler alternative scheme, which was then expected to reduce sustained speed to no less than 27 knots, and at the same time add 500 nm. of endurance. One invisible ASW feature proposed at this time was an enlarged rudder, similar to that which had so improved the turning performance of *Fletcher*s. As for the visible elements of the ASW battery, the Mk 15 was to be replaced by the potentially far more effective Weapon A launcher (Mk 108) and the six depth-charge throwers eliminated. In place of the two twin Bofors aft and No. 3 5-inch mount, there was to be a centerline quadruple Bofors, which in later proposals gave way to a twin 5-in./50, the centerline location making for greatly increased efficiency. Weight and space limitations began to be felt; when the draft characteristics were revised, the DMCC feature of the SQS-4 was dropped. However, the addition of an SQG-1 fire control sonar (for Weapon A) was proposed, and there was to be space and weight reservation for a variable-depth towed sonar, a system whose popularity rose and fell through the 1950s. By September 1954, the DDC designation had officially replaced the former DDE; at the same time the modification was extended to include the removal of both boilers in the forward fire room, for a reduction in speed to 26 knots and an increase in endurance of a thousand miles, to about 4,500 nm.; ultimately an endurance of only 4,200 nm. was expected in a Bethlehem-type (DD 421) destroyer, whereas the inherently more efficient Bath type (DD 423 class) would make about 4,400.

The DDC was also to receive modern radars, including the postwar SPS-6 air search set. The radars and sonar more than exhausted the capacity of the 100-kw diesel emergency generator built into the original destroyer, although it appears that they were not expected to exhaust the original pair of 200-kw turbogenerators; a 200-kw diesel generator was to have been installed above the oil tanks in the former forward fire room. By 1954 habitability was already an important issue, and SCB 130 provided for air conditioning of the ship.

The DDC was a mobilization prototype, and so had lower priority than new construction or, for that matter, missile conversions intended to support fast carrier operations. As for ASW, the construction of new DEs took priority; in FY 55 a total of eight were authorized. The two DDCs were dropped. Probably the last gesture towards serious use of the 1,630-tonners was a suggestion by the captain of one of the *Forrest Sherman*s (February 1959): he wanted DASH (with SQS-4/RDT and VDS over the stern rather than over the side), Mk 32 tubes, and a Hedgehog (with Mk 105 fire control) plus increased steaming radius; BuShips concluded that the cost would be three of the 5-in./38s (leaving only No. 2 gun), all of the lighter armament, and the two forward boilers. The greater cost, as compared to SCB 130, is a measure of the growth of ASW in a short time. The result was less an attractive, and nothing came of it.

These efforts were inspired by a massive perceived threat. In 1948 the General Board held extensive hearings on a proposed FY 51–60 ten-year program. For planning purposes, the known Soviet interest in Walter submarines was assumed to result in 26 operational boats by 1951, supported by 60 fast snorkels and 130 conventional types. If the Soviets went all out for submarines, by 1960 they could have 2,000, most of them superior to Type 21. ASW experts estimated that by two months into the war (D + 2) the Navy would have to field a total of 25 CLK/DDK,

526 DD, 23 escort and 2 fast light carriers, and 250 ASW submarines. These figures were based on ocean traffic as in 1942. Incredibly enough, the war programs had provided numbers of this magnitude, though the ships would have to be considered obsolete in any battle against the new type of submarine. Moreover, by 1960 many of these ships would be nearing the end of their useful lives just as the threat grew most severe. Indeed, from the late fifties onward, such block obsolescence would be the major theme of U.S. destroyer and escort programs.

A threat on the expected scale would require the intervention of masses of lesser units: subchasers, coastal convoy escorts (PC, PCE). But in view of higher submarine speeds the former 24-knot DE had to be upgraded to 30 knots, and the former 20-knot coastal escort (PC) to 25; and the latter was reassigned as a mass-production mercantile convoy escort. DEs on hand were designated "ocean escorts" or "escort vessels" and only the new DDEs were now styled "destroyer escorts."

The crash character of much of the immediate postwar ASW program was based on the assumption that the Soviets would be able very rapidly to integrate into their forces all of the German war developments. By 1950 it was clear that this had not been the case; the Soviets might have the will but they did not have the means. Although later intelligence suggested that Stalin had hoped to build up a fleet of 1,200 submarines by 1965, the reality did not come close. The 2,000-boat figure had been based on German plant figures but failed to take into account manning levels, which would be hard to maintain in peacetime. In fact, as of November 1948, ONI reported 4 confirmed and 20 probable Soviet Type 21s in the Baltic, out of a total of about 280 boats in Soviet service. The Soviets had obtained no completed Walter boats (as had the British) but they did have the central design office at Blankenburg and the Walter turbine plant. The "probable" boats were those captured incomplete in 1945.

Two years later, ONI still could report no Walter boats. As of 1 February 1950, it appeared that there were only 82 modern Soviet long-range submarines, supported by 64 medium and 109 coastal types; it was estimated that there were in addition 50 to 70 midgets and 31 obsolete boats (14 to 20 years old). Of the modern units, only 13 were snorkel types—4 Type 21, 2 Type IXC, 5 Type VIIC, and 8 of a new "B" type—presumably the first of the Soviet postwar type designated Whiskey in the West. As a *current* threat this force was not particularly impressive; the bulk of the boats, nonsnorkel, would be easy to counter with radar-equipped aircraft and World War II type surface forces. However, such an evaluation was no cause for complacency. The Soviets were building at a rate of 20 to 30 boats per year, equivalent to the German prewar output. Within 5 years they could certainly reach the thirty per *month* that German industry had attained despite heavy bombing, and it was expected that German advisors would soon begin to raise Soviet standards.

These observations changed the character of the U.S. ASW program. Their implications were drawn in a 22 April 1950 report to the CNO by Vice Admiral F.S. Low, who during World War II had commanded the specialist ASW Tenth Fleet. He saw the true significance of Soviet acquisition of German technology—that although they were not yet at a very high standard, they could choose to go to far more advanced systems whenever they liked. Hence the U.S. emphasis should be on research and development leading to prototype systems. Heavy emphasis should also be placed on the development of mobilization prototypes; for example, the mass of "mothballed" units would certainly be needed very badly in an ASW emergency. At this time war plans required a minimum of 212 DD/DE for ocean escort, and 102 more if and when Soviet submarines reached American coastal waters. Ninety more were required for fast-carrier escort duty, and 17 for Pacific forward-area patrol stations. Against this theoretical requirement, there were in full commission (FY 51) only 189 units, including 32 small ships (PC/PCE); of the latter only about 11 would be at all suitable for ocean escort. Of the major units, four would be minelayers with negligible ASW potential. In place of the five to eight escorts/convoy considered necessary, there would be perhaps three. Worse still, it would take quite some time for more escorts to appear. The 9 destroyers, 17 DEs, and 27 smaller craft assigned to Naval Reserve Training would not be ready until D + 2 months. Only the large reserve fleet could offer

real relief; but Low questioned the standard planning estimate, which assumed that a "mothballed" ship could be made mobile within a month and brought up to operational standard in another two. He recommended test recommissionings.

One major consequence of the crash-program atmosphere was an unwillingness to evaluate weapons and systems prior to undertaking expensive production; Admiral Low considered the *Norfolk* the prime example and strongly recommended cancellation of CLK-2. The *Fletcher*-class DDEs had been ordered in considerable numbers, at an estimated average cost of about $6.8 million, without any kind of evaluation; indeed, even Weapon A had not been tested properly, although 7 had been delivered and another 31 were on order. The *Gearing*s completed as DDE/DDK had been even costlier, an average of $11.3 and $16.8 million each, even though their design showed signs of poor analysis; for example, "evaluation in the attack analyzer [of the waist Mk 14 in the *Basilone* and *Epperson*] shows this a rather unfavorable [location] for a Hedgehog projector." The 11 limited *Gearing* conversions, in which a Mk 15 had replaced No. 2 gunhouse (see above), seemed to Low a far better bargain at about $2.3 million each. He suggested, too, that a pair of fixed Hedgehogs on the 01 level abeam the bridge would be a very useful supplement to the trainable projector. He pointed out that the firing of all three would produce a very broad series of three nearly tangent patterns across a destroyer's path. The cost would be small, only four 20 mm. (of very limited value) in a *Gearing*.

A major consequence of these views was the curtailment of the *Fletcher* DDE program; in a period of violently changing ASW technology, there was little point in heavy investment in what might soon be obsolete equipment—*if* the advanced ASW threat was

The *Fletcher* DDEs were little modified over their operational lives, the principal exceptions being three subjected to FRAM modernization. Here the *Taylor* is shown on 23 April 1967. She had both Weapon A and a pair of fixed Hedgehogs on her 01 level forward, with a combination of fixed, long torpedo tubes inside her deckhouse and lightweight Mk 32 tubes atop it. The small breakwater aft protects the towing mechanism for a torpedo decoy, Fanfare, which she normally streamed during ASW operations. It was the successor to the wartime Foxer.

still well in the future. In 1948 the ASW Conference was informed that ultimately the entire stockpile of *Fletcher* hulls would be turned into DDEs. By 1950 12 had been completed, of which 4 had been returned to reserve; 11 more had been authorized. Of these the President sanctioned the commencement of seven. It was a sign of the shift to R&D orientation that one was canceled in favor of a fast submerged target, which later became the USS *Albacore*. Admiral Low objected to the *Fletcher* conversions as too expensive and too time-consuming to make sense in an emergency; and in any case the absence of certain unspecified equipment would make serious evaluation impossible before FY 53.

The low *current* level of technical sophistication within the Soviet Fleet suggested the great value of relatively simple improvements throughout the U.S. Fleet. For example, the installation of two Mk 11 Hedgehogs on the 01 level forward in 45 *Gearings* was added to the Material Improvement Plan in April 1950 (FY 51). Operational Evaluation showed a substantial improvement in ASW capability at a cost of only $15,000. Such effectiveness at so low a cost impelled the Navy, even in a time of severe budget constraint, to convert the 102 active DDs and all 24 DDRs (FY 51): the refit entailed twin Hedgehogs, scanning sonar, and improved rudders. Ultimately active general purpose DDs, *Fletcher* and *Epperson* class DDEs, and the DDRs all had the twin fixed Hedgehog.

There was continuing concern as to how to turn the large mothball fleet into an effective ASW force upon mobilization. SCB 7 had some of the character of a crash design, and in fact, time-saving was an important consideration. After all, the bulk of mothballed destroyers were *Fletchers*. A proposed SCB 7A conversion was an austere *Fletcher* DDE retaining three or four 5-in./38 guns. Still later it was proposed (SCB 76) to set minimum ASW guidelines and carry them out aboard a mothballed destroyer as a mobilization experiment.

Nor was the large fleet of surviving DEs neglected. Under SCB 63 (1950) an extensive DE/ASW conversion was specified: "This conversion is considered too extensive to serve as a prototype for large scale conversion of Reserve Fleet vessels under mobilization conditions. However, in addition to improving readiness in escort vessels, these DE will provide an evaluation of certain features to be incorporated in a new construction escort now contemplated." The most noticeable "new feature" was a battery of four Mk 11 Hedgehogs on the 01 level (projectiles for 2 or 3 patterns). Such an arrangement had the virtue of permitting reattacks without the time lost by reloading; the associated steaming maneuver was a "Gitmo turn." There were also to be two of the usual fixed torpedo tubes (4 torpedoes), and facilities to lay 19-charge DC patterns (14 side throwers, one stern track) and room for at least 134 charges.

The companion mobilization prototype, SCB 63A, called for two Mk 15 projectors (6 patterns each, with ready service topside for two, plus one on the spigots).

Four DEs were converted under FY 51: the *Peterson* (DE 152, FMR), *Tweedy* (DE 532, WGT), *Lewis* (DE 535, WGT), and *Vammen* (DE 644, TE). Only the *Tweedy* had the full SCB 63 conversion, with Hedgehogs atop her relocated bridge. In the two 3-inch

The destroyer escort *Jack W. Wilke* was trials ship for the Operational Development Force; she is shown with a trainable Hedgehog forward (20 June 1952), in place of her No. 1 3-inch gun. She was not one of the special ASW conversions carried out for postwar experimental ASW group operations.

The *Tweedy* was converted to a special ASW configuration under Project SCB 63 of the FY 51 program, with four fixed Hedgehogs atop her bridge; she is shown in April 1958. Hedgehogs were relatively slow to load, so that the provision of four actually allowed her to carry out two dual-Hedgehog attacks in quick succession. Originally, she also had a massive K-gun battery, to fire 19-charge patterns, but by this time she had been reduced to six throwers. The davit visible amidships presumably fed a Mk 2 lightweight torpedo launcher.

conversions, No. 2 gun was replaced by a wide platform for two Hedgehogs; a similar platform in the *Lewis* was accommodated by the shape of the new bridge. The latter was in some ways nearly as important as the new weapons: the new consolidated control space concept called for a combined CIC/underwater battery plot, sonar control room, and conning station, all on one level. In a sense this was a physical expression of the paramount significance of detailed control during an ASW attack. A sign of the pure ASW function of these DE conversions was that they received a new sonar but retained their old air search radars; the surface search radar was replaced in view of its ASW significance.

The close-in battery was removed; in its place came the heavy ASW weapon, including generous depth-charge loads. For example, the *Lewis* was completed in 1954 with six *paired* K-guns and one single K-gun on each side, with three depth charges stowed on deck near each; the two stern tracks each contained 11 charges and two reload racks of 6 charges each, a total of 76. More conversions were proposed later; for example, early versions of the FY 53 program

showed ten SCB 63A conversions ($3.9 million each) and two completions of suspended DEs to SCB 63A standard ($6.5 million each). In both cases, lightweight torpedoes were to be added, and the new completions were to have had rapid-fire 3-in./50 guns. The two suspended units were eventually completed as DERs instead (FY 54).

New construction was not neglected; rather, it was oriented towards mobilization *prototypes*. These actually had their origins in an expected requirement for a much improved coastal escort (PC).

A formal proposal for a new PC was approved by the Second Anti-Submarine Conference in the fall of 1947:

The small PC, SC, and coastal types of past wars are outmoded because they are not large enough to carry sonar and weapons, not fast enough to catch the submarines. However, it will be necessary to have a ship to perform their functions, particularly in the escort of coastal convoys and local patrol. Such need . . . cannot be fulfilled to the extent deemed necessary by conversion of existing types. Furthermore, such a

The *Vammen* (DE 644) and *Lewis* (DE 535) were both refitted to a more austere SCB 63A standard, with two trainable Hedgehogs in No. 2 gun position and a new bridge combining ASW and conning functions on the same level. Given the design of SCB 63A, it seems likely that the two Hedgehogs were intended to fire in succession rather than together, for quick re-attack. The *Vammen* is shown well after completion of her modernization, off San Francisco on 3 December 1957, her originally massive depth-charge battery already considerably reduced.

ship should be small enough to be within the industrial capacity of the nation to produce in large numbers considering other naval requirements also. It is recommended that prototype PCs of the future be included in the 1950 shipbuilding program . . . .

SCB 51 envisaged a ship of about 1,000 tons, 25 knots, 3,000 nm. at 20 knots. The armament desired was two 3-in./50s, two trainable Hedgehogs (Mk 15), four fixed torpedo tubes, six DC throwers and two DC tracks. In effect this had to mean a steam DE of World War II type, in view of the speed, seakeeping, and armament characteristics desired. Even then the requirements for higher speed had to mean substantially increased power.

Design work began in September 1949 on the basis of the WGT type destroyer escort. At this time the requirements included a *sustained* speed of 21 knots and an endurance of 5,000 miles at 18 knots; the ASW battery would comprise two Mk 15, two tracks, 8 to 12 depth-charge projectors, and a tube for the new Mk 35 homing torpedo. Outline notes indicated a dual sonar installation, QHB and a depth-determining sonar—one or both in a bulbous bow reminiscent of present practice; and a desire for a 300-yard turning circle "with emphasis on fast response to rudder when first applied." Even Hedgehog had little tolerance for gross misestimates of target motion, although the trainable feature of Mk 15 did somewhat relax the requirements for maneuverability. There would be a one-level bridge of the type later applied to SCB 63.

The forces afloat emphasized low cost and a small crew, for mass production and operation; a speed of

The *Dealey*s were the ancestors of all postwar U.S. destroyer escorts (ocean escorts), although they were originally conceived as successors to the wartime coastal escort, the 173-foot PC. Designed for mobilization, they were relatively austere and appeared underarmed. The *Dealey* (DE 1006, above) herself, shown on trials on 28 May 1954, was unique in mounting the British Squid ahead-throwing ASW mortar, one of which is visible just forward of her bridge. The *Cromwell* (DE 1014, facing) is shown relatively late in her career; note her fiberglass-enclosed forward 3-inch gun mount, and the absence of depth-charge throwers aft, triple Mk 32 torpedo tubes having been added abreast her funnel. The *Dealey* and *Courtney* never received provision for the DASH drone helicopter. The *Van Voorhis* clearly did.

20 to 25 knots and an endurance of 4,500 nm. at 15 knots were suggested. Turning diameter should be 350 yards, battery "antisubmarine only."

By October a great deal of detail work had been done on the integrated bridge and on the selection of sensors, both considerations then relatively new in warship design. Thus, there existed detailed bridge layouts, which had to incorporate the various radar and sonar displays, but not sketch plans for the ship as a whole. This was natural: in ASW the sensors and the control system dominated. There were to be SQS-2 (improved QHB) search and SQG-1 "attack" (depth-determining) sonars in separate domes (SQG-1 forward, SQS-2 amidships) feeding into one of the new Underwater Battery Fire Control systems (Mk 105). There would also be a respectable air defense system: SPS-6B air search and SPS-4 surface/zenith search radars as well as air early warning terminal equipment.

It remained to design a hull to fit, a primary consideration being suitability for mass production. Two continuing preoccupations were propulsion and a low silhouette (to keep center of gravity low); designs incorporating a weapon thrower *behind* the bridge received serious consideration. As for propulsion, a single screw achieved early popularity in view of "efficiency, endurance, and, most of all, the saving in cost associated with one half the number of tur-

bines, gears, shafts, and propellers" (August 1950). It proved difficult to push trial speed much beyond 23 to 24 knots, even though the propulsion Code (430) promised 15,000 shp in less space than the 12,000 of wartime DEs. There was some hope that this kind of power would allow a GMT hull to reach the desired 25 knots.

This was only the most desirable of a spectrum of studies. A comparison sheet of late 1950 ranged from a 240-foot, 1,105-ton, 19.5-knot diesel, through a 22-knot modified GMT (1,205 tons, one twin 3-in./50, one Mk 15, two single TT, projectors, two tracks), up to a 320-foot type of 1,531 tons, with a 30,000 shp steam plant (29.5 knots; one twin, two single 3-in./50s, two Mk 15, four tubes). These speeds were estimated trials figures: fully loaded, 95 percent power. In each case *sustained* speed was substantially less: 18, 20.5, 26.7 knots. Endurance varied between 4,000 and 7,200 nm. at 15 knots.

No design was selected. SCB 51 served mainly to raise issues of escort design. It progressed rapidly from the new PC to a "merchant convoy escort" to escort slow (9–12 knot) convoys. By October 1950 the SCB had begun to study what it called an ocean escort, a DE (SCB 72), designed around a new and very powerful 61-spigot trainable Hedgehog, Mk 17 (on a 5-in./38 mount, weighing 22.3 tons), and the new homing torpedoes. Schemes were tried with the

projector mounted on the pilothouse, and with various combinations of 3-in./50 twin mounts and the Mk 17 forward of the pilothouse, firing over the bow. One scheme had a considerable gun armament: one 5-in./38 forward, one twin 3-in./50 aft, the Mk 17, and two fixed torpedo tubes. Others varied between one and two twin 3-in./50s. The 5-inch was rejected at a meeting with the CNO (Admiral Sherman) in January 1950. In all of these designs a primary consideration was all-around fire for the big projector—hence the unusually low silhouette adopted, which implied, for example, relatively poor vision from the bridge over the bows. Ultimately the Mk 17 was canceled in favor of a twin (British) Squid (which had been considered an alternative from the first) or, in all but the first unit, the USS *Dealey*, Weapon A. It and the Squid required special arrangements for quick reload, a defect from which Weapon A did not suffer. In the end, in the design adopted a ready-service room was installed just before the ASW projector, and the projectiles could be loaded from it with minimum interference.

The low silhouette tended to reduce top weight and hence to compensate for the rather heavy ahead-throwing ASW weapon. In the course of detail design the superstructure would be changed from steel to aluminum, which represented a substantial saving. The hull was similar in dimensions to that of the fast (24 knots) turbine DEs, but far more power, 20,000 shp, was provided.

The design selected, which became the USS *Dealey*, DE 1006, mounted 3-in./50 twins fore and aft, a heavy ASW projector abaft the forward guns, two fixed torpedo tubes, one depth-charge rack and eight DC projectors. As completed all had dropping gear for lightweight ASW torpedoes. Only DE 1006 was completed with long torpedo tubes; she also had eight DC projectors, her sisters six. In the original design, a total of six long torpedoes had been specified. However, unlike contemporary destroyers, the tubes were not described as capable of firing both antiship and antisubmarine torpedoes. DE 1006 was provided with 48 Squid rounds (8 attacks); her sisters had 48 rounds of Weapon A. Depth-charge capacity was 80 (44 in ready service); units after the prototype eliminated magazine storage of depth charges. Launchers for noise beacons (torpedo countermeasures) were contemplated, but in the end only weight and moment reservations were made, a towed noisemaker being provided instead. The sonar domes were located far aft "to reduce quenching and yet not reduce shielding from propeller noises too greatly." In order to reduce pitching, "concentrated weights have been moved as far aft as possible . . . additional stiffeners have been added forward to permit driving the ship into moderate seas." Freeboard and flare forward

were also improved for similar reasons. Compared to DE 51, SCB 72 had a slightly deeper hull so as to provide headroom in the machinery spaces and in the ASW projectile handling rooms. In the interest of maneuverability, an unusually large rudder was fitted, and the deadwood cut away.

There was only a single screw. The basic reason was producibility; everyone connected with SCB 72 was well aware of the problems encountered by the DE program. A side benefit was maximum screening of hull noise. However, some problems were encountered with the rather large, slow-turning screw. The 20,000-shp power plant was expected to yield a trial speed of 25 knots. Endurance was set at 6,000 nm. at 12 knots, as in her predecessors (which often could not really much exceed 4,000). Originally 4,500 nm. had been specified. The very long radius required an unusually great full load displacement in relation to light load. The characteristics called for 25 knots fully loaded in smooth water, 23 sustained in a moderate sea. The *Dealey*'s captain reported her good for 28 in cold water. On trials she made 27.58 knots at 1,613 tons (19,810 shp) and 26.84 knots at 1,802 tons (19,880 shp).

As in SCB 51, one problem was how to get very high power *and* good endurance in a small DE-size hull. The question of COSAG, a steam cruising plant combined with a gas turbine, was raised as early as August 1950; Newport News studied a 7,500-shp short-life gas turbine coupled to each 2,000-shp shaft of a fast DE. A companion study aimed directly at SCB 72 was a 20,000-shp single-screw escort. These studies had no immediate effect, but the perceived value of gas turbines was such that an FY 55 project (SCB 117) called for an experimental installation of two British RM 60 units in the USS *Mills*. A reduction in weight of 15 percent with an increase in power of 67 percent was expected, but the project was canceled on grounds of turbine unreliability. An earlier abortive project had been the conversion of the USS *Sutton* (DE 771, DET); plans had called for the installation of a 3,000-hp Elliott Co. gas turbine on one shaft (scheduled for delivery 24 December 1948). The Navy had no gas-turbine combatants until the advent of the *Asheville* class in the sixties; conventional steam could meet DE requirements.

Quite early in the design stage (January 1951) CinCPac asked that twin screws be substituted on reliability and survivability grounds. BuShips replied that World War II experience in single-and twin-screw warships up to and including light carriers

does not indicate any clear-cut proof that a twin-screw ship is less vulnerable than a single-screw ship. In those ships which received major damage and were subsequently salvaged, the governing factor in the successful return to bases was not the availability of a second shaft, but the tactical situation . . . . The twin-screw ship was not able to continue as an effective combat unit after sustaining major damage . . . . The Bureau does not feel, therefore, that additional cost of the twin screws can be justified for the Ocean Escort.

It was also estimated that twin screws would cost about 65 tons. However, in BuShips' view the most significant costs were in reduced rates of production of a ship whose design

> must be realistic and practical, with emphasis on simplicity to facilitate rapid and economic construction of large numbers in an emergency. In the interest of reducing engineering complexity and ship size, the speed requirement is set at the minimum necessary to provide at least a 5-knot margin over the fastest expected merchant convoy, and an adequate speed margin over submarines . . . .

This is the kind of consideration appropriate for crash production, but it does not take into account years of peacetime operation, in which machinery casualties *can* knock out one shaft without affecting the other.

Thirteen *Dealeys* were built: the prototype under FY 52, two each in FY 53/54, and eight in FY 55, after which the Schindler Destroyer Report axe fell on such "sophisticated" ships. They were a mobilization design, and to maintain a very large ASW fleet in peacetime would be to eat away at Navy manpower more urgently required elsewhere. Some indication of the success of the design might be found in its continued production in other NATO navies: five *Oslo* class in Norway, and three in Portugal. In both cases the design was somewhat modified.

DE 1006 was far from inexpensive; Navy figures prepared in 1955 show reproduction costs, at 1955 prices, of $12 million for a late *Dealey*, $10.6 for her "inexpensive" successor, and $9.2 and $9.5 million for World War II WGT and FMR types. The Schindler Committee suggested that a far more austere escort could and should be built. In June 1954, the SCB tried to describe the minimum convoy escort; "it is expected that there may be other ships in the escort unit possessing greater ASW kill probability . . . ." The characteristics emphasized endurance and detection capacity at the cost of speed and firepower. An endurance of 12,000 miles at 12 knots almost had to mean diesel power, but on the other hand sustained speed (twin screws) need not exceed 21 knots. Armament would consist of two single 3-in./50 slow fire mounts, a depth-charge track with six side throwers, and torpedo dropping gear. However, the sonar specified was the same powerful SQS-4 fitted to SCB 72. It was expected that these characteristics could be realized on no more than 1,200 tons, preferably about 900. However, special attention was to

be paid to seakeeping, since the ocean escort would have to operate in company with much larger ships. This minimum crash-production escort is very nearly a modernized World War II diesel DE.

This became SCB 131, the DE 1033 (*Claud Jones*) class. The Preliminary Design section of BuShips, Code 420, responded to these austere characteristics with a set of studies based on the *Dealey* hull and mounting ahead-throwing weapons: a DE 1006 with more fuel (endurance 7,400 nm.) and two single slow-firing 3-in./50s in place of the rapid-fire twins; one with 100 tons more fuel (10,000 nm.); and a diesel twin-screw type with or without the heavy Mk 17 projector, and with the new torpedo-dropping system in place of long torpedo tubes.

Rear Admiral Mendenhall of the SCB liked the diesel/Mk 17 design and asked for one with Weapon A; he also wondered what could be done on 300 feet, 8,000–9,000 nm. at 12 knots, 20 knots sustained. Code 420 observed that "my immediate reaction to this was that the World War Two 300-foot DE is the answer to this question." A series of single- and twin-screw steam and diesel schemes was concocted with ASW armament of two fixed Mk 11 Hedgehogs or a Mk 108, plus six depth-charge projectors, one DC track, and the torpedo-dropping system. The tradeoff was fuel weight vs. weapon weight. For example, endurance was 9,670 nm. for the steam/Mk 11 design, 9,200 for the steam/Mk 108. The diesel types were higher powered and somewhat less economical. All these schemes were based on the World War II DE hull.

However, it seemed to the designers that the light armament, large required radius, and attention to seakeeping qualities indicated a long forecastle, deep draft, narrow beam (low CG) design. A 290-foot PCE study (SCB 90) was used as a basis. This latter was a prototype for mass production, designed in the fall of 1952, for construction in FY 53. At that time it was a 756-ton vessel, 223 feet long (OA), with two 3-in./50s, two Mk 11, one DC track, and four projectors. There was provision for three lightweight torpedoes. Speed was 18.7 knots (trial) and endurance 4,000 nm. at 15 knots. This was close to the SCB 131 requirements of June 1954. Its mission was convoy escort, and in this sense it was very close to the austere DE.

The design was firm by the fall of 1954. Since the slow-firing 3-in./50 was out of production, a single rapid-firing gun was substituted; an ahead-throwing weapon was adopted, in the form either of two fixed Hedgehogs (Mk 11) or one trainable one (Mk 15). In fact these ships were provided with the fixed Hedgehogs (480 charges, 10 attacks), as well as the torpedo-dropping system (8 torpedoes), and a single depth-charge track (12 charges). The large SQS-4 sonar and an over-the-side VDS were specified, although the

Cromwell DE 1014   Nov. 1954   314'6" o.a.   *Dealey* class

Claud Jones DE 1033   May 1963   311'9¼" o.a./301' w.l.   *Claud Jones* class—By Sept. 1963, an enclosed bridge had been substituted. Later fitted with elaborate ELINT arrays.

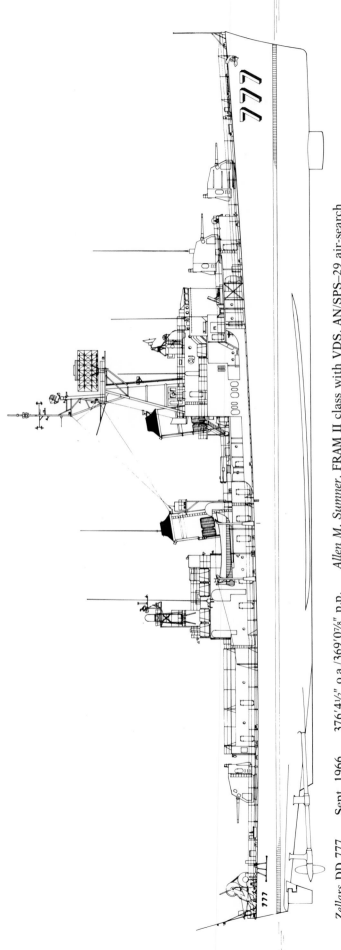

Zellars DD 777   Sept. 1966   376'4½" o.a./369'0⅞" p.p.   *Allen M. Sumner*, FRAM II class with VDS, AN/SPS–29 air-search radar

latter was not yet in production. The torpedo countermeasure was a towed device called Fanfare.

A particular problem of the design was the spread of operating speeds desired: 22 knots on trial, 12 for cruising. Diesels tended to foul at low power. One option considered was to reduce the spread in power by reducing the maximum speed to 20 knots. As an alternative, a steam plant was considered; steam engines would be lighter, more compact, and inherently quieter, as well as easier to maintain; *but* "the power range of this ship is within that for which there is more diesel manufacturing capacity than steam . . . . Since this is envisioned as a mobilization prototype . . . it is recommended that a diesel drive be required." In any case, steam could be substituted: according to BuShips (12 October 1954) "the same flexibility of power plant types that obtained in the World War Two design will be realized now." In the final design this problem of variable speed was overcome by coupling four 2,400 hp engines to the single shaft. A consideration unique to diesels was a *minimum* operating speed. For example, the FMR of World War II had a minimum speed of 10.5 knots (maximum, 21.5) on two shafts (8.7 on one).

The report of Preliminary Design (1 March 1955) noted that

> this design is to be the prototype for a trans-oceanic escort which can be produced in large numbers in the event of an emergency. To BuShips this dictated the use of Diesel machinery as the major type of propulsion machinery. The installation of this type of machinery had more influence on the design than any other single factor. The large machinery space requirement together with the SCB desire to keep the length about 300 ft. favored the adoption of an upper deck hull in order to provide adequate space for activities outside the machinery box. . . . The high freeboard associated with the upper deck hull type provides good righting arms and should enhance the seaworthiness of the design . . . . Late in the development of the design, the SCB stipulated that the design shall be such that steam turbine propulsion machinery may be substituted for the specified Diesel plant with a minimum of redesign work . . . .

A study showed that a 10,000-shp steam plant could be fitted within a length of 68 feet (105 for diesel), and a weight of 347 tons (427.5) but that the fuel rate would be 1.08 lb./shp hr (.76) so that radius would fall to 6,750 nm., on 320 tons of oil. Ironically, the bull gear of the 1033 was above the gear diameter "cross-over" point for mass production; hence "this controlling item places the same limitation on the mass-producibility of the 1033 as applies to the 1006 class." (BuShips Conference, April 1957.)

The hull form was unusual for U.S. construction, with a full underwater shape aft instead of a transom: "model tests in waves, conducted during the design of DE 1006, indicate that [this] form is subject to less speed reduction . . . . While the form selected is not quite as efficient in still water at top speed as a hull with a definite transom immersion, it is felt that its superiority at cruising speed and its anticipated superior performance in waves warrant its adoption." However, a transom *above* the waterline was adopted to simplify construction.

In August 1956, Code 420

> considered the DE 1006 a better design than the DE 1033, and that after the 1033 FY 57 ships, the Bureau should recommend the DE 1006 for future building programs. However, it should be recognized that the endurance of the 1006 is one of the major deficiencies of that design. To improve this we should recommend pressure fired boilers coupled with increased oil capacity . . . reference is made to the low speed of the 1033 and trend toward increased convoy speed. In this regard 1006 is not much better in view of the low endurance at 12 knots. The 1033 is only slightly better and could maintain a convoy speed of about 13 ½ knots for the same endurance as the 1006, namely 5800 miles. It may be a better plan to redesign 1033 to fit a 10,000 shp steam plant, carry same armament as 1006, and increase endurance by increasing fuel capacity as much as possible. . . .

The next April a BuShips conference to evaluate the DE 1033 design observed that 1006 and 1033

> are of comparable size but that DE 1033 is slower and more lightly armed. It has a larger cruising radius and probably is more sea-kindly. Cost of one ship is about 10 percent less than a ship of the 1006 class. It carries about one-half the weight of [ordnance] . . . would be relatively ineffective as a convoy escort and ASW ship due to its low speed and lack of long-range ASW weapons. . . . Studies have been conducted to improve this design . . . by lengthening the ship, increasing the installed power, removal of the variable depth sonar which has not yet been produced, substituting aluminum for steel in the upper deck and in the shell above the main deck. . . . [These improvements] would not materially affect the capabilities of the ship. Costs, however, would be increased. In the interest of providing maximum ship capability with the funds on hand, it is recommended that steps be taken to terminate construction of the DE 1033 class and to use the funds for the procurement of additional ships of the DE 1006 class.

This is not to say that the good stability and weak armament of DE 1033 did not invite improvement. In 1961, the last two ships, DE 1035/1036, received the "ASW Weapon System Mk I" consisting of the Norwegian Terne III rocket-thrown depth charge; two triple lightweight TT (Mk 32); and (in future—i.e., never) two long tubes for the Mk 37 homing torpedo. Terne was removed three years later. Sonar equipment consisted of the existing U.S. stabilized scanning sonar (SQS-31 or -32) coupled to a searchlight-type attack sonar, SQS-16, which would obtain target depth and range. Some evidence of the basic soundness of the design was the construction in Turkey, in 1967–74, of two modified (diesel-powered) units of this type.

From an ASW design point of view one might characterize the decade from 1948 to 1958 as a race between sensor and weapon performance. At first the weapons were quite obviously ahead of the sensors; Grebe was canceled as much too far ahead. But this was true even of Weapon A. In a typical tactical situation, a 10-knot submarine at 400 feet might attempt to penetrate a screen one member of which might be a 15-knot DDE, a closing rate of 833 yards/min., which meant that the submarine would remain within the 300- to 800-yard effective zone of the weapon for only half a minute: six or seven shots at most; but to fire these rounds required a ballistic solution that might take—at the very least—half a minute, after which there would be 23 seconds of dead time (13 of flight and 11 of sinking) before the depth charges reached their point of aim. In effect, even if the submarine made no attempt to evade, an attack would be fruitless were it made on a contact much inside 1,500 yards. Unfortunately, this range was at the outer limits for the advanced sonar of 1950, QHB. New tactics or new sensors were required.

Advanced ASW thinking in 1950 called for a search sonar (e.g., QHB) linked to a fire control (depth-determining) set, both feeding into a computer that could work out the submarine's underwater path in sufficient detail for a weapon with predictable underwater ballistics (Weapon A) to have a reasonable chance of hitting its target. This operation required both accurate sonars and an elaborate analog computer. In February 1950, the ship sonar code (846) indicated, in connection with SCB 51, that QHB was considered effective (at 20 knots) out to 1,800 yards. Its companion QDA searchlight (fire control, or attack) sonar was considered good to 1,500. Weapon A was said to require an accuracy in depth of ten feet at a range of 800 yards, and QDA could satisfy this requirement. The fire control system, Mk 102, was a complex affair with the then-incredible total of 2,300 vacuum tubes. Sonar data was fed in through a horizontal range computer, a depth plotter that smoothed the depth data, as well as a parallax computer to account for the separation between search and fire control sonar domes. The heart of the system was the analyzer, which computed target course and speed on a least-squares basis from up to 50 points. The operator could select the interval between points, as well as the choice of a fit to a straight or curved target course.

It is sobering to observe that a quarter-century later one can buy a pocket calculator for well under $50 that will fit more complex curves to twice as many points.

FCS Mk 102 was evaluated in 1952 at Key West aboard the DDEs Bache and Saufley, the latter with the first integrated sonar; in it, the depth determination was by a QHB turned on its side (SQG-1) so that in effect the system scanned in elevation and in bearing. The net conclusion was that the fire control system was far in advance of the sonars.

Even the simpler Mk 105 designed for the DE ASW units was sonar-limited. Thus, a system built around the new Mk 5 attack director, intended to accept data fast enough to counter medium-speed submarines at short range (1952) proved no more effective than the much slower Mk 4 (1948).

Several keys to improved sonar performance were known. One was lower frequency; to retain the same beam definition at lower frequency (and hence longer wave length) required larger sets. Thus SQS-4, originally in the 15-kc range, had a transducer four or five *feet* in diameter, compared to the 19 *inches* of QHB (25-kc range). In 1950 it was expected to deliver twice the range of QHB; and matters improved as the frequency was driven below 10 kc. For example, a 1959 training manual remarked that SQS-4 displays had markings out to 15,000 yards, and that contacts had often been held at even greater distances. By this time there was RDT, which considerably increased the energy of the beam.

The violent motion of the sea and self-noise caused more fundamental sonar problems. Studies of wartime attacks on submarines showed that, as the sea state worsened, both the range for initial contact and the number of contacts shrank substantially. For example, of 180 contacts in sea state 0 to 1, the greatest number, 76, were in the band from 800 to 1,600 yards, and 10 were found beyond 2,500 yards. In sea state 3 only 72 contacts were made, 3 of them beyond 2,500 yards. All data had been taken above 40 degrees North, an area in which sea state 3 is found about half the time; but only a quarter of all contacts were made under such conditions. In effect, a third of potential contacts were being lost; as long as nothing could be done about poor sonar performance in these seas, it would be best, in wartime, to avoid them.

A contributing factor was quenching; small ASW units "working" in a heavy sea would find their sonar transducers in bubbly water, and occasionally in air. A proposed solution was the variable depth sonar (VDS). In 1950 this was conceived as a sonar mounted on articulated rods that could be extended up to 60 feet. Preliminary tests in April 1950 showed an improvement of 83.7 percent over a conventional dome in the same ship (EPCER 849). Ultimately it was hoped that VDS would cancel out quenching, self-noise, hull turbulence—even the submarine-sheltering effect of the thermal layer—in a big enough installation. A side benefit would be the end of sonar dome damage; in World War II, DEs alone had been dry-docked about 3,500 times for dome repairs.

Other, less radical, approaches to self-noise included baffles and bubble generators; but there was also the more fundamental solution of towing a sonar in the calm water well astern of a ship. Such a system was contemplated for SCB 72. It would not be able to provide accurate ranges, but it would be employed instead for long-range search. The present TASS (Tech Assembly System) operates on a similar principle.

Neither VDS nor the proto-TASS was adopted. Instead, intense effort was applied to SQS-4, which finally promised sensor performance exceeding that of the weapons and perhaps matching that built into the fire control system.

The great range of SQS-4 required a new generation of long-range stand-off weapons without which, as Rear Admiral J.C. Daniel (DesLant) remarked, a conventional destroyer would almost have to run over a submarine before she could attack. Even at the relatively short sonar range of 6,000 yards, a 30-knot destroyer might require as much as six minutes to get into Hedgehog range, giving her target valuable evasion time. The faster the submarine, the worse the problem, since sonar contact would inevitably be lost in a high-speed run-in. Thus the advent of the new generation of submarines made the development of new ASW weapons particularly urgent. There was, however, a cost: long range required a large weapon and a launcher that would probably consume scarce centerline space on already crowded general-purpose (i.e., AAW/ASW) destroyers.

RAT (Rocket-Assisted Torpedo) was the first of the new generation of weapons. Proposed by BuOrd in 1953, it was a lightweight homing torpedo carried by a ballistic rocket to a range of about 5,000 yards. There was no longer any urgent need for depth determination; in theory the homing feature of the torpedo would make up for any evasion by the submarine while the rocket was in flight. RAT was deliberately held to a minimum of sophistication, and it could be fired from launcher arms mounted on a standard twin 5-in./38 gunhouse, elevating with the guns. For ships without 5-inch gunhouses, a simple twin launcher could replace a twin 3-in./50. The designed range was 1,500 to 5,000 yards.

An alternative solution to submarine movement while a stand-off rocket was in flight was a depth charge of huge lethal radius, which meant a nuclear depth charge. This had in any case to be a stand-off device, as otherwise its detonation would do in the destroyer as well as the submarine. In March 1953,

the Naval Ordnance Lab suggested a nuclear depth charge fired from a JATO-propelled missile atop a Talos booster; later development shrank the size of the rocket considerably. By 1955 ASROC was conceived of as a 10,000-yard ballistic rocket fired from a "pepperbox" launcher holding 12 missiles.

By this time RDT had raised the effective SQS-4 range to about 8,000 yards, which was barely enough for ASROC. However, a new sonar, SQS-23, far larger than SQS-4 (largely because of its lower frequency, about 5 kc), was expected to operate reliably at and beyond 10,000 yards: new construction in the late fifties generally incorporated a combination of ASROC and SQS-23. SQS-4 sufficed for RAT.

RAT, conceived as a simple and economical weapon, proved too inaccurate even for a homing torpedo. It was abandoned in 1957 in favor of a torpedo-carrying option for ASROC. The lesson of its inaccuracy caused the ASROC developers to increase the fin area of their missile, which in turn reduced the capacity of the "pepperbox" to eight. Given its torpedo warhead, ASROC could be improved by the upgrading of the standard U.S. lightweight ASW torpedo, which was launched from aircraft, from the racks of surface ships (later Mk 32 triple tubes), and now from ASROC.

Within the destroyer force, it was believed that even RAT would be far too massive to be accommodated aboard a standard *Gearing*-class destroyer. The Class Improvement Plan for these ships showed only SQS-4 and such short-range weapons as lightweight homing torpedoes and dual Hedgehogs. In 1956 the Atlantic Destroyer Force proposed an alternative means of stand-off delivery, a drone helicopter, initially referred to as DAT (Drone Assisted Torpedo). The CNO approved development in August 1957 as DASH (Drone A/S Helicopter). DesLant suspected that refits for RAT/ASROC would be impossible, and therefore that its SQS-4-equipped destroyers would still have almost to run down submarines, even those detected at long range. Success in vectoring manned helicopters in for ASW attacks inspired the drone concept, which DesLant believed (incorrectly, as it turned out) would require almost no ship modifications. The first experiments were made with a small manned helicopter; a Bell HUL-1 (Bell 47) first landed on the fantail of the USS *Mitscher* (DL 2) in February 1957. Similar experiments were made aboard six other destroyers; the helo pads later used by DASH were configured to take the HUL. In June 1959 the (5-gun) *Fletcher*-class destroyer *Hazelwood* completed modification with a helicopter pad (23 ½ × 69 feet with a 6-foot net along the sides) and hangar (34 × 24 × 12 feet) replacing her Number 3 and 4 guns; her tubes and her Bofors guns were landed, two triple Mk 32 TT being added in place of the two quadruple Bofors abeam the forward funnel. A torpedo workshop, aircraft fire-fighting equipment, and tanks for 2,500 gallons of aircraft fuel were also added. These modifications were typical of those required by DASH.

Late in 1955 the Kaman Corporation began a joint Army-Navy study of drone control for the existing HTK-1 training helicopter. The HTK-1 drone was first demonstrated aboard the USS *Mitscher* in May 1957; later (12 January–6 February 1959) it was tested aboard the USS *Manley* (DD 940). Fifty-nine simulated ASW missions were carried out, the drone being controlled from CIC. However, HTK-1 was only an obsolete training helicopter with a negligible payload. In April 1958, the Navy contracted with Gyrodyne Corporation for a drone version of its ultra-lightweight Rotorcycle (YRON-1) helicopter, a one-man type originally intended for observation and liaison work for the Marines. This DSN-1 (later QH 50A) drone first landed at sea (with a pilot aboard) on the USS *Mitscher* (DL 2), 1 July 1960, and on 7 December a successful drone takeoff was made from the *Hazelwood*.

The DASH system comprised an SQS-29/-30/-31/-32 (improved SQS-4) sonar for target detection and

Photographed on 17 July 1963, the *Lester* shows her FY 62 DASH conversion configuration, all K-guns having been removed, together with her after twin 3-inch gun; later some Pacific units were fitted with a single Bofors aft, apparently as a result of local initiative. The shield for her Fanfare torpedo countermeasures winch is clearly visible. The small replenishment-at-sea tripod mast atop her hangar carried at its head the vertical DASH control antenna, and a radio whip was fitted at the after end of the hangar; another DASH antenna surmounted the foremast, but is not visible here. Her lack of a variable depth sonar aft identifies her as an SQS-23 ship. The small deckhouse abaft her 3-inch/50 gun carried ready-service ammunition. Although apparently part of the large ASW modernization program of the early sixties, these DASH and sonar modernizations were not carried in the FRAM budget.

tracking, SPS-10 (search) and Mk 25 (fire control) radars, and a series of radios and signal converters to transform radar and sonar signals into a form suitable for display together in standard display devices. Both radars were to be used together to give drone position to a controller in the destroyer CIC. A specification issued 12 May 1958 called for a control system capable of putting the drone within 200 yards of a plotted submarine position at a range of 10,000 yards (400 at 20,000). Drone performance would include a cruising speed of 80 knots, an endurance of at least 25 minutes, and the capability to hover for at least 20 percent of total endurance time. The system was to provide for very quick reaction (launch within 30 seconds at most), and for low-signature (low noise, no exhaust flare at night) approach to the target. A single Mk 43 torpedo was specified.

DSN-1 was not quite up to these standards. In Operational Evaluation and Test Force trials (15 February–24 March 1961) off Key West it made 38 attacks on a radar reflector at ranges out to 9,080 yards, plus nine dummy weapon drops against a submarine out to 14,540 yards. Unfortunately, it proved unable to lift the single Mk 43 torpedo under the conditions of high temperature and humidity encountered. Even more disappointing was the low reliability of the drone, which made quick reaction impossible:

> . . . drone operations are tactically unrealistic when conducted under the necessary speed and altitude restrictions imposed. . . . The operational usefulness of the DASH system is degraded by the excessive length of time required to launch the vehicle, shift control to CIC, and move the drone to the target.

Examples of insufficient instrumentation included the use of a barometric rather than a true altimeter, which made precise control of takeoff and landing extremely difficult.

DSN-1 was only an interim type pending production of a powerful turbine-powered drone, which would carry two Mk 44 or one Mk 46 torpedo, or a single nuclear depth charge. This DSN-3 (QH 50C; DSN-2 was a developmental model) first flew in January 1962. Deliveries began on 15 November, and on 7 January 1963 the USS *Buck* (DD 761, a FRAM *Sumner*) became the first DASH ship to complete ship qualification trials. By that time many destroyers—even the *Dealey*-class DEs—were being modified for helicopter operation; other units had been modified to control DASH helicopters. Although operational evaluation aboard the USS *Hugh Purvis* (DD 709) indicated further reliability problems, the program went ahead. It would later be claimed that the program had been pressed ahead regardless of the demonstrated inadequacy of DASH drones because of pressure generated by the existence of all of those ships fitted for, but not yet supplied with, the drone. The *Hazelwood* and nearly all of the FRAMs were ready long before DASH was. A frequent comment during the subsequent GAO investigation (1970) was that the Navy had telescoped a seven-year program into three years.

A further improved drone, QH 50D, appeared in 1965 (two Mk 46). Both QH 50C and QH 50D could operate out to 28 nm., although radar tracking was inadequate beyond 15,000 yards. DASH proponents claimed that a more effective radar reflector or transponder would permit operation well beyond 20,000 yards. However, at very long (convergence zone) range a sonar such as the later SQS-26 would not be able to provide sufficiently precise data to permit an at-

The four *Claud Jones*-class escorts were the ultimate attempt to develop inexpensive mass-production ships. Slow and lightly armed, they were considered abject failures, ending their careers as electronic intelligence platforms. Under way about September 1967, the *McMorris* shows an ESM array amidships and no ASW weapons beyond Mk 32 tubes and what appears to be a depth-charge track aft.

tack without reacquisition of the submarine by the helicopter. This issue explains in large part the need for a manned attack helicopter (LAMPS) in conjunction with SQS-26 and the newer towed arrays.

DASH continued to encounter reliability problems. Thus the QH 50C operational evaluation had to be suspended for five months due to a series of drone accidents (1963). Although DASH seemed (on paper) to answer many ASW problems, in fact it was not well liked in the fleet. COs were loath to chance flying an expensive drone they considered grossly unreliable (and very much subject to electromagnetic interference), and DASH operations were not very well supported by sufficient maintenance personnel—a situation sometimes attributed to the administration of the program by the Bureau of Aeronautics, which had little use for drones. Through the sixties there were periodic attempts to improve matters, none of which were really successful. Of 746 drones built, over half were lost at sea; by 1968 one DASH was lost, on average, for every 80 hours of flight time. It was no great surprise that DoD turned down a Navy request for $31 million to continue production in FY 68. By that time about one hundred ships flew DASH drones. Two years later the only ships retaining DASH were about 50, mostly FRAM II, which had no other long-range ASW weapon.

Yet DASH could be made to work. The Japanese Navy bought only 17 and lost *none*; and a spotter version (Snoopy DASH) proved effective in Vietnam. There was also some question as to the meaning of the apparently excessive DASH failure rate. For example, Gyrodyne observed in a February 1967 letter that a 150-hour mean time to failure (as then observed) would make DASH quite competitive economically with ASROC; indeed, this figure was lower than the reliability estimate (40 failures in 1,000 51-minute flights), which had led to the selection of DASH in the first place. Here the reasoning was that a $100,000 DASH good for 150 hours (154 flights) would come out to about $650 per attack; ASROC boosters cost about $5,000 each. The problem was that these *wartime* rates bore little relation to expectations of peacetime training rates in a force supported by peacetime production. It was as though the loss rate of bombers *in training* was equated to the *combat* loss rate. Thus the statements "DASH is more economical than ASROC" and "if we keep losing them at this rate we will run out" were not contradictory.

Even as DASH was cut back in 1968, a manned helicopter program, LAMPS (Light Airborne Multi-Purpose System) was taking shape. It was to be a helicopter small enough to use a modified DASH pad, yet large enough to carry a useful load of sensors. Early versions called for magnetic anomaly detectors (MAD) to localize small contacts; these would be only modest extensions of DASH.

The manned helicopter presented far greater possibilities, however. For example, in 1968 attention was beginning to be paid Soviet antiship missiles. It was suggested that LAMPS might carry, as an alternative to ASW weapons, a pair of Sparrow air-to-air missiles plus radar and other avionics. Another concept of ASMD (antiship missile defense) called for the helicopter to carry a sea-search radar by means of which destroyer-borne weapons (Harpoon and Standard ARM) might be targeted on the prospective enemy missile launcher.

The ASW mission expanded. Besides MAD, LAMPS helicopters were to carry sonobuoys, data from which would be fed to shipboard computers via a data link.

A design competition held in 1969/70 resulted in the selection of an interim LAMPS (Mk I) helicopter in October 1970, a modified version of the Kaman UH-2 utility helicopter. At that time a contract was awarded for the conversion of ten to LAMPS configuration; ten more were awarded in July 1971. The first flew on 16 March 1971. Its equipment included an LN 66 surface-search radar, an ASQ-81 MAD, 15 sonobuoys, electronic intercept gear (ALR 54), eight flares, a data link, and provision for using a destroyer's TACAN. Armament would consist of two torpedoes. Although the Sparrow was tested, it was not made a standard weapon. Deployment began on 7 December 1971 (USS *Belknap*, DLG 26).

The SH-2 was an elderly airframe with limited potential, even though it was thoroughly rebuilt (and re-engined) for LAMPS use. A Mark II program envisaged use of the larger SH-3 with new sensors, but the Navy preferred a new airframe (LAMPS III), the Sikorsky SH-60B.

Meanwhile LAMPS is being extended to numerous escorts. Refits began under FY 72: DE 1040, 1041, 1044, 1051, 1063, 1066, 1074, 1078/1080, DEG 3; FY 73: DE 1043, 1045, 1055, 1059, 1065, 1069, 1071/1073, 1075, 1081, 1083/1088, DEG 4, 6; FY 74: DE 1049, 1053, 1054, 1056/1058, 1060, 1076, 1089/1097; FY 75: DE 1047, 1062, 1064, 1067, 1077, 1082, and DEG 1, 2, 5; FY 76: DE 1052, 1061, 1068, 1070. Of all the remaining DEs, this leaves only DE 1037/1038, 1048, and 1050 employed in towed array trials. In addition, new escorts, such as the *Spruance*-class destroyers and the *Perry*-class frigates, are designed for LAMPS. As for the larger ships, the *Belknap*s were refitted under FY 72, at least partly because they were unique among the DLGs in having full helicopter support facilities. More limited modifications were made to the DLGNs.

Both SQS-4 and SQS-23 were limited in operation to "direct propagation," that is, to more or less straight lines. However, the sea bends sound waves by refraction, and sound can bounce off its bottom to reach very distant objects. The former effect makes sound waves spread out and then converge at distant points

Variable depth sonar was one hopeful ASW development of the fifties; here the experimental destroyer escort *Maloy* prepares to launch her "fish" using her stern crane, 22 May 1963. Note her new low bridge, similar to that of the SCB 63A conversions, and the absence of nearly all of her automatic weapons.

(convergence zone). A powerful enough sonar can, in theory, reach out to successive convergence zones spaced roughly 30 miles apart. About 1955 work began on an extremely powerful sonar to take full advantage of both phenomena. This was SQS-26, a device so large that it *required* a bow mounting, where SQS-23 had fit within a 260-inch keel dome. SQS-26 was comparable in size to a 40-foot utility boat.

This was finally a sensor well in advance of existing weapons; the problem had been solved only with the development of LAMPS. Alternatives included an extended-range ASROC (which would be limited in effectiveness by submarine motion after launch), a modified DASH, or a long-range wire-guided torpedo (Mk 48). The problem of exploiting SQS-26 range explains the planned use of fixed stern torpedo tubes in ASW ships equipped with it. For SQS-4 and SQS-23 ships the equivalent was the Mk 35 torpedo, also in a fixed tube.

The other great ASW sensor advance of the decade was VDS. By the mid-fifties VDS was valued as a means of penetrating the thermal layer beneath which a submarine might hide. Early test models were streamed over the side (SQS-9); one was tested in the DDE *Saufley*, which had an asymetrical deckhouse with a cutout in the starboard side to accept the gear; the *Claud Jones* class had a similar structure. Later practice was to stream it from hoists on the fantail; the fact, the designation often applied to a VDS is really the designation for its *hoist*. Systems included a towed sonar operating off the same "stack" as the SQS-4 (in FRAM IIs), so that only one at a time could operate; a VDS associated with SQS-23 (SQA-11 hoist); and even a VDS "fish" *equivalent* to the huge SQS-23 transducer (SQA-17 hoist). A more recent development is an "independent" VDS, a sonar

with its own separate electronics (SQS-35). The SQS-35 "fish" is now often used to tow a passive array (SQR-18).

VDS experienced considerable variations in popularity, ranging from great enthusiasm (often on the part of its developers and analysts) to great disfavor among those who actually had to handle the heavy hoists and "fish" in heavy weather. It did restrict ship maneuverability; in exercises VDS ships were also limited by rules intended to prevent them from hitting submarines with their "fish." Thus, although many designs for SQS-23- and -26-equipped ships showed VDS installations, only the refitted *Forrest Sherman*s and the destroyer escorts were so fitted. In a FRAM II, VDS partly compensated for the limitations of the SQS-4-series main search sonar.

By 1958 all of the remaining World War II destroyers were considered ASW/Fire Support types; the 5- or 3-inch gun was no longer considered a serious counter to attack aircraft. Only the radar pickets retained a serious AAW role, and the ships that a decade earlier had been seen as a valuable reserve of AAW escorts no longer had any obvious role.

Meanwhile, the destroyers had lost much of their ASW effectiveness at the same time that the Soviet submarine force had progressed to large numbers of modern boats. For example, by 1957 the Soviets had built 236 of their large Whiskey class, roughly equivalent to Type 21; 22 of the larger Zulu type; and 25 Quebecs, which, with their closed-cycle propulsive systems, might be considered rough equivalents of Type 26. Construction was still proceeding at a high rate, and Soviet missile submarines were entering service.

A variety of schemes for upgrading the large existing destroyer fleet were proposed. For example, on 22 October 1958, the chairman of the SCB asked for a *Sumner/Gearing* conversion equivalent to a *Dealey*-class escort as a means of averting block obsolescence and as a means of using existing hulls. He envisaged RAT supported by Mk 32 torpedo tubes and a helicopter capability; guns were to be retained for self-defense but sacrificed if necessary to achieve ASW goals. SQS-4/RDT or SQS-23 and a VDS (if possible) were to be provided; surely all of this could be had at no less than 27 knots (loss of two boilers) and, if possible, it could be accompanied by an improvement in cruising radius. BuShips proposed that No. 2 gunhouse and all the 3-in./50s be removed; the sacrifice of No. 1 boiler room would cut maximum speed to 26 knots (sustained to 25); but endurance would rise to 6,000 nm. at 25 knots. RAT could be mounted on No. 1 gunhouse, two Mk 32s on the main deck abaft the bridge, and the helicopter could use the long cleared space on 01 level abaft the second stack. The escort would have SQS-4/RDT and (ultimately) a VDS aft; an enlarged CIC would be built up around the tripod legs.

This reconstruction was expected to add ten years to the useful life of the ship at a cost of $7.7 million (7.0 for follow-on ships). Three could be bought for the price of one of the new SQS-26-equipped DEs (1037 class, see chapter 15). Unfortunately, the conversion would be very limited at best. A study showed that one ship with SQS-26 should be the equal of *four* with SQS-4; VDS would be a requirement, not a desideratum. The helicopter would add effective ASW range—but only in suitable weather.

Something more was needed. Either the destroyers would have to undergo some less austere reconstruction, or they would have to be replaced en masse. The latter option led through a decade of abortive programs to the DX and finally the *Spruance*. The former option was the Fleet Rehabilitation and Modernization (FRAM) program.

FRAM was the result of a study on the material readiness of the fleet by a committee (W.E. Blewett, Jr., president of the Newport News Shipbuilding and Dry Dock Co.; C.H. Quackenbush, operating manager, States Marine Corp.; and R.E. Gibson, technical director of the Applied Physics Laboratory at Johns Hopkins University) formed in September 1958, at the request of the Secretary of the Navy. It concluded that "the U.S. Fleet is not in an acceptable state of readiness" and that total rehabilitation of ships of middle age, especially destroyers, should be undertaken to forestall block obsolescence. A high-level conference on 24/25 November 1958 considered the committee report and recommended the FRAM Program, in three groups:

Mark I,

A complete rehabilitation of all shipboard components (hull and machinery) which will extend the

useful life by about 8 years combined with the maximum degree of modernization that can be provided within World War II hulls as constructed.

Estimated average cost was $7.7 million per ship. Mark II,

A rehabilitation of all shipboard components (hull and machinery) sufficient to assure an effective and useful life of 5 years, together with a significant modernization of weapon systems, electronics and communications.

Estimated average cost was $4.5 million per ship. Mark III,

A complete overhaul of all components (hull and machinery) sufficient to extend the useful life approximately three years and to include highly selective alterations.

Estimated average cost was $0.9 million per ship; Mark III was dropped early in 1959.

Shipyard time was estimated at 9–12 months for Mark I, 6–7 for Mark II, and 4 months for the abortive Mark III.

Mark I, the major conversion, was restricted to the *Gearing*-class destroyers; Mark II conversions were applied to the DDRs, to the various DDE classes (including three *Fletchers*), and to the *Sumners*. Mark I was considered so major a conversion that it rated an SCB number, SCB 206; the more modest Mark II was treated formally as a major refit. The entire FRAM program was given priority "comparable to that of Polaris." Special efforts were made to restrict costs.

Original plans called for:

	FY 60	FY 61	FY 62	FY 63	TOTAL
Mark I					
DD 710	8	12	12	12	44
DDE 764	0	2	1	2	5
Mark II					
DD 692	7	11	13	14	45
DDE 764	0	1	2	3	6
DDE 445	3	3	5	7	18
DDE 719/825	0	2	2	0	4
DDR	4	9	11	12	36
DER	0	0	2	2	4
Mark III					
DD 692	0	4	4	0	8

This accounted for nearly all the active escorts built in World War II. The DEs were excluded as too small to take the new ASW sensors and weapons; presumably the few surviving *Fletchers* were excluded in view of their limited remaining life. Of the *Gearings*, only the experimental destroyers *Gyatt* and *Witek* were excluded. One other, the engineering test ship *Timmerman*, had already been scrapped.

FRAM II also extended to the ASW support aircraft carriers and to a number of other classes, including diesel submarines and APDs.

So urgent was FRAM considered that the Mark I (*Perry*, DD 844) and Mark II (*John W. Thomason*) prototypes were begun under FY 59 rather than FY 60 funds.

The program was reshuffled several times. Thus, the four DERs (SPS-30 radar and SQS-20 sonar) and one projected *Gearing* FRAM I (the *Witek*, an experimental sonar ship or EDD) were dropped in 1960 in favor of an additional five Mark II *Sumner*s. However, the *Sumner*s and *Fletcher* DDEs were a poor bargain compared to the *Gearing* FRAM Is. Hence in December 1961, 17 *Sumner*- and 15 *Fletcher*-class conversions were canceled in favor of 29 more *Gearing* FRAM I (as compared to the plan above, 10 more in FY 63, 19 in FY 64). The net result was that all but 6 DDRs became straight destroyers (26 FRAM I, 4 FRAM II); similarly all 4 of the DDE 719/825 group received FRAM I conversions. The missing ship (79 rather than 80 FRAM I conversions were done) was the *Witek*, dropped in 1960. The only Mark II *Gearing*s were, then, six DDRs, four ex-DDRs, and six ex-DDEs.

In all DD/DDR/DDE, FRAM was to provide sound isolation of the worst noise sources; hull damping in the vicinity of the sonar domes; data handling for ASW and air defense in the form of an automatic plotter; closed bridges; the new 400-cycle AC power supply; and modified SQS-4 sonars (frequency reduced to 6 or 7 kc, with a vertical beam steering feature for, in effect, depth determination). In Mark I *Gearing*s and ex-DDEs, SQS-23 was evaluated as an alternative to SQS-4 with VDS. It was selected in view of its compatibility with ASROC. In December 1958, it was estimated that a set of "black boxes" to make SQS-4 compatible with ASROC would cost $50,000, and that SQS-23s could be supplied sooner than the low-frequency version of SQS-4. Earlier BuShips had (erroneously) rejected SQS-23 as too large for the *Gearing* hull.

The thrust of the FRAM I (*Gearing*) conversion was improvement in ASW sensors and weapons: one twin 5-in./38 mount, the secondary battery, and the trainable torpedo tubes were removed to compensate for ASROC amidships, DASH aft, SQS-23 sonar, and two triple Mk 32 TT for lightweight ASW torpedoes. A Mk 111 analog Underwater Fire Control System (later replaced by Mk 114) was installed. The two fixed Mk 11 Hedgehogs were to be retained.* Initial plans called for the installation of two long (Mk 25) torpedo tubes amidships near the Mk 32s, but these were soon abandoned. A peculiarity of the design was that hangar and helicopter platform dimensions were based on the small manned HUL helicopter, which was considerably larger than DASH. There was some consideration of omitting ASROC, which in some ways duplicated DASH; but this was not done, partly because ASROC could operate in weather in which DASH

---

*In fact, they were retained only in the *Perry*, which carried her Mk 32 tubes on her fantail.

Nuclear ASW weapons can make up for a lot of inaccuracy in submarine location. ASROC, particularly when combined with a nuclear depth charge, was the white hope of the ASW force of the early sixties. Here one bursts after having been fired by the experimental destroyer *Agerholm*, 11 May 1962; this may have been the only live nuclear ASROC shot, as nuclear testing in the atmosphere was banned soon afterward. U.S. warships designed after the advent of nuclear ASROC had to be designed to stricter shock standards in view of the possibility of self-inflicted damage; the *Knox* class was the first to incorporate such requirements.

The *Meredith*, shown on 4 April 1966, was typical of FRAM I *Gearing*-class destroyers; the first few completed also retained their Hedgehogs forward on the 01 level. All carried ESM antennas aft on a short lattice mast, and later active protective ECM systems were added. Their antennas are visible on outriggers, and were probably part of the ULQ-6 deceptive ECM system. The small windows amidships are let into the ASROC control booth, and the main and fore masts carry DASH control antennas. By this time all light antiaircraft weapons had been removed, and the old destroyers had essentially no antiair capability, although they retained air-search radars and dual-purpose directors.

could not. ASROC and Mk 32 torpedo tube reloads were provided for alongside the DASH hangar; weight compensation was the elimination of the two fixed Hedgehogs forward. Habitability was improved by a limited air-conditioning installation.

The first series of conversions retained the two forward 5-inch mounts, which were closest to the director; but the forces afloat preferred to have a mount aft, so No. 2 gunhouse was removed from FY 61 and later conversions. The two triple Mk 32 tubes were mounted in its place on 01 level forward, and the Hedgehogs eliminated. However, a proposal to provide No. 3 mount with an auxiliary fire control system was dropped by the SCB on grounds of cost.

Other new features included a new foremast to carry a heavier air search antenna (SPS-29 or -37 or -40 with SPS-10 surface search above it), extensive ECM gear abaft the second funnel (with funnels raised and redesigned to carry the smoke clear); and a new and enlarged CIC between pilot house and forward stack; the bridge was enclosed.

Meanwhile another weapon was proposed for the fleet destroyers. In April 1959, General Dynamics/ Pomona proposed an interim Tartar conversion of existing fleet destroyers in which a ten-missile "pepperbox" was to be mounted on the after twin 5-in./38

or 5-in./5 mount, and a CW illuminator on the 5-inch director; the normal fire control system could then launch two Tartars into the direction in which the director was pointed where they could pick up target returns. Missile check-out equipment would replace the former 5-inch magazine. A cost of $380,000 per ship was estimated on the basis of a rate of 30 ships per year; the CNO, Admiral Burke, was enthusiastic as long as such a program did not retard FRAM.

BuShips worked up a variety of sketch schemes. In May it reported that the Tartar installation could replace either a gun mount or ASROC in FRAM I; indeed the latter was preferable as Tartar aft would seriously downgrade DASH operation in sea state 5. A more satisfactory platform would be the DDR, which in its Mark II refit was to receive no DASH and would have all three gun mounts. The short-hull *Sumner* was considered the least attractive platform in view of the proximity of Tartar to its VDS. Finally, BuShips reported that it had the *Forrest Sherman* and *Mitscher* classes under consideration as Tartar platforms; ultimately several units of both classes would receive more complete Tartar batteries.

Meanwhile BuOrd made its own study and concluded that it could fit about 12 missiles stowed ver-

Newly converted, the *Fiske* is representative of the great majority of FRAM Is, with her main battery split fore and aft. ASROC reloads were stowed in the forward end of the DASH hangar, their blow-out panels visible in this photograph, for a total of 17 rounds (9 reloads). At the time of this photograph, she had not yet been fitted with active ECM equipment, essential for survival in the face of antiship missiles such as Styx.

tically in a ring. The project died in July 1959 of cost escalation and misgivings over the sufficiency of so small a magazine capacity.

Of the *Gearing*-class DDRs, only six were retained in the DDR role. Since they were not to be primarily ASW ships, these FRAM Mark II units were given no DASH or ASROC; they retained their Hedgehogs and were fitted with the now-standard Mk 32 triple TT. The existing SQS-4 sonar was modified to incorporate RDT and coupled with a VDS. As in the Mark Is, the forefunnel was raised eight feet and the second funnel five feet and the funnel caps modified, and the new bridge and an enlarged CIC were fitted. New radars (as in Mk 1) were fitted to the foremast, and in four units a new SPS-30 replaced the former SPS-8 height-finder. All 5-inch guns were retained. However, as actually refitted, these ships did receive SQS-23 in place of SQS-4.

The four DDRs converted to FRAM II destroyers generally resembled the *Sumner* FRAM II (see below): in place of ASROC they had a pair of long Mk

25 TT to launch the Mk 37 ASW homing torpedo, and they retained all six guns.

All of the *Gearing*-class DDEs were originally to have received Mark II refits. Since these amounted to major ASW improvements, and since all of the FRAM refits could be regarded as similar ASW improvements, there was little point in retaining the DDE designation.

By this time there were three basic *Gearing* DDE classes: DDE 825/827 (ex-DDK), which mounted 3-in./70s; then DDE 719 and DDE 824 with a single Weapon A; finally the larger DDE 764 group with its trainable Hedgehog in place of No. 2 gunhouse. On the principle that minimum effort should be expended, all three types were to be given DASH, SQS-23, and Mk 32 torpedo tubes. The big ahead-throwing weapon forward—Weapon A or Mk 15 depending upon the type—was to be retained, and not even the air search radar was to be changed (except in DDE 719 and 824, the newest *Gearing* hulls, in which it was to be replaced by the new SPS-40). The fore-and-aft

The *Moale* was a typical FRAM II *Sumner*, retaining all three gun mounts and fitted with a variable depth transducer operating from the same "stack" as her modernized SQS-4 series hull sonar. The surface view, taken in 1961, shows the front of a long torpedo tube just forward of her triple Mk 32 lightweight tubes; it supplemented DASH as a long-range ASW weapon. By the time of the overhead view, March 1970, these tubes had been removed from FRAM IIs. With the failure of DASH, they were limited to short-range weapons: Hedgehog and lightweight torpedoes. They were also the principal U.S. carriers of variable depth sonar, which meant that they had no opportunity to exploit the long ranges theoretically possible with it.

gun mounts—3-in./70 or 5-in./38—were to be retained; the new ECM arrays and stacks typical of other FRAM conversions would be fitted. In DDE 825 and 827, 719 and 824, the four, fixed, long ASW torpedo tubes predating the FRAM conversion were to be retained. DDE 764s were to receive two long Mk 25 tubes amidships.

Matters turned out to be more complex, partly because, as these plans were maturing, two of the weapons upon which they were based—Weapon A and the twin 3-in./70—were on their last legs, in both cases because they were maintenance disasters. The enclosed 3-in./70, first mounted in the two DDEs only in 1957, was almost unique for the shortness of its career. In any case, the net effect of the two failures was for the Navy to decide to make standard FRAM Is of the *Epperson* (719) and *Basilone* (824). In the *Carpenter* (825) and *Robert A. Owen* (827) the two 3-in./70s were replaced by a single twin 5-in./38 gunhouse in No. 1 position; the fantail was left bare, and these two ships could be distinguished by their high bridges. Both retained the small Mk 56 directors originally associated with their 3-inch guns.

There remained 11 units classed as DDEs, in which a big Hedgehog had been mounted forward. Five (DDE 819–820, 837, 847, 871) became FRAM I destroyers. The remaining six DDEs of the *Lloyd Thomas* class (DDE 764–765, 858–861) were completed as planned to Mark II status, with two long Mk 25 and two triple, short Mk 32 torpedo tubes amidships, Hedgehog Mk 15 forward, and DASH aft.

In *Sumner*s, FRAM II comprised DASH, two Mk 25 tubes, and two triple Mk 32 tubes, a new bridge, new radar and ECM, and VDS. The former SQS-4 sonar was retained but fitted with RDT and moved forward to a more favorable location. There was no reduction in the main battery. Ultimately, however, not all were ever fitted with VDS.

Only 3 *Fletcher* DDEs (DDE 446, 447, 449) remained in the program after the 1961 reductions. Alone of the DDEs, they retained Weapon A forward, as well as their two fixed Hedgehogs; aft they were fitted with ECM gear and a DASH hangar as in other FRAMS, with funnel caps to direct stack gases away from the ECM arrays aft. Two of the four existing Mk 23 fixed torpedo tubes for long ASW torpedoes were retained, and two triple Mk 32 added. A VDS hoist was mounted on the fantail (except for DDE 447), and the former SQS-4 sonar retained (though modified). Both 5-inch guns were retained. The CIC was lengthened, but there was little change to the bridgework. All design and construction work on these three units (DDE 446, 447, 449) was done at Pearl Harbor.

As semiescorts, the APDs deserve a brief mention here. At one time six were to have been refitted (APD 60, 89, 107, 123, 127, and 135). In fact, only four (89, 119, 135; 90 was added) were modernized with enlarged command spaces forward of the bridge. In addition the *Ruchamkin* (89) and *Weiss* (135) had tripod foremasts, ECM domes, and Mk 32 torpedo tubes. In all cases the cargo boom was eliminated. More powerful sonar was fitted.

Contemporary with, but not actually a part of, the FRAM program was a series of *Dealey*-class refits from FY 62 onward. All but the *Dealey, Cromwell,* and *Courtney* received DASH, with a hangar amidships and a helo pad abaft it; the after twin 3-in./50 was landed. An SQS-23 sonar was fitted. Unrefitted units retained their SQS-4 sonar, variable depth "fish" being trailed from the fantail. Weapon A was later removed from these ships. In four Pacific Fleet units (DE 1023–1026), single Army-type 40-mm guns were installed on the fantail in 1967, reportedly as a result of local initiative. All ultimately had two triple Mk 32 lightweight torpedo tubes.

FRAM was supposed to extend the useful life of a destroyer by only five or eight years, yet in fact there were no mass scrappings when those intervals ended. The Vietnamese War precluded construction of the new destroyer, Seahawk; it was far easier to spend $10 million or less per ship than to spend three times as much or more for a new Seahawk. Present planning calls for retention of some FRAM Is well into the 1980s, so that many of them will have survived as much as a decade beyond their expected ends—even after hard service in Vietnam. All surviving units were, however, reduced to Naval Reserve training duty in 1973–75; in 1980 their usefulness is severely limited, and they cannot operate LAMPS I. Of the *Sumner*-class FRAM IIs, some completed in 1960 were not stricken until 1974/75—three times their allotted span.

Given the failure of the mass replacement programs, a new FRAM was proposed. In June 1969, the Chief of Naval Operations asked NavShips (successor to BuShips) to evaluate conversions of DD 710 as well as 931/945 (FRAM III and IV, respectively). Details have not survived, but it appears that at least LAMPS, Sea Sparrow (PDMS), and Vulcan-Phalanx (CIWS) were contemplated. Neither FRAM proved sufficiently attractive to pursue beyond the preliminary stage.

The *Dealey*-class destroyer escort *Van Voorhis* displays a standard DASH refit in this 1965 photograph, the hangar and helo pad replacing her after twin 3-inch/50 mount. Such ships also received a massive SQS-23 hull-mounted sonar, not visible here. Weapon A was still fitted at this time.

13

The Fast
Task Force Escorts

From the middle of World War II onward, the fast carrier task force has been the principal offensive arm of the U.S. Navy, and screening such forces has been a principal theme of destroyer operation and development. Generally, the threat to the carrier task force was air attack, which explains the emphasis on air defense in the *Mitscher* and *Forrest Sherman* designs. Fast task force air defense was the primary task of one of the three categories the Schindler Committee proposed for future development (see chapter 11) in May 1954. The new ship would be a logical development of the *Mitscher* concept, and like the earlier ship, would probably be designated DL ("destroyer leader"). In June, the SCB proposed instead the term "frigate," which was adopted. The new fast escorts would be comparable to the frigates of the eighteenth century or, perhaps, to the French contre-torpilleurs of the twentieth. They were not intended individually to lead lesser ships in a screen, since they would constitute the screen itself. The Schindler Committee envisaged them primarily as AAW ships "to provide limited defense against submarine and surface attack . . . to provide air control facilities . . . (and, in every fourth unit) to provide command facilities for screen commander and staff."

Thus began the construction of a series of specialized fast task force escorts, all armed with antiaircraft missiles (and thus designated DLG rather than DL) and all comparable in size to the light cruisers of former days. The U.S. Navy, indeed, was nearly unique in designating such ships as frigates; in most navies the Royal Navy's World War II revival of the frigate category for large ASW ships (comparable to destroyer escorts) was the rule. Thus for many years there was the anomaly of Soviet "cruisers" substantially smaller than U.S. DL-"frigates" and of foreign "frigates" by no means comparable to their U.S. counterparts. Finally, on 30 June 1975 the U.S. categories were revised to reflect foreign practice. The DLs were redesignated as missile cruisers (CG or CGN, depending upon their power plants) or missile destroyers (DDG, for the smaller ones). The former "ocean escorts" or "destroyer escorts" (DE and DEG) were redesignated frigates (FF, FFG). This ended the anomaly of the *Perry*-class "patrol frigate," which had originally been included in the PF category begun with the *Asheville* and *Tacoma* classes during World War II.

Given the need for a heavy antiaircraft screen to protect the fast attack carriers, the only important issue was the pace at which guns would give way to the missile systems already under crash development. At first the latter appeared to require cruiser hulls, such as the *Boston*, to support them; for example, it was only in March 1955 that the operational requirement for Terrier was formally revised to include suitability for mounting aboard destroyers and frigates. Reportedly the key figure in the very rapid transformation of the fleet in the direction of surface-to-air missiles was Chief of Naval Operations Arleigh Burke, under whose tenure it occurred. Unlike his predecessors, he had a strong surface (destroyer) background and well understood the needs and potentials of the destroyer force. He also had the

The *Farragut* was extensively modernized at the Philadelphia Navy Yard under Project SCB 243 of the FY 66 program, between 1 May 1968 and 10 March 1969. She was fitted for NTDS and Homing Terrier (both SPQ-5s were replaced by SPG-55s), and her unreliable SPS-39 three-dimensional radar was replaced by the superior SPS-48 shown. Note, too, the new TACAN antenna on her mainmast, and the ECM antennas outboard of her foremast. Within her class, she was unique in being fitted with an ASROC reload magazine, with a control cabin atop it. Most ships of this class had large NTDS-associated broadband antennas forward of their 5-inch guns; the *Farragut* has only a very small one in this 8 September 1971 photograph. She was redesignated a missile destroyer on 30 June 1975.

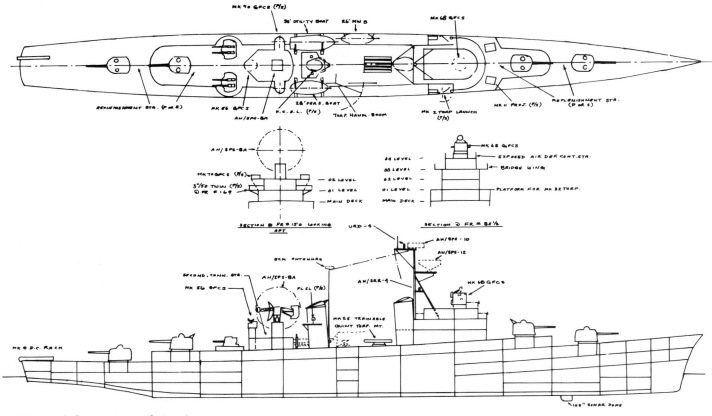

Fast task force escort (frigate)

benefit of long experience within BuOrd, where the new missile technology was being developed, and he had the advantage of a relatively long tenure during which he could put his concepts into practice. Although Admiral Burke is best known for his support of the Polaris system developments, the introduction of surface-to-air missiles on a very large scale seems, in retrospect, to have been a major achievement. It was, moreover, conducted very largely on faith, as systems moved from the drawing board almost directly into mass production. This was particularly true of Tartar. Such procedures were not indications of irresponsibility, but rather of the magnitude of the air threat as it was perceived in the late 1950s.

The missile program involved very large numbers of new ships. For example, as of September 1956, the FY 56–62 plan for missile-ship construction included two CG(N)s in FY 57 and one more in FY 60; a total of 51 DLGs (6 in FY 56, 5 in FY 57, 8 in FY 58, 9 in FY 59, 8 each in FY 60 and 61, 7 in FY 62); and 50 DDG (8 each in FY 57 and 58, 10 in FY 60 and 61, 14 in FY 62) plus missile conversions: 8 CLG (1 in FY 56, 5 in FY 57, 2 in FY 58) and four CAG (3 in FY 58, 1 in FY 59). Other objectives included the construction of one nuclear carrier annually from FY 58 onward and a program of missile submarine con-

struction. Beyond the experimental *Gyatt*, no destroyer missile conversions were envisaged: fast task force escort duty needed something far more potent than a *Gearing*. Admiral Burke was well aware of what all of this construction would cost, but he was also well aware of the emerging air threat his fleet faced, and of the need to maintain the very powerful carrier strike forces that existed. In the fall of 1956 there was, as yet, no Polaris program to drain funds from what would later be perceived as the "general purpose" arm of the Navy: the fast carriers were still the strategic as well as the limited-war striking force.

In 1954 the missiles still seemed far in the future, and the Schindler Committee asked for four 5-in./54s on a *Mitscher* hull, controlled by two directors. ASW capability was to be minimal, consisting only of Mk 32 lightweight torpedoes or their equivalent. Weapon A and even Hedgehog were specifically excluded. On the other hand, the new ship was to have excellent submarine *detection* equipment with which to warn the task force to evade: SQS-4 with dual MCC. A powerful air search radar (SPS-12) and the height finder (SPS-8) required for fighter control were also specified. "Hemispherical air search," which would have been important only for a ship operating near land, was specifically excluded, but effective picket duties with the task force required the new ship to have terminal facilities for airborne early warning aircraft. To keep up with its charges, the escort was to have "maximum seakeeping qualities," a trial speed of 34 knots, and an endurance of 5,500 nm. at 20 knots.

Speed was particularly important, and compromises such as those accepted in the design of the *Forrest Sherman*s had to be avoided. For example, a June 1954 conference on frigate design decreed that it *must* be at least 2 knots faster than the new CVA: "we must wait for final approval of CVA characteristics before setting speed for this ship." Rear Admiral Mendenhall, chairman of the SCB, wanted to know what it would take to attain 38 knots; on a quick-and-dirty basis the BuShips representatives thought a 530-foot, 80,000-shp ship or a 490-foot, 100,000-shp ship would do—and new studies of both cases were ordered. The admiral also wanted to require a radius of 1,300 nm. at 35 knots, which suggests a desire for the fast task force to be able to operate at top speed for extended periods. In fact, of course, as in previous fast-destroyer designs, more modest goals had to be adopted in the end.

The first tentative characteristics (17 May 1954) asked even more: a trial speed of 35 knots, a pair of quadruple 40-mm. AA guns (which would soon be twin 3-in./50s), as well as an ASW torpedo-launching system with six Mk 32 torpedoes, a depth-charge track (12 charges), and six depth-charge throwers. A quintuple bank of antiship torpedo tubes would be a useful means of discouraging surface attack on the task force; Samar was still well remembered after a decade. By August the thrust of the design, now designated SCB 129, had been formalized: "A predominantly anti-aircraft ship with radar picket capabilities is desired. The capability of sinking submarines is subordinate to the stressed features." The AA role was taken to require "an exposed air defense control station on a level above the Pilot House. Particular attention shall be given in the design to as near hemispherical visibility as practicable. . . ."

The torpedo pendulum swung towards long-range ASW homing torpedoes, and the quintuple mount was to be capable of launching them. There were to be no reloads, but 44 depth charges were specified. By September the side depth-charge throwers had been displaced by two fixed Hedgehogs with two sets of charges each in ready stowage and eight more (each) in a magazine. This was beginning to be a serious ASW battery.

This was a lot to cram into a 3,600-ton destroyer hull. A footnote, "by installing SQS-4 long-range detection sonar on a CLAA Class [6,000 tons plus] will give similar capabilities," suggests that the framers of these draft characteristics knew that they were pushing towards a cruiser. The single rapid-fire 5-in./54 was more than equal in firepower to a twin 5-in./38; and in weight, four of the former were equal to more than five of the latter. If electrical loads—including those required for the radar—were added in, it would seem that the main battery of a World War II AA cruiser, twelve 5-in./38s, was being demanded on a hull half the size.

The ship grew as preliminary studies progressed. In August, she was described as 5,000 tons fully loaded, 480 feet long; in September the length was 495 feet; and in October, 510 feet (and 5,300 tons). Efforts were already being made to prune back weight by eliminating the superfiring feature of No. 2 and 3 guns, and a weight study was made of eight fixed tubes as a substitute for the quintuple rotating mount. The former had the disadvantage of greater weight and length required (56 feet vs. 25) but on the other hand a fixed tube, Mk 25, was already in existence whereas a trainable one would require considerable design time. Other points in favor of the fixed tubes were that they could accommodate reloads and that torpedoes in them (and thus inside a deckhouse) could be serviced and heated—the latter particularly desirable in the cold North Atlantic. However, the tubes were—at best—secondary in an AAW ship, and the quintuple arrangement, which had lower impact on the design as a whole, prevailed.

At the end of September 1954, a BuShips comparison sheet showed that the characteristics, including quintuple torpedo tubes, could be achieved on a light displacement of 3,569 tons (vice 3,384 for DL 2; 4,761 tons on trial vice 4,441; 5,101 full load vice 4,726; length would be increased to 495 feet from the 476 of DL 2). If both the torpedo tubes and the two twin 3-in./50s were sacrificed, the main armament could be accommodated on a DL hull (which really says something about the weights of Weapon A and the 3-in./70) on a light displacement of 3,435 tons (4,516 on trial, 4,832 full load). In both cases the endurance at 20 knots was to be increased from 4,500 to 5,000 miles, and the trial speed maintained above 35 knots. As compared to a first cost of $51.5 million for DL 2 ($39 million for follow-on ships), the full SCB 129 was expected to cost $54.5 ($42) million and the restricted version $53 ($40.5) million. These are remarkably low figures in view of the spectacular combination of armament and performance demanded. They were practical partly because of improvements in machinery weight (80,000 shp in SCB 129 was to cost [wet] 1,275 tons, where 75,000 had cost [in CL 51, 1938] 1,335, and in fact DL 2 cost 1,114), and because destroyer rather than cruiser practice in hull construction was adopted. A new structural feature was the use of HY 80 steel in place of the STS formerly used over the amidships sections

The fast task force escorts were, above all, large enough to sustain high speed in rough weather so as to keep pace with carriers. Just how large is suggested by these two views of ships of the Pacific Fleet Cruiser-Destroyer Force lined up at San Diego, 4 February 1961: the radar picket destroyer *Rogers* (DDR 876), the destroyer *Brinkley Bass* (DD 887), and the frigates *Preble* (DLG 15), *Mahan* (DLG 11), *King* (DLG 10), and *Coontz* (DLG 9), the last as yet without her ASROC forward. Note the flat decks above the Terrier magazines aft, with replenishment-at-sea gear folded down. Given limited magazine capacity (40 missiles per ship), sufficient for only one major engagement, rapid replenishment was an important consideration.

of destroyers and DLs. The newer steel was regarded as considerably tougher than STS, nearly as splinter-proof, and very weldable; it was "highly desirable for the high speed rough water service for which the vessel is intended."

The ship continued to grow. A June 1955 report on the Preliminary Design listed a full load displacement of 5,249 tons and a power requirement of 85,000 shp for a speed slightly over 35 knots. The designers reported that growth resulted from "increased armament space requirements, increased fuel for endurance, and the use of machinery more conservative than the DL 2 class." To the quintuple TT had been added provision for two reloads—but now the pendulum was swinging against the long ASW torpedo, and only antisurface ship weapons (Mk 16) were to be carried.

A paradoxical element of the design was the great attention paid to sonar performance in a ship specifically *not* intended for submarine-killings. The hull lines were redrawn to allow for a deeper draft and a lower prismatic coefficient than in DL 2 (almost as low, in fact, as in DL 1). Sonar performance in the *Mitscher*s had been considered unsatisfactory, not least because of interference between the scanning sonar (QHBa) and the attack sonar SQG-1, which were mounted in tandem in separate domes. The advent of Dual MCC (introduced in DD 931, see chapter 11) permitted the use of a single dome, which could be mounted farther forward so as to avoid bubbles entrained by the stem. A more radical solution would be a bow dome. Lines with such a dome were worked out, and the final recommendation of Preliminary Design was that one ship be built with a bow dome and the others with more conventional installations to provide comparative data. Model tests suggested that whereas the conventional dome *added* about 4.7 percent to bare hull resistance at 20 knots and 1.3 percent at 35, the bow dome, acting as a small bulbous bow, *reduced* resistance by 10 and 5 percent at these speeds. There were also acoustic advantages. Bubbling, a serious source of noise in conventional domes at 20 knots—and it must be kept in mind that the fast escort would do her listening at high speed—would be abolished, although there would be more splash noise. There was some fear that the problem of the sonar emerging in rough weather would be aggravated; but on the other hand the bottom of the new dome would be rounded to take the impact of slamming back into the water.

A more conventional installation was also considered, a special rounded shape being adopted to reduce flow separation and vorticity on the after part of the dome; these effects were responsible for severe panting stresses on conventional domes. The dome dimensions suggest just what a "large" sonar meant

in 1955—100 inches long, 5 ft. 4 in. deep. By way of contrast, SQS-23, which became standard on many FRAM destroyers only four years later, was the size of a small motor boat.

Ultimately SCB 129 and its close relative, SCB 142, had hull-mounted sonars; the bow mounting was first incorporated in the frigates of the FY 58 program (SCB 172, DLG 16 class).

Even though Terrier was not officially suitable for destroyer installation, it was expected almost from the first that it would supplant the rapid-fire gun on the fast task force escort. In preparation for DLG installation, Terrier was tested at sea aboard a specially modified *Gearing*-class destroyer, the USS *Gyatt*, converted at the Boston Naval Shipyard under the FY 56 program. Conversion entailed the replacement of No. 3 5-inch gun mount and the after 40-mm. guns by a twin Terrier launcher with 14 missiles; guidance was furnished by a modified Mk 25 radar in the gun fire control system, and automatic Denny-Brown stabilizers were fitted. At the same time the remaining 40-mm. guns were replaced by 3-in./50s, and the quintuple torpedo tubes landed as weight compensation. This austere conversion, first proposed in the spring of 1954, was not intended as a prototype for further efforts. However, it inspired the destroyer force to demand Terrier rather than the new (and shorter-range) Tartar that was under development to replace the standard twin 5-in./38 or single 5-in./54 mount, and for a time repeat *Gyatt*s were proposed in the Shipbuilding Plan. The *Gyatt* herself became DDG 1, reverting to her old destroyer designation in 1962 when the missiles were removed and she became a test ship with the Operational Test and Evaluation Force.

Given the availability of Terrier, some proposed that SCB 129 include missiles; instead, a new gun-and-missile frigate was designed in parallel, as SCB 142. Characteristics were issued in January 1955. She would duplicate SCB 129 as far as possible, except for armament.

> Some members of the SCB were desirous of installing guided missile launching systems forward and aft on the DLG, but two systems of the size contemplated could not be accommodated on the DL hull. In addition, the full Board was not prepared to recommend an all-missile ship and the half Terrier-half gun armament was accepted. [Design Report, July 1955.]

A wide variety of schemes were prepared. For example, it appeared that a twin Terrier launcher could replace either the No. 3 *or* No. 4 5-in./54 gun mount, with a magazine for 24 Terriers nearby; missile guidance would be rudimentary, via a modified fire control radar on a Mk 68 director. An alternative "maximum Terrier installation" called for the removal of all guns, even the two twin 3-in./50s. Twin launchers fore and aft would be served by 48-missile magazines, and fire control would be via big SPQ-5 radars—one atop the bridge and one abaft the SPS-8 height-finder required for fighter control. The quintuple anti-surface-ship torpedo tubes and the ASW battery were to be retained in any case.

The reality was more complex. In order to handle two *simultaneous* intercepts, the missile frigate required a pair of SPQ-5 which, with one twin launcher, replaced both after 5-inch guns, as well as the space formerly reserved for the big stabilized height-finder; however, the air control role was retained in the characteristics. Moreover, missile operation required a three-dimensional radar to intermediate between the long-range search set (SPS-37) and the guidance radars. In the new frigate this was SPS-39, the first of the frequency-scanned pencil-beam sets, mounted on the foremast; a quadrupod lattice mainmast carried SPS-37 and the TACAN required for effective fighter control.

The missiles were carried in a 40-round Mk 10 launching system, consisting of two horizontal rotating rings from which rounds were carried to a "finning" space whence they were rammed onto the twin arms of the launcher proper. Excluding missiles and fluids, the Mk 10 Mod 0 of the new missile frigate weighed 123.2 tons; with forty 3,000-lb. Terriers and associated fluids, this figure rose to 178.7 tons. By way of comparison, a single 5-in./54 without ammunition weighed about 57.6 tons, so that two guns would weigh only about 115.2. Their 1,200 rounds of 5-inch ammunition would add about 54 tons, comparable to the net weight of the missiles. However, the slightly heavier missile system would involve more weight very high in the ship, and in addition the missile system required considerable electrical power, not least to operate the elaborate magazine system.

The missile system included a weapons control center forward on the 02 level below the CIC; a missile plotting room combined with the after IC and gyro room on the second platform deck aft. Missile transfer at sea and strikedown areas were provided near the missile magazine on the 01 level aft. The main deckhouse was extended 14 feet farther aft than in the original all-gun design, but 56 feet of its length was taken up with the missile-handling area, including the finning space. Thus there was a general shortage of internal volume: SCB 142 was among the first of the modern "volume critical" ships. Habitability standards had to be relaxed, as compared with those of the DL, and even so the torpedo work shop and internal stowage of two reload torpedoes had to be eliminated in favor of a mess space. The two reloads (later eliminated when the long torpedo tubes were given up) were to be stowed outboard of

the deckhouse with checkout access openings and heat circulating from within the deckhouse. Forward, the superstructure generally followed that of the DL except for the weapons control space.

Radars and the missiles high in the ship both increased weight and reduced stability. Some Preliminary Design figures (July 1955) give an idea of the evolution of the frigates (figures in parentheses are metacentric heights):

Condition	SCB 5, 1948	SCB 129	SCB 142
Light	3,377 (3.03)	3,814 (2.98)	3,893 (2.67)
Trials	4,472 (4.39)	4,905 (5.16)	4,970 (4.81)
Full Load	4,758 (4.88)	5,249 (5.89)	5,314 (5.53)

These are all design figures, hence not entirely representative of the ships as built. SCB 5, which became DD 927/DL 2, has been included to give some feeling for the growth of the frigates into the small cruiser category. Later additions to the DLG increased her displacement further: DLG 9 was completed at a light displacement of 4,186 tons, and a full load of 5,605.0.

For FY 56 the Navy was given six frigates; Admiral Carney, the CNO, personally decided that three (DLG 9–11) would be half-gun SCB 142s. Three SCB 129s (DL 6–8) were insurance against the possible failure of Terrier; but the missile was accepted for fleet use, and all were switched to the missile design during 1956. Four more of this *Farragut* class were authorized under the FY 57 program.

Meanwhile major changes were made in the ASW battery. During 1956 the torpedo pendulum swung violently away from the long-range types. For many years BuOrd had been trying to adapt the very powerful Mk 16 submarine torpedo for surface use; indeed, the quintuple tube had been included in the new DLs with this weapon in mind. Finally the bureau had to admit its failures (memo, Chief of BuOrd to CNO, 17 July 1956); worse, the new tube it had developed was too short to take the Mk 15 torpedo standard within the destroyer fleet. The Mk 37 ASW torpedo, which would fit the new tube, was considered worthless as an antiship weapon; and

> the advent of such high-priority programs as ASROC and Lulu [a nuclear depth charge], the urgent necessity to develop suitable armament for modern submarines, and the continuing heavy emphasis upon guided missiles have made it impossible to budget adequately for an effective long-range surface-to-surface torpedo.

In any case,

> in the light of current tactics it is felt that the use of long-range anti-surface ship torpedoes will be remote . . . in view of the extreme submarine threat existing,

Newly completed, the missile frigate *Farragut* displays her two Terrier guidance radars, SPQ-5s similar to those aboard contemporary missile cruisers, and suited only for beam-riding versions of the Terrier missile. They were later replaced by SPG-55s. A small antenna atop the main one formed a capture beam, guiding the missile into the main beam formed by the large microwave lens. SPQ-5 was closely related to the SPG-49 of Talos missile cruisers. Note, too, the erected underway-replenishment tripod atop the magazine, whose blast doors are visible. The funnel caps, similar to those on FRAM destroyers, were intended specifically to overcome the airborne shock wave of a nuclear explosion. Her main mast carried TACAN and an SPS-37 air-search set; her fore, an URD-4 UHF/DF and an SPS-39 electronically scanned three-dimensional radar. Also visible are a Mk 63 director for the starboard twin 3-inch/50 gun, and an active ECM antenna, the oblong mesh-covered object extending below the director tub installed aboard several frigates at this time. In this 8 December 1960 photograph the ship was still flying the Bethlehem Steel house flag, not yet having been delivered.

it is considered that the A/S phase should be emphasized.

A short-range ASW torpedo in conjunction with a standoff weapon such as RAT or ASROC would be better; BuOrd suggested the former for the new DLG. It would require a special launcher.

The lightweight Mk 32 torpedo, which had been intended for launching from simple dropping gear, was itself discarded in favor of the more effective Mk 43, which required a special (Mk 32) triple launcher. The short torpedo tubes now (1957) replaced dropping gear and also the fixed Hedgehogs originally specified.

Thus far, considerable development in ASW weapons had had little impact on the primarily AAW character of SCB 142. ASROC was another matter, as it required for its control the very large new SQS-23 sonar. The size of this device was a direct consequence of the need to pass to lower frequencies in order to achieve "a detection range of at least 10,000 yards." The SCB began to consider the deployment of ASROC in March 1957. Quite clearly, all the destroyers and frigates of FY 58 (SCB 155 and SCB 172—see below) should have ASROC. What of DLG 6? The units of this class might be completed before ASROC and SQS-23 were available in any numbers;

Little changed by almost seven years of service, the *Farragut* steamed through the North Atlantic on 22 June 1967. Note the ECM array (probably SLQ-12) at the foot of her tripod foremast, with passive ECM radomes on two levels above.

moreover, to buy ASROC for these ships would mean the sacrifice of the No. 2 5-inch gun forward—and a retreat from the predominantly AAW character of the frigate.

The advantages of ASROC, even as compared to RAT, were such that there could be little question of its adoption. Indeed, it was suggested that without ASROC the fleet would have very little chance of killing fast submarines in the numbers the Soviets would soon have; moreover, it was precisely those fast submarines that would threaten the fast carrier task force. The cost of the back-fit would be a single 5-inch gun and the adoption of the new (and massive) SQS-23 sonar, at a cost of about $2 million per ship. A hull dome rather than a bow dome was chosen because it would permit the program to proceed much faster, as BuShips was already familiar with ship characteristics with hull-mounted sonars, whereas the bow dome presented entirely new problems due to the large bulge on the bow that was expected greatly to affect shiphandling characteristics. A similar decision was taken with respect to the DDGs then under construction; FY 60 and 61 DDGs, however, incorporated a bow sonar. ASROC also required additional electrical power and the substitution of a new Mk 111 fire control system for the Mk 105 associated with the earlier underwater weapons. The increased electrical load in turn increased fuel consumption, and thus somewhat reduced endurance—a reduction more than balanced, in the case of some of the DDGs, by improved hull performance due to the bow bulge of their sonars. The DLGs derived no such benefit, however.

Delays in the ASROC program are reflected in the completion of the first few frigates with neither gun nor ASROC in No. 2 position; however, all did receive the ASROC "pepperbox" there in the end.

One might reasonably argue that the 1956/57 decision to mount ASROC in the missile frigates—the later SCB 172 project included it from the first—constituted an admission that fast nuclear submarines would ultimately be able to attack the fast task forces; certainly, American experience of the period suggested as much. Although air/missile attack was clearly still the dominant threat, something beyond mere warning of the presence of a submarine was needed. Another factor must have been the inability of the DDEs to keep up with the postwar carriers, which in 1956 were only beginning to enter service—but would dominate the carrier force by the late sixties when the new frigates would be in service.

DLG 6 was the first keel-up missile ship in the Navy, but its design showed marks of its all-gun origin. The next DLG, the *Leahy*, did not. On 31 May 1956 Admiral Sanders, chairman of the Standing Committee on the Long-Range Shipbuilding and Conversion Plan suggested to the chairman, SCB, "that Talos, Terrier, and Tartar new construction ships in FY 58 and all succeeding years be provided with missile installations forward and aft," and "that very serious consideration be given to the establishment of higher minimum missile capacities per launcher in both new construction and conversion ships. The austere and compromise arrangements that have been accepted to date, despite the space, weight, and fiscal considerations involved, leave much

The *Leahy* was surely one of the most futuristic warships of her time, with Terrier fore and aft, and combined mast-stacks ("macks"). Her bow anchor indicates a bow sonar (SQS-23 in this case).

to be desired from the standpoint of operational endurance." Hence the SCB recommended for FY 58 a double-ended missile frigate, SCB 172.

A staff proposal of October 1956 called for a ship "to screen fast task forces against enemy air, submarine, and surface threats." It would form part of the coordinated air and ASW defense system of the task force and, like its predecessors, would be expected to control aircraft. In previous classes a 5-in./54 gun had been retained to provide a residual antiship and shore bombardment capacity; Terrier had too small a warhead to be very useful—especially in small numbers—in either role. However, it now had a nuclear warhead option, and in 1956 it did not yet seem that the use of tactical nuclear weapons would be severely restricted. Hence the staff proposal listed among the missions of SCB 172 "to defend against surface threats with nuclear missiles and light calibre guns" and "to bombard with nuclear missiles."

Mk 10 Terrier launching systems were to be mounted fore and aft; the "light calibre guns" were a pair of twin 3-in./50s. The ASW battery consisted of ASROC and a pair of triple Mk 32 torpedo tubes. By replacing the forward gun with a missile launcher, the designers could double the Terrier magazine capacity to about 80 missiles. The secondary character of the ASW mission showed in the absence of reloads

for ASROC and for the short torpedo tubes; on the other hand, there was the big SQS-23 sonar required for ASROC. Performance was expected to match that of DLG 6: 35 knots on trial, 5,000 miles—later increased to 8,000 nm.—at 20 knots.

There would be the usual forest of electronics. Each twin Terrier launcher required a pair of big SPG-55 radars (backup optical fire control was also to be provided); also a big SPS-29 long-range air search radar; and the new pencil-beam SPS-39, which would take over the height-finder/intercept radar role. In addition Air Early Warning terminal gear and the usual mass of radios were required, as well as TACAN, of course, which the characteristics described as an "azimuth short-range air navigation system."

BuShips produced two sketch studies: A, with DLG 6 machinery in a modified DLG 6 hull; and B, with DLG 6 machinery in a modified DL 1 hull. The former was a forecastle type, but B was able to exceed requirements by accommodating 120 Terriers. On the other hand, neither appeared capable of making the required speeds: A would make about 34.8 knots on trial; B, despite the greater length that should have reduced her wave-making resistance, only 33.8. Both were expected to achieve the required endurance. Displacements would be, respectively, 3,970 and 5,000 tons light and 5,375 and 6,525 tons fully loaded;

Scheme B at least was certainly a light cruiser. Costs matched: $56.7 ($50.5 repeat) million for A, $66.6 ($54.2) for B; a repeat DLG 6 was expected, by comparison, to cost $45 million.

Scheme A was chosen for development, as it would be smaller and less expensive than one derived from Scheme B, although it would also fail to meet the speed requirements of the original characteristics. It was envisaged as an SCB 142 with a Terrier installation forward in lieu of the two 5-in./54s then intended for mounting there. Sacrifices, compared with the Scheme B originally favored, included a reduction in Terrier stowage from 120 to 80 rounds. The CIC would have to be enlarged very considerably, and this would almost certainly make stowage of ASROC reloads impossible.

There was some relaxation of the requirement for a speed margin over the fast carriers. The Op-05 (DCNO Air) member of the SCB commented that

> while it is recognized that a speed margin over the carriers is desirable for smart station keeping, maneuvering, disposition changes, etc., the requirement for this additional speed is rapidly disappearing. As new construction carriers join the operating forces, launch and recovery speeds will tend to recede from the high-percentage maximums currently required, except for occasional special situations. Additionally, the threat of nuclear attack and increased fleet air defense requirements has forced our dispositions to assume a considerably dispersed formation. Obviously the requirements for exact station keeping are not as stringent. In view of these lessened requirements for excess speed in escorts and the considerable increase in construction cost, it is recommended that the subject vessels be designed with no excess speed, or at most, not more than one to one and a half knots excess speed over the major combatant which they will normally escort, the aircraft carrier.

Since the 3-in./50 had only VT-fuzed ammunition and an antiaircraft fire control system, SCB 172 would have no conventional antisurface capability. This was acceptable in 1956, in view of the nuclear antisurface capability built into Terrier, and also in view of the decline in interest in antiship warfare. The interest in limited war, with its shore bombardments and amphibious landings, was still only in its infancy. Op-03 justified the retention of any guns at all:

> A determined and coordinated air attack might well saturate the available guided missile defenses and evolve into a short range melee, in which case the close-in gun battery would be highly desirable for both self-defense and task force defense. Additionally, the light gun battery is required for use against submarines forced to surface at close range as well as against light surface units which these screening ships may encounter. Since the minimum range re-

quirements for such tasks fall within the boost phase of the TERRIER missile, redesign of the TERRIER missile to provide effectiveness against targets at such short ranges does not appear to be feasible.

Circulation of the SCB 172 characteristics among the bureaus elicited the suggestion that magazine stowage for ASROC be provided, but it is not clear to what extent this represented a shift towards greater interest in ASW or simply an interest in the protection of the missiles.

Fear of sea damage to the forward launcher was a major obstacle to acceptance of any double-ended design. For example, in reference to proposals that SCB 142 be double-ended, the then chairman of the SCB, Rear Admiral Mendenhall, wrote in January 1955 that

> from a purely mechanical point of view I cannot believe that either the present or prospective launcher can long survive on the forecastle of the Frigate. . . . Our experience with the forward 5-inch mounts on destroyers has proven that they are operable. . . . There have been occasions when No. 1 mount could not be safely used but when No. 2 mount could be. . . . Under similar conditions I am sure the rocket launcher could not be used, even if it stayed aboard. . . . Loading the launcher and firing (it) in any other than favorable sea and weather conditions would be impossible. . . .

Effort therefore went into improved dryness forward, which turned out to require a prominently knuckled hull. Displacement continued to grow: 5,146 tons light, 7,588.8 fully loaded, an advance even on the huge *Norfolk*, DL 1.

Probably the single greatest contributor to the growth of the SCB 172 design, as compared to the earlier DLG 6, was the requirement for greatly increased endurance, 8,000 instead of 5,000 nm., which alone added about 800 tons of fuel. In addition, CIC and WCS (Weapon Control Space) requirements were trebled, partly to take into account the doubling of the Terrier battery. The DLG 6 propulsion plant was retained to save design cost; however, great increases in requirements for emergency electrical power encouraged the designers to consider using gas turbines instead of diesels; the class was completed with one 300-kw gas turbine and one 300-kw diesel to supplement four 1,000-kw ship service turbogenerators. The compromise between gas turbines (which were very compact) and diesels was necessary given the great uptake requirements imposed by the former.

Hull design was strongly affected by the increase in required endurance; for example, transom immersion was considerably reduced to lower power requirements at 20 knots, even though somewhat more resistance was experienced at full speed. This practice followed design experience with the SCB 131-class ocean escorts (*Claud Jones* class, see chapter

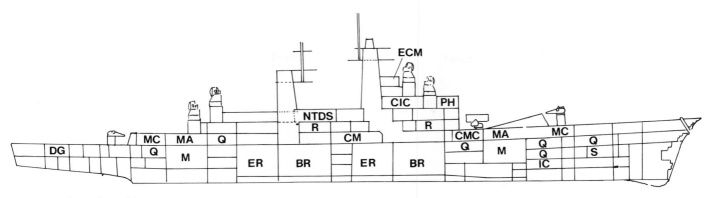

DLG 16 inboard profile

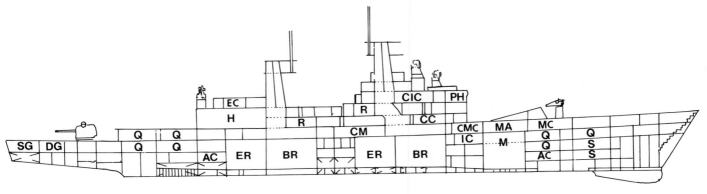

DLG 28 inboard profile

12); it was also expected to improve seakeeping. Model tests with the DLG 6 led to the form of bow bulb employed to house the big SQS-23 sonar; it was the optimum location from the point of view of resistance and also was preferred by Preliminary Design. However, care had to be taken to protect the fragile sonar dome from damage by the anchor, and in the end a steeply raked bow carried an anchor free of it. Similar practice has been followed on all later ships with bow sonars.

The general arrangement of the superstructure was determined by a combination of blast problems, the need for a very large CIC, and problems with the interference between boats, ASROC, and stacks and stack gases. Hull volume had to increase very substantially to accommodate the large forward missile magazine, a considerably larger complement, and much more fuel oil; the solution was increased length and an upper-deck hull form. Interference was sharply reduced by locating the ASROC launcher on the upper deck forward, with the loader of the forward missile launcher acting as a protective glacis, and by the introduction of "macks," combined mast-stacks.

Nine of these *Leahy* (DLG 16)-class missile frigates were built, under the FY 58 (DLG 16–18) and FY 59

programs. DLG 19–22, planned for FY 58, were deferred in June 1958 in view of funding shortages. Another DLG had been dropped in the presubmission stage. DLGN 25, the first nuclear frigate (FY 59) was essentially a nuclear version of the *Leahy* class, at least in so far as her weapon system was concerned (see chapter 14).

Three more DLGs authorized for FY 60 were deferred to FY 61 in order to release funds for Polaris. They emerged as the lead ships of a new class, which became in effect the final development of the series of DLs extending from the *Mitscher*. As first envisaged in May 1958, the FY 60 frigate was to be a repeat of the FY 58/FY 59 type with the new SQS-26 sonar, a new air search radar (SPS-13 in place of SPS-29), and dynamic roll stabilization. These features were expected to add about 700 tons to the full-load displacement and about 23 feet to the length of the ship; more importantly, it was expected that the lead ship cost would rise to $75 million ($59 million repeat) from a (1958 estimate) DLG 16 cost of $57 ($54) million; the quoted DLG 16 lead cost is low because it is really the cost of a slightly improved repeat DLG 16. The extra length and the bulbous-bow effect of SQS-26 together would cancel out any added resist-

The *Leahy*s all underwent AAW modernization under SCB Project 244; the *Leahy* is shown emerging from Philadelphia Navy Yard after completion, 14 June 1968. The major visible changes were installation of NTDS (requiring the new midships deckhouse and the communications antenna in her bows), SPS-48 on the foremast (interfacing with NTDS), and a new Mk 76 Mod 5 missile fire-control system with improved SPG-55B missile guidance radars fore and aft. Underway replenishment gear is folded down atop the after missile magazine.

ance due to the extra displacement, so that the proposed FY 60 frigate would duplicate the performance of its predecessor.

These revised characteristics were set against characteristics for a greatly improved DDG that was also proposed for FY 60 and is described below; by 1958, DDG and DLG capabilities (and costs) were not too far apart, and the two types were being lumped together in future building plans. In fact, the last of the DLGs, the *Belknap*, originated as a modified DDG.

A major development at this time was the capability to fire ASROC from a Terrier launcher, i.e., to do away entirely with considerable space and weight. A study had been requested by the chairman of the Standing Committee on Shipbuilding (30 April 1959), and that December BuOrd indicated that there would be no substantial problem. ASROC could replace Terrier on a missile-for-missile basis, except that available space would not permit ASROCs to be stowed in adjacent positions: maximum loading would be 20 missiles. On the other hand, the Tartar launcher would require extensive modification.

In view of the sacrifice in AAW capability entailed by loading with ASROC (e.g., 45 seconds to replace an ASROC on the launcher with a stowed Terrier), BuOrd considered the change most useful in double-ended ships, i.e., in the DLG 16 class.

In May 1960 the CNO suggested that the combined Terrier-ASROC feature be applied to FY 61 DLGs; space saved would be available for DASH. There was also some hope of adding SQS-26 and NTDS. These proposals were warmly supported by Commander,

Cruiser-Destroyer Force, Pacific Fleet (24 June 1960):

> The inclusion of a multipurpose Terrier launcher capable of firing ASROC is strongly endorsed. . . . The development of a dual-purpose launcher is considered a logical step toward a longer range surface launched ASW weapon. With the advent of longer range detection devices, the maximum early attack capability should be incorporated. It is therefore recommended that the proposal which provides the greatest growth potential in the development of such an increased range weapon be adopted.
>
> A capability for DASH control is an essential requirement for the DLG 16 class, as it is for any new construction which has an ASW potential, and COM-CRUDESPAC supports fully the proposal that DASH control facilities be installed. To realize the full potential of DASH, there also should be provision for complete support facilities, including hangar, landing platform and servicing equipment. However, should all of the latter not prove feasible, minimal DASH landing facilities should be provided.
>
> Installation of AN/SQS-26 in lieu of AN/SQS-23 sonar is strongly recommended in view of the anticipated bottom bounce and convergence zone capabilities and improved signal processing techniques. The longer range detection capability of the AN/SQS-26 sonar would greatly enhance the value of the ship as a part of a coordinated ASW system in the defense of a fast striking force. . . .

The CNO approved these changes to the basic DLG in July 1960, and directed that the three DLGs of FY 61 be built to the improved (SCB 172A) design. The new DLG 26 class would incorporate SQS-26, the

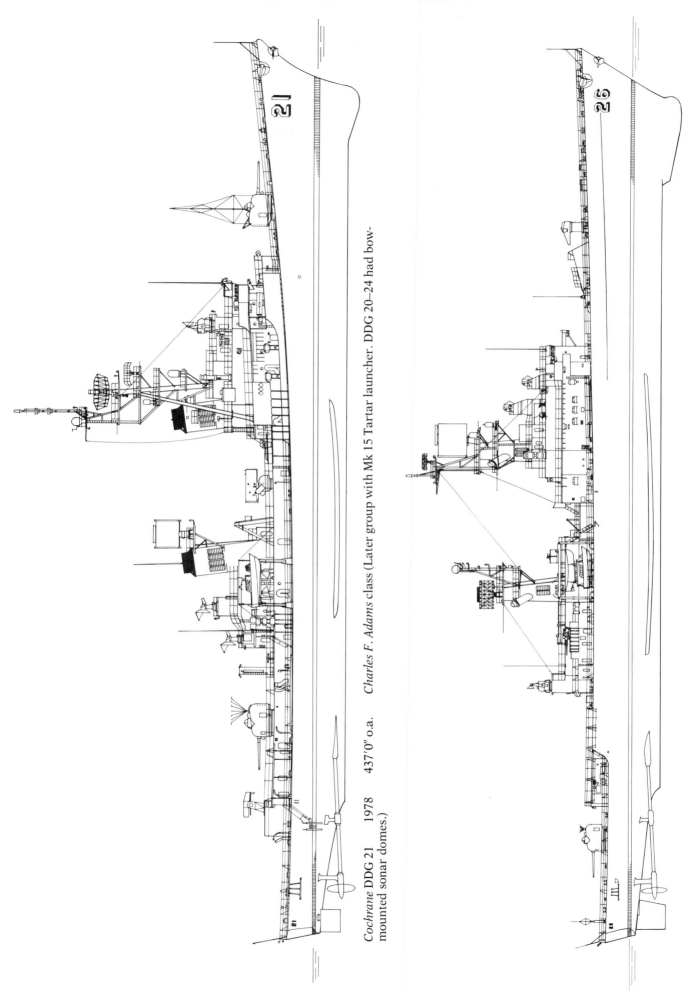

Cochrane DDG 21   1978   437'0" o.a.   *Charles F. Adams* class (Later group with Mk 15 Tartar launcher. DDG 20–24 had bow-mounted sonar domes.)

Belknap DLG 26   1965   547'0" o.a.   *Belknap* class

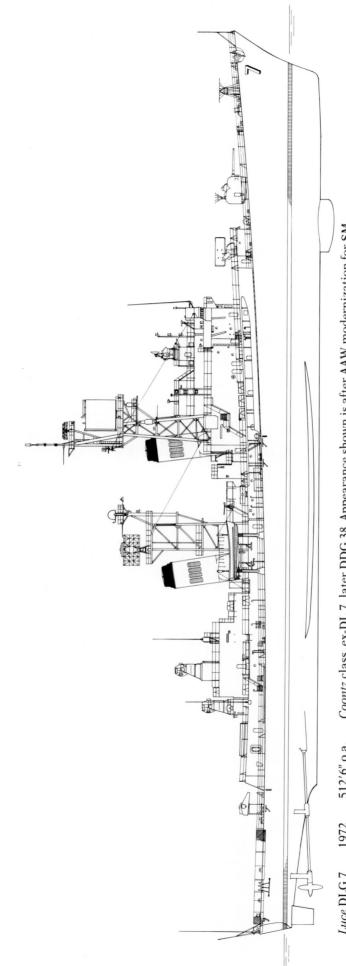

Luce DLG 7   1972   512'6" o.a.   *Coontz* class, ex-DL 7, later DDG 38. Appearance shown is after AAW modernization for SM–1(ER) missiles. Two twin 3" guns were removed in the process, but C³ and fire control were greatly improved.

In this 30 April 1969 photograph the *Belknap* does not quite resemble the austere destroyer she was originally intended to be. The helicopter pad was provided with DASH in mind, but it was large enough to accommodate substantial manned helicopters.

improved missile guidance radar (SPG-55B vice 55A), NTDS (and its associated High Capacity Communications Equipment), a hangar for three DASH (or one HU2K utility helo), and—for the first time—Terrier launchers equipped to fire ASROC in place of the familiar ASROC "pepperbox." It turned out that these changes required the insertion in the DLG 16 hull of a 14-foot section amidships, between the forward engine room and after fire room; and since the hull had considerable fore-and-aft curvature at that point, the new section could not merely be a parallel-sided plug. In addition, the superstructure was moved six feet forward (a move made possible by the elimination of ASROC) to clear the DASH landing space; the DASH hangar was incorporated in the after superstructure. The enlarged hull implied an increase in frictional resistance, which dominates ship resistance at low speeds. Hence the same fuel load sufficed only for 7,100 rather than 8,000 nm. at 20 knots. Other alterations followed from a growth in complement of 3 CPOs and 20 enlisted men.

A contract design with these characteristics was completed on 15 November 1960. But the ship finally constructed as DLG 26, the *Belknap*, turned out to be the SCB 172A design modified to match a set of more austere characteristics (SCB 212) evolved from the line of missile destroyers (DDG), themselves a kind of austere DLG (see below).

Just as destroyers continued to be planned alongside the new fast task force escorts, missile destroyers were built to fill out the numbers of the DLGs. The need for missile ships was so urgent that Tartar DDGs were ordered well before Tartar itself had flown in any form. There was, however, good reason for optimism, in that Tartar used many Terrier components. In any case, as of mid-1955 the FY 57 program did not yet include the DDG, and the LRO badly wanted at least two years' production of destroyers

to incorporate some missile, probably Terrier, to fill out the gaps in fleet air defense. Feasibility studies for the installation of Tartar in a destroyer hull began late in August 1955. The first studies were based on what amounted to a cut-down DLG 9 configuration, with two 5-in./54s *and* a RAT launcher forward, Tartar aft, quintuple torpedo tubes between the funnels, and a 10,000-yard sonar. This would amount to a drastic change from a *Forrest Sherman*—the bridge structure, for example, being moved back about 40 feet. The result would be midway between a destroyer and a frigate, and it was rejected in favor of a revision of the existing *Forrest Sherman* design. At a 15 September meeting, Admiral Mendenhall of the SCB asked that the hull and machinery of the new ship duplicate the existing type, so as to simplify production. The radar suit would include a stabilized SPS-12 for long-range air search and one of the new SPS-26 (predecessor of SPS-39) pencil-beam three-dimensional radars. The need for the latter was not yet firm, but soon would be, and there was, at first, hope that matters might be simplified by the consolidation of gun and missile fire control in a single system, then called MAGIC. This optimism, too, proved misguided.

These sketch schemes each showed one of the three 5-in./54s of the original destroyer replaced by Tartar, the nearest 3-in./50 by an underway replenishment area, and the other by RAT, using a new twin-arm launcher (with 12 missiles in reserve). RAT would require the new 10,000-yard SQS-23 sonar, and there would be six Mk 43 homing torpedoes with a Mk 27X launcher, and a single depth-charge track aft. The main battery was to be supplemented by a pair of twin 20 mm. Admiral Mendenhall rejected the placement of Tartar forward in view of heavy-weather interference. No. 3 position aft was rejected in view of restrictions it would impose on the arc of fire of the 5-inch gun aft. It was also feared that vibration due to proximity to the screws would disrupt the missiles and their launcher.

It was rather optimistically hoped that the missile destroyer might carry 20 Tartars in stowage to supplement the 40 in ready service launchers, but they were eliminated to save space and weight. Finally, an SPS-27 "hemispheric" radar was added to the electronics list; it was abandoned in favor of the simpler frequency-scanner, which could perform its role as well as that of the usual height-finder.

By December, BuShips could begin tentative calculations for DDG production under the FY 57 program. In terms of armament, the principal remaining changes were the deletion of the torpedo tubes and the replacement of RAT by ASROC, to be mounted between the funnels in place of the former torpedo tubes. Although in theory this freed up the former forward 3-in./50 position, it does not appear that any effort was made to reintroduce the light gun. As for the torpedo tubes, the SCB argued in August 1956 that ASROC (nuclear depth-charge variant) would have a significant mining effect against a cruiser at surface torpedo range, and that the 5-in./54, even with a hit probability of only 0.06 at 19,000 yards, would make 2.5 hits/barrel/minute. In a larger DLG, of course, there would also be Terrier to consider—a sure kill with its nuclear warhead, and considerable probability of damage even with its conventional one.

Hopes that the DDG would duplicate the *Forrest Sherman* hull were premature, although in the end the power plant of the earlier ship was retained, with improved access to the boilers through a two-foot lengthening of the boiler rooms. The length increase of 13 feet was justified on the basis of a need to maintain speed (which was permitted to fall half a knot to a design speed of 32.5 knots) and also in view of the need to accommodate the new SQS-23 sonar, modular CIC, and ASROC or RAT. Eighteen inches of beam were added to preserve stability, given about 600 tons more full load displacement. Hull depth was actually reduced to lower the vertical center of gravity.

There were also, of course, extensive radar arrays associated with target acquisition and designation. These did not add quite as much as they might otherwise have because DD 931 in any case had been expected to be capable of performing some radar picket duties. Some indication of the actual weight cost of Tartar and ASROC may be found in the reconstruction of four DD 931s as missile destroyers, 1965–67: Tartar replaced *both* aft 5-in./54 mounts, a much heavier mainmast was fitted, and full load displacement rose about 100 to 200 tons.

One reason for the tightness of the SCB 155 design was that it took into account the *weight* but not the

volume cost of the new missile systems. In distinct contrast to former weapon systems, missiles require large volume at a relatively low weight, so that on a given displacement, missile ships seem bloated. The volume requirements in turn drive up the weight of the ship structure, so that armament shrinks as a fraction of the ship's displacement. A NAVSEC naval architect, Philip Sims, described the SCB 155s as

> graceful and balanced; they do not seem to suffer from the bloating effect of modern weapon like other American destroyers. . . . [But] the DDGs are not consistent internally with other fleet destroyers. [They have] austere supporting systems and suffocating internal compressions—cramped crew quarters, jammed machinery spaces, and minimal support areas. . . . [They are] short-legged . . . uncomfortable to serve in and a severe problem to maintain. . . .

Sims also suggests that the DDGs were not modernized largely because of their internal congestion.

In April 1956, the issue of Tartar effectiveness from a heavily rolling ship, i.e., at low angles of elevation, was discussed. The Applied Physics Laboratory (APL) strongly suggested that Tartar be moved to the former No. 3 position (and raised to the 01 level), the alternative being to raise the existing Tartar launcher at a great cost in top weight. For blast purposes Tartar could be considered the principal destroyer air defense weapon, and its effective firing arc was calculated on the basis that the after 5-inch gun would be in the stowed position when Tartar fired. A 5 percent reduction in gun effectiveness was traded for a 10 percent improvement in overall Tartar effectiveness, particularly at low angles. Underway replenishment was simplified, compartmentation improved, and overall Tartar blast reduced. On the other hand, the lengthening of the deckhouse cut 40 tons from the original 100-ton margin; 15 tons was recovered by the elimination of the depth-charge track and the 20 mm. guns.

Twenty-three DDGs of this *C.F. Adams* class were built: 8 under FY 57, 5 under FY 58, 5 under FY 59, 3 under FY 60, and 2 under FY 61. A variety of improvements were introduced in the course of production. Thus, FY 59 and later ships (DDG 15–23) had single-arm (Mk 13) rather than twin-arm (Mk 11) Tartar launchers. FY 60 and FY 61 units (DDG 20–24) had their SQS-23 sonars bow-mounted, which change shows externally in the bow location of their anchors. Australia and West Germany both bought somewhat modified versions. The Australian units (DDG 25–27) have Ikara, an Australian ASW weapon, amidships; the German ships (DDG 28–30) have "macks."

The numbers actually built were hardly those originally envisaged. Thus the October 1956 version of the FY 58 program shows 8 DDGs; the next April,

Although initially conceived as a *Forrest Sherman* with one 5-inch gun replaced by a Tartar missile launcher, the *Charles F. Adams* class actually had a considerably larger hull, with much more freeboard forward. Note the vertical ECM array low on the forward leg of her tripod foremast, and the SPS-39 three-dimensional radar, associated with her missile system, mounted on her after funnel. The twin-arm Mk 11 Tartar launching system aft accommodated 42 missiles, but was considered unreliable.

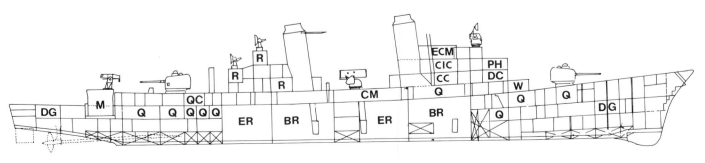

DDG 21 inboard

Later units of the *Adams* class had the improved single-arm, 40-missile Mk 13 launching system, as in the *Berkeley*, shown in 1970. Her air-search radar is SPS-40, rather than the SPS-37 of earlier ships. Jamming antennas (SLQ-12) can be discerned above a small platform flanking the enclosure between her mast legs. Note, too, the shield for a Fanfare torpedo countermeasure on her fantail, visible to the left of the missile launcher.

on the other hand, an early cut of FY 59 shows the five actually bought that year. That October the budget approved by the CNO and the Secretary of the Navy showed only 4 DDGs for FY 60.

These figures reflect the fiscal hemorrhage that was then afflicting the naval shipbuilding budget and was a continuous burden on any attempt to achieve wholesale replacement of existing ships by missile types. In August 1956, for example, the CNO had to report that the existing Shipbuilding and Conversion Plan could not be met within the funding ceiling; four DDGs and one nuclear submarine, as well as many landing craft, would have to be deferred to FY 58. Apparently it first became evident in 1958 that costs would severely disrupt the shipbuilding and conversion program. Two solutions were proposed: full-funding and end-costing. In full-funding, no new ship could be awarded unless the current shipbuilding balance sufficed to pay for the *current*

estimated cost of ships already under construction, the result being the deferment of new contracts. End-costing was introduced in FY 61. All ships in the budget, plus all not yet completed, were assigned end costs that incorporated wage and material inflation (at 5.8 percent) and allowed for design-concept evolution, but not for any changes in their original characteristics. The FY 60 program showed extensive cancellations to balance off costs. These included 2 DEs and 1 LPH that had been deferred from FY 57, as well as 4 DLGs and 2 CG conversions deferred from FY 59. In the transition to end-costing in the FY 61 program, 3 DLGs and 1 CG conversion were dropped.

The long-range program, LRO-58 which was designed in 1958, called for the end of DDG 2 production with eight ships (seven of them in FY 60), after which the solution to the numbers problem would be achieved through production of a new series of

Final units of the *Adams* class had their SQS-23 sonars in their bows, indicated in this view of the *Richard E. Byrd* by the position of her bow anchor and her more sharply raked stem.

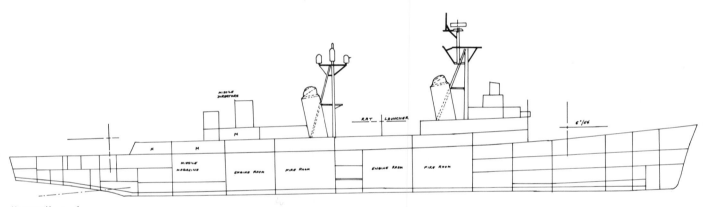

"DEG" study

missile ships armed with a new Super-Tartar—later Typhon (MR)—missile: 4 in FY 61, 8 in FY 62, 10 in FY 63, 4 in FY 64, 6 each in FY 65 and FY 66, a total of 38 units at a unit cost of $42.5 million. These ships would replace both DDGs and DLGs, since Super-Tartar would be better than Terrier. In fact, things did not work out quite that way. As early as October 1960, the CNO had retreated to a request for nine new-design DDGs (which became SCB 212) armed with Tartar or perhaps Terrier, at a unit cost of $50 million.

The Atlantic Destroyer Force, which in 1956 had enormous influence, was less than enthusiastic concerning Tartar, which it considered clearly inferior as a surface-to-air missile. In a series of Air Defense Symposia, DesLant hammered out a destroyer force "party line": there should be no further attempt to differentiate between destroyer and frigate, and instead a general purpose ship of approximately *Forrest Sherman* size should be built, armed with Terrier and with a single 5-in./54 forward, and powered, as soon as possible, by a nuclear reactor. The Terrier

requirement appears to have been inspired by the apparent success of the *Gyatt* conversion, which some in the destroyer force believed would be a prototype for mass conversion of the *Gearing*s. BuShips tried to design a Terrier DDG, but with only limited success.

Thus, an August 1956 study of a "minimum Terrier Ship" (DEG) showed that to accommodate 40 missiles as well as the new long-range ASW weapon (RAT, later ASROC) the *Forrest Sherman* hull would have to be gutted of nearly half its boiler power (reduction to 40,000 shp, 28 knots). In the proposed configuration, Terrier would replace both aft 5-in./54 guns, and RAT or ASROC the amidships torpedo tubes. The result was to cost $44 million ($36 million for follow-on ships) as compared to $40 million for DD 940. Part of the increase in cost was the big sonar required for RAT/ASROC.

This result inspired an SCB request (11 December 1956) for a study of how much DDG 2 would have to grow, were Terrier to be substituted for both Tartar and No. 2 5-inch gun; it was hoped that the result

Scheme	SCB 155	"DEG"	A	B	B-1	C	SCB 172
Light Displacement	3,210	2,650	3,370	3,690	3,800	3,550	4,470
Trial	4,180	—	4,330	5,240	5,400	4,790	6,105
Full Load	4,520	3,850	4,670	5,850	6,050	5,230	6,720
LWL	420	400	440	480	450	460	510
Beam	47	44	47	48	49	47	53
Draft (full)	15	14.5	15.5	17.5	17.5	16.5	17.6
SHP (thousands)	70	40	70	70	85	70	85
Sustained Speed	31.5	28	31.8	31.2	30.2	31.5	32.0
Endurance (20 kts)	4,300	4,000	4,300	8,000	8,000	7,000	8,000
5"/54	2	1	1	1	1	1	—
Complement	354	—	360	360	360	360	392
Lead (millions)	—	$44	$48	$49	—	—	$59
Follow-on (millions)	$34	$36	$37	$38	—	—	$42

could figure in the FY 59 program. On 9 March 1957 the chairman, SCB, asked for a Terrier DDG with endurance increased to 8,000 nm.—i.e., a fast task force escort by endurance standards then in force. These studies were presented to the Standing Committee, Shipbuilding and Conversion, and to the SCB, in May and June 1957. They are compared to SCB 155 and to SCB 172, shown above:

All of the Terrier DDGs were to have one twin launcher with the usual 40 missiles, one ASROC, and Mk 32 tubes. At the time, it was observed that "all of the studies are somewhat 'unbalanced' designs when compared to past ships in that they have excessive weather deck area for the installed armament." This "unbalance" may be taken to reflect a shift, with larger missiles, to *volume*—rather than *weight*—critical ships.

In the series above, Scheme C was included for comparison with DDG 2 modified for 6,000 nm. endurance. B-1 was an attempt to hold down length to the minimum of Scheme A without loss of speed as compared to B. No lead-ship cost is associated with DDG 2 in view of its production status in FY 59.

The next variation produced striking results. In 1957 BuShips had under advanced development a pressure-fired boiler that promised great power in a very compact package. A comparison sheet of 19 June 1957 shows:

Scheme*	F	G	H
Light Displacement	3,090	3,310	3,550
Trial	4,060	4,490	5,060
Full Load	4,400	4,920	5,640
LWL	420	440	465
Beam	47	48	48
Draft (full)	15	15.5	17
SHP (thousands)	70	70	70
Sustained Speed	31.6	31.2	30.6
Endurance (20 knots)	4,300	6,000	8,000

* Each has one 5-in./54, ASROC, twin Terrier aft.

Note that F is actually smaller than the much less capable Tartar DDG; in effect Scheme G outperforms DLG 6 on a far smaller hull. The reason they were not put into production at once was that the pressure-fired plant was not ready until somewhat later (DE 1040 class, FY 62).

In December 1957, the SCB established as its long-range policy a requirement that DLGs and DDGs have an endurance of 8,000 nm. at 20 knots. In fact, this set of standardized requirements (SCB memo 324-57) makes very little distinction between the DDG and DLG. The DLG fired Terrier, the DDG either Tartar *or* Terrier; both were to have sustained speeds of 32 knots (i.e., to have a margin of 2 knots over a 30-knot carrier).

In May 1958, the chairman of the Standing Committee circularized DesLant and CruDesPac on behalf of Admiral Burke, who noted that since the DLG cost about 50 percent more than a DDG, he urgently sought some compromise that would leave him with a large enough escort force:

In light of the development of the 26 sonar and the feeling that radars more efficient than the SPS-29/ 26 now planned for DLGs and DDGs and the thought that the DDG should have two Tartars instead of one, the SCB developed new Characteristics . . . the Chief, BuShips, in his letter of 20 May, has estimated the costs of the 1960 model DLG [SCB 172A, see above] at $75/59 million [lead/follow] compared to $54 for the 1958 follow-on, and $57–63/$41–45 million compared to a $35 million repeat DDG. . . .

For the DDG, Admiral Rose, chairman of the Standing Committee, proposed to replace a second 5-in./54 aft with Tartar, to add SQS-26 and roll stabilization, and to increase endurance to 8,000 nm. at 20 knots. The sonar and roll stabilization would require an entirely new design, whereas the additional Tartar might be bought at the cost of 15 berths. Fuel oil for 8,000 nm. would enlarge the DDG to DLG size—and cost. Meanwhile, available funds began to shrink, as the Polaris program accelerated and as pressure built for a second nuclear carrier, to follow the *Enterprise* already under construction. Thus an alternative improvement, in which DDG endurance would be increased to 6,000 nm., was also to be considered.

On 22 May BuShips reported three studies:

Scheme	DDG 2	I	II	III
Full load	4,485	4,950	5,550	6,500
LOA	432	460	485	515
Beam	47	48	50	50
Draft (over dome)	21	27	28	29
SHP (thousands)	70	70	85	85
Sustained speed	29.7	29.2	30.4	29.9
Endurance (20 knots)	4,300	4,300	6,000	8,000
Lead (millions)	$38	$51	$60	$63
Follow-on (millions)	$35	$47	$43	$45

For all practical purposes, III is a frigate; she is considerably larger than DLG 6. I, II, and III all have the FY 60 armament: two Tartar, one 5-in./54, AS-ROC, two Mk 32 tubes. All have SQS-26 and SPS-13. In fact, these revised designs were considered far too expensive, and the only new feature of the FY 60 DDG turned out to be its bow-mounted sonar. No new features appeared in the FY 61 DDG; instead, the SCB turned its attention to a radically more austere type for FY 62; in 1960 the price of a repeat DDG 2 was quoted as $41 million.

In view of the prospective improvements in Tartar, an ad hoc committee on escorts chaired by Captain D.E. Willman proposed at the same time that from FY 60 onward there be only two types, a DDG and a DE; from FY 62 onward a new and smaller missile cruiser (CG) armed with the Super-Talos (later Extended Range Typhon) missile would merge with the existing series of DLGs. At this time it was expected that a new design lead ship would appear every fourth year, staggered to get the advantages of follow-on cost reductions in the net shipbuilding budget. Moreover, given the advent of the Typhon series in the near future, it seemed wise to curtail existing programs. Thus, if the 13 DLGs already planned for the FY 58 and 59 programs were to be retained, it would be well to eliminate entirely any DLG planned for FY 60, looking toward the emergence of the Typhon DLG/CG in FY 62. DDG production incorporating Super-Tartar could begin as early as FY 61. This would allow for a new DE in FY 60 (SCB 199, see chapter 15). To some limited extent missile firepower might be maintained by the conversion of cruisers in FY 60 and 61.

Given the DDG revisions proposed for the new ships, the Super-Tartar DDG envisaged by this ad hoc escort committee would have two missile launchers, one 5-in./54, ASROC, SQS-26, torpedo tubes, and DASH, as well as a sustained speed of 32 knots, an endurance of 8,000 nm. at 20 knots, and roll stabilization, all on about 6,500 tons.

Given these depressing results, the CNO could only turn back to some form of austerity to achieve the numbers he needed. Those numbers remained, in 1959, both considerable and, apparently, unattainable: by 1959, the LRO was calling for a total of 108 DDGs in the active fleet. Austere Tartar conversions of four DL 2s and 18 *Forrest Sherman*s would provide a total of 88 DDGs and DLGs, but the obsolescence of some of these ships would make this approach to the force objective somewhat deceptive. Nor would the objective of 18 missile cruisers (CG), attendant on a total of 18 carriers, be approached effectively, even with one new-construction nuclear cruiser, the two *Boston*s, the six *Cleveland*-class conversions, and the three *Albany*s—making up a total of 12 ships.

The lesson drawn from the attempts to redesign the DDG for FY 60 appears to have been that the missile system was the chief villain; austerity applied to it might yet save the day. Bethlehem Steel tried to capitalize on this by proposing its own lightweight DDG, on a *Benson*-size hull, but it was rejected as far too cramped and ineffective. A much later development of this project, submitted in September 1961, impacted strongly on the FY 65 ASW destroyer, project Seahawk, by virtue of its advanced (COGAG) gas-turbine power plant.

A 21 August 1959 letter from the chairman of the SCB to BuShips outlined a design desired for FY 62

to explore the feasibility of a destroyer design with adequate endurance and speed for all types of operations, with an advanced ASW suite including SQS-26 sonar, but lacking the complex and costly surface and air defense armament, and also the complex electronic equipment incorporated into the DDG 2 characteristics in an attempt to provide a destroyer design priced out at approximately $25 million, so that a reasonable number of advanced ASW ships can be included in the annual building program through 1970. . . . The type of austere Tartar proposed for the DDG 931 is envisaged, possibly with an improved fire control radar, but with a minimal air search radar. Utilization of 5 in./38 mounts, removed from FRAM destroyers and completely overhauled, is suggested to provide a proven, adequate anti-surface and bombardment capability at minimum cost.

Designed tasks would be

to operate offensively and defensively against submarines as part of a coordinated ASW system; to provide a *limited* self-defense against airborne attack; to provide a *limited* gun-fire capability against surface ships and in support of amphibious assault and land forces; to exercise *limited* air control for ASW, search, patrol and rescue missions.

This might almost be a specification for the *Spruance*, which is certainly not what we would think of as a DDG. Missile armament would be limited to an austere Tartar battery with not less than 12 missiles; on the other hand, there would be DASH and four long Mk 25 tubes. Even ASROC was deleted in hopes of cutting cost; but there would be SQS-26 and roll stabilization.

This was essentially a fast DE with a missile battery. Almost as an aside, the draft characteristics called for an increase in endurance (at 20 knots) to 6,000 nm. and the possible inclusion of NTDS. Sustained speed was to be the 30 knots of previous DDGs. Endurance and speed proved controlling factors: the resulting ship was 500 tons *larger* than the more complex DDG 2, even though 300 had been saved by the adoption of pressure-fired boilers. This austere destroyer came out to no less than $57 million (lead ship; $38 million for follow-ons). A Preliminary Design work sheet showed that on $25 million all that could be had would be 50,000 shp (29–30 knots), an endurance of 4,000 nm., and possibly SQS-23. The four long tubes would be replaced by Mk 32s, so that the ship would have no long-range ASW capability *except* DASH, i.e., no effective bad-weather standoff weapon at all.

The very large but nearly unarmed hull resulting from the original SCB directive seemed unbalanced. Preliminary Design tried to return to a more conventional DDG by reducing endurance to 4,500 nm. while retaining the pressure-forced plant; on this basis a better Tartar installation could be had at the cost of the long torpedo tubes. At $56 ($40) million this cannot have seemed a great bargain. The next step, therefore, was a minimum SQS-26 ship with endurance cut to 4,000 nm. This could be had on a full load displacement of 3,450 tons and a cost of $49 ($31) million. Such a ship approximated a *Gearing* in size, and inspired the next study—a *Gearing* conversion with austere Tartar and a forecastle replacing No. 1 gun. AAW capability would become mar-

ginal at about the same time the hull would be ready for scrapping. This was by far the cheapest alternative, only about $17 million in all.

It was also possible to push matters in the other direction. If indeed a fast task force escort required the long endurance, then the large hull should be used for a better battery. In particular the twin 5-in./38s could be replaced by a pair of single 3-in./50s; the weight saved could go into a Terrier launcher with provision for firing ASROC as well. This ship would cost $67 ($49) million; it soon led to a DLG, SCB 212 (see below).

All of these costs excluded NTDS—which would, however, be essential if a ship of modest battery were to be effective in a concerted screening operation. It was estimated that NTDS and its data link *alone* would add $6.9 million to the cost of the follow-on ship in any of the cases described above.

These "destroyer spectrum" studies are shown in the table below.

D is the converted FRAM. E has Terrier/ASROC in place of Tartar. F is a very austere type (SQS-23) inspired in part by a 2,440-ton 40,000-shp DDG proposed by Bethlehem Steel. All of these (Navy) designs incorporate DASH, and A, B, and E are roll-stabilized. The main search radar would have been the relatively inexpensive SPS-40.

In his letter of transmittal to the SCB, the Chief of BuShips used this series of studies to show the futility of a long-range austere DDG. Far better to spend a little more and produce a useful task force escort. In effect the BuShips comment recalled the advice of the Schindler Committee: build only the best (in limited numbers) and a mass-production austerity type: only DLG and DE/DEG. The application of this destroyer spectrum study to the ocean escorts will be discussed in greater detail below.

The SCB tended to go along with the BuShips reasoning. On 13 May it asked for a series of five variations, all to have a 70,000 shp plant (with the option of pressure firing), an endurance of 6,000 nm. at 20

	A	B	C	D	E	F
LWL	440	420	396	383	450	380
Beam	47	47	42	42	47	42
Full Load	5,000	4,450	3,450	3,500	5,050	3,200
SHP (thousands)	70	70	50	70	70	50
Sustained Speed	30.2	30.5	29.4	29.9	30.2	29.4
Endurance	6,000	4,500	2,000	3,400	6,000	4,000
Tartar	12	40	12	12	—	12
Twin 5-in./38	1	1	1	1	—	1
Single 3-in./50	—	—	—	—	2	—
Mk 25 TT	4	—	—	—	—	—
Mk 32 TT	—	2	2	2	2	2
Lead (millions)	$57	$56	$49	$21	$67	$48
Follow-on (millions)	$38	$40	$31	$17	$49	$30

Variation	1	2	3	4	5	E
Terrier/ASROC	X	X	—	—	—	X
Tartar	—	—	X	X	X	—
5 in./54	X	—	X	—	—	—
3 in./50 (twin)	—	2	—	2	—	2 (single)
5 in./38	—	—	—	—	1	—
Mk 37 torpedo	X	—	X	—	X	—
Cost (millions)	$72/57	$68/54.5	$66.8/53.2	$63.7/51	$64.3/50.7	$67/49 (no NTDS)

knots, SQS-26, and varying armament, all on a DLG 6 hull with DLG 16 bridge structure (for increased control spaces). Armaments considered were as shown in the table above.

The SCB favored Variation 1, 6,355 tons, 29.5 knots sustained speed, $63 million for a follow-on.

According to the design history (February 1961),

with only 70,000 SHP, the longer the hull, the better the maximum speed performance even though the full load displacement increased because of increased endurance oil requirements. On this basis it appeared preferable to stick with the flush deck design concept of DLG 9–15. We began also to . . . consider machinery box requirements for a PF [pressure-fired] boiler plant. It appeared that the optimistic space picture painted by Code 430 dims materially when the requirement is imposed that a B&W boiler as well as the existing Foster Wheeler design be provided for.

Before we had resolved the question of conventional or PF boiler in a 70,000 SHP ship, the SCB indicated that they wanted an 85,000 SHP conventional boiler DLG plant since its cost is no more than the 70,000 SHP PF plant. We accordingly increased the weight of machinery plant by 100 tons . . . no additional length was required because the machinery-box length in DDG 2 and in DLG's is the same. In addition to the power plant change and a change in designation from DDG to DLG a whole series of additions came one at a time via the telephone from the SCB with no specified meetings to discuss [their] effects. These . . . included an increase in complement from 26/352 to 28/374, an additional boat, and dead stowage for 8 ASROC missiles. . . . Admiral Speck [of SCB] requested that we try to estimate the increase in ship size which would result from providing "dead storage" for 20 to 40 additional Terrier missiles . . . we finally [indicated to the SCB] that the addition of 22 [such] missiles would increase the length of the ship by 10 feet, the light displacement by about 270 tons, and the full load displacement by 340.

By this time the designers had turned to a DLG 16 hull, in which they replaced one of the Terrier launchers with a 5-in./54 gun; the other they altered by the addition of another pair of missile stowage rings ("four-ring scheme"). Now the SCB objected that the new ship would cost too much ($88/73 million), and in fact that the new DLG must come within

a $63 million cost *based on estimates for Variation 1*—and that this ship must carry more than 40 Terriers. The resulting design must be one of the earliest examples of "design to cost."

Before the new design had gone very far, the Bureau of Naval Weapons had proposed (November 1960) a "three-ring" Terrier launcher, far easier to fit into a normal hull section than the four-ring type. In this type a lower ring fed into the two upper rings associated with more conventional types; only the two upper rings could accommodate ASROC, for a potential maximum stowage of 20. A three-ring type based on SCB 172A (see above) was priced out at $84.5/69 million.

By January 1961 it was clear that SCB 172A (FY 61) and SCB 212 (FY 62) shared many common features; furthermore, the two 3-in./50 mounts of SCB 172A could be retained in SCB 212, provided they were made single rather than twin. Therefore, both designs were merged; in view of the great amount of detail work already done on SCB 172A, it proved relatively easy to produce the SCB 212 contract design by 22 March 1961. The principal changes were replacement of No. 2 Terrier launcher by a 5-in./54 gun (Mk 68 director in place of after pair of SPG-55B) and alteration of No. 1 launcher to the three-ring type, which required some internal rearrangement. The two torpedo tubes (Mk 25) of SCB 212 were angled at about 45 degrees to the centerline beneath the helicopter pad.

Dynamic roll stabilization was discarded on the basis of its cost, an increase in ship length of 7 to 10 feet. On the other hand, the decision to use a DLG 16/SCB 172A hull increased endurance from the 6,000 nm. originally asked to 7,100 nm.

There was always some question of whether a better bargain could not have been had by means of a fresh design; however, in February 1961 an SCB memo noted that a valuable consequence of adopting such a scheme was that plans were available *at once* for FY 61 (and could be used for FY 62 and probably FY 63), whereas a new design would not be ready until December. At that time it was expected that the FY 64 ships would have Typhon (see below).

Nine of these *Belknap*-class frigates were built: three (DLG 26–28) under FY 61, six under FY 62. They were the first class to incorporate NTDS and HICAPCOM from the first; in DLG 28–34 NTDS performs target designation, director designation, and weapon assignment and so replaces much of the former Weapon Designation System (WDS). Also for the first time, emergency power was supplied partly by a gas turbine (300 kw, supplementing a 500-kw emergency diesel and four 1,500-kw ship-service turbogenerators). A tenth, proposed by the Navy as DLG 35, was built instead (at congressional behest) as DLGN 35, the USS *Truxtun*, a nuclear version of the DLG 26 design (SCB 222) with the DLGN 25 power plant.

The failure of the 1962 DDG project was only another example of the escalation in missile ship cost and complexity that had plagued the Navy since the late fifties and had already severely reduced its modernization programs. There seemed little hope of reducing unit cost, but on the other hand there was a possibility that the new technology, while much more expensive on the unit level, might drastically reduce the number of units required. That was the promise of Typhon, which began life in 1958 as Super-Tartar/Super-Talos. Economies in the number of ships were to be realized through longer missile ranges and, at the same time, a reduction in the size of the individual missile installation. Thus, a Tartar-sized Super-Tartar (later Typhon MR) was to replace both Tartar and Terrier; a Terrier-sized Super-Talos employing advanced ram-jet technology would replace Talos. Ship size might not fall, but each ship would be able to accommodate many more weapons, as well as a new and very powerful guidance radar, SPG-59.

Probably the most depressing lesson of the Typhon project was that the weapons themselves were at best a very minor contribution to ship size and cost. For example, the 1958 studies included a Super-Tartar DDG, which would not even incorporate the phased-array radar of larger Typhon ships. It soon grew to 7,250 tons fully loaded. Typhon alone could not take full credit for this growth: there was also the new SQS-26 sonar and NTDS.

In November 1958, the LRO commented to the chairman of the Standing Committee that quite probably Super-Talos would not be compatible with a DLG, and that a ship carrying it would look much more like a missile cruiser, both in size and in cost. It would be necessary to build Super-Tartar DDG/DLG in numbers, with smaller numbers of Super-Talos CGs. At this time it appeared that Super-Talos would become available in FY 62 or 63, so that it would be wise to suspend any plans for new Talos construction, although conversions might still be wise. As of February 1959 the basic carrier task force of the late 1960s, i.e., the force for which the Navy was then planning, was envisaged as two carriers, two missile cruisers (Talos or Super-Talos), and six DLGs or DDGs, all of which were to have Super-Tartar or

fore-and-aft Terrier. The basic minimum unit for a non-carrier force would be a pair of DDGs or DEGs for an underway replenishment group or an ASW carrier group. Very large numbers of new ships would be required, since the existing DDGs would become obsolete with the advent of Super-Tartar; it was already known that the latter would hardly fit the constricted DDG hull.

The failure of Typhon left the fleet with a residue of new weapon-system technology that well over a decade later became the basis for Aegis. However, the missile technology that produced in Super-Tartar a missile capable of Terrier performance finally accomplished the elimination of the earlier large missile and the merging of DDG and DLG categories: all missile-escort designs developed after the *Belknaps* incorporated the new version of Tartar, with its improved performance. They show, more clearly than any other missile-ship design, the enormous predominance of sensors and command and control systems in determining the size of modern warships.

With the demise of Typhon, attention turned to the deficiencies of the existing "3-T" missiles; indeed, funds freed by the cancellation of Typhon were applied to a "3-T" "get-well" program. Secretary of Defense McNamara was reluctant to approve new missile-ship construction, but he did hope to help make up the numbers through conversion of existing all-gun destroyers (*Forrest Sherman* class) and frigates (the large *Norfolk* and the smaller *Mitschers*). BuShips had studied conversions of these classes as early as 1959, at the same time that Convair had proposed a more austere 12-round Tartar for *Gearings* undergoing FRAM.

Schemes prepared in November 1959 called for ASROC in place of the two Mk 108s aft in the *Norfolk*. An SPS-37 air search radar would be mounted on her pilothouse, and the SPS-30 height-finder would be on a mack built up from her second funnel, with two missile guidance radars abaft it. DASH would fly off the fantail. Tartar or an austere Terrier (20 missiles) would replace No. 3 gunhouse. Costs of $19 or $27 million were estimated. An alternative would be a full 40-missile Terrier system aft, without ASROC, and with the more advanced SPS-39 height-finder (January 1961: $31 million). SQS-23 sonar would have been fitted in each case.

The *Mitscher* design called for Tartar in place of No. 1 5-inch gun (all the 3-inch would be removed) with the two missile radars on the pilothouse. Both funnels would be transformed into macks, and a hangar for DASH would be built up abaft the second funnel. Radars would have been SPS-39 (forward) and SPS-37 (aft). The cost would have been $35 million ($41 million for the analogous Terrier conversion).

Much less could be done with the destroyers. The alternatives considered were more or less AAW oriented: a 12-Tartar single-arm launcher aft, but VDS and Mk 25 TT in the fantail ($16 million), or else a 40-missile launcher without the ASW features ($17 million). In each case SQS-23 sonar and SPS-40 (air search) and SPS-39 (intercept) radars were to be fitted. All 3 inch and No. 2 and 3 5-in./54s would be removed.

In January 1963, the Secretary of Defense announced that the conversion program would be carried out over the next three years: 2 DLs and 5 DDs to Tartar DDGs in FY 64, the remaining pair of DDGs and 13 DDs to Tartar DDGs in FY 65, and the *Norfolk* to a Terrier DLG in FY 66. Congress appropriated $183 million to begin this program in FY 64: but the Navy asked for a more effective radar suit in the DD conversions (SPS-37 and SPS-48; SPS-40 in DDG 34) and existing funds covered only four conversions (DD 936, 932, 949, 947 became DDG 31–34). As completed, these ships had ASROC mounted between their second stack and a built-up reload magazine structure (presumably initially intended as a DASH hangar; ASROC occupied the flight deck) upon which a single missile guidance radar perched. The fifth *Forrest Sherman*, DD 933, received ASW modernization: SQS-23, 3-inch guns removed, ASROC in place of No. 2 5-in./54. A deckhouse was added between the stacks, and (as in the missile ships) two Mk 32s were mounted on the 01 level forward.

DLs 2 and 3 became DDGs 35 and 36, with ASROC and a reload magazine in place of the forward twin 3-in./70 and a 40-missile Tartar launcher in place of the after 3-in./70; both 5-in./54s were retained. As in the destroyers, radar (SPS-37 and SPS-48) was mounted on quadrupods rather than macks. There were two SPG-51C illuminators. By this time the DLs had already received SQS-23 as part of their CIPs. DASH had replaced their after 3-in./70s, the SPS-8 radar being relocated to hangar top. The Weapon A

and 3-in./70 on the 01 level forward were not disturbed during these 1960–62 refits.

All was not well with the Tartar missile system; DoD found itself reluctant to authorize the remaining 16 conversions of the program. They were deferred and then dropped, and plans were made to provide ASW modernization for the *Forrest Shermans* remaining: five each in FY 67 and FY 68, three more in FY 69. As for DL 5, she had received the prototype of the new SQS-26 sonar in 1961. Now her sister (DL 4) followed suit (1966). Otherwise, these ships remained in their previous configuration, with DASH aft. ASROC was not fitted even after Weapon A and the 3-in./70 had been cleared from the 01 level forward. The *Norfolk* had served as test ship for AS-ROC (in place of her after Weapon As) and toward the end of her career had all of her Weapon As removed. As a test ship she was not considered worth extensive modernization.

Of the *Forrest Shermans*, two conversions were authorized for FY 67 and six for FY 68; but five programmed for FY 70/71 were dropped as too costly, and the FY 68 conversion of DD 942 was canceled in April 1969.

Great attention was also paid to updating the existing missile force, particularly the missile frigates. In February 1965, Secretary McNamara could report that over the previous two and a half years the kill probability and readiness rate of Terrier had been doubled, with similar but less spectacular improvements evident in Tartar. The first four frigates were originally built to fire the beam-riding Terrier; all later ones operated the more effective semiactive homing variant. Under the FY 66 program, all four were modified to operate the homing weapon, their SPQ-5A radars replaced by the SPG-55 of later Terrier installations. Fourteen other frigates were to be modernized, with the installation of NTDS and the advanced SPS-48 three-dimensional radar. Their fire control radars were also improved. In the *Farraguts*,

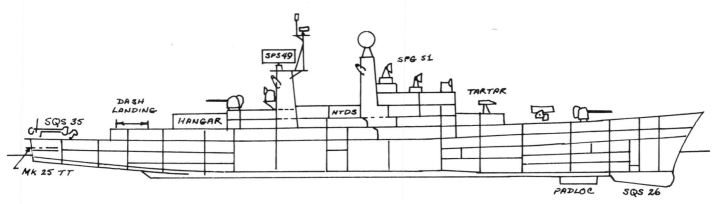

FY 66 DDG

this AAW modernization was visible in a superstructure extension to accommodate NTDS; larger ship-service turbogenerators were also fitted. The *Farragut*, the first to be modernized, received a magazine for ASROC reloads at the base of her forward superstructure; the others were not so fitted. By the end of the decade all ten ships also had the two-dome active/passive SQQ-23 Pair sonar system in place of their original SQS-23. Refits were completed in 1970–77.

The *Leahy* class was refitted in 1967–72, receiving improved missile fire control systems (SPG-55B), SPS-48, and NTDS; the similar *Bainbridge* was refitted and modernized in 1974–76, these ships receiving a single-dome variant of SQQ-23 in place of their existing SQS-23 as a separate modernization item.

Meanwhile, new construction lagged badly; in view of the troubles of the "3-T" series, McNamara was reluctant to approve any new starts—despite the inclusion of a massive DDG program in Navy long-range planning. For example, LRO-63 projected the construction of 23 DDGs in FY 66–71.

The CNO outlined requirements for the new generation on 15 March 1963: a ship to carry SQS-26 and two Mk 32 torpedo tubes; a Mk 13 Tartar launcher (40 missiles) with SPS-48 and SPS-10 radars; an endurance increased to 5,000 nm. at 20 knots; and a sustained speed of 30 knots. A series of variations in the long-range ASW suit was to be considered.

   A. VDS, Extended Range ASROC (ERA)
   B. VDS, DASH, two Mk 25 long torpedo tubes (4 torpedoes)
   C. ASROC with 8 reloads
   D. DASH and two Mk 25 tubes
   E. VDS and ERA
   F. VDS and ERA with a more advanced fire control system

A consolidated weapons control system was to be incorporated in several cases. The results of these studies were discouraging: even the relatively unsophisticated Case E required 4,994 tons (light; 6,666 tons fully loaded), and an 85,000 shp plant to exceed 30 knots sustained speed. Plans to build an FY 66 DDG were dropped, partly in view of the opposition of Secretary McNamara.

The long-range requirement was not. In January 1965, the SCB began to develop characteristics for a new DDG to be built under the FY 67 program. The primary objectives of the design were to be (i) improved command and control through integration of weapons direction and NTDS; (ii) improved weapon capability through a new Tartar D missile system with back-up target designation capability through the Mk 68 gun director; (iii) reduced overhaul requirement via improved propulsive machinery and Tartar D; (iv) reduced manning.

COSAG, COGAG, and 1,200 psi steam power plants were all considered; COSAG was rejected on the grounds that it combined the maintenance problems of high-pressure steam with an increase in required specialist personnel. Hence the SCB chose COGAG. However, on 12 August the CNO opted for an all-steam plant, which BuShips advised him should be of the derated (600 psi) type. Preliminary Characteristics of 31 August 1965 reflected this choice.

The result, once again, was a very large ship: 515 feet long, 7,250 tons fully loaded—in fact, not far from a DLG in size. Superficially, the FY 67 DDG has the same characteristics as its predecessor of a decade before: Tartar aft, two 5-in./54s, ASROC. In fact the 5-in./54s were the slow-firing lightweight models, equal in theory to half a heavy 5-in./54. In consequence the weight of fixed battery had actually declined; dramatic changes were to be found in the sensors and in the engineering department.

In the sensor suit, SQS-26 replaced the SQS-23 sonar. A measure of the relative size of these devices was the weight of salt water carried in their domes: 28 vs. 102 tons. Operationally, the later sonar has much greater range, achieved through higher power and lower frequency. The same requirement for longer range appears in the much larger three-dimensional radar of the later design. Finally the FY 67 DDG incorporated NTDS. It was no great surprise that DDG FY 67 required a 6,000 kw electrical plant compared to 2,000 in DDG 2. Such a plant was equivalent to 8,000 shp; in effect, DDG FY 67 was to be capable of putting out 83,000 shp, DDG 2 only about 72,300.

This disparity only begins to explain the far heavier power plant required by the later ship. Another important factor was the abandonment of high-pressure, high-temperature steam. The U.S. Navy had pressed for higher and higher steam conditions since the late thirties, not least in order to achieve low fuel consumption. In the postwar DD 931, steam pressure reached 1,200 psi at 950 degrees, and these conditions were repeated in DDG 2. Unfortunately, the 1,200-psi boilers tended to break down in service, and the Navy had to retreat to 600 psi/850 degrees, the conditions of World War II construction. More space had to be allowed for maintenance as well; in the end the machinery space of DDG FY 67 was 172 feet long, where 144 had sufficed for its predecessor; in fact, 144 had sufficed for 80,000 shp (and 2,000 kw) in DD 927/DL 2.

Even so, failures of 1,200-psi steam plants had given steam a bad name as a maintenance risk. The Secretary of the Navy reopened the propulsion question, and on 11 January 1966 BuShips proposed a simple-cycle gas turbine (i.e., not a regenerative cycle). The Secretary of the Navy approved this choice on 14 April 1966. Factors in Secretary Nitze's decision ap-

Table 13–1. Missile Destroyer Studies

	DDG FY 66	DDG FY 67 (STEAM)	DDG FY 67 (COGAG) August 1966	DXG BASELINE	DG/Aegis 30 August 1974
LOA			552–6		
LWL	500	515	525	538	488
Beam	54	57	60	54.7	53
Draft (full)	17.8	18.5	19.2		16.2
SHP	85,000	75,000	85,000	68,000	70,000
Speed				30	29.4
Endurance/20	5,000	5,000	7,000	6,000	5,000
Tartar	1(40)	1(40)	1(40)	1(40)	1(64)
ASROC	1	1	1		—(DP LCHR)
Mk 32 TT	2	2	2		2
Long ASW TT	2 Mk 25				
5-in./54	2 LW	2 LW	2 LW	1 LW	—
CIWS	—	—	—	—	2
NTDS	Yes	Yes	Yes		
Hull	1,971	2,356	2,978.2	2,480.6	1,909.9
Propulsion	943	886	680.7	909.8	509.2
Electrical	211	227	283.7	351.0	333.1
C³	215	411	424.6	318.9	211.1
Auxiliaries	535	660	559.0	626.1	519.7
Outfit	381	480	501.5	356.4	356.9
Armament	149	161	159.9	149.5	138.2
Margin	589	568	585.6	519.2	397.7
Light Ship	4,994	5,748	6,173.2	5,711.6	4,375.8
Loads	1,672	1,715	2,276.8	2,100.4	1,508.5
Full Load	6,666	7,463	8,450	7,812	5,884.3
Complement	22/367		23/337	27/264	

pear to have included the advanced state of gas-turbine development worldwide. Advantages over conventional steam included a higher degree of ship availability, rapid starting and acceleration, lower noise levels (for sonar operation) and, perhaps most importantly, greatly reduced manning levels. In addition, the light weight of a gas turbine made it possible to stow more fuel (and hence to realize a greater endurance) on a given displacement. In fact, given reduced machinery weight, a gas turbine could drive a ship 7,000 nm. at 20 knots on about the same displacement required for 5,000 nm. for a steam plant. BuShips resisted this change because it would increase cost (for redesign) and delay; a gas turbine could be tested aboard one of the destroyer escorts already in production. In fact, one of the FY 68 ships of that type was selected as a test bed for the regenerative gas turbine (see chapter 15), but it was never built.

By July the new DDG was 525 feet long on the waterline, 8,450 tons fully loaded. Her endurance had grown to 7,000 miles, and her shp to 85,000; but even so, the displacement seemed a very high price to pay for a single-ended missile ship with ASROC, SQS-26, VDS, and a full radar suit. One unusual feature of the design was its two-level machinery arrangement, with the base-load gas turbines on the main deck. Ultimately they were to be replaced by more economical regenerative units, and with the main deck arrangement this backfit could be accomplished without drydocking. In addition, the elements of the base-load system below the main deck were located at the extreme ends of the machinery box, so that a hit flooding any three of the five machinery spaces (which included a 20-foot separation space between the two boost units) would leave the ship with motive power. The location of the base-load turbines high in the ship also facilitated quiet operation, as in cruising operation the only working units below the main deck would be electric motors and reduction gears. However, at this time there was strong sentiment in Congress that any warship over 7,000 tons should have nuclear power. Although Secretary McNamara supported the FY 67 DDG program (in part as a prelude to the DXG program), the gas-turbine DDG was not authorized for FY 67. In-

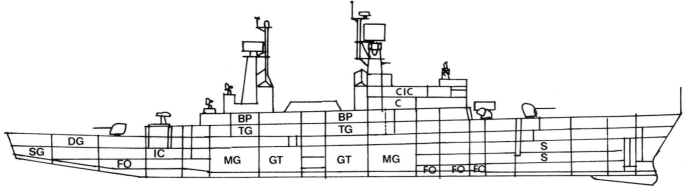

DDG FY 67

stead, Congress bought two nuclear DLGs, one in FY 67 and one in FY 68: the *California* and *South Carolina.*

For FY 68, then, drastic weight reduction was in order. The chairman of the SCB looked toward a reduction to 7,800 tons to be achieved by a variety of drastic reductions. Endurance would be cut by 1,000 nm., to about 6,000 nm.; the base turbines would be lowered to the hold; headroom would be cut from the desired 6 foot 10 inches to something over the 6-foot-3-inch mandatory minimum; even the emergency generator might be deleted. This was a very desperate program; at one point even deletion of the Masker silencer was contemplated. By December 1966, the designers (now known as NavShips rather than BuShips) had cut the ship down to 7,983 tons, just below the magic 8,000-ton figure. Preliminary design began on this basis in January 1967; in March the Secretary of the Navy directed NavShips to advance the procurement schedule to permit contract award as early as the third quarter of FY 68, i.e., the first three months of 1968. That would only have been possible either by using the already-completed Gibbs & Cox preliminary design of DDG FY 67 (8,450 tons) or by awarding the new ship on a sole-source basis to a selected shipyard, with an estimated cost of about $8 million.

The design effort ended in June 1967. Congress had effectively decided the issue by buying nuclear DLGNs, and OSD intended to buy a large standardized class of missile ships it now called DXG; indeed, as early as the late fall of 1966 Secretary McNamara had proposed termination of the new DDG design. That no DXG would be built, at least for a decade, was hardly obvious at the time (see chapter 15). Whether the demise of DDG FY 67/68 is to be blamed on Admiral Rickover's success in achieving congressional authorization for two nuclear, rather than two conventional, missiles or whether it was much more a matter of the best (DXG) being the mortal enemy of perfectly good enough is by no means clear.

The nuclear vs. conventional issue was much more sharply drawn in the next round of surface missile escorts, the Aegis ships. For FY 68 a drastic weight-reduction program was attempted extending even to deletion of the Masker silencer, but once more no hulls were authorized. The elimination of the Tartar DDG once more did not eliminate the need for fleet air defense; and if rising ship costs made it difficult to pay for DDGs, they certainly did not spare the more complex nuclear frigates.

The new ASMS (Advanced Surface Missile System) that became the present Aegis was first conceived in 1963, as it became clear that Typhon would soon die of excess cost. It was hoped that some new system might combine the antisaturation concepts of Typhon with the less-expensive solid-state hardware already in prospect. Development was protracted, partly because of the far greater urgency of curing the existing "3-T" systems entering combat in Vietnam. Thus, no prime contractor was selected until 1969, when the system officially became RCA's Aegis. As with Typhon, the cost of the Aegis system is concentrated in its advanced radar and fire control computer systems; the missile is a modified version of the Standard Missile that succeeded Tartar.

In 1969 the only ongoing missile ship program was DXGN, DXG having been dropped. ASMS was designed for installation, then, in a nuclear destroyer/cruiser of about 10,000 tons. At the time it was generally accepted that each carrier required four missile escorts, and that the escorts for a nuclear carrier should be nuclear. Thus, nine DLGN in all (one reserve) were required for two all-nuclear task groups. However, with the advent of ASMS the need for new carrier escorts rose dramatically; by 1970 a total buy of as many as 23 DXGNs was in prospect, most of them equipped with ASMS. In the event, ASMS development did not keep up with the new frigate program, and the four units ultimately built as DLGN (later CGN) 38–41 did not receive Aegis.

Now Admiral Zumwalt became Chief of Naval Operations. He was determined to increase the number of combatant ships by ruthlessly paring away irrelevant unit costs, as in the *Perry*-class FFG (see chapter 15). Design discipline was to be enforced by a combination of displacement and unit-cost limits backed by limits on personnel aboard ship and by rigorous reviews of proposals for shipboard equipment, including not only weapons but also sensors and combat system computers. A study by the Navy's "think tank," the Center for Naval Analysis, showed a need for 18 to 35 Aegis ships by the early 1980s; at the same time, Zumwalt resolved to reverse the cost trend in strike forces by reversing the general trend toward making those forces all-nuclear.

On August 1971 he requested that the Chief of Naval Materiel prepare a plan for Aegis deployment in very large numbers; he hoped that advances in miniaturization would permit a substantial saving in ship size compared to DXGN. As in the FFG, cost and size estimates derived from feasibility studies were deliberately rounded down: thus the initial $120 to $180 million became a firm limit of $100 million in FY 73 dollars, and displacement was to be limited to 5,000 tons. By way of comparison, the contemporary FFG (then called PF) design was set at $45 million and 3,400 tons. In neither case were the limits met; in the case of the Aegis ship, the $100 million equates to about $600 or $650 million, and by way

of comparison, CG 48, the follow-on Aegis cruiser, is to cost about $820 million; these figures suggest the brutal effect of inflation over the past seven years, with its debilitating consequences for the shipbuilding program.

The evolution of the austere Aegis ship (DG) demonstrated that in warships capability is never inexpensive. Of 139 computer runs of the first series, only one alternative fell within the allowed bounds, and it was too austere even for Admiral Zumwalt: it would have had a single Mk 22 launcher (with only 16 missiles, as in a *Brooke*-class DEG), no two-dimensional radar, no ASW capability at all, no Harpoon fire control system, no digital data links (and, therefore, no ability to make use of task force data resources). Admiral Zumwalt was now forced upward to 6,000 tons and $125 million.

Even within these limits, the DG design varied considerably. At first it was to have an austere sonar suit and provision for landing, but not stowing, a helicopter. The missile launcher would be the new Mk 26 Mod 1, which could fire ASROC as well as the Standard missile; austerity measures included the deletion of the SPS-49 two-dimensional radar. Those objecting said that so valuable a ship should have at

This is one version of DG/Aegis, sketched in 1972 when the ship was limited to $150 million in FY 72 dollars. Note the limitation to two illuminators and the single Mk 26 launching system, with gas turbine propulsion. The demise of DG/ Aegis has been blamed variously on proponents of nuclear propulsion and on the rather limited capabilities of the austere ship actually proposed.

least two launchers, and the design was recast to show two Mk 13 launchers, with 40 missiles each—but without ASROC capability. LAMPS and an SPS-49 were added, and by early 1973 the DG displaced 6,161 tons fully loaded and was to cost $136.1 million (follow-on ship), both of which figures exceeded Admiral Zumwalt's limits.

This was not entirely satisfactory. Although compact, the Mk 13 launcher severely limited the dimensions of the missiles it could accommodate, and thus left little room for growth in the Standard missile, or indeed for replacement of that weapon by some alternative, such as a blended rocket-ramjet then being discussed. Nor was it suited to nuclear weapons, which in earlier SAM systems had been considered an important means of breaking up mass attacks. Thus, early in 1973 DG development shifted once more to the Mk 26, this time in its Mod 2 (64-missile) version. The DG now fell within the displacement limit (5,884 tons fully loaded), although its estimated cost rose to about $200 million, which merely foreshadowed the explosive cost escalation to come.

Even so, DG/Aegis did appear to be the minimum platform that could support a vital means of Fleet Air Defense, and it progressed to Preliminary Design, with procurement scheduled for FY 77. In effect, the choice of conventional power for the platform for the major Fleet Air Defense system of the 1980s challenged the continuation of nuclear escort construction; in May 1973, Secretary of the Navy John Warner ordered a study of a nuclear Aegis ship. At that time the Navy's version of the Five-Year Shipbuilding Program showed procurement of a new class of nuclear escorts from FY 79 onward, presumably to replace the first nuclear frigate, the *Bainbridge*; the Secretary noted that, given the plan to buy DGs as well, it might be wise to consider the feasibility of a single new class of nuclear-powered surface combatants.

This was a return to the original ASMS/DXGN plan. In retrospect it seems fortunate that DG/Aegis was abandoned, as—miniaturization or not—it was not very easy to squeeze 10,000 tons worth of combat system into a 5,000-ton hull. If anything, the growth of the DDG 47/CG 47 Aegis platform suggests as much. The series of nuclear Aegis ship concepts is described in chapter 14.

Given the cost of the nuclear cruiser ultimately preferred by the CNO, OSD demanded a mix of nuclear and non-nuclear ships. In the presentation to Secretary of Defense Schlesinger that initiated the Aegis shipbuilding program, Admiral Hayward requested a total of 8 strike cruisers (nuclear), plus 16 conventionally powered Aegis ships to be derived from the existing *Spruance* hull. The lead DDG would

be authorized under the FY 77 program, the lead strike cruiser under FY 78. In fact, Congress became deadlocked between supporters of nuclear and non-nuclear ships, and neither project was approved for FY 77. DDG 47, the lead Aegis ship, was finally approved in FY 78; the strike cruisers suffered a political death that is described in the next chapter.

The contract for the lead ship, DDG 47, was awarded to Litton 22 September 1978 and the ship laid down on 21 January 1980 for completion in January 1983. By this time DXG had grown so large that it was redesignated a cruiser, CG 47 (USS *Ticonderoga*), in January 1980. This was no more than an expression of the general shift from DLG to CG designations, as well as of the merger of the DDG and DLG lines of development. However, it was also rather controversial, as the congressional action of 1974 (since rescinded) appeared to require special justification for the construction of any non-nuclear major combatant, such as a cruiser.

The CG 47 design is perhaps the best expression of the inherent flexibility of the original *Spruance* design; the additions for Aegis eat up virtually all of the enormous margin originally designed into the ship. This is hardly the Aegis design considered briefly early in the program, which would have had only a single Mk 26 launcher and two illuminators. CG 47 has launchers fore and aft, with four illuminators, and her SPY-1A radar is split fore and aft in part for greater survivability.

In 1981 CG 47 seems destined for a considerable production run, with later ships provided with greater missile capacity through the introduction of vertical (box) launching systems to replace the current highly mechanized type. It also appears that some reversion to the "high-low" concept of the Zumwalt years is envisaged, as current programs include a future DDGX or DDX. This is to be a wholly new design, substantially smaller than the Aegis ship, and it will probably need a new combat system, similar, perhaps, in concept to that of the larger ship, but simpler and less capable. It is difficult to avoid the fear that once again the dimly perceived future system will be the mortal enemy of the current one, that the well-known defects of current or near-term practice will not serve to make a paper system far more attractive than it should be, in the face of a sharply increasing air threat. CG 47 still carries the enmity of many within the naval ship design community, who consider the entire CF/CD process that produced the *Spruance* tainted, and who feel that the Navy can do far better inhouse, beginning afresh. That the fresh approach may take far too long, and that CG 47 may be relatively inexpensive because of the effort already sunk in the basic design, are issues yet to be resolved as this is written.

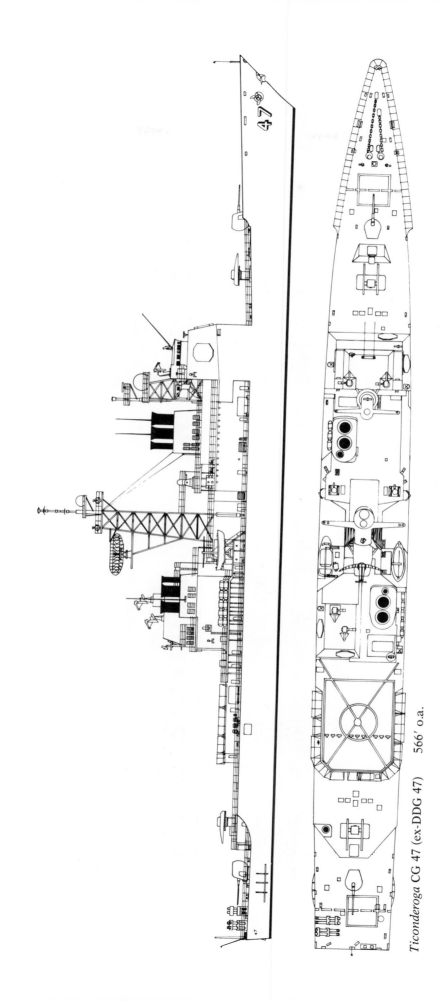

Ticonderoga CG 47 (ex-DDG 47)   566' o.a.

Success and apparent failure: in this sketch the successful Aegis platform, *Ticonderoga* (CG 47), steams alongside the abortive Aegis nuclear cruiser, CGN 42, canceled by the Carter Administration. The *Ticonderoga* represents the outer limit to what could be accommodated in the basic *Spruance* hull; she has bulwarks forward to compensate for badly reduced freeboard. Note the difference in phased-array panel configurations, and the armored box launchers for cruise missiles carried just forward of the nuclear cruiser's bridge. CGN 42 was herself considered an austere alternative to the proposed nuclear strike cruiser, or CSGN.

Among the first of the fast task force escorts, the *Dahlgren* (DLG 12) and *William V. Pratt* (DLG 13) complete at Philadelphia, 31 December 1959. A mothballed *Iowa*-class battleship lies in the background. These DLGs, extremely large destroyers for their day, were reclassified as missile destroyers (DDG) rather than cruisers in 1975.

The USS *Dewey* was the first of her class in the Mediterranean. Here she shows her SPQ-5A missile-guidance radars, with an SPS-39 three-dimensional set on the foremast and SPS-29 (air search) and TACAN on the lattice mainmast. Small radomes forward carried ESM antennas.

14

Nuclear Destroyers
and Frigates

Destroyers have always presented unusually severe problems in propulsion design. From their inception until after World War II, the emphasis was on high speed, hence maximum power at minimum engine weight. Fuel weight to meet endurance requirements was of lesser import, particularly since destroyers were often designed, before the war, to meet specific standard (i.e., unfueled) displacements. In wartime, however, high sustained speed and great endurance proved far more important. The trial condition came to include a full load of fuel, so that the combination of light, (dry) machinery and good fuel economy came to determine even trial speed. Under these circumstances, nuclear power became a natural candidate for destroyer propulsion, perhaps even more so than for larger surface ships with inherently greater steaming endurance. However, during the first postwar decade nuclear power plants remained far too heavy for destroyer or even cruiser application. The new submarine plants were relatively low powered. For example, as unofficially reported, even the Submarine Advanced Reactor (SAR, later redesignated S4G), developed specially for the large, fast *Triton*, developed only about 17,000 shp per shaft, where wartime destroyers had required 60,000, and the postwar frigates, 80,000.

It was, therefore, a considerable feat of engineering for the nuclear frigate *Bainbridge* to be completed in 1962 with a power of 60,000 shp, using two D2G reactors. Moreover, it appears that the basic D2G design was sufficiently advanced for it to be used in all subsequent nuclear frigates (now cruisers); an

upgraded version was to have powered the abortive strike cruiser (CSGN), essentially a much-enlarged frigate. The *Bainbridge* represented a political as well as a technological triumph, in that at the time of her conception she was supported only by the staff of the Atlantic Destroyer Force, which had practically pressed her upon a reluctant Chief of Naval Operations. Opposition was based almost entirely upon the high cost associated with nuclear power, given the very general feeling that above all the fleet needed large numbers of new destroyers to replace the aging World War II fleet. Advocates of nuclear power argued successfully that the need to fuel frequently, which appeared inseparable from retention of conventional (fossil-fuel) plants, so reduced the value of conventional destroyers as to balance off the difference in cost. This controversy has continued to the present.

In effect, a nuclear power plant imposes an "overhead" on a warship design, in size, complexity of design, and cost of construction. Just how great it is depends upon the sophistication of nuclear plant design and also on the size and cost of the combat system built into the ship. The larger and more complex the combat system, the larger its direct and indirect costs, and consequently the smaller the difference between the size and cost of nuclear and conventional versions of the ship to accommodate it. For example, the choice of nuclear power in some versions of the abortive Typhon frigate had far less impact than it had in more conventional, simpler ships. The same might well be true for an Aegis ship. There

The *Bainbridge* was the prototype U.S. nuclear frigate, the first of a rather controversial series of ships. Here she cruises in the Pacific, September 1968. The small white object on her fantail is her FANFARE (torpedo countermeasures) winch in its small spray shield, and the marking on the fantail is for helicopter replenishment rather than for landing.

is, however, another factor at work. A nuclear ship is inherently extremely capable, and the greater size implicit in nuclear warship design can support a larger (and more expensive) combat system than may at first be desired. It is therefore tempting to upgrade the combat system to take advantage of the larger hull that must in any case be purchased, and such an upgrade is rational, given the advantages of nuclear endurance at high speed. The result is a cost escalation only very loosely associated with the adoption of nuclear power. Thus, to some extent nuclear power appears to carry a larger cost than is indeed the case.

Nuclear destroyer design presents unusual problems for the naval architect. The designer of a conventional ship can make up for unexpected changes in weight during construction by adjusting the large amounts of liquid fuel and even feed water that his plant requires. Considerable errors in estimated weights and centers of gravity can be overcome, given sufficient fuel tankage. In a nuclear ship, on the other hand, liquids are relatively scarce and, moreover, cannot be adjusted at will. The propelling plant itself consists of a few highly concentrated weights, and the remainder of the design must be carefully balanced around them. There are also issues of arrangement. There must be clear deck space permitting access to the reactor for servicing and for refueling. Radiation standards require, for example, that areas around the reactors cannot be used for accommodations, and indeed fore-and-aft access may be a problem in itself. Moreover, given the delicate balances in a nuclear ship, design is relatively complex, and there are strong pressures to accept repeat designs rather than trade a lengthy new design period for relatively marginal improvements.

Reactor design itself is so complex that the naval architect never has more than a few nuclear plants among which to choose. He may wish to use an undefined power plant with flexible horsepower (and, say, fixed weight per shp) in his initial calculations, but in fact he must choose his power plant and let that choice very largely determine the size of his ship, a procedure opposite to the conventional case. It must be admitted, however, that this formulation overstates the flexibility of choice in conventional cases. Gas turbines are also modular, although the choice may be somewhat wider because the individual units are somewhat smaller. As for conventional steam plants, there is considerable pressure, in any new design, to repeat some existing one either in whole or in part. On the other hand, it appears to be a far simpler matter to overload a conventional plant than to attain some increase in the rating of a nuclear plant. Yet in 1975, when the CSGN required a considerably uprated D2G plant, the upgrading report-

edly involved the turbines rather than the reactor proper, which had considerable powering margin designed into it.

The Bureau of Ships began a study of a nuclear destroyer, or DDN, as early as August 1953. This was about the time the very large, fast submarine radar picket *Triton* was entering Preliminary Design, and both projects were to have employed the same Submarine Advanced Reactor (SAR). The destroyer was to have had roughly the characteristics of the contemporary *Forrest Sherman*, except for its power plant. It proved unacceptable, as the power plant alone was estimated to weigh about as much as a World War II destroyer. The project was dropped in September, and Rear Admiral Rickover commented that any DDN project was premature. Even so, that December Admiral Robert B. Carney, the CNO, asked the Bureau of Ships for estimates for a nuclear destroyer and a large submarine.

The DDN was largely a reaction to strong sentiment within OpNav and the fleet favoring some advance on the 4,500 nm. endurance expected for the new *Forrest Shermans*. Gas turbines appeared to present a considerable potential for high power with light weight, albeit coupled with high fuel consumption and, perhaps, a short operating lifetime. In 1954, Preliminary Design sketched a series of destroyers with combined gas-turbine and steam (base) plants (COSAG). By designing the steam plant for maximum efficiency at cruising speed, and accepting a very limited dash capability (about 1,000 nm., equal, however, to the high-speed endurance of existing ships) the designers could achieve their goal of about 6,000 nm. at 20 knots on substantially the same displacement as the *Forrest Sherman*. An important point favoring the COSAG concept was statistical evidence that in normal wartime operation destroyers operated only relatively rarely at speeds above that provided by the base plant. On the other hand, COSAG was complex. For example, the gas turbines did not burn standard bunker (steam) fuel oil.

It was natural to extend this concept to the nuclear destroyer, replacing the steam base plant with *Triton* reactors, but retaining the three aircraft-type (J-40) gas turbines of the COSAG studies. The result proved somewhat disappointing; a CONAG sketch design of September 1954 approximated frigate size; even so it was smaller than a pure nuclear ship. The subject was temporarily closed.

Nevertheless, it must have appeared to many that the transition to nuclear power for destroyers and other surface warships was no more than a matter of time. In January 1955, Preliminary Design prepared a long series of sketch designs for a committee appointed by Admiral Leggett, Chief of the Bureau of Ships, to consider future Navy shipbuilding re-

The *Bainbridge* was essentially a nuclear version of the *Leahy* class. The boxy deckhouse just forward of her lattice mainmast presumably was intended to accommodate her NTDS, although at this time (4 September 1968) she had not been fitted with the SPS-48 three-dimensional radar of the AAW modernizations, nor does she show the usual NTDS-associated antenna forward. Her forward radar antenna is an improved planar array for her original SPS-39.

quirements. This Committee of Fifteen included such bureau luminaries as Admirals Cochrane, Wheelock, Morgan, and Mumma. The series of sketches they saw included not only numerous nuclear submarines, but also a series of destroyers and frigates, and even a nuclear DER. Destroyer, DDR, and DDG sketches were based on a 4,800-ton (light; 5,200 fully loaded), 460-foot (LOA) hull, and were expected to cost almost twice as much as conventional ships. For example, with a *Forrest Sherman* battery the DDN would cost about $50 million, vs $30 million for the conventional destroyer. The frigate (conventional and missile) was based on a 7,160-ton (8,000-ton full load), 575-foot hull, which would carry about the same battery as the 3,600-ton (5,200 full load) DL 6/DLG 9 class then in the design stage. Again, costs were not quite twice those of conventional ships: $76.5 vs. $42.8 million for the all-gun DL(N), $80 vs $46.5

million for the DLG(N). No particular reactor seems to have been used as a basis for the design, although at this time there was an effort to develop the powerful system later used in the carrier *Enterprise* and the cruiser *Long Beach*.

On 17 August Admiral Arleigh Burke became CNO. He was deeply committed to long-term fleet modernization, looking toward the eventual end of the large surviving force of World War II-built ships. His wartime experience in destroyers and his recent service as ComDesLant had, if anything, sensitized him to the requirements of the destroyer force. His considerable experience in the Bureau of Ordnance gave him an unusual grasp of the possibilities inherent in guided missiles and nuclear weapons. Moreover, as a captain on the General Board staff in 1948, he had been deeply involved in long-range studies of the Navy's future. The day after his installation, he asked the Bureau of Ships to indicate the feasibility of installing nuclear plants in a frigate (DLG), a missile cruiser, and an attack carrier. It is conceivable that he was prompted by the Committee of Fifteen report, which may well have circulated within OpNav, and particularly within the new Long-Range Objectives group (Op-93). In any case, the bureau replied in September that although the cruiser and carrier were certainly feasible, the destroyer was not. The smallest destroyer the bureau could provide with nuclear power would be a large frigate about 540 feet long, of 8,500 tons (fully loaded). It would be somewhat larger than the existing *Norfolk*, powered by half a carrier plant. Even this size estimate proved extremely optimistic, and the frigate became the nuclear cruiser *Long Beach* (17,350 tons).

There was another source of pressure for a nuclear destroyer. Rear Admiral John C. Daniel relieved Admiral Burke as ComDesLant on 17 January 1955, bringing with him a staff with considerable Pacific wartime experience, i.e., quite sensitive to the problem of short destroyer endurance. Beginning in July, Admiral Daniel began to press for what he called the "destroyer of the future." In contrast to the new Navy policy (enunciated by the Schindler Committee) of specialization and a defensive role, he looked toward a destroyer quite capable of taking offensive action—and nuclear powered for sufficient endurance. He saw specialization, apart from the destroyer-DE distinction, as an unfortunate error. DesLant felt that destroyers should have the first priority among surface warships for nuclear power, and that a nuclear destroyer should be included in the FY 59 program. Indeed, it would be possible to accept a slow destroyer (25 knots), although of course 30 knots would be best; these were *sustained* speeds. Note that even the low sustained speed would make for a much higher cruising speed than the standard 20 knots. The new destroyer should be about the size of a *Forrest Sherman*, sacrificing two 5-in./54s for Terrier (Tartar was not acceptable), ASROC, and a new drone ASW helicopter, which became DASH.

ComCruDesPac disagreed. He and his staff suspected that a nuclear destroyer would cost the equivalent of three or even four conventional ships. However, Admiral Daniel writes, "we believed that in time of war one nuclear would be equal to three steam driven. We did not believe it to be as big as the *Bainbridge*—it just grew in size as the plans progressed." He had the great advantage of proximity to Admiral Burke who, although he was not a supporter, was at least quite willing to listen. Moreover, when Admiral Rickover visited Woods Hole, the DesLant staff met him and enlisted his support. In particular, Rickover began a project to investigate a lightweight reactor for destroyers, which he desig-

nated D1G. At first it appeared that the prospective new technology of organic coolants would permit the kind of weight saving that would result in a *Forrest Sherman*-size nuclear ship; ultimately, that proved impossible, although the destroyer reactor program did produce a system quite appropriate to a frigate, the D2G.

Admiral Daniel recalls writing weekly letters to Admiral Burke, gradually winning him over. In January 1957, Preliminary Design began two parallel nuclear destroyer projects. One was the DesLant DDN, which required an extremely light reactor; the other was a nuclear missile frigate, which was to accommodate *Leahy*-class (SCB 172) armament on a 6,000-ton, 30-knot hull. It became the *Bainbridge*. The DesLant DDN, however, proved impracticable. A pure DDN with two SARs would make only 27 knots, and even so it would displace about 4,300 tons light (4,700 fully loaded). Alternatives included a 3,300-tonner with *Forrest Sherman* armament and two SARs (27 knots) and a series of CONAGs, which appeared to permit a closer approach to DesLant goals. For example, on 3,500 tons light (4,300 fully loaded) Preliminary Design could provide one SAR (now designated S4G) plus six 7,000-shp gas turbines, for a cruising speed (all nuclear) of 22 knots and a dash speed of 30; dash endurance was 1,000 nm. One advantage of the CONAG concept was that it could incorporate existing (submarine) reactors and therefore faced no greater developmental risk. However, it was rejected in favor of the pure nuclear ship, which was far larger. All-nuclear power permitted a change in tactics. For example, an all-nuclear task force would be able to maintain high speed, with the associated relative immunity from submarine attack, while cruising, whereas a conventional force would have to approach within about 500 nm. of the target zone before its high-speed dash in and out.

Admiral Burke appears to have expected that the DesLant goals would prove impossible to meet, and that a DLGN would be the closest possible approach. For example, in a 26 January 1957 letter to BuShips he wrote that "There is being exerted considerable pressure by the destroyer sailors for a small nuclear power plant suitable for a ship of about 5,000 tons or less. The difficulties which are ahead of us in getting such a plant are recognized, but the need is great and the payoff would also be great. . . ." In fact, he imposed a 6,000-ton limit on the new DLGN study.

A first batch (30 January 1957) showed that to achieve 30 knots on 6,000 tons fully loaded, with SCB 172 battery, would require a plant weighing no more than two SARs but generating the much higher power appropriate to a frigate. Light displacement would be 5,377 tons. A somewhat more realistic estimate of reactor weight led to a ship of 6,918 tons (6,285

Details of the newly completed *Bainbridge* are visible in this 1962 photograph, including URD-4, TACAN, SPS-39 (with IFF at its lower edge), SPS-10, and the usual trio of radar direction-finders on her foremast; note, too, what appears to be a diesel generator exhaust for her emergency generating plant. The lattice mainmast carries an SPS-37 for air search and a pair of SLQ-12 jammers. The small conical antenna pointing towards her SPG-55 missile guidance radars atop her forward superstructure was a standard missile telemetry unit, generally turned in the direction of flight. Note, too, the ASROC replenishment crane (no reloads were carried) which hinged outward from the bridge face.

light). Preliminary Design commented that it would probably have excessive deck area for the battery envisaged. As an indication of the "overhead" associated with nuclear power, a ship with a similar power plant but *Forrest Sherman* armament would still come to 6,813 tons (full load; 6,171 tons light). In each case, length would be 520 feet, compared to 510 for a *Leahy*. Alternatively, if the new reactor weight were accepted, and the 6,000-ton limit retained, speed would have to be sacrificed. In fact, even the figure on which these designs were based was considered unrealistic; in May Captain McQuilkin of BuShips wrote Admiral Daniel that the DDN was many years off, that even 6,800 or 6,900 was at best a target for five years off, and that the bureau was struggling to reduce reactor weights in the face of stiffening radiation shielding requirements.

The 6,000-ton limit had to be abandoned. BuShips thought 7,600 tons (7,000 light) a realistic goal, with 7,300 (6,695 light) possible at a lower limit of reactor weight. This was well above the initial requirement, but not so far above as to be rejected. By late April, the DLGN had been fixed at 7,600 tons fully loaded (6,900 light); cost was expected to be $108 million for the lead ship. By way of comparison, at the end of December 1956 it was expected that the lead SCB 172 would cost $59 million ($49 million for repeat

ships). In fact, in common with virtually all of the high-technology ships of the period, the *Bainbridge* suffered from considerable cost inflation: ultimately she cost about $163.6 million. Even before this, the cost of the nuclear ship was impressive.

There were several reasons for the increased size of the nuclear ship. Her power plant, although still less powerful than that of a conventional DLG, had a higher net center of gravity, required a somewhat larger machinery box, and required more personnel—7 officers and 158 enlisted men in the Engineering Department, compared to 4 officers and 116 enlisted men in a steam DLG. Thus, the *Bainbridge* hull was lengthened: first, to maintain a favorable speed-length ratio in the face of reduced power; second, to accept the longer machinery box; third, to accept the increased complement and also to provide spaces to make up for those that could not be used in view of radiation levels around the machinery. In addition, the hull had to be made beamier to make up for the higher CG of the nuclear plant.

In hopes of cutting her cost if not her size, the SCB in July asked BuShips to consider a possible alternative mixed plant, boosted either by a gas turbine or by a conventional steam turbine. The gas turbine was immediately rejected, as it had about twice the fuel rate of the oil-fired boiler plant; the bureau worked up three schemes for combined steam and nuclear (CONAS) ships, employing a single D2G reactor and either *Forrest Sherman* or small boilers. In this way a ship the size of the *Bainbridge* might achieve a full-power endurance of as much as 3,000 nm., while acceptance of an endurance of 1,000 nm. would reduce size and cost somewhat. For example, the 3,000-nm. ship (6,160 light, 7,780 full load tons) would cost $89 million for the lead ship, and $74 million for follow-ons, compared to $108/93 million for the *Bainbridge*, as then estimated. By way of comparison, the FY 58 DLG (SCB 172) was estimated at $59/49 million. The bureau commented that of course the combined-plant ship would be slower than the all-nuclear, and would have limited full-power endurance; "the advantages to be gained . . . are mainly monetary, a saving of about $20 million per ship. However, a combined plant would not have the fundamental advantage of nuclear power, namely sustained full power operation without refueling. Consequently, it would not allow a true evaluation of nuclear power for destroyer type (frigate) application." This did not quite kill the combined plant. For example, in January 1959 Rear Admiral Horacio Rivero, Director of the Long-Range Objectives Group (Op-93), asked that the question of the combined plant be reopened. He did not question the value of nuclear warships, but feared that high costs would "unacceptably reduce the numbers of new ships procurable. Despite this need for restraint, the Navy will be under increasing pressure to place nuclear power in more surface ships. Specific pressures have already been applied for nuclear power in destroyers; these will increase as the approaching completion of a nuclear carrier points up the shortage of compatible support ships. Also, by failing to place nuclear power in ASW ships, we make the latter vulnerable to those who view the SSN as the only "modern" answer to the submarine problem."

> The only all-nuclear high-speed destroyer BuShips can now build is the DLGN. This was quoted at $93 million for follow ships at a time when the DLG with identical armament and electronics was quoted at $49 million. The price of the latter is now $59 million. There is no reason to believe the $44 million differential for nuclear power has decreased significantly. We may thus fairly price DLGN follow ships at $100 million or more. The super (TYPHON) missile programs do not promise any reduction in the armament element of the DLGN cost. The addition of POLARIS has been proposed in some quarters. . . . The DLGN as presently conceived does not appear to be a promising approach to nuclear-powered destroyers in any numbers likely to satisfy either the pressures or ultimate Navy needs.

One of the major BuShips objections to the combined steam plant had been that nuclear boilers pro-

duced saturated steam, whereas the additional oil-fired plant would produce high-pressure super-heated steam; there would, then, have to be two main steam systems per engine room. Admiral Rivero proposed a retreat to low-pressure steam for the oil plant. "Op-93 suggests that in terms of the practical requirements, a combined plant may buy (at half the added cost) perhaps 80 percent as much of *that added endurance which we really need*, as the full nuclear plant buys. Furthermore, it may be procurable in much larger numbers. . . ." Admiral F. V. H. Hilles, director of the Surface Warfare Division, Op-34, concurred: he was "confident that marine reactor development will soon give us a propulsive plant that will meet power, weight, and cost specifications for destroyer types, and that, circa 1970, all combatant ships will be coming off the ways with fully nuclear plants. Whe considering the minimum 20-year life expected of a destroyer one is reluctant to build hermaphrodites as an interim measure. On the other hand, the oil-fired DLGs, DDGs, and DEs projected for the future shipbuilding programs will also have to last for 20 years, but will be viewed as relics during the latter half of their lives when nuclear ships come into abundance. Op-34 therefore concurs with Op-93 that another study should be made of a combined plant with the objective of possible application to DLGs, DDGs and DEs of the 1962–1965 shipbuilding programs. . . ." He suggested a return to CONAG.

A new BuShips study ended this line of investigation. It was indeed possible to devise a mixed plant, but that would be far more complex than might otherwise be imagined. Although $20 million might be saved, the lead ship of a new program would have to cost about $10 million more than a repeat *Bainbridge* (February 1960). For example, for the combined nuclear and steam plant it would be necessary to integrate oil-firing and the reactor proper; although the result was both expensive and heavy, a separate boiler would be even worse. A gas turbine would require about four times as much intake air and stack uptake area as a steam plant and would require, too, a special reversible gear box or a controllable-pitch reversing propeller; neither was as yet available. Moreover, long life and reliability would prohibit the use of a lightweight aircraft-type engine. A pressure-fired steam plant would offer some space and weight savings, but would require development of a new generation of steam turbines capable of using both saturated and superheated steam, no mean achievement. "It should be noted that the best of the combined plant schemes is bigger and far more costly than the DLG 16 but offers no improvement in endurance at high speed. Also, when the oil is gone from the combined plant ship, it has only one power source, a single reactor."

There were considerable pressures for repeat

*Bainbridge*s; DesLant, for example, had been looking for a new generation of destroyers, not merely an experimental prototype. Admiral Daniel's successor, Rear Admiral E. B. Taylor, strongly advocated inclusion of a follow-on ship in the FY 60 program. Based on the usual reduction in cost for such a ship, he estimated in October 1958 that it would only displace one and a fraction destroyer types of equal armament capability.

> The importance of getting on with the destroyer nuclear propulsion program is considered by COMDESLANT to overshadow the question of numbers of destroyers in the small range of numbers we are currently considering. While the relative operational merits of nuclear and oil fire destroyers are still speculative, it is a fair conclusion that one of the former will always be worth more than one of the latter. The Destroyer Forces urgently need a limited number of nuclear-powered ships to get a start on solving the numerous operational, maintenance, and training problems expected to arise with the advent of nuclear propulsion. We need to find out in actual operations just how valuable nuclear propulsion is to destroyers and to an OTC, in order to make sound decisions on future shipbuilding programs. . . ."

Navy planners waxed and waned in their enthusiasm for quick construction of nuclear ships. For example, in 1957 a policy of annual construction of a nuclear carrier (which proved impractical) was promulgated. The nuclear carrier required nuclear escorts, and a fleet of 6 CGNs and 16 DLGNs (plus 6 CVANs) was projected for 1957. It was entirely impossible to build, given the high costs of such ships and also the costs of new programs such as Polaris. Op-93, charged with long-range planning within realistic cost guidelines, projected in 1959 (LRO-59) that by 1974 the Navy should be able to operate two nuclear strike forces; an associated shipbuilding plan called for the construction of 1 CVAN, 1 CGN, and 1 DLGN during FY 63–67. In December 1960 the director of Op-93, then Rear Admiral T. H. Moorer, commented that a more definite program was needed. He observed that nuclear warships could be developed either by the construction of integrated nuclear forces or by concentration on particular types. The DLGN seemed particularly worthwhile, any such program would have to be large enough (for tactical reasons) to make nuclear construction economical. Moreover, if in fact two DLGNs cost about as much as three DLGs, the sacrifice in numbers would be far less severe than in the case of a CGN or an attack carrier. Also, with the advent of Typhon, the DLGN would be very nearly as capable as a cruiser. He foresaw the construction of a DLGN in FY 63, followed by two in FY 64, three in FY 65, and four in FY 66. Conventional DLG construction would cease after two in FY 63 and one in FY 64.

Admiral Moorer commented, too, that increasing pressure from the fleet seemed sure to produce a workable DDN in the near future, with a single reactor of new design. It would have a sustained speed of at least 27 knots, and the cost ratio to a conventional destroyer would fall to the range of 1.1 to 1.3.

In fact, progress was rather slow. For FY 62 the Navy requested only conventional frigates, the *Belknap* class, but Congress substituted a nuclear ship for one of them. The nuclear design group, Code 1500, argued for a repeat *Bainbridge*, on the theory that any major redesign would create an undue delay. OpNav, however, considered the major improvements inherent in the *Belknap*, particularly the SQS-26 sonar, too valuable to forego.

The compromise solution was to maintain the *Bainbridge* hull as far as possible, while accepting the alterations necessary to accommodate the much larger SQS-26 bow dome. This required that the Terrier-ASROC launcher be mounted aft rather than forward, which was expected to save about $3 million as compared to the configuration adopted for the *Belknap* class. In view of limited hull depth right aft, the three-ring magazine had to be moved farther forward, and a new Mod of the Mk 10 launching system, with a longer rammer, designed; that proved a minor annoyance. The only important operational limitation was that ASROC could not be launched into the forward arc best covered by the SQS-26 sonar, but that was accepted in the interest of producing a new design more quickly, by using as much of the *Bainbridge* design as possible. The new ship became, in effect, a nuclear equivalent to the *Belknap* class, using a slightly modified *Bainbridge* hull—as the *Belknap* used a modified *Leahy* hull.

In June 1961, Moorer examined the issue of future cruiser, destroyer, and escort programs over the FY 63–69 period. He looked toward an objective of one cruiser per deployable CVA, designed primarily around a very long range surface-to-air missile, albeit with some surface-to-surface capability, as well as three frigates per deployable CVA and three per division of Marine assault lift. The latter goal would require 14 frigates beyond the 7 already programmed for FY 62, towards a 1972 goal, and according to the latest LRO all 14 were to be nuclear. The costs of the program were worrisome. At first all had been carried as DLGN (Terrier), the program calling for the continuation of Terrier production until Typhon was ready. Each would cost $110 million, compared to $75 million for a DLG. Worse, it was estimated that the Typhon ship would cost $192 million for a lead ship, $153 million for a follow-on; "financing the number of ships required . . . appears doubtful."

Moreover, the LRO projected no further destroyer production (then generally understood to be 30-knot,

The modernized *Bainbridge* steams off the California coast in April 1979. She shows the characteristic NTDS broadband HF radio antenna forward, as well as an SPS-48 three-dimensional radar on her foremast, and a revised mainmast with a LAMPS data link antenna and UHF/DF at its peak; the *Bainbridge* was fitted to operate LAMPS helicopters under the FY 74 program at Puget Sound. Note, too, the replacement of her former twin 3-inch/50s by quadruple Harpoon missile launchers, and the erected underway replenishment tripod atop her after missile magazine. The quarter view was taken upon her completion in April 1977; note the ULQ-6 deceptive ECM antennas abreast her bridge.

4,000–5,000-ton general-purpose warships) and instead looked towards a continuation of the 27-knot FY 62 DEG 1 class, of the FY 62 DE (*Garcia* class), and, tentatively, of a DEK with manned helicopters; later the DE might evolve

toward increased versatility without major increase in size or manning, through provision of lightweight SAM, an SSM capability, and speed approaching 30 knots, while remaining primarily an ASW ship. Improved power plants and hull designs, developments arising from SURIC and sonars of new types, are all visualized as potential contributors to increasing DE capability *without* increasing size, and hopefully with reduced personnel requirements.

It is considered desirable to restate the foregoing in order to combat the current tendency to let available nuclear power plants dictate the characteristics of ships, and thereby the missions and tasks of those ships, and in turn the composition and operating concepts of future task forces. While nuclear propulsion is a key consideration to be kept in mind at all stages of future force planning, the sound approach is to proceed in the reverse of the order stated, i.e., from concepts and composition to missions and tasks to Characteristics, making the plant, whenever possible, adapt *to* the desired Characteristics. Numerical requirements and fiscal limitations also make this approach preferable.

Nonetheless, in order to derive full benefit from nuclear power, it is necessary to consider how we can best use the available nuclear plants, with minimum disruption of our projected concepts. . . . The *Long Beach* plant is the only plant capable today of driving a frigate or cruiser of more than 8,000 tons at 30 knots. It requires a ship of about 15,000 tons displacement. It adds some $50 million to the cost of a conventional ship, if the latter must be one of 15,000 ton size. It probably adds *more* to the cost of a ship which, with conventional power, could be of lesser tonnage. There is some reason to suppose that the CG (Typhon) requirement *could* be met in a CG of 11,000 tons, e.g., by a reduction to a 7,000 element radar.

The *Bainbridge* plant is able to drive a 7,000-ton ship at 30 knots but speed falls off . . . when, as in the recently proposed DLGN (Typhon), over 2,000 tons of displacement and the Typhon radar power demand must be added.

The Navy has now committed itself to use, when developed, a plant providing the *Bainbridge* power output from a single reactor, presumably with a considerable saving in space, weight, and cost . . . this plant has been conceived of as a *destroyer* (i.e., *DD*) plant. However, as noted above, LRO-61 states no objective for further *DD* construction, and this plant is clearly incompatible, in size or cost of ship resulting, with the family of small relatively inexpensive *DE* types called for in large numbers. . . . This plant may be available for the FY 65 program, probably not sooner.

There is the possibility that *half* of the *Bainbridge*

plant, i.e., one reactor and one turbine, might prove adaptable to a size of ship not clearly incompatible with, though considerably slower and much more costly than, the types of DEs visualized for the future. It is not believed that this has been thoroughly studied. . . .

Moorer feared that if care were not taken in the nuclear program, and if the new single reactor (which he expected for FY 65) were not incorporated in a new and more austere DLGN, the costs might well kill off the CGN, leaving the Navy with no new first-rate AAW ship, while "we may be forced to schedule a DDN, not now called for in the LRO, in order to use the new reactor to which we are committed; each such ship will cost us two of the smaller ASW ships now projected."

In fact, the DE(N) idea was not entirely new. In 1957 a special committee of the National Academy of Sciences met to discuss the implications of nuclear submarines, both U.S. and, prospectively, Soviet. This Nobska study is generally remembered for its recommendation for Polaris. However, it also reviewed the state of ASW in the face of nuclear submarines; recommendations included the quick development of a nuclear ASW torpedo—and the design of a nuclear destroyer escort, perhaps incorporating the new lightweight reactor then being developed for the abortive aircraft nuclear propulsion program.

Thus in March 1958, the SCB asked BuShips to sketch DE(N). The result, that August, would carry the then-current DE battery and sensors (SQS-26, ASROC, three DASH, a twin 3-in./50) on 3,200 tons (full load), and would make 23 knots. The reactor contemplated was not specified, and the project proceeded no further. However, the following month the bureau sent the Standing Committee on the Shipbuilding and Conversion Program notes on possible ships for the FY 61–66 programs, including both a DDGN and a DEG(N). The latter was rather impressive, with Tartar, ASROC, DASH, and a sustained speed of 27 knots. Again, it did not appear in the actual building programs. Although its great endurance would have been a considerable asset, numbers were far too important in ASW, given the limited area a single ship could control.

Ultimately, Admiral Burke chose to give destroyers priority in the extension of nuclear power to surface ships, as extensions in their endurance would provide the greatest military advantages. This philosophy was continued by his successor, Admiral Anderson. A study made late in 1962 or early in 1963 set 8,000 tons as the lower limit for an effective nuclear escort; in March 1963, Admiral Anderson made it CNO policy

to support the nuclear propulsion of surface ships larger than 8,000 tons, and to support R&D aimed at making reductions in the cost and other improvements in naval nuclear propulsion plants to enable nuclear power to be introduced on a wider scale in surface warships. Specifically, the orderly introduction of nuclear propulsion in surface ships will be continued by programming future construction of all aircraft carriers and frigates with nuclear power, recognizing potential physical and personnel limitations. . . .

This policy was justified to OSD on the ground that the successful round-the-world cruise of the *Enterprise*, *Long Beach*, and *Bainbridge* proved the advantages of nuclear power.

On this basis, Secretary of the Navy Fred Korth proposed in an April 1963 memorandum that all carriers beginning with CVAN 67 be nuclear powered, including those planned as conventional ships for FY 65 and FY 67. All future frigates were to be nuclear powered beginning with the lead Typhon ship in FY 65, which had already been approved as nuclear, and continuing with two DLGNs in FY 66, three in FY 67, and two in FY 68, which were being carried in the OSD program as conventional. Moreover, specific proposals were to be prepared for a new nuclear-powered guided-missile destroyer to be funded in FY 66 and to be followed by annual building programs. "This DDGN will be suitable both for carrier task force support and for independent types of operations. It is noted that there are questions, including those from OSD, yet to be resolved on this ship type, and that there are no new DDGs or DDGNs currently in the OSD approved Navy Ship Construction Program." It is clear from an accompanying paper that the DDGN was what became DLGN 36, the *South Carolina* class; it was described in his paper as a DDGN (augmented) and had twice the missile battery of the DDG. Augmentation was sensible in view of the considerable cost already sunk in a nuclear power plant that would be the same for either the "augmented" 10,400-ton ship or the 9,000-ton base DDGN. In effect, the demise of the Typhon system meant the demise of what the DLGN or DLG had become, a second-rate nuclear cruiser; all subsequent missile-ship construction had fallen back into the former DDG category, upgraded considerably from the *Adams* class. Indeed, the DDG cited in the Anderson papers came to 7,300 tons, not far from a DLG (Terrier).

In the event, Secretary of Defense McNamara proved recalcitrant, and the nuclear program did not develop nearly as quickly as might have been expected. The secretary feared, among other things, that escorts in general were growing far too quickly in size and in cost. Moreover, in line with his preference for numbers to express precisely concepts such as greater effectiveness, he continued to demand detailed studies showing the relative cost and value of

nuclear warships. It is not entirely clear to what extent the design studies of this period reflect the requirements of these studies, and to what extent they reflect Admiral Anderson's determination to build a nuclear escort force.

For example, the projects for a faster (30 knot) DE and for a DE(N) appear to have been associated, at least in their nonpropulsion elements; on the other hand, in the late fall of 1963 the Center for Naval Analysis requested data on nuclear and conventional escorts as part of its nuclear carrier study. The weapon system contemplated was a six-illuminator Improved Tartar with two Mk 13 launchers. This DDG(N) would displace 9,717 tons fully loaded, and would be powered by a full pair of D2G reactors, as in the *Bainbridge*. The cost was estimated at $142 million ($172 million lead ship), and nonmissile armament was to include one 5-inch lightweight gun, an ASROC box, two torpedo tubes for Mk 37s and the usual pair of triple lightweight tubes for homing torpedoes. DASH facilities would be limited to a platform, controls, and a hangar for three drones or one UH-2. BuShips estimated that a comparable DDG would displace 9,660 tons fully loaded, but would cost only $97 million ($122 million lead). As an alternative, the bureau considered a single-screw DEG(N), powered by a derated plant in which one main coolant loop was deleted and the two reactors placed back to back to economize on length and shielding—a practice the bureau considered unwise in such expensive units. Full load displacement did fall to 7,600 tons and cost to $114 million ($146 lead), but there was a considerable cost in speed, and the proposed design deleted one of the two Tartar launchers, one of the three NTDS computers (and seven of the seventeen displays), as well as the long-range two-dimensional air search radar of the other schemes. Tartar channels were also reduced from six to two. This was austerity with a vengeance, but even so the cost of the nuclear ship considerably exceeded that of a DDG quite equivalent to the larger DDG(N) in capabilities.

The *Truxtun* was the last of the Terrier-armed frigates. As she was being built, a new missile system, Typhon, was reaching the point at which it appeared to be ready for deployment. For the first time the cost and complexity of the system was entirely dominated by its radar and computers. Indeed, the Typhon system design represented a conscious attempt to trade off cost per missile for electronics. Economies were to be realized by a combination of a reduction in the *number* of missile ships (through much longer missile ranges realized largely through more sophisticated guidance systems) and at the same time a reduction in the size of the individual missile installation. Countervailing tendencies would include

The *Truxtun* carried the *Belknap* battery and systems, including NTDS and SPS-48; note the broadband antenna forward. She is shown newly completed in 1967.

the size of the very long range radar required, the need to stow more missiles for each of a small number of launchers, and advances in ASW weapons and sensors—which, although unrelated to the AAW system, would drive up ship size and cost. Ultimately, the size of Typhon ships was dominated by the size and power requirements of the big SPG-59 electronically steered acquisition and tracking radar. It existed in two versions, one with 3,400 radiating elements and one with 10,000. These figures translated into power requirements of, respectively, 2,500 and 5,000 kw, which would entail substantial reductions of cruising range in a conventionally powered ship. Some idea of scale is given by the observation that it was the smaller array that was fitted to the *Norton Sound* in 1964.

A series of feasibility studies was started in November 1958 for conventionally powered destroyers, frigates, and cruisers. All would be *fleet* air defense ships, which was taken to mean NTDS, a high sustained speed, and an 8,000 nm. endurance at 20 knots. ASROC and two Mk 32 torpedo tubes supported by SQS-26 were also demanded. The performance requirements alone, far in excess of those demanded of contemporary fast escorts, would in themselves have guaranteed substantial increases in hull size.

Thus, for example, the DDG began as an expanded DDG 2 and ended as an enlarged DLG 16 of 7,250 tons (full load); even then it could not accommodate the big SPG-59. The DLG came to 11,400 tons, at an estimated cost of $151 million (lead; $130 million for follow-on ships), and the cruiser to 15,900 tons ($206/ 184 million). By way of comparison, in 1958 it was estimated that DDG 2, if included in the FY 60 program, would cost $35 to $38 million; DLG 16 would come to $54 to $57 million. In each case the precise cost would depend upon the number of repeat ships.

What was most striking was the way in which the inclusion of the new missile system pushed each type into the next: DDG became DLG, DLG became CG. At this time it was expected that the earliest Typhon construction would be for FY 62; decisions to proceed would be required by July 1959 for the cruiser and by October for the DDG or DLG. In fact, progress on the missile system did not justify inclusion of any Typhon ships prior to the FY 63 program.

A new cycle of studies now began, still with conventional propulsion. The DLG was now characterized by its 3,400-element radar; it carried one launcher for a long-range missile (the Terrier-sized replacement for Talos) and two for medium-range weapons (Tartar replacements with Terrier performance) with, respectively, 40 and 80 missiles; SQS-26, ASROC, and NTDS. Full load displacement would be 8,700 tons. Even with this large a hull, endurance was only 7,000 nm.; with the SPS-59 on, it was reduced to 6,600 nm., and even this figure required that the radar be operated at reduced power 90 percent of the time and at full power only 10 percent. Thus, the DLG required an SPS-43 conventional air search radar to complement the fire control set. The inferior endurance of all the conventional Typhon designs soon led to the evaluation of nuclear power. Although the latter would add even more to the cost of the ships, the SCB felt that this addition would be a minor one, given the cost already sunk in the Typhon system.

In March 1961, the SCB met to consider a CG (Typhon) and decided to pursue CG(N) and DLG(N) types, the latter to be based on the 560-foot, 8,700-ton design of January 1961 described above. The CNO formally requested a Typhon DLG(N) of about 9,000 tons on 11 May; it became the FY 63 Typhon DLG(N), SCB 227. In his formal request, the CNO asked that LR missile stowage, which included ASROC, be expanded beyond 40 missiles, and that a 5-inch gun be included. A sustained speed of 30 knots was required. Both pure nuclear and nuclear/gas turbine (CONAG) variants, all descended from the 560-foot DLG, were considered. On 25 August 1961, BuShips reported three frigates and a 16,100-ton nuclear cruiser. The frigate characteristics were:

Scheme	F	G	L
	Nuclear	CONAG	Nuclear
LWL	580	626	560
Beam	61	61	60
Draft (over sonar)	30	30	—
Full Load	9,700	11,500	9,260
Sustained Speed	28	30/27	28
LR Missiles	1(60)	1(60)	—
MR Missiles	2(80)	2(80)	2(80)
5-inch./38		2	2
Complement	501	573	539
Cost* (millions)	$192/153	$217/171	$186/148

* In cost, first figure is lead ship, second is follow-on.
Missiles: first figure is the number of launchers.

CONAG was attractive only because with the only nuclear plant available, the dual D2G, the speed requirement could not be met. Thus, in Scheme G a 30,000 shp gas-turbine plant was added; the growth in hull could, in turn, accommodate facilities for AAW sector control and enough fuel for 2,200 nm. at 30 knots. However, CONAG remained unattractive because it did not provide simplicity of operation and because it denied the ship the advantage of sustained

high-speed operation. Note, however, that unlike the earlier CONAG studies, in this one the nuclear plant provided most of the power even at high speed. Scheme L was too austere, considering its cost; in September 1961, characteristics for SCB 227 based on Scheme F were issued. They included two Mk 32 and two Mk 25 torpedo tubes, as well as a hangar for three DASH drones or one HU2K helicopter. By January 1962, the 5-inch battery had been shaved to a single centerline 5-inch/38 or one lightweight 5-in./54, then in the discussion stage. Early suggestions to include roll stabilization were rejected on grounds of weight and cost.

The new ship would be extremely costly, but on the other hand Typhon promised great effectiveness. Thus, on 5 September 1961, Admiral Speck, chairman of the SCB, described the AAW effectiveness of a Typhon DLG as "of an entirely different order of magnitude" than that of a Terrier frigate;

> the Typhon radar and the long and medium range launchers give the Typhon frigate a greater AAW effectiveness in a 9,500-ton ship than a 16,000-ton Talos/Tartar ship. . . . The Typhon weapon system has a well-defined capability against air-launched, surface-launched, or sub-surface launched missiles because of the quick reaction time which applies not only to the first target but also to each succeeding target because of the Typhon radar ability to track and guide several missiles concurrently.

Speck strongly recommended that a Typhon ship be included in the FY 63 program, that it be in the 9,500-ton class, and that it be redesignated a cruiser.

The ship grew in the course of design, so that by April 1962 she was expected to displace 10,825 tons (trial) on a waterline length of 600 feet. This lengthening solved the speed problem so that she was expected to make 30.25 knots on trial (29.15 sustained). The LR and one MR launcher were forward, with the remaining MR launcher aft alongside the DASH hangar (rather than abaft, as in the original Scheme F). Overriding considerations in this unusual arrangement were:

—Maximum separation of SPG-59 from the large communications antenna; the SCB wanted the SPG-59 at the fore end of the superstructure;
—The SCB wanted one of the MR launchers aft;
—The DASH hangar and helo pad had to be aft;
—The communications antenna had to be so located as to minimize interference with missile arcs of fire.

The solution adopted was to locate the SPG-59 over the machinery space and the communications antenna over the DASH hangar aft; this in turn pushed the DASH hangar so far aft as to necessitate the peculiar side-by-side arrangement, which the Bureau

An artist's conception of the abortive Typhon nuclear missile frigate, drawn in 1961, shows the Terrier-sized long-range ramjet and the Tartar-sized medium-range rocket missile. The conical structure is the SPG-59 radar, with its transmitter at the top and three receivers at its base; a conventional two-dimensional air-search radar was to have been mounted atop the mainmast. Both it and a shorter radio mast display the conical wire antennas that were then being introduced for broadband operation so as not to have excessive multiplication of antennas.

of Naval Weapons approved—although originally it had wanted a centerline position and had gone so far as to approve a launcher *between* DASH pad and hangar. The gun was also located aft, in part because it would have required a director interfering with the SPG-59—and its personnel would have been exposed to radiation hazards from the radar proper. Another peculiarity of the design was the decision to move the LR launcher abaft the forward MR launcher, although the former was the primary weapon and might, therefore, have been expected to have the greatest command. One factor was the fore-and-aft weight distribution, an important issue in a nuclear ship design.

As of January 1962, the Navy program called for a prototype DLGN in FY 63, followed by two less-expensive DLGs in FY 64, and ultimately for a total of seven Typhon ships. However, sensor development lagged, and the DLGN was dropped from the FY 63 budget after $190 million had been appropriated for it. Of this sum, $121 million was diverted to a program for curing the faults of the "3-T" missiles Typhon was being developed to replace, and to other missile ships.

For FY 64 the SCB tried to reduce prototype costs so as to avoid cancellation of the entire Typhon program. Thus, it tried to remain within limits of $180 million and a full load displacement of 10,000 tons. The 560-foot DLG and an updated 580-foot DLGN were to be used as bases for an austere design that, in March 1962, appeared to be a 580-foot, 10,900-ton, 30-knot DLG (endurance 7,000 nm. at 20 knots, i.e.,

less than that of contemporary DLGs). Any attempt to increase endurance only made matters worse. For example, 8,000 nm. (SPG-59 turned off; 7,500 with mixed operation, and 6,600 nm. with the SPG-59 on full power continuously) cost (in June) 11,400 tons fully loaded, and $185 million. This was unacceptable, and by October the SCB was willing to cut endurance to 6,000 nm. (5,500/4,800 with the SPG-59 turned on) in order to reduce the size of the DLG to 10,300 tons (8,300 light) and $181/157.5 million.

Virtually every other means of shaving size and cost was tried. For example, in one scheme the LR launcher was eliminated entirely and an ASROC pepperbox substituted, which saved 20 feet of length, 700 tons, and about $7 million. An alternative was to abandon all ASW weapons except ASROC and to replace the SQS-26 sonar with the far less effective SQS-23; this saved only 400 tons and about $2 million. Even these two reductions, a terrible loss of effectiveness, saved only 20 feet, 800 tons, and less than $10 million. The only other austerity measure was a reduction in endurance fuel; the sacrifice of 2,000 nm. bought 10 feet of length and 800 tons, but saved almost no money because most of the cost of the ship went into weapons and sensors, not ship steel. Finally, pressure-fired boilers were tried; they saved only 300 tons and actually added to the cost, which was not surprising.

Indeed, any reduction at all was rather dismal in a $180-million ship, at a time when $40 million seemed a great deal to pay for a DDG. On the other hand, the lower the cost of the Typhon prototype, the better the chance that the system would enter service. In September 1962, the SCB issued tentative characteristics for SCB 243: endurance was reduced to 6,000 nm. with the big radar turned off, LR magazine capacity cut to 40. Savings were, however, small, and the SCB began to return to the larger DLG, with an 8,000 nm. endurance (590-foot length, 11,335 tons fully loaded, $184.3 million for the lead ship; 7,500 nm. endurance with the SPG-59 at low power 90 percent of the time). A major consideration in the design was the requirement for two 2,500-kw turbogenerators devoted to the SPG-59.

The SCB presented this last scheme, which had been developed in November 1962, to the CNO as the best buy, but by January 1963 Secretary of Defense Robert S. McNamara had decided to defer procurement pending system progress. Efforts within BuShips shifted back to the DLGN, and SCB 227 was revived for the FY 65 program. The design was renumbered SCB 240.65 under a new numbering system. The complement now included a unit commander and his staff.

	SCB 227	SCB 240.65
LWL	600	650
Beam	62	64
Draft (keel)	20–6	21
Light Displacement	9,951	10,000
Full Load	10,902	12,000
Sonar	SQS-26	SQS-26/VDS
Air Search Radar	SPS-43A	SPS-49
LR	1(60)	1(60)
MR	2(80)	1(80)
DASH	Yes	No
Complement	601	743

Cost figures are not available. What seems most to have impressed the Secretary of Defense about these ships was their great size, primarily a consequence of the *volume* of electronics—and of electronic operators, maintainers, spare parts. Much of the cost was electronics, too; for example, a BuShips comparison sheet of 18 June 1962 shows the cost of the lead Weapons Control System Mk 2/SPG-59 at $43.8 million, as compared to $5.7 million for an LR or $4.7 million for an MR launcher.

Secretary McNamara decided that Typhon was too expensive, and on 13 December 1963 he informally deleted the DLGN from the FY 65 program; the entire Typhon program was canceled shortly thereafter. This was by no means to be taken as a sign of loss of interest in fleet air defense; from FY 66 onward the Secretary of Defense tried to convince the Congress to authorize new DDGs that were really equivalent to the earlier DLGs. At the same time he permitted the Navy to begin work on a new Advanced Surface Missile System (ASMS), which was to combine Typhon techniques with new and less-expensive electronic technology. It became Aegis.

With the demise of Typhon, a gap opened in U.S. missile escort production. A series of conventional DDGs was proposed, but Congress preferred further DLGNs equivalent to the DDGNs of the 1963 Korth memorandum. Indeed, the next two, DLGN 36 (the *California*, FY 67) and DLGN 37 (*South Carolina*, FY 68), were essentially nuclear equivalents of the abortive FY 66 DDG. Long-lead items for each were bought under the previous-year programs, FY 66 and FY 67. A third ship, DLGN 38, partly funded in FY 68, was dropped in favor of a new DXGN design; she would have been built with FY 69 funds. The ancestry of these ships shows in their mack-like masts to carry electronic gear. Like the new (abortive) DDG, they were armed with Standard, the advanced version of Tartar, which now had performance equivalent to that of the earlier Terriers—and a far higher launch rate. They were very expensive, and by the late sixties Secretary McNamara was unwilling to spend funds already limited by the expense of the Vietnam War. Indeed, the ships were built only because of congressional pressure: the Secretary of Defense did not release funds for them until March 1968.

The design originally called for two heavy 5-in./ 54s, as opposed to the lightweight Mk 45 of the DDG designs, two single-arm Mk 13 launchers, an ASROC pepperbox with reloads stowed in a magazine forward of it, two Mk 32 and two Mk 25 torpedo tubes, the latter in the transom. Construction was slow, largely because only one yard, Newport News, was qualified to build nuclear surface ships. Thus, although both frigates were ordered in June 1968, they did not enter service until 1974/75. Their design changed: the lightweight 5-inch gun replaced the former rapid-fire type, the transom torpedo tubes were discarded with the demise of the surface-launched Mk 48 torpedo, and the fantail was strengthened for a helicopter pad, albeit with no hangar. As in previous nuclear frigate designs, they were powered by a pair of D2Gs, although reportedly the later version employed in these ships provided greatly increased range. This improvement might better be characterized as longer reactor core life, since from an operational point of view all nuclear endurance is effectively infinite. However, reactor core replacement is both expensive and time-consuming, and how often it must be done determines to a large extent how often a nuclear warship must be withdrawn from service for a large refit. By extension, it determines how many nuclear warships must be built to provide a given level of operational ships. The improvement in the DLGN 36 reactor, which increased endurance by about a factor of three, thus was quite significant.

The nuclear cruiser *South Carolina* is shown late in 1974, as completed. She has a fully symmetrical missile installation, with two guidance channels fore and aft, and 40 missiles in each of her two Mk 13 launching systems. Her forward superstructure carries, in addition, the SPG-60 tracking radar of her Mk 86 fire-control system, which adds an additional missile control channel. The radome aft accommodates the SPQ-9 track-while-scan surface fire-control radar. The fore topmast carries LAMPS data link antennas and a UHF/DF; there is no helicopter hangar. SPG-51D missile-control radars are part of the digital Tartar D system.

Among other things, it encouraged a new attitude toward hull design, which was manifested in the next DLGN design.

That is, in a conventional ship the hull is designed to minimize resistance at cruising speed, about 20 knots, to achieve maximum endurance. Such a design exacts a performance penalty at maximum speed, and in fact it is necessary to balance power plant efficiency at cruising speed against the need for much more power at maximum. However, a plant that can operate indefinitely at cruising speed permits a hull design optimized for the high-speed end of the per-

formance envelope. The greater the nuclear endurance, the less important is a penalty of a few percent at cruising speed and, by extension, the better the high-speed performance for fixed power output. Similar reasoning applies to trade-offs between stability and speed performance, where a nuclear ship can accept a resistance penalty at cruising speed that would be entirely out of bounds for a conventional design.

A new DLGN design effort began in 1967 towards the end of the DX/DXG cycle of fleet escort studies. When a nuclear version of DXG was introduced into the Major Fleet Escort Study, it appeared that four DXGNs could replace the six conventional escorts of a fast carrier. Secretary of Defense McNamara decided to support two all-nuclear carrier task groups, for which a total of eight operational DLGNs would be required, with another to permit one to be in overhaul at any one time. At first four new ships were proposed (two FY 70, two FY 71), and then a fifth— the cruiser *Long Beach* having been eliminated as a carrier escort, presumably because of her potential value as a fleet flagship. In fact, at this time there were a total of four nuclear carriers in prospect. Secretary McNamara proposed to use conventional escorts for two of them. If he chose to provide nuclear ships for all 4, that would require 7 more DLGNs, to get an average of 15 on line at any one time. For the 20 percent of the time when all four CVANs would be on line, a total of 16 DLGNs would be required, i.e., 12 new ones. The secretary argued that the ten-year cost of seven new DLGNs would be $1.6 billion, vs. $1.1 billion for the equivalent force of nine new DLGs. The nuclear ships would save an additional $75 to $80 million in logistics, but he doubted that their nuclear endurance was worth $400 million. Others in the Navy felt quite differently, and proposed the extension of nuclear power to further carrier strike groups. They argued that limited DLG endurance was an important limitation on carrier strike group effectiveness; indeed, it might well be more profitable to put reactors in the DLGs than in the carrier, which had a large inherent endurance. Thus, by 1970 a program of 23 DXGNs was being proposed. With such a large production run in mind, it was logical to provide for the new surface-to-air missile system (ASMS, now Aegis) in later ships.

As in previous ambitious nuclear surface-ship programs, this one ran afoul of the fiscal considerations of the office of the Secretary of Defense, who in May 1971 suspended the program at the first three units, a contract for which was signed with Newport News that December. Long-lead items for DLGN 38 had already been approved under the FY 69 budget (procurement in FY 70) and the same pattern was followed for DLGN 39 and 40 (FY 70/71 and FY 71/72). Congress, generally a strong supporter of nuclear propulsion, reversed the OSD decision and appropriated long-lead items for DLGN 41 in FY 74 (procurement FY 75) and for DLGN 42 in FY 75. However, the procurement of this fifth ship was stopped in FY 76 because she would not receive Aegis and would therefore be obsolescent. In effect, the DLGNs, which by the end of 1975 were designated cruisers, were to be succeeded by the much larger strike cruisers (CSGN) and by Aegis-armed conventionally powered destroyers, which themselves graduated to the cruiser class in 1980.

The DXGN study began on the basis of DXG armament slightly improved, i.e., lightweight 5-in./54 guns fore and aft, ASROC abaft the usual magazine (as in DLGN 36), and one Mk 13 launcher aft. NAVSEC estimated that such a ship could be built on a waterline length of 540 feet and a full load displacement of 8,720 tons, which compared to the 570 feet and 10,150 tons of the *California*. There were many efforts at austerity: for example, DXGN would not have division commander facilities. The new design seemed so economical that in January 1968 the Secretary of Defense proposed that DLGN 37 be built to it. This plan, however, was abandoned to avoid delays in laying down the ship.

In fact, it was never entirely clear that the best DXGN would duplicate the DXG battery. Thus, although the Navy Major Fleet Escort study showed that single-ended missile ships appeared to be most cost effective, there were instances in which double-ended units would be valuable for their ability to provide sustained fire against, for example, fighter-bomber attacks. Ships with only 40 weapons would become magazine-limited. In turn, the double-ender might be suited to independent operations. It was a prime candidate for nuclear power in view both of its size as well as of the requirement for long and unreplenished endurance. The study considered such ships worthwhile despite their cost, partly in view of the reduction in underway replenishment groups and their escorts that would result.

Despite considerable OSD pressures for austerity, DXGN began quite early to grow beyond a nuclear DXG. Adoption of the Mk 26 Tartar/ASROC launcher permitted elimination of the separate ASROC pepperbox and its magazine forward—for which a second Mk 26 was substituted; now DXGN was, for all practical purposes, a double-ender. It was hoped that at least some ships would be able to incorporate ASMS. This required provision for the considerable top weight associated with the deckhouse supporting the Aegis phased-array fire control radar. Thus, although DXGN approached DLGN 36 size, it could not use the same hull: a new hull form was chosen in October 1968. This was a major step, given the problems of hull design for any nuclear ship. Compared to the Mk 13 of the earlier design, the Mk 26 actually saved some length (although DLGN 38 grew, in the end, to 560 feet). However, it reduced the number of air-defense weapons carried. A Mk 13 launcher accommodates 40 missiles, all SAMs, whereas a Mk 26 Mod 1 holds 44—including the ASROCs not accommodated because of the deletion of their specialized launcher and magazine.

The new design incorporated a new ESM system (small ship Shortstop, in the design phase) as well as an improved reactor system. Initial weight estimates suggested that length might be reduced to as little as 540 feet, but the designers suspected that so short a weather deck might prove insufficient (for armament, electronics, boats, underway replenishment, and a helicopter pad aft) and opted for a 550-foot hull at a cost of 3 tons; ultimately, ten more feet were added. With a new hull form, they could choose either a forecastle or a flush (two-deck) type. The former was preferred for easier handling of weapons and stores, particularly in underway replenishment; for greater freeboard for helicopter operation; and for a lower silhouette, with some superstructure functions transferred to the hull. Costs included an additional weight of 200 tons, as well as somewhat poorer vision over the bow, an intangible factor. The two-deck hull was, therefore, selected. An increased prismatic coefficient was accepted to reduce hull size and to increase water-plane inertia, the latter to balance off the top weight for which provision had to be made (ASMS). There was some penalty in terms of power required for cruising speed, but that was quite acceptable in view of the long reactor core life.

LAMPS entered service quite late in the DLGN 38 design process, but even so a requirement for a hangar and helo pad had to be levied. The solution chosen was quite neat: this late, the superstructure could not be moved about, but there was unused hull space right aft within the hull. A dual-purpose elevator and door were provided to transport the single helicopter between hangar and fantail. In practice this idea proved unfortunate. Located right aft, the helicopter suffered from maximum hull vibration and motion. The seal between door and deck leaked badly and required frequent replacement. This experience led to a considerable rearrangement in the next series of DLGN designs, the CSGNs.

These nuclear escorts were subject to considerable cost inflation. In December 1968, while DXGN was still an "economy" design with only one Mk 13, it was expected to cost $220 ($180 follow-on) million, a saving of about $40 million over additional DLGN 36s. In fact, DLGN 36/37 cost only $219/186 million. On the other hand, DXGN evolved into DLGN 38 (*Virginia* class), by no means an austere ship. Total end costs rose spectacularly, partly due to inflation: $279 million for DLGN 38, $257 million for DLGN 39 (which suggests the true follow-on cost in a still relatively uninflated economy), then $270 million for DLGN 40. The long gap between DLGN 40 and DLGN 41 resulted in a rise in the later ship to $337 million. In 1975, it appeared that DLGN 42, were she to be built, would cost $368 million.

By that time there was a new nuclear frigate program in sight. The Aegis system had originally been designed for installation in late units of the DXGN type. However, when Admiral Elmo F. Zumwalt, Jr.,

became CNO he decided instead on a new class of extremely austere gas-turbine destroyers, then designated DG/Aegis. This project continued until 1974, when Admiral Zumwalt was replaced as CNO by Admiral James Holloway III, who canceled it in favor of a nuclear platform. In fact, the nuclear alternative had been explored even earlier. In the process of program planning in the spring of 1973, the Secretary of the Navy, reviewing the Tentative POM (Program Objectives Memorandum) for FY 75, asked that the feasibility of building a single new class of nuclear-powered surface combatants capable of providing area defense for carriers be investigated. Issues to be considered included the impact of such a program on the force level of surface combatants, with particular regard to the coming need to replace all of the *Charles F. Adams*-class DDGs.

It proved impossible simply to place Aegis aboard a DLGN 38 hull; a new nuclear frigate, tentatively designated DG(N), was designed instead. It was to have two Mk 26 Mod 2 (64 missile) launchers as compared to the one of DG/Aegis, and would operate two LAMPS III helicopters (one in DG/Aegis). Other advantages would include an additional missile-control console and, perhaps most significantly, four rather than two slaved illuminators for terminal missile guidance. All of this was not inexpensive: in January 1974 DG(N) displaced 9,961 tons (light) and 10,708 tons fully loaded.

This tentative DG(N) design was the result of a long series of studies beginning with the rather austere DG payload and the standard two-reactor (DG2) propulsive plant. The cost of nuclear propulsion itself shows in this base-line case: 9,144 tons (light) or 9,695 tons fully loaded, 530 feet long. In effect, the addition of an extra launcher, which would have been extremely expensive in the conventional design, was overshadowed by the design overhead associated with the nuclear plant. Alternatively, one might say that the decision to accept nuclear power automatically made an austere weapon system unattractive; in fact, other analyses suggested that the one-launcher DG did not make full use of the Aegis system potential, and so was not as economical as had been hoped.

The DLGN (Aegis) project continued through the spring of 1974, but was stopped that July. The new CNO looked upon it as insufficiently offensive, and redefined it as a strike cruiser (CSGN) capable of independent surface operations. The combination of a very high capacity air (i.e., antimissile) defense system (Aegis) with nuclear power for unlimited endurance made for a surface combatant that might well be able to operate, alone, in many medium-threat areas. With the development of antiship (Harpoon) and long-range tactical or strategic (Tomahawk) ship-launched cruise missiles, such a ship might

Although superficially similar to the earlier *South Carolina* type, the *Virginia*-class missile cruiser *Texas* (above and facing) actually had rather different capabilities, having descended from the *Spruance* AAW version. Thus, her forward missile-launching system is Mk 26 Mod 0, accommodating only 24 missiles and intended primarily for ASROC; note that both SPG-51D missile-guidance radars are located aft (for her Mk 26 Mod 1 launching system, with its 44 missiles), leaving her only an SPG-60 tracker forward, which is shared with her 5-inch battery for antiaircraft fire. The white square forward is a target for helicopter underway replenishment. These ships have a helicopter hangar sunk in their fantails; its door/elevator reportedly leaks badly and is not well liked.

well have a useful offensive role, again in the absence of a carrier. ASW self-defense might be handled by shipboard LAMPS supported by the new towed array, which would permit effective operation even at a high cruising speed. Moreover, with VSTOL in prospect such a cruiser might be able to provide some minimal level of effective air support. She would not replace a carrier task group, but would be able to replace some of its functions in areas of relatively low or medium threat. For example, she would be able to engage Soviet forces in many areas of the world without any necessity for fragmenting the limited number of carrier groups. Her land attack missiles would present a threat that the Soviets would be forced to counter, even at the cost of fragmenting their own forces more customarily targeted against carriers, and thus the mere existence of cruisers capable of independent operations would tend to reduce the effectiveness of the Soviet anticarrier offensive. The strike cruiser would of course be valuable as an air-defense unit of the carrier force, and indeed the increase in size associated with increased

offensive capabilities would permit the relatively inexpensive addition of flagship facilities—sorely needed with the coming departure from service of existing conventional cruisers and with the failure of a project to build a class of new flagships. Finally, the strike cruiser could form the nucleus of an independent Surface Action Group (SAG).

The only problem was, of course, money. Critics of the CSGN concept argued, ultimately successfully, that the new capability she provided was not worth its cost; that, for example, although Aegis would make a major contribution to task force air defense, it alone could not assure protection in an increasingly hostile worldwide environment. Certainly, less expensive specialized Aegis destroyers might prove as effective within the carrier task group: hence the interest in a class of conventional DDGs to complement the Aegis CSGN. The counterargument was that nuclear endurance was essential for carrier escorts, and that there was little point in building two separate classes of nuclear surface combatants, one for independent operations and one for carrier groups. In part, the

issue was one of overheads. Nuclear power plants are expensive, and impose some constructional costs of their own. Aegis was another expensive system. It might be argued that once these two costs were accepted, it was a false economy to forego other advantages; indeed, even that once Aegis was accepted, nuclear power was relatively inexpensive. On the other hand, most of those involved in the Aegis program had been veterans of Typhon, and most of them must have suspected that the costs associated with nuclear power had edged Secretary McNamara into his decision to cancel the system. Clearly such an argument might be irrational, but equally clearly there was little point in designing a magnificent and rational ship and weapon system that OSD would shrink from financing.

At first the CSGN was little more than an Aegis DLGN with provision for surface-to-surface weapons in low-impact topside cannisters: two quadruple Harpoon and two quadruple Tomahawk launchers. There were also to be two LAMPS helicopters, necessary to keep one operational during independent missions. The fantail location having proven unsuccessful, they were placed in a topside hangar, with a helo pad abaft it at the ideal three-quarters point along the ship's length. To save length, they were stowed side by side. The after Mk 26 launcher was placed abaft and below the helo pad to avoid interference with it. In this form the new design passed its DSARC (Defense Systems Acquisition Review Council) I review in November 1974. As completed in May 1975, this Concept Design called for a 580-foot, 12,700-ton (full load) ship. In a presentation to Secretary of Defense James Schlesinger that set up the Aegis shipbuilding program, Admiral J.T. Holloway III, the CNO, requested a total of 8 strike cruisers, plus another 16 conventionally powered Aegis ships to be derived from the existing *Spruance* hull; they became DDG 47/CG 47. The lead DDG would be funded under the FY 77 program, and the lead strike cruiser under FY 78. In fact, Congress became deadlocked between supporters of nuclear and non-nuclear ships, and neither project was approved for FY 77. However, Congress did appropriate $371 million to begin to convert the existing *Long Beach* to a prototype CSGN. It was estimated that a further $164 million in FY 78 and $248 million in FY 79 would have been required, but the Ford Administration canceled the conversion on 17 January 1977. Shortly afterwards President Carter killed the entire project.

By that time it had grown considerably beyond the ex-DLGN category. In July 1975, PMS 403, responsible for Aegis ships, asked for the new variant, which would incorporate an 8-in./55 lightweight gun as well as CBW and ballistic protection, and provision to provide VSTOLs as well as LAMPS helicopters. The twin D2G power plant would have to be upgraded to maintain the usual speed of about 30 knots in the face of considerable growth in displacement. The result was far closer to a classical cruiser than to a destroyer; for example, Admiral R. C. Gooding, Coordinator of Shipbuilding, stated that "all in all the strike cruiser will be the most survivable surface combatant we have built since World War Two . . . the CSGN will be armored over her radar equipment; her CIC will be below the waterline. . . ."

Between September and December 1975, Preliminary Design studied means of improving survivability by an increase in the usual separation between the two engine rooms, as well as a superstructure rearrangement in which all four phased-array radar faces might be concentrated in a single structure rather than split, as in the original non-nuclear DG and the original CSGN projects. These questions were actually closely connected, since the arrangement of engine rooms had to allow for vertical access to the reactors, at least for re-coring. The greater their physical separation, the greater the survivability of the ship, and the additional compartment meant a distance between engine rooms of as much as 15 percent of the total length of the ship. Achievement of this separation was, in turn, much facilitated by the decision to concentrate the entire SPY-1 radar in a single structure placed between the engine rooms. However, the desire to concentrate the radar had been a matter of deck space limitations, a strong effect on the CSGN design. Concentration reduced alignment errors between faces and between the SPY-1 and the slaved illuminators; it cut cable lengths; it reduced electronic vulnerability and at the same time improved access through the ship. Some weight saved was put into further ballistic protection.

The 8-inch gun had to be placed so as to maximize its coverage without degrading the ship's AAW capability; moreover, missiles on their launch rails had to be protected from gun ejecta. The position to the fore of the forward Mk 26 also had the advantage of providing over-bow cover against pop-up targets: the guided 8-inch shells should add significantly to the ship's close-in air defense capability.

In this form the CSGN expanded to a waterline length of 666 feet and a fully loaded displacement of 17,172 tons. There was a proposal for an even larger version. Reuven Leopold, Technical Director of the Naval Ship Engineering Center, suggested increasing the air capability of the CSGN by providing an angled flight deck, with VSTOL aircraft to be hangared at flight deck level in an expanded island superstructure. He reasoned that ship steel was relatively inexpensive, and that his modification would entail little or no increase in the expensive components of the ship—Aegis and the nuclear plant. His "Mark II" design came to 24,648 tons fully loaded, and could support two helicopters, six VSTOL aircraft, as well as two Tomahawk and four Harpoon launchers, and the two Mk 26 Mod 2 of the basic CSGN. It received some considerable support within OpNav, but died with the Mark I version in 1977.

The incoming Carter Administration did not quite kill off the nuclear Aegis program, at least not immediately. It suggested that a new class of nuclear cruisers of more modest dimensions be built, perhaps one per nuclear carrier, or four in all. The new ship was tentatively designated CGN 42, and harked back to the nuclear Aegis studies of 1973. It was slightly larger than the *Virginia* class, at 12,185 rather than 10,500 tons; speed would have fallen by about a knot. The Aegis system required greatly increased complement (634 rather than 527), and there would have been two LAMPS helicopters, rather than the one of the earlier frigate/cruiser. CGN 42 was also to have received the towed array. Compared to the strike cruiser, she lacked VSTOL, the 8-inch gun (although there were to have been 5-inch/54s), and some missile capacity: although the launchers would be Mk 26, they would be the 44-weapon Mod 1 rather than the 64-weapon Mod 2, for a loss of 40 missiles. Four quadruple launchers for Harpoon or Tomahawk were to have been accommodated.

The CGN 42 design was strongly influenced by CSGN experience. For example, the gun, abaft the forward missile launcher in DLGN 38, was moved forward of it. The helicopters were moved out of the hull, as in the CSGN, and indeed important driving forces in the design were the location of the flight deck and the decreasing hull depth aft. At first it appeared that weight and moment considerations would preclude the placement of more than two quadruple Harpoon launchers, but careful attention to detail permitted the addition of a pair of quadruple Tomahawks forward. The location of all the cannisters on deck would make reloading at sea after underway replenishment relatively simple. As for the choice of the Mod 1 launcher, as the CGN was being designed the Navy was also working on a new Vertical Launch System, which would accommodate 64 missiles of up to Tomahawk size in the space normally occupied by a Mk 26 Mod 1. In fact, the CGN 42 was not quite as close to full CSGN capability as this suggests. For example, she was not nearly as survivable and she could not accommodate such flag facilities as the highly automated TSC, the Tactical Support Center. Even so, she was an extremely powerful warship.

The CGN 42 would cost about $500 million more than a repeat *Virginia*, much of that assignable to the Aegis system proper. As such, she became increasingly attractive as an item to cut in a very tight defense budget. Thus, the first Carter Five-Year Shipbuilding Plan of FY 79–83 showed one per year (with Admiral Holloway suggesting that as many as two per carrier might be required). The program announced in March 1978 showed only one, and that one in FY 83. Sometime that fall the CGN 42 program was canceled entirely. Secretary of Defense Harold Brown stated that a single unit would cost two DDG 47s, which would provide about the same air defense capability. This argument was particularly attrac-

tive to a Carter Administration determined to cease building nuclear carriers. In fact, the Secretary's figures may well have been somewhat biased. It now appears that the first CGN 42 would have cost about $1.2 billion (FY 80) compared to $800 million for a DDG 47. However, follow-on cruisers would surely have cost considerably less, whereas the FY 80 DDG *is* a follow-on.

Thus, in February 1981, the United States Navy has no nuclear escorts under either design or construction. However, the pendulum may be swinging back in their direction. A new nuclear carrier, CVN 71, is to be built (FY 80 authorization), and there is some considerable prospect of another. Perhaps as importantly, the first Soviet nuclear surface combatant, the *Kirov*, rather larger than the CSGN, began sea trials in the summer of 1980. Her appearance may well undercut those critics of nuclear surface ships who ask why no other country has proceeded in the same direction; the prospective appearance of a Soviet nuclear carrier later this decade may well have a similar effect on carrier critics.

15

The New Escorts: SCB 199, Seahawk, DX, FFG

Antisubmarine warfare is very much a game of numbers, given the relatively poor performance of long-range submarine detectors and the consequent inefficiency of convoy tactics, both of which shaped the evolution of the U.S. ASW force through the 1960s. The consistent policy from about 1950 onward was to build a two-tier ("high-low") force: mass-production convoy escorts for the numbers, quality escorts for hunter-killer operations that might exploit World War II-style distant (e.g., HF/DF) contacts. By the late 1950s the hunter-killer concept had become materially more attractive with the success of the SOSUS system of bottom-moored passive arrays, but the essential balance between it and the convoy escorts remained, with a third tier of ASW escorts required for fast task force protection, now that the Soviets had fast nuclear submarines capable of shadowing and attacking such formations.

The Schindler Committee report of 1954 can be read as a statement of this policy: it would be necessary to maintain the utmost discipline in order to hold down the cost and complexity of the mass-production escorts, while quality ASW ships might be had by converting existing destroyer hulls. In view of the relative immunity of really fast formations, the production of very fast ASW ships seemed an unwise dilution of assets that might better be spent to protect the fast task force against the primary threat, air attack. Developments from 1957 on can be read as the gradual downfall of the "low" end of the ASW "high-low" mix; the *Perry* class and the new (1980) FFX are attempts to revive it. As for the high

end, the weapon and sensor developments that doomed the low end also made the proposed destroyer conversion impractical, leading to the construction of substantial numbers of specialized quality ASW escorts.

The viability of the low end of the mix always depended upon the extent to which an existing or proposed mass-production hull could support a minimally acceptable suit of sensors and the weapons to match. Through the fifties, continual advances in the performance of Soviet submarines were matched by U.S. advances in sonars and weapons, but the new equipment demanded larger and larger platforms. Thus, the SQS-4 of the early fifties might be grouped with RAT and with the Mk 37 torpedo; the SQS-23 of the late fifties with ASROC; and the SQS-26 of the early sixties—the most powerful surface ship sonar of all—with an extended-range ASROC, with the Mk 48 torpedo, and, most effectively, with the manned LAMPS helicopter. In practice, the austere convoy escort of the Schindler Committee, the *Claud Jones* (SCB 131), could accommodate SQS-4 but not a weapon to match. The FRAM program showed that the largest World War II mass-production destroyer, the *Gearing*, was marginally capable of supporting the SQS-23/ASROC combination; however, by the late fifties SQS-26 was considered the future standard. Moreover, by that time it was clear that the remaining lives of hulls built in World War II were limited at best, and that the mass production of new destroyers or destroyer-like ships would soon be essential.

Although both of these ships have about the same displacement, the *Perry* looks much larger, thanks to its longer, narrow hull and its much higher freeboard, for better seakeeping. The *Garcia*-class escort is the *Brumby*, refitting at Bath as *Perry* was being completed.

This issue of numbers *and* quality has dominated destroyer thinking since about 1960. The postwar Navy had never been able to buy ships in anything like the numbers bought in World War II, but through the fifties mobilization projects such as the DE ASW conversions, the *Fletcher* DDE, and the DDC promised sufficient numbers for a war emergency. It also appeared that there might be enough time to mass-produce new escorts such as the *Claud Jones* or *Dealey*. By the late fifties, however, the U.S. image of war had turned more and more toward massive exchanges of thermonuclear weapons, and mobilization concepts had become less and less popular: any new war would be fought with existing weapons and existing forces. Wars short of massive strategic exchange probably would not evoke the kind of mobilization response that had characterized World War II and had been expected through the 1950s. Again, any future war would have to be fought very largely with existing forces, augmented, perhaps, by called-up ready reserves.

Unfortunately, the shipbuilding budget shrank just as the need for a large new escort program became urgent. From FY 57 onward, rapid escalation in the cost of high-technology fast task force ships sharply limited numbers, and the new escorts would themselves incorporate considerable high technology in such forms as the SQS-26 sonar. The Polaris crash program also constricted shipbuilding funds, and the emergency FRAM program, while it did stave off disaster, also delayed escort replacement; by the time it had been completed, the decision to fight the Vietnam War on a "guns *and* butter" basis had been made. There would be no massive naval shipbuilding program associated with that war, although the war itself used up the rebuilt but aging gun-and-ASW destroyers.

The decline of the mass-production escort did not begin as such. Rather, it began as no more than an attempt to adapt the existing (satisfactory) mass-production design, the *Dealey*, to new ASW conditions. The key piece of technology was the new SQS-26 bottom-bounce sonar which, it was hoped, would overcome the immense problem of submarine detection in bad thermal gradients. The *Dealey* seaworthiness and good engineering performance made it the basis for the characteristics of a new escort, which would be needed in large numbers. Work on the FY 60 escort began in March 1958, first consideration going to hull and below-decks arrangement to accommodate the new sonar. ASROC would exploit its long range and make up for the low speed of the escort relative to the new submarines. The SCB also wanted three DASH helicopters as an alternative ASW delivery system, capable of hitting beyond ASROC range. The new study was designated SCB 199, as it was clearly more than a modified SCB 72. Early estimates suggested that the hull would be only slightly enlarged (325 feet long, 2,000 tons fully loaded, capable of 25 knots) and that, in comparison with the *Dealey*, SCB 199 might trade three of the original four 3-in./50 guns for greater ASW effectiveness, a very natural expression of priorities.

However, considerable increases were made at the SCB working level: dynamic stabilization, two more 3-inch guns, a better fire control system, better helicopter facilities, even air control facilities. By October 1958 it was estimated that SCB 199 would displace 1,640 tons light (the *Dealey*: about 1,270). Armament would be one twin and one single 3-in./50 (aft), ASROC, two triple lightweight torpedo tubes (Mk 32) for homing torpedoes, and three DASH. It was anticipated that a VDS would ultimately replace the after gun; much later (1964–65) a pair of long Mk 25 torpedo tubes for Mk 48 torpedoes were proposed to replace this gun, but this plan, too, proved abortive.

These improvements cost performance. The initial estimate of 25 knots was already at least a knot slower than the nominal ASW task force with which the new ocean escort was to operate, and this difference was significant even though the helicopter would obviate high-speed runs over the target submarine. Speed "in a moderate sea" now fell to 24 knots, and endurance to 4,000 nm. at 15 knots. One study showed that by adopting a new hull form (350 feet long on the waterline) and redistributing weights, at no significant increase in cost, about 0.7 knots could be gained; this change was incorporated in the design.

The 24-knot speed of SCB 199 was not entirely popular, particularly since the submarine threat of the future was imagined, in 1958, as a 30-knot, deep-diving nuclear submarine. Thus in May 1959, the chairman of the SCB, Rear Admiral Denys W. Knoll, asked the Bureau of Ships to investigate the feasibility and cost of a 30-knot DE of SCB 199 size; "future escorts, with the capability to match speed expected of new submarine designs, would be very attractive if obtainable without improving main propulsion machinery and boilers within the existing hull design." In fact, the bureau concluded that 27 knots could be obtained within a 350-foot SCB 199 hull, using a new pressure-fired boiler and a 35,000 shp DDG 2 plant, at a cost of $24.5 million (lead ship; $19.5 follow-on) compared to $21/$17 million for SCB 199. The 30-knot DE would be a far more difficult proposition, requiring a new pressure-fired boiler and a new turbine of 50,000 shp; length would grow to 385 feet and cost to $31.5/$22.5 million. BuShips had produced a 7,500-hp pressure-fired boiler in 1952, and had been running a 17,500-hp unit since September 1956. It was therefore prepared to propose

The *Bronstein*s were the smallest ships that could accommodate the massive SQS-26 bow sonar: the name ship is shown in drydock at San Diego, 5 December 1963.

the 27-knot DE for the FY 61 program. An FY 60 proposal seemed unwise given the need to reprice a ship already submitted to Congress, whereas an FY 61 ship could be proposed as such. At this time BuShips contemplated only a single experimental prototype (EDE) in the FY 61 program.

Thus, despite early pressure for increased DE speed, two ships were built to the original *Bronstein*-class (DE 1037, or SCB 199) design under the FY 60 program.

Op-34 favored the 27-knot escort. It was somewhat skeptical of the need for higher speed, given the fact that the DE would escort transoceanic convoys; "the sub must come to the convoy and must perforce put himself within range of the DE's ASROC. In order to make successful attack on a sub, the DE must maintain contact. No known surface ship sonar has the ability to detect satisfactorily at over 30 knots. Maximum speed should be close to 30 knots in any case, and the 27-knot figure refers to a sustained speed which is 80 percent of full power. During at least 50 percent of most ocean voyages, sea conditions will preclude use of 30-knot speeds." If a 30-knot escort were really needed, it seemed to Op-34 that reconfigured 1,630-ton destroyers (*Benson*s) would be a far more realistic option.

In any case, although the 27-knotter was 15 percent more expensive than the 24-knot ship, it would be 28 percent cheaper than the 30-knotter.

The Long Range Objectives Group (Op-93) was far more skeptical. The increase of 3 knots would not bring the new DE into the speed range of carrier forces, and it seemed that for hunter-killer operations this speed increase was coming at a very high price. LRO-59 called for 130 new escorts in the next decade, which seemed to preclude anything beyond minimum cost. Similarly, the Undersea Warfare Division (Op-312) noted that the most important objective was to build SQS-26 sonar into as many new ships as possible. Eight 27-knot ships would cost the same as nine of 24 knots; only the jump to 30 knots would be worth any great increase in DE cost: "until it is possible to utilize a boiler capable of 30 knots and in view of the comments given it is recom-

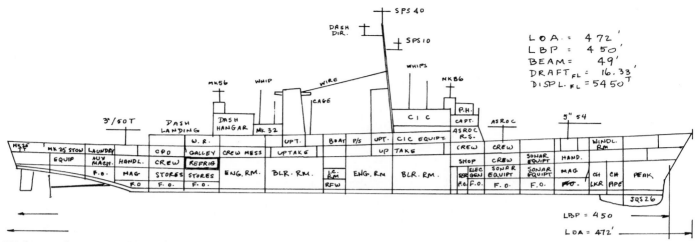

High-speed DE—Study No. 15-64, D. Winter, 6/10/64

mended that no further changes be made to the Characteristics of this class."

In fact, the SCB working level did recommend that one of the FY 61 DEs be powered by pressure-fired boilers, for a speed of 27 knots. On 4 March 1960 the SCB 199 characteristics were modified to incorporate a specific requirement for a pressure-fired plant in at least one ship of the FY 61 program. This SCB 199A (*Garcia* class) design became the basis for both FY 61 ships (DE 1040 and 1041), as well as 15 ships built under FY 62 (DE 1043–1045 and DEG 1–3) and FY 63 (DE 1046–1051 and DEG 4–6) programs. Given the potential for high speed, the original SCB 199 hull began to grow, and the ocean escort came closer and closer to a destroyer, a development actively promoted by BuShips.

The key to this development, pressure firing, was expected to save about 50 percent of space and weight as compared to a conventional system. Half the power of a *Forrest Sherman*, about 35,000 shp, could fit the space that in a conventional DE produced 20,000 shp on the basis of a 600-pound plant. A pressure-fired boiler employs a gas turbine to drive a supercharger; it benefits from better heat transfer characteristics, employing high velocity gases of combustion at greater densities. Additional benefits include improved shock resistance and reduced maintenance requirements. Generally, a distillate fuel such as diesel fuel or aircraft fuel (JP-5) was burned, to minimize deposits and pressure drop.

Even the original SCB 199 (*Bronstein* class) design was not too far from a slow destroyer; despite the effort to economize and so to promote mass production, it was by no means an inexpensive escort. In March 1959, an alarmed SCB asked BuShips to investigate the design of a mass-production convoy escort, in effect the minimum hull that would support an SQS-26 and sustain 15 knots, approximately the speed of a convoy. Preliminary Design sought a

compromise between minimum cost and low self-noise, and investigated both a 1959 and what it considered a feasible 1969 minimum ocean escort. One alternative was to mount SQS-26 in the hull of a standard cargo ship, a C3, locating the machinery as far aft as possible to limit noise interference. The deep draft of the merchant hull would be an important advantage. The alternative conventional naval design came to 1,700 tons, and would be powered by 4,000 hp diesels, for an endurance of 4,500 nm. at 15 knots. Armament would consist of one triple tube for six Mk 44 torpedoes and one twin 40-mm. gun, and it was expected that such a ship could be mass-produced for $8 million, compared to $17 million for a repeat *Dealey*. A nuclear submarine escort, which would cost $41 million, was also considered: it would have the advantages of a significant attack capability, better sonar performance, and immunity from air attack.

For 1969, Preliminary Design looked toward 20-knot convoys, given studies showing a rise in the average speed of merchant ships. Extrapolation suggested that the minimum warship would grow to 1,800 tons and would require gas-turbine propulsion; her cost would almost double, to $15 million, and her endurance would be about 3,000 nm. at 20 knots. The big merchant ship, about ten times as large, would still be the best bargain, since there would be an existing hull and only the $3 million electronics and weapons suit would have to be added. An additional $0.5 million would buy DASH. These mobilization estimates only showed that even austerity was expensive, and they were soon abandoned. In 1981 they are interesting only because in some important ways they foreshadow the current FFX concept: a minimum sensor platform.

Given the failure of such concepts, and the escalating cost of full missile-armed destroyers, some elevation of the ocean escort to near-destroyer status

The *McCloy* steams in Narragansett Bay, 4 May 1970, still in much her original configuration, except for the usual ULQ-6 jamming antennas arrayed vertically just abaft her mack. Her fantail shows a single 3-inch/50 and the shield of her Fanfare torpedo countermeasure; later these ships were fitted with large towed arrays. These ships generally turn about 18 inches by their bows.

was attractive; even austere ocean escorts would never be bought in vast numbers in any case, and the existing destroyer force was aging very rapidly. An 11 January 1960 meeting of the Standing Committee on Shipbuilding and Conversion concluded that any new general-purpose destroyer would displace 5,000 to 6,000 tons; lesser displacements would have to imply specialized ships, while for "super weapon" (Typhon) ships 7,000 to 9,000 tons would be required. The meeting concluded that numbers could be achieved only through an upgrade of the ocean escort, a possibility raised by the success of the pressure-fired boiler. Thus Admiral Thach, commander of the experimental ASW Task Force ALFA, was "inclined to lean toward a single-purpose ship, possibly the Project 199 DE." He stated his preference for a 27–30 knot ship, "but he felt that a compromise with the money situation appeared necessary so that he would accept 25." The Chief of Staff, Destroyers, Atlantic concurred with Admiral Thach and indicated a desire for two destroyer classes: an ASW ship with limited air defense (SCB 199 with missile) and an AAW ship with limited ASW capability, a DLG 16. BuOrd then raised the possibility of using a combined Terrier/ASROC launcher, which ultimately made DLG 26 practical (see chapter 13).

The meeting concluded with a shopping list of future destroyer types: a Tartar or perhaps Terrier DDG with DASH but not ASROC, for task force escort; a DE with SQS-26, DASH, and the pressure-fired boiler (for speed); and a double-ended Talos CG, which the committee doubted would survive the budget process.

BuShips pushed these studies further; gradually its Chief, R. Adm. R.K. James, became convinced that in future the destroyer fleet would consist of

Seen from aft in 1972, the *Bronstein* shows the large area required to support the DASH helicopter system.

only two classes, a DLG/DDG and a DEG. The DDG will be too expensive to replace, in numbers, the World War II destroyers. However, maintaining an effective escort force for the strike fleet does not require replacement of old destroyers in numbers, if the effectiveness of individual ships is sufficiently advanced. This situation forces a new look at our DE type, because on it will fall many of the tasks previously undertaken by our World War II destroyers. The job of projecting naval surface power to all corners of the earth and throughout vast ocean areas requires a design which can be built in large numbers. This DEG would have a good capability to fight submarines and to protect itself against air attack but would not be assigned the task of staying with and protecting fast carrier task forces. . . .

In March 1960, James recommended for the FY 62 program a 27-knot DEG based on SCB 199: an "austere Tartar" forward would be combined with a twin 3-in./50 aft, DASH would operate from a cut-away fantail, and ASROC would be mounted amidships.

This effort was already well under way. As early as August 1959, the SCB had emphasized the operational requirement for a missile-type destroyer with maximum ASW but limited surface and air self-defensive power. The Atlantic and Pacific destroyer forces concurred in January 1960; in fact, the provision of missile air defense for the DE had been urged by Rear Admiral Daniel (DesLant) as early as December 1956. Thus, although it seemed unlikely to BuShips that any DEG would be authorized for FY 61, there were strong indications that one might be wanted for FY 62. Since the pressure-fired boiler would require redesign in any case, Preliminary Design felt that a feasibility study of a missile ship was in order. Tartar seemed the best guess for the missile; if it could be incorporated in the new hull, no redesign would be needed for the FY 62 program, and the entire escort program might be speeded. Moreover, if desired, the all-gun ships might be retrofitted with the missile, a concept that foreshadowed the later DX/DXG idea. This was very much a BuShips initiative: although the SCB was interested in a missile, it still thought in terms of the Army's point-defense Mauler, then under development and in fact destined for the FY 64 escort, the *Knox* class.

The result was a hybrid, halfway between escort and destroyer. "It was felt," according to the Design Report,

that the DE could take on some of the functions of the destroyer types particularly if a missile capability was provided. Reports have come in that the DE 1006 operators like their ships very much but would like more speed to keep up with the ASW carriers. This would make the ships definitely task force es-

corts. As a result of the above, it was decided to provide fuel for the 4,000 nm. endurance at 20 knots instead of the 15 knots stated in the Characteristics. . . .

The higher endurance speed was characteristic of destroyers and fast task force escorts, and 4,000 nm. at 20 knots was equivalent to about 5,000 at the 15 knots of SCB 199.

The key to commonality was the location of the DASH helo pad and hangar aft. If it were located on the main deck with a 3-inch gun superfiring over it, there would be sufficient hull depth aft to take the Tartar, and the deckhouse could shrink to the size of that in SCB 199. However, BuWeps, responsible for the drone, demanded relocation to the 01 level; the after gun was returned to the main deck, and Tartar had to be located forward. ASROC, with no requirement for below-deck facilities, could be moved aft. In this form the DEG would have only a single 3-inch gun, and thus could use a Mk 63 instead of a heavy Mk 56 fire control system. In addition, the DEG mounted six long Mk 25 torpedo tubes aft. Both DE and DEG were to have DASH, ASROC, and two triple Mk 32 tubes.

In this design the DEG version dominated, because in effect the DE was a DEG with the heavy Tartar removed and replaced by a much lighter twin 3-in./50. Similarly, although all *Spruances* (except for the ex-Iranian *Kidd* class) were built as ASW-only destroyers, the fact that an alternative DDG version was required in turn dominated their arrangement and even the choice of their size.

Work on SCB 199A, which became the *Garcia* (DE 1040) class, began on the basis of SCB 199 armament (e.g., three 3-in./50s) and greatly increased power, which in turn implied a wholly new hull design. A length of 368 feet would have duplicated the displacement-length ratio of SCB 199, which was already considered not quite optimal, and increases to 385 and 400 feet (waterline) each appeared to confer a gain of half a knot. Preliminary Design chose 375 feet (398 overall). On this basis Tartar would cost an additional 5 feet of length and half a foot of beam as well as 80 tons of full load displacement, for a total of 3,030 tons, if the customary 4 percent margin were to be retained.

There was a problem: in 1960 there was an arbitrary 3,000-ton limit on ships that might be designated "DE." Rear Admiral Speck, chairman of the SCB, affirmed his desire for commonality to reduce design costs and at the same time to permit Tartar to be backfitted, but he could not accept the elimination of the future growth margin. On the other hand, the Bureau of Ships could not design a missile DE within the 3,000-ton limit.

The *Garcia* was the prototype for 62 large ocean escorts. Note the cut-out in her transom for long torpedo tubes, and the ASROC reloading crane folded back across the front of her bridge.

In a 1975 photograph, the *O'Callahan* shows an enlarged hangar permitting her to accommodate a LAMPS helicopter. The inclined portion of her bridge front leads to an ASROC reload magazine.

Admiral Speck's solution was to develop an all-gun ocean escort of 2,950 tons; the design history goes on to say that

> when Admiral Speck determines that the time is proper to propose the missile carrying Ocean Escort he will do so on the basis of modifying the FY 61, 380 ft. LWL gun ship by increasing the full load displacement 80 tons and making other basic design changes only in the areas of the hull directly affected by substitution of a missile installation for part of the gun battery. The Bureau of Ships will not mention the potential missile capability of the FY 61 DE in any descriptive brochures unless Rear Admiral Speck requests such a statement. . . .

The missile/gun DE was announced at an SCB meeting in October 1960, when the board voted to adopt a main (gun) battery of two single 5-in./38 enclosed mounts, which were essential to Admiral James's concept of the ocean escort as austere destroyer. They were to be controlled by a Mk 56 fire control system. In the course of the subsequent contract design, the hull grew by another ten feet to 390 feet (waterline) and the beam grew from 41.1 to 43.7 feet; full load displacement rose from 3,085 tons in the gun version to 3,498 tons, and from 3,136 tons in the DEG to 3,525 tons at the end of contract design. It was expected that at 35,000 shp the gun-armed DE would make a sustained speed of 27.43 knots at 3,500 tons; in fact the *Garcia*s were good for 30 knots on trial.

The all-gun DE 1040 (*Garcia*) class was designated SCB 199A, the gun-and-missile DEG 1 (*Brooke*) class, SCB 199B. In the latter, Tartar replaced the after 5-in./38, and an SPS-39 frequency-scanned three-dimensional radar replaced the two-dimensional (air search) SPS-40. Each had ASROC, two lightweight Mk 32 torpedo tubes, and two long Mk 24/25 torpedo tubes in the transom for wire-guided torpedoes. A small hangar could accommodate two DASH drones or one manned HUL helicopter, and SCB 199B had a 16-missile Mk 22 launcher for its Tartars.

By this time the ocean escort was the length and displacement of a long-hull destroyer. She was clearly *not* a crash-production ship, yet she still retained the single shaft originally intended for mass production. Another interesting survival was the splinter armor amidships. The Preliminary Design Report (28 November 1960) observes that "the stress values have reached the destroyer level, therefore, it is recommended that the hull girder material in the middle half length of the ship be changed from MS (Mild Steel) to HTS (High Tensile Steel). This is in conformance with destroyer practice." That the rationale of "destroyer practice" had been splinter protection had been quite forgotten.

SCB 199A/B were unique among postwar destroyers in being designed by Bethlehem Steel rather than by Gibbs & Cox. For some time Bethlehem had been trying to reenter the field of detail design; in 1959, for example, it produced an unsuccessful design for an austere DDG. The return to Gibbs & Cox for SCB 199C, the next ocean escort, was to have important implications for propulsion design in the U.S. Navy.

At the outset, it was assumed that future U.S. destroyer escorts would all be missile-armed, so that SCB 199B rather than 199A would be the basis for future development. Other important elements in the evolution of the new escort were Design Work Study, an attempt to reduce manning through more efficient ship design, and CSED (Consolidated Ships Electronic Design), an attempt to consolidate antennas for more efficient electronic design. The final design showed only partial CSED, reflected in the space for a "billboard" surrounding the single mack, which was to have carried a dual ECM/UHF antenna. The design was characterized by a conscious attempt to cut topside clutter, consolidate commissary spaces, and improve habitability. For example, one of the anchors was suspended from the keel so as not to foul the SQS-26 sonar. Twin instead of triple Mk 32 torpedo tubes were adopted to consolidate the tubes, DASH hangar, and torpedo reloads, thereby gaining flexibility in distributing weapons between DASH and the torpedo tubes. As in earlier ships, two Mk 25 long tubes were to be mounted in the transom, but they were separated to avoid interference between guidance wires and a planned VDS installation. Machinery manning was to be reduced by consolidating spaces to reduce watch-keeping. For example, the usual ship-service turbogenerators were replaced by diesels in a separate space to achieve a single machinery space; the diesels were combined with the IC room in one (forward auxiliary) space to reduce manning.

Work began in May 1962 on the basis of alternative batteries of missiles or guns; the long-range program then called for the construction of as many as ten DEGs in FY 64 and three in later years. However, they were soon priced out of the program. In January 1963, Secretary of Defense McNamara explained the abandonment of DEG construction: the FY 62 DEG cost about $31 million, $6 million more than the DE, whereas the proposed FY 64 DEG would cost $11 million more than an equivalent DE; "the substantial increase in the number of guided missile destroyers will fully meet the Navy's requirements for missile ships of the destroyer and escort classes. . . ."

Thus, in November 1962 further development of the design was intended to produce a DE, not a DEG. However, so much work had already been done that the result could have no more than a single 5-inch gun. Thus, the sketch design as it existed at that time called for a single 5-in./38 gun forward, a Sea Mauler point-defense missile aft, ASROC, and an SQA-13 VDS. Length had grown to 395 feet. The SCB went further: if there were to be no Tartar and only a single gun, that might best be a rapid-fire 5-in./54 Mk 42, more than equivalent (in theory) to two single 5-in./38s; the Mk 56 director was replaced by a Mk 37 better suited to surface fire. Later, the more modern Mk 68 of destroyer and missile-destroyer type would be substituted. The new escort was to have DASH, and the Design Work Study effort provided an automated reloader for ASROC, a feature that shows externally

Brooke-class missile escorts had a 16-missile Mk 22 launcher in place of the after 5-inch/38 of the *Garcia* class, and a three-dimensional (SPS-39) radar in place of the two-dimensional SPS-40 of the ocean escorts. There was only a single missile-guidance channel, provided by one SPG-51 facing aft. Note the cut-out for long torpedo tubes in the transom.

The *Marvin Shields* (DE 1066) and *Roark* (DE 1053) are typical of the *Knox* class, with a point-defense missile system (for which space and weight was reserved from the first) finally installed aft, and LAMPS replacing the original DASH. They are almost unique among American escorts in having only twin rather than triple Mk 32 tubes, and theirs are enclosed in the after superstructure, a single torpedo magazine feeding both the helicopter and the tubes. The diminutive Mk 115 missile director is mounted atop the telescopic hangar, and countermeasures antennas are fixed abreast the large "mack."

as an angled base to the bridge structure. This feature was applied retroactively to the previous FY escorts, DE 1047–1051 and DEG 4–6.

By this time the combat system, i.e., the combination of display devices and computers in CIC, was becoming quite as important as the actual choice of sensors and weapons. Remarkably, the new NTDS technology was never extended to most of the ocean escorts; only the two *Garcia*-class escorts *Voge* and *Koelsch* received prototype ASW command and control systems. All of the other SCB 199s had to make

do with hand-plotting techniques in CIC. At the time, it undoubtedly appeared that such methods could suffice for a slowly developing ASW situation, but experience with the extensive computer installations in the newer escorts (*Spruances* and *Perrys*) suggests otherwise. One officer went so far as to say that the sheer volume of data involved in AAW and ASW engagements is quite comparable, the chief difference being the duration of the engagement and thus, in effect, the rate at which data must be processed.

This SCB 199C was derived from a DEG even though

a redesign based instead on DE 1040 would have been smaller. The Chief of Naval Operations preferred to use the increased size of the basic hull to buy a more capable ship, but even so the new *Knox* class (DE 1052) is generally criticized as far too weak. Increased capability purchased in this fashion included an increase of 500 nm. in endurance, a modification to the characteristics that survived the later retreat to a more conventional power plant and undoubtedly contributed to the growth, compared to the *Garcia*, of the final DE 1052 design.

The contract for detail design was awarded on 9 December 1963 to Gibbs & Cox, who proceeded to cast doubt on the wisdom of proceeding with pressure-fired boilers on what would soon become a very large program. In 1964, a total of 17 ships under construction were scheduled to receive such plants: 10 DE 1040s, 6 DEGs, and an experimental escort, USS *Glover*, AGDE 1, which generally resembled a DE 1040 except for her shrouded propeller.* Late in December, Francis W. Gibbs advised the Chief of the Bureau of Ships against using pressure-fired boilers and suggested that the new escort be redesigned; it is ironic that he, who had introduced the destroyer force to high pressure-high temperature steam, stopped what many considered the next logical step in steam plant development. In any case, bidding on the ships was stopped in January 1964, and the bureau advised the competitors that the boilers would be changed to the conventional 1,200-pound type.

Redesign began almost at once and was complete by January 1965. The original pressure-fired ship had a relatively full midship section to accommodate a pair of boilers side by side, but this arrangement was now abandoned and a slacker section (CX 0.81 instead of 0.837) adopted. Length was increased 20 feet to 415 feet on the waterline (438 overall) and displacement rose to 3,947 tons. Some internal rearrangement was necessary to maintain survivability against flooding, and ultimately the machinery spaces were divided into an auxiliary machinery space (30 feet), a boiler room (40 feet), and an engine room (30 feet). Of four 750-kw generators, three occupied the auxiliary room and one was fitted in the engine room. With the abandonment of pressure firing, the primary fuel reverted from diesel or distillate to bunker oil, and it was no longer worthwhile to employ diesel rather than turbogenerators. The final arrangement, then, was three turbogenerators and one emergency diesel generator aft with automatic starting.

SCB 199C was the largest postwar class of U.S. escorts prior to the *Perry* class, 46 ships being completed with an annual buy of up to 16 units: DE 1052–1061 were ordered under the FY 64 program, DE

1062–1077 under FY 65, DE 1078–1087 under FY 66, DE 1088–1097 under FY 67, and DE 1098–1107 under FY 68. The first units were built by several yards: Todd (Seattle and San Pedro), Lockheed, Avondale. However, it was generally recognized that a mass-production series built in one yard would be considerably more economical, and all ships from DE 1078 (*Joseph Hewes*) onward were awarded to Avondale Shipyards.

In fact, the ambitious series of 56 units authorized was not completed, as the FY 68 ships were never built. DE 1099–1107 were deferred in 1968 to permit a shift to DX/DXG (DE 1102–1107) and to cover cost overruns in nuclear submarines. DE 1101 was to have been a gas-turbine test ship, but she seemed unnecessary in view of other construction; DE 1098 was deferred early in 1969. On the other hand, five DEG variants of the basic DE 1052 design were built in Spain with U.S. assistance as DEG 7–11. They have Tartar aft and actually incorporate the Mk 25 tubes; they would seem to correspond roughly to the original work-studied DEG—fitted, however, with conventional boilers.

Externally, the *Knox* (DE 1052) class differed from earlier ocean escorts in having a much taller mack; and aft, it had space and weight reserved for Sea Mauler. In theory, the single gun retained would be more than adequate. Unfortunately, the 5-in./54 had a propensity to jam, which made the idea of a one-gun destroyer escort seem particularly unfortunate. Matters were only compounded when, in 1965, Mauler was canceled on technological grounds. DE 1052 was subject to abuse as an absurdly slow "destroyer" totally dependent upon a single shaft and a single gun, a kind of reductio ad absurdum of technological sophistication.

A more fundamental point was that DE 1052 was attacked, not because she was a poor ASW ship—she was not—but because she was not a general-purpose destroyer. A single gun made sense if the gun was in any case a standby weapon; but the DEs were judged within the fleet on the basis of their performance on the gun-line off Vietnam, on a service for which they had not been intended.

The big hull of SCB 199C did leave considerable leeway for improvement. A DASH hangar replaced the discarded Sea Mauler, and when DASH was discarded, enough weight was available for the small helo pad to be expanded to take the much heavier manned LAMPS (see chapter 11). The *Knox* class was, however, widely criticized for deck wetness, due to low freeboard and a lack of hull flare, which limited its capability in a seaway; waves often damaged both the 5-inch gun and the relatively fragile ASW pepperbox. Bulwarks and spray strakes, the solution advocated for many years by NAVSEC, were added be-

---

* AGDE 1 was redesignated DE 1098, 1 October 1979.

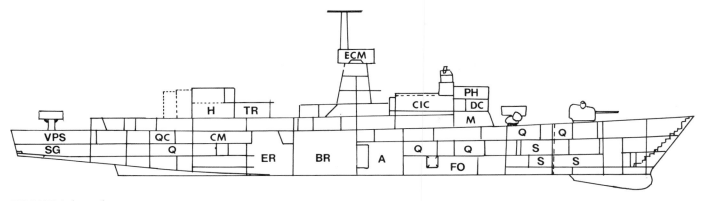

FF 1052 inboard

Always criticized as too wet in the past, the *Knox*-class escorts are being modified for improved seakeeping, with bow bulwarks and spray strakes; the *Bagley* is shown, on 12 February 1979.

ginning in 1979, the *Bagley* (DE 1069) being the first unit fitted.

The much more compact successor to Sea Mauler was BPDMS, Basic Point Defense Missile System, an adaptation of the air-launched Sparrow. It was first tested in 1967 aboard the *Bradley* (DE 1041); this system was extended to 31 ships in 1971–75 (DE 1052–1069, 1071–1083); in addition, DE 1070 was used to test the Improved Point Defense Missile System (NATO Sea Sparrow). The remaining 14 ships were scheduled to receive Sea Chaparral, a version of the air-launched Sidewinder. This was not done, but in 1981 it appears that they may be fitted instead with the new 24-round General Dynamics RAM missile, which is also partly based on Sidewinder. BPDMS was not extended to earlier escorts; for example, the unit tested aboard DE 1041 was later shifted to the carrier *Forrestal*.

As this is written, the ASW pendulum has swung against long surface-launched torpedoes, and the

1052s show no tubes in their transoms, although they do have space reserved for torpedo rooms. Installation of VDS on 25 ships (DE 1052, 1056, 1063–1071, 1073–1076, 1078–1097) began in 1972; these units trail their SQS-35 "fish" from cuts in the transom between the spaces originally reserved for long torpedo tubes. From FY 80 onward the VDS units are being fitted to tow the SQR-18A tactical towed array.

A basic change in the DE mission may stem from their ability to fire Harpoon antiship missiles from modified cells of their ASROC pepperboxes. Generally the port pair of cells is modified, and each ship carries two Harpoons in the launcher and two in the magazine; the first ship to be fitted was DE 1091, in 1976. A few ships, including DE 1068 and DE 1075, were modified to fire the interim Standard-ARM antiship missile (two in the launcher, two in the magazine). It becomes tempting to destroyer operators to assume an offensive role and to discard such defensive functions as ASW screening, and now, for the first time since 1945, they have an enemy *fleet* against which to strike.

Although the *Garcia* and *Knox* classes ultimately came to approach destroyer size and capability, in 1961 the new ocean escorts were still a category apart from fleet destroyers and FRAMs. Clearly, too, the FRAMs then being rebuilt would require replacement within the decade. The FRAM replacement program became Project Seahawk, which at one point called for the design and construction of a 40-knot destroyer with a wide range of advanced ASW weapons and sensors. Although Seahawk itself was never built, the systems developed for it have, in many cases, been incorporated into its successor, the *Spruance*.

The origin of the new ASW destroyer program may be traceable to a May 1959 memorandum from the Long-Range Objectives Group to the chairman of the Standing Committee on the Long-Range Shipbuilding and Conversion Plan. The LRO considered the DDG and DLG classes then under construction deficient: their SQS-23 sonars would be inadequate against a post-1965 submarine threat; their Terriers and Tartars would be inadequate after 1965; and their endurance was too short. It seemed unwise to invest $360 to $370 million in obsolescent designs; redesign would be expensive, however. It would probably involve SQS-26 ($12 million for a lead ship, $2 million for a follow-on); DASH and NTDS would cost even more, perhaps as much as $40 million in the lead ship. Even then there would still be the issue of the obsolescent missile—Typhon was, after all, expected shortly. The LRO suggested that the AAW emphasis of FY 57–60 programs had been due to the availability of surface-to-air missiles at the same time that air defense had been perceived as critical (1955–56). Thus, ASW might be emphasized in tbe FY 61–62 programs as new systems such as SQS-26 and DASH came into service, with a swing back to AAW in FY 63–64 to take advantage of what was then described as Super-Tartar.

The two alternatives for FY 61 were SCB 199, too slow for the fast task force, and, to complement it, a 32-knot destroyer with a long endurance (6,000 nm. at 20 knots), fin-stabilized for seakeeping, and intended both to support the fast task force and to operate with hunter-killer forces. It would have SQS-26, DASH, the Mk 37 guided torpedo, space and weight provision for VDS, and one or two 5-in./54s for shore bombardment and operation in "TNT" wars in the absence of any satisfactory shore-bombardment missile. Guns were no longer an effective means of air defense: the new ship would have an austere SAM, either a reduced-capacity Tartar (one illuminator, 10–20 rounds) or else space and weight for a new point defense system, perhaps one based on the Army's Mauler or on the air-to-air Sidewinder. In the interest of low cost, there would be no provision for NTDS except for ASW functions. A cost of $30–32 million ($38–40 million lead ship) was expected, compared to $62–77 million for a "Super-Tartar" DDG. In view of the very long range and great effectiveness expected of the latter, the LRO suggested that of 31 DDGs planned for FY 62–66, at least 18 might well be replaced by the new ASW destroyer. As yet there was no sense of urgency, no sense of the imminent disintegration of the destroyer force with the retirement of the mass of war-built *Sumners* and *Gearings*. That did not come for another two years; in 1959 the Navy's primary problem was how to afford sufficient high-technology escorts to protect its fast carriers and to fill out its hunter-killer ASW forces.

In September 1961 the LRO again called for the design of a new ASW destroyer. About 70 or more ships would be required in FY 65–70 to replace the aging FRAMs, and efforts would have to be concentrated on minimizing unit cost and manning. Considerable effort had recently been spent in automating submarine (SUBIC) and surface ship (SURIC) control; the LRO looked towards manning reductions in ship control, CIC operation, engineering, and weapons, for increased combat efficiency with decreased ship size. Emphasis would be placed on integrating weapons, information, and command and control—all goals that were quite as glamorous then as they are today. Speed, seakeeping, endurance, and self-maintenance would match destroyer characteristics, although the new ships would not generally operate within carrier strike forces. One hope for size reduction would be the replacement of the conventional cylindrical sonar transducer by a conformal array; this became a specific development objective. So important was the new project that the CNO, Admiral George E. Anderson, made the chairman of the SCB personally responsible for its success; he was to report major problems directly to the CNO.

Conformal sonar was particularly valued as a means of improving seakeeping, as a hull form could be chosen for its speed or seakeeping qualities and the sonar molded to it. Under SCB 191, a conformal array was to be tested on the hull of the light cruiser *Spokane* (CLAA 120). The construction of the test ship *Glover* was pressed ahead for trials of more conventional sonars, in particular for tests of interference between a conventional bow sonar, an independent VDS, a depth sounder, and underwater communications gear. Another sonar candidate was PADLOC (Passive Detection and Localization), which figured in several destroyer projects of this period, and which generally required a second sonar dome.

FRAM replacement implied some non-ASW missions, most notably the destruction of surface ship and shore targets, e.g., in support of amphibious operations. It seemed unlikely that any gun would confer much antiaircraft firepower; the new destroyer would, therefore, be fitted with what amounted to a surface-only gun, the new lightweight Mk 45 5-in./ 54. Air defense would be by missile.

The original directive to the SCB to begin work on a new ASW destroyer (23 September 1961) was followed by a request for feasibility studies (23 January 1962); a steering group for Seahawk was formed by the SCB on 23 April 1962. A technical development plan dated 9 March called for about 30 units under the FY 65–67 program and 40–70 improved versions from FY 68 onward. These figures were dictated by the number of existing destroyers that required replacement; they correspond roughly to the number of FRAM *Gearings*. The program would be an enormous one; BuShips, for example, suspected that it would not fall far short of $9.5 billion, a worrying figure in a period of relatively tight budgets.

As conceived in 1961 and early 1962, Seahawk was essentially a platform for the wide range of new ASW sensors and weapons then under development. As for propulsion, the principal emphasis was on improved quieting at a somewhat increased cruising speed, 25 rather than 20 knots, in view of the increased search speed to be expected with new sonars. The maximum speed of about 30 knots was well within the then-current state of the art, and its adequacy is suggested by the adoption of a similar standard in the *Spruance* design five years later. Indeed, it could be argued that a revised SCB 199A might come very close to meeting the new Seahawk goals. For example, in December 1961 the BuShips Machinery Branch completed a study of a CODAG plant of about 37,000 shp, which would have driven a DE at about 30 knots. Early Seahawk studies within BuShips were premised on this sort of performance, and driven by a requirement for maximum reliability and minimum manning levels. Four alternatives evolved, three for a single-shaft and one for a two-shaft plant. Scheme A called for three 3,800-bhp base-plant diesels and one 23,600-shp gas turbine, with a controllable-reversible pitch (CRP) propeller for reversing and three 750-kw gas-turbine ship-service generators. In Scheme B two of the gas-turbine generators were replaced by diesel units of similar rating, and in Scheme C they were replaced by three 500-kw diesels. In each case a sustained speed of 27.7 knots was expected, i.e., DE performance. On the other hand, endurance rose well above DE figures, to 5,700 nm. at 20 knots in the schemes combining the gas-turbine main power plant with the economical diesel generators, and using diesels for cruising performance. A fourth scheme, D, combined two 3,800-bhp diesels and one 20,400-shp gas turbine on each shaft, for a sustained speed estimated at 31 knots and an endurance of 5,850 nm. at 20 knots. In each case machinery-box length was fixed at 100 feet and oil stowage at 620 tons; given the fact that such a ship might well spend most of her time cruising at 20 knots or below, the efficiency of the diesel base plant would make for great endurance.

The Bureau of Ships was not entirely enthusiastic about the whole concept: a large ASW surface ship would probably have an advanced version of SQS-26 in a large, deep bow dome, an extensive passive array, and a large VDS on her stern. Even this arrangement would suffer from cavitation, quenching, water aeration, and in 1961 VDS was far from problem-free. There would have to be, too, some type of missile—the DEGs had not yet priced themselves out of business. The cost would probably be exacted in speed and seakeeping. Admiral James wrote that:

in view of these technical facts of life and the size of the total program envisaged, I cannot but wonder if the time has not come when we should seriously question the wisdom of continuing to emphasize the surface ship as our primary ASW vehicle . . . we are trying to accomplish the job "the hard way," expending a tremendous effort to get our sonars deep in the water where the acoustic problems will disappear . . . there is no question but that a surface ship is not a good sonar platform nor, indeed, is it likely that we will ever succeed in making it somewhat more than marginal. A submarine, on the other hand, represents a near optimum sonar platform. . . . Few dare to express [this conclusion] openly, for it is not a generally palatable subject. . . . [The submarine] does have two disadvantages at the present, communications and cost . . . I would not propose that the submarine be assigned as the sole ASW vehicle. Some surface types would inevitably be required for use in shallow waters, for escorting convoys in areas where air attack is possible . . . and in other multi-purpose roles. I do espouse the submarine as the *primary* vehicle. . . .

The LRO view was that Admiral James was too impressed with detection capability, too little with kill capability at long range—for which the submarine required the SUBROC nuclear weapon, whereas the surface ship might deploy a helicopter. In any case, a great deal of planned ASW spending was already shifting to submarines, which could perform extremely effectively in the barrier role.

Indeed, from 1961 onward the character of U.S. ASW strategy began to shift against the traditional need for large numbers of surface ships. Advanced nuclear attack submarines in barriers could exact considerable attrition as Soviet submarines surged into the North Atlantic shipping lanes, and as they attempted to return to their bases for replenishment. The evolving SOSUS network could direct long-range ASW aircraft and destroyer-carrier-hunter-killer (HUK) forces against submarines at sea in the North Atlantic; as shore-based aircraft performance improved, even the HUK units became less important: the overall efficacy of the SOSUS/patrol plane system increased sharply. Thus the balance of the ASW effort would shift from escort operations to offensive patrol, with escort ships employed as a back-up. By the mid to late sixties, therefore, the special ASW task groups (HUK groups), which had been used to fill mid-ocean areas not efficiently covered by shore-based aircraft, shifted to direct support of fast carrier task forces, which were now increasingly threatened by Soviet nuclear submarines. In this new situation, it might be argued, many fewer convoy escorts would be required, not merely because each one would be more effective, but also because it could be said that even in their absence relatively few submarines would survive for long. On the other hand, escort would remain important in some cases; for example, while the loss of fairly large numbers of merchant ships very early in a war might be tolerated, the same could hardly be said of carriers or of their underway replenishment groups or, for that matter, of vital resupply convoys for a European war. The net effect of this shift, then, was to reduce the requirement for very large numbers of high-quality surface ASW ships just as the FRAMs began to vanish, and so to lessen the extreme urgency of programs such as Seahawk and the later DX.

Even so, new-generation destroyers were clearly in order. The Seahawk program (SCB 239) called for a prototype to be funded under the FY 65 program, laid down in the last quarter of FY 67 for launch in 1968 and delivery in the summer of 1969. The fully integrated combat system would be ready only in mid-1971; the prototype would, then, be little more than a platform with which to obtain basic information on the performance of the new hull form at sea and on the propulsion plant and the sonar.

As of August 1962, BuShips looked toward a 1963 DEG design that would be phased into the Seahawk program. One possibility was a hull large enough to accept the Seahawk sensors and battery as well as an integrated combat system, but initially armed with the usual DEG battery. It was expected that DE and DEG construction would continue through the FY 65 program, the latter to include the prototype Seahawk I. Seahawk II production would begin in the FY 68 program with a prototype, all FY 69 ships being Seahawk IIs with improved electronics.

The primary effort went into ASW improvements; it was assumed that the existing DE would be able to search at 17 knots, and Seahawk was to realize a 50 percent improvement—to 25 knots. Endurance speed would, therefore, rise to 25 knots from the usual 20. Seahawk I would be able to realize this search speed in Sea State 2 (1965); the improved Seahawk II would operate in Sea State 4. The latter would

also realize a 60 percent improvement in ASW weapon range, to 16,000 yards; a 100 percent improvement in periscope detection; increased reliability (as SQS-26 was beginning to be troublesome); 50 percent better automated sonar target classification; and integration of sensors, fire control, and weapons (ASW only in Seahawk I, but all systems in Seahawk II). For better sonar cover beneath thermal layers, Seahawk I would incorporate an independent VDS; Seahawk II would have fully integrated sonars, provisionally designated SQQ-20.

SQQ-20 was never fully defined, but it was expected to employ an immense VDS "fish" as large as SQA-17—i.e., as large as an SQS-23 transducer—to fill the shadow region under the hull as well as to permit penetration of the thermal layer. A very high standard of contact-keeping was demanded.

In 1962, NTDS was very new and much was expected of automated displays for improved decision making. It was hoped that automation would reverse the trend in manning growth. For example, if 25 percent could be saved relative to a FRAM, as much as $16.8 million might be saved over the 20-year life of a Seahawk, at $10,000 per man-year; comparable saving relative to a DEG would be about $6.2 million. Annual operating cost would also be sharply reduced by the use of more reliable electronics, as well as by new engines requiring much lower manning: aircraft-type gas turbines and diesels with reliable lifetimes between overhaul of as much as 4,000 to 5,000 hours.

Effort was initially concentrated on the choice of weapons and sensors. For example, there was a choice between Advanced Tartar and the new (developmental) Sea Mauler, the former promising as much as four times the range and a much better kill probability, at a high cost in ship impact. It was argued that Seahawks would be quite valuable, and that they would not be escorted by specialized AAW ships. Moreover, to adopt the smaller Sea Mauler would not make the ship much smaller, given requirements for seakeeping, speed, and endurance. Even so, the more austere Sea Mauler was ultimately adopted, with Tartar as a back-up. Early units would mount a twin 3-in./50 in place of Sea Mauler.

Detailed characteristics issued in October 1962 envisaged a net improvement in mission capability of about 30 percent relative to a DEG, with a cruising speed of 25 knots and a maximum (boost) speed of 30. The ship would be able to sustain 25 knots in Sea State 5 without losing capability. Preliminary machinery studies were based on a 420-foot, 4,175-ton hull, with 80,000 shp on two shafts and an endurance of 4,500 nm. at 20 knots—all figures not too far from those realized in the big ocean escorts, given very compact high-powered machinery. The alternative plants were CODAG and COGAG-E, i.e., gas-turbine cruise and boost with turboelectric coupling to permit easy reversing. In each case a maximum of about 34 knots (30 with the VDS streamed) was expected. CODAG promised an endurance of 4,500 nm. at 20 knots, but only 1,900 at 25 (since its base speed would be 22.5 knots), whereas COGAG, with a higher base speed (25.8 knots) could promise 3,100 at 25 knots, 4,500 at 20.

Although Project Seahawk was concerned primarily with new ship control and ASW sensor technology, Admiral Anderson himself was concerned with the performance of the new ship. He felt that the state of the art was not being pushed far enough with respect to propulsion, and looked toward an endurance of 5,000 nm. at the new endurance speed of 25 knots (rather than 4,000 nm. at 20 knots) and a burst speed of 40 knots. In fact, most of the new sensor

technology fell by the wayside, as it was far too ambitious; Seahawk ultimately became synonymous with the design of a 40-knot gas-turbine destroyer. There was as yet no particular operational justification for very high speed, and indeed a Speed Requirements Study Panel would not be formed until February 1964, by which time Seahawk had been put back to FY 66, with preliminary characteristics due in the spring of 1964. Sustained speeds ranging from 25 to 39 knots were to be considered, as well as the impact of conventional steam, COSAG, COGAG, and CODAG plants.

It appears in retrospect that this shift to much higher speed performance can be traced at least in part to a Bethlehem Steel design project for a very high speed destroyer. With the completion of the DE 1040 (SCB 199A) detail design, Bethlehem had on its staff a large but idle destroyer design group. As early as February 1962, Bethlehem proposed a very high

Table 15–1. Seahawk Variants

	Steam	Steam	COGAG	CODAG	COGAG
		July 1963		March 1964	
LWL	470	480	450	488	
Beam	52.1	51.5	49.9	53.0	
Draft	18.2	18.6	16.8	15.3	
SHP	120,000	120,000*	121,900	126,900	125,900
Sustained	36.7	36.6	39.8	39.4	38.3
Endurance	4,000/25	5,000/25	4,580/25	4,000/25	4,000/25
Hull	1,612	1,865	1,481	2,012	
Propulsion	1,210	1,138	507	926	
Electrical	163	166	121	251	
C³	248	249	245	336	
Auxiliaries	515	530	363	399	
Outfit	351	358	404	260	
Armament	84	84	84	119	
Margin	373	383	319	430	
Light Ship	4,556	4,773	3,524	4,733	
Full Load	6,360	6,630	5,280	5,829	6,150

* Pressure-fired boilers.

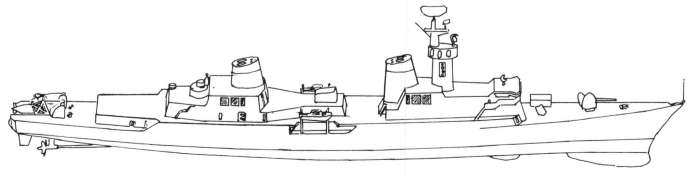

Seahawk   Flush-deck CODAG scheme submitted by Bethlehem Steel (Scheme AA)

speed COGAG destroyer, only to have BuShips reject it as risky and as offering insufficient advantages. There was no established requirement for a very fast destroyer, and the Seahawk project was far more concerned with reduced manning and with quiet operation at sonar search speed. However, very high speed has an abiding fascination; Bethlehem's vice president in charge of shipbuilding approached the CNO directly, telling him that the company could design a 40-knot DE. The CNO bit, and in effect shifted Seahawk from an ASW system platform to an attempt to propel existing systems at much increased speed.

By this time the DEs were coming very close to Seahawk requirements, apart from speed, and it is difficult to avoid the impression that as the program continued, speed became more and more important as a means of differentiating Seahawk from the SCB 199 series that it was intended to succeed in production.

By 1964 considerable machinery development had already been completed. In February 1963, hull and machinery study contracts were let to Bethlehem Steel and to Gibbs & Cox. By July both had demonstrated that no conventional, or even pressure-fired, steam plant could provide the kind of performance the Navy wanted within any dimensions it would readily accept. This would have been less than surprising had the history of DD 927 been better known. In 1963, the only kind of plant with enough output per unit weight and volume was a gas turbine—which had the grave disadvantage of high fuel consumption. Hence, a combined gas turbine/boost and steam or diesel base plant seemed indicated. A future possibility was a regenerative gas turbine in which exhaust gas would be used to heat intake air, but this was too far in the future to be considered for the prototype ship. As for the boost turbine, in 1963 there was only one aircraft turbine available in the 25,000-shp class (and that was only in the design stage); two in the 12,500- to 15,000-shp class were in production. BuShips ranked the four most attractive power plants:

(a) COGAG with a regenerative gas turbine as base and (gas) turboelectric drive for silence. Problems included the volume and weight associated with the electric motors. A "new device," probably superconducting motors, was to be considered as a solution.

(b) COGAG, (gas) turboelectric *geared* drive. It was expected that gear noise would predominate below 15 knots, so the preference for (i) was serious.

(c) CODAG with four 7,500-bhp diesels, two per shaft, and two-speed gearing into a main bull gear. These diesels would be either a Fairbanks-Morse 6-cylinder type already under commercial development or an MAN 24-cylinder type being sponsored by the German Navy. (c) was considered very nearly equivalent to (ii) in overall merit.

(d) CODAG with one 15,000-bhp diesel per shaft. This was rejected; no such diesel was in existence or under development; in any case, it was harder to make an effective clutch for so large an engine, not to mention the lack of redundancy.

In view of the technical problems associated with its first choice, BuShips chose to bet on (b) or (c). The boost turbine would be the FT4A, a version of the J75 Air Force engine then running at 20,000 bhp but expected ultimately to reach 25,000.

Some idea of what Seahawk might have produced is given by a pair of Gibbs & Cox/Bethlehem studies. The 1963 report on propulsion alternatives favored a COGAG plant, three gas turbines per shaft (one FT4A base, two boost), 110,000 shp for 38.2 knots. This would require 3,600 tons *light* and 5,350 fully loaded. Even those figures seem to have been optimistic. In March 1964, Gibbs & Cox produced a detailed preliminary design for a CODAG ship of no less than 4,733 tons *light* displacement; full load was estimated at 5,590 tons, and at 488 feet the ASW destroyer (or fast DE) was coming close to a DLG. Had it materialized, it might well have been derided as grossly underarmed: such critiques rarely take into account the mass of sensors so important in modern operations. Thus, the Gibbs & Cox sketch of this design shows two very large sonar domes (one presumably for passive devices) as well as the large VDS aft.

One thing Seahawk would *not* have been derided for would have been performance. Four diesels and four gas turbines (boost plant) were expected to provide 126,900 shp, for a maximum speed of 39.4 knots; on diesels alone, with the VDS streamed, Seahawk would make 24.3 knots. Of course, it might have seemed slightly excessive to pay so very much for a 40-knot DE. The preferred COGAG alternative would have been even worse: 6,150 tons, 38.3 knots on a total of 125,900 shp provided by six gas turbines.

Opinion within the fleet was by no means unanimous as to the virtues of Seahawk. For example, ComDesLant was willing to forego the VDS and to accept SQS-26 bottom-bounce/convergence zone performance for below-layer detection, but he feared evolving Soviet surface-to-surface and air-to-surface missile capability. He considered DASH superior to ASROC at long range, *if* it could be improved to provide for target reacquisition through a self-contained MAD, a radar beacon, and Lorelei. The last was a sonar buoy that DASH could drop, and that might serve as a reference point by which the drone could be guided to its target. LAMPS would provide this reacquisition capability; a 1964 report observed that "manned or drone helicopters offer the only early potential for ASW weapon delivery beyond 20,000 yards." ComDesLant wanted the Mk 37 guided torpedo for use against deep-diving submarines, and

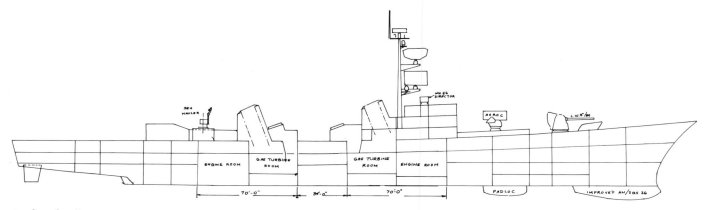

Seahawk—"recommended ship—COGAG"

also preferred Tartar to Sea Mauler, not least for its antiship potential. Moreover, the Tartar launcher could be modified to fire ASROC. He considered 30 knots a minimum for any ship designed to fight 30-knot submarines; in an endorsement, CinCLant noted that the new ASW carrier scheduled for FY 68 (and not, in fact, built), was to make 30 knots, and that her escort required a 5-knot speed margin, for a target of 35 knots.

The Commander, ASW Forces Atlantic did not consider Seahawk an ASW-optimized ship at all, but rather a continuation of the trend towards larger and costlier ships:

> Recent ASW studies have uniformly pointed out the serious shortage of ASW escorts and have recommended that first priority should be assigned to increasing the number of surface escorts . . . a smaller and less sophisticated ASW escort than is now specified for SEAHAWK will be required. A stronger and more effective ASW capability can be achieved through a larger number of medium sized escorts, rather than a lesser number of more highly sophisticated escorts. . . . The size and cost of SEAHAWK can be reduced to that necessary for a modestly expensive, rapidly built escort by eliminating the requirement for much of the redundancy in weapon systems and unrealistic propulsion system requirements. . . .

The detailed speed analysis took into account the new ASW conditions: in many cases Seahawk would be responding to an initial datum provided by some external system such as SOSUS, and its efficacy would depend upon how quickly it might search the area around the datum. In addition, the advent of long-range sonar detection (e.g., via convergence-zone performance of SQS-26 and later sonars) would make dash performance to investigate distant contacts valuable. It could be argued that a ship making contact on a convergence-zone target would have to bring that target within direct-path range before it might hope to attack, and therefore that high dash speed would be extremely valuable. (In the absence of such performance, it has been necessary to provide the destroyer with a long-range helicopter, LAMPS, capable of reacquiring the target at convergence-zone range, but that solution was not yet in sight in 1964.) The special panel on speed concluded that the 25-knot sonar search speed would increase effective search area by 50 percent, with a corresponding improvement in the probability that the ship would reacquire a contact around a datum. For example, a ship arriving one hour late at a datum, faced with a 25-knot submarine, and enjoying a 20-nm. sonar sweep width would achieve a net probability of contact within eight hours of 38 percent (25 knots) versus 25 percent (17 knots).

Dash speed would be valuable only if the ship could accelerate very rapidly from cruise to maximum speed, in which case the panel considered 35 knots a useful target speed. It used the problem of convergence-zone detection followed by a dash out to investigate to evaluate alternative dash speeds. An increase in maximum speed from 34 to 38 knots would buy about half as much increased effectiveness as the increase from 25 to 34 at about the same cost, two gas turbines. In either case, the adoption of propellers suited to very high speed operation might not be compatible with silencing.

The shift in emphasis from ASW systems to propulsion was not entirely popular. For example, the Directorate of Defense Research and Engineering (DDR&E) in the Office of the Secretary of Defense (OSD), which was financing Seahawk as an advanced project, began to question its urgency, since at least the early Seahawk platforms would be little more than advanced DEs, and would not incorporate new sensors. Within the Navy, the powerful ASW R&D community (which had probably been responsible for the Seahawk concept in the first place), became disenchanted; the formation of the special panel on Seahawk speed probably reflects this problem. DDR&E increasingly demanded reversion to system development efforts. By February 1964, DDR&E

wanted yet another review of the propulsion system choice and strongly favored reversion to a conventional steam plant. It is possible that this decision was affected by the strong pronuclear bias of some DDR&E officers, formerly closely associated with the naval nuclear program. In effect, this choice delayed the introduction of a propulsion system, the gas turbine, which would have competed with nuclear power.

What really killed Seahawk as a concept, however, was the shift from ASW systems to propulsion; DDR&E increasingly asked whether this choice had ever been appropriate, given the undeveloped state of many important sensors. In accordance with the systems approach that was then dominant within OSD, DDR&E suggested an overall review of ASW practice that would include not only surface ships but also aircraft (both carrier and land-based) and submarines. At almost the same time the Bureaus of Ships, Weapons, and Aeronautics were all combined under a single Naval Materiel (NavMat) organization. Seahawk was assigned to a new NavMat program manager, who was established as "Program Manager for ASW," to reflect his much broader responsibilities. In his statement on the FY 66 program (February 1965) Secretary of Defense McNamara wrote Seahawk's obituary: "because some of the basic technology required for this ship was yet to be developed, we are concentrating on the required systems. The results of these separate developments may, where possible, be back-fitted to currently operational or programmed ASW ships as well as applied to a future high performance DE optimized for all ASW tasks." Some within OSD suspected, too, that little could be hoped for in the way of a new sonar system when the existing SQS-26 was not yet operating to its full potential. DE 1052 procurement continued. About a year elapsed before the ASW destroyer concept was revived, and participants in the DX program that produced the *Spruance* class disclaimed any direct link with Seahawk. The indirect link was the variety of system projects that Seahawk spawned, some of which have seen fruition aboard the *Spruances*.

Had it been built, the Seahawk ship would probably have been subject to many of the criticisms currently leveled at the *Spruance*. It would have been large, although not as large as the current ship: a length of 420 feet and a displacement of about 4,200 tons were envisaged. Visible armament would have been limited to one lightweight 5-in./54 forward and Sea Mauler or a twin 3-in./50 aft, with a hangar and pad for an extended-range DASH and a launcher for an improved ASROC. There would also have been tubes for short-range (Mk 46) and long-range (Mk 48) homing torpedoes. Only the very high speed of the new ship might have mollified its critics.

By 1964, the distinction between Seahawk and the large ocean escorts was no longer very great, and the CNO looked at an upgraded DE 1052 as an alternative to the special Seahawk hull. On 17 March 1964 he requested a series of studies: a 30-knot quick-reaction power plant for FY 66; Seahawk propulsion in FY 68 units (with maximum speed approaching 35 knots); and Seahawk electronics in units to be built under the FY 71 program. This 30- to 35-knot DE study was followed almost immediately by one for a DEG(N) or DE(N); Admiral Anderson clearly found the existing DE unsatisfactory.

Table 15–2. Alternatives to the *Knox* Class

	FAST DE 5 June 1964	DE FY 68 July 1966	DE FY 68 August 1966
LWL	450	507	440
Beam	49	54.8	47.5
Draft	16.3		
SHP	70,000	40,000	40,000
Sustained	30		27
Endurance	4,500/20		6,000/20
5-in./54	1 LW	2 RF	1 RF
3-in./50 Twin	1	—	—
BPDMS	—	—	Space and weight
ASROC	1	1	1
Mk 32 TT	2	2	2
Mk 25 TT	2	2	2
Hull	1,650	2,210	1,567
Propulsion	840	614	354
Electrical	150	180	212
C³	240	263	224
Auxiliaries	410	526	392
Outfit	340	382	309
Armament	95	261	147
Margin	415	444	320
Light Ship	4,180	4,880	3,535
Loads	1,310		1,650
Full Load	5,490		5,185
Plant	DDG 2	3 Boiler 2 Shaft	COGAG (E) 1 Shaft

BuShips tried a DDG 2 plant (which alone gives some idea of how the DE hull had grown) as well as gas turbines in various forms: COSAG (DE 1006 steam plant as base), CODAG, COGAG. In June, it reported to the CNO a study derived from an all-steam (70,000-shp) DDG 2 plant in a modified DE 1052 hull: 4,140 tons light, 5,450 full load, and 450 feet long (472 overall). Even this rather large ship sufficed only for one 5-in./54 lightweight gun, ASROC, DASH (with a hangar), two long torpedo tubes in the transom, and two short triple tubes (Mk 32). The SQS-26 of DE

1052 would be supplemented by a new independent VDS, SQS-35. The hull stabilizer of DE 1052 would be retained, and there would be space and weight reservation for a short-range self-defense missile and for the integrated digital underwater fire control system being developed under Seahawk. Ships completed before the missile was ready would have a twin 3-in./50 aft instead. The result was not far from Seahawk, and had a price to match: $58 million for a lead ship, $37 million for repeat ships (FY 66). This seemed high in comparison to less than $20 million for a DE 1052, and the project did not get far.

A November 1964 study of a 35-knot DE called for COGAG propulsion, as in Seahawk; the power plant would consist of four regenerative gas turbines as a base, four FT4A as a boost plant. A 4,330-ton (light; 5,605 full load) hull would be required.

This proposal also died, but the DE was a *destroyer* replacement, and its speed remained a problem. In the spring of 1966 the new Naval Ship Engineering Center (NAVSEC) began (apparently on its own initiative) to work up proposals for a new DE for FY 68. The SCB's reactions tended toward either (i) a FRAM replacement or (ii) a two-gun DE. Behind both requirements lay the failure of Seahawk: (i) was taken to mean a fast twin-screw ship biased toward AAW, (ii) a type with more "payload" than DDG FY 67, already a very substantial ship. A June 1966 NAVSEC memo observed that "we are being pushed towards a cruiser." One way out was to use single-shaft CO-GAG machinery to achieve 30 knots on one shaft with little expansion of the machinery box. A common hull and machinery arrangement would be used for both DE and DD.

The DE would have SQS-26 and VDS (SQS-35), two 5-in./54s (one aft pending replacement by BPDMS), ASROC, DASH, and long and short ASW torpedoes, the former firing through the transom. In the destroyer, DASH would be replaced by an austere Tartar launcher, and the two-dimensional air search radar of the DE replaced by a pencil-beam type suitable for missile operation. The stern tubes and VDS would be eliminated as weight compensation.

This common hull concept must have influenced the DX/DXG project, which was just getting under way in the fall of 1966.

Meanwhile the FY 68 DE project concentrated on questions of propulsion. Some very powerful single-shaft plants were considered. For example, in July a 60,000-shp COGAG plant based on the 25,000-shp FT4A was worked up; most of the sketch schemes were based on 40,000-shp plants. The latter could be accommodated within roughly the dimensions of DE 1052, but on the other hand they could not push speed much above 27 knots. A major advantage of COGAG turned out to be fuel economy: a 5,400-ton

(full load) COGAG-type could achieve 6,000 nm. at 20 knots, a 5,320-ton type with 600 psi boilers, only 5,000. The higher pressure (1,200 psi) steam plant could achieve nearly the same result (4,500 nm.) on only 4,050 tons. Fuel economy would, however, come at a high price: the COGAG DE would cost $70.1 million ($44 repeat) vs. $65.4 ($44.2) for psi steam. By this time the going rate for repeat DE 1052s was $29.8 million (a lower price quoted above excludes electronics and weapons).

Efforts were also made to find an optimum battery. By 1966, BuOrd favored a pair of lightweight 5-in./54s, quite adequate for shore bombardment and lighter, together, than one rapid-firing 5-in/54. The slower firing type made sense if air defense was to be relegated, for the most part, to a missile system (BPDMS). In the armament schemes studied, where two full (rapid-fire) 5-in./54s were specified, one was to be replaced by BPDMS when that system became available.

Although these studies produced no ships—the FY 68 DEs were canceled, and in any case there is no evidence that they would have differed significantly from those of FY 64–67—almost certainly these armament studies affected the choice of battery for DX/DXG (*Spruance*).

The demise of Seahawk did not eliminate the block obsolescence problem, which indeed only worsened with time: by 1966 it was evident that many of the missile ships converted from World War II cruisers would soon have to be retired. The *Spruance* class represents a partial solution to this problem, constrained, like every other postwar escort program, by sharp escalation in unit cost. It differs from all the other programs in that it was conceived, not within OpNav, but instead within the Office of the Secretary of Defense (OSD), an organization that often fought the Navy on other ship-procurement issues. Remarkably, too, although there is an obvious connection with Seahawk, no direct connection exists, and many of those within OSD who first proposed what became the *Spruance* had had no direct contact with the earlier program. DX/DXG, the new destroyer, was conceived within OASD(SA), the System Analysis or program-planning arm of OSD, in connection with the coming end of the only existing escort program, the DE 1052. There was a common perception that general-purpose force levels were falling, and recent studies in shipbuilding had convinced Russ Murray of OASD(SA) that the key to future efficiency was large-scale production in a single yard, with standardization strongly enforced. An informal internal OSD memo proposed a modular program combining a new general-purpose destroyer with the DDG that the Navy was then demanding, for a total

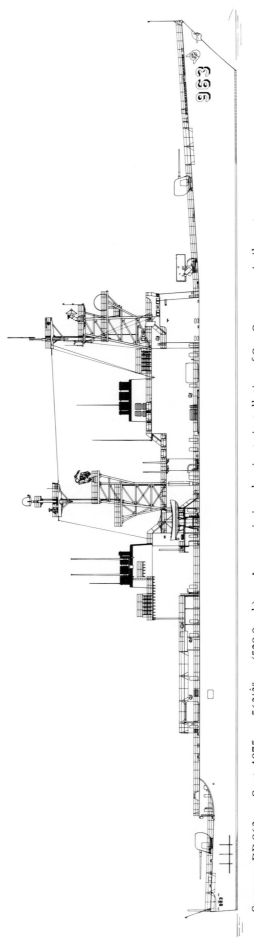

Spruance DD 963   Sept. 1975   563'3" o.a.(529.0 w.l.)   As commissioned, prior to installation of Sea Sparrow missile system, ECM gear, etc. Well at starboard quarter later filled in, folding helo safety nets forward deleted. On early trials did not have windbreak bulwark above pilothouse.

of about 90 ships averaging the extraordinarily low price of $22 million. The cost estimate was based on DE 1052 experience and hopes of benefits to be derived from a long production run. Once Systems Analysis had convinced the Navy that this was a desirable program, tensions between the two organizations began to rise, the Navy wanting the optimum general-purpose combat suit, while OSD looked toward large numbers and a very low unit cost.

In its formal presentation OASD(SA) emphasized the need for new missile ships, as none had been authorized since FY 62, given the "3-T" problems and the failure of Typhon. The Navy would not be permitted to build its FY 68 DDGs at a cost of $167 million (two ships), nor would it receive a $151 million DLGN that year. On the other hand, for FY 68 the Secretary of Defense requested $30 million for contract definition of a new guided missile destroyer or escort, tentatively designated DXG, and also for a new ASW escort, DX. The final Draft Memorandum for the President (16 November 1966, which was approved) observed that "this joint funding will permit investigation of the desirability of various degrees of commonality between the DX and the DXG." From the beginning, the new program was identified as a major fleet escort, which in the parlance of the day meant a missile escort.

Thus, the Decision Memorandum summarized the current missile escort force, consisting of 12 cruisers, 30 frigates, 31 destroyers, and 6 destroyer escorts, which would provide 4 ships per carrier (15 carriers) as well as 2 for each of 4 ASW carrier groups "which might operate independently in areas subject to enemy air attack, and 11 additional ships for other missions such as the protection of amphibious groups, underway replenishment groups, and convoys. . . ." It appeared that the 79-ship force would be adequate, but the CNO held out for 100, and Secretary McNamara "encouraged" further analysis on his part. In any case, the existing missile force was beginning to age, and the missile cruisers would soon have to be retired in view of their very high annual operating costs and, in most cases, their obsolescence. The DEGs were marginal at best. Secretary McNamara wished "to replace these ships with a new class which would not only be far more effective, but would also be relatively inexpensive to procure and to operate."

There was also an ongoing analysis of ASW escort force requirements, the program in the fall of 1966 calling for an average of 12 DE 1052 per year. OSD wished to reduce this to 10 annually, for a total of 60 rather than 70 in FY 67–72. OSD further championed the new gas turbine, and the Navy intended to make one of its FY 68 DEs an experimental gas-turbine escort (AGDE), possibly with advanced features such as a regenerative cycle. DX was, then,

conceived at first as little more than a DE, and hardly fast enough for carrier operations. Its single gun would be unsatisfactory for shore bombardment.* In the fall of 1967, however, after the completion of several studies, including the Navy's Major Fleet Escort effort, OSD commented that

> we already have enough modern DE to meet the inventory requirement derived from the new analysis. Thus, the DX should be changed from a DE type to a 30-knot ASW ship with better guns than the DE, so that we can also meet the inventory requirement for ships to escort attack carriers or provide fire support. The DX will now be a more direct—but much more capable descendent of the old World War Two destroyers which it will, in part, replace.

Now mixed covering forces of DX and DXG were contemplated, given the conclusions of the Major Fleet Escort study, and in another context Secretary McNamara could indicate that the total number of escorts per carrier was set by ASW screening requirements, whereas it appeared that fewer missile launchers per carrier would be required. The non-missile DX would, then, cut the net cost of the carrier task force.

The original (1966) OSD concept called for the construction of 18 DXGs and 75 DXs in FY 69–74 at a total program cost of about $2.4 billion.

> As one alternative, the two classes could share identical hulls, and differ only in weapon systems. This would take maximum advantage of standardization, and of the economies of large scale production. However, if the requirements of the DXG were to result in such an oversized DX as to more than offset the advantages of commonality, it might be preferable to build two separate classes of ships. Between these two extremes, there are possibilities of having various degrees of commonality . . . such as common bow and stern sections with midbodies specialized. . . . they might use a modular design so that major components, such as the surface-to-air missile system, could be installed en bloc. This would be particularly desirable if the DX and DXG share a common hull. However, even with separate classes the modular concept should result in more rapid construction, since the systems would be more nearly ready to operate prior to installation. In future years, the ships could be modernized more rapidly and inexpensively . . . .

Procurement was to be on a total package basis, with a single private contractor creating the design and then building all units. One effect of this decision was that a company with no previous preliminary design experience had to create a new destroyer design from scratch. Clauses in the design contract em-

---

* The second gun was needed to fire flares for night operations.

The *Paul F. Foster* (DD 964, above) and *Comte de Grasse* (DD 974, facing) illustrate the major design features of the *Spruance* class, including a helicopter pad in very nearly the optimum position three-quarters of the way aft, and the Mk 86 gun fire-control system on the heavy foremast, with the SPS-40 air-search radar on the lattice mainmast. The NATO Sea Sparrow point-defense launcher looks tiny abaft the helicopter platform; it is controlled by a Mk 91 director atop the large hangar. The two stub antennas folded down right aft are broadband whips; note also the three broadband antennas carried atop the two masts. Plans to install SQS-35 VDS sonars were abandoned, although ultimately these ships will be fitted with towed arrays.

phasizing particular factors drove the design. For example, the *Spruance* is exceptionally quiet because the design requirement specified a very high standard of quieting, and because Litton believed that improvement in that direction would help it win the competition. The total package concept also emphasized the actual production of the ships, which meant that Litton built a computerized shipyard for them. Mass-production concepts shaped the design to some extent; for example, the *Spruances* have no deck camber.

Later, the principle would be formulated as a limitation in risks inherent in the ship by adopting well-proven systems but leaving space for later replacement by types as yet only conceptual. Quite early in the DX/DXG program the ships were designed de-

liberately with a later *modernization* in mind, a concept entirely new to warship design. This was seen as occurring about once in ten years, and required design margins. A later development, after considerable commonality between DX and DXG had been accepted, was *conversion:* a change in the threat might make DDGs more valuable than DD (ASW), in which case it would be well to be able to transform the new DD into an "AAW Area Defense Escort"—which in one phrase says that the DDG had become a frigate.

A Special Study Group on Implementing a DX/DXG Program (23 September 1966) called for a five-year program of 103 ships (18 DXGs, 85 DXs),to replace 250 elderly escorts. Concept formulation was to be complete by June 1967, contract definition by December 1968, and the first units would be ready

early in 1973. In this study, as in the original OASD(SA) proposal, the DXG was an FY 67 DDG, i.e., the latest available design. The DX was a DXG "deconverted," i.e., reduced, to a DE 1052 standard of weapons. It appeared that, on average, DXG would cost $57.2 million, and DX, $40.8, for a program cost of $4.5 billion. This seemed very expensive to OASD, who proposed (October) instead of DX a repeat DE 1052 ($19.7 million).

So large a program merited review on the Secretary of Defense level, in the form of a major fleet escort study (November 1966); a program of 75 DXs (DE 1052) and 17 DXGs was envisaged. Later these numbers were changed to 49 DXs and 33 DXGs by counting the greater endurance of six programmed DXGNs (including a DLGN 36-class ship of FY 68).

In line with the total package policy, a Concept Formulation Plan was promulgated in February 1967. It began by restating the problem: in FY 67–75 8 cruisers and 156 destroyers would be stricken. Programmed additions would be only 1 nuclear frigate, 56 ocean escorts, and 2 DEGs; net losses would include 12 8-inch guns, 24 6-inch, and 723 5-inch, as well as 3 Talos and 4 Terrier launchers. Fully half of the heavy fire support capability and 57 percent of flagship facilities would go. A multipurpose destroyer was required to "operate offensively, independently or with strike, amphibious, or ASW forces to shield them, replenishment groups, and military and mercantile convoys against air, surface, and submarine threats"; and "to detect and destroy missiles, aircraft, and submarines alone or as part of a coor-

dinated system; destroy surface targets at close range; provide fire support; destroy shore targets at close range; exercise limited air control for ASW, Search and Rescue and patrol; blockade; and provide limited unit commander accommodation." Hopes for economy of scale in procurement, standardization in series production, lower manning, and provision for future update were all expressed. The Concept Formulation Plan cited the speed requirements for CVA escort, as well as the reliability problems later brought to public notice in the 1971 DE 1052 controversy. It required a new analytic study, however, to convince the Secretary of Defense. This the CNO issued in June 1967.

The new Major Fleet Escort study compared a DE (A), DDG (B),and DLG (C). A was DE 1052; B, the FY 67 DDG; and C, a double-ended Tartar frigate of 8,000 tons. The study showed that beyond a level of three to four escorts per CVA, it was *less* expensive to add pure ASW escorts *if* they could sustain 30 knots or better. This speed requirement was reinforced by a Maritime Administration study predicting a trend in the mid-seventies toward 30-knot merchant ships, and by the usual argument in favor of fast ships to run down fast submarines. It turned out that in addition, B, a single-ended Tartar D ship, was more cost effective than the double-ender C, which had been favored at first. Finally, the study showed that, for this new generation of task force escorts, a minimum endurance of 6,000 nm. was set by geography.

Hence, an ASW/shore-support destroyer (DX 2) and an AAW/ASW DDG (DXG 1) were proposed: 40 of the former, 20 of the latter. Estimated unit prices were about $31.5 million for the DX, and $42.6 million for the DXG. Subsequent studies by Op-96 (long-range plans) recommended more of both types, up to 58 DXs and 36 DXGs (July 1967). By August, the DX was also seen as a replacement for the abortive fire support ship (LFS), using a new 175-mm. gun. At that time a displacement of about 7,000 tons was expected.

A DX/DXG Ship Development Plan was drawn up in October 1967 by a panel headed by Admiral Sonenshein of NavShips. It endorsed the single contractor idea, and also came out in favor of a movement toward lower ship costs via a reduction in the number of different classes and a consequent increase in production runs. A desire for lower manning was reminiscent of Seahawk.

The paper went on to analyze speed, gun, and range requirements. Speed requirements were dominated by the need to screen 30-knot fast carriers; indeed, it was assumed that the vulnerability of carriers on transit increased sharply below 28 knots. This consideration alone would rule out the ocean escorts as carrier ASW screens. The other speed requirements did not: ASW group with a CVS, 27 knots; fast logistics group or fast convoy, 26 knots; amphibious force, 20 knots. An old argument, the need to counter fast submarines, was also used at this time to justify high speed.

It was clear by this time that, as the Chief of BuShips had foreseen in 1960, any new DDG was really a slightly austere frigate; the specified endurance of 6,000 miles at 20 knots was therefore no surprise. As for the gun, the choice was between the lightweight 5-in./54 and a more powerful weapon in development, a lightweight 175-mm./60 (which later became the abortive Mk 71 8-in./55). Both guns were roughly equivalent in operation against a fixed or slow target; on the other hand, the heavier gun could destroy such fortifications as pillboxes, a consideration of some consequence in view of the coming demise of most U.S. cruisers. The suggested solution was a provision for replacement of one of the 5-inch guns by a 175 after completion.

A very important suggestion was "modular" design, in which one basic hull might accept modules such as a SAM, flag facilities, or ASW. It was fully understood that any such concept implied substantial size, but that did not have to mean great cost; the example of a 150,000-ton Japanese supertanker built for only $41.2 million was cited. This argument is reminiscent of one made by William F. Gibbs in connection with the *Forrest Sherman* design. At a September 1951 BuShips meeting he stated his disappointment in the low sustained speed (31 knots) accepted:

The conclusion was reached that the Navy did not want to pay for the increase in speed in terms of a ship's size . . . but the cheapest thing by far in a ship is the steel hull . . . the Bureau could obtain the speed desired in this ship, provided the armament was left alone, i.e., fixed, and the design then completed to give the speed and endurance required. Unfortunately, the thinking seems to be that when a large ship is designed it must be loaded up with offensive weapons, with a resultant enormous increase in cost. . . .

Finally, the panel urged immediate authorization of two FY 67 DDGs to test a variety of DX/DXG components: Tartar D, gas turbines, modular command and control spaces.

Characteristics of the DX were finally set by a presidential memo of January 1968, calling for "30 knots for CVA escort, two guns for fire support." Both the DX and DXG were to be capable of a sustained sea speed of 30 knots in Sea State 4; previously the requirement had been for speed in a calm sea. Sea State 4 could be read as "North Atlantic," which made sense for strike operations against the Soviet Union. The 6,000-mile endurance was also specified. Other characteristics would include:

	DX	DXG
Displacement	6,000	7,000 tons (approx)
Sonar	SQS-26	SQS-26
VDS	SQS-35	
	ASROC	ASROC
	Two Triple Mk 35	Two Triple Mk 32
Helicopter	Facilities	Platform
SAM	BPDMS	Tartar D
Air Search	SPS-40A	SPS-49
Three-D Radar	—	SPS-48B
Sea Search	SPS-55	SPS-55
5-in./54 LW Guns	2	1

A *conversion* of the DX to DXG had to be simple and economical. Some DX features would have to be removed at that time; in order of preference, candidates for removal were the SPS-40, BPDMS, the SQS-35, the enclosed helicopter hangar, and one gun. It was assumed that the conversion would entail replacement of the ASROC launcher with a combined ASROC/Tartar launcher. The lightweight gun was chosen over the more conventional type because manning would roughly double the life-cycle cost of the more sophisticated weapon, with only minor improvements in action against fast surface targets, none against fixed or slow ones.

At this time it was hoped that contracts for the lead DX and DXG could be awarded in August 1969 and December 1970, respectively, for delivery in March 1973 and September 1974.

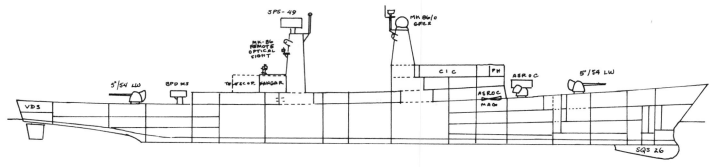

DX/DXG notional ship B (ASW)

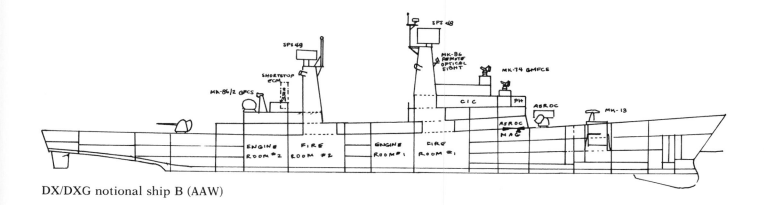

DX/DXG notional ship B (AAW)

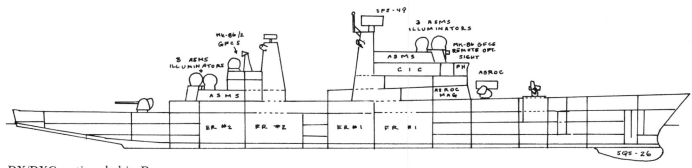

DX/DXG notional ship B

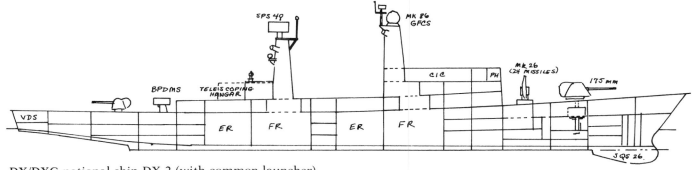

DX/DXG notional ship DX 2 (with common launcher)

The procedure followed by the Navy was to sketch a series of notional ships ("base-line designs") that would test the feasibility of proposed performance standards; only the latter would be transmitted to the bidders. These studies indicated quite early that the DX would be an exceptionally large destroyer. The reason was not hard to find. Although the DX had roughly the armament of a DE, it had to be *convertible* to a DDG, which was, as we have seen, very nearly a frigate. That meant that the DX had to look very much like a disarmed DLG. In addition, the DX would fall heir to the combat system automation originally designed for Seahawk, which would increase costs without providing any obvious improvement in firepower.

An additional pressure towards greater size was the severe performance requirement. Even had internal space requirements not proven decisive, the demand for sustained speed in Sea State 4 could not have been satisfied by a materially shorter ship. A consequence of the specification of speed in a *rough* sea was that estimation of required power was difficult; note that all of the other destroyers were rated at sustained speed at 80 percent power in a calm sea, with some fixed percentage margin to take account of weather, hull fouling, etc. A former employee of Litton has suggested that the design proved overconservative in this regard. It is worth remarking here that the modular character of gas turbines tends to reinforce the growth brought on by a very conservative power estimate: a 20 percent rise in power required could demand an extra turbine, in this case a 33 percent increment in power.

The greatest effect was exercised by the prospective conversion to DXG. At first this entailed no more than the replacement of the ASROC and one 5-in./54 by a single-arm Tartar/ASROC launcher, perhaps even the very austere Mk 22. This was generally in line with the requirement posed for DXGN. It was estimated by NAVSEC that such a ship, steam-powered, could be had on about 5,700 tons (light), which proved surprisingly accurate in the end.

The ship actually built was far more powerful than that originally envisaged, however. It incorporates in its modernization/conversion plan the new Mk 26 twin-arm Tartar/Harpoon/ASROC launcher, which is built in three sizes: 24 (Mod 0), 44 (Mod 1), and 64 (Mod 2) missiles. In the end, potential alterations called for a DDG version with a Mk 26 Mod 0 forward in place of the usual ASROC pepperbox and a Mod 1 aft in place of the smaller PDMS (Sea Sparrow) pepperbox. Moreover, it was expected that the DDG would retain *both* guns of the original DD; one (forward) might be replaced by an 8-in./55. It must be kept in mind that this is essentially the armament of a missile cruiser, CGN (formerly DLGN) 38; that,

although it is not mounted, hull volume and weight had to be provided for it from the beginning. Thus, for example, the forward ASROC loads from a magazine below it, because provision had to be made for a magazine beneath the Mk 26 launcher. Similarly, the PDMS seems to require a disproportionate amount of space mainly because that is really the length absorbed by a Mk 26 Mod 1 launcher. A less visible space consideration is extra rack space for DDG electronics; even so, in its ASW version, the new destroyer has an extraordinary level of automation: about half its cost goes for electronics. In fact, this is the first U.S. warship with a completely digital C^3 system. By way of comparison, in DG/Aegis only about 15 percent of acquisition cost was to have been spent on electronics.

The Request for Proposals, which the Navy had hoped to distribute to potential builders on 1 December 1967, in fact went out the next 15 February. Under the total package concept, each bidder had to bid, first, on concept definition (contracts awarded 3 July 1968), and then on development production (awarded 23 June 1970). Contract definition was essentially preliminary design and had to be completed by early spring of 1969; the Navy would use the CD submissions to narrow the field of entrants so as to request DP proposals by 3 April 1969. All of these dates represented some slippage on the original proposal; for example, it had been hoped that the CD contract would be awarded in April 1968 and the production contract the following May. In fact, this slippage caused Congress to reject a Navy request for the first five DXs under FY 69. Another congressional problem was an attempt by supporters of an all-nuclear surface force who wanted the DXGN program passed to block CD/CF (formulation) funds.

Contractors were asked to bid on runs of 30, 40, and 50 DXs, and 25 and 35 DXGs. In early 1968, it was expected that all DXs would have been delivered by 31 December 1977, all DXGs by one year later.

CD contracts were awarded to Newport News, to Avondale (who had much DE 1052 experience), to Todd Shipyards, to General Dynamics (Quincy), to Litton Industries (Ingalls), and to Bath Iron Works. The competitors were narrowed to General Dynamics, Litton, and Bath for the DP stage, and Litton was awarded a contract for 30 destroyers in June 1970.

The contest rules emphasized life-cycle costing, and there was a strong drive towards gas turbines. The latter came only in modular units with very nearly fixed power, and a designer perfectly willing to settle for, say, 65,000 shp would have to go to 80,000 if limited to 20,000-shp units. In the interest of fuel economy and low acquisition cost, Litton chose a relatively long hull that could be driven at 30 knots by only three LM-2500 engines, each of about 20,000 shp. For cruising operation one turbine could turn both shafts by means of an electric coupling, a complex mechanism. In this form the Litton design won the contest, but the Navy almost immediately demanded that the coupling be abandoned in favor of a fourth engine. Had Litton begun with 80,000 shp, it would have been able to accept a much smaller ship, so that the result was somewhat oversized, even on the basis that DX size was driven by DXG requirements.

An invisible contributor to ship size was a strong requirement for silencing; the Navy contract actually called for a bonus for better silencing than specified. Litton rejected cruise diesels (CODOG) for this reason. Similarly, the Litton design incorporated gas-turbine rather than diesel ship-service generators: in a gas-turbine ship, there is no excess steam to turn a generator integral with the main power plant, so some auxiliary power plant has to be provided.

No DXGs were ordered, partly in view of the greater efficiency of the DLGNs. The 30 *destroyers* ordered were considered potential DDGs in view of their inherent capacity for modernization and conversion.

Ironically, this large and apparently roomy fast escort turns out to be distinctly tight. Her designer, Reuven Leopold, once described her as determined in length by her subsystems: two sets of gas turbines en echelon, two 5-inch LW guns, ASROC (space for Mk 26), a helicopter pad *and* hangar, and BPDMS/Mk 26. In fact, the 5-inch gun forward has been pushed as far forward as it will go; space is required for a magazine, for the bow anchor, and for the big SQS-26 (now redesignated SQS-53 in a re-engineered version) sonar. It happened that the length required for all of these systems—not to mention superstructure blocks and uptakes—actually exceeded the optimum for the required speed.

One space—and weight—saver was adopted: controllable reversible-pitch propellers (CRPP). A serious problem of all-gas-turbine power plants had been reversing, i.e., going astern. Unlike a steam turbine, a gas turbine cannot incorporate special "astern" stages—or, at least, cannot easily incorporate them. Hence most all-gas-turbine designs had envisaged *turboelectric* drive, which was heavy and space-consuming but had the virtue of permitting full astern power. A controllable-pitch propeller was a far more elegant solution, but it entailed some technological risk, as CRPP had never previously been applied to so powerful a plant.

As built, the new destroyer (the *Spruance*, DD 963) presents an impressive, if apparently underarmed, profile, with a pair of 5-in./54 LW guns, ASROC (with the unusually large magazine capacity of 16 reload missiles), PDMS (not installed at first), two LAMPS helicopters, and the usual pair of triple Mk 32 tubes. Provision has been made for CIWS and for chaff launchers, both antimissile defense measures, and Harpoon (in canisters) has been added.

The basic design provides for both *modernization* and an AAW *conversion* (i.e., to DDG). In the former version, the forward 5-in./54 was to be replaced by a lightweight 8-in./55, and 8 Harpoons in canisters were to be added, as well as CIWS. A Mk 26 Mod 0 launcher would replace the ASROC pepperbox, with no loss of rounds (24 in. magazine vs. 8-inch box plus 16 stowed). However, there would clearly be a *capability* to use the Mk 26 for AAW weapons. *Conversion* would entail, in addition, a Mk 26 Mod 1 in place of the PDMS aft; a new gun fire control system; a continuous wave illumination; and an SPS-48 radar in place of the less capable SPS-40B of the basic ship.

A total of 30 ships were ordered in FY 70–75: 3 in June 1970; 6 in January 1971; 7 in January 1972; 7 in January 1974; and the last 7 in January 1975. Throughout, the program was plagued by cost escalation, so that an original target of $2,506 million rose to an (estimated) final cost of $3,730 million—i.e., a rise from an average of $83.5 to about $124.3 million per ship. By 1976, even that seemed reasonable for so large a ship, and the Congress asked for four more in the FY 77 budget. They were not ultimately approved, but a thirty-first ship was funded under the FY 78 program (DD 997), and proposals for repeat construction (to use Litton's existing automated yard) appear periodically. There is a fair chance, in 1981, that the DDGX currently proposed will have considerable commonality with the *Spruance*. In addition, the Aegis platform ultimately selected is a modified *Spruance* (see chapter 13).

As for the DXG, it was ordered, not by the U.S. Navy but by Iran, which originally asked for six but then cut the order to four in view of escalation to a unit price of $330 million. With the fall of the Shah, the new Iranian government was more than willing to part with these expensive ships, which the Imperial Navy had termed cruisers rather than destroyers. All four were bought under the FY 79 Supplemental Appropriation for a total of $1.35 billion, a bargain at current rates (in FY 79 six FFG 7 cost $1.2 billion) to become the *Kidd* (DDG 993) class.

Neither the DD 963 program nor the DLGN 38 program could make up for the loss of the enormous fleet of World War II destroyers. On 9 September 1970 the new CNO, Admiral Zumwalt, initiated a new destroyer type feasibility study "to examine a new class ship which would be optimized for essentially one mission of either ASW, AAW, on surface warfare, with common hull and propulsion config-

USS *Kidd* (DDG 993)

urations. All ship types would have an ASW capability but only the ASW version would be optimized for ASW . . . equipments should be kept relatively simple and the use of complex hardware and software systems should be avoided." This new type became the *Oliver Hazard Perry* class (FFG 7, originally designated patrol frigate, PF 109).

Admiral Zumwalt was concerned, above all, with the drastic erosion in numbers, particularly in less-sophisticated ships such as the FRAMs. As early as 1963, he had published an article in the *Proceedings* of the U.S. Naval Institute calling for a "high-low" mix of more and less sophisticated destroyers (though not in precisely those words) and in 1970 he sought to put that policy into effect. He was almost certainly deeply affected by his experience with DX/DXG, since as head of Systems Analysis within the Navy he had conducted the Major Fleet Escort study, and later indicated that he considered the *Spruance*s an unfortunately sophisticated response to the numbers

problem. This orientation goes far to explain the ruthless attention to cost inherent in the FFG 7 design. To some extent, too, Admiral Zumwalt suspected that as long as he could get the hulls, his successors would be able to obtain funds to add essential systems to them, whereas a high initial cost would merely foreclose the option of regaining the numbers the Navy had enjoyed until the late 1960s.

It was Admiral Zumwalt's personal style to confront problems in the bluntest possible way, to emphasize his differences rather than his links to past doctrine and procedure. Thus, he coined the phrase "high-low" to characterize his policy of deliberately building unsophisticated ships for some missions, and his critics suggested that in fact he would be sending Americans to die in inferior warships. What they ignored, and what he generally failed to publicize, was that until the end of the 1960s there had always been a "low" end of the escort force, since otherwise the country could hardly have afforded

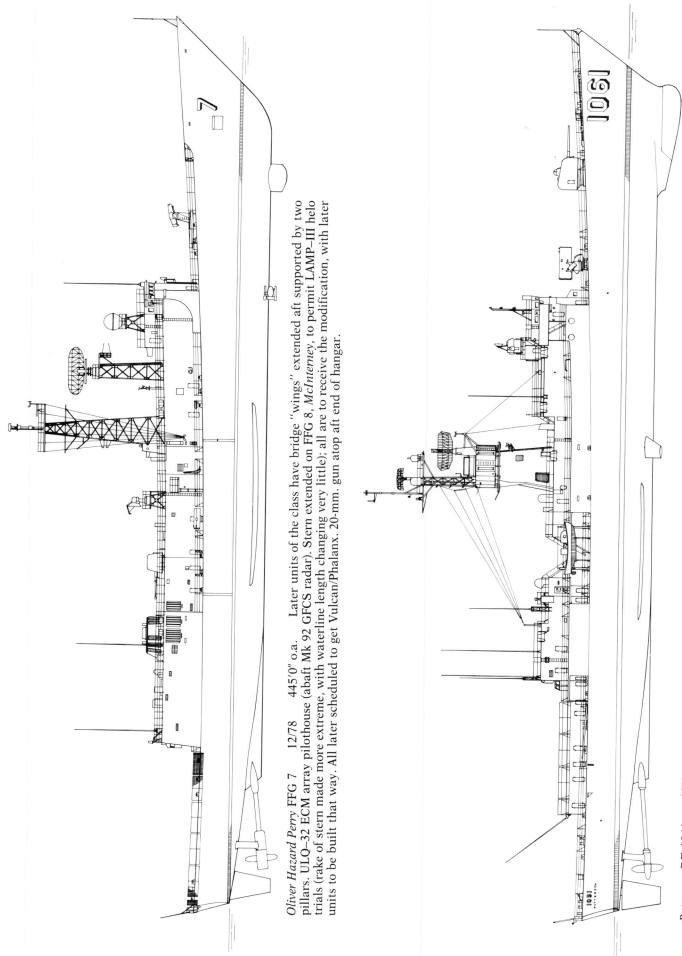

Oliver Hazard Perry FFG 7   12/78   445'0" o.a.   Later units of the class have bridge "wings" extended aft supported by two pillars. ULQ–32 ECM array pilothouse (abaft Mk 92 GFCS radar). Stern extended on FFG 8, *McInerney*, to permit LAMP–III helo trials (rake of stern made more extreme, with waterline length changing very little); all are to receive the modification, with later units to be built that way. All later scheduled to get Vulcan/Phalanx. 20-mm. gun atop aft end of hangar.

Patterson DE 1061   3/70—as commissioned   438' o.a./415' w.l.   *Knox* class (As completed, with small helicopter hangar, no Sea Sparrow, no VDS, no ECM(ULQ–6), etc.

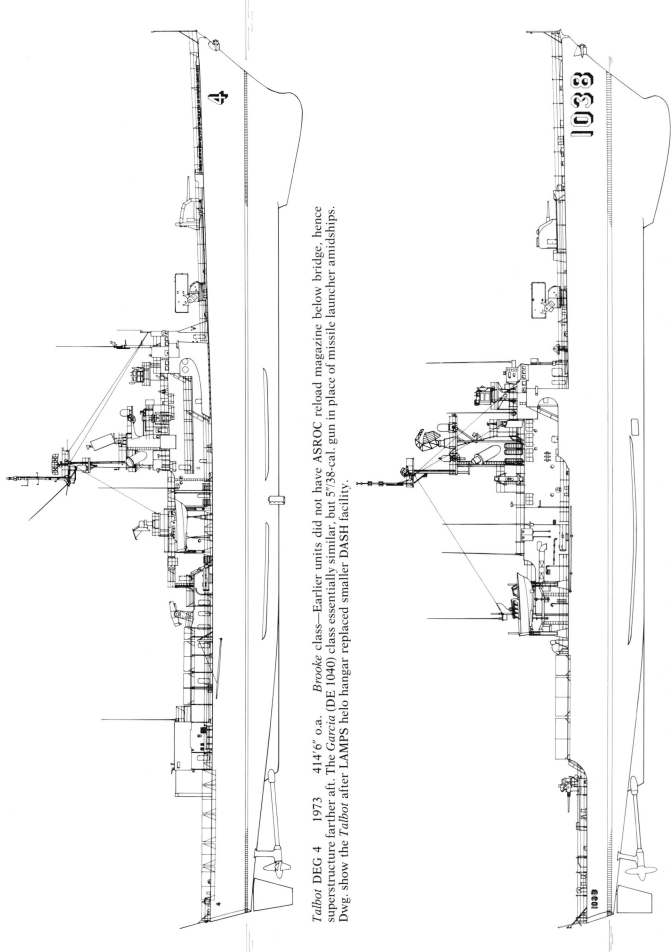

Talbot DEG 4 1973 414'6" o.a.   *Brooke* class—Earlier units did not have ASROC reload magazine below bridge, hence superstructure farther aft. The *Garcia* (DE 1040) class essentially similar, but 5"/38-cal. gun in place of missile launcher amidships. Dwg. show the *Talbot* after LAMPS helo hangar replaced smaller DASH facility.

McCloy DE 1038   1972   371'6" o.a.   *Bronstein* class—after 3" gun later replaced by passive acoustic array

The *Brooke*-class missile frigate *Talbot* was used to test the *Perry*-class weapon suit; she is shown at Roosevelt Roads, 6 December 1974. At that time a Mk 75 76-mm. OTO-Melara gun had replaced her 5-inch/38, and she had the radome of the Dutch-designed Mk 92 fire-control system aft, with a Separate Tracking and Illuminating Radar (STIR) on her fantail.

sufficient numbers. This was somewhat obscured by the composition of the "low" end; after World War II, when new fast task force escorts were built, the large number of war-built destroyers, decidedly the "high" end in World War II, had quite rapidly become the "low" end of the mix.

Given its initial publicity as a "low"-end ship, the *Perry*-class frigate has attracted considerable criticism; it appears relatively unarmed, and its boxy superstructure is often derided. This is at least as much a case of the invisibility of modern weapon systems as it is of economy measures. A *Perry* carries the same SAM as a DDG, and has the same two-channel capability—supported by a vastly more powerful computer system, and by an Automatic Detection and Tracking radar, for very quick reaction. It has no data link, but it does have provision for the later installation of one. In ASW, its main battery is often invisible: two LAMPS helicopters in that boxy hangar, prosecuting contacts the ship can make with its towed array. Like the *Spruance*, the *Perry* has the computer power for a modern ASW command and control system—which the numerous (and better endowed, in terms of sonar) SCB 199s, on the whole, lack.

The transition from visible to much less visible weapon systems is perhaps the dominant theme of modern warship development, and it seems unfortunate that the *Perry* class (and the larger *Spruance*) have suffered so badly in view of it. It is still common, for example, to note only the number of guns and missile launchers, not even the number of fire control channels (illuminators) or the number of missiles in a magazine. Thus, the *Perry* is most easily—and most misleadingly—identified, not with the popular DDG, but rather with the "lemon," the DEG.

A key to the evolution of the FFG was the great degree of standardization the U.S. Navy had achieved in major naval missiles by 1970. With the availability

of the Mk 26 Tartar/ASROC launcher, and the great success of late models of Tartar, a true AAW/ASW ship was entirely feasible. The advent of Harpoon, a sophisticated antiship weapon compatible with Tartar/ASROC launchers, meant that in the near term the surface warfare role, too, could be filled by a ship armed primarily with missiles. Thus, abandonment of the shore bombardment mission, which alone required a substantial gun, could result in a substantial cost and weight saving.

By this time, the total package idea had been dropped and the ship design function returned to the Navy, in the form of the Naval Ship Engineering Center, NAVSEC. By 31 December 1970 NAVSEC had completed feasibility studies suggesting that austere escorts could be built at a cost of $40 to $50 million each. From the first, Admiral Zumwalt, the Chief of Naval Operations, sought to control the usual cost and size escalation; Admiral Franke Price, Op-36, was placed in charge of the program, and, given the attention to cost control, he was often referred to as "design to Price." The initial studies encouraged Admiral Zumwalt to set limits of 3,400 tons and $45 million, both of which represented reductions from the feasibility figures of 3,700 tons, $50 million; in addition, Admiral Zumwalt demanded a reduction in complement to 185, about 30 percent below the usual estimate. There was some small irony here, in that the original displacement limit appears to have originated in a series of errors, due to the complexity of displacement adjustments for alternative weapon suits. Thus, the estimate from which he worked appeared to show that a satisfactory ship might be built on about 3,450 tons, and it was entirely reasonable to assume that 50 tons might be saved in Preliminary Design.

Given the collapse of the FRAMs, the new program was extremely urgent, and it was pressed ahead relatively quickly. Thus, the results of the feasibility

The newly completed frigate *Perry* is shown in December 1977. Much of the boxiness of her appearance can be blamed on a decision half-way through her design to add a second LAMPS helicopter, requiring a much wider hangar. Unlike the *Spruance*, she has diesel generators, the exhaust stack for which is visible just behind her lattice mainmast. The considerable separation between her Mk 92 radome and the STIR tracker-illuminator farther aft is a survivability feature, since it is unlikely that a single hit would destroy both missile-guidance channels. The large search radar is the new SPS-49, which is replacing the earlier metric-wavelength sets in missile cruisers and which is to be fitted to the *Ticonderoga* class. Later units in this class will have enlarged fantails and hangars modified to accommodate the LAMPS III helicopter. The choice of diesel over gas-turbine generators reflected a lessened interest in self-noise reduction for a ship initially conceived more as an AAW than as an ASW combatant. However, all *Perry*s are to be fitted with the towed array, and the capacity to carry two helicopters makes them major ASW ships. Reportedly the towed array is less subject to ship self-noise interference than is a hull sonar. Later units will be fitted with fin stabilizers.

study were presented to the CNO on 1 December 1970; he approved proceeding to the conceptual phase; on 13 March 1971, the Ship Acquisition Plan Manager (SHAPM) reported that a lead ship might be built as early as the FY 73 program. Characteristics, particularly those of the weapon system, were not yet firm; they were approved by Admiral Zumwalt on 6 May, at which time he also approved procurement of the lead ship in FY 73 and of follow-on ships beginning not in FY 74, as would have been usual, but instead in FY 75, to take advantage of experience with the lead ship. Two weeks later, he selected the single-shaft gas-turbine propulsion system, at the same time choosing (temporarily) a more sophisticated sonar (SQS-23). Ultimately, however, the simpler Raytheon 1160B (SQS-56) was adopted. The NAVSEC base-line design was begun on 1 June and official characteristics promulgated on 1 July. After that the only two important design changes were a major change in the helicopter facilities (November) and an alteration in the machinery plant (April 1972). As in many earlier designs, Gibbs & Cox carried out the detail design; Bath was selected as lead yard in April 1973, and the first ship, FFG 7 (*Oliver Hazard Perry*), ordered on 30 October 1973. Fabrication began in March 1975, and she was commissioned on 30 November 1977, the first of more than 50 units authorized to date.

From the first, the new escort was thought of as an austère destroyer. Her mission was defined essentially as transatlantic escort for fast (20-knot) convoys or, alternatively, static picket duty for about ten days around a point a thousand miles from base. Ultimately, these requirements were boiled down to the old DD/DDG 4,500-mile endurance at 20 knots. Sustained speeds in the DE (27-knot) and DD (30-knot) range were considered.

ASW and AAW variants were expected to differ in that the AAW escort was to perform area air defense, the ASW variant only local; whereas the ASW escort was expected to "detect, classify, track or localize, and attack and kill a nuclear submarine at long ranges and when attempting to penetrate its screen sector," the AAW escort could accomplish these tasks only at relatively short ranges. In effect, this would most likely mean a difference in sonars. In both cases torpedo detection and decoy were required.

Two hulls that seemed adaptable to these requirements were DE 1052 and the new Coast Guard *Hamilton* class; but study showed that neither was so very easy to redesign as not to justify a fresh design.

Although some of the earliest sketch studies showed steam plants, gas turbines were chosen very early. Several alternatives were considered, including COGOG (one Rolls Royce Tyne for cruise, two LM-2500 for boost) and COGAG. The LM-2500 of the *Spruance*

class was clearly favored for commonality, but the Pratt and Whitney FT4A was considered a backup. Thus, by January 1971 ASW and AAW variants of a twin-screw COGOG plant (48,500 shp, 30 knots) hull had been developed, on a displacement of 3,362 tons fully loaded ($37 million for follow-on ships). A single-shaft COGAG plant (half a *Spruance* plant, in fact) turned out to be less expensive, and was expected to cost only one knot in speed; displacement was estimated as 2,949 tons fully loaded ($33.8 million). Since the gas turbines had fixed power outputs, once they had been chosen the speed of the ship was set. It gradually fell as displacement rose, the current announced figure being 28.5 knots.

The single shaft was adopted on cost grounds, but justified on the basis of extensive experience with the big DEs, which appeared to show a reliability only 3 percent less than that of a twin-shaft plant. As for battle damage, World War II experience was held to show that in the majority of cases (17 out of 30) destroyers hit by torpedoes broke up and sank at once, in which case the value of a second shaft would indeed be academic. Of the 13 destroyers that did not break up, only 3 got away with no more than severe flooding: seven were severely (structurally) damaged, and three had to be towed home for scrapping. It seemed to NAVSEC that anything short of a torpedo hit could best be dealt with by burying the engines deep in the ship, that the single-shaft itself would be a relatively minor source of vulnerability. In addition, two "outboard" motors (podded retractable units) were provided to bring home a crippled frigate; they were designed for 5 to 6 knots in a calm sea.

A great variety of weapons and sensors was considered. The ASW ship, for example, was equipped with a Mk 16 ASROC/Harpoon pepperbox, LAMPS, two of the usual Mk 32 tubes, the new TACTAS towed array (SQR-18/19), and a new commercial sonar, the Edo 610E. Replacing the pepperbox with the new Mk 26 universal launcher would cost 3,480 tons fully loaded (twin screw), and the addition of emergency point defense (Sea Sparrow) to the basic ship would cost an increase to 3,430. Other alternatives were the addition of a 5-in./54 (3,500 tons) and SQS-26 in place of the small sonar (3,578 tons).

The AAW base-line design called for a Mk 26 launcher firing Harpoon and the Standard missile as well as two Vulcan-Phalanx Close-In Weapon Systems (20-mm. guns); ASW weapons might be limited to a pair of Mk 32 tubes. Gradually it became clear that as long as the design included a moderate sonar and the Mk 26 launcher, it could combine the AAW and ASW tasks. The issue of sonar selection was solved by the observation that although SQS-26 was the most capable available sonar, force levels showed there were already enough in the fleet; the new escort was to *supplement* existing ships. The new towed array, already in the conceptual stage, may have been seen as an inexpensive way to obtain an effective submarine detector without any need for a very expensive keel-mounted sonar. The next most attractive sonar was the SQQ-23, an improved SQS-23 incorporating passive detection capability. It was adopted, but in a meeting its cost gave rise to questions. When Admiral Zumwalt shifted from one helicopter to two, he also ordered the shift to a much smaller sonar, a Raytheon type, which became the SQS-56 of the present *Perry* class. It appears, however, that strength has been built into the keel to permit a later return to the SQQ-23 or to some other larger sonar.

LAMPS was added to the ASW suit on the strength of analyses done in the course of the *Spruance* design; an incidental element of these escort studies was that ASROC per se added very little to the effectiveness of a LAMPS/SQS-23 ship, whereas the long range afforded by the towed array would be wasted without the manned helicopter. Well into contract design only a single helicopter was envisaged, with a pad at the optimum position about three-quarters of the way aft, and split uptakes. However, a second LAMPS was specified in November 1971, so that at least one would always be available. The hangar had to be very considerably enlarged and moved aft; the helo pad was moved to the stern, and the uptakes were consolidated.

This last represented a very considerable shift in priorities, as the original FFG was much much more an AAW than an ASW ship. To many, for example, the choice in favor of diesel (rather than gas-turbine) ship-service generators was a choice, not merely in favor of economy, but also against silencing. Unlike a keel sonar, however, the towed array operates well away from the noise generated by the ship, its efficacy depends much more on signal processing than on silencing. It can be argued, then, that the chief sacrifice made by economizing on silencing and by choosing a very small sonar is in a combination of below-layer detection and vulnerability to potential Soviet developments in silencing their own submarines.

AAW capability was a compromise between stiffening operational requirements and cost constraints. For example, at first the AAW version of the frigate was to have had an SPS-52 frequency-scanned three-dimensional radar, a type generally mounted in DDGs. The frigate as completed has instead the SPS-49 long-range two-dimensional type, and indeed is unique among U.S. missile ships in having no inherent height-finding capability. Other economies were effected in the choice of CIC equipment—for example, in the

number of computers and in the deletion of the NTDS automated data link, although provision was made for its later installation.

By May 1971, the CNO Executive Board had selected a weapon suit for the frigate: the Dutch Mk 87 fire control system with STIR (Separate Tracking and Illuminating Radar, for a second fire control channel), and the Mk 13 missile launcher, more compact than the twin-arm Mk 26. Its selection became possible when ASROC was given up. Tartar C was to be a hedge against failure of the Dutch system. The gun battery was to be a single 35-mm. Oerlikon in an OTO Melara twin mounting, with the heavier 76-mm. OTO Melara gun as a fall-back. In fact, a more capable version of the Dutch fire control system, the Mk 92 Mod 4, was adopted, also with a STIR, and the gun was the fall-back 76 mm., with space and weight provided for later installation of the 20-mm. Vulcan-Phalanx. The choice of the heavier gun was made partly out of a desire to have some means of handling attacking vessels short of the expenditure of a half-million-dollar missile; there was also some question of the effectiveness of the short bursts available from the lighter gun. However, the 76-mm. weapon is not capable of firing laser-guided rounds, which have made even the slow-firing lightweight 5-in./54 potentially an effective adjunct to AAW. In effect, then, the *Perry* approximates a DDG in missile firepower: unlike a DEG (now FFG) she has 40 Tartar/Standard missiles.

Survivability features were not lost in the attempt to cut costs. One example is the "get-home" propulsive pod; another is the extent to which the gas-turbine engines are buried in the hull to protect them from splinter damage. Unofficial reports credit these ships with ¾-inch aluminum-alloy armor over magazine spaces, ⅝-inch steel over the main engine-control room, and ¾-inch in Kevlar plastic armor over vital electronics and command spaces. On the other hand, they continue the U.S. practice of using aluminum deckhouses to save weight, a practice often criticized for its contribution to surface-ship vulnerability.

The new FFG is very similar in size, and slightly faster than the *Knox* (DE 1052); in effect, it trades sonar sophistication and a big 5-inch gun for an enhanced missile capability. Compared to DD 963, the FFG 7 design began as an austere mass-production type in which design margins would be cut to the bone and "state of the art" systems used to hold down costs. All of the weapons that can go into the hull are already there, which is why armament accounts for about a fifth of acquisition cost (about 15 percent for DD 963—but in the latter case *electronics* is the driving cost).

The "off the shelf" philosophy extended to elaborate tests of the PF combat system. In the summer of 1974, DEG 4 was fitted with what amounted to a complete system: an OTO Melara 76-mm. gun in No. 1 position, a Mk 92 fire control system atop the helicopter hangar, and STIR radar right aft. The SQS-56 sonar was tested in the USS *Glennon* (DD 840).

The FFG was one of the earliest examples of design-to-cost: its target price was $45.7 million for follow-on ships. Unfortunately, inflation and a general tendency to disregard the requirements of austerity raised costs very rapidly. The original 50-ship program of 1974 ($3.2 billion, $64 million average cost) was expected, only a year later, to cost $6.8 billion (56 ships, $121.4 million each): a rise of $2.2 billion attributed to inflation and program delays, 726 million for six more ships, and $386 million for changes in design—such as a fourth diesel generator.

As costs rose, Congress became skeptical. A buy of seven ships scheduled for FY 75 was cut to three (FFG 8–10). In FY 76, a request for 10 more ships (to bring the class to 14) was cut to 6 (FFG 11–16); and by this time the 50-ship program was expected to cost $8.5 billion. The Navy kept trying to catch up to its originally projected building rate of 8 ships per year, and for FY 77 requested 12 ($143 million *each*). On the other hand, the basic value of the design was such that Australia ordered four modified units. Two Australian ships were built as FFG 17–18, and the FY 77 buy was cut to eight ships, FFG 19–26. This finally did establish a steady rate of eight per year: FFG 27–34 in FY 78, FFG 36–43 in FY 79 (FFG 35 is Australian), FFG 44–50 (FFG 44 is Australian) in FY 80, and six more (FFG 50–55) in FY 81. FFG 50 was later canceled to pay for Indian Ocean operations. Late in 1980 plans called for construction of the last FFG 7 in FY 82, but ultimately two were included in that year's budget. The Carter Administration planned to commence the new FFX class in FY 84. The latter is to be even more austere than FFG 7, and is to cost half as much, with a smaller displacement. Some would be commissioned directly into the Naval Reserve Force, replacing elderly FRAMs and providing an ASW mobilization base. FFX is sometimes referred to as an "ASW corvette." A tentative (and unofficial) Reagan Administration shipbuilding plan published in September 1981 called instead for construction of a more austere version of the FFG 7, with two in each of FY 83–85, and three in each of FY 86 and FY 87. Throughout its production life the FFG

has been a victim of very rapid cost escalation, with consequent sharp reductions in actual, as opposed to planned, procurement. For example, the Five-Year Shipbuilding Plan submitted in January 1979 called for the construction of 19 FFGs under the FY 81–84 programs; a year later that had been cut to 15. In 1978, the Navy planned a total of 48 units (for a net buy of 76 including Australian ships) during FY 79–84, as compared to a total of 22 currently planned, for a final buy of 52, again including Australian ships.

Cost-cutting during construction left gaps in the FFG weapon system that will be filled during refits. For example, the class is designed to operate the LAMPS I helicopter, and will require considerable enlargement of its helo pad to accept the LAMPS III that will enter service during FY 85. Beginning with the FY 79 ships, helicopter support equipment will be incorporated upon completion, including fin stabilization, the RAST helicopter recovery system. These ships will also be the first to be completed with the towed array, which is to be backfitted to earlier ships. All are ultimately to be backfitted with Vulcan-Phalanx, SLQ-32 ECM, and the Mk 36 Super-RBOC chaff launcher system (the latter not fitted as standard until FFG 27). Ironically, the intense efforts to hold down weight did not always hold down cost. For example, the hull was a composite of HY-80 and mild steel—rather than all mild steel—as a weight saver, but composite construction was more expensive. Nor did it prove possible to hold down displacement: the original FFG 7 came to 3,648 tons fully loaded including a 50-ton service-life margin, and it was expected that FY 79 and later ships would exceed 3,700 tons.

The FFG designation is itself new. The new escort was originally designated "patrol frigate" (PF), probably to dissociate it from the *Knox*-class destroyer escort, which was in considerable disrepute in 1971. The PF designation had first been introduced during World War II, and had been applied postwar to very small escorts of Italian design built for transfer abroad. Clearly, however, there was something unsatisfactory in calling a 3,500-ton escort and an 11,000-ton missile cruiser "frigates"—especially when no other navy in the world did so. Thus, the frigate category was extended to cover all of the DEs in 1975, the missile ships becoming FFGs, the pure ASW types FFs. The missile cruisers became DDGs and CGs (see chapter 13).

16

The Future

In 1981 the United States is designing new classes of destroyers and frigates that may well remain in production through the end of the century, and by their existence will testify to the continued viability of the destroyer concept. The 80-year history of the destroyer suggests some of the conflicts that will shape the new DDGX and FFX designs and some of the pitfalls that their developers may attempt to avoid. Both ships are already embroiled in controversy, which is no stranger to destroyer development. In particular, the precise role of the destroyer remains uncertain. Is it primarily a screening ship for carrier battle groups and other high-value units, its characteristics determined by the threats they face and the performance of the ships it screens? Or is the destroyer the smallest independent combatant, capable of surviving attack by lesser naval powers and of destroying their warships?

In principle, any surface combatant has capabilities in four distinct warfare areas: antiair, antisurface, antisubmarine, and gunfire against shore targets. In fact, however, important judgments must be made as to the requirements for capability in each area. For example, a ship that must survive saturation air attacks probably requires an Aegis-like phased-array radar and mid-course guided missiles, whereas ships in lower-threat areas may make do with systems comparable with Tartar/Standard or even with point-defense or close-in defense weapons. Part of the choice is based on a judgment as to whether the weapons attacking the ship have nuclear warheads, i.e., on how near a near miss the ship can tolerate.

The type and number of antiship weapons depend upon some perception of the role of the destroyer. If she is to operate within a carrier battle group, any sacrifice made for antiship weapons may be undesirable, since the carrier attack aircraft will make a far greater contribution to the antiship potential of the fleet as a whole. On the other hand, if developments in ship-borne antiaircraft weapons make non-carrier Surface Action Groups (SAGs) viable, then the antiship battery of the individual destroyer or cruiser becomes extremely important. To some extent, too, the value of such weapons depends upon perceptions of the threat the United States Navy faces. Since 1945 that threat has come overwhelmingly from submarines and from land-based aircraft. The ability to destroy Soviet surface combatants is useful, but not as vital as the ability to neutralize the other, dominant elements of the Soviet fleet. However, the Soviet threat now appears to be shifting towards a capability to fight surface-to-surface actions against the United States, in which case antiship weapons should become far more important to us.

The new Vertical Launching System (VLS) is an important step toward providing the cruiser-destroyer force with a dual antiair/antisurface capability. In contrast to existing single- or twin-arm systems, a vertical launcher permits immediate random selection of any of a variety of weapons; the existing systems encounter delays when a weapon not in the ready-service position is selected. At first the VLS was designed only to accommodate the Standard antiaircraft missile and the Harpoon medium-range antiship weapons, but in 1980 the decision was made to add three feet to its depth in order to accommodate the long-range Tomahawk, which is effective against both land (strategic) and sea (tactical) targets. By adopting the VLS in the new generation of missile cruisers and destroyers, the Navy is avoiding any rigid choice between antiair and antiship capabilities.

If the destroyers, particularly those in SAGs, are to have any effective antiship capability at very long range, the Navy as a whole will have to provide considerable targeting support. The Soviets are already doing so, but then again they consider U.S. surface ships (particularly carrier battle groups) their primary targets. Soviet ships are not, however, the primary targets of the U.S. fleet; the primary role of the U.S. Navy has been, and continues to be, the maintaining of free passage across the world's oceans, to permit attacks on the periphery of the Soviet land mass, and to support her allies in peace and in war. To invest heavily in sea surveillance capable of detecting only the least-effective element of the three-dimensional Soviet naval threat might well be counterproductive. There is some cause for hope, however. U.S. national intelligence groups already routinely collect considerable data on Soviet naval movements, and properly integrated, their outputs can provide some of the elements of a dedicated ocean surveillance system. The use of such data for targeting has already been tested in a submarine context, in Outlaw Shark.

There are also important issues to be addressed in antisubmarine warfare. For some time the Navy has emphasized offensive ASW supported by SOSUS (Sound Surveillance System) and prosecuted by long-range patrol aircraft. In theory, attrition by barrier submarines and by the aircraft will suffice, over time, to keep merchant ship losses down to acceptable levels, particularly if the merchant ships are concentrated in low-risk areas. Only unique units, the loss of which the Navy cannot afford (such as carriers and underway replenishment groups), then require close escort as a back-up to the attrition forces. It follows that destroyer and escort production numbers can be held down.

Perhaps the central issue, then, is the viability of SOSUS and the systems it supports. SOSUS is a passive system, and it is effective because its sensitivity and the quality of its signal processing have kept step with or gone beyond Soviet progress in submarine silencing. It is not clear that this happy situation will be permanent, nor is it clear that the Soviets will find it difficult to disable SOSUS at the outbreak of a war. In either case the situation may well revert to what it was in World War II, and extensive merchant convoying will be required. Numerous studies, some of them mentioned in chapter 15, have shown the immense cost of true convoy tactics in the absence of SOSUS or some equivalent. That the towed array, which is the great hope of future surface ASW success, is a passive system (in effect a miniature SOSUS) must also be a cause for some disquiet, in that it, too, depends upon the cooperation of potential targets. The towed array is particularly attractive because of the very limited demands it places upon its platform: limited space, limited quieting, some computer space that can be almost anywhere

aboard ship, and helicopter support facilities for contact prosecution.

Finally, there is the continued role of the gun. Missiles remain unsatisfactory for the area bombardment of ill-defined shore targets. Moreover, with a laser designator (or with IR-guided ammunition) gunfire may be far less expensive per hit than a missile, and may therefore be extremely attractive for targets at relatively short range. The perceived value of gunfire has gyrated wildly. With Pacific experience in mind, the Navy was unwilling to abandon the 5-inch gun in the *Mitscher*s. However, as limited-war scenarios faded in importance and the nuclear-armed carrier task group became almost all-important, it was possible to arm the *Leahy*s entirely with missiles; in theory they could destroy shore targets with nuclear-armed Terriers. Vietnam experience showed that in some wars destroyers would operate primarily as offshore gun platforms delivering harrassing fire; it is not surprising, then, that the destroyer designed during the Vietnam War, the *Spruance*, was provided with two austere 5-inch guns and also with provision for replacing one of them with an 8-inch weapon. In the aftermath of Vietnam, shore bombardment is less and less popular, and for a time it was not clear whether the new DDGX was to have a 5-inch gun at all. Descriptions of its mission include attack against shore targets, but that appears to mean attack by long-range weapons such as Tomahawk. The decision to arm the FFG 7 class with a 3-inch weapon useful primarily against aircraft would seem to have been part of the same trend; it is ironic that the 5-inch gun with a guided projectile will probably be far more effective in the same role.

A review of destroyer design since World War I shows a continuing concern that the growth of the ships will preclude their production in sufficient numbers; again and again attempts (often grossly unsuccessful) have been made to assure austerity of design. The current FFG 7 is, thus, only the latest of a very long line of "low-end" destroyers. Efforts to add sufficient equipment to make it effective (and, incidentally, to demolish the cost limits originally envisaged) also have many forebears, the *Belknap* story being only the most vivid. In 1981 austerity is once again the great hope, as the number of destroyers and frigates has been recognized as quite insufficient, particularly in view of the coming obsolescence of the first postwar generation (*Forrest Sherman* and *Adams* classes). The Aegis destroyer, which began as the austere DXG, graduated to *Spruance* size, and was then recognized for what it was, a full missile cruiser. Now something more limited is being planned.

There are two major new design projects. One is

DDGX, which is to replace the aging destroyers from FY 85 onward. Its target cost is $500 million in FY 80 dollars, compared to $800 million for a repeat CG 47; it is to operate within the carrier battle group and also as a SAG unit. As envisaged in 1980, the DDGX was to be armed with the VLS, its antiaircraft missiles guided with the assistance of a multi-function array radar, in effect a less-expensive, less-capable version of the SPY-1 carried by Aegis ships. For close-in defense there will be Vulcan-Phalanx Gatling guns fore and aft, and there will also be a single gun mount, originally an OTO-Melara 76-mm. type but later the lightweight 5-in./54. For ASW there will be a lightweight sonar and, presumably, a com-bination of the towed array and a helicopter pad. However, congressional briefings on the DDGX design did not include specific mention of either of these latter systems. It remains to be seen whether the DDGX will be totally optimized in the direction of antiair warfare, with a small sonar for self-defense only.

The proposed FFX has a rather different function. It was conceived initially as a replacement for the aging FRAM destroyers operating in the Naval Reserve Force (NRF); the Navy's judgment is that the new destroyers and frigates are far too complex for NRF operation. In the tradition of World War II and early postwar destroyer escorts, the FFX is to be a

The DDGX is to be the next major U.S. destroyer class. It will include some features of the larger and more expensive *Ticonderoga*, as well as improved passive protection—officially described as including over 130 tons of fragmentation protection for vital electronic, machinery, and magazine spaces. The CIC and radio rooms will be located within the hull in contrast to current practice, and the ship will be designed to withstand "more than twice the blast overpressure" of earlier classes to enable her to operate in a nuclear environment. A citadel system will protect the crew against radiation, fallout, and chemical attack, with air locks leading into the citadel and all internal air filtered. Although the currently planned DDGX hull is not a direct derivative of the *Spruance* hull, the DDGX will share the quieting and infrared suppression features of the earlier ship. The hull itself is to be a new, wide, waterplane type with better inherent surviv-ability and improved seakeeping performance. Candidate engine systems include a mixed plant in which gas turbine exhaust heat would be extracted to generate steam for added effective power. The preliminary design shown here is 479 feet long, and 60 feet in beam, with a displacement of about 8,500 tons. Armament consists of a single lightweight gun forward, with vertical launchers fore and aft (32 launch cells forward and 64 aft) as well as eight Harpoon amidships and the usual pair of triple lightweight torpedo tubes aft. Unlike the *Ticonderoga*, the DDGX has all four faces of her modified SPY-1 radar concentrated forward, together with two of her three SPG-62 illuminators. She has no independent long-range air-search radar, however. The sonar is an SOS-53C, and there is design provision for a towed array aft. Helicopter facilities are to be limited to a landing and refueling pad; there is no hangar. Although they are not shown here, the DDGX is to have two Phalanx 20-mm. guns aft alongside her vertical launcher. First delivery is scheduled for 1989 as of this writing. In 1982, the DDGX was formally redesignated DDG 51.

mobilization design, ruthlessly limited in complexity. In fact, she is feasible primarily because of the limited demands imposed by the combination of a towed array and a helicopter for contact prosecution; the FFX will have little or no capability beyond these two systems. Among present foreign warships, the FFX is perhaps most closely comparable to the British Type 22 frigate, which appears to the unschooled eye even more underarmed than the *Perry* class.

In fact, the FFX has an important historical forebear, the 173-foot PC of World War II. The PC was originally proposed in 1937 as a training ship for the NRF, a replacement for aging World War I Eagle Boats. In wartime it would release destroyers for more arduous duty. This rationale was sufficient to justify a considerable building program, as the PC did not obviously duplicate destroyer functions. Thus it did not encounter the opposition experienced by the DE program; PCs were available in numbers early enough to fight in the more intense phase of the Battle of the Atlantic—although the austerity of their design made them inadequate operationally. Hopefully the FFX can do better.

In 1980 the Carter Administration's Five-Year Defense Plan called for one FFX in FY 83 and four in FY 85, following the now-standard program of a one-year pause after the prototype in a new class. Its official wartime mission was described as the escort of economic (merchant) convoys, a function that had been abandoned in the late 1950s due to the limited numbers of ships available.

The FFX is encountering considerable opposition. It will have to be an extremely austere ship, the target cost being about half that of a *Perry*. Many critics have argued that it will be so austere that it will be worthless; they do not believe that a combination of the towed array and one or two helicopters alone will suffice, even in ASW. Since some of the most vocal of the critics served on the Reagan Administration's preelection advisory panels, there is some considerable chance that the FFX program will either be scrapped entirely or will be redirected toward increased capability (i.e., towards something very much like an FFG 7 with, perhaps, somewhat less sophisticated equipment). Certainly the history of destroyer design (and of the design of other classes of warship) suggests strongly that the internal discipline necessary to make austerity and cost-control work is extremely difficult to maintain. This is particularly the case as governmental power becomes more diffuse, so that there are more and more ways to overcome the strong vetos needed to maintain limited cost goals. By late 1981, it appeared that FFX would be abandoned in favor of a somewhat simplified FFG 7.

In 1981 the United States may be on the verge of its greatest increase in defense spending since the Korean War. A long period of neglect has left the Navy, and particularly the cruiser-destroyer force, at its lowest strength in many years. In some important ways the situation recalls that of 1939: reconstruction is already occurring, but at a very slow pace. Designs exist, but there is as yet no determination to build them in vast numbers. In 1940 the United States made a mobilization decision, and chose to build, not the most austere destroyer it could design, but rather the ship in production—the extremely powerful *Fletcher*. Three years of intense naval war in the Pacific proved the wisdom of this decision. The *Spruance* and the CG 47 may well find themselves in a similar position, with the DDGX redefined as a modified *Spruance*, and the FFX as a slightly redesigned *Perry*. There will be intense pressures to go instead to new special mobilization ships, or to wait for the maturity of new systems. If history is any indication, any decision in that direction will be sadly misguided; the need will be for numbers, and the iron law of mobilization is that only what is already in production can be produced fast enough. Hopefully the experience of 80 years of destroyer design and production will contribute to the appropriate decisions now.

Notes to Tables

Three series of data tables have been compiled: very complete ones for ships of wartime or prewar construction, or that were stricken before 1980; less comprehensive ones for the conventionally powered ships of the current fleet; and corresponding to the most severe security restrictions of all, the least complete tables refer to the nuclear fleet. The tables of modern types also incorporate the new system of weight breakdowns (which emphasizes the new roles of C^3 and of electrical systems) introduced in the mid-1950s. *Fletcher* data is included for comparison. Note that the *endurance* figures in the modern tables refer to the characteristics according to which these ships were designed and thus bear little resemblance to operational figures.

Data are *representative* of each class as built and, where possible, as subject to standard modification. Displacement and loading data are taken from inclining experiment reports, and the names and dates refer to those reports.

Where two trial figures are given, they refer to separate runs at light and heavy displacements, as noted. Trial endurance is a prewar figure; the wartime figure takes into account practices such as split-plant operation, which considerably reduced effective endurance. The design figure is that stated in the characteristics. Ammunition supply *per* weapon (averaged) is given in parentheses (note, however, that it was limited to a standard allowance prewar); in the case of helicopters such as LAMPS or DASH, it is the number of weapons available (which in a few cases are pooled with the Mk 32 torpedo tubes).

Generator capacity is given in kw, and is AC unless otherwise noted. The notation "132 AC/40 DC" refers to two generators, one of 132 kw (AC) and one of 40 kw (DC) run off the same auxiliary turbine. Steam conditions are given in boiler pressure (psi)/temperature (F.).

Weight data in parentheses are designed as opposed to returned (i.e., actual) weights. In many cases the returned weights of the ship in light condition do not match the light ship displacement deduced from the inclining experiment, and the figure *below* the light ship weight is that found upon inclining. The same convention applies when the light ship weight breakdown refers to a sister ship of the one inclined; such instances are noted.

Among the weights, the margin is a designer's figure. Applied to returned weights, it is the (very small) weight still remaining to be placed aboard at the time of the final weight report. Machinery liquids include lubricating oil and fuel oil "in the system," i.e., not in storage tanks. Fog oil is for smoke screens. Note that prewar standard displacements were computed on the basis of a "normal," or design, condition, with 2/3 stores and other loads (except ammunition) aboard. In wartime this condition was no longer computed and only maximum or full loads are given.

For modern ships, no breakdown of loads is given, due to security classification.

All weights are in long tons of 2,240 lbs.

Stability data refer to the loading noted. GM is metacentric height, GZ maximum righting arm (with corresponding angle in parentheses) and the range is the range of stability.

Name *Bainbridge* (DD 1)
Date As built
LOA 249'9⅞"
LWL 244'2⅞"
Beam 23'5"
Depth 14'0"
CB 0.43
C⊗ 0.703
CW 0.627
SHP (trial) 8,000
Speed (trial) 28.45
At (tons) 452
Endurance (trial) 2,100/12†

Endurance (war)
Main Battery 2 3-in/50, 5 6-pdr (57 mm)
GFCS None
Torpedo Tubes 2 18-in (4)
TFCS None
Complement 3/72
Design Displacement 420.0
Design STD
Design Full Load 630.9
Boilers 4 Thornycroft
Steam Conditions 250 psi
SSTG 1 5 DC

Diesel Generators
SHP (design) 8,000
Speed (design) 28.0
Fuel Capacity (design) 212.3
Endurance (design)
Tactical Diameter (yds/kts) 250/22
AA Battery None
AA FCS None
Hedgehog None
D.C. Tracks None
D.C. Projectors None
Sonar None

WEIGHTS

	Normal	Full Load
Hull	165.2	(139.5)
Fittings	26.1	(14.7)
Eqpmt & Outfit	11.7	(8.5)
Armament	10.1	(14.3)
Machy (dry)	200.4	(187.1)
Margin		
Ballast		
Light Ship	413.5	(364.1)
Machy Liquid	14.5	14.5*
Complement	6.9	6.9
Ammo		9.2
Stores & PW		16.3
Lube Oil		
Standard		
RFW		
Fuel Oil	25.0	250.2
Diesel Oil		
Fog Oil		
Displacement		710.5
Draft	(450T) 6–9	
GM		
GZ		
Range		

Name *Hopkins* (DD 6)
Date As built
LOA 244'0"
LWL 238'9"
Beam 23'1½"
Depth 23·1½"
Depth 14' 5½"
CB
C⊗
CW
SHP (trial) 8,456
Speed (trial) 29.02
At (tons) 467
Endurance (trial)

Endurance (war)
Main Battery 2 3-in/50, 6 6-pdr (57 mm)
GFCS None
Torpedo Tubes 2 18-in (4)
TFCS None
Complement 3/75
Design Displacement 408
Design STD
Design Full Load
Boilers 4 Thornycroft
Steam Conditions
SSTG 1 5 DC

Diesel Generators None
SHP (design) 7,000
Speed (design) 29
Fuel Capacity (design) 150
Endurance (design)
Tactical Diameter (yds/kts) 400/23
AA Battery None
AA FCS None
Hedgehog None
D.C. Tracks None
D.C. Projectors None
Sonar None

WEIGHTS

	Normal	Full Load
Hull	186.9	
Fittings	22.5	
Eqpmt & Outfit	15.8	
Armament	12.9	
Machy (dry)	186.8	
Margin		
Ballast		

*Includes RFW.
†Cruising radius (Robinson, 1920).

Light Ship	424.9	
Machy Liquid	17.9	17.9
Complement	3.3	
Ammo	1.7	10.1
Stores & PW	4.1	14.9
Lube Oil		

Standard		
RFW		38.1
Fuel Oil	25.	153.6
Diesel Oil		
Fog Oil		

Displacement	476.9	659.5
Draft		
GM		
GZ		
Range		

Name *Lawrence* (DD 8)
Date As built
LOA 246′3″
LWL 240′10″
Beam 22′2½″
Depth 19′9″
CB 0.428
C⊗ 0.808
CW 0.682
SHP (trial) 8,400
Speed (trial) 28.41
At (tons) 412
Endurance (trial)

Endurance (war)
Main Battery 7 6-pdr (57 mm)
GFCS None
Torpedo Tubes 2 18-in (4)
TFCS None
Complement 3/75
Design Displacement 400
Design STD
Design Full Load
Boilers 4 Normand
Steam Conditions
SSTG 1 5 DC (to 10 kw 1912)

Diesel Generators None
SHP (design) 8,400
Speed (design) 30
Fuel Capacity (design) 115
Endurance (design)
Tactical Diameter (yds/kts)
AA Battery None
AA FCS None
Hedgehog None
D.C. Tracks None
D.C. Projectors None
Sonar None

WEIGHTS

	Normal	Full Load
Hull } Fittings }	133	
Eqpmt & Outfit	12	
Armament	15	
Machy (dry)	182	
Margin		
Ballast		

Light Ship		
Machy Liquid	12	
Complement		
Ammo		
Stores & PW		
Lube Oil		

Standard		
RFW		
Fuel Oil	34	116
Diesel Oil		
Fog Oil		

Displacement	400	505
Draft	6–2	
GM	4.2	
GZ	2.3 (50)	
Range	Over 90	

Name *Truxtun* (DD 14)
Date As built
LOA 259'6"
LWL 248'0"
Beam 22'3½"
Depth 13'4"
CB
C⊗ 0.663
CW 0.620
SHP (trial) 8,300
Speed (trial) 29.58
At (tons) 486
Endurance (trial)

Endurance (war)
Main Battery 2 3-in/50, 6 6-pdr (57 mm)
GFCS None
Torpedo Tubes 2 18-in (4)
TFCS None
Complement 3/75
Design Displacement 433
Design STD
Design Full Load
Boilers 4 Thornycroft
Steam Conditions 240 psi
SSTG 1 5 DC

Diesel Generators None
SHP (design) 8,300
Speed (design) 30
Fuel Capacity (design) 232
Endurance (design)
Tactical Diameter (yds/kts) 503/24 (*Whipple*)
AA Battery None
AA FCS None
Hedgehog None
D.C. Tracks None
D.C. Projectors None
Sonar None

WEIGHTS

	Normal	Full Load
Hull	199.5	
Fittings	22.7	
Eqpmt & Outfit	15.0	
Armament	12.3	
Machy (dry)	206.9*	
Margin		
Ballast		
Light Ship	456.4	
Machy Liquid		
Complement	3.3	7.3
Ammo	1.6	11.2
Stores & PW	4.1	37.0
Lube Oil		
Standard		
RFW		11.6
Fuel Oil	25.0	171.0
Diesel Oil		
Fog Oil		
Displacement	490.4	694.5
Draft		
GM		
GZ		
Range		

"Flivvers"

Name *Smith* (DD 17)
Date As built
LOA 293'10½"
LWL 289'0"
Beam 26'0¼"
Depth 16'4¾"
CB 0.407
C⊗ 0.649
CW 0.662
SHP (trial) 9,946
Speed (trial) 28.35
At (tons) 716

Endurance (trial) 2,000/18
Endurance (war)
Main Battery 5 3-in, 2 0.30 cal
GFCS None
Torpedo Tubes 3 × 1 (6)
TFCS None
Complement 4/83
Design Displacement 700
Design STD
Design Full Load
Boilers 4 Mosher
Steam Conditions

SSTG 2 5 (Conv. to 10 kw 1914) DC
Diesel Generators None
SHP (design) 10,000
Speed (design) 28
Fuel Capacity (design) 304
Endurance (design) 2,800/10†
Tactical Diameter (yds/kts) 676/25
AA Battery None
AA FCS None
Hedgehog None
D.C. Tracks None
D.C. Projectors None
Sonar None

WEIGHTS

	Normal	Full Load
Hull	238.4	(252.8)
Fittings	28.4	(27.4)
Eqpmt & Outfit	20.0	(16.1)
Armament	20.7	(19.9)
Machy (dry)	249.8	(237.0)
Margin		(19.3)
Ballast		

*Includes liquids.
†Cruising radius (Robinson, 1910).

	Normal	Full Load
Light Ship	557.3	(550.9)
Machy Liquid		
Complement		
Ammo	12.6	
Stores & PW	30.4*	
Lube Oil		
Standard	600.3	
RFW	11.7	
Fuel Oil	285.6	
Diesel Oil		
Fog Oil		
Displacement	897.6	
Draft	8–0½	
GM	3.24	
GZ		
Range		

Name *Paulding* (DD 22)
Date As designed
LOA 293'10½"
LWL 289'0"
Beam 26'1½"
Depth 16'4¾"
CB 0.41
C⊗ 0.66
CW 0.67
SHP (trial) 17,393
Speed (trial) 32.8
At (tons) 887
Endurance (trial) 3,343/15, 2,642/20

Endurance (war)
Main Battery 5 3-in/50
GFCS None
Torpedo Tubes 6 (3 × 2) 18-in
TFCS None
Complement 4/82
Design Displacement 742
Design STD
Design Full Load
Boilers 4 Normand
Steam Conditions
SSTG 2 5 (to 10 kw 1914) DC

Diesel Generators None
SHP (design) 12,000
Speed (design) 29.5
Fuel Capacity (design) 241
Endurance (design) 3,000/16†
Tactical Diameter (yds/kts) 860/25
AA Battery None
AA FCS None
Hedgehog None
D.C. Tracks None
D.C. Projectors None
Sonar None

WEIGHTS

	Normal	Full Load
Hull	253.3	(249.6)
Fittings	31.7	(29.6)
Eqpmt & Outfit	18.2	(17.4)
Armament	21.3	(20.1)
Machy (dry)	258.3	(242.9)
Margin		
Ballast		(23.6)
Light Ship	582.8	(583.1)
Machy Liquid		24.8
Complement		9.1
Ammo		6.6
Stores & PW		28.3
Lube Oil		
Standard		
RFW		14.7
Fuel Oil		230.8
Diesel Oil		
Fog Oil		
Displacement		897.1
Draft		
GM		
GZ		
Range		

*Includes complement.
†Cruising radius (Robinson, 1920).

Name *Perkins* (DD 26)
Date April, 1912
LOA 293'10"
LWL 289'0"
Beam 26'1½"
Depth
CB 0.414
C⊗ 0.666
CW 0.649
SHP (trial) 11,668
Speed (trial) 29.76
At (tons) 765
Endurance (trial) 1,864/15, 1,470/20

Endurance (war)
Main Battery 5 3-in/50
GFCS None
Torpedo Tubes 6 (3 × 2) 18-in
TFCS None
Complement 4/79
Design Displacement 742
Design STD
Design Full Load
Boilers 4 Yarrow
Steam Conditions
SSTG 2 5 (to 10 kw 1914) DC

Diesel Generators None
SHP (design) 12,000
Speed (design) 29.5
Fuel Capacity (design)
Endurance (design)
Tactical Diameter (yds/kts)
AA Battery None
AA FCS None
Hedgehog None
D.C. Tracks None
D.C. Projectors None
Sonar None

WEIGHTS

	Normal	Full Load
Hull	223.0	
Fittings	38.0	
Eqpmt & Outfit	19.1	
Armament	21.2	
Machy (dry)	300.5	
Margin		
Ballast		
Light Ship	601.8	
	(604)	
Machy Liquid	23.4	23.4
Complement	9.1	9.1
Ammo		6.6
Stores & PW		36.9
Lube Oil		
Standard		
RFW		15.0
Fuel Oil		246.7
Diesel Oil		
Fog Oil		
Displacement	757	902
Draft		
GM	2.76	3.01
GZ		
Range		

Name *Trippe* (DD 33)
Date March, 1911
LOA 293'10"
LWL 289'0"
Beam 26'1½"
Depth 16'4¾"
CB 0.412
C⊗ 0.663
CW 0.6699
SHP (trial) 14,978
Speed (trial) 30.89
At (tons) 883
Endurance (trial) 2,175/15, 1,913/20

Endurance (war)
Main Battery 5 3-in/50
GFCS None
Torpedo Tubes 6 18-in (3 × 2)
TFCS None
Complement 4/85
Design Displacement 742
Design STD
Design Full Load
Boilers 4 Normand
Steam Conditions
SSTG 2 5 (to 10 kw 1914) DC
Diesel Generators None

SHP (design)
Speed (design)
Fuel Capacity (design)
Endurance (design)
Tactical Diameter (yds/kts)
AA Battery None
AA FCS None
Hedgehog None
D.C. Tracks None
D.C. Projectors None
Sonar None
Note: Weight breakdown is
    taken from the *Walke* (DD 34)

WEIGHTS

	Normal	Full Load
Hull	256.1	
Fittings	33.5	
Eqpmt & Outfit	22.9	
Armament	20.9	
Machy (dry)	298.8	
Margin		
Ballast		

Light Ship	632.2	
Machy Liquid	28.8	28.8
Complement	9.1	9.1
Ammo	11.4	11.4
Stores & PW	18.3	27.5
Lube Oil	0.9	1.3

Standard		
RFW	3.0	14.7
Fuel Oil	92.5	224.8
Diesel Oil	4.0*	6.2*
Fog Oil		
Displacement	720	880
Draft	8'2½"	9'3¾"
GM	2.80	2.72
GZ	1.25 (45–30)	1.32 (43–0)
Range	95–0	93–30

Name *Henley* (DD 39)
Date As built
LOA 293'10½"
LWL 289'0"
Beam 26'4½"
Depth 16'4⅜"
CB 0.410
C⊗ 0.650
CW 0.670
SHP (trial) 13,472
Speed (trial) 29.5
At (tons) 891
Endurance (trial)

Endurance (war)
Main Battery 5 3-in, 2 0.30 MG
GFCS None
Torpedo Tubes 6 (3 × 2) 18-in
TFCS None
Complement
Design Displacement 742
Design STD
Design Full Load
Boilers 4 Yarrow
Steam Conditions
SSTG 2 5 (to 10 kw 1914) DC

Diesel Generators
SHP (design)
Speed (design) 29.5
Fuel Capacity (design)
Endurance (design) 3,000/15
Tactical Diameter (yds/kts) 685/25
  (*Fanning*)
AA Battery None
AA FCS None
Hedgehog None
D.C. Tracks None
D.C. Projectors None
Sonar None

WEIGHTS

	Normal	Full Load
Hull	256.7	
Fittings	37.2	
Eqpmt & Outfit	26.0	
Armament	21.1	
Machy (dry)	291.8	
Margin		
Ballast		

Light Ship	632.8	
	(621.7)	
Machy Liquid	23.8	23.8
Complement	8.9	8.9
Ammo		11.8
Stores & PW		41.1
Lube Oil		

Standard		
RFW		14.6
Fuel Oil		246.7
Diesel Oil		
Fog Oil		
Displacement	778.6	927.8
Draft		
GM	2.88	2.78
GZ		
Range		

*Galley coal.

"Thousand Tonners"

Name *Downes* (DD 45)
Date February, 1915
LOA 305'3"
LWL 300'0"
Beam 30'4"
Depth 17'1⅛"
CB .423
C⊗ .683
CW .662
SHP (trial) 14,254
Speed (trial) 29.14
At (tons) 1,057 (*Duncan*)
Endurance (trial)

Endurance (war)
Main Battery 4 4-in/50
GFCS None
Torpedo Tubes 8 (4 × 2)18-in
TFCS None
Complement 5/93
Design Displacement 1,010
Design STD
Design Full Load
Boilers 4 Yarrow
Steam Conditions
SSTG 2 10 DC (later 2–25 DC)

Diesel Generators None
SHP (design) 16,000
Speed (design) 29.0
Fuel Capacity (design) 307.6
Endurance (design)
Tactical Diameter (yds/kts) 847/25 (*Aylwin*)
AA Battery None
AA FCS None
Hedgehog None
D.C. Tracks None
D.C. Projectors None
Sonar None

WEIGHTS

	Normal	Full Load
Hull	340.9	(319.0)
Fittings	52.0	(38.8)
Eqpmt & Outfit	45.0	(31.3)
Armament	33.0	(32.7)
Machy (dry)	353.5	(353.4)
Margin		
Ballast		
Light Ship	824.4	(775.2)
	(805.2)	
Machy Liquid	33.5	33.5
Complement	10.0	10.0
Ammo	20.8	20.8
Stores & PW	21.0	31.7
Lube Oil	1.4	2.1
Standard		
RFW	12.1	18.1
Fuel Oil	205.1	307.6
Diesel Oil	4.0*	6.0*
Fog Oil		
Displacement	1,113.3	1,235.1
Draft	9'9⅞"	10'6⅛"
GM	4.02	3.53
GZ	1.97 (41–30)	1.73 (38–15)
Range	92–0	83–45

Name *McDougal* (DD 54)
Date May, 1914
LOA 305'3"
LWL 300'0"
Beam 30'4"
Depth
CB
C⊗
CW
SHP (trial) 16,974
Speed (trial) 30.70
At (tons) 1,021
Endurance (trial)

Endurance (war)
Main Battery 4 4-in/50
GFCS None
Torpedo Tubes 8 (4 × 2) 21-in
TFCS None
Complement 8/93
Design Displacement 1,050
Design STD
Design Full Load
Boilers 4 Normand
Steam Conditions
SSTG 2 10 DC (later 2–25)

Diesel Generators
SHP (design) 17,000
Speed (design) 29.0
Fuel Capacity (design) 327
Endurance (design)
Tactical Diameter (yds/kts)
AA Battery None
AA FCS None
Hedgehog None
D.C. Tracks None
D.C. Projectors None
Sonar None

WEIGHTS

	Normal	Full Load
Hull		(323.4)
Fittings		(43.1)
Eqpmt & Outfit		(25.6)
Armament		(30.5)
Machy (dry)		(320.9)
Margin		
Ballast		

*Galley coal.

Light Ship	(718.7)	(743.5)
Machy Liquid	32.0	32.0
Complement	10.0	10.0
Ammo	22.9	22.9
Stores & PW	28.1	41.7
Lube Oil	0.7	1.1
Standard	811.8	
RFW	12.5	18.7
Fuel Oil	218.4	327.5
Diesel Oil		
Fog Oil		
Displacement	1,043	1,172
Draft	9'4¾"	10'7¾"
GM	4.16	3.64
GZ	2.07 (40–20)	1.78 (39–0)
Range	93–0	86–12

Name *Tucker* (DD 57)
Date April, 1916
LOA 315'3"
LWL 310'0"
Beam 29'10"
Depth 17'1¹⁄₁₆"
CB 0.443
C⊗ 0.749
CW 0.630
SHP (trial) 16,399
Speed (trial) 29.56
At (tons) 1,103
Endurance (trial)

Endurance (war)
Main Battery 4 4-in/50
GFCS None
Torpedo Tubes 8 (4 × 2) 21-in
TFCS None
Complement 5/94
Design Displacement 1,090
Design STD
Design Full Load
Boilers 4 Yarrow
Steam Conditions
SSTG 2 25 DC

Diesel Generators None
SHP (design) 17,000
Speed (design) 29.5
Fuel Capacity (design) 290
Endurance (design) 2,500/20
Tactical Diameter (yds/kts)
AA Battery None
AA FCS None
Hedgehog None
D.C. Tracks None
D.C. Projectors None
Sonar None

WEIGHTS

	Normal	Full Load
Hull	335.4	(340.9)
Fittings	58.1	(51.5)
Eqpmt & Outfit	44.5	(41.7)
Armament	37.2	(25.0)
Machy (dry)	333.1	(336.3)
Margin		(0.2)
Ballast		
Light Ship	768.3	(795.6)
	(811.4)	
Machy Liquid	31.2	31.2
Complement	10.1	10.1
Ammo	31.6	31.6
Stores & PW	25.2	37.8
Lube Oil	1.3	2.0
Standard	910.8	
RFW	15.3	23.0
Fuel Oil	206.1	309.2
Diesel Oil		
Fog Oil		
Displacement	1,132.3	1,256.7
Draft	9'7⅛"	10'4¹³⁄₁₆"
GM	2.55	2.29
GZ	1.64 (46)	1.46 (42–50)
Range	93–36	88–40

Name *Rowan* (DD 64)
Date August, 1916
LOA 315′3¼″
LWL 310′0″
Beam 29′8¼″
Depth 17′7½″
CB 0.452
C⊗ 0.761
CW 0.635
SHP (trial) 17,964
Speed (trial) 29.57
At (tons) 1,135
Endurance (trial)

Endurance (war)
Main Battery 4 4-in/50
GFCS None
Torpedo Tubes 12 (4 × 3) 21-in
TFCS None
Complement 5/95
Design Displacement
Design STD
Design Full Load
Boilers 4 Yarrow
Steam Conditions
SSTG 2 25 DC

Diesel Generators None
SHP (design) 17,000
Speed (design) 29.5
Fuel Capacity (design)
Endurance (design)
Tactical Diameter (yds/kts)
AA Battery None
AA FCS None
Hedgehog None
D.C. Tracks None
D.C. Projectors None
Sonar None

WEIGHTS

	Normal	*Full Load*	
Hull		(341.5)	
Fittings		(55.1)	
Eqpmt & Outfit		(44.7)	
Armament		(38.2)	*Allen* (DD 66),
Machy (dry)		(333.7)	(November,
Margin		(0.8)	1944)
Ballast			48.9
Light Ship	(825.6)	(814.0)	930.8
Machy Liquid	31.2	31.2	37.7
Complement	10.2	10.2	15.5
Ammo	39.7	39.7	51.0
Stores & PW	23.1	34.7	40.8
Lube Oil	1.3	2.0	2.2
Standard	931.1		1,078.0
RFW	15.4	23.1	18.9
Fuel Oil	206.1	309.2	335.6
Diesel Oil			
Fog Oil			
Displacement	1,152.3	1,275.6	1,433.1
Draft	9.7	10.5	11′4¾″
GM	2.48	2.21	1.78
GZ	1.6 (45–0)	1.41 (44–0)	1.11 (36.9)
Range	92–48	87–12	75.4

Flush Deckers

Name *Gwin* (DD 71)
Date April, 1920
LOA 315′6″
LWL 310′0″
Beam 30′7″
Depth 19′8½″
CB 0.51
C⊗ 0.86
CW 0.65
SHP (trial) 19,930
Speed (trial) 30.29
At (tons) 1,192
Endurance (trial)

Endurance (war)
Main Battery 4 4-in/50
GFCS None
Torpedo Tubes 12 (4 × 3) 21-in
TFCS None
Complement 5/95
Design Displacement 1,120
Design STD
Design Full Load
Boilers 4 Yarrow
Steam Conditions
SSTG 2 25 DC

Diesel Generators None
SHP (design) 18,500
Speed (design) 30.0
Fuel Capacity (design) 205
Endurance (design) 2,500/20
Tactical Diameter (yds/kts)
AA Battery 2 1-pdr
AA FCS None
Hedgehog None
D.C. Tracks 2
D.C. Projectors 1 Y-Gun
Sonar None

WEIGHTS

	Normal	*Full Load*
Hull	367.7	(367.0)
Fittings	60.8	(59.2)
Eqpmt & Outfit		(33.7)
Armament	40.7	(40.7)
Machy (dry)		(364.9)*
Margin		(3.2)
Ballast		

*Includes liquids.

Light Ship		(868.7)
Machy Liquid	35.0	35.0
Complement	11.8	11.8
Ammo	37.0	37.0
Stores & PW	34.6	51.9
Lube Oil	0.9	1.3
Standard		
RFW	18.4	27.6
Fuel Oil	180.0	270.0
Diesel Oil		
Fog Oil		
Displacement	1,262.1	1,379.0
Draft	8'9¾"	9'5½"
GM	1.66	1.54
GZ	1.67 (53–0)	1.72 (52–40)
Range	107–30	109–30

Bath Type

Name *Wickes* (DD 75)
Date June, 1918
LOA 314'4"
LWL 310'0"
Beam 30'11½"
Depth 20'7¾"
CB .47
C⊗ .75
CW .68
SHP (trial) 24,610
Speed (trial) 35.34
At (tons) 1,149
Endurance (trial) 3,800/15, 2,850/20

Endurance (war)
Main Battery 4 4-in/50 (100)
GFCS None
Torpedo Tubes 12 (4 × 3) 21-in
TFCS None
Complement 6/108
Design Displacement 1,160
Design STD
Design Full Load
Boilers 4 Normand
Steam Conditions 265 psi
SSTG 2 25 DC

Diesel Generators None
SHP (design) 24,200
Speed (design) 35.0
Fuel Capacity (design) 225 (275 emergency)
Endurance (design) 2,500/20
Tactical Diameter (yds/kts) 770/15, 810/25
AA Battery 2 1-pdr
AA FCS None
Hedgehog None
D.C. Tracks 2
D.C. Projectors None
Sonar None

WEIGHTS

	Normal	Full Load	*Jacob Jones* (DD 130) (as Escort, Nov, 1941: 6 3-in DP, 6 21-in TT, 5.50, 1Y-Gun)	*Blakeley* (DD 150) (Sept, 1942: One BLR removed. 4 4-in, 6 21-in TT, 6 20-mm, 6 DC Projectors, Max load condition)
Hull		(367.1)		
Fittings		(59.7)		
Eqpmt & Outfit		(37.8)		
Armament		(40.7)		
Machy (dry)		(387.0)		
Margin		—		
Ballast		—		16.9
Light Ship	(885.3)	(892.2)		1,016.2
Machy Liquid	43.0	43.0		38.0
Complement	11.7	11.7		15.2
Ammo	36.3	36.3		49.5
Stores & PW	32.6	46.7		67.3
Lube Oil	0.9	1.4		
Standard				
RFW	16.2	24.3		40.7
Fuel Oil	182.7	274.0		390.3
Diesel Oil				
Fog Oil				
Displacement	1,208.6	1,322.6		1,597
Draft	9'3⅛"	9'10½"		11'4¼"
GM	2.13	1.95		1.81
GZ				1.37 (47.5)
Range				Over 90

Bethlehem Type

Name *Kimberly* (DD 80)	Endurance (war)	Diesel Generators None
Date April, 1918	Main Battery 4 4-in/50 (100)	SHP (design) 27,000
LOA 314'4½"	GFCS None	Speed (design) 35.0
LWL 310'0"	Torpedo Tubes 12 (4 × 3) 21-in	Fuel Capacity (design) 225 (275 emergency)
Beam 30'11½"	TFCS None	Endurance (design) 2,500/20
Depth	Complement	Tactical Diameter (yds/kts)
CB 0.47	Design Displacement 5/95	AA Battery 2 1-pdr
C⊗ 0.75	Design STD	AA FCS None
CW 0.68	Design Full Load	Hedgehog None
SHP (trial) 27,350	Boilers 4 Yarrow	D.C. Tracks 2
Speed (trial) 34.81	Steam Conditions 265 psi	D.C. Projectors None
At (tons) 1,236	SSTG 2 25 DC	Sonar None
Endurance (trial)		

WEIGHTS

	Normal	Full Load
Hull		
Fittings		
Eqpmt & Outfit		
Armament		
Machy (dry)		
Margin		
Ballast		
Light Ship	(919.8)	
Machy Liquid	46.6	46.6
Complement	10.2	10.2
Ammo	39.1	39.1
Stores & PW	20.6	20.6
Lube Oil	1.4	2.0
Standard		
RFW	14.0	21.0
Fuel Oil	150.0	225.0
Diesel Oil		
Fog Oil		
Displacement	1,201.7	1,294.8
Draft	9'2⅝"	9'8⅝"
GM	2.03	2.09
GZ	1.23 (50–45)	1.38 (51–50)
Range	101–0	106–0

Name *Preble* (DD 345)	Endurance (war)	Diesel Generators
Date April, 1927	Main Battery 4 4-in/50	SHP (design) 27,000
LOA 314'4"	GFCS Mk 8	Speed (design) 35
LWL 310'0"	Torpedo Tubes 12 (4 × 3) 21-in	Fuel Capacity (design) 225 (371 emergency)
Beam 30'10½"	TFCS Mk 11	Endurance (design) 2,500/20
Depth 20'8"	Complement	Tactical Diameter (yds/kts) 750/25
CB 0.478	Design Displacement	AA Battery 1 3-in/23
C⊗ 0.753	Design STD	AA FCS
CW 0.680	Design Full Load	Hedgehog
SHP (trial) 24,890	Boilers 4 Normand	D.C. Tracks 2
Speed (trial) 35.51	Steam Conditions	D.C. Projectors 1 Y-Gun
At (tons) 1,107	SSTG 2 25 DC	Sonar None
Endurance (trial)		

WEIGHTS

	Normal	Full Load	
Hull	430.2		*McCormick*
Fittings	65.5		(DD 223)
Eqpmt & Outfit	36.8		(March, 1942:
Armament	49.4		6 3-in/50, 4 20-mm,
Machy (dry)	364.4		6 DC projectors,
Margin			2 DC tracks)
Ballast			30

Light Ship	946.3 (991.0)		1,054
Machy Liquid	46.6	46.6	37
Complement	11.8	11.8	16
Ammo	45.3	45.3	50
Stores & PW	28.7	39.1	55
Lube Oil	2.9	4.3	3
Standard	1,126.3		1,215
RFW	14.0	21.0	24
Fuel Oil	150.0	225.0	460
Diesel Oil	0.3*	0.5*	
Fog Oil			
Displacement	1,290.7	1,388.7	1,699
Draft	9'8¹³⁄₁₆"	10'3¹⁄₁₆"	11'11"
GM	1.41	1.36	1.52
GZ	0.87 (45–38)	0.91 (44–35)	1.06 (43)
Range	83–5	84–0	90

Farragut Class

Name *Farragut* (DD 348)
Date April, 1934
LOA 341'3"
LWL 334'0"
Beam 34'3"
Depth 19'8"
CB 0.522
C⊗ 0.838
CW 0.744
SHP (trial) 40,353
Speed (trial) 36.6
At (tons) 1,613
Endurance (trial) 8,968/12

Endurance (war) 5,980/12, 3,710/20 (2,150 tons)
Main Battery 5 5-in/38 (100)
GFCS Mk 33
Torpedo Tubes 8 (2 × 4) 21-in
TFCS Mk 27
Complement 10/150
Design Displacement 1,711
Design STD 1,500
Design Full Load
Boilers 4 Yarrow
Steam Conditions 400/648
SSTG 132 AC/45 AC, 2 30 DC

Diesel Generators None
SHP (design) 42,800
Speed (design) 36.5
Fuel Capacity (design) 600
Endurance (design) 6,500/12 (est. 7,700/12)
Tactical Diameter (yds/kts) 850/35.5
AA Battery 4 .50
AA FCS None
Hedgehog None
D.C. Tracks 2 (14)†
D.C. Projectors None
Sonar QC

WEIGHTS

	Normal	Full Load	
Hull	458.6	(528)	
Fittings	81.7	(102)	
Eqpmt & Outfit	45.4	(43)	*Aylwin* (DD 355)
Armament	96.7	(93)	(September,
Machy (dry)	566.0	(695)	1944:
Margin			Complement:
Ballast			22/248)
Light Ship	1,248.4 (1,211.9)	(1,365)	1,367.9
Machy Liquid	44.6	44.6	54.4
Complement	16.8	16.8	28.8
Ammo	46.0	46.0	105.4
Stores & PW	32.7	57.2	69.3
Lube Oil	5.9	8.8	6.9
Standard	1,357.9		
RFW	25.0	77.6	67.1
Fuel Oil	200.0	600.1	606.4
Diesel Oil	1.0*	1.0*	1.0
Fog Oil			
Displacement	1,583.9	2,063.8	2,307.2
Draft	9'7³⁄₈"	11'6½"	12'6¾"
GM	2.76	2.37	1.63
GZ	1.34 (38)	1.49 (39.5)	
Range	77.25	87.50	

*Gasoline.
†Mounted 1936; 300-lb charges. On DD 350–355 as built.

Porter Class

Name *Porter* (DD 356)
Date June, 1936
LOA 381'0½"
LWL 372'0"
Beam 36'10⅝"
Depth 21'0"
CB 0.487
C⊗ 0.796
CW 0.753
SHP (trial) 51,127/47,271
Speed (trial) 38.19/37.17
At (tons) 2,132/2,180
Endurance (trial) 8,710/15 (2,157 tons)

Endurance (war) 6,380/12, 4,080/15 (2,700 tons)
Main Battery 8 5-in/38 (100)
GFCS Mk 35
Torpedo Tubes 8 21-in (16)
TFCS Mk 27
Complement 13/193
Design Displacement 2,131
Design STD 1,850
Design Full Load
Boilers 4 B&W
Steam Conditions 400/645
SSTG 2 200 AC

Diesel Generators 2 70
SHP (design) 50,000
Speed (design) 37
Fuel Capacity (design) 646
Endurance (design) 7,800/12
Tactical Diameter (yds/kts)
AA Battery 8 (2 × 4) 1.1-in, 2 .50
AA FCS None
Hedgehog None
D.C. Tracks 2 (14)*
D.C. Projectors None
Sonar QC

WEIGHTS

	Normal	Full Load	
Hull }	834.7	(677)	
Fittings }		(100)	
Eqpmt & Outfit		(51)	*Selfridge*
Armament	140.4	(149)	(DD 357)
Machy (dry)	641.9	(630)	(March,
Margin		(49)	1944)
Ballast			
Light Ship	(1,689)	(1,664)	1,750
Machy Liquid	52.5	52.5	59
Complement	24.8	24.8	34
Ammo	64.3	64.3	172
Stores & PW	41.3	68.8	78
Lube Oil	1.5	3.8	5
Standard	1,873.4		
RFW	39.3	84.5	84
Fuel Oil	235.0	651.4	651
Diesel Oil	6.0	24.3	24
Fog Oil			
Displacement	2,154	2,663	2,857
Draft	11'5½"	13'2¼"	13'9¾"
GM	2.17	2.42	2.67
GZ	0.92 (34.16)	1.23 (37.46)	1.40 (37.9)
Range	61.40	73.40	80.7

Somers Class (DD 381, 383, 394–396)

Name *Sampson* (DD 394)
Date July, 1938
LOA 381'6"
LWL 372'0"
Beam 36'10¼"
Depth 21'0"
CB 0.482
C⊗ 0.795
CW 0.747
SHP (trial) 53,271
Speed (trial) 38.56
At (tons) 2,179
Endurance (trial) 10,540/15 (2,143 tons)

Endurance (war) 7,020/12, 6,030/15, 4,250/20 (2,750 tons)
Main Battery 8 5-in/38 (112)
GFCS Mk 35
Torpedo Tubes 12 21-in
TFCS Mk 27
Complement 10/225
Design Displacement 2,130
Design STD 1,850
Design Full Load
Boilers 4 FW & B&W
Steam Conditions 600/850
SSTG 2 200/50

Diesel Generators 2 100
SHP (design) 52,000
Speed (design) 37.5
Fuel Capacity (design) 619.1
Endurance (design) 7,500/15
Tactical Diameter (yds/kts) 1,240/20, 860/30
AA Battery 8 (2 × 4) 1.1-in, 4 0.50
AA FCS None
Hedgehog None
D.C. Tracks 2 (14)*
D.C. Projectors None
Sonar QCE

*300–16 charges.

WEIGHTS

	Normal	Full Load	
Hull	744.9	(683.4)	
Fittings	137.1	(106.5)	
Eqpmt & Outfit	58.4	(53.5)	*Jouett* (DD 396)
Armament	197.8	(161.1)	(Feb, 1942:
Machy (dry)	706.2	(702.7)	8 20-mm, 6 DC projectors,
Margin		(6.8)	2 DC tracks)
Ballast			20
Light Ship	(1,839.8)	(1,685.7)	1,855
Machy Liquid	28.2	28.2	45
Complement	27.5	27.5	33
Ammo	72.4	72.4	167
Stores & PW	43.2	74.4	82
Lube Oil	2.5	3.8	9
Standard	2,013.6		
RFW	40.0	84.3	84
Fuel Oil	230.0	611.9	611
Diesel Oil	10.0	24.2	24
Fog Oil			
Displacement	2,293.6	2,766.6	2,901
Draft	11'11"	13'5¼"	13'11½"
GM	2.0	2.16	2.08
GZ	0.87 (33)	1.08 (35)	1.05 (34.4)
Range	63	73	72.4

Mahan Class

Name *Mahan* (DD 364)	Endurance (war) 6,940/12, 4,360/20 (2,200 tons)	Diesel Generators 1 25/1.25
Date April, 1936	Main Battery 5 5-in/38 (100)	SHP (design) 46,000
LOA 341'3"	GFCS Mk 33	Speed (design) 37
LWL 334'0"	Torpedo Tubes 12 21-in	Fuel Capacity (design) 550
Beam 35'6⅛"	TFCS Mk 27	Endurance (design) 6,500/12
Depth 19'8"	Complement 8/150	Tactical Diameter (yds/kts) 870/30
CB 0.481	Design Displacement 1,725	AA Battery 4 .50
C⊗ 0.808	Design STD 1,500	AA FCS None
CW 0.748	Design Full Load	Hedgehog None
SHP (trial) 44,477	Boilers 4 B&W & FW	D.C. Tracks 2 (14)*
Speed (trial) 37.8	Steam Conditions 400/700†	D.C. Projectors
At (tons) 1,749	SSTG 2 132 AC/40 DC	Sonar QC
Endurance (trial) 7,300/12		

WEIGHTS

	Normal	Full Load	
Hull	481.9	(489)	*Case* (DD 370)
Fittings	127.1	(105)	(November,
Eqpmt & Outfit	50.5	(45)	1943: 40-mm
Armament	105.6	(103)	guns; CIC,
Machy (dry)	595.5	(587)	ram bow,
Margin		(9)	new sound
Ballast			dome.)
Light Ship	1,360.6 (1,313.0)	(1,338)	1,443
Machy Liquid	58.6	58.6	58
Complement	20.6	20.6	28
Ammo	52.8	52.8	136
Stores & PW	38.7	54.3	66
Lube Oil	4.2	3.6	7

†Note: Original machinery design was for 825 DEG superheat,
52,000 SHP, 39 kts.
*300-lb charges.

Standard	1,487.9		1,738
RFW	25.0	58.3	58
Fuel Oil	201.0	522.2	523
Diesel Oil	3.6	19.3	19
Fog Oil			
Displacement	1,717.6	2,102.6	2,328
Draft	10'7⅜"	12'3¾"	13'1¼"
GM	3.30	3.05	2.39
GZ	1.72 (38.8)	1.74 (38.4)	1.13 (32.9)
Range	85.2	92.3	73.7

Name *Downes* (DD 375)
Date November, 1934
LOA 341'4"
LWL 334'0"
Beam 35'5"
Depth
CB
C⊗
CW
SHP (trial)
Speed (trial)
At (tons)
Endurance (trial)

Endurance (war)
Main Battery 4 5-in/38 (364)
GFCS Mk 37
Torpedo Tubes 8 21-in (2 × 4)
TFCS Mk 27
Complement 16/235
Design Displacement
Design STD
Design Full Load
Boilers 4 B&W & FW
Steam Conditions 400/700
SSTG 2 200 AC/40 DC
Diesel Generators 1 25

SHP (design)
Speed (design)
Fuel Capacity (design)
Endurance (design)
Tactical Diameter (yds/kts)
AA Battery 4 (2 × 2) 40-mm, 6 20-mm
AA FCS Mk 51
Hedgehog None
D.C. Tracks 2
D.C. Projectors 6
Sonar
Note: As rebuilt at Mare Island

WEIGHTS

	Normal	Full Load
Hull		
Fittings		
Eqpmt & Outfit		
Armament		
Machy (dry)		
Margin		
Ballast		
Light Ship	1,434	
Machy Liquid	58	
Complement	29	
Ammo	116	
Stores & PW	64	
Lube Oil	7	
Standard	1,708	
RFW	58	
Fuel Oil	480	
Diesel Oil	19	
Fog Oil		
Displacement	2,265	
Draft	12'10¾"	
GM	2.72	
GZ	1.35 (35.6)	
Range	81.1	

Dunlap Class

Name *Dunlap* (DD 384)
Date July, 1938
LOA 341'5"
LWL 334'0"
Beam 35'0"
Depth
CB 0.481
C⊗ 0.802
CW 0.738
SHP (trial) 45,452
Speed (trial) 39.09
At (tons) 1,741 (*Fanning*)
Endurance (trial)

Endurance (war)
Main Battery 5 5-in/38 (100)
GFCS Mk 33
Torpedo Tubes 12 21-in
TFCS Mk 27
Complement 8/150
Design Displacement 1,725
Design STD
Design Full Load
Boilers 4 B&W & FW
Steam Conditions 400/700
SSTG 2 132 AC/40 DC
Diesel Generators 1 25

SHP (design) 46,000
Speed (design) 37
Fuel Capacity (design)
Endurance (design)
Tactical Diameter (yds/kts)
AA Battery 4 .50
AA FCS None
Hedgehog None
D.C. Tracks 2 (14)*
D.C. Projectors None
Sonar QC
Note: Weight breakdown
for *Fanning* (DD 385)

WEIGHTS

	Normal	Full Load
Hull	505.8 ⎫	(573.6)
Fittings	102.5 ⎭	
Eqpmt & Outfit	57.6	(45.0)
Armament	105.3	(105.9)
Machy (dry)	613.3	(647.1)†
Margin		
Ballast		
Light Ship	1,384.5	
	(1,425.8)	
Machy Liquid	57.0	57.0
Complement	20.5	20.5
Ammo	65.0	65.0
Stores & PW	39.3	59.0
Lube Oil	2.3	3.4
Standard	1,609.9	
RFW	25.0	58.2
Fuel Oil	194.0	521.6
Diesel Oil	6.0	19.2
Fog Oil		
Displacement	1,835	2,230
Draft	2.26	2.62
GM	11'1¹³⁄₁₆"	12'9³⁄₁₆"
GZ	1.20 (38)	1.47 (37)
Range	69	85

Gridley Class (DD 380, 382, 400, 401)

Name *Gridley* (DD 380)
Date April, 1937
LOA 341'4¼"
LWL 334'0"
Beam 35'6½"
Depth 19'7⅞"
CB 0.488
C⊗ 0.804
CW 0.748
SHP (trial) 47,265/53,073
Speed (trial) 38.99/38.7
At (tons) 1,774/1,992
Endurance (trial) 7,735/15 (1,771 tons)

Endurance (war) 5,520/12, 4,910/15, 3,660/20 (2,150 tons)
Main Battery 4 5-in/38 (100)‡
GFCS Mk 33
Torpedo Tubes 16 21-in
TFCS Mk 27
Complement 8/150
Design Displacement 1,738
Design STD 1,500
Design Full Load
Boilers 4 Yarrow
Steam Conditions 565/700
SSTG 2 132 AC/40 DC

Diesel Generators 1 80/3
SHP (design) 44,000
Speed (design) 37
Fuel Capacity (design) 562.8
Endurance (design) 6,500/12
Tactical Diameter (yds/kts)
AA Battery 4 .50
AA FCS None
Hedgehog None
D.C. Tracks 2 (14)†
D.C. Projectors None
Sonar QC

*300-lb charges.
†Including liquids.
‡Two base ring (enclosed), two pedestal mounts.

WEIGHTS

	Normal	Full Load	
Hull	523.2	(484.4)	
Fittings	114.6		
Eqpmt & Outfit	41.7		
Armament	115.0		
Machy (dry)	662.6		*Craven*
Margin			(DD 382)
Ballast			(November, 1943)
Light Ship	1,457.1		1,517
	(1,429.6)		
Machy Liquid	43.0	43.0	49.0
Complement	19.2	19.2	26.0
Ammo	56.3	56.3	124.0
Stores & PW	37.2	58.1	67.0
Lube Oil	4.2	6.4	5.0
Standard	1,589.5		1,788
RFW	25.0	65.1	56.0
Fuel Oil	194.0	524.9	525.0
Diesel Oil	25.3	37.9	37.0
Fog Oil			
Displacement	1,815.7	2,218.7	2,406
Draft	11'1½"	12'8½"	13'5½"
GM	2.58	2.67	2.18
GZ	1.14 (33.8)	1.26 (34.4)	
Range	67.3	76.2	

Bagley Class

Name *Bagley* (DD 386)
Date July, 1937
LOA 341'3⅝"
LWL 334'
Beam 35'6⅛"
Depth 19'8"
CB 0.475
C⊗ 0.782
CW 0.729
SHP (trial) 47,191
Speed (trial) 36.8
At (tons) 1,969 (*Blue*, DD 387)
Endurance (trial)

Endurance (war) as *Mahan* class
Main Battery 4 5-in/38 (100)
GFCS Mk 33
Torpedo Tubes 16 21-in
TFCS Mk 27
Complement 8/150
Design Displacement 1,726
Design STD 1,500
Design Full Load
Boilers 4 B&W & FW
Steam Conditions 400/700
SSTG 2 132 AC/40 DC

Diesel Generators 1 80
SHP (design) 46,000†
Speed (design) 37
Fuel Capacity (design) 509.0
Endurance (design) 6,500/12
Tactical Diameter (yds/kts) 880/30
AA Battery 4 .50
AA FCS
Hedgehog
D.C. Tracks 2 (14)*
D.C. Projectors
Sonar QC

WEIGHTS

	Normal	Full Load	
Hull			
Fittings			
Eqpmt & Outfit			
Armament			
Machy (dry)			
Margin			
Ballast			
Light Ship	1,407.0		
Machy Liquid	62.7	62.7	
Complement	19.4	19.4	
Ammo	93.4	93.4	
Stores & PW	36.9	55.4	
Lube Oil	4.9	7.4	

*300-lb charges.

†Originally designed for 50,000 shp, but reduction in steam temperature from 825 to 700 degrees reduced performance.

Standard	1,624.3	
RFW	38.9	58.3
Fuel Oil	336.6	503.8
Diesel Oil	24.9	37.4
Fog Oil		
Displacement	2,025	2,245
Draft	11'11⅜"	12'9½"
GM	2.63	2.57
GZ	1.38 (36)	1.38 (36)
Range	76–0	83–0

Benham Class

Name *Benham* (DD 397)
Date September, 1938
LOA 341'4¼"
LWL 334'0"
Beam 35'5¾"
Depth 19'7⅞"
CB 0.480
C⊗ 0.810
CW 0.741
SHP (trial) 50,220/49,250
Speed (trial) 40.86/37.9
At (tons) 1,738/2,038
Endurance (trial) 9,500/15 (1,762 tons)

Endurance (war) 5,390/12, 4,860/15, 3,600/20 (2,300 tons)
Main Battery 4 5-in/38 (100)*
GFCS Mk 33
Torpedo Tubes 16 21-in
TFCS Mk 27
Complement 9/175
Design Displacement 1,725
Design STD 1,500
Design Full Load
Boilers 3 B&W
Steam Conditions 600/700–715
SSTG 2 132 AC/40 DC

Diesel Generators 1 80 AC/1.9 DC
SHP (design) 50,000
Speed (design) 38.8
Fuel Capacity (design) 530.0
Endurance (design) 6,500/12
Tactical Diameter (yds/kts)
AA Battery 4 .50
AA FCS None
Hedgehog None
D.C. Tracks 2 (10)†
D.C. Projectors None
Sonar QCE

WEIGHTS

	Normal	Full Load	Stack (DD 406) (April, 1942: 6 20-mm, 6 D.C. projectors, 2 D.C. tracks)	Sterett (DD 407) (July, 1945 Anti-Kamikaze armament refit)
Hull	535.7	(499.8)		
Fittings	130.8	(102.2)		
Eqpmt & Outfit	45.4	(47.0)		
Armament	118.0	(116.0)		
Machy (dry)	684.1	(633.2)		
Margin		(10.5)		
Ballast				
Light Ship	1,513.9 (1,491.3)	(1,408.7)	1,599.1	1,577.0
Machy Liquid	44.9	44.9	42.6	41.2
Complement	19.1	19.1	24.7	17.9
Ammo	68.2	68.2	138.4	87.3
Stores & PW	29.9	62.3	74.8	76.4
Lube Oil	2.8	4.2	8.5	8.5
Standard	1,656.2			
RFW	25.0	39.0	39.7	39.7
Fuel Oil	194.0	484.0	483.9	484.0
Diesel Oil	12.5	37.4	36.9	29.0
Fog Oil				8.6
Displacement	1,887.7	2,250.4	2,449.0	2,369.6
Draft	11'5"	12'10⅜"	13'7½"	13'3¾"
GM	2.22	2.47	2.42	2.34
GZ	0.99 (33)	1.16 (33)	1.10 (29.4)	1.07 (31.5)
Range	62–30	72–30	72.6	71.0

*Plus total of 100 illuminating rounds.
†600-lb charges (or 14 × 300-lb).

Sims Class

Name *Anderson* (DD 411)
Date April, 1939
LOA 348'3⅛"
LWL 341'4¼"
Beam 36'1⅛"
Depth 19'8"
CB 0.493
C⊗ 0.810
CW 0.756
SHP (trial) 51,387/51,138
Speed (trial) 38.75/36.91
At (tons) 1,948/2,230
Endurance (trial)

Endurance (war) 5,640/12, 3,660/20 (2,350 tons)
Main Battery 5 5-in/38 (150)*
GFCS Mk 37
Torpedo Tubes 12 21-in (3 × 4)
TFCS Mk 27
Complement 10/182
Design Displacement 1,770
Design STD 1,570
Design Full Load 1,960.5
Boilers 3 B&W
Steam Conditions 600/700–715
SSTG 2 150 AC/40 DC

Diesel Generators 1 100 AC/2.5 DC
SHP (design) 50,000
Speed (design) 35
Fuel Capacity (design) 500
Endurance (design) 6,500/12
Tactical Diameter (yds/kts) 843/30
AA Battery 4 .50
AA FCS None
Hedgehog None
D.C. Tracks 2 (10)†
D.C. Projectors None
Sonar QC

WEIGHTS

	Normal	Full Load	*Buck* (DD 420) (June, 1940, with 8 TT, ballast. Normal cond.)	*Anderson* (DD 411) (May, 1943: 4 40-mm, 2 DC projectors. 366 rounds per 5-in. Complement 16/249.)
Hull	589.9	(537.6)		
Fittings	132.7	(100.0)		
Eqpmt & Outfit	44.7	(48.0)		
Armament	139.5	(130.6)		
Machy (dry)	687.5	(607.7)		
Margin	4.4	(10.4)		
Ballast			39.1	40.7
Light Ship	1,598.6 (1,570.6)	(1,434.3)	1,650.0	1,635.0
Machy Liquid	46.5	46.5	41.0	44.0
Complement	20.0	20.0	21.6	28.0
Ammo	55.4	55.4	66.8	142.0
Stores & PW	63.1	63.1	48.7	71.0
Lube Oil	3.7	3.7	7.0	8.0
Standard	1,759.3		1,835.1	
RFW	35.3	53.1	35.4	53
Fuel Oil	298.0	443.9	298.0	459
Diesel Oil	24.3	36.9	24.3	37
Fog Oil				
Displacement	2,116.8	2,293.1	2,193.0	2,477
Draft	12'0¼"	12'8⁵⁄₁₆"	12'3¾"	13'4½"
GM	2.19	2.37	2.76	2.73
GZ	0.98 (31–30)	1.08 (32)	1.30 (32–42)	1.20 (32.2)
Range	61–30	66–30	72–48	74.2

Benson Class

Name *Mayo* (DD 422)
Date June, 1941
LOA 348'1¹³⁄₁₆"
LWL 341'3⅜"
Beam 36'2⅛"
Depth 19'7⅞"
CB 0.495
C⊗ 0.801
CW 0.747
SHP (trial) 51,390
Speed (trial) 37.89
At (tons) 2,065
Endurance (trial)

Endurance (war) 5,580/12, 3,880/20
(2,400 tons)
Main Battery 5 5-in/38 (100)‡
GFCS Mk 37
Torpedo Tubes 5 21-in
TFCS Mk 27
Complement 9/182
Design Displacement 2,030
Design STD 1,620
Design Full Load
Boilers 4 B&W
Steam Conditions 618/700–750
SSTG 2 200 AC/40 DC

Diesel Generators 1 100
SHP (design) 50,000
Speed (design) 35
Fuel Capacity (design) 500
Endurance (design) 6,500/12
Tactical Diameter (yds/kts) 960/30
AA Battery 10 .50
AA FCS
Hedgehog
D.C. Tracks 2 (12)§
D.C. Projectors 1 Y-Gun (10)
Sonar QC

*Plus total of 100 illuminating.
†600-lb charges (or 14 × 300-lb).
‡Plus total of 120 illuminating rounds.
§600-lb charges.

WEIGHTS

	Normal	Full Load	(August, 1944: 40-mm guns installed; 8 20-mm in place of after TT. 460 rounds per 5-in gun. Complement 17/228.)	Laffey (DD 459) (March, 1942: 4 (1 × 4) 1.1-in, 5 20-mm, 5 21-in TT, 6 projectors, 2 DC tracks.)
Hull	629.9	(567.8)		
Fittings	134.2	(129.1)		
Eqpmt & Outfit	49.6	(50.0)		
Armament	134.5	(131.6)		
Machy (dry)	693.6	(659.8)		
Margin		(0.1)		
Ballast	41.0		41.1	41.6
Light Ship	1,679.8 (1,696)	(1,533.4)	1,732	1,600.0
Machy Liquid	52	52	63	41.9
Complement	20	20	26	26.7
Ammo	91	91	128	114.9
Stores & PW	52	78	83	91.5
Lube Oil			4	3.3
Standard	1,911			1,878.3
RFW	36	57	57	57.3
Fuel Oil	308	441	458	441.2
Diesel Oil	26	39	40	38.4
Fog Oil				
Displacement	2,281	2,474	2,591	2,415.1
Draft	12'7¾"	13'4½"	13'9¾"	13'1¼"
GM	2.56	2.78	2.79	3.17
GZ	1.18 (31.4)	1.25 (33.2)	1.23 (33.5)	1.50 (36)
Range	69.1	75.7	77	84

Gleaves Class

Name Niblack (DD 424)
Date July, 1940
LOA 348'3⅝"
LWL 341'0"
Beam 36'1⅛"
Depth 19'7⅞"
CB
C⊗
CW
SHP (trial) 50,200
Speed (trial) 36.5
At (tons) 2,220
Endurance (trial)
Endurance (war) 5,250/12, 3,630/20 (2,450 tons)

Main Battery 5 5-in/38 (100)*
GFCS Mk 37
Torpedo Tubes 10 21-in
TFCS Mk 27
Complement 9/199
Design Displacement 1,817
Design STD 1,630
Design Full Load 2,060
Boilers 4 B&W
Steam Conditions 615/825
SSTG 2 200 AC/40 DC
Diesel Generators 1 100 AC/2.5 DC
SHP (design) 50,000
Speed (design) 35

Fuel Capacity (design) 441.0
Endurance (design) 6500/12
Tactical Diameter (yds/kts) 700/25
AA Battery 6 .50
AA FCS None
Hedgehog None
D.C. Tracks 2 (10)†
D.C. Projectors None
Sonar QCJ
Note: Weight breakdown refers to
Bristol (DD 453), delivered as
a duplicate of DD 423–424 but
without No. 3 5-in gun.

WEIGHTS

	Normal	Full Load	
Hull	607.2		
Fittings	142.9		
Eqpmt & Outfit	45.6		(March, 1945, with 4 40-mm, 6 DC projectors)
Armament	134.0		
Machy (dry)	699.0		
Margin			
Ballast	41.76		42
Light Ship	1,669.7 (1,654.8)		1,741
Machy Liquid	41.9	41.9	52
Complement	21.5	21.5	26
Ammo	50.6	50.6	126
Stores & PW	64.2	79.5	85
Lube Oil	5.8	8.7	4

*Plus total of 120 illuminating rounds.
†600-lb charges.

Standard	1,838.8		
RFW	32.3	48.5	49
Fuel Oil	302.0	453.0	453
Diesel Oil	24.4	36.6	23
Fog Oil			13
Displacement	2,197.5	2,395.0	2,572
Draft	12'4"	13'2"	13'8¼"
GM	2.76	2.88	2.69
GZ	1.28 (32.8)	1.33 (33.1)	
Range	72.4	77.3	

Fletcher Class

Name *Fletcher* (DD 445)
Date June, 1942
LOA 376'6"
LWL 369'0"
Beam 39'8"
Depth 22'8"
CB 0.499
C⊗ 0.799
CW 0.756
SHP (trial) 60,000
Speed (trial) 35.1
At (tons) 2,800
Endurance (trial) 4,800/15, 4,150/20

Endurance (war) 4,900/12, 4,490/15, 3,480/20 (2,850 tons)
Main Battery 5 5-in/38 (605)
GFCS Mk 37
Torpedo Tubes 10 21-in
TFCS
Complement 9/264
Design Displacement 2,700†
Design STD 2,110
Design Full Load
Boilers 4 B&W
Steam Conditions 615/850
SSTG 2 250AC/40DC

Diesel Generators 1 100
SHP (design) 60,000
Speed (design) 37.8
Fuel Capacity (design) 491
Endurance (design) 6,500/15
Tactical Diameter (yds/kts) 950/30
AA Battery 2 (1 × 2) 40-mm, 6 20-mm
AA FCS Mk 51
Hedgehog None
D.C. Tracks 2 8 (26)*
D.C. Projectors 6 (30)
Sonar QC

WEIGHTS

	Normal	Full Load	
Hull	739.6	(770.5)	
Fittings	126.7	(137.1)	
Eqpmt & Outfit	53.1	(72.4)	*Leutze*
Armament	161.8	(147.4)	(DD 481)
Machy (dry)	786.7	(821.6)	(March, 1944:
Margin		(16.0)	10 40-mm,
Ballast			7 20-mm)
Light Ship	1,868.0	(1,965.0)	1,974.6
Machy Liquid	75.7		72.7
Complement	27.9		37.0
Ammo	190.8		203.1
Stores & PW	109.6		113.2
Lube Oil	4.6		5.5
Standard	2,276.6		2,406.1
RFW	66.9		66.9
Fuel Oil	492.3		492.3
Diesel Oil	40.2		40.2
Fog Oil			
Displacement	2,871.0		3,005.5
Draft	13'5⅜"		13'10¾"
GM	3.94		3.27
GZ	2.07 (38.6)		1.65 (34)
Range	82–30		72.5

*600-lb charges.
†Original figure was 2,550 tons; increase due to inclusion of mobilization supply of ammunition.

Sumner Class

Name *Barton* (DD 722)
Date December, 1943
LOA 376′6″
LWL 369′0″
Beam 40′10″
Depth 23′0″
CB 0.520
C⊗ 0.830
CW
SHP (trial) 67,108
Speed (trial) 35.82
At (tons) 2,882
Endurance (trial) 5,100/15, 4,000/20

Endurance (war) 4,620/12, 4,220/15, 3,240/20 (3,100 tons)
Main Battery 6 5-in/38
GFCS Mk 37
Torpedo Tubes 10 21-in
TFCS Mk 27
Complement 11/325
Design Displacement 2,890
Design STD 2,290
Design Full Load
Boilers 4 B&W
Steam Conditions 565/850
SSTG 2 400 AC/50 DC

Diesel Generators 2 100
SHP (design) 60,000
Speed (design) 36.5
Fuel Capacity (design) 538
Endurance (design) 6,500/15
Tactical Diameter (yds/kts) 700/30
AA Battery 12 (2 × 2, 2 × 4) 40-mm, 11 20-mm
AA FCS Mk 51
Hedgehog None
D.C. Tracks 2 (26)
D.C. Projectors 6 (30)
Sonar QGA (QCL/QCJ interim)

WEIGHTS

	Normal	Full Load	
Hull	840.1	(787.2)	
Fittings	169.7	(144.2)	
Eqpmt & Outfit	61.6	(70.3)	
Armament	240.2	(205.6)	*John W.*
Machy (dry)	823.1	(845.5)	*Thomason* (DD 760)
Margin		(27.3)	(FRAM II,
Ballast			April, 1964)
Light Ship	2,134.6* (2,069.2)	(2,080)	2,345
Machy Liquid	70.6		
Complement	39.8		33.4
Ammo	217.9		110.9
Stores & PW	132.4		104.5
Lube Oil	5.7		11.6
Standard	2,535.6		
RFW	71.1		71.1
Fuel Oil	503.9		496.6
Diesel Oil	35.1		25.2†
Fog Oil			1.2‡
Displacement	3,145.4		3,210
Draft	13′10¾″		14′1¼″
GM	3.68		3.10
GZ	1.97 (37.1)		
Range	74.6		

Gearing Class

Name *Charles R. Ware* (DD 865)
Date July, 1945
LOA 391′0″
LWL 383′0″
Beam 40′10″
Depth 23′0″
CB 0.540
C⊗ 0.830
CW
SHP (trial) 65,464
Speed (trial) 33.82
At (tons) 3,195 (*Forrest Royal*, DD 872, 1946)
Endurance (war) 6,370/12, 5,690/15, 4,380/20 (3,300 tons)

Main Battery 6 5-in/38
GFCS Mk 37
Torpedo Tubes 5 21-in
TFCS Mk 27
Complement 11/325
Design Displacement 3,160
Design STD 2,450
Design Full Load
Boilers 4 B&W
Steam Conditions 565/800
SSTG 2 400AC/50DC
Diesel Generators 2 100
SHP (design) 60,000
Speed (design) 34.5

Fuel Capacity (design) 708
Endurance (design)
Tactical Diameter (yds/kts) 725/30
AA Battery 16 (2 × 2, 3 × 4) 40-mm, 20 (10 × 2) 20-mm
AA FCS Mk 51
Hedgehog None
D.C. Tracks 2 (26)
D.C. Projectors 6 (30)
Sonar QGA
Note: Light ship weights are a Gibbs & Cox estimate but appear to be based on returned weights of DD 865.

*Weights for DD 692.
†JP-5 for DASH.
‡DASH drone.

WEIGHTS

	Normal	Full Load	
Hull	871.3		
Fittings	175.4		
Eqpmt & Outfit	64.5		
Armament	239.7		*Keppler*
Machy (dry)	929.6		(DD 765)
Margin			(FRAM II,
Ballast			Sept., 1961)
Light Ship	2,280.6		2,342
	(2,203)		
Machy Liquid	77.2		
Complement	36.4		35.1
Ammo	183.1		70.9
Stores & PW	132.0		133.2
Lube Oil	5.7		11.8
Standard	2,637.4		
RFW	71.1		71.0
Fuel Oil	740.1		727.1
Diesel Oil	21.8		23.7*
Fog Oil	11.9		1.3†
Displacement	3,482		3,416
Draft	14'4¾"		14'2⅛"
GM	3.55		3.69
GZ	1.86 (36.6)		
Range	72.8		

Name *Cony* (DDE 508)
Date
LOA *Fletcher* Hull
LWL
Beam
Depth
CB
C⊗
CW
SHP (trial)
Speed (trial)
At (tons)
Endurance (trial)

Endurance (war)
Main Battery 2 5-in/38
GFCS Mk 37
Torpedo Tubes 4 Mk 23 (fixed)
TFCS UBFCS Mk 100
Complement
Design Displacement
Design STD
Design Full Load
Boilers
Steam Conditions
SSTG 2 350AC/40DC

Diesel Generators 1 100
SHP (design) 60,000
Speed (design)
Fuel Capacity (design)
Endurance (design)
Tactical Diameter (yds/kts) 630/30
AA Battery 4 (2 × 2) 3 in/50, 8 (4 × 2) 20-mm
AA FCS Mk 56
Hedgehog 1 Mk 15, 1 Mk 108
D.C. Tracks
D.C. Projectors None
Sonar QHB

WEIGHTS

	Normal	Full Load	
Hull			
Fittings			
Eqpmt & Outfit			
Armament			
Machy (dry)			
Margin			
Ballast			
Light Ship			
Machy Liquid			
Complement			
Ammo			
Stores & PW			
Lube Oil			

*JP-5.
†For DASH.

Standard
RFW
Fuel Oil
Diesel Oil
Fog Oil

Displacement
Draft
GM
GZ
Range

Name *Epperson* (DDE 719)
Date
LOA *Gearing* Hull
LWL
Beam
Depth
CB
C⊗
CW
SHP (trial)
Speed (trial)
At (tons)
Endurance (trial)

Endurance (war)
Main Battery 4 (2 × 2) 5-in/38
GFCS Mk 37
Torpedo Tubes 4 (Fixed) Mk 23
TFCS UBFCS Mk 100
Complement
Design Displacement
Design STD
Design Full Load
Boilers
Steam Conditions
SSTG

Diesel Generators
SHP (design)
Speed (design)
Fuel Capacity (design)
Endurance (design)
Tactical Diameter (yds/kts)
AA Battery 4 (2 × 2) 3-in/50, 14 (7 × 2) 20-mm
AA FCS Mk 56, Mk 63
Hedgehog 1 Weapon A, 2 Mk 15
D.C. Tracks 1
D.C. Projectors
Sonar QHB

WEIGHTS

	Normal	Full Load
Hull	891	
Fittings	185	
Eqpmt & Outfit	74	
Armament	216	
Machy (dry)	895	
Margin		
Ballast		
Light Ship	2,261	
Machy Liquid		
Complement		
Ammo		
Stores & PW		
Lube Oil		

Standard
RFW
Fuel Oil
Diesel Oil
Fog Oil

Displacement
Draft
GM
GZ
Range

Name *Carpenter* (DDE 825)
Date
LOA *Gearing* Hull
LWL
Beam
Depth
CB
C⊗
CW
SHP (trial)
Speed (trial)
At (tons)
Endurance (trial)

Endurance (war)
Main Battery 4 (2 × 2) 3-in/70
GFCS Mk 56
Torpedo Tubes 4 Mk 23
TFCS UBFCS Mk 100
Complement
Design Displacement
Design STD
Design Full Load
Boilers
Steam Conditions
SSTG

Diesel Generators
SHP (design)
Speed (design)
Fuel Capacity (design)
Endurance (design)
Tactical Diameter (yds/kts)
AA Battery 8 (4 × 2) 20-mm
AA FCS 1 Mk 63
Hedgehog 2 Weapon A (48)
D.C. Tracks 1
D.C. Projectors
Sonar QHB

WEIGHTS

	Normal	Full Load
Hull	915	
Fittings	188	
Eqpmt & Outfit	74	
Armament	109	
Machy (dry)	896	
Margin		
Ballast		
Light Ship	2,182	
Machy Liquid		
Complement		
Ammo		
Stores & PW		
Lube Oil		
Standard		
RFW		
Fuel Oil		
Diesel Oil		
Fog Oil		
Displacement		
Draft		
GM		
GZ		
Range		

Name *Norfolk* (DL 1)
Date August, 1959
LOA 540'0"
LWL 520'0"
Beam 53'6"
Depth 34'6"
CB 0.571
CO 0.805
CW 0.707
SHP (trial) 76,158/77,514
Speed (trial) 33.23/32.64
At (tons) 6,360/6,980
Endurance (trial)

Endurance (war)
Main Battery 8 (4 × 2) 3-in/70 (1,110)
GFCS Mk 56
Torpedo Tubes 8 ASW Mk 24 (30)
TFCS UBFCS Mk 102
Complement 42/504
Design Displacement 6,626
Design STD 5,518
Design Full Load
Boilers 4 B&W
Steam Conditions 1,200/950
SSTG 4 750AC
Diesel Generators 2 300

SHP (design) 80,000
Speed (design)
Fuel Capacity (design) 1,180
Endurance (design) 6,000/20
Tactical Diameter (yds/kts) 800/30
AA Battery 16 (8 × 2) 20-mm
AA FCS 2 Gunar
Hedgehog 4 Weapon A (88)
D.C. Tracks None
D.C. Projectors None
Sonar QHB/SQG-1
Note: Battery as designed; she had 3-in/50 as completed.

WEIGHTS

	Normal	Full Load
Hull	2,627.4	(2,403.7)
Fittings	519.8	(530.9)
Eqpmt & Outfit	180.5	(199.3)
Armament	222.2	(284.0)
Machy	1,448.1	(1,372.0)
Margin	200.0	(213.0)
Ballast		

Light Ship	5,003.0
	(4,955.7)
Complement	58.9
Ammo	205.7
Stores & PW	322.8
Lube Oil	12.4
Standard	5,555.5
RFW	128.3
Fuel Oil	1,229.9
Diesel Oil	91.7
Fog Oil	1.6*
Displacement	7,315
Draft	18'11⅞"
GM	4.97
GZ	
Range	

Name *Mitscher* (DL 2)
Date May, 1960
LOA 490'0"
LWL 476'0"
Beam 47'6"
Depth 28'0"
CB 0.497
C⊗ 0.800
CW 0.756
SHP (trial) 75,862
Speed (trial) 34.84
At (tons) 4,550
Endurance (trial)

Endurance (war)
Main Battery 2 5-in/54 (700)
GFCS Mk 67
Torpedo Tubes 4 Mk 24 (10)
TFCS UBFCS Mk 102
Complement 28/345
Design Displacement 4,472 (trial)
Design STD 3,670
Design Full Load 4,758
Boilers 4 FW
Steam Conditions 1,200/950
SSTG 4 500AC
Diesel Generators 2 300

SHP (design) 80,000
Speed (design) 36.5
Fuel Capacity (design) 720
Endurance (design) 4,500/20
Tactical Diameter (yds/kts) 540/20, 600/30
AA Battery 4 (2 × 2) 3-in/70 (1,000),
 8 (4 × 2) 20-mm
AA FCS Mk 56
Hedgehog 2 Weapon A (88)
D.C. Tracks 1 (12)
D.C. Projectors None
Sonar QHB/SQG-1
Note: Battery as designed; she had 3-in/50 as built.

WEIGHTS

	Normal	Full Load
Hull		(1,504)
Fittings		(301)
Eqpmt & Outfit		(112)
Armament		(291)
Machy (dry)		(1,076)
Margin		(100)
Ballast		
Light Ship	(3,330.8)	(3,384)
Complement	38.9	
Ammo	146.8	
Stores & PW	114.4	
Lube Oil	10.6	
Standard	3,641.5	
RFW	72.6	
Fuel Oil	740.3	
Diesel Oil	44.4	
Fog Oil		
Displacement	4,855	
Draft	14'7⅞"	
GM	5.76	
GZ		
Range		

*Gasoline.

Destroyer Escorts

Name *Brennan* (DE 13) (GMT)*
Date January, 1943
LOA 289'5"
LWL 283'6"
Beam 35'0"
Depth 18'9"
CB 0.518
C⊗ 0.81
CW 0.75
SHP (trial) 6,000
Speed (trial) 21.5

At (tons) 1,436 (*Andres*, DE 45)
Endurance (trial)
Endurance (war) 4,150/12
Main Battery 3 3-in/50
GFCS Mk 51
Torpedo Tubes None
TFCS None
Complement 15/183
Design Displacement 1,436
Design STD 1,140
Design Full Load 1,430

Boilers None
Steam Conditions
SSTG
Diesel Generators 2 200/40 (2 100 emergency)
SHP (design) 6,000
Speed (design) 19
Fuel Capacity (design) 198
Endurance (design) 6,000/12
Tactical Diameter (yds/kts) 280/16†
AA Battery 2 40-mm, 9 20-mm
AA FCS Mk 51
Hedgehog 1
D.C. Tracks 2
D.C. Projectors 8
Sonar QC series

WEIGHTS

	Normal	Full Load
Hull		(490)
Fittings		(108)
Eqpmt & Outfit		(57)
Armament		(31)
Machy (dry)		(353)
Margin		(30)
Ballast		
Light Ship	(1,023)	(1,069)
Machy Liquid	8	8
Complement	21	21
Ammo	88	88
Stores & PW	39	59
Lube Oil	13	20
Standard	1,192	
RFW		
Fuel Oil		
Diesel Oil	131	197
Fog Oil		
Displacement	1,323	1,416
Draft	9'7½"	10'0⅞"
GM	3.95	4.00
GZ	1.92 (37.7)	2.02 (37.9)
Range	74.3	76.7

Name *Bowers* (DE 637) (TE)‡
Date January, 1944
LOA 306'0"
LWL 300'0"
Beam 36'9"
Depth 20'0"
CB
C⊗
CW
SHP (trial) 12,200
Speed (trial) 23.7
At (tons) 1,673 (*Buckley*, DE 51)
Endurance (trial) 4,920/15

Endurance (war) 4,940/12, 4,490/15,
    3,360/20 (1,700 tons)
Main Battery 3 3-in/50
GFCS Mk 51
GFCS 3 21-in
TFCS None
Complement 15/198
Design Displacement 1,650
Design STD 1,400
Design Full Load 1,740
Boilers 2 "D" Express
Steam Conditions 435/750
SSTG 2 300/40

Diesel Generators None
SHP (design) 12,000
Speed (design) 24
Fuel Capacity (design) 350
Endurance (design) 6,000/12
Tactical Diameter (yds/kts) 350/18†
AA Battery 2 (1 × 2) 40-mm, 8 20-mm
AA FCS Mk 51
Hedgehog 1
D.C. Tracks 2
D.C. Projectors 8
Sonar QC series

WEIGHTS

	Normal	Full Load
Hull		(587)
Fittings		(125)
Eqpmt & Outfit		(62)
Armament		(38)
Machy (dry)		(441)
Margin		(30)
Ballast		

*DE 1–50, 256–280, 301–315, 516–530
†From model test.
‡DE 51–98, 153–161, 198–223, 563–578, 633–644, 665–673, 675–683, 693–705, 789–800

Light Ship	(1,147.7)	(1,283)
Machy Liquid	14.6	14.6
Complement	22.3	22.3
Ammo	130.0	130.0
Stores & PW	39.7	59.5
Lube Oil	3.0	4.5
Standard	1,357.3	
RFW	19.6	29.8
Fuel Oil	273.6	358.7
Diesel Oil	1.9	1.9
Fog Oil		
Displacement	1,147.7	1,652.4
Draft	8'3¼"	10'6½"
GM	3.87	3.96
GZ	1.56 (37–0)	2.03 (39–0)
Range	67–0	76–0

Name *Cannon* (DE 99) (DET)*
Date Estimates (March, 1943)
LOA 306'0"
LWL 300'0"
Beam 36'10"
Depth 20'0"
CB
C⊗
CW
SHP (trial) 5,150
Speed (trial) 20.2
At (tons) 1,525 (*Levy*, DE 162)
Endurance (trial)

Endurance (war) 10,800/12, 6,700/18
Main Battery 3 3-in/50
GFCS Mk 51
Torpedo Tubes 3 21-in
TFCS None
Complement 15/201
Design Displacement 1,525
Design STD 1,240
Design Full Load 1,620
Boilers Diesel
Steam Conditions
SSTG None

Diesel Generators 200/40, 2 (1 in some ships) 100 emergency
SHP (design) 6,000
Speed (design) 21
Fuel Capacity (design)
Endurance (design) 6,000/12
Tactical Diameter (yds/kts) 350/20†
AA Battery 2 (1 × 2) 40-mm, 8 20-mm
AA FCS Mk 51
Hedgehog 1
D.C. Tracks 2
D.C. Projectors 8
Sonar QCS-1

WEIGHTS

	Normal	Full Load
Hull	528	
Fittings	104	
Eqpmt & Outfit	62	
Armament	38	
Machy (dry)	356	
Margin	30	
Ballast		
Light Ship	1,120	
Machy Liquid	22	22
Complement	21	21
Ammo	74	74
Stores & PW	72	72
Lube Oil		
Standard	1,309	
RFW		
Fuel Oil		
Diesel Oil	211	316
Fog Oil		
Displacement	1,518	1,623
Draft	10'0¼"	10'5¾"
GM	4.51	4.69
GZ		
Range		

*DE 99–128, 162–197, 739–788
†From model test.

Name *Edsall* (DE 129) (FMR)*
Date
LOA 306'0"
LWL 300'0"
Beam 36'10"
Depth 20'6"
CB 0.480
C⊗ 0.800
CW 0.750
SHP (trial)
Speed (trial) 20.9
At (tons)
Endurance (trial) 10,800/12

Endurance (war) 9,100/12
Main Battery 3 3-in/50
GFCS Mk 51
Torpedo Tubes 3 21-in
TFCS None
Complement 8/201
Design Displacement 1,490
Design STD 1,200
Design Full Load 1,590
Boilers None
Steam Conditions
SSTG None

Diesel Generators 2 200/40, 2 100
SHP (design) 6,000
Speed (design) 21
Fuel Capacity (design) 312
Endurance (design) 6,000/12
Tactical Diameter (yds/kts) 300/20
AA Battery 2 (1 × 2) 40-mm, 8 20-mm
AA FCS Mk 51
Hedgehog 1
D.C. Tracks 2
D.C. Projectors 8
Sonar QC series

WEIGHTS

	Normal	Full Load
Hull		(526)
Fittings		(104)
Eqpmt & Outfit		(62)
Armament		(38)
Machy (dry)		(345)
Margin		(30)
Ballast		
Light Ship	(1,016.6)	(1,105)
Machy Liquid	36.5	
Complement	21.9	
Ammo	107.6	
Stores & PW	86.2	
Lube Oil	13.0	
Standard	1,281.8	
RFW		
Fuel Oil		
Diesel Oil	319.9	
Fog Oil		
Displacement	1,601.6	
Draft	10'4¾"	
GM	4.62	
GZ		
Range		

Name *Holt* (DE 706) (TEV)†
Date May, 1944
LOA 306'0"
LWL 300'0"
Beam 36'11½"
Depth 20'0"
CB
C⊗
CW
SHP (trial)
Speed (trial)
At (tons)
Endurance (trial)

Endurance (war) 5,050/12, 4,470/15,
3,330/20 (1,650 tons)
Main Battery 2 5-in/38
GFCS Mk 51
Torpedo Tubes 3 21-in
TFCS None
Complement 12/192
Design Displacement 1,650
Design STD 1,450
Design Full Load 1,810
Boilers 2 CE
Steam Conditions 435/750
SSTG 2 300AC/40DC

Diesel Generators None
SHP (design) 12,000
Speed (design) 24.0
Fuel Capacity (design) 354.5
Endurance (design) 6,000/12
Tactical Diameter (yds/kts)
AA Battery 4 (2 × 2) 40-mm, 10 20-mm
AA FCS Mk 51
Hedgehog 1 (230)
D.C. Tracks 2 12-charge (60)
D.C. Projectors 8 (40)
Sonar QBF

WEIGHTS

	Normal	Full Load
Hull		(587)
Fittings		(121)
Eqpmt & Outfit		(443)
Armament		(85)
Machy (dry)		(61)
Margin		(30)
Ballast		

*DE 129–152, 238–255, 316–338, 382–401
†DE 224–237, 281–300, 579–632, 645–664, 674, 684–692, 706–738, 905–1005

Light Ship	(1,223.8)	(1,327)
Machy Liquid	16.6	16.6
Complement	21.0	21.0
Ammo	113.9	113.9
Stores & PW	57.7	57.7
Lube Oil	2.2	2.2
Standard	1,435.2	
RFW	19.5	28.4
Fuel Oil	229.4	348.3
Diesel Oil	1.3	1.9
Fog Oil		
Displacement	1,685	1,814
Draft	10'8¼"	11'3"
GM	4.19	4.41
GZ	2.19 (40)	2.39 (40.5)
Range	79.3	84.2

Name *John C. Butler* (DE 339)(WGT)*
Date March, 1944
LOA 306'0"
LWL 300'0"
Beam 36'10"
Depth 20'6"
CB 0.505
C⊗ 0.800
CW 0.750
SHP (trial)
Speed (trial) 24.15
At (tons)
Endurance (trial)

Endurance (war) 4,650/12
Main Battery 2 5-in/38
GFCS Mk 51
Torpedo Tubes 3 21-in
TFCS
Complement 14/201
Design Displacement 1,600
Design STD 1,350
Design Full Load 1,745
Boilers 2 "D" Express
Steam Conditions 435/750
SSTG 2 200/40

Diesel Generators None
SHP (design) 12,000
Speed (design) 24
Fuel Capacity (design) 347
Endurance (design) 6,000/12
Tactical Diameter (yds/kts) 395/25
AA Battery 4 (2 × 2) 40-mm, 10 20-mm
AA FCS Mk 51
Hedgehog 1
D.C. Tracks 2
D.C. Projectors 8
Sonar QC series

WEIGHTS

	Normal	Full Load
Hull		(587)
Fittings		(121)
Eqpmt & Outfit		(61)
Armament		(85)
Machy (dry)		(475)
Margin		
Ballast		
Light Ship	(1,101.2)	(1,329)
Machy Liquid	26.0	
Complement	22.9	
Ammo	124.9	
Stores & PW	86.8	
Lube Oil	4.8	
Standard	1,366.6	
RFW	29.3	
Fuel Oil	347.5	
Diesel Oil	1.8	
Fog Oil		
Displacement	1,745.2	
Draft	11'0"	
GM	4.2	
GZ	2.26 (40)	
Range	80.3	

*DE 339–381, 402–515, 531–562, 801–904

Name *Fletcher*
(DD 445)
LOA 376'6"
LWL 369'0"
Beam 37'8"
Draft (full) 13'5⅜"
Depth 22'8"
Hull 735
Propulsion 690
Electrical 73
C³ 70
Auxiliaries 183
Outfit 139

Armament 140
Margin
Light Ship 2,035
Loads 871
Full Load 2,906
SHP (design) 60,000
Speed (design)
SHP (trial)
Speed (trial)
At (tons)
Endurance 6,500/12
SSTG
Emerg Gen

MFCS (UBFCS)
GFCS Mk 37, Mk 51
NTDS No
SAM
ASROC
Sonar QC
Mk 32
Long ASW TT 10 21-in
DASH
5-in/54 5 5-in/38
3-in/50 2 40-mm
Complement 9/264

Name *Forrest Sherman*
(DD 931)
LOA 418'6"
LWL 407'0"
Beam 44'11½"
Draft (full) 15'0⅜"
Depth 25'2"
Hull 952
Propulsion 720
Electrical 114
C³ 89
Auxiliaries 363
Outfit 220
Armament 276

Margin
Light Ship 2,734
Loads 2,182
Full Load 4,916
SHP (design) 70,000
Speed (design) 33
SHP (trial) 71,500/71,500
Speed (trial) 33.93/34.97
At (tons) 3,650/3,295
Endurance 4,500/20
SSTG
Emerg Gen 2 100 DG
MFCS (UBFCS) (Mk 105)

GFCS Mk 68, Mk 56
NTDS No
SAM
ASROC 2 Hedgehog
Sonar SQS-4
Mk 32
Long ASW TT 4
DASH
5-in/54 3
3-in/50 2 × 2
Complement
Trials Refer to *Decatur*
(DD 936)

Name *Charles F. Adams*
(DDG 2)
LOA 437
LWL 420
Beam 47
Draft (full) 15
Depth 25
Hull 1,217.9
Propulsion 831.4
Electrical 122.3
C³ 176.0
Auxiliaries 375.2
Outfit 271.4
Armament 258.2

Margin 25.0
Light Ship 3,277.4
Loads 1,248.1
Full Load 4,525.5
SHP (design) 70,000
Speed (design)
SHP (trial) 72,050/70,610
Speed (trial) 33.46/34.06
At (tons) 4,335/4,100
Endurance 4,500/20
SSTG 4 500
Emerg Gen 2 100 DG
MFCS (UBFCS)
    (ASROC FCG Mk 111) Mk 74

GFCS Mk 68
NTDS No
SAM Tartar (42)
ASROC 1 (8)
Sonar SQS-23
Mk 32 2 (6)
Long ASW TT
DASH
5-in/54 2
3-in/50
Complement 18/320
Trials Refer to *R.E. Byrd*
(DDG 23)

Name *Spruance*
(DD 963)
LOA 563.3
LWL 529
Beam 55
Draft (full) 20.5
Depth
Hull 3,079.6
Propulsion 761.0
Electrical 285.5
C³ 353.5
Auxiliaries 739.1
Outfit 453.5
Armament 153.8

Margin
Light Ship 5,825.9
Loads 1,974.1
Full Load 7,800.0
SHP (design) 80,000
Speed (design) 30
SHP (trial) 80,000
Speed (trial) 32.5
At (tons) 7,800
Endurance 6,000/20
SSTG 3 200
Emerg Gen
MFCS (UBFCS) (Mk 116)

GFCS Mk 86
NTDS Yes
SAM
ASROC 1 (24)
Sonar SQS-53
Mk 32 2 (14)
Long ASW TT
DASH LAMPS
5-in/54 2 LW
3-in/50
Complement 24/272

Name *Farragut*
(DLG 6)
LOA 512'6"
LWL 490'0"
Beam 52'4"
Draft (full) 17'9"
Depth
Hull 1,759
Propulsion 899
Electrical 169
C³ 209
Auxiliaries 497
Outfit 327

Armament 284
Margin
Light Ship 4,167
Loads 1,481
Full Load 5,648
SHP (design) 85,000
Speed (design) 32
SHP (trial) 85,350/84,870
Speed (trial) 33.09/33.72
At (tons) 5,450/5,010
Endurance 5,000/20
SSTG 4 750
Emerg Gen 2 300 DG

MFCS Mk 76
GFCS Mk 68
NTDS No
SAM Terrier (40)
ASROC 1 (8)
Sonar SQS-23
Mk 32 2 (12)
Long ASW TT
DASH
5-in/54 1 (560)
3-in/50 2 × 2 (636)
Complement 23/337
Trials Refer to *Farragut*

Name *Leahy*
(DLG 16)
LOA 533'0"
LWL 510'0"
Beam 53'4"
Draft (full) 19'0½"
Depth
Hull 2,308
Propulsion 943
Electrical 216
C³ 339
Auxiliaries 588
Outfit 356
Armament 372

Margin
Light Ship 5,146
Loads 2,444
Full load 7,590
SHP (design) 85,000
Speed (design) 32
SHP (trial) 82,780
Speed (trial) 32.08
At (tons) 7,170
Endurance 8,000/20
SSTG 4 1000
Emerg Gen 2 750 DG
MFCS Mk 76

GFCS Mk 63
NTDS No
SAM Terrier (2 × 40)
ASROC 1 (16)
Sonar SQS-23
Mk 32 2 (12)
Long ASW TT
DASH
5-in/54
3-in/50 2 × 2 (636)
Complement 25/352
Trials Refer to *Reeves*
(DLG 24)

Name *Belknap*
(DLG 26)
LOA 547'0"
LWL 524'0"
Beam 54'9"
Draft (full) 18'1⅝"
Depth 38'6"
Hull 2,462
Propulsion 944
Electrical 221
C³ 372
Auxiliaries 615
Outfit 425
Armament 320

Margin
Light Ship 5,409
Loads 2,481
Full Load 7,890
SHP (design) 85,000
Speed (design) 32
SHP (trial) 85,950/84,380
Speed (trial) 33.26/33.61
At (tons) 7,610/6,975
Endurance 7,100/20
SSTG 4 1500
Emerg Gen 1 500 DG,
1 500 GTG

MFCS Mk 76
GFCS Mk 68
NTDS No
SAM Terrier (60)
ASROC w/Terrier
Sonar SQS-26
Mk 32 2 (6)
Long ASW TT 2 (10)
DASH Yes
5-in/54 1 (600)
3-in/50 2 × 1 (600)
Complement 23/365
Trials Refer to *Belknap*

Name *Ticonderoga*
(CG 47)
LOA 563'0"
LWL 529'0"
Beam 55'0"
Draft (full) 31'0"
Depth
Hull 3,319
Propulsion 767
Electrical 311
C³ 467
Auxiliaries 797
Outfit 444

Armament 306
Margin 148
Light Ship 6,560
Loads 2,350
Full Load 8,910
SHP (design) 80,000
Speed (design) 30
SHP (trial)
Speed (trial)
At (tons)
Endurance 6,000/20
SSTG
Emerg Gen

MFCS Aegis Mk 7
GFCS Mk 86
NTDS Yes
SAM SM-2 (2 × 44)*
ASROC None
Sonar SQS-56
Mk 32 2 (24)
Long ASW TT
DASH LAMPS
5-in/54 2 LW (600)
3-in/50
Complement 31/312

---

*Plus Harpoon (8).

Name *Dealey*
(DE 1006)
LOA 315'0"
LWL 308'0"
Beam 36'8"
Draft (full) 11'10⅜"
Depth
Hull 595
Propulsion 244
Electrical 51
C³ 48
Auxiliaries 152
Outfit 160

Armament 64
Margin
Light Ship 1,314
Loads 563
Full Load 1,877
SHP (design) 20,000
Speed (design) 27
SHP (trial) 19,880/19,810
Speed (trial) 26.84/27.58
At (tons) 1,802/1,613
Endurance 6,000/12
SSTG 2 300
Emerg Gen 1 100 DG

UBFCS Mk 105
GFCS Mk 63
NTDS No
SAM No
ASROC 2 Squid†
Sonar SQS-4
Mk 32 No
Long ASW TT No
DASH No
5-in/54 No
3-in/50 2 × 2
Complement 12/161

Name *Claud Jones*
(DE 1033)
LOA 312'
LWL 301'
Beam 38'
Draft (full) 12'11"
Depth
Hull 595.1
Propulsion 244.1
Electrical 51.0
C³ 47.9
Auxiliaries 151.9
Outfit 159.6
Armament 64.4

Margin
Light Ship 1,314
(1,297)
Loads 602.5
Full Load 1,916.5
SHP (design) 8,700
Speed (design) 21.5
SHP (trial) 8,852/9,037
Speed (trial) 21.6/22.15
At (tons) 1,720/1,550
Endurance 7,000/12
SSTG 3 200 DG
Emerg Gen
UBFCS Mk 105

GFCS Mk 70
NTDS No
SAM No
ASROC 2 Hedgehog
Sonar SQS-4
Mk 32
Long ASW TT No
DASH No
5-in/54 No
3-in/50 2 × 1
Complement 12/159
Trials Refer to
John R. Perry
(DE 1034)

Name *Bronstein*
(DE 1037)
LOA 372'
LWL 350'
Beam 41'
Draft (full) 23'*
Depth
Hull 800.6
Propulsion 294.4
Electrical 81.4
C³ 115.5
Auxiliaries 249.4
Outfit 163.0
Armament 69.6

Margin
Light Ship 1,791.7
(1,882)
Loads 841
Full Load 2,723
SHP (design) 20,000
Speed (design) 26
SHP (trial)
Speed (trial)
At (tons)
Endurance 4,000/15
SSTG 2 500, 1 600
Emerg Gen 1 500 DG
UBFCS Mk 111

GFCS Mk 56
NTDS No
SAM No
ASROC 1 (8)
Sonar SQS-26
Mk 32 2 (18)
Long ASW TT 2 (8)
DASH No
5-in/54 No
3-in/50 1 × 2, 1 × 1 (300)
Complement 13/178

Name *Garcia*
(DE 1040)
LOA 414'
LWL 390'
Beam 44'
Draft (full) 24'*
Depth 30'
Hull 1,110.5
Propulsion 351.6
Electrical 105.0
C³ 148.7
Auxiliaries 312.9
Outfit 220.2
Armament 98.3

Margin 92.6
Light Ship 2,440.8
Loads 930.6
Full Load 3,371.4
SHP (design) 35,000
Speed (design) 27
SHP (trial) 34,260/34,460
Speed (trial) 29.0/29.60
At (tons) 3,320/2,990
Endurance 4,000/20
SSTG 2 500
Emerg Gen 2 500 DG
UBFCS Mk 114

GFCS Mk 56
NTDS No
SAM No
ASROC 1 (16)
Sonar SQS-26
Mk 32 2 (18)
Long ASW TT 2 (8)
DASH Yes
5-in/54 2 5 in/38 (350)
3-in/50 No
Complement 13/196
Trials Refer to *Brumby*
(DE 1044)

*Includes sonar dome.
† All others in class had Mk 108 (Alfa).

Name *Knox*
(DE 1052)
LOA 438'
LWL 415'
Beam 47'
Draft (full) 15'
Depth
Hull 1,424.3
Propulsion 437.8
Electrical 135.4
C³ 211.8
Auxiliaries 382.9
Outfit 279.7
Armament 148.6

Margin
Light Ship 3,020.4
Loads 1,045.5
Full Load 4,065.9
SHP (design) 35,000
Speed (design) 27
SHP (trial) 35,170/35,920
Speed (trial) 28.80/29.22
At (tons) 4,120/3,760
Endurance 4,500/20
SSTG 3 750
Emerg Gen 1 750 DG
UBFCS Mk 114

GFCS Mk 68
NTDS No
SAM BPDMS
ASROC 1 (16)
Sonar SQS-26
Mk 32 2 (6)
Long ASW TT 2 (8)
DASH Yes (12)
5-in/54 1 (600)
3-in/50
Complement 13/211
Trials Refer to *Meyerkord*
(DE 1058)

Name *Brooke*
(DEG 1)
LOA 414'
LWL 390'
Beam 44'
Draft (full) 24*
Depth 30'
Hull 1,232
Propulsion 348
Electrical 105
C³ 176
Auxiliaries 332
Outfit 288
Armament 111

Margin
Light Ship 2,710
Loads 716
Full Load 3,426
SHP (design) 35,000
Speed (design) 27
SHP (trial)
Speed (trial)
At (tons)
Endurance 4,000/20
SSTG 2 500
Emerg Gen 2 500 DG
(UBFCS) Mk 114

GFCS Mk 56†
NTDS No
SAM Tartar (16)
ASROC 1 (16)
Sonar SQS-26
Mk 32 2 (6)
Long ASW TT No
DASH Yes
5-in/54 1 5-in/38
3-in/50
Complement 14/214

Name *Oliver Hazard Perry*
(FFG 7)
LOA 445'
LWL 408'
Beam 47.4'
Draft (full) 14.4'
Depth
Hull 1,243.4
Propulsion 262.3
Electrical 188.7
C³ 98.7
Auxiliaries 450.4
Outfit 310.0
Armament 94.5

Margin
Light Ship 2,647.9
Loads 838.0
Full Load 3,485.9
SHP (design) 40,000
Speed (design) 28.5
SHP (trial) 41,360
Speed (trial) 30.6
At (tons) 3,320
Endurance "over 4,000/20"
SSTG 4 750 GTG
Emerg Gen
UBFCS Panel Mk 309

GFCS Mk 92
NTDS No
SAM SM-1 (40)
ASROC No
Sonar SQS-56
Mk 32 2 (24)
Long ASW TT No
DASH LAMPS
5-in/54
3-in/50 1 (OTO-M 3-in/62)
Complement 14/162

Name *Bainbridge*
Displacement
Light 7,250 (6,900)
Full 7,982 (7,600)
LOA 565
LWL 540 (530)

Beam 56 (56)
Draft 19'5" (18'5")
Terrier 2 (80)
Std (MR)
Harpoon
Tomahawk

5-in/55
5-in/54
3-in/50 2 twin
Mk 32 2 (6)
ASROC 1 (8)
Complement 459

Note: figures in parentheses refer to the preliminary estimate of 24 April 1957, and illustrate the extent of growth during detail design.

Name *Truxtun*
Displacement
Light 8,149
Full 8,927
LOA 564'
LWL 540'

Beam 57'10"
Draft 19.9'
Terrier 1 (60)
Std (MR)
Harpoon
Tomahawk

5-in/55
5-in/54 1 Mk 42 (600)
3-in/50 2 single
Mk 32 2 (6)
ASROC
Complement 490

Note: Drafts are all for full load condition, and do not include sonar domes; all of these ships were powered by pairs of D2G, and were capable of about 30 knots. Actual speeds and powers have not been released.

* Includes sonar dome.
† And MFCS Mk 74.

Name *Virginia*
Displacement
Light
Full 10,150
LOA 596'
LWL 570'

Beam 61'
Draft 20'6"
Terrier
Std (MR) 2 (80)
Harpoon
Tomahawk

5-in/55
5-in/54 2 Mk 45 (600)
3-in/50
Mk 32 2 (16)
ASROC 1 (24)
Complement 540

Note: Drafts are all for full load condition, and do not include sonar domes; all of these ships were powered by pairs of D2G, and were capable of about 30 knots. Actual speeds and powers have not been released.

Name *California*
Displacement
Light
Full 11,000
LOA 585'
LWL 560'

Beam 63'
Draft 21'
Terrier
Std (MR) 2 (88)
Harpoon
Tomahawk

5-in/55
5-in/54 2 Mk 45 (600)
3-in/50
Mk 32 2 (14)
ASROC
Complement 442

Note: Drafts are all for full load condition, and do not include sonar domes; all of these ships were powered by pairs of D2G, and were capable of about 30 knots. Actual speeds and powers have not been released.

Name DG (N)
Baseline
Displacement
Light 9,144
Full 9,695
LOA
LWL 530'

Beam 61.2'
Draft 20.1'
Terrier
Std (MR) 1 (64)
Harpoon
Tomahawk

5-in/55
5-in/54
3-in/50
Mk 32 2
ASROC
Complement

Note: Drafts are all for full load condition, and do not include sonar domes; all of these ships were powered by pairs of D2G, and were capable of about 30 knots. Actual speeds and powers have not been released.

Name DG(N)
As of 1/74
Displacement
Light 9,961
Full 10,708
LOA
LWL 550'

Beam 62.2'
Draft
Terrier
Std (MR) 2 (128)
Harpoon
Tomahawk

5-in/55
5-in/54
3-in/50
Mk 32 2
ASROC
Complement

Note: Drafts are all for full load condition, and do not include sonar domes; all of these ships were powered by pairs of D2G, and were capable of about 30 knots. Actual speeds and powers have not been released.

Name CSGN
of 3/75
Displacement
Light 11,800
Full 12,700
LOA
LWL 580

Beam 66
Draft 22
Terrier
Std (MR) 2 (128)
Harpoon (quads) 2
Tomahawk (quads) 2

8-in/55
5-in/54 2 Mk 45
3-in/50
Mk 32 2
Mk 24
Helo 2 LAMPS
VTOL

Name CSGN
of 12/75
Displacement
Light 15,902
Full 17,172
LOA 709'7"
LWL 666

Beam 76.6
Draft 22.3
Terrier
Std (MR) 2 (128)
Harpoon (quads) 2
Tomahawk (quads) 2

8-in/55 1
5-in/54 1 Mk 45
3-in/50
Mk 32 2
Mk 24
Helo 2 LAMPS/VSTOL
VTOL

Name CSGN Mk II	Draft 30′1″	5-in/54
Displacement	Terrier	3-in/50
Light 22,070	Std (MR) 2 (128)	Mk 32 2
Full 24,648	Harpoon (quads) 4	Mk 24
LOA 730	Tomahawk (quads) 2	Helo 2 LAMPS
LWL 666	8-in/55 2	VTOL 6
Beam 80′10″ (130 ext)		

Name CGN 42	Draft 18′0″	5-in/54 2 Mk 45
Displacement	Terrier	3-in/50
Light 11,144	Std (MR) 2 (88)	Mk 32 2
Full 12,118	Harpoon (quads) 4	Mk 24
LOA 588	Tomahawk (quads)	Helo 2 LAMPS
LWL 560	8-in/55	VTOL
Beam 62′6″		

The destroyer *Craven* is shown at Mare Island on 23 November 1943 after a wartime refit. She and her three sisters were unique among wartime destroyers in never being fitted with 40-mm., anti-aircraft guns. Prewar, they had differed from the very similar *Bagley* (DD 386) class in having less prominent deckhouses between their funnels and their after superstructures, carrying their large searchlights amidships rather than aft. Clearly visible here are the usual wartime fittings: depth charges aft and K-guns and roller racks abeam the after superstructure, floater nets on the after side of the 20-mm. gun tubs amidships. Note, too, the rather prominent venturis built into the sides of the bridge wings, to keep them clear of wind. The air-search radar is an SC-1.

Building Yards

Amer	American Shipbuilding, Lorain, Ohio
Avon	Avondale
Bath	Bath Iron Works
BethHi	Bethlehem Steel, Hingham
BethQ	Bethlehem Steel, Quincy (Fore River)
BethSF	Bethlehem Steel, San Francisco (Union Iron Works)
BethSI	Bethlehem Steel, Staten Island (United Shipyards)
BethSP	Bethlehem Steel, San Pedro
BethSQ	Bethlehem Steel, Squantum (Destroyer Plant)
BosNY	Boston Navy Yard
Brown	Brown Shipbuilding
CharNY	Charleston Navy Yard
Cramp	Cramp Shipyard
Defoe	Defoe
Dravo	Dravo, Wilmington
DravoP	Dravo, Pittsburgh
Fed	Federal, Kearny
FedN	Federal, Newark
Gas	Gas Engine Company
Gulf	Gulf Shipbuilding, Chickasaw
HH	Harlan and Hollingsworth
Ing	Ingalls, Pascagoula (now Litton)
Lock	Lockheed
MINY	Mare Island Navy Yard
MD	Maryland Steel Company, Sparrows Point
NL	Neafie & Levy
NN	Newport News
NorNY	Norfolk Navy Yard
NYNY	New York Navy Yard
NYSB	New York Shipbuilding Corp., Camden
Orange	Consolidated Shipbuilding, Orange, Texas
PHNY	Philadelphia Navy Yard
PS	Puget Sound Bridge & Dredge
PSNY	Puget Sound Navy Yard
SeaTac	Seattle-Tacoma (later Todd)
Tampa	Tampa
Todd	Todd Pacific
ToddSP	Todd San Pedro
Trigg	Trigg
WPS	Western Pipe and Steel

Fates

BU	Broken Up
CG	Coast Guard
Coll	Collision
Conv	Conversion
Exptl	Experimental
MDAP	Military Defense Assistance Program
NRF	Naval Reserve Force ship
Rcn	Recommissioned
Rem	Remainder
Res	Decommissioned (reserve)
ROK	Republic of Korea
RN	Royal (British) Navy
WD(K)	Irreparably damaged by Kamikaze
WGER	Federal Republic of Germany
WL(C)	War loss by collision
WL(E)	War loss by explosion
WL(G)	War loss by gunfire
WL(M)	War loss by mine
WL(T)	War loss by torpedo

		LD/Launch	Comm	Decomm	Fate
1	Bainbridge NL	15 Aug 99 27 Aug 01	24 Nov 02	3 Jul 19	Str 15 Sep 19
2	Barry NL	2 Sep 99 22 Mar 02	24 Nov 02	28 Jun 19	Str 15 Sep 19
3	Chauncey NL	2 Dec 99 26 Oct 01	20 Nov 02		WL(G) 19 Nov 17
4	Dale Trigg	12 Jul 99 24 Jul 00	20 Nov 02	9 Jul 19	Str 15 Sep 19
5	Decatur Trigg	26 Jul 99 26 Sep 00	19 May 02	20 Jun 19	Str 15 Sep 19
6	Hopkins HH	2 Feb 99 24 Feb 02	23 Sep 03	20 Jun 19	Str 2 Oct 19
7	Hull HH	22 Feb 99 21 Jun 02	20 May 03	7 Jul 19	Str 15 Sep 19
8	Lawrence BethQ	10 Apr 99 7 Nov 00	14 Apr 03	20 Jun 19	CTB–8; str 15 Sep 19
9	Macdonough BethQ	21 Apr 99 24 Dec 00	5 Sep 03	3 Sep 19	CTB–9; str 7 Nov 19
10	Paul Jones BethSF	20 Apr 99 14 Jun 02	14 Dec 03	29 Jul 19	Str 15 Sep 19
11	Perry BethSF	21 Apr 99	14 Dec 03	2 Jul 19	Str 15 Sep 19
12	Preble BethSF	21 Apr 99 2 Mar 01	14 Dec 03	11 Jul 19	Str 15 Sep 19
13	Stewart Gas	24 Jun 00 10 May 02	17 Dec 02		Str 15 Sep 19
14	Truxtun MD	13 Nov 99 15 Aug 01	11 Sep 02	7 Jul 19	Str 15 Sep 19; merchant service (banana carrier)
15	Whipple MD	13 Nov 99 15 Aug 01	21 Oct 02	28 May 19	Str 15 Sep 19; merchant service (banana carrier); BU 1956
16	Worden MD	13 Nov 99 15 Aug 02	31 Dec 02	13 Jul 19	Str 15 Sep 19; merchant service (banana carrier)
17	Smith Cramp	18 Mar 08 20 Apr 09	26 Nov 09	15 Mar 19	Str 19; sold 20 Dec 21; BU
18	Lamson Cramp	18 Mar 08 16 Jun 09	10 Feb 10	15 Jul 19	Str 15 Sep 19; sold 21 Nov 19; BU
19	Preston NYSB	28 Apr 08 14 Jul 09	24 Dec 09	17 Jul 19	Str 15 Sep 19; sold 21 Nov 19; BU
20	Flusser Bath	3 Aug 08 20 Jul 09	28 Oct 09	14 Jul 19	Str 15 Sep 19; sold 21 Nov 19; BU

		LD/Launch	Comm	Decomm	Fate
21	*Reid* Bath	3 Aug 08 17 Aug 09	3 Dec 09	Aug 19	Str 15 Sep 19; BU
22	*Paulding* Bath	24 Jul 09 12 Apr 10	29 Sep 10	Aug 19	CG Apr 24–Oct 30; str 28 Jun 34
23	*Drayton* Bath	19 Aug 08 22 Aug 10	29 Oct 10	17 Nov 19	Str 8 Mar 35
24	*Roe* NN	18 Jan 09 24 Jul 09	17 Sep 10	1 Dec 19	CG Jun 24–Oct 30; str 28 Jun 34
25	*Terry* NN	8 Feb 09 21 Aug 09	18 Oct 10		CG Jun 24–Oct 30; str 28 Jun 34
26	*Perkins* BethQ	22 Mar 09 9 Jul 10	18 Nov 10	5 Dec 19	Str 8 Mar 35
27	*Sterett* BethQ	22 Mar 09 12 May 10	15 Dec 10	9 Dec 19	Str 8 Mar 35
28	*McCall* NYSB	8 Jun 09 4 Jun 10	23 Jan 11	12 Dec 19	CG Jun 24–Oct 30; str 28 Jul 34
29	*Burrows* NYSB	19 Jun 09 23 Jun 10	21 Feb 11	12 Dec 19	CG Apr 24–May 31; str 5 Jul 34
30	*Warrington* Cramp	21 Jun 09 18 Jun 10	20 Mar 11	30 Jun 22	Str 8 Mar 35
31	*Mayrant* Cramp	22 Apr 09 23 Apr 10	12 Jul 11	12 Dec 19	Str 8 Mar 35
32	*Monaghan* NN	1 Jun 10 18 Feb 11	12 Jul 11	4 Nov 19	CG Jun 24–May 31; str 5 Jul 34
33	*Trippe* Bath	12 Apr 10 20 Dec 10	23 Mar 11		CG Jun 24–May 31; str 5 Jul 34
34	*Walke* BethQ	5 Mar 10 3 Nov 10	22 Jun 11	12 Dec 19	Str 8 Mar 35
35	*Ammen* NYSB	29 Mar 10 30 Sep 10	23 May 11	11 Dec 19	CG Apr 24–May 31; str 5 Jul 34
36	*Patterson* Cramp	27 Apr 10 29 Apr 11	11 Oct 11	1919	CG Apr 24–Oct 30; str 28 Jun 34
37	*Fanning* NN	29 Apr 11 11 Jan 12	21 Jun 12	24 Nov 19	CG Jun 24–Nov 30; str 28 Jun 34
38	*Jarvis* NYSB	1 Jul 11 4 Apr 12	22 Oct 12	26 Nov 19	Str 8 Mar 35
39	*Henley* BethQ	17 Jul 11 3 Apr 12	6 Dec 12	12 Dec 19	CG May 24–May 31; str 5 Jul 34
40	*Beale* Cramp	8 May 11 30 Aug 12	30 Aug 12	25 Oct 19	CG Apr 24–Oct 30; str 28 Jun 34
41	*Jouett* Bath	7 Mar 11 15 Apr 12	25 May 12	24 Nov 19	CG Apr 24–May 31; str 5 Jul 34
42	*Jenkins* Bath	24 Mar 11 29 Apr 12	15 Jun 12	31 Oct 19	Str 8 Mar 35

"Thousand Tonners"

		LD/Launch	Comm	Decomm	Fate
43	*Cassin* Bath	1 May 12 20 May 13	9 Aug 13	7 Jun 22	CG Jun 24–Jun 32; str 5 Jul 34
44	*Cummings* Bath	21 May 12 6 Aug 13	19 Sep 13	23 Jun 22	CG Jun 24–May 32; str 5 Jul 34
45	*Downes* NYSB	27 Jun 12 8 Nov 13	11 Feb 15	6 Jun 22	CG Apr 24–May 31; str 5 Jul 34
46	*Duncan* BethQ	17 Jun 12 5 Apr 13	30 Aug 13	9 Aug 21	Str 8 Mar 35
47	*Aylwin* Cramp	7 Mar 12 23 Nov 12	17 Jan 14	23 Feb 21	Str 8 Mar 35
48	*Parker* Cramp	11 Mar 12 8 Feb 13	30 Dec 13	6 Jun 22	Str 8 Mar 35
49	*Benham* Cramp	14 Mar 12 22 Mar 13	20 Jan 14	7 Jul 22	Str 8 Mar 35
50	*Balch* Cramp	7 May 12 21 Dec 12	26 Mar 14	20 Jun 22	Str 8 Mar 35
51	*O'Brien* Cramp	8 Sep 13 20 Jul 14	22 May 15	9 Jun 22	Str 8 Mar 35
52	*Nicholson* Cramp	8 Sep 13 19 Aug 14	30 Apr 15	26 May 22	Str 7 Jan 36
53	*Winslow* Cramp	1 Oct 13 11 Feb 15	7 Aug 15	5 Jun 22	Str 7 Jan 36
54	*McDougal* Bath	29 Jul 13 22 Apr 14	16 Jun 14	26 May 22	CG Jun 24–Jun 33; str 1934
55	*Cushing* BethQ	23 Sep 13 16 Jan 15	21 Aug 15	7 Aug 20	Str 7 Jan 36

No. Name / Builder				
56 *Ericsson* NYSB	10 Nov 13 22 Aug 14	14 Aug 15	16 Jun 22	CG Jun 24–May 32; str 5 Jul 34
57 *Tucker* BethQ	9 Nov 14 4 May 15	11 Apr 16		CG Mar 26–Jun 33; str 24 Oct 36
58 *Conyngham* Cramp	27 Jun 14 8 Jul 15	21 Jan 16	23 Jun 22	CG Jun 24–Jun 33; str 5 Jul 34
59 *Porter* Cramp	24 Feb 14 26 Jul 15	17 Apr 16	23 Jun 22	Str 7 Jan 36
60 *Wadsworth* Bath	23 Feb 14 29 Apr 15	23 Jul 15	3 Jun 22	Str 7 Jan 36
61 *Jacob Jones* NYSB	3 Aug 14 29 May 15	10 Feb 16		WL(T) 6 Dec 17
62 *Wainwright* NYSB	1 Sep 14 12 Jun 15	12 May 16		CG Apr 26–Apr 34; str 5 Jul 34
63 *Sampson* BethQ	21 Apr 15 4 Mar 16	27 Jun 16	25 Jun 21	Str 7 Jan 36
64 *Rowan* BethQ	10 May 15 23 Mar 16	19 Aug 16	19 Jun 22	Str 7 Jan 36
65 *Davis* Bath	7 May 15 15 Aug 16	5 Oct 16	20 Jun 22	CG Mar 26–Jun 33; str 5 Jul 34
66 *Allen* Bath	10 May 15 5 Dec 16	24 Jan 17 23 Jun 25 23 Aug 40	22 Jun 22 Mar 28 15 Oct 45	Str 45
67 *Wilkes* Cramp	11 Mar 15 18 May 16	10 Nov 16	26 Jun 22	CG Mar 26–Apr 34; str 5 Jul 34

"Flush Deckers"

No. Name / Builder				
68 *Shaw* MINY	7 Feb 16 9 Dec 16	9 Apr 17	21 Jun 22	CG Mar 26–Jun 33; str 5 Jul 34
69 *Caldwell* MINY	9 Dec 16 10 Jul 17	1 Dec 17	27 Jun 22	Str 7 Jan 36
70 *Craven* NorNY	20 Nov 17 29 Jun 18	19 Oct 18 9 Aug 40	15 Jun 22 23 Oct 40	*Conway* 12 Nov 39; HMS *Lewes*, scuttled May 46
71 *Gwin* SeaTac	21 Jun 17 22 Dec 17	18 Mar 20	28 Jun 22	Str 25 Jan 37
72 *Conner* Cramp	16 Oct 16 21 Aug 17	12 Jan 18 23 Aug 40	21 Jun 22 23 Oct 40	HMS *Leeds*; Res Apr 45; BU Mar 47
73 *Stockton* Cramp	16 Oct 16 17 Jul 17	26 Nov 17 16 Aug 40	26 Jun 22 23 Oct 40	HMS *Ludlow*; Res Jun 45; BU May 45
74 *Manley* Bath	22 Aug 16 23 Aug 17	15 Oct 17 1 May 30	14 Jun 22 19 Nov 45	AG–28 Nov 38; APD–1 Aug 40; DD–74 Jun 45; str 5 Dec 45
75 *Wickes* Bath	26 Jun 17 25 Jun 18	31 Jul 18	23 Oct 40	HMS *Montgomery*; Res Feb 44, BU Mar 45
76 *Philip* Bath	1 Sep 17 25 Jul 18	24 Aug 18 25 Feb 30 30 Sep 39	29 May 22 2 Apr 37 23 Oct 40	HMS *Lancaster*; Res Jul 45; BU Feb 47
77 *Woolsey* Bath	1 Nov 17 17 Sep 18	30 Sep 18		Coll 26 Feb 21
78 *Evans* Bath	28 Dec 17 30 Oct 18	11 Nov 18 1 Apr 30 30 Sep 39	29 May 22 31 Mar 37 23 Oct 40	HMS *Mansfield*, Royal Norwegian Navy (RNorN) Dec 40–Mar 42; Res Oct 43; sold Oct 44; BU
79 *Little* BethQ	18 Jun 17 11 Nov 17	6 Apr 18 4 Nov 40	5 Jul 22 —	APD–4 Aug 40; WL(G) 5 Sep 42
80 *Kimberly* BethQ	21 Jun 17 14 Dec 17	26 Apr 18	30 Jun 22	Str 25 Jan 37
81 *Sigourney* BethQ	25 Aug 17 16 Dec 17	15 May 18 23 Aug 40	26 Jun 22 26 Nov 40	HMS *Newport* RNorN Mar–Jun 42; Res Jul 45, BU 47
82 *Gregory* BethQ	25 Aug 17 27 Jan 18	1 Jun 18 4 Nov 40	7 Jul 22 —	APD–3 Aug 40; WL(G) 5 Sep 42
83 *Stringham* BethQ	19 Sep 17 30 Mar 18	2 Jul 18 11 Dec 40	2 Jun 22 10 Nov 45	APD–6 18 Aug 40; Str 5 Dec 45
84 *Dyer* BethQ	26 Sep 17 13 Apr 18	1 Jul 18 —	7 Jun 22 —	Str 7 Jan 36
85 *Colhoun* BethQ	19 Sep 17 21 Feb 18	13 Jun 18 11 Dec 40	28 Jun 22 —	APD–2 Aug 40; WL(B) 30 Aug 42
86 *Stevens* BethQ	20 Sep 17 13 Jan 18	24 May 18	16 Jun 22	Str 7 Jan 36
87 *McKee* BethSF	29 Oct 17 23 Mar 18	7 Sep 18	16 Jun 22	Str 7 Jan 36
88 *Robinson* BethSF	31 Oct 17 28 Mar 18	19 Oct 18 23 Aug 40	3 Aug 22 26 Nov 40	HMS *Newmarket*; Res Jul 45; BU 46
89 *Ringgold* BethSF	20 Oct 17 14 Apr 18	14 Nov 18 23 Aug 40	17 Jun 22 26 Nov 40	HMS *Newark*; BU 47

No.	Name	Builder				Disposition
90	*McKean*	BethSF	12 Feb 18 4 Jul 18	25 Feb 19 11 Dec 40	19 Jun 22	APD–5 Aug 40; WL(T) 17 Nov 43
91	*Harding*	BethSF	12 Feb 18 4 Jul 18	24 Jan 19	1 Jul 22	Str 7 Jan 36
92	*Gridley*	BethSF	1 Apr 18 4 Jul 18	8 Mar 19	22 Jun 22	Str 25 Jan 37
93	*Fairfax*	MINY	10 Jul 17 15 Dec 17	6 Apr 18	26 Nov 40	HMS *Richmond*; USSR *Zhivuchi* 16 Jul 44; ret Jun 49; BU 49
94	*Taylor*	MINY	15 Oct 17 14 Feb 18	1 Jun 18 1 May 30	21 Jun 22 23 Sep 38	Str 6 Dec 38
95	*Bell*	BethQ	16 Nov 17 14 Jan 19	31 Jul 18	21 Jun 22	Str 25 Jan 37
96	*Stribling*	BethQ	14 Dec 17 29 May 18	16 Aug 18	26 Jul 22	DM–1 17 Jul 20; str 1 Dec 36; tgt 28 Jul 37
97	*Murray*	BethQ	22 Dec 17 8 Jun 18	21 Aug 18	1 Jul 22	DM–2 17 Jul 20; str 7 Jan 36
98	*Israel*	BethQ	26 Jan 17 22 Jun 18	21 Aug 18	7 Jul 22	DM–3 17 Jul 20; str 25 Jan 37
99	*Luce*	BethQ	9 Feb 18 29 Jun 18	11 Sep 18	31 Jan 31	DM–4 17 Jul 20; str 7 Jan 36
100	*Maury*	BethQ	25 Feb 18 4 Jul 18	23 Sep 18	19 Mar 30	DM–5 17 Jul 20; str 22 Oct 30
101	*Lansdale*	BethQ	20 Apr 18 21 Jul 18	26 Oct 18 1 May 30	25 Jun 22 24 Mar 31	DM–6 17 Jul 20; str 25 Jan 37
102	*Mahan*	BethQ	4 May 18 4 Aug 18	24 Oct 18	1 May 30	DM–7 17 Jul 20; str 22 Oct 30
103	*Schley*	BethSF	29 Oct 17 28 Mar 18	20 Sep 18 3 Oct 40	1 Jun 22 10 Nov 45	APD–14 Jan 43; DD–103 Jul 45; str 5 Dec 45
104	*Champlin*	BethSF	29 Oct 17 7 Apr 18	11 Nov 18	7 Jun 22	Str 19 May 36; tgt 12 Aug 36
105	*Mugford*	BethSF	20 Dec 17 14 Apr 18	25 Nov 18	7 Jun 22	Str 19 May 36
106	*Chew*	BethSF	2 Jan 18 26 May 18	12 Dec 18 14 Oct 40	1 Jun 22 15 Oct 45	Str 1 Nov 45
107	*Hazelwood*	BethSF	24 Dec 17 22 Jun 18	20 Feb 19	15 Nov 30	Str 5 Jun 35
108	*Williams*	BethSF	25 Mar 18 4 Jul 18	18 Apr 19 6 Nov 39	7 Jun 22 24 Sep 40	HMS *St. Clair*; res Aug 44; hulk; str Oct 46
109	*Crane*	BethSF	7 Jan 18 4 Jul 18	18 Apr 19 18 Dec 39	7 Jun 22 14 Nov 45	Str 19 Dec 45
110	*Hart*	BethSF	8 Jan 18 4 Jul 18	26 May 19	1 Jun 31	DM–8 17 Jul 20; str 11 Nov 31
111	*Ingraham*	BethSF	12 Jan 18 4 Jul 18	15 May 19	29 Jun 22	DM–9 17 Jul 20; str 1 Dec 36; tgt 23 Jul 37
112	*Ludlow*	BethSF	7 Jan 18 9 Jun 18	23 Dec 18	24 May 30	DM–10 17 Jul 20; str 18 Nov 30
113	*Rathburne*	Cramp	12 Jul 17 27 Dec 17	24 Jun 18 —	2 Nov 45	APD–25 May 44; DD–113 Jun 45; str 24 Oct 45
114	*Talbot*	Cramp	12 Jul 17 20 Feb 18	20 Jul 18 31 May 30	31 Mar 23 9 Oct 45	APD–7 Oct 42; DD–114 Jul 45; str 24 Oct 45
115	*Waters*	Cramp	26 Jul 17 9 Mar 18	8 Aug 18 4 Jun 30	28 Dec 22 12 Oct 45	APD–8 Oct 42; DD–115 Aug 45; str 24 Oct 45
116	*Dent*	Cramp	30 Aug 17 23 Mar 18	9 Sep 18 15 May 30	7 Jun 22 4 Dec 45	APD–9 Mar 43; str 3 Jan 46
117	*Dorsey*	Cramp	18 Sep 17 9 Apr 18	16 Sep 18 1 Mar 30	9 Mar 23	DMS–1 Nov 40; grounded 9 Oct 45; str 3 Jan 46
118	*Lea*	Cramp	18 Sep 17 29 Apr 18	2 Oct 18 1 May 30 30 Sep 39	22 Jun 22 7 Apr 37 20 Jul 45	Str 13 Aug 45
119	*Lamberton*	NN	1 Oct 17 30 Mar 18	22 Aug 18 15 Nov 30	30 Jun 22 13 Dec 45	AG–21 Apr 32; DMS–2 Nov 40; AG–21 May 45; str 28 Jan 47
120	*Radford*	NN	2 Oct 17 5 Aug 18	30 Sep 18	9 Jun 22	Str 19 May 36; tgt 5 Aug 36
121	*Montgomery*	NN	2 Oct 17 23 Mar 18	26 Jul 18 30 Aug 31 25 Sep 39	6 Jun 22 7 Dec 37 23 Apr 45	DM–17 Jan 31; WD(M) 17 Oct 44; str 28 Apr 45
122	*Breese*	NN	10 Nov 17 11 May 18	23 Oct 18 1 Jun 31 25 Sep 39	17 Jun 22 12 Nov 37 15 Jan 36	DM–18 Jan 31; sold 16 May 46
123	*Gamble*	NN	12 Nov 17 11 May 18	28 Nov 18 24 May 30 25 Sep 39	17 Jun 22 22 Dec 37 1 Jun 45	DM–15 Jun 30; WD(K) 17 Feb 45; scuttled 16 Jul 45
124	*Ramsay*	NN	21 Dec 17 8 Jun 18	14 Feb 19 2 Jun 30 25 Sep 39	30 Jun 22 14 Dec 37 19 Oct 45	DM–16 Jun 30; AG–98 Jun 45; str 13 Nov 45

No. Name / Builder				Notes
125 *Tattnall* / NYSB	1 Dec 17 5 Sep 18	26 Jun 19 1 May 30	15 Jun 22 17 Dec 45	APD–19 Jul 43; str 8 Jan 46
126 *Badger* / NYSB	9 Jan 18 24 Aug 18	29 May 19 Jan 30	May 22 20 Jul 45	Str 30 Aug 45
127 *Twiggs* / NYSB	23 Jan 18 28 Sep 18	28 Jul 19 20 Feb 30	24 Jun 22 23 Oct 40	HMS *Leamington*; USSR *Zhiguchi* 16 Jul 44; ret Jan 50; BU 52
128 *Babbitt* / NYSB	19 Feb 18 30 Sep 18	24 Oct 19 4 Apr 30	15 Jun 22 25 Jan 46	AG–102 Jun 45; str 25 Feb 46
129 *De Long* / NYSB	21 Feb 18 29 Oct 18	20 Sep 19	—	Grounded 1 Dec 21; str 25 Sep 22
130 *Jacob Jones* / NYSB	21 Feb 18 20 Nov 18	20 Oct 19 1 May 30	24 Jun 22	WL(T) 28 Feb 42
131 *Buchanan* / Bath	29 Jun 18 2 Jan 19	20 Jan 19 10 Apr 30 30 Sep 39	7 Jun 22 9 Apr 37 9 Sep 40	HMS *Campbeltown*; Polish Navy 41; WL 28 Mar 42 St. Nazaire (destroyed drydock lock)
132 *Aaron Ward* / Bath	1 Aug 18 10 Apr 19 —	21 Apr 19 May 30 30 Sep 39	Jun 22 Apr 37 9 Sep 40	HMS *Castleton*; Res Mar 45; BU 48
133 *Hale* / Bath	7 Oct 18 29 May 19	12 Jun 19 1 May 30 30 Sep 39	22 Jun 22 9 Apr 37 9 Sep 40	HMS *Caldwell*; Res Feb 44; BU 45
134 *Crowninshield* / Bath	5 Nov 18 24 Jul 19	6 Aug 19 12 May 30 30 Sep 39	7 Jul 22 8 Apr 37 9 Sep 40	HMS *Chelsea*; USSR *Dyerzki*, 16 Jul 44; ret Jun 49; BU 49
135 *Tillman* / CharNY	29 Jul 18 7 Jul 19	30 Apr 21 1 May 30 30 Aug 40	3 Jul 22 15 Jun 39 26 Nov 40	HMS *Wells*; Res Feb 44; BU 45
136 *Boggs* / MINY	15 Nov 17 25 Apr 18	23 Sep 18 19 Dec 31	29 Jun 22 30 Mar 46	IX–36 Aug 31; AG–19 Sep 31; DMS–3 Nov 40; sold 27 Nov 46
137 *Kilty* / MINY	15 Dec 17 25 Apr 18	2 Apr 18 18 Dec 39	5 Jun 22 2 Nov 45	IX–37 Aug 31; APD–15 Jan 43; str 16 Nov 45
138 *Kennison* / MINY	14 Feb 18 8 Jun 18	17 Dec 18 18 Dec 39	22 Jun 22 23 Nov 45	AG–83 Oct 44; str 5 Dec 45
139 *Ward* / MINY	15 May 18 1 Jun 18	24 Jul 18 13 Feb 41	21 Jun 21 —	APD–16 Jan 43; WL(K) 7 Dec 44
140 *Claxton* / MINY	25 Apr 18 14 Jan 19	13 Sep 19 22 Jan 30	18 Jun 22 5 Dec 40	HMS *Salisbury*; Res Dec 43; sold Oct 44
141 *Hamilton* / MINY	8 Jun 18 15 Jan 19	7 Nov 19 20 Jan 30	20 Jul 22 16 Oct 45	DMS–18 Oct 41; AG–111 Jun 44; str 1 Nov 45
142 *Tarbell* / Cramp	31 Dec 17 28 May 18	27 Nov 18 29 May 30	8 Jun 22 20 Jul 45	Str 13 Aug 45
143 *Yarnall* / Cramp	2 Feb 17 19 Jan 18	29 Nov 18 19 Apr 30 4 Oct 39	22 May 22 30 Dec 36 23 Oct 40	HMS *Lincoln*; RNorN Feb 42; USSR *Druzhny* (spares) Aug 44; ret Aug 52; BU 52
144 *Upshur* / Cramp	19 Feb 18 4 Jul 18	23 Dec 18 2 Jun 30 4 Oct 39	15 May 22 22 Dec 36 2 Nov 45	AG–103 Jun 45; str 16 Nov 45
145 *Greer* / Cramp	24 Feb 18 1 Aug 18	31 Dec 18 31 Mar 30 4 Oct 39	22 Jun 22 13 Jan 37 19 Jul 45	Str 13 Aug 45
146 *Elliot* / Cramp	23 Feb 18 4 Jul 18	25 Jan 19 8 Feb 30	22 May 22 12 Oct 45	DMS–4 Nov 40; AG–104 Jun 45; str 24 Oct 45
147 *Roper* / Cramp	19 Mar 18 17 Aug 18	15 Feb 19 18 Mar 30	14 Dec 22 15 Sep 45	APD–20 Oct 43; str 11 Oct 45
148 *Breckinridge* / Cramp	11 Mar 18 17 Aug 18	27 Feb 19 May 30 Sep 39	30 Jun 22 Sep 36 30 Nov 45	AG–112 Jun 45; str 19 Dec 45
149 *Barney* / Cramp	26 Mar 18 5 Sep 18	14 Mar 19 1 May 30 4 Oct 39	30 June 22 Nov 36 30 Nov 45	AG–113 Jun 45; str 19 Dec 45
150 *Blakeley* / Cramp	26 Mar 18 19 Sep 18	8 May 19 16 Oct 39	29 Jun 22 21 Jul 45	Str 13 Aug 45
151 *Biddle* / Cramp	22 Apr 18 3 Oct 18	22 Apr 19 16 Oct 39	20 Jun 22 5 Oct 45	AG–114 Jun 45; str 24 Oct 45
152 *Du Pont* / Cramp	2 May 18 22 Oct 18	30 Apr 19 1 May 30 16 Oct 39	19 Apr 22 14 Jan 37 2 May 46	AG–80 Sep 44; str 5 Jun 46
153 *Bernadou* / Cramp	4 Jun 18 7 Nov 18	19 May 19 1 May 30 Oct 39	1 Jul 22 Sep 36 17 Jul 45	Str 13 Aug 45
154 *Ellis* / Cramp	8 Jul 18 30 Nov 18	7 Jun 19 1 May 30 16 Oct 39	17 Jun 22 16 Dec 36 31 Oct 45	AG–115 Jun 45; str 16 Nov 45

155 *Cole* Cramp	25 Jun 18 11 Jan 19	19 Jun 19 1 May 30 16 Oct 39	10 Jul 22 7 Jan 27 1 Nov 45	AG–116 Jun 45; str 16 Nov 45
156 *J. Fred Talbott* Cramp	8 Jul 18 14 Dec 18	30 Jun 19 1 May 30	18 Jan 23 21 May 46	AG–81 Sep 44; str 19 Jun 46
157 *Dickerson* NYSB	25 May 18 12 Mar 19	3 Sep 19 1 May 30	25 Jun 22 4 Aug 45	APD–21 Aug 43; WD(K) 2 Apr 45; scuttled 4 Apr 45
158 *Leary* NYSB	6 Mar 18 18 Dec 18	5 Dec 19 1 May 30	29 Jun 22 —	WL(T) 24 Dec 43
159 *Schenck* NYSB	26 Mar 18 23 Apr 19	30 Oct 19 1 May 30	9 Jun 22 17 May 46	AG–8 2 Sep 44; str 5 Jun 46
160 *Herbert* NYSB	4 Apr 18 8 May 19	21 Nov 19 1 May 30	27 Jun 22 25 Sep 45	APD–22 Dec 43; str 24 Oct 45
161 *Palmer* BethQ	29 May 18 18 Aug 18	22 Nov 18 7 Aug 40	31 May 22 7 Jan 45	DMS–5 Nov 40; WL(T) 7 Jan 45
162 *Thatcher* BethQ	8 Jun 18 31 Aug 18	14 Jan 19	24 Sep 40	HMCS *Niagara*, Res Sep 45; sold May 46
163 *Walker* BethQ	18 Jun 18 14 Sep 18	31 Jan 19	7 Jun 22	str 28 Mar 38
164 *Crosby* BethQ	23 June 18 28 Sep 18	24 Jan 19 18 Dec 39	7 Jun 22 28 Sep 45	APD–17 Jan 43; str 24 Oct 45
165 *Meredith* BethQ	26 Jun 18 22 Sep 18	29 Jan 19 —	28 Jun 22 —	Str 7 Jan 36
166 *Bush* BethQ	4 Jul 18 27 Oct 18	19 Feb 19 —	21 Jun 22 —	Str 7 Jan 36
167 *Cowell* BethQ	15 Jul 18 23 Nov 18	17 Mar 19 17 Jun 40	27 Jun 22 23 Sep 40	HMS *Brighton;* USSR *Zharki* Jul 44; ret Mar 49; BU 49
168 *Maddox* BethQ	20 Jul 18 27 Oct 18	10 Mar 19 17 Jun 40	14 Jun 22 23 Sep 40	HMS *Georgetown;* USSR *Zhostki* Aug 44; ret Sep 52; BU 52; last serving flush decker
169 *Foote* BethQ	7 Aug 18 14 Dec 18	21 Mar 19 2 Jul 40	6 Jul 22 23 Sep 40	HMS *Roxborough;* USSR *Dob-lestny* Aug 44; ret Feb 49; BU 49
170 *Kalk* BethQ	17 Aug 18 21 Dec 18	29 Mar 19 17 Jun 40	10 Jul 22 23 Sep 40	HMS *Hamilton,* Rcn Oct 40; ret Jun 45; sold Jul 45
171 *Burns* BethSF	15 Apr 18 4 Jul 18	7 Aug 19	2 Jun 30	DM–11 Mar 21; sold 22 Apr 32
172 *Anthony* BethSF	18 Apr 18 10 Aug 18	19 Jun 19	30 Jun 22	DM–12 Jul 20; str 1 Dec 36; tgt 22 Jul 37
173 *Sproston* BethSF	20 Apr 18 10 Aug 18	11 Jul 19	15 Aug 22	DM–13 Jul 20; str 1 Dec 36; tgt 20 Jul 37
174 *Rizal* BethSF	26 Jun 18 21 Sep 18	28 May 19	20 Aug 31	DM–14 Jul 20; str 11 Nov 31
175 *Mackenzie* BethSF	4 Jul 18 29 Sep 18	25 Jul 19 6 Nov 39	27 May 22 24 Sep 40	HMCS *Annapolis;* Res 45; sold 21 Jun 45
176 *Renshaw* BethSF	8 May 18 21 Sep 18	31 Jul 19	27 May 22	Str 19 May 36
177 *O'Bannon* BethSF	12 Nov 18 28 Feb 19	27 Aug 19	27 May 22	Str 19 May 36
178 *Hogan* BethSF	25 Nov 18 12 Apr 19	28 Jan 20 7 Aug 40	27 May 22 11 Oct 45	DMS–6 Nov 40; AG–105 Jun 45; str 1 Nov 45; tgt 8 Nov 45
179 *Howard* BethSF	9 Dec 18 26 Apr 19	28 Jan 20 29 Aug 40	27 May 22 30 Nov 45	DMS–7 Nov 40; AG–106 Jun 45; str 19 Dec 45
180 *Stansbury* BethSF	9 Dec 18 16 May 19	8 Jan 20 29 Aug 40	27 May 22 11 Dec 45	DMS–8 Nov 40; AG–107 Jun 45; str 3 Jan 46
181 *Hopewell* NN	19 Jan 18 8 Jun 18	21 Mar 19 17 Jun 40	17 Jul 22 23 Sep 40	HMS *Bath;* RNorR, Jan 41; WL(T) 19 Aug 41
182 *Thomas* NN	23 Mar 18 4 Jul 18	25 Apr 19 17 Jun 40	30 Jun 22 23 Sep 40	HMS *St. Albans;* RNorN Apr 41; USSR *Dostoiny,* Jul 44; ret Mar 49; BU 49
183 *Haraden* NN	30 Mar 18 4 Jul 18	7 Jun 19 4 Dec 39	17 Jul 22 24 Sep 40	HMCS *Columbia;* grounded, 25 Feb 44; hulk; Res Jun 45; sold Aug 45
184 *Abbot* NN	5 Apr 18 4 Jul 18	19 Jul 19 17 Jun 40	5 Jul 22 23 Sep 40	HMS *Charlestown* WD(C) Dec 44; Res Jan 45; BU 48
185 *Bagley* NN	11 May 18 19 Oct 18	27 Aug 19 17 Jun 40	12 Jul 22 23 Sep 40	*Doran* 22 Dec 39; HMS *St. Marys;* Res Sep 44; BU 45
186 *Clemson* NN	11 May 18 5 Sep 18	29 Dec 19 12 Jul 40	30 Jun 22 12 Oct 45	AVP–17 Nov 39; AVD–4 Aug 40; DD–186 Dec 43; APD–31 Mar 44; DD–186 Jul 45; str 24 Oct 45
187 *Dahlgren* NN	8 Jun 18 20 Nov 18	6 Jan 20 25 Oct 32	30 Jun 22 14 Dec 45	AG–91 Mar 45; str 8 Jan 46
188 *Goldsborough* NN	8 Jun 18 20 Nov 18	26 Jan 20 1 Jul 40	14 Jul 22 11 Oct 45	AVP–18 Nov 39; AVD–5 Aug 40; DD–188 Dec 43; APD–32 Mar 44; DD–188 Jul 45; str 24 Oct 45

189 *Semmes*	10 Jul 18	21 Feb 20	17 Jul 22	CG Apr 32–Apr 34; AG–24 Jul
NN	21 Dec 18	20 Apr 34	21 Jun 46	35; str 3 Jul 46
190 *Satterlee*	10 Jul 18	23 Dec 19	11 Jul 22	HMS *Belmont*, WL(T)31 Jan 42
NN	21 Dec 18	18 Dec 39	8 Oct 40	
191 *Mason*	10 Jul 18	28 Feb 20	3 Jul 22	HMS *Broadwater*, WL(T) 18 Oct
NN	8 Mar 19	4 Dec 39	8 Oct 40	41
192 *Graham*	7 Sep 18	13 Mar 20	31 Mar 22	Coll 16 Dec 21
NN	22 Mar 19			
193 *Abel P. Upshur*	20 Aug 18	23 Nov 20	7 Aug 22	NRF Mar 28–Oct 30; CG Nov 30–
NN	14 Feb 20	4 Dec 39	9 Sep 40	May 34; HMS *Clare*; Res Aug 45; BU 46
194 *Hunt*	20 Aug 18	30 Sep 20	11 Aug 22	HMS *Broadway*; Res Aug 45; BU
NN	14 Feb 20	Dec 39	8 Oct 40	47
195 *Welborn C. Wood*	24 Sep 18	14 Jan 21	8 Aug 22	CG Oct 30–May 34; HMS *Chesterfield*; Res Jan 45; BU 47
NN	6 Mar 20	4 Sep 39		
196 *George E. Badger*	24 Sep 18	28 Jul 20	11 Aug 22	CG Oct 30–May 34; AVP–16 Oct
NN	6 Mar 20	8 Jan 40	3 Oct 45	39; AVD–3 Aug 40; DD–196 Nov 43; APD–33 Apr 44; DD 196 Jul 45; str 24 Oct 45
197 *Branch*	25 Oct 18	26 Jul 20	11 Aug 22	HMS *Beverly*; WL(T) 11 Apr 43
NN	19 Apr 19	4 Dec 39	8 Oct 40	
198 *Herndon*	25 Nov 18	14 Sep 20	6 Jun 22	CG Sep 30–May 34; HMS
NN	31 May 19	4 Dec 39	9 Sep 40	*Churchill*; USSR *Dyeyatelni* Jul 44; WL(T) 16 Jan 45
199 *Dallas*	25 Nov 18	29 Oct 20	26 Jun 22	*Alexander Dallas* Mar 45; str 13
NN	31 May 19	14 Apr 25	25 Mar 39	Aug 45
		25 Sep 39	28 Jul 45	
206 *Chandler*	19 Aug 18	5 Sep 19	20 Oct 22	DMS–9 Nov 45; AG–108 Jun 45;
Cramp	19 Mar 19	31 Mar 30	21 Dec 45	str 5 Dec 45
207 *Southard*	18 Aug 18	24 Sep 19	7 Feb 22	DMS–10 Nov 40; grounded 9 Oct
Cramp	31 Mar 19	6 Jan 30	15 Dec 45	45; str 8 Jan 46
208 *Hovey*	7 Sep 18	2 Oct 19	1 Feb 23	DMS–11 Nov 40; WL(K) 6 Jan
Cramp	26 Apr 19	20 Feb 30		45
209 *Long*	23 Sep 18	20 Oct 19	30 Dec 22	DMS–12 Nov 40; WL(K) 6 Jan
Cramp	26 Apr 19	29 Mar 30	—	45
210 *Broome*	8 Oct 18	31 Oct 19	30 Dec 22	AG–96 May 45; sold 20 Nov 46
Cramp	14 May 19	5 Feb 30	20 May 46	
211 *Alden*	24 Oct 18	24 Nov 19	24 Jan 23	sold 30 Nov 45
Cramp	7 Jun 19	8 May 30	20 Jul 45	
212 *Smith Thompson*	24 Mar 19	10 Dec 19	15 May 36	Coll 14 Apr 36; str 19 Mar 36;
Cramp	14 Jul 19	—	—	scuttled 25 Jul 36
213 *Barker*	30 Apr 19	27 Dec 19	18 Jul 45	Sold 30 Nov 45
Cramp	11 Sep 19	—	—	
214 *Tracy*	30 Apr 19	9 Mar 20	16 Jan 46	DM–19 Jan 37; str 7 Feb 46
Cramp	12 Aug 19			
215 *Borie*	30 Apr 19	24 Mar 20	—	WL(C) 2 Nov 43
Cramp	4 Oct 19	—	—	
216 *John D. Edwards*	21 May 19	6 Apr 20	28 Jul 45	Str 13 Aug 45
Cramp	18 Oct 19			
217 *Whipple*	12 Jun 19	23 Apr 20	9 Nov 45	AG–117 Jun 45; str 5 Dec 45
Cramp	6 Nov 19			
218 *Parrott*	23 Jul 19	11 May 20	16 Jun 44	Coll 2 May 44; sold 5 Apr 47
Cramp		—		
219 *Edsall*	15 Sep 19	26 Nov 20	—	WL(G) 1 Mar 42
Cramp	29 Jul 20			
220 *MacLeish*	19 Aug 19	2 Aug 20	11 Mar 38,	AG–87 Jan 45; str 13 Nov 46
Cramp	18 Dec 19	25 Sep 39	8 Mar 46	
221 *Simpson*	9 Oct 19	3 Nov 20	29 Mar 46	AG–97 May 46; str 19 Jun 46
Cramp	28 Apr 20	—		
222 *Bulmer*	11 Aug 19	16 Aug 20	16 Aug 46	Sold 19 Feb 47
Cramp	22 Jan 20	—	—	
223 *McCormick*	11 Aug 19	30 Aug 20	14 Oct 38	AG–118 Jun 45; str 24 Oct 45
Cramp	14 Feb 20	26 Sep 39	4 Oct 45	
224 *Stewart*	9 Sep 19	15 Sep 20	—	Scuttled 2 Mar 42; Japanese P–
Cramp	4 Mar 20	—	—	102; Ret Oct 45; str 23 May 46; tgt 24 May 46
225 *Pope*	9 Sep 19	27 Oct 20	—	WL(G, B) 1 Mar 42
Cramp	23 Mar 20	—	—	
226 *Peary*	9 Sep 19	22 Oct 20	—	WL(B) 19 Feb 42
Cramp	6 Apr 20	—	—	
227 *Pillsbury*	23 Oct 19	15 Dec 20	—	WL(G) 1 Mar 42
Cramp	3 Aug 20	—	—	
228 *Ford*	11 Nov 19	30 Dec 20		*John D. Ford* 17 Nov 21; AG–119
Cramp	2 Sep 20			Jun 45; str 16 Nov 45

229	*Truxtun*	3 Dec 19	16 Feb 21		Grounded 18 Feb 42
	Cramp	28 Sep 20	—		
230	*Paul Jones*	23 Dec 19	19 Apr 21	5 Nov 45	AG–120 Jun 45; str 28 Nov 45
	Cramp	30 Sep 20	—		
231	*Hatfield*	10 Jun 18	16 Apr 20	13 Jan 31	WD(K) 6 Jan 45; sold 30 Jan
	NYSB	17 Mar 19	1 Apr 32	28 Apr 38	46
			25 Sep 39	13 Dec 46	
232	*Brooks*	11 Jun 18	18 Jun 20	20 Jan 31	WD(K) 6 Jan 45; sold 30 Jan
	NYSB	24 Apr 19	18 Jun 32	2 Sep 38	46
			25 Sep 39	2 Aug 45	
233	*Gilmer*	25 Jun 18	30 Apr 20	31 Aug 38	APD–11 Oct 42; str 25 Feb 46
	NYSB	24 May 19	25 Sep 39	5 Feb 46	
234	*Fox*	25 Jun 18	17 May 20	2 Feb 31	AG–85 Oct 44; str 19 Dec 45
	NYSB	12 Jun 19	1 Apr 32	16 Sep 38	
			25 Sep 39	29 Mar 45	
235	*Kane*	3 Jul 18	11 Jun 20	31 Dec 30	APD–18 Jan 43; str 25 Feb 46
	NYSB	12 Aug 19	1 Apr 32	28 Apr 38	
			23 Sep 39	24 Jan 46	
236	*Humphreys*	31 Jul 18	21 Jul 20	10 Jan 30	APD–12 Oct 42; DD–236 Jul 45;
	NYSB	28 Jul 19	13 Jun 32	14 Sep 39	str 13 Nov 46
			26 Sep 39	26 Oct 45	
237	*McFarland*	31 Jul 18	30 Sep 20	8 Nov 45	AVD–14 Aug 40; DD–237 Dec 43;
	NYSB	30 Mar 20	—		str 19 Dec 45
238	*James K. Paulding*	31 Jul 18	30 Sep 20	10 Feb 31	Str 25 Jan 37
	NYSB	20 Apr 20			
239	*Overton*	30 Oct 18	30 Jun 32	3 Feb 31	APD–23 Aug 43; str 13 Aug 45
	NYSB	10 Jul 19	1932	20 Nov 37	
			26 Sep 39	28 Jul 45	
240	*Sturtevant*	23 Nov 18	21 Sep 20	30 Jan 31	WL(M) 26 Apr 42
	NYSB	29 Jul 20	9 Mar 32	20 Nov 35	
			26 Sep 39	—	
241	*Childs*	19 Mar 19	22 Oct 20	10 Dec 45	AVP–14 Jul 38; AVD–1 Aug 40;
	NYSB	15 Sep 20	—		str 3 Jan 46
242	*King*	28 Apr 19	16 Dec 20	10 Mar 31	str 16 Nov 45
	NYSB	14 Oct 20	13 Jun 32	21 Sep 38	
			26 Sep 39	23 Oct 45	
243	*Sands*	22 Mar 19	10 Nov 20	13 Feb 31	ADP–13 Oct 42; str 1 Nov 45
	NYSB	28 Oct 19	21 Jul 32	15 Sep 38	
			26 Sep 39	19 Oct 45	
244	*Williamson*	27 Mar 19	29 Oct 20	8 Nov 45	AVP–15 Jul 38; AVD–2 Aug 40;
	NYSB	16 Oct 19	—	—	DD–244 Dec 43; str 19 Dec 45
245	*Reuben James*	2 Apr 19	24 Sep 20	20 Jan 31	AVP–16 Aug 39; canc Oct 39;
	NYSB	4 Oct 19	9 Mar 32	—	WL(T) 31 Oct 41
246	*Bainbridge*	27 May 19	9 Feb 21	23 Dec 30	Str 13 Aug 45; sold 30 Nov 45
	NYSB	12 Jun 20	5 Sep 33	20 Nov 37	
			26 Sep 39	21 Jul 45	
247	*Goff*	16 Jun 19	19 Jan 21	13 Jan 31	Str 13 Aug 45
	NYSB	2 Jun 20	2 Mar 32	21 Jul 45	
248	*Barry*	26 Jul 19	28 Dec 20	20 Dec 32	APD–29 Jan 44; WD(K) 24 May
	NYSB	28 Oct 20	20 Jun 33	—	45; WL(K) 21 Jun 45
249	*Hopkins*	30 Jul 19	21 Mar 21	21 Dec 45	DMS–13 Nov 40; str 8 Jan 46
	NYSB	26 Jun 20			
250	*Lawrence*	14 Aug 19	18 Apr 21	6 Jan 31	Str 13 Nov 45
	NYSB	10 Jul 20	13 Jun 32	13 Sep 38	
			26 Sep 39	24 Oct 45	
251	*Belknap*	3 Sep 18	28 Apr 19	28 Jun 22	AVD–8 Aug 40; WD(K) 11 Jan
	BethQ	14 Jan 19	22 Nov 40	4 Aug 45	45; Str 13 Aug 45
252	*McCook*	11 Sep 18	30 Apr 19	30 Jun 22	HMCS *St. Croix*; WL(T) 30 Sep
	BethQ	31 Jan 19	18 Dec 39	24 Sep 40	43
253	*McCalla*	25 Sep 18	19 May 19	30 Jun 22	HMS *Stanley*; WL(T) 19 Dec 41
	BethQ	28 Mar 19	18 Dec 39	23 Oct 40	
254	*Rodgers*	25 Feb 18	22 Jul 19	20 Jul 22	HMS *Sherwood*; Res May 43;
	BethQ	26 Apr 19	18 Dec 39	23 Oct 40	beached as tgt 30 Nov 43; BU
					45
255	*Ingram*	15 Oct 18	28 Jun 19	24 Jun 22	*Osmond Ingram* 11 Nov 19; AVD–
	BethQ	28 Feb 19	22 Nov 40	8 Jan 46	9 Aug 40; DD–255 Nov 43; APD–
					35 Jun 44; str 21 Jan 46
256	*Bancroft*	4 Nov 18	30 Jun 19	11 Jul 22	HMCS *St. Francis*; coll 14 Jul 45,
	BethQ	21 Mar 19	18 Dec 39	24 Sep 40	under tow for scrap
257	*Welles*	13 Nov 18	2 Sep 19	15 Jun 22	HMS *Cameron*, WD(B) 5 Dec 40;
	BethSQ	8 May 19	6 Nov 39	9 Sep 40	hulk for shock trials Jul 42—Aug
					43; BU Nov 44

258	*Aulick*	3 Dec 18	26 Jul 19	27 May 22	HMS *Burnham*, Res Dec 44; BU 48
	BethQ	11 Apr 19	18 Jun 39	8 Oct 40	
259	*Turner*	21 Dec 18	24 Sep 19	7 Jun 22	Str 5 Aug 36; water barge. CIC training ship *Moosehead* (IX–98) Feb 43–Mar 46; str 17 Apr 46
	BethQ	17 May 19			
260	*Gillis*	27 Dec 18	3 Sep 19	26 May 22	AVD–12 Aug 40; str 1 Nov 45
	BethQ	29 May 19	28 Jun 40	15 Oct 45	
261	*Delphy*	20 Apr 18	30 Nov 18	—	Grounded 8 Sep 23
	BethSQ	18 Jul 18			
262	*McDermut*	20 Apr 18	27 Mar 19	22 May 29	Str 11 Nov 31
	BethSQ	6 Jul 18			
263	*Laub*	20 Apr 18	17 Mar 19	15 Jun 22	HMS *Burwell*, Res Jan 45; BU 47
	BethSQ	25 Aug 18	18 Dec 39	8 Oct 40	
264	*McLanahan*	20 Apr 18	5 Apr 19	Jun 22	HMS *Bradford*, accom ship Jun 43; sold 46
	BethSQ	22 Sep 18	18 Dec 39	8 Oct 40	
265	*Edwards*	20 Apr 18	24 Apr 19	8 Jun 22	HMS *Buxton*, Rcn for training Nov 43; Res Jun 45; sold Jun 45
	BethSQ	10 Oct 18	18 Dec 39	8 Oct 40	
266	*Greene*	3 Jun 18	9 May 19	17 Jun 22	AVD–13 Aug 40; DD–266 Nov 43; APD–36 Feb 44; grounded 9 Oct 45; str 5 Dec 45
	BethSQ	2 Nov 18	28 Jun 40	24 Nov 45	
267	*Ballard*	3 Jun 18	5 Jun 19	17 Jul 22	AVD–10 Aug 40; sold 23 May 46
	BethSQ	7 Dec 18	25 Jun 40	5 Dec 45	
268	*Shubrick*	3 Jun 18	7 Jul 19	8 Jun 22	HMS *Ripley*, Res Feb 44; BU 45
	BethSQ	31 Dec 18	18 Dec 39	26 Nov 40	
269	*Bailey*	3 Jun 18	27 Jun 19	15 Jun 22	HMS *Reading*, Res Jul 45; BU 45
	BethSQ	5 Feb 19	30 Sep 39	26 Nov 40	
270	*Thornton*	3 Jun 18	15 Jul 19	24 May 22	AVD–11 Aug 40; WD(C) 5 Apr 45; str 13 Aug 45
	BethSQ	22 Mar 19	5 Mar 41	2 May 45	
271	*Morris*	20 Jul 18	21 Jul 19	15 Jun 22	Str 19 May 36
	BethSQ	12 Apr 19			
272	*Tingey*	8 Aug 18	25 Jul 19	24 May 22	Str 19 May 36
	BethSQ	24 Apr 19			
273	*Swasey*	27 Aug 18	8 Aug 19	10 Jun 22	HMS *Rockingham*, WL(M) 27 Sep 44
	BethSQ	7 May 19	18 Dec 39	26 Nov 10	
274	*Meade*	24 Sep 18	8 Sep 19	25 May 22	HMS *Ramsey*, Res Jun 45; BU 47
	BethSQ	24 May 19	18 Dec 39	26 Nov 40	
275	*Sinclair*	11 Oct 18	8 Oct 19	25 May 21	Light tgt No. 3 (IX–37) Nov 30; str 5 Jun 35
	BethSQ	2 Jun 19	27 Sep 23	1 Jun 30	
276	*McCawley*	2 Nov 18	22 Sep 19	7 Jun 22	Str 13 Aug 30
	BethSQ	14 Jun 19	27 Sep 23	1 Apr 30	
277	*Moody*	9 Dec 18	10 Dec 19	2 Jun 30	Str 3 Nov 30
	BethSQ	28 Jun 19			
278	*Henshaw*	3 Jan 19	10 Dec 19	11 Mar 30	Str 22 Jul 30
	BethSQ	28 Jun 19			
279	*Meyer*	6 Feb 19	17 Dec 19	15 May 29	Str 25 Nov 30
	BethSQ	18 Jul 19			
280	*Doyen*	24 Mar 19	17 Dec 19	25 Feb 30	Str 12 Jul 30
	BethSQ	26 Jul 19			
281	*Sharkey*	14 Apr 19	28 Nov 19	1 May 30	Str 22 Oct 30
	BethSQ	12 Aug 19			
282	*Toucey*	26 Apr 19	9 Dec 19	1 May 30	Str 22 Oct 30
	BethSQ	5 Sep 19			
283	*Breck*	8 May 19	1 Dec 19	1 May 30	Str 22 Oct 30
	BethSQ	5 Sep 19			
284	*Isherwood*	24 May 19	4 Dec 19	1 May 30	Str 22 Oct 30
	BethSQ	10 Sep 19			
285	*Case*	3 Jun 19	8 Dec 19	1 May 30	Str 22 Oct 30
	BethSQ	21 Sep 19			
286	*Lardner*	16 Jun 19	10 Dec 19	1 May 30	Str 22 Oct 30
	BethSQ	29 Sep 19			
287	*Putnam*	30 Jun 19	18 Dec 19	1 May 30	Str 22 Oct 30; MV *Teapa* (banana carrier) 31–32; Army freighter 42–45; banana carrier 47–51; sold May 55
	BethSQ	30 Sep 19			
288	*Worden*	30 Jun 19	24 Feb 20	1 May 30	Str 22 Oct 30; MV *Tabasco* 31; grounded 33
	BethSQ	24 Oct 19			
289	*Flusser*	21 Jul 19	25 Feb 20	1 May 30	Str 22 Oct 30
	BethSQ	7 Nov 19			
290	*Dale*	28 Jul 19	16 Feb 20	1 May 30	Str 22 Oct 30; MV *Masaya* (banana carrier) 31–42; Army freighter 42–43; WL(B) 28 Mar 43
	BethSQ	19 Nov 19			
291	*Converse*	13 Aug 19	28 Apr 20	1 May 30	Str 22 Oct 30
	BethSQ	28 Nov 19			

292	*Reid*	9 Sep 19	3 Dec 19	1 May 30	Str 22 Oct 30
	BethSQ	15 Oct 19			
293	*Billingsley*	8 Sep 19	1 Mar 20	1 May 30	Str 22 Oct 30
	BethSQ	10 Dec 19			
294	*Charles Ausburn*	11 Sep 19	23 Mar 20	1 May 30	Str 22 Oct 30
	BethSQ	18 Dec 19			
295	*Osborne*	23 Sep 19	17 May 20	1 May 30	Str 22 Oct 30; MV *Matagalpa* 31–42 (banana carrier); Army freighter 42; burned 27 Jun 42
	BethSQ	29 Dec 19			
296	*Chauncey*	17 Jun 18	25 Jun 19	—	Grounded 8 Sep 23
	BethSF	29 Sep 19			
297	*Fuller*	4 Jul 18	28 Feb 20	—	Grounded 8 Sep 23
	BethSF	5 Dec 18			
298	*Percival*	4 Jul 18	31 Mar 20	6 Apr 30	Str 18 Nov 30
	BethSF	5 Dec 18			
299	*John Francis Burnes*	4 Jul 18	1 May 20	25 Feb 30	Str 22 Jul 30
	BethSF				
300	*Farragut*	4 Jul 18	4 Jun 20	1 Apr 30	Str 22 Jul 30
	BethSF	10 Nov 18			
301	*Somers*	4 Jul 18	23 Jun 20	10 Apr 30	Str 18 Nov 30
	BethSF	21 Nov 18			
302	*Stoddert*	4 Jul 18	30 Jun 20	10 Jan 33	Light tgt No. 1 (IX–35) 5 Nov 30; AG–18 Jun 31; DD–302 Apr 32; str 5 Jun 35
	BethSF	8 Jan 19			
303	*Reno*	4 Jul 18	23 Jul 20	18 Jan 30	Str 8 Jul 30
	BethSF	22 Jan 19			
304	*Farquhar*	13 Aug 18	5 Aug 20	20 Feb 30	Str 18 Nov 30; barracks ship New London 1930–31
	BethSF	18 Jan 19			
305	*Thompson*	14 Aug 18	16 Aug 20	4 Apr 30	Str 22 Jul 30; bar and restaurant 1931–44; bombing tgt 44
	BethSF	19 Jan 19			
306	*Kennedy*	25 Sep 18	28 Aug 20	1 May 30	Str 18 Nov 30
	BethSF	15 Feb 19			
307	*Paul Hamilton*	25 Sep 18	24 Sep 20	20 Jan 30	Str 8 Jul 30
	BethSF	21 Feb 19			
308	*William Jones*	2 Oct 18	30 Sep 29	24 May 30	Str 13 Aug 30
	BethSF	9 Apr 19			
309	*Woodbury*	3 Oct 18	30 Oct 20	—	Grounded 8 Sep 23
	BethSF	6 Feb 19			
310	*S.P. Lee*	31 Dec 18	30 Oct 20	—	Grounded 8 Sep 23
	BethSF	22 Apr 19			
311	*Nicholas*	11 Jan 19	23 Nov 20	—	Grounded 8 Sep 23
	BethSF	1 May 19			
312	*Young*	28 Jan 19	29 Nov 20	—	Grounded 8 Sep 23
	BethSF	8 May 19			
313	*Zeilin*	20 Feb 19	10 Dec 20	22 Jan 30	Str 8 Jul 30
	BethSF	28 May 19			
314	*Yarborough*	27 Feb 19	31 Dec 20	29 May 30	Str 3 Nov 30
	BethSF	20 Jun 19			
315	*La Vallette*	14 Apr 19	24 Dec 20	19 Apr 30	Str 22 Jul 30
	BethSF	15 Jul 19			
316	*Sloat*	18 Jan 19	30 Dec 20	2 Jun 30	Str 28 Jan 35, tgt 26 Jun 35
	BethSF	14 May 19			
317	*Wood*	23 Jan 19	28 Jan 21	31 Mar 30	Str 22 Jul 30
	BethSF	28 May 19			
318	*Shirk*	13 Feb 19	5 Feb 21	8 Feb 30	Str 22 Jul 30; damage control training hulk 30–31; BU 31
	BethSF	20 Jun 19			
319	*Kidder*	5 Mar 19	7 Feb 21	18 Mar 30	Str 22 Jul 30
	BethSF	10 Jul 19			
320	*Selfridge*	28 Apr 19	17 Feb 21	8 Feb 30	Str 3 Nov 30
	BethSF	25 Jul 19			
321	*Marcus*	20 May 19	23 Feb 21	31 May 30	Str 28 Jan 35; tgt 25 Jun 35
	BethSF	22 Aug 19			
322	*Mervine*	28 Apr 19	1 Mar 21	4 Jun 30	Str 3 Nov 30
	BethSF	11 Aug 19			
323	*Chase*	5 May 19	10 Mar 21	15 May 30	Str 13 Aug 30
	BethSF	2 Sep 19			
324	*Robert Smith*	13 May 19	17 Mar 21	1 Mar 30	Str 12 Jul 30
	BethSF	19 Sep 19			
325	*Mullany*	3 Jun 19	29 Mar 21	1 May 30	Str 18 Nov 30
	BethSF	9 Jul 20			
326	*Coghlan*	25 Jun 19	31 Mar 21	1 May 30	Str 22 Oct 30
	BethSF	16 Jun 20			
327	*Preston*	19 Jul 19	13 Apr 21	1 May 30	Str 6 Nov 31; strength tests; sold 23 Aug 32
	BethSF	7 Aug 20			
328	*Lamson*	13 Aug 19	19 Apr 21	1 May 30	Str 22 Oct 30
	BethSF	1 Sep 20			

329 *Bruce* BethSF	30 Jul 19 20 May 20	29 Sep 20	1 May 30	Str 6 Nov 31; strength tests; sold Aug 32
330 *Hull* BethSF	13 Sep 20 18 Feb 21	26 Apr 21	31 Mar 30	Str 22 Jul 30
331 *Macdonough* BethSF	24 May 20 15 Dec 20	30 Apr 21	8 Jan 30	Str 8 Jul 30
332 *Farenholt* BethSF	13 Sep 20 9 Mar 21	10 May 21	20 Feb 30	Str 12 Jul 30
333 *Sumner* BethSF	27 Aug 19 24 Nov 20	27 May 21	5 Feb 30	Str 18 Nov 30; barracks New London; sold 34
334 *Corry* BethSF	15 Sep 20 28 Mar 21	25 May 21	5 Feb 30	Str 22 Oct 30
335 *Melvin* BethSF	15 Sep 20 11 Apr 21	31 May 21	8 May 30	Str 3 Nov 30
336 *Litchfield* MINY	15 Jan 19 12 Aug 19	12 May 20	5 Nov 45	AG–95 Mar 45; str 28 Nov 45
337 *Zane* MINY	15 Jan 19 12 Aug 19	15 Feb 21 25 Feb 30	1 Feb 23 15 Dec 45	DMS–14 Nov 40; AG–109 Jun 45; str 8 Jan 46
338 *Wasmuth* MINY	12 Aug 19 15 Sep 20	16 Dec 21 11 Mar 30	26 Jul 22 —	DMS–15 Nov 40; foundered 29 Dec 42
339 *Trever* MINY	12 Aug 19 15 Sep 20	3 Aug 22 2 Jun 30	17 Jan 23 23 Nov 45	DMS–16 Nov 40; AG–110 Jun 45; str 5 Dec 45
340 *Perry* MINY	15 Sep 20 29 Oct 21	7 Aug 22 1 Apr 30	17 Jan 23 —	DMS–17 Nov 40; WL(M) 13 Sep 44
341 *Decatur* MINY	15 Sep 20 29 Oct 21	9 Aug 22 —	28 Jul 45	Str 13 Aug 45
342 *Hulbert* NorNY	18 Nov 18 28 Jun 19	27 Oct 20 2 Aug 40	17 Oct 34 2 Nov 45	AVP–19 Nov 39; AVD–6 Aug 40; DD–342 Dec 43; str 28 Nov 45
343 *Noa* NorNY	18 Nov 18 28 Jun 19	15 Feb 21 1 Apr 40	11 Nov 34 —	APD–24 Aug 43; WL(C) 12 Sep 44
344 *William B. Preston* NorNY	18 Nov 18 9 Aug 19	23 Aug 20 14 Jun 40	15 Oct 34 6 Dec 45	AVP–20 Nov 39; AVD–7 Aug 40; str 3 Jan 46
345 *Preble* Bath	12 Apr 19 8 Mar 20	19 Mar 20 —	7 Dec 45	DM–20 Jun 37; AG–99 Jun 45; str 3 Jan 46
346 *Sicard* Bath	18 Jun 19 20 Apr 20	9 Jun 20 —	21 Nov 45	DM–21 Jun 37; AG–100 Jun 45; str 19 Dec 45
347 *Pruitt* Bath	25 Jun 19 2 Aug 20	2 Sep 20 —	16 Nov 45	DM–22 Jun 37; AG–101 Jun 45; str 5 Dec 45

"1500 Ton" Destroyers

348 *Farragut* BethQ	20 Sep 32 15 Mar 34	18 Jun 34	23 Oct 45	Sold 14 Aug 47
349 *Dewey* Bath	16 Dec 32 28 Jul 34	4 Oct 34	19 Oct 45	Sold 20 Dec 46
350 *Hull* NYNY	7 Mar 33 31 Jan 34	11 Jan 35		Typhoon 18 Dec 44
351 *Macdonough* BosNY	15 May 33 22 Aug 34	15 Mar 35	22 Oct 45	Sold 20 Dec 46
352 *Worden* PSNY	29 Dec 32 27 Oct 34	15 Jan 35		WL (grounded) 12 Jan 43
353 *Dale* NYNY	10 Feb 34	17 Jun 35	16 Oct 45	Sold 20 Dec 46
354 *Monaghan* BosNY	21 Nov 33 9 Jan 35	19 Apr 35		Typhoon 18 Dec 44
355 *Aylwin* PHNY	23 Sep 33 10 Jul 34	1 Mar 35	6 Oct 45·	Sold 20 Dec 46
364 *Mahan* BethSI	12 Jun 34 15 Oct 35	18 Sep 36		WD(K) 7 Dec 44; scuttled by gunfire, torpedoes (DD–723)
365 *Cummings* BethSI	26 Jun 34 11 Dec 35	25 Nov 36	14 Dec 45	Sold 17 Jul 47
366 *Drayton* Bath	20 Mar 34 26 Mar 36	1 Sep 36	9 Oct 45	Sold 20 Dec 46
367 *Lamson* Bath	20 Mar 34 17 Jun 36	21 Oct 36		Bikini: sunk 2 Jul 46
368 *Flusser* Fed	4 Jun 34 28 Sep 35	1 Oct 36	16 Dec 46	Sold 6 Jan 48
369 *Reid* Fed	25 Jun 34 11 Jan 36	2 Nov 36		WL(K) 11 Dec 44
370 *Case* BosNY	19 Sep 34	15 Sep 36	13 Dec 45	Sold 31 Dec 47
371 *Conyngham* BosNY	19 Sep 34 14 Sep 35	4 Nov 36	20 Dec 46	Tgt 2 Jul 48
372 *Cassin* PHNY	1 Oct 34 28 Oct 35	21 Aug 36	17 Dec 45	Sold 25 Nov 47; had been destroyed at Pearl Harbor and new hull built

No. Name / Yard				
373 *Shaw* / PHNY	1 Oct 34 / 28 Oct 35	18 Sep 36	2 Oct 45	WD (grounded) 2 Apr 45; sold 1946
374 *Tucker* / NorNY	15 Aug 34 / 26 Feb 36	23 Jul 36		WL(M) 4 Aug 42 (U.S. minefield)
375 *Downes* / NorNY	15 Aug 34 / 22 Apr 36	15 Jan 37	17 Dec 45	Sold 18 Nov 47; had been destroyed at Pearl Harbor and new hull built
376 *Cushing* / PSNY	15 Aug 34 / 31 Dec 35	28 Aug 36		WL(G,T) 13 Nov 42
377 *Perkins* / PSNY	15 Nov 34 / 31 Dec 35	18 Sep 36		WL(C) 29 Nov 43 (Australian troop ship)
378 *Smith* / MINY	27 Oct 34 / 20 Feb 36	19 Sep 36	28 Jun 46	Str 25 Feb 47
379 *Preston* / MINY	27 Oct 34 / 22 Apr 36	27 Oct 36		WL(G,T) 15 Nov 42
380 *Gridley* / BethQ	3 Jun 35 / 1 Dec 36	24 Jun 37	18 Apr 46	Str 25 Feb 47; sold 20 Aug 47
382 *Craven* / BethQ	3 Jun 35 / 25 Feb 37	2 Sep 37	19 Apr 46	Str 25 Feb 47; sold 2 Oct 47
384 *Dunlap* / BethSI	10 Apr 35 / 18 Apr 36	12 Jun 37	14 Dec 45	Sold 31 Dec 47
385 *Fanning* / BethSI	10 Apr 35 / 18 Sep 36	8 Oct 37	14 Dec 45	Sold 6 Jan 48
386 *Bagley* / NorNY	31 Jul 35 / 3 Sep 36	12 Jun 37	14 Jun 46	Sold 3 Oct 47
387 *Blue* / NorNY	25 Sep 36 / 27 May 37	14 Aug 37		WD(T) 22 Aug 42; scuttled 23 Aug 42
388 *Helm* / NorNY	25 Sep 35 / 27 May 37	16 Oct 37	26 Jun 46	Str 25 Feb 47; sold 2 Oct 47
389 *Mugford* / BosNY	28 Oct 35 / 21 Oct 36	16 Aug 37	29 Aug 46	Bikini; sunk 22 Mar 48
390 *Ralph Talbot* / BosNY	28 Oct 35 / 31 Oct 36	14 Oct 37	28 Aug 46	Bikini; sunk 8 Mar 48
391 *Henley* / MINY	28 Oct 35 / 12 Jan 37	14 Aug 37		WL(T) 3 Oct 43
392 *Patterson* / PSNY	23 Jul 35 / 6 May 37	22 Sep 37	8 Nov 45	Str 25 Feb 47
393 *Jarvis* / PSNY	21 Aug 35 / 6 May 37	27 Oct 37		WL(T) Aug 42
397 *Benham* / Fed	1 Sep 36 / 16 Apr 38	2 Feb 39		WD(T) 15 Nov 42; scuttled (gunfire, DD–433)
398 *Ellet* / Fed	3 Dec 36 / 11 Jun 38	17 Feb 39	29 Oct 45	Str 13 Nov 45; sold 1 Aug 47
399 *Lang* / Fed	5 Apr 37 / 27 Aug 38	30 Mar 39	16 Oct 45	Sold 20 Dec 45
400 *McCall* / BethSF	17 Mar 36 / 20 Nov 37	22 Jun 38	30 Nov 45	Str 27 Jan 47
401 *Maury* / BethSF	24 Mar 36 / 14 Feb 38	5 Aug 38	19 Oct 45	Str 1 Nov 45; sold 23 May 46
402 *Mayrant* / BosNY	15 Apr 37 / 14 May 38	19 Sep 39	28 Aug 46	Bikini; sunk 4 Apr 48
403 *Trippe* / BosNY	15 Apr 37 / 14 May 38	1 Nov 39	28 Aug 46	Bikini; sunk 3 Feb 48
404 *Rhind* / PHNY	22 Sep 37 / 28 Jul 38	10 Nov 39	28 Aug 46	Bikini; sunk 22 Mar 48
405 *Rowan* / NorNY	25 Jun 37 / 5 May 38	23 Sep 39		WL(T) 11 Sep 43
406 *Stack* / NorNY	25 Jun 37 / 5 May 38	20 Nov 39	28 Aug 46	Bikini; sunk 24 Apr 48
407 *Sterett* / CharNY	12 Feb 36 / 27 Oct 38	15 Aug 39	2 Nov 45	Sold 10 Aug 47
408 *Wilson* / PSNY	22 Mar 37 / 12 Apr 39	5 Jul 39	28 Aug 46	Bikini; sunk 8 Apr 48
409 *Sims* / Bath	13 Jul 37 / 8 Apr 39	1 Aug 39		WL(T) 7 May 42
410 *Hughes* / Bath	15 Sep 37 / 17 Jun 39	21 Sep 39		Bikini; sunk 16 Oct 48
411 *Anderson* / Fed	14 Nov 37 / 4 Feb 39	19 May 39		Bikini 2 Jul 46
412 *Hammann* / Fed	17 Jan 38 / 4 Feb 39	11 Aug 39		WL(T) 7 Jun 42
413 *Mustin* / NN	20 Dec 37 / 8 Dec 38	15 Sep 39	29 Aug 46	Bikini; sunk 18 Apr 48
414 *Russell* / NN	20 Dec 37 / 8 Dec 38	3 Nov 39	15 Nov 45	Str 28 Nov 45; sold 28 Sep 47

415 *O'Brien* BosNY	31 May 38 20 Oct 39	2 Mar 40		WD(T) 15 Sep 42; broke up 19 Oct 42 en route to U.S. for repairs
416 *Walke* BosNY	31 May 38 20 Oct 39	27 Apr 40		WL(G,T) 14 Nov 42
417 *Morris* NorNY	7 Jun 38 1 Jun 38	5 Mar 40	9 Nov 45	WD(K) 6 Apr 45; str 28 Nov 45
418 *Roe* CharNY	23 Apr 38 21 Jun 39	5 Jan 40	30 Oct 45	Str 16 Nov 45; sold 1 Aug 47
419 *Wainwright* NorNY	7 Jun 38 1 Jun 39	15 Apr 40	26 Aug 46	Bikini; sunk 2 Jul 48
420 *Buck* PHNY	6 Apr 38 22 May 39	15 May 40		WL(T) 9 Oct 43

"1850–Ton" Leaders

356 *Porter* NYSB	18 Dec 33 12 Dec 35	25 Aug 36		WL(T) 26 Oct 42
357 *Selfridge* NYSB	18 Dec 33 18 Apr 36	25 Nov 36	15 Oct 45	Sold 19 Nov 46
358 *McDougal* NYSB	18 Dec 33 17 Jul 36	23 Dec 36	24 Jun 46	AG–126 Sep 45; NRF 1947–49; str 15 Aug 49
359 *Winslow* NYSB	18 Dec 33 21 Sep 36	17 Feb 37	28 Jun 50	AG–127 Sep 45; str 5 Dec 57; sold 23 Feb 59
360 *Phelps* BethQ	2 Jan 34 18 Jul 35	26 Feb 36	6 Nov 45	Str 28 Jan 47
361 *Clark* BethQ	2 Jan 34 15 Oct 35	20 May 36	23 Oct 45	Sold 29 Mar 46
362 *Moffett* BethQ	2 Jan 34 11 Dec 35	28 Aug 36	2 Nov 45	Str 28 Jan 47
363 *Balch* BethQ	16 May 34 24 Mar 36	20 Oct 36	19 Oct 45	Sold 1946
381 *Somers* Fed	27 Jun 35 13 Mar 37	1 Dec 37	13 Oct 45	Str 28 Jan 47
383 *Warrington* Fed	10 Oct 35 15 May 37	9 Feb 38		Storm 13 Sep 44
394 *Sampson* Bath	8 Apr 36 16 Apr 38	19 Aug 38	8 Nov 45	Sold 1946
395 *Davis* Bath	28 Jul 36 20 Jul 38	9 Nov 38	19 Oct 45	Sold 24 Nov 47
396 *Jouett* Bath	26 Mar 36 24 Sep 38	25 Jan 39	1 Nov 45	Sold 1946

Benson-Livermore Class

421 *Benson* BethQ	16 May 38 15 Nov 39	25 Jul 40	18 Mar 46	Taiwan 26 Feb 54 (*Lo Yang*); str 1 Nov 74
422 *Mayo* BethQ	16 May 38 26 Mar 40	18 Sep 40	18 Mar 46	Str 1 Dec 70
423 *Gleaves* Bath	16 Mar 38 9 Dec 39	14 Jun 40	8 May 46	Str 1 Nov 69; plan for memorial (Smithsonian) canc; sold 29 Jun 72
424 *Niblack* Bath	8 Aug 38 18 May 40	1 Aug 40	Jun 47	Str 31 Jul 68; test hulk for new method of dry-docking 68–73; sold 16 Aug 73
425 *Madison* BosNY	19 Dec 38 20 Oct 39	6 Aug 40	13 Mar 46	Str 1 May 68; tgt Oct 69
426 *Lansdale* BosNY	19 Dec 38 30 Oct 39	17 Sep 40		WL(T) 20 Apr 44
427 *Hilary P. Jones* CharNY	16 Nov 38 14 Dec 39	7 Sep 40	6 Feb 47	Taiwan 26 Feb 54 (*Han Yang*)
428 *Charles F. Hughes* PSNY	3 Jan 39 16 May 40	5 Sep 40	18 Mar 46	Str 1 May 68; tgt Mar 69
429 *Livermore* Bath	6 Mar 39 3 Aug 40	7 Oct 40	24 Jan 47	NRF 47–50; grounded 30 Jul 49; Str 19 Jul 56; spares and test hulk 56–58; sold 3 Mar 61; BU 17 Aug 61
430 *Eberle* Bath	12 Apr 39 14 Sep 40	4 Dec 40	3 Jun 46	NRF 47–50; Greece Jan 51 (*Niki*); re-rated escort 70; BU 74
431 *Plunkett* Fed	1 Mar 39 9 Mar 40	17 Jul 40	3 May 46	Taiwan 16 Feb 59 (*Nan Ying*); Str 1 Nov 74
432 *Kearny* Fed	1 Mar 39 9 Mar 40	13 Sep 40	7 Mar 46	Str 1 Jun 71
433 *Gwin* BosNY	1 Jun 39 25 May 40	15 Jan 41		WL(T) 13 Jul 43
434 *Meredith* BosNY	1 Jun 39 24 Apr 40	1 Mar 41		WL(T,B) 15 Oct 42

435 *Grayson* CharNY	17 Jul 39 2 Aug 40	14 Feb 41	4 Feb 47	Str 1 Jun 71
436 *Monssen* PSNY	12 Jul 39 16 May 40	14 Mar 41		WL(G) 13 Nov 42
437 *Woolsey* Bath	9 Oct 39 12 Feb 41	7 May 41	13 Jun 46	Str 1 Jul 71
438 *Ludlow* Bath	18 Dec 39 11 Nov 40	5 Mar 41	20 May 46	NRF 47–50; Greece 22 Jan 51 (*Doxa*); escort 70; BU 72
439 *Edison* Fed	18 Mar 40 23 Nov 40	31 Jan 41	18 May 46	Str 1 Apr 66; sold Dec 66
440 *Ericsson* Fed	18 Mar 40 23 Nov 40	31 Mar 41	15 Mar 46	Str 1 Jun 70; tgt
441 *Wilkes* BosNY	1 Nov 39 31 May 40	22 Apr 41	4 Mar 46	Str 1 Mar 71
442 *Nicholson* BosNY	1 Nov 39 31 May 40	3 Jun 41 17 Jul 50	26 Feb 46 15 Jan 51	NRF 1946–50; Italy 11 Jun 51 (*Aviere*); exptl ship 71
443 *Swanson* CharNY	15 Nov 39 2 Nov 40	29 May 41	6 Mar 46	Str 1 Mar 71
444 *Ingraham* CharNY	15 Nov 39 15 Feb 41	17 Jul 41		WL(G) 22 Aug 42
453 *Bristol* Fed	2 Dec 40 25 Jul 40	22 Oct 41		WL(T) 12 Oct 43
454 *Ellyson* Fed	2 Dec 40 25 Jul 41	28 Nov 41	19 Oct 54	DMS–19 Nov 44; Japan 20 Oct 54 (*Asakaze*); Taiwan 6 Aug 70 (spares)
455 *Hambleton* Fed	16 Dec 40 26 Sep 41	22 Dec 41	15 Jan 55	DMS–20 Nov 44; str 1 Jun 71
456 *Rodman* Fed	2 Dec 40 26 Sep 41	27 Jan 41	28 Jul 55	DMS–21 Nov 44; Taiwan 28 Jul 55 (*Hsieng Yang*); grounded 22 May 70; repl by ex-*Macomb*; sold 4 Apr 73.
457 *Emmons* Bath	14 Nov 40 23 Aug 41	5 Dec 41		DMS–22 Nov 44; WL(K) 7 Apr 45
458 *Macomb* Bath	3 Sep 40 23 Sep 41	26 Jan 42	19 Oct 54	DMS–23 Nov 44; Japan 19 Oct 54 (*Hatakaze*); Taiwan 6 Aug 70 (spares) but repl ex-*Rodman* (*Hsieng Yang*)
459 *Laffey* BethSF	13 Jan 41 30 Oct 41	31 Mar 42		WL(T,G) 13 Nov 42
460 *Woodworth* BethSF	13 Jan 41 30 Oct 41	31 Mar 42 21 Nov 50	11 Apr 46	NRF 47–50; Italy 11 Jun 51 (*Artigliere*); str Jan 71
461 *Forrest* BosNY	6 Jan 41 14 Jun 41	13 Jan 42	30 Nov 45	DMS–24 Nov 44; WD(K) 27 May 45; str 9 Dec 45
462 *Fitch* BosNY	6 Jan 41 14 Jun 41	3 Feb 42	24 Feb 56	DMS–25 Nov 44; str 1 Jul 71; tgt
463 *Corry* CharNY	4 Sep 40 28 Jul 41	18 Dec 41		WL(M) 6 Jun 44
464 *Hobson* CharNY	14 Nov 40 8 Sep 41	22 Jan 42		DMS–26 Nov 44; coll 26 Apr 52
483 *Aaron Ward* Fed	11 Feb 41 22 Nov 41	4 Mar 42		WL(B) 7 Apr 43
484 *Buchanan* Fed	11 Feb 41 22 Nov 41	21 Mar 42 11 Dec 48	21 May 46 28 Apr 49	Turkey 29 Apr 49 (*Gelibolu*); BU 74
485 *Duncan* Fed	31 Jul 41 20 Feb 42	16 Apr 42		WL(G) 12 Oct 42
486 *Lansdowne* Fed	31 Jul 41 20 Feb 42	29 Apr 42	2 May 46	Turkey 10 Jun 49 (*Gaziantep*); BU 74
487 *Lardner* Fed	15 Sep 41 20 Mar 42	13 May 42	16 May 46	Turkey 10 Jun 49 (*Gemlik*)
488 *McCalla* Fed	15 Sep 41 20 Mar 42	27 May 42	17 May 46	Turkey 29 Apr 49 (*Giresun*)
489 *Mervine* Fed	3 Nov 41 3 May 42	17 Jun 42	27 May 49	DMS–31 May 45; str 31 Jul 68
490 *Quick* Fed	3 Nov 41 3 May 42	3 Jul 42	28 May 49	DMS–32 May 45; str 15 Jan 72
491 *Farenholt* BethSI	11 Dec 40 19 Nov 41	2 Apr 42	26 Apr 46	Str 1 Jun 71
492 *Bailey* BethSI	29 Jan 41 19 Dec 41	11 May 42	2 May 46	Str 1 May 68; tgt
493 *Carmick* SeaTac	29 May 41 8 Mar 42	28 Dec 42	13 Feb 54	DMS–33 Jun 45; str 1 Jul 71
494 *Doyle* SeaTac	26 May 41 17 Mar 42	27 Jan 43	19 May 55	DMS–34 Jun 45; str 1 Jul 71
495 *Endicott* SeaTac	1 May 41 5 Apr 42	25 Feb 43	17 Aug 55	DMS–35 May 45; str 1 Nov 69

		LD/Launch	Comm	Decomm	Fate
496	McCook SeaTac	1 May 41 20 Apr 42	15 Mar 43	27 May 49	DMS–36 May 45; str 15 Jan 72
497	Frankford SeaTac	5 Jun 41 17 May 42	31 Mar 43	4 Mar 46	Str 1 Jun 71
598	Bancroft BethQ.	1 May 41 31 Dec 41	30 Apr 42	1 Feb 46	Str 1 Jun 71
599	Barton BethQ	30 May 41 31 Jan 42	29 May 42		WL(T) 13 Nov 42
600	Boyle BethQ	31 Dec 41 15 Jun 42	15 Aug 42	29 Mar 46	Str 1 Jun 71
601	Champlin BethQ	31 Jan 42 25 Jul 42	12 Sep 42	31 Jan 47	Str 2 Jan 71
602	Meade BethSI	25 Mar 41 15 Feb 42	22 Jun 42	17 Jun 46	Str 1 Jun 71
603	Murphy BethSI	19 May 41 29 Apr 42	27 Jul 42	9 Mar 46	Str 1 Nov 70
604	Parker BethSI	9 Jun 41 12 May 42	31 Aug 42	31 Jan 47	Str 1 Jul 71
605	Caldwell BethSF	24 Mar 41 15 Jan 42	10 Jun 42	24 Apr 46	Str 1 May 65
606	Coghlan BethSF	28 Mar 41 12 Feb 42	10 Jul 42	31 Mar 47	Str 1 Jul 71
607	Frazier BethSF	5 Jul 41 17 Mar 42	30 Jul 42	15 Apr 46	Str 1 Jul 71
608	Gansevoort BethSF	16 Jun 41 11 Apr 42	25 Aug 42	1 Feb 46	Str 1 Jul 71; tgt 23 Mar 72
609	Gillespie BethSF	16 Jun 41 1 Nov 42	18 Sep 42	17 Apr 46	Str 1 Jul 72; tgt
610	Hobby BethSF	30 Jun 41 4 Jun 42	18 Nov 42	1 Feb 46	Str 1 Jul 71; tgt 28 Jun
611	Kalk BethSF	30 Jun 41 18 Jul 42	17 Nov 42	3 May 46	Str 1 Jun 68; tgt Mar 69
612	Kendrick BethSP	1 May 41 2 Apr 42	12 Sep 42	31 Mar 47	Str 1 May 66; tgt 2 Mar 66
613	Laub BethSP	1 May 41 28 Apr 42	24 Oct 42	2 Feb 46	Str 1 Jul 71
614	Mackenzie BethSP	29 May 41 27 Jun 42	21 Nov 42	4 Feb 46	Str 1 Jul 71; tgt
615	McLanahan BethSP	29 May 41 2 Sep 42	19 Dec 42	2 Feb 46	Str 1 Jul 71
616	Nields BethQ	15 Jun 42 1 Oct 42	15 Jan 43	25 Mar 46	Str 15 Sep 71
617	Ordronaux BethQ	25 Jul 42 9 Nov 42	13 Feb 43	Jan 47	Str 1 Jul 71
618	Davison Fed	26 Feb 42 19 Jul 42	11 Sep 42	24 Jun 49	DMS–37 Jun 45; str 15 Jan 71
619	Edwards Fed	26 Feb 42 19 Jul 42	18 Sep 42	11 Apr 46	Str 1 Jul 71
620	Glennon Fed	25 Mar 42 26 Aug 42	8 Oct 42		WL(M) 8 Jun 44
621	Jeffers Fed	25 Mar 42 26 Aug 42	5 Nov 42	23 May 55	DMS–27 Nov 44; str 1 Jul 71
622	Maddox Fed	7 May 42 15 Sep 42	31 Oct 42		WL(B) 10 Jul 43
623	Nelson Fed	7 May 42 15 Sep 42	26 Nov 42	Jan 47	Str 1 Mar 68
624	Baldwin SeaTac	19 Jul 41 15 Jun 42	30 Apr 43	20 Jun 46	Grounded 16 Apr 61; scuttled 5 Jun 61
625	Harding SeaTac	22 Jul 41 28 Jun 42	25 May 43	2 Nov 45	DMS–28 Nov 44; WD(K) 16 Apr 45; str 16 Nov 45
626	Satterlee SeaTac	10 Sep 41 17 Jul 42	1 Jul 43	16 Mar 46	Str 1 Dec 70
627	Thompson SeaTac	22 Sep 41 15 Jul 42	10 Jul 43	23 May 55	DMS–38 May 45; str 1 Jul 71
628	Welles SeaTac	27 Sep 41 7 Sep 42	16 Aug 43	4 Feb 46	Str 1 Mar 68
632	Cowie BosNY	18 Mar 41 27 Sep 41	1 Jun 42	21 Apr 47	DMS–39 May 45; str 1 Dec 70
633	Knight BosNY	18 Mar 41 27 Sep 41	23 Jun 42	19 Mar 47	DMS–40 Jun 45; str 1 Dec 66; tgt 27 Oct 67
634	Doran BosNY	14 Jun 41 10 Dec 41	4 Aug 42	29 Jan 47	DMS–41 May 45; str 15 Jan 72
635	Earle BosNY	14 Jun 41 10 Dec 41	1 Sep 42	17 May 47	DMS–42 Jun 45; str 1 Dec 69

	LD/Launch	Comm	Decomm	Fate
636 *Butler* PHNY	16 Sep 41 12 Feb 42	15 Aug 42	8 Nov 45	DMS–29 Nov 44; WD(K) 25 May 45; str 28 Nov 45
637 *Gherardi* PHNY	16 Sep 41 12 Feb 42	15 Sep 42	17 Dec 55	DMS–30 Nov 44; str 1 Jun 71
638 *Herndon* NorNY	26 Aug 41 2 Feb 42	20 Dec 42	8 May 46	Str 1 Jul 71; tgt 23 May 72
639 *Shubrick* NorNY	17 Feb 42 18 Apr 42	7 Feb 43	19 Oct 45	WD(K) 29 May 45; sold 28 Sep 47
640 *Beatty* CharNY	1 May 41 20 Dec 41	7 May 42		WL(B,T) 6 Nov 43
641 *Tillman* CharNY	1 May 41 20 Dec 41	4 Jun 42	16 Mar 46	Str 1 Jun 70
645 *Stevenson* Fed	23 Jul 42 11 Nov 42	15 Dec 42	27 Apr 46	Str 1 Jun 68
646 *Stockton* Fed	24 Jul 42 11 Nov 42	11 Jan 43	15 May 46	Str 1 Jul 71
647 *Thorn* Fed	15 Nov 42 28 Feb 43	1 Apr 43	6 May 46	Str 1 Jul 71; tgt Aug 74
648 *Turner* Fed	15 Nov 42 28 Feb 43	16 Apr 43		WL(E) 3 Jan 44

***Fletcher* Class**

	LD/Launch	Comm	Decomm	Fate
445 *Fletcher* Fed	2 Oct 41 3 May 42	30 Jun 42 3 Oct 49	15 Jan 47	Str 1 Aug 69 (DDE); possible memorial (Smithsonian) canc; sold 22 Feb 72
446 *Radford* Fed	2 Oct 41 3 May 42	22 Jul 42 17 Oct 49	17 Jan 46 10 Nov 69	Str 10 Nov 69 (DDE)
447 *Jenkins* Fed	27 Nov 41 21 Jan 42	31 Jul 42 2 Nov 51	1 May 46	Str 2 Jul 69 (DDE)
448 *LaVallette* Fed	27 Nov 41 21 Jun 42	12 Aug 42	16 Apr 46	Str 1 Feb 72; Peru Jul 72 (spares)
449 *Nicholas* Bath	3 Mar 41 19 Feb 42	4 Jun 42 19 Feb 51	12 Jun 46	Str 30 Jan 70 (DDE)
450 *O'Bannon* Bath	3 Mar 41 14 Mar 42	26 Jun 42 19 Feb 51	21 May 46 3 Jan 70	Str 1 Jan 70; DDE Mar 49; memorial canc; sold 6 Jun 72
451 *Chevalier* Bath	30 Apr 41 11 Apr 42	20 Jul 42	—	WD(T,C) 6 Oct 43; scuttled
465 *Saufley* Fed	27 Jan 42 19 Jul 42	9 Aug 42 15 Dec 49	12 Jun 46 29 Jan 65	Str 1 Sep 66; tgt 20 Feb 68 (DDE)
466 *Waller* Fed	12 Feb 42 15 Aug 42	1 Oct 42 5 Jul 50	46 15 Jul 70	NRF 56; str 15 Jul 69; tgt 2 Feb 70 (DDE)
467 *Strong* Bath	30 Apr 41 17 May 42	7 Aug 42	—	WL(T) 5 Jul 43
468 *Taylor* Bath	28 Aug 41 7 Jun 42	28 Aug 42 3 Dec 51	31 May 46 3 Jun 69	(DDE) Italy 2 Jul 69 (*Lanciere*) (spares); str Jan 71
469 *De Haven* Bath	27 Sep 41 28 Jun 42	21 Sep 42	—	WL(B) 1 Feb 43
470 *Bache* BethSI	19 Nov 41 7 Jul 42	14 Nov 42 1 Oct 51	4 Feb 46 1 Mar 68	Grounded 6 Feb 68; str 1 Mar 68 (DDE)
471 *Beale* BethSI	19 Dec 41 24 Aug 42	23 Dec 42 2 Jan 51	11 Apr 46 20 Sep 68	Str 1 Oct 68; tgt 24 Jun 69 (DDE)
472 *Guest* BosNY	27 Sep 41 20 Feb 42	15 Dec 42 —	4 Jun 46	Brazil 5 Jun 59 (*Para*)
473 *Bennett* BosNY	10 Dec 41 16 Apr 42	9 Feb 43 —	18 Apr 46	Brazil 15 Dec 59 (*Paraiba*)
474 *Fullam* BosNY	10 Dec 41 16 Apr 42	9 Feb 43 —	15 Jan 47 —	A-Test 1 Jun 62; sunk 7 Jul 62
475 *Hudson* BosNY	20 Feb 42 3 Jun 42	13 Apr 43 —	31 May 46	Str 1 Dec 72
476 *Hutchins* BosNY	27 Sep 41 20 Feb 42	17 Nov 42 —	30 Nov 45 —	WD(K) 27 Apr 45; sold 19 Jan 48
477 *Pringle* CharNY	31 Jul 41 2 May 42	15 Sep 42	—	WL(K) 16 Apr 45
478 *Stanly* CharNY	15 Sep 41 12 May 42	15 Oct 42 —	15 Jan 47	Str 1 Dec 70
479 *Stevens* CharNY	30 Dec 41 24 Jun 42	1 Feb 43 —	28 Sep 46	Str 1 Dec 72
480 *Halford* PSNY	3 Jun 41 29 Oct 42	10 Apr 43 —	15 May 46 —	Str 1 May 68
481 *Leutze* PSNY	3 Jun 41 29 Oct 42	4 Mar 44 —	6 Dec 45	WD(K) 6 Apr 45; str 3 Jan 46
498 *Philip* Fed	7 May 42 13 Oct 42	21 Nov 42 30 Jun 50	Jan 47 30 Sep 68	Str 1 Oct 68 (DDE); sunk in storm en route to BU, 2 Feb 72

		LD/Launch	Comm	Decomm	Fate
499	*Renshaw*	7 May 42	5 Dec 42	Feb 47	Str 14 Feb 70 (DDE)
	Fed	13 Oct 42	Jun 50	14 Feb 70	
500	*Ringgold*	25 Jun 42	30 Dec 42	23 Mar 46	WGER 14 Jul 59 (Z–2)
	Fed	11 Nov 42	—	—	
501	*Schroeder*	25 Jun 42	1 Jan 43	29 Apr 46	Str 1 Oct 72
	Fed	11 Nov 42	—	—	
502	*Sigsbee*	22 Jul 42	23 Jan 43	13 Apr 46	Str 1 Dec 74
	Fed	7 Dec 42	—	—	
507	*Conway*	5 Nov 41	9 Oct 42	25 Jun 46	NRF; str 15 Nov 69; tgt 26 Jun (DDE)
	Bath	16 Aug 42	8 Nov 50	—	
508	*Cony*	24 Dec 41	30 Oct 42	18 Jun 46	NRF; str 2 Jul 69; tgt 20 Mar 70 (DDE)
	Bath	20 Aug 42	17 Nov 49	—	
509	*Converse*	23 Feb 42	20 Nov 42	23 Apr 46	Spain 1 Jul 59 (*Almirante Valdes*)
	Bath	30 Aug 42	—	—	
510	*Eaton*	17 Mar 42	4 Dec 42	21 Jun 46	NRF post-Korea; str 2 Jul 69; tgt 27 Mar 70 (DDE)
	Bath	20 Sep 42	11 Dec 51	—	
511	*Foote*	14 Apr 42	22 Dec 42	18 Apr 46	Str 1 Oct 71
	Bath	11 Oct 42	—	—	
512	*Spence*	18 May 42	8 Jan 43	—	Typhoon 18 Dec 44
	Bath	27 Oct 42			
513	*Terry*	8 Jun 42	27 Jan 43	13 Aug 46	Str 1 Apr 74; Peru (spares) 18 Jul 74
	Bath	22 Nov 42	—	—	
514	*Thatcher*	29 Jun 42	10 Feb 43	18 Nov 45	WD(K) 19 Jul 45; sold 23 Jan 48
	Bath	6 Dec 42	—	—	
515	*Anthony*	17 Aug 42	26 Feb 43	17 Apr 46	WGER 17 Jan 58 (Z 1); res Feb 72 (spares); DDE conv canc
	Bath	20 Dec 42	—	—	
516	*Wadsworth*	18 Aug 42	16 Mar 43	18 Apr 46	WGER 6 Oct 59 (Z–3)
	Bath	10 Jan 43	—	—	
517	*Walker*	31 Aug 42	3 Apr 43	31 May 46	(DDE); Italy 2 Jul 64 (*Fante*)
	Bath	31 Jan 43	15 Sep 50	2 Jul 69	
518	*Brownson*	15 Feb 42	3 Feb 43	—	WL(T) 26 Dec 43
	BethSI	24 Sep 42	—		
519	*Daly*	29 Apr 42	10 Mar 43	18 Apr 46	Str 1 Dec 74
	BethSI	24 Oct 42	6 Jul 51	2 May 60	
520	*Isherwood*	12 May 42	12 Apr 43	1 Feb 46	Peru 8 Oct 61 (*Guise*)
	BethSI	24 Nov 42	5 Apr 57	11 Sep 61	
521	*Kimberly*	27 Jul 42	22 May 43	5 Feb 47	Taiwan 1 Jun 67 (*An Yang*)
	BethSI	4 Feb 43	8 Feb 51	16 Jan 54	
522	*Luce*	24 Aug 42	21 Jun 43	—	WL(K) 4 Mar 45
	BethSI	6 Mar 43	—	—	
526	*Abner Read*	30 Oct 41	5 Feb 43	—	WL(K) 1 Nov 44
	BethSF	18 Aug 42	—	—	
527	*Ammen*	29 Nov 41	12 Mar 43	15 Apr 46	Coll 19 Jul 60 (DD–730) en route to decomm; str 1 Sep 60
	BethSF	17 Sep 42	5 Apr 51		
528	*Mullany*	15 Jan 42	10 May 43	14 Feb 46	NRF post-Korea; Taiwan 6 Oct 71 (*Ching Yang*)
	BethSF	10 Oct 42	8 Mar 51	6 Oct 71	
529	*Bush*	12 Feb 42	10 May 43	—	WL(K) 6 Apr 45
	BethSF	27 Oct 42			
530	*Trathen*	18 Jul 42	28 May 43	18 Jan 46	Str 1 Nov 72; tgt
	BethSF	22 Oct 42	1 Aug 51	11 May 65	
531	*Hazelwood*	11 Apr 42	18 Jun 43	18 Jan 46	NRF post-Korea; str 1 Dec 74
	BethSF	20 Nov 42	12 Sep 51	19 Mar 65	
532	*Heermann*	8 May 42	6 Jul 43	12 Jun 46	Argentina 14 Aug 61 (*Brown*)
	BethSF	5 Dec 42	12 Sep 51	20 Dec 57	
533	*Hoel*	4 Jun 42	29 Jul 43	—	WL(G) 25 Oct 44
	BethSF	19 Dec 42			
534	*McCord*	17 Mar 42	19 Aug 43	15 Jan 47	Str 1 Oct 7
	BethSF	10 Jan 43	1 Aug 51	9 Jun 54	
535	*Miller*	18 Aug 42	31 Aug 43	19 Dec 45	Str Dec 72
	BethSF	15 Feb 43	19 May 51	30 Jun 64	
536	*Owen*	17 Sep 42	20 Sep 43	10 Dec 46	Str 15 Apr 73
	BethSF	21 Mar 43	17 Aug 51	27 May 58	
537	*The Sullivans*	10 Oct 42	30 Sep 43	19 Dec 45	NRF post-Korea; str 1 Dec 74
	BethSF	4 Apr 43	—	—	
538	*Stephen Potter*	27 Oct 42	21 Oct 43	21 Sep 45	Str 1 Dec 74
	BethSF	28 Apr 43	29 Mar 51	21 Apr 58	
539	*Tingey*	22 Oct 42	25 Nov 43	Mar 46	NRF post-Korea; str 1 Nov 65; tgt May 66
	BethSF	28 May 43	27 Jan 51	30 Nov 63	
540	*Twining*	20 Nov 42	1 Dec 43	14 Jun 46	NRF 47–50, also post-Korea; Taiwan 16 Aug 71 (*Kwei Yang*)
	BethSF	11 Jul 43	10 Jun 50	1 Jul 71	
541	*Yarnall*	5 Dec 42	30 Dec 43	15 Jan 47	Taiwan 10 Jun 68 (*Kuen Yang*)
	BethSF	25 Jul 43	31 Aug 50	30 Sep 58	
544	*Boyd*	2 Apr 42	8 May 43	15 Jan 47	Turkey 1 Oct 69 (*Iskenderun*)
	BethSP	29 Oct 43	24 Nov 50	1 Oct 69	

	LD/Launch	Comm	Decomm	Fate
545 *Bradford*	28 Apr 42	12 Jun 43	11 Jul 46	Greece 28 Sep 62 (*Thyella*)
BethSP	12 Dec 42	27 Oct 50	28 Sep 61	
546 *Brown*	27 Jun 42	10 Jul 43	1 Aug 46	Greece 27 Sep 62 (*Navarinon*)
BethSP	21 Feb 43	27 Oct 50	9 Feb 62	
547 *Cowell*	7 Sep 42	23 Aug 43	22 Jul 46	NRF post-Korea; Argentina 17
BethSP	18 Mar 43	21 Sep 51	17 Aug 71	Aug 71 (*Almirante Storni*)
550 *Capps*	12 Jun 41	23 Jun 43	15 Jan 47	Spain 15 May 57 (*Lepanto*)
Gulf	31 May 42	—	—	
551 *David W. Taylor*	12 Jun 41	18 Sep 43	17 Aug 46	Spain 15 May 57 (*Almirante Ferrandiz*)
Gulf	4 Jul 43	—	—	
552 *Evans*	21 Jul 41	11 Dec 43	7 Nov 45	WD(K) 11 May 45; sold 11 Feb 47
Gulf	4 Oct 42	—	—	
553 *John D. Henley*	21 Jul 41	2 Feb 44	30 Apr 46	Str 1 May 68
Gulf	15 Nov 42	—	—	
554 *Franks*	8 Aug 42	30 Jul 43	31 May 46	Brazil 59
SeaTac	7 Dec 42			
555 *Haggard*	27 Mar 42	31 Aug 43	1 Nov 45	WD(K) 29 Apr 45; sold 46
SeaTac	9 Feb 43	—		
556 *Hailey*	11 Apr 42	30 Sep 43	27 Jan 46	Brazil 20 Jul 61 (*Pernambuco*)
SeaTac	9 Mar 43	27 Apr 51	3 Nov 60	
557 *Johnston*	6 May 42	27 Oct 43	—	WL(G) 25 Oct 44
SeaTac	25 Mar 43	—	—	
558 *Laws*	19 May 42	18 Nov 43	10 Dec 46	Str 15 Apr 73
SeaTac	22 Apr 43	2 Nov 51	30 Mar 64	
559 *Longshaw*	16 Jun 42	4 Dec 43	—	WL(K) 3 May 45
SeaTac	4 Jun 43	—	—	
560 *Morrison*	30 Jun 42	18 Dec 43	—	WD (grounded) 18 May 45; further damaged by shore batteries; destroyed
SeaTac	4 Jul 43	—	—	
561 *Prichett*	20 Jul 42	15 Jan 44	14 Mar 46	Italy 10 Jan 70 (*Geniere*)
SeaTac	31 Jul 43	17 Aug 51	10 Jan 70	
562 *Robinson*	12 Aug 42	31 Jan 44	12 Jun 46	Str 1 Dec 74
SeaTac	28 Aug 43	3 Aug 51	1 Apr 64	
563 *Ross*	7 Sep 42	21 Feb 44	4 Jun 46	Str 1 Dec 74
SeaTac	18 Sep 43	27 Oct 51	6 Nov 59	
564 *Rowe*	7 Dec 42	13 Mar 44	20 Sep 51	Str 1 Dec 74
SeaTac	30 Sep 43	31 Jan 47	6 Nov 59	
565 *Smalley*	9 Feb 43	31 Mar 44	Jan 47	Str 1 Apr 65
SeaTac	29 Oct 43	3 Jul 51	30 Sep 57	
566 *Stoddard*	10 Mar 43	15 Apr 44	Jan 47	Str 1 Jun 75
SeaTac	19 Nov 43	Nov 50	26 Sep 69	
567 *Watts*	26 Mar 43	29 Apr 44	12 Apr 46	Str 1 Feb 74
SeaTac	31 Dec 43	6 Jul 51	26 Sep 69	
568 *Wren*	24 Apr 43	24 Apr 43	13 Jul 46	Str 1 Dec 74
SeaTac	29 Jan 44	7 Sep 51	Oct 63	
569 *Aulick*	14 May 41	27 Oct 42	18 Apr 46	Greece 21 Aug 59 (*Sfendoni*)
Orange	2 Mar 42			
570 *Charles Ausburne*	14 May 41	24 Nov 42	18 Apr 46	WGER 12 Apr 60 (Z–6); Res Dec 67; BU 69
Orange	16 Mar 42	—	—	
571 *Claxton*	25 Jun 41	8 Dec 42	18 Apr 46	WGER 15 Dec 59 (Z–4)
Orange	1 Apr 42	—	—	
572 *Dyson*	25 Jun 41	30 Dec 42	31 Mar 47	WGER 17 Feb 60 (Z–5)
Orange	15 Apr 42			
573 *Harrison*	25 Jul 41	25 Jan 43	1 Apr 46	Str 1 May 68; Mexico 19 Aug 70 (*Cuauthemoc*)
Orange	7 May 42			
574 *John Rodgers*	25 Jul 41	9 Feb 43	25 May 46	Str 1 May 68; Mexico 19 Aug 70 (*Cuitlahuac*)
Orange	7 May 42			
575 *McKee*	2 Mar 42	31 Mar 43	25 Feb 46	BU Oct 72
Orange	2 Aug 42			
576 *Murray*	16 Mar 42	20 Apr 43	27 Mar 46	Str 1 Jun 65 (DDE)
Orange	16 Aug 42	2 Jan 51	May 65	
577 *Sproston*	1 Apr 42	19 May 43	18 Jan 46	Str 1 Oct 68 (DDE)
Orange	31 Aug 42	15 Sep 50	30 Sep 68	
578 *Wickes*	15 Apr 42	16 Jun 43	20 May 46	Str 1 Nov 72; tgt 8 Apr 74
Orange	13 Sep 42			
579 *William D. Porter*	7 May 42	6 Jul 43	—	WL(K) 10 Jun 45
Orange	27 Sep 42	—	—	
580 *Young*	7 May 42	31 Jul 43	31 Mar 46	Str 1 May 68; tgt 16 Apr 70
Orange	11 Oct 42	—	—	
581 *Charrette*	20 Feb 42	18 May 43	15 Jan 47	Greece 16 Jun 59 (*Velos*)
BosNY	3 Jun 42	—	—	
582 *Conner*	16 Apr 42	8 Jun 43	5 Jul 46	Greece 15 Sep 59 (*Aspis*)
BosNY	18 Jul 42	—	—	
583 *Hall*	16 Apr 42	6 Jul 43	10 Dec 46	Greece 9 Feb 60 (*Lonchi*)
BosNY	18 Jul 42			

	LD/Launch	Comm	Decomm	Fate
584 *Halligan* BosNY	9 Nov 42 19 Mar 43	19 Aug 43 —	— —	WL(M) 26 Mar 45
585 *Haraden* BosNY	9 Nov 42 19 Mar 43	16 Sep 43 —	2 Jul 46 —	Str 1 Nov 72; tgt
586 *Newcomb* BosNY	19 Mar 43 4 Jul 43	10 Nov 43 —	20 Nov 45 —	WE(K) 6 Apr 45; str 28 Mar 46
587 *Bell* CharNY	30 Dec 41 24 Jun 42	4 Mar 43 —	14 Jun 46 —	Str 1 Nov 72; tgt 11 May 75
588 *Burns* CharNY	9 May 42 8 Aug 42	3 Apr 43 —	25 Jun 46 —	Str 1 Nov 72; tgt 20 Sep 74
589 *Izard* CharNY	9 May 42 8 Aug 42	15 May 43 —	31 May 46 —	Str 1 May 68
590 *Paul Hamilton* CharNY	20 Jan 43 7 Apr 43	25 Oct 43 —	24 Sep 45 —	Str 1 May 68
591 *Twiggs* CharNY	20 Jan 43 7 Apr 43	4 Nov 43 —	— —	WL(T) 16 Jun 45
592 *Howorth* PSNY	26 Nov 41 10 Jan 43	3 Apr 44 —	30 Apr 46 —	Str 1 Jun 61; tgt 8 Mar 62
593 *Killen* PSNY	26 Nov 41 10 Jan 43	4 May 44 —	9 Jul 46 —	Str 1 Jan 63; tgt (A); static tgt Roosevelt Roads 63-, repl APD–39
594 *Hart* PSNY	10 Aug 43 25 Sep 44	4 Nov 44 —	31 May 46 —	Str 15 Apr 73
595 *Metcalfe* PSNY	10 Aug 43 25 Sep 44	18 Nov 44 —	Mar 46 —	Str 2 Jan 71
596 *Shields* PSNY	10 Aug 43 25 Sep 44	8 Feb 45 15 Jul 50	14 Jun 46 1 Jul 72	Str 1 July 72; Brazil 6 July 72 (*Maranhao*); NRF 1946–50 and post-1963
597 *Wiley* PSNY	10 Aug 43 25 Sep 44	22 Feb 45 —	9 Aug 46 —	Str 1 May 68
629 *Abbot* Bath	21 Sep 42 17 Feb 43	23 Apr 43 26 Feb 51	21 May 46 26 Mar 65	Str 1 Dec 74
630 *Braine* Bath	12 Oct 42 7 Mar 43	23 Apr 43 6 Apr 51	26 Jul 46 17 Aug 71	NRF post-Korea; Argentina 17 Aug 71 (*Domecq Garcia*)
631 *Erben* Bath	28 Oct 42 21 Mar 43	28 May 43 19 May 51	31 May 46 27 Jun 58	ROK May 63 (*Chung Mu*)
642 *Hale* Bath	23 Nov 42 4 Apr 43	15 Jun 43 24 Mar 51	15 Jan 47 30 Jul 60	Colombia 23 Jan 61 (*Antioquia*)
643 *Sigourney* Bath	7 Dec 42 24 Apr 43	29 Jun 43 7 Sep 51	20 Mar 46 1 May 60	
644 *Stembel* Bath	21 Dec 42 8 May 43	16 Jul 43 9 Nov 51	31 May 46 27 May 58	Argentina 7 Aug 61 (*Rosales*)
649 *Albert W. Grant* CharNY	30 Dec 42 29 May 43	24 Nov 43 —	16 Jul 46 —	Str 14 Apr 71
650 *Caperton* Bath	11 Jan 43 22 May 43	30 Jul 43 6 Jul 46	6 Apr 51 27 Apr 60	Str 1 Dec 74
651 *Cogswell* Bath	1 Feb 43 5 Jun 43	17 Aug 43 7 Jan 51	30 Apr 46 1 Oct 69	Turkey 1 Oct 69 (*Izmit*)
652 *Ingersoll* Bath	18 Feb 43 28 Jun 43	31 Aug 43 4 May 51	19 Jul 46 Jan 70	Str 20 Jan 70; tgt for Pt. Mugu replaced APD–131; sunk 19 May 74
653 *Knapp* Bath	8 Mar 43 10 Jul 43	10 Jul 43 3 May 51	5 Jul 46 4 Mar 57	Str 6 Mar 72
654 *Bearss* Gulf	14 Jul 42 25 Jul 43	25 Jul 43 7 Sep 51	31 Jan 47	NRF post-Korea; str 1 Dec 74
655 *John Hood* Gulf	12 Oct 42 25 Oct 43	7 Jun 44 3 Aug 51	3 Jul 46	Str 1 Dec 74
656 *Van Valkenburgh* Gulf	15 Nov 42 19 Dec 43	2 Aug 44 8 Mar 51	15 Apr 46 21 Oct 53	Turkey 28 Feb 67 (*Izmir*); spares 73
657 *Charles J. Badger* BethSI	24 Sep 42 3 Apr 43	23 Jul 43 10 Sep 51	10 May 46 20 Dec 57	Chile 27 May 74 (spares)
658 *Colahan* BethSI	24 Oct 42 3 May 43	23 Aug 43 16 Dec 50	14 Jun 46 1 Aug 66	NRF 47–50, also post-Korea; str 1 Aug 66; tgt 18 Dec 66
659 *Dashiell* Fed	1 Oct 42 6 Feb 43	20 Mar 43 3 May 51	30 Mar 46 29 Apr 60	Str 1 Dec 74
660 *Bullard* Fed	16 Oct 42 28 Feb 43	9 Apr 43 —	20 Dec 46	Str 1 Dec 72
661 *Kidd* Fed	16 Oct 42 28 Feb 43	23 Apr 43 28 Mar 51	10 Dec 46 19 Jun 64	Str 1 Dec 74
662 *Bennion* BosNY	19 Mar 43 4 Jul 43	14 Dec 43 —	20 Jun 46 —	Str 15 Apr 71
663 *Heywood L. Edwards* BosNY	4 Jul 43 6 Oct 43	26 Jan 44 —	1 Jul 46 —	Japan 10 Mar 59 (*Ariake*); ret 10 Mar 74; ROK (spares)

	LD/Launch	Comm	Decomm	Fate
664 *Richard P. Leary* BosNY	4 Jul 43 / 6 Oct 43	23 Feb 44 / —	10 Dec 46 / —	Japan 10 Mar 59 (*Yugure*); ROK (spares) Mar 74
665 *Bryant* CharNY	30 Dec 42 / 29 May 43	4 Dec 43	15 Jan 47	Tgt 24 Aug 69
666 *Black* Fed	14 Nov 42 / 28 Mar 43	21 May 43 / 18 Jul 51	5 Aug 46 / 69	Str 21 Sep 69
667 *Chauncey* Fed	14 Nov 42 / 28 Mar 43	31 May 43 / 18 Jul 50	19 Dec 45 / 14 May 54	Str 1 Oct 72
668 *Clarence K. Bronson* Fed	9 Dec 42 / 18 Apr 43	11 Jun 43 / 7 Jun 51	16 Jul 46 / 29 Jun 60	Turkey 14 Jan 67 (*Istanbul*)
669 *Cotten* Fed	8 Feb 43 / 12 Jun 43	24 Jul 43 / 3 Jul 51	15 Jul 46 / 2 May 60	Str 1 Dec 74
670 *Dortch* Fed	2 Mar 43 / 20 Jun 43	7 Aug 43 / 4 May 51	19 Jul 46 / 13 Dec 57	Argentina 1 Aug 61 (*Espora*)
671 *Gatling* Fed	3 Mar 43 / 20 Jun 43	19 Aug 43 / 4 Jun 51	16 Jul 46 / 2 May 60	Str 1 Dec 74
672 *Healy* Fed	4 Mar 43 / 4 Jul 43	3 Sep 43 / 3 Aug 51	11 Jul 46 / 11 Mar 58	Str 1 Dec 74
673 *Hickox* Fed	12 Mar 43 / 4 Jul 43	10 Sep 43 / 19 May 51	10 Dec 46 / 20 Dec 57	ROK 11 Nov 68 (*Pusan*)
674 *Hunt* Fed	31 Mar 43 / 1 Aug 43	22 Sep 43 / 31 Oct 51	15 Dec 45 / 30 Dec 63	Str 1 Dec 74
675 *Lewis Hancock* Fed	31 Mar 43 / 1 Aug 43	29 Sep 43 / 19 May 51	10 Jan 46 / 18 Dec 57	Brazil 26 Aug 67 (*Piaui*); spares Nov 73
676 *Marshall* Fed	19 Apr 43 / 29 Aug 43	16 Oct 43 / 27 Apr 51	Dec 45	NRF post-Korea; str 19 Jul 69
677 *McDermut* Fed	14 Jun 43 / 17 Oct 43	19 Nov 43 / 29 Dec 50	15 Jan 47 / 16 Dec 63	Str 1 Apr 65
678 *McGowan* Fed	30 Jun 43 / 14 Nov 43	20 Dec 43 / 6 Jul 51	30 Apr 46 / 30 Nov 60	Spain 1 Dec 60 (*Jorge Juan*)
679 *McNair* Fed	30 Jun 43 / 14 Nov 43	30 Dec 43 / 6 Jul 51	28 May 46 / 30 Dec 63	NRF post-Korea; str 1 Dec 74
680 *Melvin* Fed	6 Jul 43 / 17 Oct 43	24 Nov 43 / 26 Feb 51	31 May 46 / 13 Jan 54	Str 1 Dec 74
681 *Hopewell* BethSP	29 Oct 42 / 2 May 43	30 Sep 43 / 28 Mar 51	15 Jan 47 / 2 Jan 70	Str 2 Jan 70; tgt 11 Feb 72
682 *Porterfield* BethSP	12 Dec 42 / 13 Jun 43	30 Oct 43 / 27 Apr 51	46 / 7 Nov 69	Str 1 Mar 75
683 *Stockham* BethSF	19 Dec 42 / 25 Jun 43	11 Feb 44 / 14 Nov 51	46 / 2 Sep 57	Str 1 Dec 74
684 *Wedderburn* BethSF	10 Jan 43 / 1 Aug 43	9 Mar 44 / 21 Nov 50	March 46 / 69	NRF 46–50; str 1 Oct 69
685 *Picking* BethSI	24 Nov 42 / 1 Jun 43	21 Sep 43 / 26 Jan 51	20 Dec 45 / 4 Dec 69	Str 1 Mar 75
686 *Halsey Powell* BethSI	4 Feb 43 / 30 Jun 43	25 Oct 43 / 27 Apr 51	10 Dec 46 / —	NRF post-Korea; ROK 27 Apr 68 (*Seoul*)
687 *Uhlmann* BethSI	6 Mar 43 / 30 Jul 43	22 Nov 43 / 23 May 50	14 Jun 46 / 15 Jul 72	NRF 47–50; post 1969; str 15 Jul 72; last active *Fletcher*
688 *Remey* Bath	22 Mar 43 / 25 Jul 43	30 Sep 43 / 14 Nov 51	10 Dec 46 / 30 Dec 63	Str
689 *Wadleigh* Bath	5 Apr 43 / 7 Aug 43	19 Oct 43 / 3 Oct 51	Jan 47 / 28 Jun 62	Chile 26 Jul 62 (*Blanco Encalada*)
690 *Norman Scott* Bath	26 Apr 43 / 28 Aug 43	5 Nov 43 / —	30 Apr 46 / —	Str 15 Apr 73
691 *Mertz* Bath	10 May 43 / 11 Sep 43	19 Nov 43	23 Apr 46	Str Oct 70
792 *Callaghan* BethSP	21 Feb 43 / 1 Aug 43	27 Nov 43 / —	—	WL (K) 28 Jul 45
793 *Cassin Young* BethSP	18 Mar 43 / 12 Sep 43	31 Dec 43 / 8 Sep 51	28 May 46 / 29 Apr 60	Str 1 Dec 74
794 *Irwin* BethSP	2 May 43 / 31 Oct 43	14 Feb 44 / 26 Feb 51	31 May 46 / 10 Jan 58	Brazil 10 May 68 (*Santa Catarina*); spares Nov 73
795 *Preston* BethSP	13 Jun 43 / 12 Dec 43	20 Mar 44 / 26 Jan 51	24 Apr 46 / 69	Turkey 15 Nov 69 (*Icel*)
796 *Benham* BethSI	3 Apr 43 / 30 Aug 43	20 Dec 43 / 24 Mar 51	18 Oct 46 / 15 Dec 60	Peru (*Villar*)
797 *Cushing* BethSI	3 May 43 / 30 Sep 43	17 Jan 44 / 17 Aug 51	3 Feb 47 / 8 Nov 60	Brazil 20 Jul 61 (*Parana*)
798 *Monssen* BethSI	1 Jun 43 / 30 Oct 43	14 Feb 44 / 31 Oct 51	30 Apr 46 / Sep 57	Grounded 6 Mar 62; str 1 Feb 63; sold 21 Oct 63, BU
799 *Jarvis* SeaTac	7 Jun 43 / 14 Feb 44	3 Jun 44 / 8 Feb 51	29 Jun 46 / 24 Oct 60	Spain 3 Nov 60 (*Alcala Galiano*)
800 *Porter* SeaTac	6 Jul 43 / 13 Mar 44	24 Jun 44 / 3 Jul 46	9 Feb 51 / 10 Aug 53	Str 1 Oct 72

		LD/Launch	Comm	Decomm	Fate
801	*Colhoun*	3 Aug 43	8 Jul 44	—	WD (K) 6 Apr 45; scuttled same day
	SeaTac	10 Apr 44	—		
802	*Gregory*	31 Aug 43	29 Jul 44	15 Jan 47	Str 1 May 66; non-operable training ship (named *Indoctrinator*) San Diego 66–71; tgt, but ran aground in storm 4 Mar 71; retained as experimental hulk
	SeaTac	8 May 44	27 Apr 51	1 Feb 64	
803	*Little*	13 Sep 43	19 Aug 44	—	WL (K) 3 May 45
	SeaTac	22 May 44	—	—	
804	*Rooks*	27 Oct 43	2 Sep 44	11 Jun 46	Chile 26 Jul 62 (*Cochrane*)
	SeaTac	6 Jun 44	19 May 51	26 Jul 62	

Sumner Class

		LD/Launch	Comm	Decomm	Fate
692	*Allen M. Sumner*	7 Jul 43	26 Jan 44	15 Aug 73	NRF 1971; str 15 Aug 73; memorial/sea school, Baltimore
	Fed	15 Dec 43			
693	*Moale*	5 Aug 43	28 Feb 44	2 Jul 73	NRF 1970; str 2 Jul 73
	Fed	16 Jan 44	—		
694	*Ingraham*	4 Aug 43	10 Mar 44		Greece 15 Jun 71 (*Miaoulis*)
	Fed	16 Jan 44			
695	*Cooper*	30 Aug 43	27 Mar 44	—	WL (T) 3 Dec 44
	Fed	9 Feb 44			
696	*English*	19 Oct 43	4 Jul 44		NRF post-Korea; str 15 May 70; Taiwan 11 Aug 70 (*Hui Yang*)
	Fed	27 Feb 44			
697	*Charles S. Sperry*	19 Oct 43	17 May 44		NRF 1969; str 15 Dec 73; Chile 8 Jan 74 (*Ministro Zenteno*)
	Fed	13 Mar 44			
698	*Ault*	15 Nov 43	31 May 44	31 May 50	NRF 1970; str 16 Jul 73; sold 30 Apr 74
	Fed	26 Mar 44	15 Nov 50	2 Jul 73	
699	*Waldron*	16 Nov 43	8 Jun 44	17 May 50	NRF 1970; Colombia (*Santander*)
	Fed	26 Mar 44	20 Nov 50	30 Oct 73	
700	*Haynsworth*	16 Dec 43	22 Jun 44	19 May 50	NRF post-Korea; str 30 Jan 70; Taiwan 12 May 70 (*Yuen Yang*)
	Fed	15 Apr 44	22 Sep 50		
701	*John W. Weeks*	17 Jan 44	21 Jul 44		NRF post-Korea; str 12 Aug 70; tgt 19 Nov 70
	Fed	21 May 44			
702	*Hank*	17 Jan 44	28 Aug 44		NRF 1963; str 1 Jul 72; Argentina (*Segui*)
	Fed	21 May 44			
703	*Wallace L. Lind*	14 Feb 44	9 Sep 44		NRF 1971; str 4 Dec 73; ROK (*Dae Gu*)
	Fed	14 Jun 44			
704	*Borie*	29 Feb 44	21 Sep 44		NRF 1969; str 1 Jul 72; Argentina (*Bouchard*)
	Fed	4 Jul 44			
705	*Compton*	29 Mar 44	4 Nov 44	27 Sep 72	NRF 1964; Brazil (*Matto Grosso*)
	Fed	17 Sep 44			
706	*Gainard*	28 Mar 44	23 Nov 44		NRF post-Korea; str 26 Feb 71; Iran 19 May 71 but repl by DD–780; sold 26 Mar 74, BU
	Fed	17 Sep 44			
707	*Soley*	18 Apr 44	8 Dec 44		Grounded Jan 70; str 13 Feb 70; tgt 18 Sep 70
	Fed	8 Sep 44			
708	*Harlan R. Dickson*	23 May 44	15 Feb 44		NRF 1968; str 1 Jul 72; sold 18 May 73
	Fed	17 Dec 44			
709	*Hugh Purvis*	23 May 44	1 Mar 45	15 Jun 72	Turkey (*Zafer*) 1 Jul 72
	Fed	17 Dec 44			
722	*Barton*	24 May 43	30 Dec 43	22 Jan 47	Str 1 Oct 68; tgt 8 Oct 69
	Bath	10 Oct 43	11 Apr 49		
723	*Walke*	7 Jun 43	21 Jan 44	30 May 47	Str 1 Feb 74; tgt
	Bath	27 Oct 43	5 Oct 50	30 Nov 70	
724	*Laffey*	28 Jun 43	8 Feb 44	30 Jun 47	Str 29 Mar 75
	Bath	21 Nov 43	26 Jan 51		
725	*O'Brien*	12 Jul 43	25 Jan 44	4 Oct 47	Str 18 Feb 72; tgt 13 Jul 72
	Bath	8 Dec 43	5 Oct 50		
726	*Meredith*	26 Jul 43	14 Mar 44	—	WL (M, B) 8/9 Jun 44
	Bath	21 Dec 43	—	—	
727	*De Haven*	9 Aug 43	31 Mar 44	71	NRF 1971; ROK 5 Dec 73 (*Inchon*)
	Bath	9 Jan 44			
728	*Mansfield*	28 Aug 43	14 Apr 44	4 Feb 71	Argentina 4 Jun 74 (spares)
	Bath	29 Jan 44			
729	*Lyman K. Swenson*	11 Sep 43	2 May 44	12 Feb 71	Taiwan 6 May 74 (spares)
	Bath	12 Feb 44			
730	*Collett*	11 Oct 43	16 May 44	18 Dec 70	Argentina 4 Jun 74 (spares)
	Bath	5 Mar 44			
731	*Maddox*	28 Oct 43	2 Jun 44		NRF 1969; Taiwan 6 Jul 72 (*Po Yang*)
	Bath	19 Mar 44			
732	*Hyman*	22 Nov 43	16 Jun 44		NRF post-Korea; str 14 Nov 69; sold 13 Oct 70
	Bath	8 Apr 44			

		LD/Launch	Comm	Decomm	Fate
733	Mannert L. Abele Bath	12 Sep 43 23 Apr 44	7 Apr 44		WL(K) 12 Apr 45
734	Purdy Bath	22 Dec 43 7 May 44	18 Jul 4		NRF 1966; str 2 Jul 73; BU
735	Robert H. Smith Bath	10 Jan 44 25 May 44	4 Aug 44 —	May 47	Str 26 Feb 71 (DM–23)
736	Thomas E. Fraser Bath	31 Jan 43 10 Jun 44	23 Aug 44 —	30 Jun 55	Str 1 Nov 70 (DM–24)
737	Shannon Bath	14 Feb 44 24 Jun 44	8 Sep 44 —	30 Jun 55	Str 1 Nov 70 (DM–25)
738	Harry F. Bauer Bath	6 Mar 44 9 Jul 44	22 Sep 44	12 Mar 56	Str 15 Aug 71 (DM–26)
739	Adams Bath	20 Mar 44 23 Jul 44	10 Aug 44	29 Jan 47	Str 1 Dec 70 (DM–27)
740	Tolman Bath	10 Apr 44 13 Aug 44	27 Oct 44	29 Jan 47	Str 1 Dec 70 (DM–28)
741	Drexler BethSI	24 Apr 44 3 Sep 44	31 Aug 44		WL (K) 27 May 45
744	Blue BethSI	30 Jun 43 28 Nov 43	20 Mar 44 14 May 49	14 Feb 47 27 Jan 71	Str 1 Feb 74; tgt
745	Brush BethSI	30 Jul 43 28 Dec 43	17 Apr 44		Taiwan 9 Dec 69 (Hsiang Yang)
746	Taussig BethSI	30 Aug 43 25 Jan 44	20 May 44	1 Dec 70	Taiwan 6 May 74 (spares)
747	Samuel N. Moore BethSI	30 Sep 43 23 Feb 44	24 Jun 44		NRF; Taiwan 9 Jun 69 (Heng Yang)
748	Harry E. Hubbard BethSI	30 Oct 43 24 Mar 44	22 Jul 44		Str 17 Oct 69; sold Jul 70
749	Henry A. Wiley BethSI	28 Nov 43 21 Apr 44	31 Aug 44	29 Jan 47	Str 15 Oct 70 (DM–29)
750	Shea BethSI	28 Dec 43 20 May 44	30 Sep 44	9 Apr 58	Str 1 Sep 73; last DM (DM–30)
751	J. William Ditter BethSI	25 Jan 44 4 Jul 44	28 Oct 44	28 Sep 45	Str 11 Oct 45; WD (K) 6 Jun 45 (DM–31)
752	Alfred A. Cunningham BethSI	23 Feb 44 3 Aug 44	23 Nov 44 5 Oct 50	12 May 47 24 Feb 71	Str 1 Feb 74; tgt
753	John R. Pierce BethSI	24 Mar 44 1 Sep 44	30 Dec 44		NRF 1965; str 2 Jul 73; BU
754	Frank E. Evans BethSI	21 Apr 44 3 Oct 44	3 Feb 45 15 Sep 50	14 Dec 49	Coll 30 Jun 69 (HMAS Melbourne); stern salvaged; tgt 10 Oct 69
755	John A. Bole BethSI	20 May 44 1 Nov 44	3 Mar 45	6 Nov 70	Taiwan 6 May 74 (spares)
756	Beatty BethSI	4 Jun 44 30 Nov 44	31 Mar 45		NRF 1968; Venezuela 14 Jul 72 (Carabobo)
757	Putnam BethSF	11 Jul 43 26 Mar 44	12 Oct 44 Oct 50	1949	NRF 1969; str 6 Aug 73; BU
758	Strong BethSF	25 Jul 43 23 Apr 44	8 Mar 45		Brazil 31 Oct 73 (Rio Grande de Norte)
759	Lofberg BethSF	11 Apr 43 12 Aug 44	26 Apr 45	15 Jan 71	Taiwan 6 May 74 (spares)
760	John W. Thomason BethSF	21 Nov 43 30 Sep 44	11 Oct 45	8 Dec 70	Taiwan 6 May 74 (spares)
761	Buck BethSF	1 Feb 44 11 Mar 45	28 Jun 46		NRF 1971; Brazil 16 Jul 73 (Alagoas)
762	Henley BethSF	8 Feb 44 8 Apr 45	8 Oct 46 23 Sep 50	15 Mar 50	NRF 1964; str 2 Jul 73; BU; last active non-FRAM destroyer
770	Lowry BethSP	1 Aug 43 6 Feb 44	23 Jul 44 27 Dec 50	30 Jun 47	NRF 1969; Brazil 31 Oct 73 (Espiritu Santo)
771	Lindsey BethSP	12 Sep 43 5 Mar 44	20 Aug 44	25 May 46	Str 1 Oct 70 (DM–32)
772	Gwin BethSP	31 Oct 43 9 Apr 44	30 Sep 44	3 Apr 58	(DM–33); to Turkey 22 Oct 71 (Muavenet)
773	Aaron Ward BethSP	12 Dec 43 5 May 44	28 Oct 44	28 Sep 45	WD (K) 3 May 45; str 11 Oct 45 (DM–34)
774	Hugh W. Hadley BethSP	6 Feb 44 16 Jul 44	25 Nov 44	—	WD (K) 11 May 45; str 8 Jan 46; sold 2 Sep 47
775	Willard Keith BethSP	5 Mar 44 29 Aug 44	27 Dec 44 23 Oct 50	47	NRF 1963; Colombia 1 Jul 72 (Caldas)
776	James C. Owens BethSP	4 Sep 44 1 Oct 44	17 Feb 43 20 Sep 50	3 Apr 50 16 Jul 73	NRF 1971; Brazil 16 Jul 73 (Sergipe)
777	Zellars Todd	24 Dec 43 19 Jul 44	25 Oct 44	19 Mar 71	NRF; Iran 19 Mar 71 (Babr)

	LD/Launch	Comm	Decomm	Fate
778 *Massey*	14 Jan 44	24 Nov 44	69	NRF 1969; str 17 Sep 72; BU
Todd	19 Aug 44			
779 *Douglas H. Fox*	31 Jan 44	26 Dec 44	21 Apr 50	NRF 1969; Chile 8 Jan 74 (*Ministro Portales*)
Todd	30 Sep 44	15 Nov 50	15 Dec 73	
780 *Stormes*	25 Jul 43	27 Jan 45	Sep 50	Iran 16 Feb 72 (*Palang*)
Todd	4 Nov 44	Aug 50	5 Dec 70	
781 *Robert K. Huntington*	29 Feb 44	3 Mar 45	21 Oct 73	NRF 1971; Venezuela 31 Oct 73 (*Falcon*)
Todd	5 Dec 44			
857 *Bristol*	5 May 44	17 Mar 45		Taiwan 2 Dec 69 (*Hwa Yang*)
BethSP	29 Oct 44			

Gearing Class

	LD/Launch	Comm	Decomm	Fate
710 *Gearing*	10 Aug 44	3 May 45		NRF 1970; FRAM I; str 2 Jul 73
Fed	18 Feb 45			
711 *Eugene A. Greene*	17 Aug 44	8 Jun 45		DDR 1952; FRAM I; 31 Aug 72 to Spain (*Churruca*)
Fed	18 Mar 45			
712 *Gyatt*	7 Sep 44	2 Jul 45		DDG 1956; no FRAM; NRF; str 22 Oct 69; tgt 11 Jun 70
Fed	15 Apr 45			
713 *Kenneth D. Bailey*	21 Sep 44	31 Jul 45		DDR 1953; FRAM II; 1 Feb 74 to Iran (spares)
Fed	17 Jun 45			
714 *William R. Rush*	19 Oct 44	21 Sep 45		DDR 1953; FRAM I; str 1 Jul 74; Korea (*Kang Won*)
Fed	8 Jul 45			
715 *William W. Wood*	22 Nov 44	24 Nov 45		DDR 1953; FRAM I; str 1 Dec 76
Fed	29 Jul 45			
716 *Wiltsie*	13 Mar 45	12 Jan 46		FRAM I; 23 Jan 76 to Pakistan (*Tariq*)
Fed	31 Aug 45			
717 *Theodore E. Chandler*	23 Apr 45	22 Mar 46		FRAM I; str 1 Apr 75
Fed	20 Oct 45			
718 *Hamner*	25 Apr 45	12 Jul 46		FRAM I
Fed	24 Nov 45			
719 *Epperson*	20 Jun 45	19 Mar 49		DDE; FRAM I; str 1 Dec 75; Pakistan (*Taimur*)
Fed	22 Dec 45			
720 *Castle*	11 Jul 45			Canc 11 Dec 45 (60.3%); sold 29 Aug 55
Fed				
721 *Woodrow R. Thompson*	1 Aug 45			Canc 11 Dec 45 (53.3%); sold 29 Aug 55
Fed				
742 *Frank Knox*	8 May 44	11 Dec 44		DDR 1945; FRAM II; 23 Jan 71 Greece
Bath	17 Sep 44			
743 *Southerland*	27 May 44	22 Dec 44		DDR 1945; FRAM I
Bath	5 Oct 44			
763 *William C. Lawe*	12 Mar 44	18 Dec 46		FRAM I
BethSF	21 May 45			
764 *Lloyd Thomas*	26 Mar 44	21 Mar 47		DDE 1949; FRAM II; 12 Oct 72 to Taiwan (*Dang Yang*)
BethSF	5 Oct 45			
765 *Keppler*	23 Apr 44	23 May 47		DDE 1949; FRAM II; 1 Jul 72 to Turkey (*Tinaztepe*)
BethSF	24 Jun 46			
766 *Lansdale*	2 Apr 44			Canc 7 Jan 46; bow rem to repair DD–884, May 56
BethSF	20 Dec 46			
767 *Seymour D. Owens*	3 Apr 44			Canc 7 Jan 46; bow rem to repair DD–838, Nov 51
BethSF	24 Feb 47			
768 *Hoel*	21 Apr 44			Canc 13 Sep 46; BU on slip
BethSF				
769 *Abner Read*	21 May 44			Canc 13 Sep 46; BU on slip
BethSF				
782 *Rowan*	25 Mar 44	31 Mar 45		FRAM I; 18 Dec 75 to Pakistan
Todd	29 Dec 44			
783 *Gurke*	1 Jul 44	12 May 45		FRAM I; str 20 Jan 76
Todd	15 Feb 45			
784 *McKean*	15 Sep 44	9 Jun 45		FRAM I
Todd	31 Mar 45			
785 *Henderson*	27 Oct 44	4 Aug 45		FRAM I; str 1 Oct 80
Todd				
786 *Richard B. Anderson*	1 Dec 44	26 Oct 45		FRAM I; str 20 Dec 75; Taiwan (*Kai Yang*)
Todd	7 Jul 45			
787 *James E. Kyes*	27 Dec 44	8 Feb 46		FRAM I; 31 Mar 73 to Taiwan (*Chien Yang*)
Todd	4 Aug 45			
788 *Hollister*	18 Jan 45	26 Mar 46		FRAM I; str 31 Aug 79; tgt
Todd	9 Oct 45			
789 *Eversole*	21 Mar 45	10 Jul 46		FRAM I; 11 Jul 73 to Turkey (*Gayret*)
Todd	8 Jan 46			
790 *Shelton*	31 May 45	21 Jun 46		FRAM I; 31 Mar 73 to Taiwan (*Lao Yang*)
Todd	8 Mar 46			

		LD/Launch	Comm	Decomm	Fate
791	Seaman / Todd	10 Jul 45 / 20 May 46			Canc 7 Jan 46; hulk sold 12 Sep 61
805	Chevalier / Bath	12 Jun 44 / 29 Oct 44	9 Jan 45		DDR 1945; FRAM II; 2 Jun 75 to Korea (Chung Buk)
806	Higbee / Bath	26 Jun 44 / 12 Nov 44	27 Jan 45		DDR 1945; FRAM I; str 15 Jul 79
807	Benner / Bath	10 Jul 44 / 20 Nov 44	13 Feb 45		DDR 1945; FRAM II; str 1 Feb 74; tgt
808	Dennis J. Buckley / Bath	24 Jul 44 / 20 Dec 44	2 Mar 45		FRAM I: str 2 Jul 73
817	Corry / Orange	5 Apr 45 / 28 Jul 45	27 Feb 46		DDR 1954; FRAM I; str 1 Oct 80
818	New / Orange	14 Apr 45 / 18 Aug 45	5 Apr 46		FRAM I; 1 Jul 76 to Korea (Taejon)
819	Holder / Orange	23 Apr 45 / 25 Aug 45	18 May 46		FRAM I; str 1 Oct 76
820	Rich / Orange	16 May 45 / 5 Oct 45	3 Jul 46		FRAM I; str 15 Dec 77
821	Johnston / Orange	5 Jun 45 /	23 Aug 46		FRAM I; str 1 Oct 80
822	Robert H. McCard / Orange	20 Jun 45 / 9 Nov 45	26 Oct 46		FRAM I; str 1 Oct 80
823	Samuel B. Roberts / Orange	27 Jun 45 / 30 Nov 45	20 Dec 46		FRAM I; str 2 Nov 70; tgt 14 Nov 71
824	Basilone / Orange	7 Jul 45 / 21 Dec 45	26 Jul 49		DDE; FRAM I; str 1 Nov 77
825	Carpenter / Orange	30 Jul 45 / 30 Dec 45	15 Dec 49		DDE; FRAM I; str 1 Oct 80
826	Agerholm / Bath	10 Sep 45 / 30 Mar 46	20 Jun 46		FRAM I; str 1 Dec 78; tgt
827	Robert A. Owens / Bath	29 Oct 45 / 15 Jul 46	5 Nov 49		DDE; FRAM I;
828	Timmerman / Bath	1 Oct 45 / 15 May 51	26 Sep 52		Machinery test ship, later AG–152 (Jan 54); str 4 Apr 58
829	Myles C. Fox / Bath	14 Aug 44 / 13 Jan 45	20 Mar 45		DDR 1945; FRAM I
830	Everett F. Larson / Bath	4 Sep 44 / 28 Jan 45	6 Apr 45		DDR 1945; FRAM II; 2 Jun 75 to Korea (Jeong Buk)
831	Goodrich / Bath	18 Sep 44 / 25 Feb 45	24 Apr 45		DDR 1945; FRAM II; str 1 Feb 74; Turkey (spares)
832	Hanson / Bath	7 Oct 44 / 11 Mar 45	11 May 45		DDR 1945; FRAM I; 31 Mar 73 to Taiwan (Liao Yang)
833	Herbert J. Thomas / Bath	30 Oct 44 / 25 Mar 45	29 May 45		DDR 1945; FRAM I; 1 Feb 74 to Taiwan (spares, commissioned as Han Yang)
834	Turner / Bath	13 Nov 44 / 8 Apr 45	12 Jun 45		DDR 1945; FRAM II; str 26 Sep 69
835	Charles P. Cecil / Bath	2 Dec 44 / 22 Apr 45	29 Jun 45		DDR 1945; FRAM I
836	George K. MacKenzie / Bath	21 Dec 44 / 13 May 45	13 Jul 45		FRAM I; str 1 Oct 76; tgt
837	Sarsfield / Bath	15 Jan 45 / 27 May 45	31 Jul 45		FRAM I; 1 Oct 76 to Taiwan (Te Yang)
838	Ernest G. Small / Bath	30 Jan 45 / 9 Jun 45	21 Aug 45		DDR 1952; FRAM II; Taiwan 13 Apr 71 (Fu Yang)
839	Power / Bath	26 Feb 45 / 30 Jun 45	13 Sep 45		FRAM I; 1 Oct 76 to Taiwan (Shen Yang)
840	Glennon / Bath	12 Mar 45 / 14 Jul 45	4 Oct 45		FRAM I; str 1 Oct 76
841	Noa / Bath	26 Mar 45 / 30 Jul 45	2 Nov 45		FRAM I; 2 Jun 75 to Spain (Blas de Lezo)
842	Fiske / Bath	9 Apr 45 / 8 Sep 45	28 Nov 45		DDR 1952; FRAM I; str 1 Oct 80
843	Warrington / Bath	23 Apr 45 / 27 Sep 45	20 Dec 45		FRAM I; str 17 Jul 72; WD(M) 17 Jul 72; Taiwan (spares), bow for ex-DD–857
844	Perry / Bath	14 May 45 / 25 Nov 45	17 Jan 46		FRAM I; str 2 Jul 73 (first FRAM I)
845	Baussell / Bath	28 May 45 / 19 Nov 45	7 Feb 46		FRAM I; str 30 May 78
846	Ozbourn / Bath	16 Jun 45 / 22 Dec 45	5 Mar 46		FRAM I; str 1 Jun 75

		LD/Launch	Comm	Decomm	Fate
847	*Robert L. Wilson* Bath	2 Jul 45 5 Jan 46	25 Apr 46		FRAM I; str 30 Sep 74
848	*Witek* Bath	16 Jul 45 2 Feb 46	25 Apr 46		No FRAM; str 17 Sep 68; tgt 4 Jun 69
849	*Richard E. Kraus* Bath	31 Jul 45 2 Mar 46	23 May 46		FRAM I; 1 Jul 76 to Korea (*Kwang Ju*)
850	*Joseph P. Kennedy, Jr.* BethQ	2 Apr 45 26 Jul 45	15 Dec 45		FRAM I; str 2 Jul 73; memorial
851	*Rupertus* BethQ	2 May 45 21 Sep 45	8 Mar 46		FRAM I; 10 Jul 73 to Greece (*Kontouriotis*)
852	*Leonard F. Mason* BethQ	6 Aug 45 4 Jan 46	28 Jun 46		FRAM I; str 2 Nov 76; Taiwan (*Lai Yang*)
853	*Charles H. Roan* BethQ	27 Sep 45 15 Mar 46	2 Sep 46		FRAM I; 21 Sep 73 to Turkey (*Cakmak*)
858	*Fred T. Berry* BethSP	16 Jul 44 28 Jan 45	12 May 45		DDE 1949; FRAM II; str 15 Sep 70, scuttled after tests, 4 May 72
859	*Norris* BethSP	29 Aug 44 25 Feb 45	9 Jun 45		DDE 1949; FRAM II; 1 Feb 74 to Turkey (spares, commissioned as *Kocatepe* to repl DD–861)
860	*McCaffery* BethSP	1 Oct 44	26 Jul 45		DDE 1949; FRAM II; str 30 Sep 73
861	*Harwood* BethSP	29 Oct 44 24 May 45	28 Sep 45		NRF 1971; DDE 1949; FRAM II; 1 Feb 73 to Turkey (*Kocatepe*); WL (Turkish aircraft, in error) 7 Jul 74
862	*Vogelgesang* BethSI	3 Aug 44 15 Jan 45	28 Apr 45		FRAM I
863	*Steinaker* BethSI	1 Sep 44 13 Feb 45	26 May 45		DDR 1953; FRAM I
864	*Harold J. Ellison* BethSI	3 Oct 44 14 Mar 45	23 Jun 45		FRAM I
865	*Charles R. Ware* BethSI	1 Nov 44 12 Apr 45	21 Jul 45		FRAM I; str 2 Dec 74
866	*Cone* BethSI	30 Nov 44 10 May 45	18 Aug 45		FRAM I
867	*Stribling* BethSI	15 Jan 45 8 Jun 45	29 Sep 45		FRAM I; str 1 Jul 76
868	*Brownson* BethSI	13 Feb 45 7 Jul 45	17 Nov 45		FRAM I; str 30 Sep 76
869	*Arnold J. Isbell* BethSI	14 Mar 45 6 Aug 45	5 Apr 46		FRAM I; 12 Mar 73 to Greece (*Sachtouris*)
870	*Fechteler* BethSI	12 Apr 45 19 Sep 45	2 Mar 46		DDR 1953; str 11 Sep 70; BU
871	*Damato* BethSI	10 May 45 21 Nov 45	27 Apr 46		FRAM I; str 1 Oct 80
872	*Forrest Royal* BethSI	8 Jun 45 17 Jan 46	29 Jun 46		FRAM I; 1 Feb 73 to Turkey (*Adatepe*)
873	*Hawkins* Orange	14 May 44 7 Oct 44	10 Feb 45		DDR 1945; FRAM I; str 1 Oct 79
874	*Duncan* Orange	22 May 44 27 Oct 44	25 Feb 45		DDR 1945; FRAM II; str 1 Sep 73; tgt, replaced ex-DD–652 at Pt. Mugu
875	*Henry W. Tucker* Orange	29 May 44 8 Nov 44	12 Mar 45		DDR 1945; FRAM I; 3 Dec 73 to Brazil (*Marcilio Dias*)
876	*Rogers* Orange	3 Jun 44 20 Nov 44	26 Mar 45		DDR 1945; FRAM I; str 1 Oct 80
877	*Perkins* Orange	19 Jun 44 7 Dec 44	4 Apr 45		NRF 1971; DDR 1945; FRAM II; 15 Jan 73 to Argentina (PY)
878	*Vesole* Orange	3 Jul 44 29 Dec 44	23 Apr 45		DDR 1945; FRAM I; str 1 Dec 76
879	*Leary* Orange	11 Aug 44 20 Jan 45	7 May 45		DDR 1945; FRAM I; 2 Jun 75 to Spain (*Langara*)
880	*Dyess* Orange	17 Aug 44 26 Jan 45	21 May 45		NRF 1971; DDR 1945; FRAM I; str 1 Oct 80
881	*Bordelon* Orange	9 Sep 44 3 Mar 45	5 Jun 45		DDR 1945; FRAM I; str 1 Feb 77; Iran (spares)
882	*Furse* Orange	23 Sep 44 9 Mar 45	10 Jul 45		DDR 1945; FRAM I; 2 Jun 72 to Spain (*Gravina*)
883	*Newman K. Perry* Orange	10 Oct 44 17 Mar 45	26 Jul 45		DDR 1945; FRAM I; str 1 Oct 80
884	*Floyd B. Parks* Orange	30 Oct 44 31 Mar 45	31 Aug 45		FRAM I; str 2 Jul 73

	LD/Launch	Comm	Decomm	Fate
885 *John R. Craig* Orange	17 Nov 44 14 Apr 45	20 Aug 45		FRAM I; str 27 Jul 79; tgt
886 *Orleck* Orange	28 Nov 44 12 May 45	15 Sep 45		FRAM I
887 *Brinkley Bass* Orange	20 Dec 44 26 May 45	1 Oct 45		FRAM I; 3 Dec 73 to Brazil (*Mariz E. Barros*)
888 *Stickell* Orange	5 Jan 45 16 Jun 45	31 Oct 45		DDR 1953; FRAM I; 1 Jul 72 to Greece (*Kanaris*)
889 *O'Hare* Orange	27 Jan 45 22 Jun 45	29 Nov 45		DDR 1953; FRAM I; 2 Jun 75 to Spain (*Mendez Nunez*)
890 *Meredith* Orange	27 Jan 45 28 Jun 45	31 Dec 45		FRAM I; str 29 Jun 79; Turkey (spares)

Forest Sherman Class

	LD/Launch	Comm	Decomm	Fate
931 *Forrest Sherman* Bath	27 Oct 53 5 Feb 55	9 Nov 55		
932 *John Paul Jones* Bath	18 Jan 54 7 May 55	5 Apr 56		DDG Sep 67 (DDG–32)
933 *Barry* Bath	15 Mar 54 1 Oct 55	31 Aug 56		
936 *Decatur* BethQ	13 Sep 54 15 Dec 55	7 Dec 56		DDG Apr 67 (DDG–31)
937 *Davis* BethQ	1 Feb 55 28 Mar 56	28 Feb 57		
938 *Jonas Ingram* BethQ	15 Jun 55 8 Jul 56	19 Jul 57		
940 *Manley* Bath	10 Feb 55 12 Apr 56	1 Feb 57		
941 *Du Pont* Bath	11 May 55 8 Sep 56	1 Jul 57		
942 *Bigelow* Bath	6 Jul 55 2 Feb 57	8 Nov 57		
943 *Blandy* BethQ	29 Dec 55 19 Dec 56	26 Nov 57		
944 *Mullinnix* BethQ	5 Apr 56 18 Mar 57	7 Mar 58		
945 *Hull* Bath	12 Sep 56 10 Aug 57	3 Jul 58		
946 *Edson* Bath	3 Dec 56 1 Jan 58	7 Nov 58		NRF Apr 77
947 *Somers* Bath	4 Mar 57 30 May 58	3 Apr 59		DDG Feb 68 (DDG–34)
948 *Morton* Ing	4 Mar 57 23 May 58	26 May 59		
949 *Parsons* Ing	17 Jun 57 19 Aug 58	29 Oct 59		DDG Nov 67 (DDG–33)
950 *Richard S. Edwards* PS	20 Dec 56 24 Sep 57	5 Feb 59		
951 *Turner Joy* PS	30 Sep 57 5 May 58	3 Aug 59		

Charles F. Adams Class

	LD/Launch	Comm	Decomm	Fate
2 *Charles F. Adams* Bath	16 Jun 58 8 Sep 59	10 Sep 60		Originally DDG 952
3 *John King* Bath	25 Aug 58 30 Jan 60	4 Feb 61		
4 *Lawrence* NYSB	27 Oct 58 27 Feb 60	6 Jan 62		
5 *Claude V. Ricketts* NYSB	18 May 59 4 Jun 60	5 May 62		
6 *Barney* NYSB	18 May 59 10 Dec 60	11 Aug 62		
7 *Henry B. Wilson* Defoe	28 Feb 58 23 Apr 59	17 Dec 60		
8 *Lynde McCormick* Defoe	4 Apr 58 9 Sep 60	3 Jun 61		
9 *Towers* Todd	1 Apr 58 23 Apr 59	6 Jun 61		
10 *Sampson* Bath	2 Mar 59 9 Sep 60	24 Jun 61		

Note: DD–935 was ex-German T–35, acquired 1945, trans to France 1947 (spares); DD–934 was ex-Japanese *Hanazuki*.
DD–939 was ex-German Z–39, acquired 1945, trans to France 1948 (spares); became floating pier.
DD–960, –961 were built in Japan with U.S. MDAP funds (*Akizuki, Teruzuki*); DD–962 was HMS *Charity* bought for Pakistan as *Shah Jehan* (trans 16 Dec 58).

		LD/Launch	Comm	Decomm	Fate
11	*Sellers*	3 Aug 59	28 Oct 61		
	Bath	9 Sep 60			
12	*Robison*	23 Apr 59	9 Dec 61		
	Defoe	27 Apr 60			
13	*Hoel*	1 Jun 58	16 Jun 62		
	Defoe	4 Aug 60			
14	*Buchanan*	23 Apr 59	7 Feb 62		
	Todd	11 May 60			
15	*Berkeley*	1 Jun 60	15 Dec 62		
	NYSB	29 Jul 61			
16	*Joseph Strauss*	27 Dec 60	20 Apr 63		
	NYSB	9 Dec 61			
17	*Conyngham*	1 May 61	13 Jul 63		
	NYSB	19 May 62			
18	*Semmes*	18 Aug 60	10 Dec 62		
	Avon	20 May 61			
19	*Tattnall*	14 Nov 60	13 Apr 63		
	Avon	26 Aug 61			
20	*Goldsborough*	3 Jan 61	9 Nov 63		
	PS	15 Dec 61			
21	*Cochrane*	31 Jul 61	21 Mar 64		
	PS	18 Jul 62			
22	*Benjamin Stoddert*	11 Jun 62	12 Sep 64		
	PS	8 Jan 63			
23	*Richard E. Byrd*	12 Apr 61	7 Mar 64		
	Todd	6 Feb 62			
24	*Waddell*	6 Feb 62	28 Aug 64		
	Todd	26 Feb 63			

Spruance Class

		LD/Launch	Comm	Decomm	Fate
963	*Spruance*	17 Nov 72	20 Sep 75		
	Ing	10 Nov 73			
964	*Paul F. Foster*	6 Feb 73	21 Feb 76		
	Ing	23 Feb 74			
965	*Kinkaid*	19 Apr 73	10 Jul 76		
	Ing	25 May 74			
966	*Hewitt*	23 Jul 73	25 Sep 76		
	Ing	24 Aug 74			
967	*Elliott*	15 Oct 73	22 Jan 76		
	Ing	19 Dec 74			
968	*Arthur W. Radford*	14 Jan 74	16 Apr 77		
	Ing	1 Mar 75			
969	*Peterson*	29 Apr 74	9 Jul 77		
	Ing	21 Jun 75			
970	*Caron*	1 Jul 74	1 Oct 77		
	Ing	24 Jun 75			
971	*David R. Ray*	23 Sep 74	19 Nov 77		
	Ing	23 Aug 75			
972	*Oldendorf*	27 Dec 74	4 Mar 78		
	Ing	21 Oct 75			
973	*John Young*	17 Feb 75	20 May 78		
	Ing	7 Feb 76			
974	*Comte de Grasse*	4 Apr 75	5 Aug 78		
	Ing	26 Mar 76			
975	*O'Brien*	9 May 75	3 Dec 77		
	Ing	8 Jul 76			
976	*Merrill*	16 Jun 75	11 Mar 78		
	Ing	1 Sep 76			
977	*Briscoe*	21 Jul 75	3 Jun 78		
	Ing	15 Dec 76			
978	*Stump*	25 Aug 75	19 Aug 78		
	Ing	29 Jan 77			
979	*Conolly*	29 Sep 75	14 Oct 78		
	Ing	19 Feb 77			
980	*Moosbrugger*	3 Nov 75	16 Dec 78		
	Ing	23 Jul 77			
981	*John Hancock*	16 Jan 76	1 Mar 79		
	Ing	29 Oct 77			

Note: DDG 26, DDG 27 were built for Australia. DDG 28–30 were built for West Germany. DDG 31–36 were conversions of existing DD and DL hulls. DDG 37–46 are former DLG 6–15.

		LD/Launch	Comm	Decomm	Fate
982	Nicholson	20 Feb 76	12 May 79		
	Ing	11 Nov 77			
983	John Rodgers	12 Aug 76	14 Jul 79		
	Ing	25 Feb 78			
984	Leftwich	12 Nov 76	25 Aug 79		
	Ing	8 Apr 78			
985	Cushing	27 Dec 76	21 Sep 79		
	Ing	17 Jun 78			
986	Harry W. Hill	3 Jan 77	11 Nov 79		
	Ing	10 Aug 78			
987	O'Bannon	21 Feb 77	15 Dec 79		
	Ing	25 Sep 78			
988	Thorn	29 Aug 77	16 Feb 80		
	Ing	14 Nov 78			
989	Deyo	14 Oct 77	22 Mar 80		
	Ing	27 Jan 79			
990	Ingersoll	5 Dec 77	12 Apr 80		
	Ing	10 Mar 79			
991	Fife	6 Mar 78	31 May 80		
	Ing	1 May 79			
992	Fletcher	24 Apr 78	12 Jul 80		
	Ing	16 Jun 79			
993	Kidd	26 Jun 78	27 Jun 81		
	Ing	11 Aug 79			
994	Callaghan	23 Oct 78	6 Jul 81		
	Ing	1 Dec 79			
995	Scott	12 Feb 79	8 Sep 81		
	Ing	1 Mar 80			
996	Chandler	7 May 79	20 Mar 82		
	Ing	24 May 80			
997	Hayler	27 Mar 82			
	Ing				

DL/DLG/CG

DL

1	Norfolk	1 Sep 49	4 Mar 53	15 Jan 70	Str 1 Nov 73; BU
	NYSB	29 Dec 51			
2	Mitscher	3 Oct 49	15 May 53	1 Jun 78	Originally DD–927; DDG–35 Jun 68; str 1 Jun 78
	Bath	26 Jan 52			
3	John S. McCain	24 Oct 49	12 Oct 53	29 Apr 78	Originally DD–928; DDG–36 Sep 69; str 29 Apr 78
	Bath	12 Jul 52			
4	Willis A. Lee	1 Nov 49	28 Sep 54	Dec 69	Originally DD–929; str 15 May 72; BU
	BethQ	26 Jan 52			
5	Wilkinson	1 Feb 50	29 Jul 54	19 Dec 69	Originally DD–930; str 1 May 74; BU
	BethQ	23 Apr 52			

DLG

6	Farragut	3 Jun 57	10 Dec 60		
	BethQ	18 Jul 58			
7	Luce	1 Oct 57	20 May 61		
	BethQ	11 Dec 58			
8	Macdonough	15 Apr 58	4 Nov 61		
	BethQ	9 Jul 59			
9	Coontz	1 Mar 57	15 Jul 60		
	PSNY	6 Dec 58			
10	King	1 Mar 57	17 Nov 60		
	PSNY	6 Dec 58			
11	Mahan	31 Jul 57	25 Aug 60		
	MINY	7 Oct 59			
12	Dahlgren	1 Mar 58	8 Apr 61		
	PHNY	16 Mar 60			
13	William V. Pratt	1 Mar 58	4 Nov 61		
	PHNY	16 Mar 60			
14	Dewey	10 Aug 57	7 Dec 59		
	Bath	30 Nov 58			
15	Preble	16 Dec 57	9 May 60		
	Bath	23 May 59			

CG

16	Leahy	3 Dec 59	4 Aug 62		
	Bath	1 Jul 61			
17	Harry E. Yarnell	31 May 60	2 Feb 63		
	Bath	9 Dec 61			

		LD/Launch	Comm	Decomm	Fate
18	*Worden*	19 Sep 60	3 Aug 63		
	Bath	2 Jun 62			
19	*Dale*	6 Sep 60	23 Nov 63		
	NYSB	28 Jul 62			
20	*Richmond K. Turner*	9 Jan 61	13 Jun 64		
	NYSB	6 Apr 63			
21	*Gridley*	15 Jul 60	25 May 63		
	PS	31 Jul 61			
22	*England*	4 Oct 60	7 Dec 63		
	Todd	6 Mar 62			
23	*Halsey*	26 Aug 60	20 Jul 63		
	MINY	15 Jan 62			
24	*Reeves*	1 Jul 60	15 May 64		
	PSNY	12 May 62			
25	*Bainbridge*	15 May 59	6 Oct 62		
	BethQ	15 Apr 61			
26	*Belknap*	5 Feb 62	7 Nov 64		
	Bath	20 Jul 63			
27	*Josephus Daniels*	23 Apr 62	8 May 65		
	Bath	2 Dec 63			
28	*Wainwright*	2 Jul 62	8 Jan 66		
	Bath	25 Apr 64			
29	*Jouett*	25 Sep 62	3 Dec 66		
	PSNY	30 Jun 64			
30	*Horne*	12 Dec 62	15 Apr 67		
	MINY	30 Oct 64			
31	*Sterett*	25 Sep 62	8 Apr 67		
	PSNY	30 Jun 64			
32	*William H. Standley*	29 Jul 63	9 Jul 66		
	Bath	19 Dec 64			
33	*Fox*	15 Jan 63	28 May 66		
	Todd	21 Nov 64			
34	*Biddle*	9 Dec 63	21 Jan 67		
	Bath	2 Jul 65			
35	*Truxtun*	17 Jun 63	27 May 67		
	NYSB	19 Dec 64			
36	*California*	23 Jan 70	16 Feb 74		
	NN	22 Sep 71			
37	*South Carolina*	1 Dec 70	25 Jan 75		
	NN	1 Jul 72			
38	*Virginia*	19 Aug 72	11 Sep 76		
	NN	14 Dec 74			
39	*Texas*	18 Aug 73	10 Sep 77		
	NN	9 Aug 75			
40	*Mississippi*	22 Feb 75	5 Aug 78		
	NN	31 Jul 76			
41	*Arkansas*	17 Jan 77	18 Oct 80		
	NN	21 Oct 78			
47	*Ticonderoga*	21 Jan 80			
	Ing	16 May 81			
48	———	Dec 81			
	Ing				

DEs

		LD/Launch	Comm	Decomm	Fate
1	*Bayntun*	5 Apr 42	20 Jan 43		RN; ret 22 Aug 45; sold 22 Feb 47
	BosNY	27 Jun 42			
2	*Bazely*	5 Apr 42	18 Feb 43	20 Aug 45	RN; ret 20 Aug 45; BU May 46
	BosNY	27 Jun 42			
3	*Berry*	22 Sep 42	15 Mar 43		RN; ret 15 Feb 46
	BosNY	23 Nov 42			
4	*Blackwood*	22 Sep 42	27 Mar 43		RN; WL(T) 15 Jun 44
	BosNY	23 Nov 42			
5	*Evarts*	17 Oct 42	15 Apr 43	2 Oct 45	Sold 12 Jul 46
	BosNY	7 Dec 42			
6	*Wyffels*	17 Oct 42	21 Apr 43	25 Sep 45	China (*Tai Kang*); BU 72
	BosNY	7 Dec 42			
7	*Griswold*	27 Nov 42	28 Apr 43	19 Nov 45	Str 5 Dec 45; sold 27 Nov 46
	BosNY	28 Apr 42			
8	*Steele*	27 Nov 42	4 May 43	28 Nov 45	Sold 2 Dec 46
	BosNY	9 Jan 43			
9	*Carlson*	27 Nov 42	10 May 43	10 Dec 45	Sold 17 Oct 46
	BosNY	9 Jan 43			

		LD/Launch	Comm	Decomm	Fate
10	*Bebas* BosNY	27 Nov 42 9 Jan 43	15 May 43	18 Oct 45	Sold 8 Jan 47
11	*Crouter* BosNY	8 Dec 42 26 Jan 43	25 May 43	30 Nov 45	Sold 25 Nov 46
12	*Burges* BosNY	8 Dec 42 26 Jan 43	2 Jun 43		RN; ret 27 Feb 46
13	*Brennan* MINY	28 Feb 42 22 Aug 42	20 Jan 43	9 Oct 45	Str 24 Oct 45; sold 12 Jul 46
14	*Doherty* MINY	28 Feb 42 24 Aug 42	6 Feb 43	14 Dec 45	Str 8 Jan 46; sold 26 Dec 45
15	*Austin* MINY	14 Mar 42 25 Sep 42	13 Feb 43	21 Dec 45	Str 8 Jan 46; sold Feb 47
16	*Edgar G. Chase* MINY	14 Mar 42 26 Sep 42	20 Mar 43	16 Oct 45	Sold 18 Mar 47
17	*Edward C. Daly* MINY	1 Apr 42 21 Oct 42	3 Apr 43	20 Dec 45	Str 8 Jan 46; sold 8 Jan 47
18	*Gilmore* MINY	1 Apr 42 22 Oct 42	17 Apr 43	29 Dec 45	Str 21 Jan 46; sold 1 Feb 47
19	*Burden R. Hastings* MINY	15 Apr 42 20 Nov 42	1 May 43	25 Oct 45	Str 13 Nov 45; sold 1 Feb 47
20	*Le Hardy* MINY	15 Apr 42 21 Nov 42	15 May 43	25 Oct 45	Str 13 Nov 45; sold 26 Dec 46
21	*Harold C. Thomas* MINY	30 Apr 42 18 Dec 42	31 May 43	26 Oct 45	Str 28 Nov 45; sold 25 Nov 46
22	*Wileman* MINY	30 Apr 42 19 Dec 42	11 Jun 43	16 Nov 45	Str 28 Nov 45; sold 8 Jan 47
23	*Charles R. Greer* MINY	7 Sep 42 18 Jan 43	25 Jun 43	2 Nov 45	Sold 1 Feb 47
24	*Whitman* MINY	7 Sep 42 19 Jan 43	3 Jul 43	16 Nov 45	Sold 31 Jan 47
25	*Wintle* MINY	1 Oct 42 18 Feb 43	10 Jul 43	14 Nov 45	Str 28 Nov 45; sold 25 Jul 47
26	*Dempsey* MINY	1 Oct 42 19 Feb 43	24 Jul 43	22 Nov 45	Str 28 Nov 45; sold 18 Apr 47
27	*Duffy* MINY	29 Oct 42 16 Apr 43	5 Aug 43	9 Nov 45	Str 28 Nov 45; sold 16 Jun 47
28	*Emery* MINY	29 Nov 42 17 Apr 43	14 Aug 43	15 Nov 45	Str 28 Nov 45; sold 21 Jul 47
29	*Stadtfeld* MINY	26 Nov 42 17 May 43	26 Aug 43	10 Nov 45	Str 28 Nov 45; sold 22 Jul 47
30	*Martin* MINY	26 Nov 42 18 May 43	4 Sep 43	19 Nov 45	Str 5 Dec 45; sold 15 May 46
31	*Sederstrom* MINY	24 Dec 42 15 Jun 43	11 Sep 43	15 Nov 45	Str 28 Nov 45; sold 21 Jan 48
32	*Fleming* MINY	24 Dec 42 16 Jun 43	18 Sep 43	10 Nov 45	Str 28 Nov 45; sold 29 Jan 48
33	*Tisdale* MINY	23 Jan 43 28 Jun 43	11 Oct 43	12 Oct 45	Str 28 Nov 45; sold 9 Feb 48
34	*Eisele* MINY	23 Jan 43 29 Jun 43	18 Oct 43	16 Nov 45	Str 28 Nov 45; sold 29 Jan 48
35	*Fair* MINY	24 Feb 43 27 Jul 43	23 Oct 43	17 Nov 45	Str 28 Nov 45; trans to U.S. Army 20 May 47 for use by Canada in experiments in Caribbean; ret 1948; sold 1949
36	*Manlove* MINY	24 Feb 43 28 Jul 43	8 Nov 43	16 Nov 45	Str 28 Nov 45; sold 4 Dec 47
37	*Greiner* PSNY	7 Sep 42 20 May 43	18 Aug 43	19 Nov 45	Str 5 Dec 45; sold 10 Feb 46
38	*Wyman* PSNY	7 Sep 43 3 Jun 43	1 Sep 43	21 Dec 45	Str 8 Jan 46; sold 16 May 47
39	*Lovering* PSNY	7 Sep 42 18 Jun 43	17 Sep 43	16 Oct 45	Str 1 Nov 45; sold 31 Dec 46
40	*Sanders* PSNY	7 Sep 42 18 Jun 43	1 Oct 43	12 Dec 45	Str 8 Jan 46; Sold 8 May 47
41	*Brackett* PSNY	12 Jan 43 1 Aug 43	18 Oct 43	23 Nov 45	Sold 22 May 47
42	*Reynolds* PSNY	12 Jan 43 1 Aug 43	1 Nov 43	45	Sold 28 Apr 47
43	*Mitchell* PSNY	12 Jan 43 1 Aug 43	17 Nov 43	29 Dec 45	Str 29 Dec 45; sold 11 Dec 45
44	*Donaldson* PSNY	12 Jan 43 1 Aug 43	1 Dec 43	5 Dec 45	Sold 2 Jul 46
45	*Andres* PHNY	12 Feb 42 24 Jul 42	15 Mar 43	18 Oct 45	Sold Feb 46

	LD/Launch	Comm	Decomm	Fate
46 *Drury* PHNY	12 Feb 42 24 Jul 42	4 Dec 43	22 Oct 45	RN; ret 20 Aug 45; sold Jun 46
47 *Decker* PHNY	1 Apr 43 24 Jul 42	3 May 43	28 Aug 45	China (*Tai Ping*); WL(T) 14 Nov 54
48 *Dobler* PHNY	1 Apr 42 24 Jul 42	17 May 43	2 Oct 45	Str 24 Oct 45; sold 12 Jul 46
49 *Doneff* PHNY	1 Apr 42 24 Jul 42	10 Jun 43	22 Dec 45	Str 21 Jan 46; sold 9 Jan 47
50 *Engstrom* PHNY	1 Apr 42	21 Jun 43	19 Dec 45	Str 8 Jan 46; sold 26 Dec 46
51 *Buckley* BethHI	21 Jul 42 9 Jan 43	30 Apr 43	3 Jul 46	DER conv 1945; str 1 Jun 68; sold 69
52 *Bentinck* BethHI	29 Jun 42 22 Aug 42	19 May 43		RN; ret 5 Jan 46; sold 26 May 46
53 *Charles Lawrence* BethHI	1 Aug 42 16 Feb 43	31 May 43		APD–37 23 Oct 44
54 *Daniel T. Griffin* BethHI	7 Sep 42 25 Feb 43	9 Jun 43		APD–38 23 Oct 44
55 *Byard* BethHI	15 Oct 42 13 Mar 43	18 Jun 43	—	RN; ret 20 Dec 45
56 *Donnell* BethHI	27 Nov 42 13 Mar 43	26 Jun 43	23 Oct 45	WD(T) 3 May 44; IX–182 15 Jul 44; sold 29 Apr 46
57 *Fogg* BethHI	4 Dec 42 20 Mar 43	7 Jul 43	27 Oct 47	DER conv 45; str 1 Apr 65; sold Jan 66
58 *Calder* BethHI	11 Dec 42 27 Mar 43	15 Jul 43		RN; ret 19 Oct 45
59 *Foss* BethHI	31 Dec 42 10 Apr 43	23 Jul 43	30 Oct 57	EDE 1949; str 1 Nov 65; tgt(T)
60 *Gantner* BethHI	31 Dec 42 17 Aug 43	23 Jul 43	—	APD–42 23 Feb 45
61 *Duckworth* BethHI	16 Jan 43 1 May 43	4 Aug 43	—	RN; ret 17 Dec 45
62 *George W. Ingram* BethHI	6 Feb 43 8 May 43	11 Aug 43	—	APD–43 23 Feb 45
63 *Ira Jeffery* BethHI	13 Feb 43 15 May 43	15 Aug 43	—	APD–44 23 Feb 45
64 *Duff* BethHI	22 Feb 43 29 May 43	23 Aug 43	—	RN; ret 22 Aug 45
65 *Lee Fox* BethHI	1 Mar 43 29 May 43	30 Aug 43	—	APD–45 23 Feb 45
66 *Amesbury* BethHI	8 Mar 43 5 Jun 43	31 Aug 43	—	APD–46 23 Feb 45
67 *Essington* BethHI	15 Mar 43 19 Jun 43	7 Sep 43	—	RN; ret 19 Oct 45
68 *Bates* BethHI	29 Mar 43 6 Jun 43	12 Sep 43		APD–47, 31 Jul 44
69 *Blessman* BethHI	22 Mar 43 19 Jun 43	19 Sep 43		APD–48, 31 Jul 44
70 *Joseph E. Campbell* BethHI	29 Mar 43 26 Jun 43	23 Sep 43		APD–49, 24 Nov 44
71 *Affleck* BethHI	5 Apr 43 30 Jun 43	29 Sep 43	—	RN; WD(T) 26 Dec 44; sold in UK 24 Jan 47; merchant hulk *Nostra Senora de la Luz* to 1954
72 *Aylmer* BethHI	12 Apr 43 10 Jul 43	20 Sep 43		RN; ret 5 Nov 45; sold 20 Jun 47
73 *Balfour* BethHI	19 Apr 43 10 Jul 43	7 Oct 43		RN; ret 25 Oct 46; sold 28 Oct 46
74 *Bentley* BethHI	26 Apr 43 17 Jul 43	13 Oct 43		RN; ret 5 Nov 45; sold 20 Jun 47
75 *Bickerton* BethHI	3 May 43 24 Jul 43	17 Oct 43		RN; WD(T); scuttled 22 Aug 44
76 *Bligh* BethHI	10 May 43 31 Jul 43	22 Oct 43		RN; ret 12 Nov 45; sold 13 Jun 46
77 *Braithwaite* BethHI	10 May 43 31 Jul 43	13 Nov 43		RN; ret 13 Nov 45
78 *Bullen* BethHI	17 May 43 7 Aug 43	25 Oct 43		RN; WL(T) 6 Dec 44
79 *Bryon* BethHI	24 May 43 14 Aug 43	30 Oct 43		RN; ret 24 Nov 45
80 *Conn* BethHI	2 Jun 43 21 Aug 43	31 Oct 43		RN; ret 26 Nov 45

		LD/Launch	Comm	Decomm	Fate
81	Cotton	2 Jun 43	8 Nov 43		RN; ret 5 Nov 45
	BethHI	21 Aug 43			
82	Cranstoun	9 Jun 43	13 Nov 43		RN; ret 3 Dec 45
	BethHI	28 Aug 43			
83	Cubitt	9 Jun 43	17 Nov 43		RN; ret 4 Mar 46
	BethHI	11 Sep 43			
84	Curzon	23 Jun 43	20 Nov 43		RN; ret 27 Mar 46
	BethHI	18 Sep 43			
85	Dakins	23 Jun 43	23 Nov 43		RN; sold in Holland 9 Jan 47; BU Greece
	BethHI	18 Sep 43			
86	Deane	30 Jun 43	26 Nov 43		RN; ret 4 Mar 46
	BethHI	29 Sep 43			
87	Ekins	5 Jul 43	29 Nov 43		RN; WD(M) 16 Apr 45; sold in Holland 1947
	BethHI	2 Oct 43			
88	Fitzroy	24 Aug 43	16 Oct 43		RN; ret 5 Jan 46
	BethHI	1 Sep 43			
89	Redmill	14 Jul 43	30 Nov 43		RN; ret 20 Jan 47
	BethHI	2 Oct 43			
90	Retalick	21 Jul 43	8 Dec 43		RN; ret 25 Oct 45
	BethHI	9 Oct 43			
91	Halsted	10 Jul 43	3 Nov 43		RN; WD(T) 11 Jun 44, hulk; sold 1 Nov 46 in Holland (BU)
	BethHI	14 Oct 43			
92	Riou	4 Aug 43	14 Dec 43		RN; ret 25 Feb 46
	BethHI	23 Oct 43			
93	Rutherford	4 Aug 43	16 Dec 43		RN; ret 25 Oct 45
	BethHI	23 Oct 43			
94	Cosby	11 Aug 43	20 Dec 43		RN; ret 4 Mar 46
	BethHI	30 Oct 43			
95	Rowley	18 Aug 43	22 Dec 43		RN; ret 12 Nov 45
	BethHI	30 Oct 43			
96	Rupert	25 Aug 43	24 Dec 43		RN; ret 20 Mar 46
	BethHI	31 Oct 43			
97	Stockham	25 Aug 43	28 Dec 43	—	RN; ret 15 Feb 46; str 12 Mar 46; BU 15 Jun 48
	BethHI	31 Oct 43			
98	Seymour	1 Sep 43	23 Dec 43	—	RN; ret 5 Jan 46
	BethHI	1 Nov 43			
99	Cannon	14 Nov 43	26 Sep 43	19 Dec 44	Brazil (Baependi); res 65; BU 73
	Dravo	25 May 43			
100	Christopher	7 Dec 42	23 Oct 43	19 Dec 44	Brazil (Benevente); res 65
	Dravo	19 Jun 43			
101	Alger	2 Jan 43	12 Nov 43	10 Mar 45	Brazil (Babitonga); BU 64
	Dravo	8 Jul 43			
102	Thomas	16 Jan 43	21 Nov 43	13 Mar 47	China 11 Jan 49 (Tai Ho)
	NorNY	31 Jul 43			
103	Bostwick	6 Feb 43	1 Dec 43	30 Apr 46	China 14 Dec 48 (Tai Tsang)
	Dravo	30 Aug 43			
104	Breeman	20 Mar 43	12 Dec 43	26 Apr 46	China 29 Oct 48 (Tai Hu); res Dec 72; pier ramp
	NorNY	4 Sep 43			
105	Burrows	24 Mar 43	19 Dec 43	14 Jun 46	Holland 1 Jun 50 (Van Amstel); ret Dec 67; sold Feb 68
	Dravo	2 Oct 43			
106	Senegalais	24 Apr 43	2 Jan 44	—	France; str May 64; sold Oct 65 (ex-Corbesier)
	Dravo	1 Nov 43			
107	Algerien	13 May 43	23 Jan 44		France; str May 64; 1 sold Nov 65 (ex-Cronin)
	Dravo	7 Nov 43			
108	Tunisien	23 Jun 43	11 Feb 44		France; str May 64; BU (ex-Crosley)
	Dravo	7 Dec 43			
109	Marocain	7 Sep 43	239 Feb 44		France; str May 64, BU
	Dravo	1 Jan 44			
110	Hova	25 Sep 43	18 Mar 44		France; str May 64; BU
	Dravo	22 Jan 44			
111	Somali	23 Oct 43	9 Apr 44		France
	Dravo	2 Feb 44			
112	Carter	19 Nov 43	3 May 44	10 Apr 46	China 14 Dec 48 (Tai Chao); res Nov 72; BU
	Dravo	29 Feb 44			
113	Clarence L. Evans	23 Dec 43	25 Jun 44	29 May 47	France 29 Mar 52 (Barbere); BU
	Dravo	22 Mar 44			
129	Edsall	2 Jul 42	10 Apr 43	11 Jun 46	Str 1 Jun 68; sold
	Orange	1 Nov 42			
130	Jacob Jones	26 Jun 42	29 Apr 43	26 Jul 46	Str 2 Jan 71
	Orange	1 Nov 42			

	LD/Launch	Comm	Decomm	Fate
131 *Hammann* Orange	10 Jul 42 13 Dec 42	17 May 43	24 Oct 45	Str 1 Oct 72
132 *Robert E. Peary* Orange	30 Jun 42 3 Jan 43	31 May 43	13 Jun 47	Str 1 Jul 66; sold 6 Sep 67
133 *Pillsbury* Orange	18 Jul 42 10 Jan 43	7 Jun 43 15 Mar 55	47 20 Jun 60	DER–133 Aug 54; str 1 Jul 65; sold
134 *Pope* Orange	14 Jul 42 12 Jan 43	25 Jun 43	17 May 46	Str 2 Jan 71
135 *Flaherty* Orange	7 Nov 42 17 Jan 43	26 Jun 43	17 Jun 46	Str 1 Apr 65; sold 4 Nov 66
136 *Frederick C. Davis* Orange	9 Nov 42 24 Jan 43	14 Jul 43	—	WL(T) 24 Apr 45
137 *Herbert C. Jones* Orange	30 Nov 42 19 Jan 43	21 Jul 43	2 May 47	Str 1 Jul 72
138 *Douglas L. Howard* Orange	8 Dec 42 24 Jan 43	29 Jul 43	17 Jun 46	Str 1 Oct 72
139 *Farquhar* Orange	14 Dec 42 13 Feb 43	5 Aug 43	14 Jun 46	Str 1 Oct 72
140 *J.R.Y. Blakely* Orange	16 Dec 42 7 Mar 43	16 Aug 43	14 Jun 46	Str 2 Jan 71; sold
141 *Hill* Orange	21 Dec 42 28 Feb 43	16 Aug 43	7 Jun 46	Str 1 Oct 72
142 *Fessenden* Orange	4 Jan 43 9 Mar 43	25 Aug 43 4 Mar 52	24 Jun 46 30 Jun 60	DER–142 Oct 51; str 1 Sep 66; tgt 20 Dec 67
143 *Fiske* Orange	4 Jan 43 14 Mar 43	25 Aug 43	—	WL(T) 2 Aug 44
144 *Frost* Orange	13 Jan 43 21 Mar 43	30 Aug 43	18 Jun 46	Str 1 Apr 65; sold 29 Dec 66
145 *Huse* Orange	11 Jan 43 23 Apr 43	30 Aug 43 3 Aug 51	27 Mar 46 Jun 65	Str 1 Aug 73; sold 11 Jun 74; NRF 60–65
146 *Inch* Orange	19 Jan 43 4 Apr 43	8 Sep 43	17 May 46	Str 1 Oct 72
147 *Blair* Orange	19 Jan 43 6 Apr 43	13 Sep 43 5 Oct 51 2 Dec 57	28 Jun 46 13 Nov 56	DER–147 Dec 57; str 1 Dec 72; sold
148 *Brough* Orange	22 Jan 43 10 Apr 43	18 Sep 43	22 Mar 46	Str 1 Nov 65; sold 13 Oct 66
149 *Chatelain* Orange	25 Jan 43 21 Apr 43	22 Sep 43	14 Jun 46	Str 1 Aug 73
150 *Neunzer* Orange	29 Jan 43 27 Apr 43	27 Sep 43	Jan 47	Str 1 Jul 72
151 *Poole* Orange	13 Feb 43 8 May 43	29 Sep 43	Jan 47	Str 2 Jan 71
152 *Peterson* Orange	28 Feb 43 15 May 43	29 Sep 43 2 May 52	1 May 46	ASW conversion; Str 1 Aug 73
153 *Reuben James* NorNY	7 Sep 42 6 Feb 43	1 Apr 43	11 Oct 47	DER conv 45; str 30 Jun 68; explosive tests Dahlgren 68–71; tgt 1 Mar 71
154 *Sims* NorNY	7 Sep 42 6 Feb 43	24 Apr 43		APD–50 7 Sep 44
155 *Hopping* NorNY	15 Dec 42 10 Mar 43	21 May 43		APD–51 7 Sep 44
156 *Reeves* NorNY	7 Feb 43 22 Apr 43	9 Jun 43		APD–52 7 Sep 44
157 *Fechteler* NorNY	7 Feb 43 22 Apr 43	1 Jul 43		WL(T) 5 May 44
158 *Chase* NorNY	16 Mar 43 24 Apr 43	18 Jul 43		APD–54 24 Nov 44
159 *Laning* NorNY	23 Apr 43 4 Jul 43	1 Aug 43	—	APD–55 24 Nov 44
160 *Loy* NorNY	23 Apr 43 4 Jul 43	12 Sep 43	—	APD–56 24 Nov 44
161 *Barber* NorNY	27 Apr 43 20 May 43	10 Oct 43	—	APD–57 24 Nov 44
162 *Levy* FedN	19 Oct 42 26 Mar 43	13 May 43	4 Apr 47	
163 *McConnell* FedN	19 Oct 42 28 Mar 43	28 May 43	29 Jun 46	Str 1 Oct 72
164 *Osterhaus* FedN	11 Nov 42 8 Apr 43	12 Jun 43	26 Jun 46	Str 1 Nov 72
165 *Parks* FedN	11 Nov 42 8 Apr 43	23 Jun 43	Mar 46	Str 1 Jul 72

	LD/Launch	Comm	Decomm	Fate
166 *Baron* FedN	30 Nov 42 9 May 43	5 Jul 43	26 Apr 46	Uruguay 3 May 52 (*Uruguay*)
167 *Acree* FedN	30 Nov 42 9 May 43	19 Jul 43	1 Apr 46	Str 1 Jul 72
168 *Amick* FedN	30 Nov 42 27 May 43	26 Jul 43	16 May 47	Japan 14 Jun 55 (*Asahi*)
169 *Atherton* NorNY	14 Jan 43 27 May 43	29 Aug 43	10 Dec 45	Japan 14 Jun 55 (*Hatsuhi*)
170 *Booth* NorNY	30 Jan 43 21 Jun 43	19 Sep 43	4 Mar 46	Philippines 15 Dec 67 (*Datu Kalantiaw*)
171 *Carroll* NorNY	30 Jan 43 21 Jun 43	24 Oct 43	19 Jun 46	Str 1 Aug 65; sold 29 Dec 66
172 *Cooner* FedN	22 Feb 43 23 Jul 43	21 Aug 43	25 Jun 46	Str 1 Jul 72
173 *Eldridge* FedN	22 Feb 43 25 Jul 43	27 Aug 43	17 Jun 46	Greece 15 Jan 51 (*Lion*)
174 *Marts* FedN	26 Apr 43 8 Aug 43	3 Sep 43	20 Mar 45	Brazil (*Bocaina*)
175 *Pennewill* FedN	26 Apr 43 8 Aug 43	15 Sep 43	1 Aug 44	Brazil (*Bertioga*); BU 64
176 *Micka* FedN	3 May 43 22 Aug 43	23 Sep 43	14 Jun 46	Str 1 Aug 65; sold 15 May 67
177 *Reybold* FedN	3 May 43 22 Aug 43	29 Sep 43	15 Aug 44	Brazil (*Bauru*); res 11 Jul 72; BU
178 *Herzog* FedN	17 May 43 5 Sep 43	6 Oct 43	1 Aug 44	Brazil (*Beberibe*); grounded Feb 66; BU
179 *McAnn* FedN	17 May 43 5 Sep 43	11 Oct 43	15 Aug 44	Brazil (*Bracui*)
180 *Trumpeter* FedN	7 Jun 43 19 Sep 43	16 Oct 43	5 Dec 47	Str 1 Aug 73; tgt
181 *Straub* FedN	7 Jun 43 19 Sep 43	25 Oct 43	17 Oct 47	Str 1 Aug 73
182 *Gustafson* FedN	5 Jul 43 3 Oct 43	1 Nov 43	26 Jun 46	Holland 23 Oct 50 (*Van Ewijck*); ret 15 Dec 67; sold Feb 68
183 *Samuel S. Miles* FedN	5 Jul 43 3 Oct 43	4 Nov 43	28 Mar 46	France 12 Aug 50 (*Arabe*); BU 68
184 *Wesson* FedN	29 Jul 43 17 Oct 43	11 Nov 43	25 Jul 46	Italy 10 Jan 51 (*Andromeda*); str Jan 72; BU
185 *Riddle* FedN	29 Jul 43 17 Oct 43	17 Nov 43	8 Jun 46	France 12 Aug 50 (*Kabyle*); str May 64; BU
186 *Swearer* FedN	12 Aug 43 31 Oct 43	24 Nov 43	27 Aug 47	France 12 Aug 50 (*Bambara*); str May 64; BU
187 *Stern* FedN	12 Aug 43 31 Oct 43	1 Dec 43	26 Apr 46	Holland 3 May 51 (*Van Zijill*); ret 15 Dec 67; sold Feb 68
188 *O'Neill* FedN	26 Aug 43 14 Nov 43	6 Dec 43	2 May 46	Holland 23 Oct 50 (*Duboir*); ret 15 Dec 67; sold Feb 68
189 *Bronstein* FedN	26 Aug 43 14 Nov 43	13 Dec 43	5 Nov 45	Uruguay 3 May 52 (*Artigas*)
190 *Baker* FedN	9 Sep 43 28 Nov 43	23 Dec 43	4 Mar 46	France 29 Mar 52 (*Malgache*); res 1 Jan 69; sunk 70
191 *Coffman* FedN	9 Sep 43 28 Nov 43	27 Dec 43	30 Apr 46	Str 1 Jul 72; sold 73
192 *Eisner* FedN	23 Sep 43 12 Dec 43	1 Jan 44	5 Jul 46	Holland 1 Mar 50 (*De Zeeuw*); ret 15 Dec 67; sold Feb 68
193 *Garfield Thomas* FedN	23 Sep 43 12 Dec 43	24 Jan 44	27 Mar 47	Greece 15 Jan 51 (*Panthir*)
194 *Wingfield* FedN	7 Oct 43 30 Dec 43	28 Jan 44	26 Aug 47	France 20 Oct 50 (*Sakalave*)
195 *Thornhill* FedN	7 Oct 43 20 Dec 43	1 Feb 44	17 Jun 47	Italy 10 Jan 51 (*Aldebaran*)
196 *Rinehart* FedN	21 Oct 43 1 Jan 44	12 Feb 44	17 Jul 46	Holland 1 Jun 50 (*De Bitter*); ret 15 Dec 67; sold Feb 68
197 *Roche* FedN	21 Oct 43 9 Jan 44	21 Feb 44	—	WD(M) 22 Sep 45; scuttled 11 Mar 46
198 *Lovelace* NorNY	22 May 43 4 Jul 43	7 Nov 43	22 May 46	Str 1 Jul 67; tgt 25 Apr 68
199 *Manning* CharNY	15 Feb 43 1 Jun 43	1 Oct 43	15 Jan 47	Str 31 Jul 68; sold
200 *Neuendorf* CharNY	15 Feb 43 1 Jun 43	18 Oct 43	14 May 46	Str 1 Jul 67; sold 30 Nov 67
201 *James E. Craig* CharNY	15 Apr 43 22 Jul 43	1 Nov 43	2 Jul 46	Str 30 Jun 68; tgt Feb 69

		LD/Launch	Comm	Decomm	Fate
202	*Eichenberger*	15 Apr 43	17 Nov 43	14 May 46	Str 1 Dec 72
	CharNY	22 Jul 43			
203	*Thomason*	5 Jun 43	10 Dec 43	22 May 46	Str 30 Jun 68; sold
	CharNY	23 Aug 43			
204	*Jordan*	5 Jun 43	17 Dec 43	19 Dec 45	Sold Jul 47; conv to DER canc 18 Jul 45; collision 18 Sep 45 off Miami (SS *John Sherman*)
	CharNY	23 Aug 43			
205	*Newman*	8 Jun 43	26 Nov 43	—	APD–59 5 Jul 44
	CharNY	9 Aug 43			
206	*Liddle*	8 Jun 43	6 Dec 43	—	APD–60 5 Jul 44
	CharNY	9 Aug 43			
207	*Kephart*	12 May 43	7 Jan 44	—	APD–61 5 Jul 44
	CharNY	6 Sep 43			
208	*Cofer*	12 May 43	19 Jan 44	—	APD–62 5 Jul 44
	CharNY	6 Sep 43			
209	*Lloyd*	26 Jul 43	11 Feb 44	—	APD–63 5 Jul 44
	CharNY	23 Oct 43			
210	*Otter*	26 Jul 43	21 Feb 44	47	Str 1 Nov 69; tgt 6 Jul 70
	CharNY	23 Oct 43			
211	*Hubbard*	11 Aug 43	6 Mar 44		APD–53 1 Jun 45
	CharNY	11 Nov 43			
212	*Hayter*	11 Aug 43	16 Mar 44	—	APD–80 1 Jun 45
	CharNY	11 Nov 43			
213	*William T. Powell*	26 Aug 43	28 Mar 44	17 Jan 58	DER conv 45; str 1 Nov 65; sold 3 Oct 66
	CharNY	27 Nov 43			
214	*Scott*	1 Jan 43	20 Jul 43	3 Mar 47	APD–64 Aug 44, later canc; str 1 Jul 65
	PHNY	3 Apr 43			
215	*Burke*	1 Jan 43	20 Aug 43	—	APD–65 24 Jan 45
	PHNY	3 Apr 43			
216	*Enright*	22 Feb 43	21 Sep 43	—	APD–66 21 Jan 45
	PHNY	29 May 43			
217	*Coolbaugh*	22 Feb 43	15 Oct 43	21 Feb 59	NRF 59 onward; str 1 Jul 72; sold 73
	PHNY	29 May 43			
218	*Darby*	22 Feb 43	15 Nov 43	28 Apr 47	NRF 59–62; str 23 Sep 68; tgt 24 May 70
	PHNY	29 May 43	24 Oct 50	58	
219	*J. Douglas Blackwood*	22 Feb 43	15 Dec 43	20 Apr 46	Str 30 Jan 70; tgt 20 Jul 70; NRF 58–61, 62–70
	PHNY	29 May 43	5 Feb 51	1 Aug 58	
			2 Oct 61	1 Aug 62	
220	*Francis M. Robinson*	22 Feb 43	15 Jan 44	20 Jun 60	Str 1 Jul 72
	PHNY	1 May 43			
221	*Solar*	22 Feb 43	15 Feb 44	—	Conv to DER canc 18 Jul 45; explosion 30 Apr 46; scuttled 9 Jun 46
	PHNY	29 May 43			
222	*Fowler*	5 Apr 43	15 Mar 44	28 Jun 46	Str 1 Jul 65; sold 29 Dec 67
	PHNY	3 Jul 43			
223	*Spangenberg*	5 Apr 43	15 Apr 44	18 Oct 47	DER conv 45; str 1 Nov 65; sold 3 Oct 66
	PHNY	3 Jul 43			
224	*Rudderow*	15 Jul 43	15 May 44	15 Jan 47	Str 1 Nov 68; sold
	PHNY	14 Oct 43			
225	*Day*	15 Jul 43	10 Jun 44	16 May 46	Str 30 Jun 68; tgt Mar 69
	PHNY	14 Oct 43			
226	*Crosley*	16 Oct 43			APD–87
	PHNY	12 Feb 44			
227	*Cread*	16 Oct 43			APD–88
	PHNY	12 Feb 44			
228	*Ruchamkin*	14 Feb 44			APD–89
	PHNY	15 Jun 44			
229	*Kirwin*	14 Feb 44			APD–90
	PHNY	16 Jun 44			
230	*Chaffee*	26 Aug 43	9 May 44	15 Apr 46	Grounded 5 Nov 45; sold 29 Jun 48; mach to Cal Maritime Acad for training
	CharNY	27 Nov 43			
231	*Hodges*	9 Sep 43	27 May 44	22 Jun 46	Sold 73
	CharNY	9 Dec 43			
232	*Kinzer*	9 Sep 43			APD–91
	CharNY	9 Dec 43			
233	*Register*	27 Oct 43			APD–92
	CharNY	20 Jan 44			
234	*Brock*	27 Oct 43			APD–93
	CharNY	20 Jan 44			
235	*John Q. Roberts*	15 Nov 43			APD–94
	CharNY	11 Feb 44			

		LD/Launch	Comm	Decomm	Fate
236	*William M. Hobby* CharNY	15 Nov 43 11 Feb 44			APD–95
237	*Ray K. Edwards* CharNY	1 Dec 43 19 Feb 44			APD–96
238	*Stewart* Brown	15 Jul 42 22 Nov 42	31 May 43	27 Mar 46	Str 1 Oct 72; memorial at Galveston, Texas
239	*Sturtevant* Brown	15 Jul 42 3 Dec 42	16 Jun 43 3 Aug 51 5 Oct 57	24 Mar 46 31 Oct 46 Jun 60	DER–239 1 Nov 56; str 1 Dec 72; sold 20 Sep 73
240	*Moore* Brown	20 Jul 42 20 Dec 42	1 Jul 43	30 Jun 47	Str 1 Aug 73; tgt 22 Apr 74
241	*Keith* Brown	4 Aug 42 21 Dec 42	19 Jul 43	20 Jul 46	Str 1 Nov 72
242	*Tomich* Brown	15 Sep 42 28 Dec 42	27 Jul 43	20 Sep 46	Str 1 Nov 72
243	*F. Richard Ward* Brown	30 Sep 42 6 Jan 43	5 Jul 43	13 Jun 46	Str 2 Jan 71; sold
244	*Otterstetter* Brown	9 Nov 42 19 Jan 43	6 Aug 43 6 Jun 52	21 Sep 46 20 Jun 60	DER–251 Dec 51; str 1 Aug 74; tgt
245	*Sloat* Brown	21 Nov 42 21 Jan 43	16 Aug 43	6 Aug 47	Str 2 Jan 71; sold
246	*Snowden* Brown	7 Dec 42 19 Feb 43	23 Aug 43 6 Jun 51 2 Oct 61	Mar 46 Aug 60 1 Aug 62	Str 23 Sep 68; tgt 27 Jun 68; NRF 60–68
247	*Stanton* Brown	7 Dec 42 21 Feb 43	7 Aug 43	2 Jun 47	Str 1 Dec 70; sold
248	*Swasey* Brown	30 Dec 42 18 Mar 43	31 Aug 43	15 Mar 46	Str 1 Nov 72
249	*Marchand* Brown	3 Dec 42 30 Mar 43	8 Sep 43	25 Apr 47	Str 2 Jan 71; sold
250	*Hurst* Brown	27 Jan 43 1 Apr 43	30 Aug 43	1 May 46	Str 1 Dec 72; Mexico 1 Oct 73 (*Commodore Manuel Azueta*)
251	*Camp* Brown	27 Jan 43 16 Apr 43	16 Sep 43 31 Jul 56	1 May 46 13 Feb 51	DER–251 Dec 55; Vietnam (*Tran Hung Dao*); Philippines (*Rajah Lakandula*)
252	*Howard D. Crow* Brown	6 Feb 43 16 Apr 43	27 Sep 43 6 Jul 51	22 May 46	Str 23 Sep 68; sold
253	*Pettit* Brown	6 Feb 43 28 Apr 43	23 Sep 43	6 May 46	Str 1 Aug 73; tgt 30 Sep 74
254	*Ricketts* Brown	16 Mar 43 10 May 43	5 Oct 43	17 Apr 46	Str 1 Nov 72
255	*Sellstrom* Brown	16 Mar 43 12 May 43	12 Oct 43 1 Oct 56	Apr 46 Jun 60	DER–255 1956; str 1 Nov 65; sold Apr 67
256	*Seid* BosNY	10 Jan 43 22 Feb 43	11 Jun 43	7 Dec 45	Str 8 Jan 46; sold 8 Jan 47
257	*Smartt* BosNY	10 Jan 43 22 Feb 43	18 Jun 43	5 Oct 45	Sold Aug 48
258	*Walter S. Brown* BosNY	10 Jan 43 22 Feb 43	25 Jun 43	4 Oct 45	Sold Aug 48
259	*William C. Miller* BosNY	10 Jan 43 22 Feb 43	2 Jul 43	17 Dec 45	Str 8 Jan 46; sold 18 Apr 47
260	*Cabana* BosNY	27 Jan 43 10 Mar 43	9 Jul 43	9 Jan 46	Str 21 Jan 46; sold 13 May 47
261	*Dionne* BosNY	27 Jan 43 10 Mar 43	16 Jul 43	18 Jan 46	Str 7 Feb 46; sold 12 Jun 47
262	*Canfield* BosNY	23 Feb 43 6 Apr 43	22 Jul 43	21 Dec 45	Str 8 Jan 46; sold 12 Jun 47
263	*Deede* BosNY	23 Feb 43 6 Apr 43	29 Jul 43	9 Jan 46	Str 21 Jan 46; sold 12 Jun 47
264	*Elden* BosNY	23 Feb 43 6 Apr 43	4 Aug 43	18 Jan 46	Str 7 Feb 46; sold 12 Jul 47
265	*Cloues* BosNY	23 Feb 43 6 Apr 43	10 Aug 43	26 Nov 45	Str 5 Dec 45; sold 22 May 47
266	*Capel* BosNY	11 Mar 43 22 Apr 43	16 Aug 43		RN; WL(T) 26 Dec 44
267	*Cooke* BosNY	11 Mar 43 22 Apr 43	16 Aug 43		RN; ret 3 Jun 47; sold
268	*Dacres* BosNY	7 Apr 43 14 Apr 43	28 Aug 43		RN; ret 26 Jan 46; sold 14 Dec 46
269	*Domett* BosNY	7 Apr 43 3 Sep 43	3 Sep 43		RN; ret 3 Jun 47; sold
270	*Foley* BosNY	7 Apr 43 19 May 43	8 Sep 43		RN; ret 22 Aug 45; sold 19 Jun 46

		LD/Launch	Comm	Decomm	Fate
271	*Garlies* BosNY	7 Apr 43 19 May 43	13 Sep 43	10 Oct 45	RN; ret 20 Aug 45; sold 18 Jul 47; BU
272	*Gould* Dosny	23 Apr 43 4 Jun 43	18 Sep 43		RN; WL(T) 1 Mar 44
273	*Grindall* BosNY	23 Apr 43 4 Jun 43	23 Sep 43		RN; ret 20 Aug 45; str 1 Nov 45
274	*Gardiner* BosNY	20 May 43 8 Jul 43	28 Sep 43		RN; ret 12 Feb 46; sold 10 Dec 46
275	*Goodall* BosNY	20 May 43 8 Jul 43	4 Oct 43		RN; WL(T) 29 Apr 45
276	*Goodson* BosNY	20 May 43 8 Jul 43	9 Oct 43		RN; WD(T) 25 Jun 44; ret 21 Oct 44; sold 9 Jan 47
277	*Gore* BosNY	20 May 43 8 Jul 43	14 Oct 43		RN; ret 2 May 46; sold 10 Jun 47
278	*Keats* BosNY	5 Jun 43 17 Jul 43	19 Oct 43		RN; ret 27 Feb 46
279	*Kempthorne* BosNY	5 Jun 43 17 Jul 43	23 Oct 43		RN; ret 20 Aug 45
280	*Kingsmill* BosNY	9 Jul 43 13 Aug 43	29 Oct 43	26 Oct 45	RN; ret 22 Aug 45; str 16 Nov 45; sold 17 Feb 47
281	*Arthur L. Bristol* CharNY	1 Dec 43 19 Feb 44			APD–97
282	*Truxtun* CharNY	13 Dec 43 9 Mar 44			APD–98
283	*Upham* CharNY	13 Dec 43 9 Mar 44			APD–99
301	*Lake* MINY	22 Apr 43 18 Aug 43	5 Feb 44	3 Dec 46	Sold 14 Dec 46
302	*Lyman* MINY	22 Apr 43 19 Aug 43	19 Feb 44	5 Dec 46	Sold 14 Dec 46
303	*Crowley* MINY	24 May 43 22 Sep 43	25 Mar 44	3 Dec 45	Sold 21 Dec 46
304	*Rall* MINY	24 May 43 23 Sep 43	8 Apr 44	11 Dec 45	WD(K) 12 Apr 45; Str 3 Jan 46; sold 18 Mar 47
305	*Halloran* MINY	21 Jun 43 14 Jan 44	27 May 44	2 Nov 45	Str 38 Nov 46; Sold 7 Mar 47
306	*Connolly* MINY	31 Jun 43 15 Jan 44	8 Jul 44	22 Nov 45	Sold 20 May 46
307	*Finnegan* MINY	5 Jul 43 22 Feb 44	19 Aug 44	27 Nov 45	Sold Jun 46
316	*Harveson* Orange	9 Mar 43 22 May 43	12 Oct 43 12 Feb 51	9 May 47 30 Jun 60	DER–316 Feb 51; str 1 Dec 66
317	*Joyce* Orange	8 Mar 43 26 May 43	30 Sep 43 28 Feb 51	1 May 46 17 Jun 60	DER–317 Feb 51; str 1 Dec 72
318	*Kirkpatrick* Orange	15 Mar 43 5 Jun 43	23 Oct 43 23 Feb 52	1 May 46 24 Jun 60	DER–318 Oct 51; str 1 Aug 74
319	*Leopold* Orange	24 Mar 43 12 Jun 43	18 Oct 43		WL(T) 10 Mar 44
320	*Menges* Orange	22 Mar 43 15 Jun 43	26 Oct 43	Jan 47	Str 2 Jan 71; sold
321	*Mosley* Orange	6 Apr 43 26 Jun 43	30 Oct 43	15 Mar 46	Str 2 Jan 71; sold
322	*Newell* Orange	5 Apr 43 29 Jun 43	30 Oct 43 20 Aug 57	20 Nov 45 21 Sep 68	CG Jul 51–Jun 54 (WDE–422); DER–322 Nov 56; str 23 Sep 68; used in the movie *Tora Tora Tora* Jan Apr 69; sold for BU 15 Dec 71 Taiwan
323	*Pride* Orange	12 Apr 43 3 Jul 43	13 Nov 43	26 Apr 46	CG Jul 51–Jun 54 (WDE–423); str 2 Jan 71; sold
324	*Falgout* Orange	26 May 43 24 Jul 43	15 Nov 43 30 Jun 55	18 Apr 47	CG Aug 51–May 54 (WDE–424); DER–324 Oct 54; str 1 Jun 75; tgt
325	*Lowe* Orange	24 May 43 28 Jul 43	22 Nov 43 55	1 May 46 20 Sep 68	CG Jul 51–Jun 54 (WDE–425); DER–325 55; str 23 Sep 68; sold
326	*Gary* Orange	15 Jun 43 21 Aug 43	27 Nov 43 2 Aug 57	7 Mar 47 22 Oct 73	*Thomas J. Gary* 1 Jan 45; DER–326 1 Nov 56; 22 Oct 73 Tunisia (*President Bourguiba*)
327	*Brister* Orange	14 Jun 43 24 Aug 43	30 Nov 43 2 Jul 56	4 Oct 46	DER–327 Jul 56; str 23 Sep 68; sold 3 Nov 71 Taiwan

		LD/Launch	Comm	Decomm	Fate
328	*Finch*	29 Jun 43	13 Dec 43	4 Oct 46	CG Aug 51–Apr 54 (WDE–428);
	Orange	28 Aug 43	17 Sep 56	1 Oct 73	DER–328 Aug 56; str 1 Feb 74; tgt
329	*Kretchmer*	28 Jun 43	13 Dec 43	20 Sep 46	CG Jun 51–Aug 54 (WDE–429);
	Orange	31 Aug 43	22 Sep 56	1 Oct 73	DER–329 Sep 56; str 30 Sep 73; sold 14 May 74
330	*O'Reilly*	29 Jul 43	28 Dec 43	15 Jun 46	DE(A/S); str 15 Jan 71; sold 10
	Orange	14 Nov 43			Apr 72
331	*Koiner*	26 July 43	27 Dec 43	4 Oct 46	CG Jun 51–May 54 (WDE–431);
	Orange	5 Sep 43	26 Aug 55	68	DER–331 Sep 54; str 23 Sep 68; sold 3 Sep 69
332	*Price*	24 Aug 43	12 Jan 44	16 May 47	DER–332 21 Oct 55;
	Orange	30 Oct 43	1 Aug 56	30 Jun 60	
333	*Strickland*	23 Aug 43	10 Jan 44	15 Jun 46	DER–333 Dec 51; Str 1 Oct 72
	Orange	2 Nov 43	2 Feb 52	17 Jun ?	
334	*Forster*	31 Aug 43	25 Jan 44	15 Jun 46	CG Jun 51–May 54 (WDE–434);
	Orange	13 Nov 43	23 Oct 56		DER–334 Oct 55; Vietnam 25 Sep 71 (*Tran Khanh Du*)
335	*Daniel*	30 Aug 43	24 Jan 44	12 Apr 46	Str 15 Jan 71
	Orange	16 Nov 43			
336	*Roy O. Hale*	13 Sep 43	3 Feb 44	11 Jul 36	DER–338 Dec 55; str 1 Aug 74
	Orange	20 Nov 43	29 Jan 57	15 Jul 63	
337	*Dale W. Peterson*	25 Oct 43	17 Feb 44	27 Mar 46	Str 2 Jan 71
	Orange	22 Dec 43			
338	*Martin H. Ray*	27 Oct 43	28 Feb 44	Mar 46	Str 1 May 66; sold 30 Mar 67
	Orange	23 Dec 43			
339	*John C. Butler*	5 Oct 43	31 Mar 44	26 Jun 46	Str 1 Jun 70; tgt
	Orange	12 Nov 43	27 Dec 50	18 Dec 57	
340	*O'Flaherty*	4 Oct 43	8 Apr 44	Jan 47	Str 1 Dec 72
	Orange	14 Dec 43			
341	*Raymond*	3 Nov 43	15 Apr 44	24 Jan 47	NRF 59 onward; str 1 Jul 72
	Orange	8 Jan 44	27 Apr 51	22 Sep 58	
342	*Richard W. Suesens*	1 Nov 43	26 Apr 44	15 Jan 47	Str 15 Mar 72
	Orange	11 Jan 44			
343	*Abercrombie*	8 Nov 43	1 May 44	15 Jun 46	Str 1 May 67; tgt 7 Jan 68
	Orange	14 Jan 44			
344	*Oberrender*	8 Nov 43	11 May 44	11 Jul 45	WD(K) 9 May 45; str 25 Jul 45;
	Orange	18 Jan 44			tgt 6 Nov 45
345	*Robert Brazier*	16 Nov 43	18 May 44	16 Sep 46	Str 1 Jan 68; tgt 9 Jan 69
	Orange	22 Jan 44			
346	*Edwin A. Howard*	15 Nov 43	25 May 44	25 Sep 46	Str 1 Dec 72; sold 73
	Orange	25 Jan 44			
347	*Jesse Rutherford*	22 Nov 43	31 May 44	21 Jun 46	Str 1 Jan 68; tgt 8 Dec 68
	Orange	20 Jan 44			
348	*Key*	14 Dec 43	5 Jun 44	9 Jul 46	Str 1 Mar 72
	Orange	12 Feb 44			
349	*Gentry*	13 Dec 43	14 Jun 44	2 Jul 46	Str 15 Jan 72
	Orange	15 Feb 44			
350	*Traw*	19 Dec 43	20 Jun 44	7 Jun 46	Str 1 Aug 67; tgt 17 Aug 68
	Orange	12 Feb 44			
351	*Maurice J. Manuel*	22 Dec 43	30 Jun 44	20 May 46	Str 1 May 66; tgt Aug 66
	Orange	19 Feb 44	27 Apr 51	30 Oct 57	
352	*Naifeh*	29 Dec 43	4 Jul 44	27 Jun 46	NRF 59 onward; str 1 Jan 66;
	Orange	29 Feb 44	26 Jan 51	17 Jun 60	tgt Jul 66
353	*Doyle C. Barnes*	11 Jan 44	13 Jul 44	15 Jan 47	Str 1 Dec 72; sold 12 Sep 73
	Orange	4 Mar 44			
354	*Kenneth M. Willett*	10 Jan 44	19 Jul 44	24 Oct 46	NRF 59 onward; str 1 Jul 72; tgt
	Orange	7 Mar 44	25 May 51	26 Feb 59	Mar 74
355	*Jaccard*	25 Jan 44	26 Jul 44	30 Sep 46	Str 1 Nov 67; tgt 4 Oct 68
	Orange	18 Mar 44			
356	*Lloyd E. Acree*	24 Jan 44	1 Aug 44	10 Oct 46	Str 15 Jan 72; sold 16 Jun 73
	Orange	21 Mar 44			
357	*George E. Davis*	15 Feb 44	11 Aug 44	26 Aug 46	NRF 51–54; str 1 Dec 72; sold 2
	Orange	8 Apr 44	11 Jul 51	11 Nov 54	Jan 74
358	*Mack*	14 Feb 44	16 Aug 44	11 Dec 46	Str 15 Mar 72; sold 13 Jun 73
	Orange	11 Apr 44			
359	*Woodson*	7 Mar 44	24 Aug 44	15 Jan 47	NRF 57–62; str 1 Jul 65; sold 16
	Orange		19 May 51	11 Aug 62	Aug 66
360	*Johnnie Hutchins*	6 Mar 44	28 Aug 44	14 May 46	NRF 46–58; str 1 Jul 72; sold 5
	Orange	2 May 44	23 Jun 50	25 Feb 58	Feb 74
361	*Walton*	21 Mar 44	4 Sep 44	31 May 46	Str 23 Sep 68; tgt 7 Aug 69
	Orange	20 May 44	26 Jan 51		
362	*Rolf*	20 Mar 44	7 Sep 44	3 Jun 46	Str 1 Dec 72; sold 11 Sep 73
	Orange	23 May 44			

	LD/Launch	Comm	Decomm	Fate
363 *Pratt* Orange	11 Apr 44 1 Jun 44	18 Sep 44	14 May 46	Str 15 Mar 72; sold 15 Jan 73
364 *Rombach* Orange	10 Apr 44 6 Jun 44	20 Sep 44	9 Jan 58	NRF 46–58; str 1 Mar 72; sold 19 Dec 72
365 *McGinty* Orange	3 May 4 5 Aug 44	25 Sep 44 28 Mar 51 2 Oct 61	15 Jan 47 19 Sep 59 1 Aug 62	NRF 59–61, 62–68; str 23 Sep 68; sold 27 Oct 69
366 *Alvin C. Cockrell* Orange	1 May 44 8 Aug 44	7 Oct 44 27 Jun 51	2 Jul 46	Str 23 Sep 68; tgt 19 Sep 69
367 *French* Orange	May 44 17 Jun 44	9 Oct 44	29 May 46	Str 15 May 72; sold 20 Sep 73
368 *Cecil J. Doyle* Orange	12 May 44 1 Jul 44	16 Oct 44	2 Jul 46	Str 1 Jul 67; tgt
369 *Thaddeus Parker* Orange	23 May 44 26 Aug 44	25 Oct 44 21 Sep 51	31 May 46 1 Sep 67	NRF post-Korea; str 1 Sep 67; sold 9 Jul 68
370 *John L. Williamson* Orange	22 May 44 29 Aug 44	31 Oct 44	14 Jun 46	Str 15 Sep 70; sold
371 *Presley* Orange	6 Jun 44 19 Aug 44	7 Nov 44	20 Jun 46	Str 30 Jun 68; sold
372 *Williams* Orange	5 Jun 44 22 Aug 44	11 Nov 44	4 Jun 46	Str 1 Jul 67; tgt 29 Jun 68
382 *Ramsden* Brown	26 Mar 43 24 May 43	19 Oct 43 10 Dec 57	13 Jun 46 23 Jun 60	CG Apr 51–Jun 54 (WDE–482); DER–382 Nov 56; tgt
383 *Mills* Brown	26 Mar 43 26 May 43	12 Oct 43 3 Oct 57	14 Jun 46 27 Oct 70	DER–383 Oct 57; NRF 68–
384 *Rhodes* Brown	19 Apr 43 29 Jun 43	25 Oct 43 1 Aug 55	13 Jun 46 10 Jul 63	DER–384 Aug 55
385 *Richey* Brown	19 Apr 43 30 Jun 43	30 Oct 43	Jan 47	CG Apr 52–Jun 54 (WDE–485); str 30 Jun 68; tgt Jul 69
386 *Savage* Brown	30 Apr 43 15 Jul 43	29 Oct 43 18 Feb 55	13 Jun 46 17 Oct 69	DER–386 Sep 54;
387 *Vance* Brown	30 Apr 43 16 Jul 43	1 Nov 43 5 Oct 56	27 Feb 46 10 Oct 69	CG May 51–Jun 54 (WDE–487); DER–387 Nov 56
388 *Lansing* Brown	15 May 43 2 Aug 43	10 Nov 43 18 Dec 56	25 Apr 46 21 May 65	CG Jun 52–Jun 54 (WDE–488); DER–388 Oct 55; str 1 Feb 74
389 *Durant* Brown	15 May 43 1 Aug 43	16 Nov 43 8 Dec 56	27 Feb 46	CG May 51–Jun 54 (WDE–489); DER–389 Dec 55; str 1 Apr 74; tgt
390 *Calcaterra* Brown	28 May 43 16 Aug 43	17 Nov 43 12 Sep 55	1 May 46 2 Jul 73	DER–390 Oct 54; str 2 Jul 73; sold 14 May 74
391 *Chambers* Brown	28 May 43 17 Aug 43	22 Nov 43 1 Jun 55	22 Apr 46 20 Jun 60	CG Jun 52–Jul 54 (WDE–491); DER–391 Oct 54
392 *Merrill* Brown	1 Jul 43 29 Aug 43	27 Nov 43	1 May 46	Str 2 Apr 72; sold 74
393 *Haverfield* Brown	1 Jul 43 30 Aug 43	29 Nov 43 4 Jan 55	30 Jun 17	DER–393 Sep 54; str 2 Jun 69; sold 15 Dec 71
394 *Swenning* Brown	17 Jul 43 13 Sep 43	1 Dec 43	25 Sep 47	Str 1 Jul 72
395 *Willis* Brown	17 Jul 43 14 Sep 43	10 Dec 43	12 Sep 47	Str 1 Jul 72
396 *Janssen* Brown	4 Aug 43 10 Oct 43	18 Dec 43	12 Apr 46	Str 1 Jul 72
397 *Wilhoite* Brown	4 Aug 43 5 Oct 43	16 Dec 43 29 Jan 55	19 Jun 46 2 Jul 69	DER 1955; str 2 Jul 69; sold 19 Jul 72
398 *Cockrill* Brown	31 Aug 43 29 Oct 43	24 Dec 43	21 Jun 46	Str 1 Aug 73; tgt
399 *Stockdale* Brown	31 Aug 43 30 Oct 43	31 Dec 43	18 Apr 47	Str 1 Jul 72; tgt
400 *Hissem* Brown	6 Oct 43 26 Oct 43	13 Jan 44 31 Aug 56	15 Jun 46 15 May 70	DER–400 Aug 56; str 1 Jun 75; tgt
401 *Holder* Brown	6 Oct 43 27 Nov 43	18 Jan 44	—	WL(T) 11 Apr 44; part used to repair *Menges*; rest sold 20 Jun 47
402 *Richard S. Bull* Brown	18 Aug 43 16 Nov 43	26 Feb 44	Mar 46	Str 30 Jun 68; tgt 4 Jun 69
403 *Richard M. Rowell* Brown	18 Aug 43 17 Nov 43	9 Mar 44	2 Jul 46	Str 30 Jun 18; sold
404 *Eversole* Brown	15 Sep 43 3 Dec 43	21 Mar 44		WL(T) 28 Oct 44
405 *Dennis* Brown	15 Sep 43 4 Dec 43	20 Mar 44	31 May 46	Str 1 Dec 72; sold 73

		LD/Launch	Comm	Decomm	Fate
406	Edmonds	1 Nov 43	3 Apr 44	31 May 46	Str 15 May 72
	Brown	17 Dec 43	28 Feb 51		
407	Shelton	1 Nov 43	4 Apr 44	—	WL(T) 3 Oct 44
	Brown	18 Dec 43			
408	Straus	18 Nov 43	6 Apr 44	15 Jan 47	Str 1 May 66; tgt
	Brown	30 Dec 43			
409	La Prade	18 Nov 43	20 Apr 44	11 May 46	Str 15 Jan 72
	Brown	31 Dec 43			
410	Jack Miller	29 Nov 43	13 Apr 44	1 Jun 46	Str 30 Jun 68; sold
	Brown	10 Jan 44			
411	Stafford	29 Nov 43	19 Apr 44	16 May 46	Str 15 Mar 72
	Brown	11 Jan 44			
412	Walter C. Wann	6 Dec 43	2 May 44	31 May 46	Str 30 Jun 68; sold
	Brown	19 Jan 44			
413	Samuel B. Roberts	6 Dec 43	28 Apr 44	—	WL(G) 25 Oct 44
	Brown	20 Jan 44			
414	Le Ray Wilson	20 Dec 43	10 May 44	15 Jan 47	Str 15 May 72
	Brown	28 Jan 44	28 Mar 51	30 Jan 59	
415	Lawrence C. Taylor	20 Dec 43	13 May 44	23 Apr 46	Str 1 Dec 72; sold 73
	Brown	29 Jan 44			
416	Melvin R. Nawman	3 Jan 44	16 May 44	23 Apr 46	NRF post-Korea; str 1 Jul 72
	Brown	16 Feb 44	28 Mar 51	30 Aug 60	
417	Oliver Mitchell	3 Jan 44	14 Jun 44	24 Apr 46	Str 15 Mar 72
	Brown	8 Feb 44			
418	Tabberer	12 Jan 44	23 May 44	24 Apr 46	NRF post-Korea; str 1 Jul 72
	Brown	3 Feb 44	7 Apr 51	May 60	
419	Robert F. Keller	12 Jan 44	17 Jun 44	24 Apr 46	Str 1 Jul 72; sold 73; NRF 46–
	Brown	19 Feb 44	31 Mar 50	21 Sep 59	50, 59 onward
			2 Oct 61	1 Aug 62	
420	Leland E. Thomas	21 Jan 44	19 Jun 44	3 May 46	Str 1 Dec 72; sold 11 Sep 73
	Brown	28 Feb 44			
421	Chester T. O'Brien	21 Jan 44	3 Jul 44	2 Jul 46	NRF 59 onward; str 1 Jul 72;
	Brown	29 Feb 44	28 Mar 51	21 Feb 59	sold 28 Mar 74
422	Douglas A. Munro	31 Jan 44	11 Jul 44	15 Jan 57	Str 1 Dec; tgt
	Brown	8 Mar 44	28 Feb 51	24 Jun 60	
423	Dufilho	31 Jan 44	21 Jul 44	14 May 46	Str 1 Dec; sold 73
	Brown	9 Mar 44			
424	Haas	23 Feb 44	2 Aug 44	31 May 46	Str 1 Dec; sold 6 Sep 67
	Brown	20 Mar 44	19 May 51	24 Jan 58	
438	Corbesier	4 Nov 43	31 Mar 44	2 Jul 46	Str 1 Dec 72; sold 3 Dec 73
	FedN	13 Feb 44			
439	Conklin	4 Nov 43	21 Apr 44	17 Jan 46	Str 1 Oct 70; sold 12 May 72
	FedN	13 Feb 44			
440	McCoy Reynolds	18 Nov 43	2 May 44	31 May 46	Portugal (Corte Real); sold Nov
	FedN	22 Feb 44	28 Mar 51	7 Feb 57	68 for BU
441	William Seiverling	2 Dec 43	1 Jun 44	21 Mar 47	Str 1 Dec 72; sold 20 Sept 73
	FedN		27 Dec 50		
442	Ulvert M. Moore	2 Dec 43	18 Jul 44	22 May 46	Str 1 Dec 65; tgt 13 Jul 66
	FedN	7 Mar 44	27 Jan 51	10 Oct 58	
443	Kendall C. Campbell	16 Dec 43	31 Jul 44	31 May 46	Str 15 Jan 72; sold 15 Nov 73
	FedN	19 Mar 44			
444	Goss	16 Dec 43	26 Aug 44	15 Jun 46	NRF 59 onward; str 1 Mar 72;
	FedN	19 Mar 44	27 Dec 50	10 Oct 58	sold 20 Nov 72
445	Grady	3 Jan 44	11 Sep 44	2 Jul 46	NRF 47–50; sold Jun 69
	FedN	2 Apr 44	1 Aug 50	18 Dec 57	
446	Charles E. Brannon	13 Jan 44	1 Nov 44	21 May 46	NRF 46 onward; str 23 Sep 68;
	FedN	23 Apr 44	21 Nov 50	18 Jun 60	sold 27 Oct 69
447	Albert T. Harris	13 Jan 44	29 Nov 44	26 Jul 46	NRF post-Korea; str 23 Sep 68;
	FedN	16 Apr 44	27 Apr 51		tgt 9 Apr 69
448	Cross	19 Mar 44	8 Jan 45	14 Jun 46	NRF 51–58; str 1 Jul 66; sold 5
	FedN	4 Jul 44	6 Jun 51	2 Jan 58	Mar 68
449	Hanna	22 Mar 44	27 Jan 45	31 May 46	NRF post-Korea; str 1 Dec 72;
	FedN	4 Jul 44	27 Dec 50	11 Dec 59	sold 3 Dec 73
450	Joseph E. Connolly	6 Apr 44	28 Feb 45	20 Jun 46	Str 1 Jun 70; tgt 24 Feb 72
	FedN	6 Aug 44			
508	Gilligan	18 Nov 43	12 May 44	2 Jul 46	NRF 47–50, also 59 onward; str
	FedN	22 Feb 44	15 Jul 50	31 Mar 59	1 Mar 72
509	Formoe	3 Jan 44	5 Oct 44	27 May 46	Portugal 27 May 46 (Diogo Cao)
	FedN	2 Apr 44	27 Jun 51	7 Feb 57	
510	Heyliger	27 Apr 44	24 Mar 45	20 Jun 46	Str 1 May 66; tgt 69
	FedN	6 Aug 44	28 Mar 51	2 Jan 58	

	LD/Launch	Comm	Decomm	Fate
516 *Lawford* BosNY	9 Jul 43 13 Aug 43	3 Nov 43		RN; WL(B) 8 Jun 44
517 *Louis* BosNY	9 Jul 43 13 Aug 43	9 Nov 43		RN; ret 20 Mar 46; sold 17 Jun 46
518 *Lawson* BosNY	9 July 43 13 Aug 43	15 Nov 43		RN; ret 20 Mar 46; sold 31 Jan 47
519 *Paisley* BosNY	18 July 43 30 Aug 43	20 Nov 43		RN; ret 20 Aug 45
520 *Loring* BosNY	18 Jul 43 30 Aug 43	27 Nov 43		RN; ret 7 Jan 47; sold
521 *Hoste* BosNY	14 Aug 43 24 Sept 43	3 Dec 43		RN; ret 22 Aug 45; sold 7 May 46
522 *Moorson* BosNY	14 Aug 43 24 Sept 43	16 Dec 43		RN; ret 25 Oct 45; str 5 Dec 45; sold 12 July 46
523 *Manners* BosNY	14 Aug 43 24 Sept 43	6 Dec 43		RN; WD(T) 26 Jan 45; ret 8 Nov 45; str 19 Dec 45; sold 3 Dec 46; BU Greece
524 *Mounsey* BosNY	14 Aug 43 24 Sept 43	23 Dec 43		RN; ret 27 Feb 46; str 28 Mar 46; sold 8 Nov 46
525 *Inglis* BosNY	25 Sept 43 2 Nov 43	29 Dec 43		RN; ret 20 Mar 46; sold Sep 47
526 *Inman* BosNY	25 Sept 43 2 Nov 43	13 Jan 44		RN; ret 1 Mar 46; sold Nov 46
527 *O'Toole* BosNY	25 Sept 43 2 Nov 43	22 Jan 44	18 Oct 45	Sold Mar 46
528 *John J. Powers* BosNY	25 Sept 43 2 Nov 43	29 Feb 44	16 Oct 45	Sold Feb 46
529 *Mason* BosNY	14 Oct 43 17 Nov 43	20 Mar 44	12 Oct 45	Str 1 Nov 45; sold 18 Mar 47
530 *John M. Bermingham* BosNY	14 Oct 43 17 Nov 43	8 Apr 44	12 Oct 45	Sold Mar 46
531 *Edward H. Allen* BosNY	31 Aug 43 7 Oct 43	16 Dec 43 26 Feb 51	10 May 46 9 Jan 58	Str 1 Jul 72; sold 5 Feb 74
532 *Tweedy* BosNY	31 Aug 43	12 Feb 44 2 Apr 52	10 May 46 Jun 69	NRF post-Korea; str 30 Jun 69; tgt May 70; was ASW conversion
533 *Howard F. Clark* BosNY	8 Oct 43 8 Nov 43	25 May 44	15 Jul 46	Str 15 May 72; sold 6 Sep 73
534 *Silverstein* BosNY	8 Oct 43 8 Nov 43	14 Jul 44 28 Feb 51	15 Jan 47 30 Jan 59	Str 1 Dec 72; sold 3 Dec 73
535 *Lewis* BosNY	3 Nov 43 7 Dec 43	5 Sep 44 28 Mar 52	1 May 46 27 May 60	Str 1 Jan 66; tgt Mar 66; was ASW conversion
536 *Bivin* BosNY	3 Nov 43 7 Dec 43	31 Oct 44	15 Jan 47	Str 30 Jun 68; tgt 17 Jul 69
537 *Rizzi* BosNY	3 Nov 43 7 Dec 43	26 Jun 45 28 Mar 51	18 Jun 46 28 Feb 58	Str 1 Aug 72; sold 5 Feb 74
538 *Osberg* BosNY	3 Nov 43 7 Dec 43	10 Dec 45 26 Feb 51	47 Sep 57	Str 1 Aug 72; sold 5 Feb 74
539 *Wagner* BosNY	8 Nov 43 27 Dec 44	22 Nov 55	Mar 60	Str 1 Nov 74; tgt
540 *Vandivier* BosNY	8 Nov 43 27 Dec 43	11 Oct 55	Jun 60	Str 1 Nov 74; tgt
541 *Sheehan* BosNY	8 Nov 43 —			Canc 7 Jan 46
542 *Oswald A. Powers* BosNY	18 Nov 43 17 Dec 43			Canc 7 Jan 46; sold 2 Jul 46
543 *Groves* BosNY	9 Dec 43			Canc 5 Sep 44
544 *Alfred Wolf* BosNY	9 Dec 43			Canc 5 Sep 44
563 *Spragge* BethHI	15 Sep 43 16 Oct 43	14 Jan 44		RN; ret 28 Feb 46
564 *Stayner* BethHI	22 Sep 43 6 Nov 43	30 Dec 43		RN; ret 24 Nov 45
565 *Thornborough* BethHI	22 Sep 43 13 Nov 43	31 Dec 43		RN; ret 29 Jan 47; sold Holland
566 *Trollope* BethHI	29 Sep 43 20 Nov 43	10 Jan 44		RN; WD (T) 6 July 44; ret 24 Dec 45; sold 9 Jan 47; BU at Troon, Scotland May 51
567 *Tyler* BethHI	6 Oct 43 20 Nov 43	14 Jan 44		RN; ret 12 Nov 45; sold 23 May 46

		LD/Launch	Comm	Decomm	Fate
568	Torrington	22 Sep 43	18 Jan 44		RN; ret 11 Jun 46; sold 7 Nov 47
	BethHI	27 Nov 43			
569	Narbrough	6 Oct 43	21 Jan 44		RN; ret 4 Feb 46; sold 5 Nov 46
	BethHI	27 Nov 43			
570	Waldegrave	16 Oct 43	25 Jan 44		RN; ret 3 Dec 45; sold 5 Nov 46
	BethHI	4 Dec 43			
571	Whitaker	20 Oct 43	28 Jan 44		RN; WD(T) 1 Nov 44; ret 10 Mar; sold 9 Jan 47 England
	BethHI	12 Dec 43			
572	Holmes	27 Oct 43	31 Jan 44		RN; ret 7 Feb 46; sold Oct 47
	BethHI	18 Dec 43			
573	Hargood	27 Oct 43	7 Feb 44		RN; ret 23 Feb 46; str 12 April 46; sold 7 May 47
	BethHI	18 Dec 43			
574	Hotham	5 Nov 43	8 Feb 44		RN; fitted as floating power station for Singapore but used as guardship Hong Kong; ret UK late 46 for conv to gas turb power; conv canc 1954; ret 13 Mar 56, BU England
	BethHI	21 Dec 43			
575	Ahrens	5 Nov 43	12 Feb 44	24 June 46	Str 1 Apr 65; sold 20 Jun 67
	BethHI	21 Dec 43			
576	Barr	5 Nov 43	15 Feb 44	—	APD–39 31 Jul 44
	BethHI	28 Dec 43			
577	Alexander J. Luke	5 Nov 43	19 Feb 44	18 Oct 47	DER conv 45; str 1 May 70; tgt 22 Oct 70
	BethHI	28 Dec 43			
578	Robert I. Paine	5 Nov 43	26 Feb 44	21 Nov 47	DER conv 45; str 1 Jun 68; sold Taiwan 10 Jul 68 (Tai Yuan); last of Rudderow class
	BethHI	30 Dec 43			
579	Riley	20 Oct 43	13 Mar 44	15 Jan 47	Str 15 Jan 72
	BethHI	29 Dec 43			
580	Leslie L.B. Knox	7 Nov 43	22 Mar 44	15 June 46	Str 1 Mar 72; tgt 16 Nov 72
	BethHI	8 Jan 44			
581	McNulty	17 Nov 43	31 Mar 44	2 Jul 46	Str 30 June 66; sold May 69
	BethHI	8 Jan 44			
582	Metivier	24 Nov 43	7 Apr 44	1 Jun 46	Str 1 Nov 65; sold 19 Sept 66; NRF 46–50
	BethHI	12 Jan 44			
583	George A. Johnson	24 Nov 43	15 Apr 44	31 May 46	Str 30 Jun 68; tgt 11 Nov 69
	BethHI	12 Jan 44	29 Sep 50	Sep 57	
584	Charles J. Kimmel	1 Dec 43	20 April 44	15 Jan 47	NRF 46–50; NRF 58 onward; str 1 May 65; sold 11 Mar 66, largest U.S. warship on Great Lakes
	BethHI	15 Jan 44			
585	Daniel A. Joy	1 Dec 43	28 Apr 44	7 Feb 49	Str 1 Nov 69
	BethHI	15 Jan 44	5 May 50	65	
586	Lough	8 Dec 43	2 May 44	24 Jun 46	NRF 46–50; str 1 Dec 72
	BethHI		22 Jan 44		
587	Thomas F. Nickel	15 Dec 43	9 Jun 44	31 May 46	Str 1 Dec 66; tgt 16 May 67
	BethHI	22 Jan 44	22 Sep 50	22 Feb 58	
588	Peiffer	21 Dec 43	15 Jun 44	1 Jun 46	Str 15 May 72
	BethHI	26 Jan 44			
589	Tinsman	21 Dec 43	26 Jun 44	11 May 46	
	BethHI	29 Jan 44			
590	Ringness	23 Dec 43			APD–100
	BethHI	5 Feb 44			
591	Knudson	23 Dec 43			APD–101
	BethHI	5 Feb 44			
592	Rednour	30 Dec 43			APD–102
	BethHI	12 Feb 44			
593	Tollberg	30 Dec 43			APD–103
	BethHI	12 Feb 44			
594	William J. Pattison	4 Jan 44			APD–104
	BethHI	15 Feb 44			
595	Myers	15 Jan 44			APD–105
	BethHI	15 Feb 44			
596	Walter B. Cobb	15 Jan 44			APD–106
	BethHI	23 Feb 44			
597	Earle B. Hall	19 Jan 44			APD–107
	BethHI	1 Mar 44			
598	Harry L. Corl	19 Jan 44			APD–108
	BethHI	1 Mar 44			
599	Belet	26 Jan 44			APD–109
	BethHI	3 Mar 44			
600	Julius A. Raven	26 Jan 44			APD–110
	BethHI	3 Mar 44			
601	Walsh	27 Feb 45			APD–111
	BethHI	28 Apr 45			
602	Hunter Marshall	9 Mar 45			APD–112
	BethHI	5 May 45			

		LD/Launch	Comm	Decomm	Fate
603	*Earhart*	20 Mar 45			APD–113
	BethHI	12 May 45			
604	*Walter S. Gorka*	3 Apr 45			APD–114
	BethHI	26 May 45			
605	*Rogers Blood*	12 Apr 45			APD–115
	BethHI	2 June 45			
606	*Francovich*	19 Apr 45			APD–116
	BethHI	5 Jun 45			
633	*Foreman*	9 Apr 43	22 Oct 43	28 June 46	Str 1 May 65; sold
	BethSF	1 Aug 43			
634	*Whitehurst*	21 Mar 43	19 Nov 43	27 Nov 46	NRF post-Korea; str 12 Jul 69;
	BethSF	5 Sep 43	1 Sep 50	25 Jul 62	tgt
635	*England*	4 Apr 43	10 Dec 43	15 Oct 45	APD–41 Jul 43 canc; sold 26 Nov
	BethSF	26 Sep 43			45 due WD (K)
636	*Witter*	28 Apr 43	29 Dec 43	29 Oct 45	APD–58 Mar 45 canc; sold 2 Dec
	BethSF	17 Oct 43			46
637	*Bowers*	28 May 43	27 Jan 44		APD–40 25 Jun 45
	BethSF	31 Oct 43			
638	*Willmarth*	25 Jun 43	13 Mar 44	26 Apr 46	Str 66; sold 1 Jul 68
	BethSF	21 Nov 43			
639	*Gendreau*	1 Aug 43	17 Mar 44	13 Mar 48	Str 1 Dec 72
	BethSF	12 Dec 43			
640	*Fieberling*	19 Mar 44	11 Apr 44	13 Mar 48	Str 1 Mar 72
	BethSF	2 Apr 44			
641	*William C. Cole*	5 Sep 43	12 May 44	28 Apr 48	Str 1 Mar 72
	BethSF	29 Dec 43			
642	*Paul G. Baker*	26 Sep 43	25 May 44	3 Feb 47	Str 1 Dec 69
	BethSF	12 Mar 44			
643	*Damon M. Cummings*	17 Oct 43	29 Jun 44	3 Feb 47	Str 1 Mar 72
	BethSF	18 Apr 44			
644	*Vammen*	1 Aug 43	27 Jul 44	3 Feb 47	Str 12 Jul 69; tgt; was ASW
	BethSF	21 May 44	15 Feb 52		conversion
665	*Jenks*	12 May 43	19 Jan 44	26 Jun 46	APD–67 canc; str 1 Feb 66; sold
	Dravo	11 Sept 43			3 Sep 68
666	*Durik*	22 Jan 43	24 Mar 44	15 June 46	APD–68 canc; str 1 Jun 65; sold
	Dravo	11 Sep 43			30 Jan 67
667	*Wiseman*	26 July 43	4 Apr 44	31 Jan 47	NRF 59–61, 62–?; str 15 Apr 73
	Dravo	6 Nov 43	50	16 May 59	
			2 Oct 61	1 Aug 62	
668	*Yokes*	22 Aug 43			APD–69
	Orange	27 Nov 43			
669	*Pavlic*	21 Sep 43			APD–70
	Orange	18 Dec 43			
670	*Odum*	15 Oct 43			APD–71
	Orange	19 Jan 44			
671	*Jack C. Robinson*	10 Nov 43			APD–72
	Orange	8 Jan 44			
672	*Bassett*	28 Nov 43			APD–73
	Orange	15 Jan 44			
673	*John B. Gray*	18 Dec 43			APD–74
	Orange	18 Mar 44			
674	*Joseph M. Auman*	8 Nov 43			APD–117
	Orange	5 Feb 45			
675	*Weber*	22 Feb 43	30 Jun 43	15 Dec 44	APD–75
	BethQ	1 May 43			
676	*Schmitt*	22 Feb 43	24 Jul 43	27 Jun 44	APD–76
	BethQ	29 May 43			
677	*Frament*	1 May 43	15 Aug 43	15 Dec 44	APD–77
	BethQ	28 Jun 43			
678	*Harmon*	31 May 43	31 Aug 43	25 Mar 47	Str 1 Aug 65; sold 30 Jan 67
	BethQ	25 Jul 43			
679	*Greenwood*	29 Jun 43	25 Sep 43	1958	NRF post-Korea; str 20 Feb 67;
	BethQ	21 Aug 43	2 Oct 61	1966	sold 6 Sep 67
680	*Loeser*	27 Jul 43	10 Oct 43	28 Mar 49	NRF post-Korea; str 23 Sep 68;
	BethQ	11 Sep 43	9 Mar 51	22 Sep 68	sold
681	*Gillette*	24 Aug 43	27 Oct 43	Dec 46	Str 1 Dec 72
	BethQ	25 Sep 43	—	—	
682	*Underhill*	16 Sep 43	15 Nov 43	—	WL(T) 24 Jul 45
	BethQ	15 Oct 43			
683	*Henry R. Kenyon*	29 Sep 43	30 Nov 43	3 Feb 47	Str 1 Dec 69
	BethQ	30 Oct 43	—	—	

		LD/Launch	Comm	Decomm	Fate
684	*De Long*	19 Oct 43	31 Dec 43	Jan 46	NRF post-Korea; APD–137 canc;
	BethQ	23 Nov 43	7 Feb 51	8 Aug 69	str 8 Aug 69; tgt 19 Feb 70
685	*Coates*	8 Nov 43	24 Jan 44	30 Jan 70	NRF post-Korea; APD–138 canc;
	BethQ	12 Dec 43	7 Feb 51		str 30 Jan 70; tgt 19 Sep 71
686	*Eugene E. Elmore*	27 Nov 43	4 Feb 44	31 May 46	Str 30 June 68; sold May 69
	BethQ	23 Dec 43	—	—	
687	*Kline*	27 May 44			APD–120
	BethQ	27 Jun 44			
688	*Raymon W. Herndon*	12 Jun 44			APD–121
	BethQ	15 Jul 44			
689	*Scribner*	29 Jun 44			APD–122
	BethQ	1 Aug 44			
690	*Alexander Diachenko*	18 Jul 44			APD–123
	BethQ	15 Aug 44			
691	*Horace A. Bass*	3 Aug 44			APD–124
	BethQ	12 Sep 44			
692	*Wantuck*	17 Aug 44			APD–125
	BethQ	25 Sep 44			
693	*Bull*	15 Dec 42	12 Aug 43		APD–78 31 Jul 44
	Defoe	25 Mar 43			
694	*Bunch*	22 Feb 43	21 Aug 43		APD–79 31 Jul 44
	Defoe	29 May 43			
695	*Rich*	27 Mar 43	1 Oct 43		WL (M) 8 Jun 44
	Defoe	22 Jun 43			
696	*Spangler*	28 Apr 43	31 Oct 43	8 Oct 58	NRF 58 onward; str 1 Mar 72;
	Defoe	15 Jul 43			sold 20 Nov 72
697	*George*	22 May 43	20 Nov 43	8 Oct 58	NRF 58 onward; str 1 Nov 69;
	Defoe	4 Aug 43			sold
698	*Raby*	7 Jun 43	7 Dec 43	22 Dec 53	NRF post-Korea; str 1 Jun 68
	Defoe	4 Sep 43			
699	*Marsh*	23 June 43	12 Jan 44	16 Aug 58	Str 15 Apr 71; NRF 58–61, 62-
	Defoe	25 Sep 43	15 Dec 61	69	69
700	*Currier*	21 Jul 43	1 Feb 44	4 Apr 60	Str 1 Dec 66; tgt Jul 67
	Defoe	14 Oct 43			
701	*Osmus*	17 Aug 43	23 Feb 44	15 Mar 47	Str 1 Dec 72
	Defoe	4 Nov 43			
702	*Earl V. Johnson*	7 Sep 43	18 Mar 44	18 Jun 46	Str 1 May 67; sold 3 Sep 68
	Defoe	24 Nov 43			
703	*Holton*	28 Sep 43	1 May 44	31 May 46	Str 1 Nov 71
	Defoe	15 Dec 43			
704	*Cronin*	19 Oct 43	5 May 44	31 May 46	DEC–704 Sep 50; str 1 Jun 70;
	Defoe	5 Jan 44	9 Feb 51	4 Dec 53	tgt
705	*Frybarger*	8 Nov 43	18 May 44	30 Jun 47	DEC–705 Oct 50; str 1 Dec 72
	Defoe	25 Jan 44	6 Oct 50	9 Dec 54	
706	*Holt*	28 Nov 43	9 Jun 44	2 July 46	ROK 16 Jun 63
	Defoe	15 Feb 44			
707	*Jobb*	20 Dec 43	4 Jul 44	13 May 46	Str 1 Nov 69; sold
	Defoe	4 Mar 44			
708	*Parle*	8 Jan 44	29 Jul 44	10 Jul 46	Str 1 Jul 70: tgt 27 Oct 70; NRF
	Defoe	25 Mar 44	2 Mar 51	Jul 62	59–70; last active WW II DE
709	*Bray*	27 Jan 44	4 Sep 44		APD–139 16 Jul 45
	Defoe	15 Apr 44			
710	*Gosselin*	17 Feb 44			APD–126
	Defoe	4 May 44			
711	*Begor*	6 Mar 44			APD–127
	Defoe	24 May 44			
712	*Cavallaro*	28 Mar 44			APD–128
	Defoe	15 June 44			
713	*Donald W. Wolf*	17 Apr 44			APD–129
	Defoe	22 Jul 44			
714	*Cook*	7 May 44			APD–130
	Defoe	26 Aug 44			
715	*Walter X. Young*	27 May 44			APD–131
	Defoe	30 Sep 44			
716	*Balduck*	17 Jun 44			APD–132
	Defoe	27 Oct 44			
717	*Burdo*	26 Jul 44			APD–133
	Defoe	25 Nov 44			
718	*Kleinsmith*	30 Aug 44			APD–134
	Defoe	27 Jan 45			
719	*Weiss*	4 Oct 44			APD–135
	Defoe	17 Feb 45			

		LD/Launch	Comm	Decomm	Fate
720	*Carpellotti*	31 Oct 44			APD–136
	Defoe	10 Mar 45			
721	*Don O. Woods*	1 Dec 43			APD–118
	Orange	19 Feb 44			
722	*Beverly W. Reid*	5 Jan 44			APD–119
	Orange	4 Mar 44			
739	*Bangust*	11 Feb 43	30 Oct 43	17 Nov 46	Peru 21 Feb 52 (*Castilla*)
	WPS	6 Jun 43			
740	*Waterman*	24 Feb 43	30 Nov 43	31 May 46	Peru 18 Oct 49 (*Aguirre*)
	WPS	20 Jun 43			
741	*Weaver*	13 Mar 43	31 Dec 43	3 Jul 47	Peru 18 Oct 49 (*Rodriguez*)
	WPS	4 July 43			
742	*Hilbert*	23 Mar 43	4 Feb 44	19 Jun 46	Str 1 Aug 72; sold 15 Oct 73
	WPS	18 Jul 43			
743	*Lamons*	10 Apr 43	29 Feb 44	14 Jun 46	Str 1 Aug 72; sold 15 Oct 73
	WPS	1 Aug 43			
744	*Kyne*	16 Apr 43	4 Apr 44	17 June 46	NRF 46 onward; str 1 Aug 72; sold 1 Nov 73
	WPS	15 Aug 43			
745	*Snyder*	28 Apr 43	5 May 44	46	NRF 46–57; str 1 Aug 72; sold
	WPS	29 Aug 43	May 50	5 May 60	
746	*Hemminger*	8 May 43	30 May 44	17 June 46	NRF 46–50; Thailand 22 July 59 (*Pin Klao*)
	WPS	12 Sep 43	1 Dec 50	21 Feb 58	
747	*Bright*	9 Jun 43	30 June 44	19 Apr 46	France 11 Nov 50 (*Touareg*); str May 64; sold 65
	WPS	26 Sep 43			
748	*Tills*	23 June 43	8 Aug 44	Jun 46	NRF 46–50; NRF post-Korea to 58; str 23 Sep 68; tgt 3 Apr 69
	WPS	3 Oct 43	21 Nov 50	23 Sep 68	
749	*Roberts*	7 Jul 43	2 Sep 44	3 Mar 46	NRF 46–50, 64–68; str 23 Sep 68; tgt
	WPS	14 Nov 43	13 Aug 50	1 Oct 64	
750	*McClelland*	21 Jul 43	19 Sep 44	15 May 46	NRF 47–59; str 1 Aug 72; sold 1 Nov 73
	WPS	28 Nov 43	14 Jul 50	12 Sep 60	
751	*Gaynier*	4 Aug 43			Canc 1 Sep 44
	WPS	30 Jan 44			
752	*Curtis W. Howard*	18 Aug 43			Canc 1 Sep 44
	WPS	—			
753	*John J. VanBuren*	31 Aug 43			Canc 1 Sep 44
	WPS	16 Jan 44			
754	—	14 Sep 43			Canc 2 Oct 43
	WPS	—			
755	—	27 Sep 43			Canc 2 Oct 43
	WPS	—			
763	*Cates*	1 Mar 43	15 Dec 43	28 Mar 47	France 11 Nov 50 (*Soudanais*); str May 64; sold 65
	Tampa	10 Oct 43			
764	*Gandy*	1 Mar 43	7 Feb 44	17 June 46	Italy 10 Jan 51 (*Altair*); BU 71
	Tampa	12 Dec 43			
765	*Earl K. Olsen*	9 Mar 43	10 Apr 44	17 June 46	NRF 46–50; str 1 Aug 72: sold 15 Oct 73
	Tampa	13 Feb 44	21 Nov 50	25 Feb 58	
766	*Slater*	9 Mar 43	1 May 44	26 Sep 47	Greece 15 Mar 51 (*Aetos*)
	Tampa	13 Feb 44			
767	*Oswald*	1 Apr 43	12 June 44	30 Apr 46	Str 1 Aug 72
	Tampa	25 Apr 44			
768	*Ebert*	1 Apr 43	12 Jul 44	14 Jun 46	Greece 1 Mar 51 (*Ierax*)
	Tampa	11 May 44			
769	*Neal A. Scott*	1 June 43	31 Jul 44	30 April 46	Str 1 June 68; sold
	Tampa	4 June 44			
770	*Muir*	1 Jun 43	30 Aug 44	Sep 47	ROK 2 Feb 56 (*Kyongki*)
	Tampa	4 Jun 44			
771	*Sutton*	23 Aug 43	12 Dec 44	19 Mar 48	ROK 2 Feb 56 (*Kangwon*)
	Tampa	6 Aug 44			
772	*Milton Lewis*	23 Aug 43			Canc 1 Sep 44
	Tampa	6 Aug 44			
773	*George M. Campbell*	14 Oct 43			Canc 11 Sept 44
	Tampa	—			
774	*Russell M. Cox*	14 Dec 43			Canc 1 Sep 44
	Tampa	—			
789	*Tatum*	22 Apr 43	22 Nov 43	15 Nov 46	APD–81 15 Dec 44
	Orange	7 Aug 43			
790	*Borum*	28 Apr 43	30 Nov 43		APD–82 canc; str 1 Aug 65; sold Apr 67
	Orange	14 Aug 43			
791	*Maloy*	10 May 43	13 Dec 43	28 May 65	APD–83 canc; EDE; str 1 Jun 65; sold 11 Mar 66
	Orange	18 Aug 43			

		LD/Launch	Comm	Decomm	Fate
792	*Haines* Orange	17 May 43 26 Aug 43	27 Dec 43		APD–84 15 Dec 44
793	*Runels* Orange	7 Jun 43 4 Sep 43	3 Jan 44		APD–85 15 Dec 44
794	*Hollis* Orange	5 Jul 43 11 Sep 43	24 Jan 44		APD–86 15 Dec 44
795	*Gunason* Orange	9 Sep 43 16 Oct 43	1 Feb 44	13 Mar 48	Str 1 Sep 73; last WW II DE on register; tgt 28 Jul 74
796	*Major* Orange	16 Aug 43 23 Oct 43	12 Feb 44	13 Mar 48	Str 1 Dec 72; sold 27 Nov 73
797	*Weeden* Orange	18 Aug 43 27 Oct 43	19 Feb 44 26 May 50	9 May 46 26 Feb 58	NRF 46–50; str 30 Jun 68; sold 27 Oct 69
798	*Varian* Orange	27 Aug 43 6 Nov 43	29 Feb 44	15 Mar 46	Str 1 Dec 71; sold 2 Jan 74
799	*Scroggins* Orange	4 Sep 43 6 Nov 43	30 Mar 44	28 Feb 47	Str 1 Jul 65; sold 5 Apr 67
800	*Jack W. Wilke* Orange	18 Oct 43 18 Dec 43	7 Mar 44	24 May 60	Str 1 Aug 71; sold 1 Feb 74
1006	*Dealey* Bath	15 Dec 52 8 Nov 53	3 Jun 54	28 Jul 72	Uruguay 28 Jul 72 (*18 de Julio*)
1014	*Cromwell* Bath	3 Aug 53	24 Nov 54		Str 5 Jul 73 for transfer to New Zealand; BU instead
1015	*Hammerberg* Bath	12 Nov 53 20 Aug 54	2 Mar 55		Str 14 Dec 73; BU
1021	*Courtney* Defoe	2 Sep 54 2 Nov 55	24 Sep 56		Str 14 Dec 73; BU
1022	*Lester* Defoe	2 Sep 54 5 Jan 56	14 Jun 57		Str 14 Dec 73; BU
1023	*Evans* PS	8 Apr 55 14 Sep 55	14 Jun 57		NRF Sep 68; str 3 Dec 73; BU
1024	*Bridget* PS	19 Sep 55 24 Apr 56	24 Oct 57		NRF Sep 68; str 12 Nov 73; BU
1025	*Bauer* BethSF	1 Dec 55 4 Jun 57	21 Nov 57		NRF Sep 68; str 3 Dec 73; BU
1026	*Hooper* BethSF	4 Jan 56 1 Aug 57	18 Mar 58		NRF Sep 68; str 6 Jul 73; BU ex-*Gatch*
1027	*John Willis* NYSB	5 Jul 55 4 Feb 56	21 Feb 57		Str 14 Jul 72; BU
1028	*Van Voorhis* NYSB	29 Aug 55	22 Apr 57		Str 1 Jul 72 (BU, spares)
1029	*Hartley* NYSB	31 Oct 55 26 Jan 57	26 Jun 57		Str 8 July 72 for transfer to New Zealand; to Colombia instead Jul 72 (*Boyaca*)
1030	*Joseph K. Taussig* NYSB	3 Jan 56	10 Sep 57		Str 1 Jul 72 (BU, spares)
1033	*Claud Jones* Avon	1 Jun 57 27 May 58	10 Feb 59		Indonesia 16 Dec 74 (*Mongidisi*)
1034	*John R. Perry* Avon	1 Oct 57 29 July 58	5 May 59		Indonesia 20 Feb 73 (*Samadikun*)
1035	*Charles Berry* Avon	29 Oct 58 17 Mar 59	25 Nov 59		Indonesia 31 Jan 74 (*Martadinata*)
1036	*McMorris* Avon	5 Nov 58 26 May 59	4 Mar 60		Indonesia 16 Dec 74 (*Ngurah Rai*)
1037	*Bronstein* Avon	15 May 61 31 Mar 62	15 Jun 63		
1038	*McCloy* Avon	15 Sep 61 9 Jun 62	21 Oct 63		
1040	*Garcia* BethSF	16 Oct 62 31 Oct 63	21 Dec 64		
1041	*Bradley* BethSF	17 Jan 63 26 Mar 64	15 May 65		
1043	*Edward McDonnell* Avon	1 Apr 63 15 Feb 64	15 Feb 65		
1044	*Brumby* Avon	1 Aug 63 6 Jun 64	5 Aug 65		
1045	*Davidson* Avon	20 Sep 63 2 Oct 64	7 Dec 65		
1047	*Voge* Defoe	21 Nov 63 4 Feb 65	25 Nov 66		
1048	*Sample* Lock	19 Jul 63 28 Apr 64	23 Mar 68		

Note: DE 1007–1013, 1016–1019 were built in France (MDAP); DE 1020, 1031 built in Italy (MDAP); DE 1032, 1039, and 1042 were built in Portugal (MDAP).

		LD/Launch	Comm	Decomm	Fate
1049	*Koelsch*	19 Feb 64	10 Jun 67		
	Defoe	8 Jun 65			
1050	*Albert David*	29 Apr 64	19 Oct 68		
	Lock	19 Dec 64			
1051	*O'Callahan*	19 Feb 64	13 Jul 68		
	Defoe	20 Oct 65			
1052	*Knox*	5 Oct 65	12 Apr 69		
	Todd	19 Nov 66			
1053	*Roark*	5 Feb 66	22 Nov 69		
	Todd	24 Apr 67			
1054	*Gray*	19 Nov 66	4 Apr 70		
	Todd	3 Nov 67			
1055	*Hepburn*	1 Jun 66	3 Jul 69		
	ToddSP	25 Mar 67			
1056	*Connole*	23 Mar 67	30 Aug 69		
	Avon	20 Jul 68			
1057	*Rathburne*	8 Jan 68	16 May 70		
	Lock	2 May 69			
1058	*Meyerkord*	1 Sep 66	28 Nov 69		
	ToddSP	15 Jul 67			
1059	*W.S. Sims*	10 Apr 67	3 Jan 70		
	Avon	4 Jan 69			
1060	*Lang*	25 Mar 67	28 Mar 70		
	ToddSP	17 Feb 68			
1061	*Patterson*	12 Oct 67	14 Mar 70		
	Avon	3 May 69			
1062	*Whipple*	24 Apr 67	22 Aug 70		
	Todd	12 Apr 68			
1063	*Reasoner*	6 Jan 69	31 Jul 71		
	Lock	1 Aug 70			
1064	*Lockwood*	3 Nov 67	5 Dec 70		
	Todd	5 Sep 68			
1065	*Stein*	1 Jun 70	8 Jan 72		
	Lock	19 Dec 70			
1066	*Marvin Shields*	12 Apr 68	10 Apr 71		
	Todd	23 Oct 69			
1067	*Francis Hammond*	15 Jul 67	25 Jul 70		
	ToddSP	11 May 68			
1068	*Vreeland*	20 Mar 68	13 Jun 70		
	Avon	14 Jun 69			
1069	*Bagley*	22 Sep 70	9 May 72		
	Lock	24 Apr 71			
1070	*Downes*	5 Sep 68	28 Aug 71		
	Todd	13 Dec 69			
1071	*Badger*	17 Feb 68	1 Dec 70		
	Todd	7 Dec 68			
1072	*Blakely*	3 Jun 68	18 Jul 70		
	Avon	23 Aug 69			
1073	*Robert E. Peary*	20 Dec 70	23 Sep 72		
	Lock	23 Jun 71			
1074	*Harold E. Holt*	11 May 68	26 Mar 71		
	ToddSP	3 May 69			
1075	*Trippe*	29 Jul 68	19 Sep 70		
	Avon	1 Nov 69			
1076	*Fanning*	7 Dec 68	23 Jul 71		
	ToddSP	24 Jan 70			
1077	*Ouellet*	15 Jan 69	12 Dec 70		
	Avon	17 Jan 70			
1078	*Joseph Hewes*	15 May 69	27 Feb 71		
	Avon	7 Mar 70			
1079	*Bowen*	11 Jul 69	22 May 71		
	Avon	2 May 70			
1080	*Paul*	12 Sep 69	14 Aug 71		
	Avon	20 Jun 70			
1081	*Aylwin*	13 Nov 69	18 Sep 71		
	Avon	20 Aug 70			
1082	*Elmer Montgomery*	23 Jan 70	30 Oct 71		
	Avon	21 Nov 70			
1083	*Cook*	20 Mar 70	18 Dec 71		
	Avon	23 Jan 71			
1084	*McCandless*	4 Jun 70	18 Mar 72		
	Avon	20 Mar 71			

		LD/Launch	Comm	Decomm	Fate
1085	Donald B. Beary	24 Jul 70	22 Jul 72		
	Avon	22 May 71			
1086	Brewton	2 Oct 70	8 Jul 72		
	Avon	24 Jul 71			
1087	Kirk	4 Dec 70	9 Sep 72		
	Avon	25 Sep 71			
1088	Barbey	5 Feb 71	11 Nov 72		
	Avon	4 Dec 71			
1089	Jesse L. Brown	8 Apr 71	17 Feb 73		
	Avon	18 Mar 72			
1090	Ainsworth	11 Jun 71	31 Mar 73		
	Avon	15 Apr 72			
1091	Miller	6 Aug 71	30 Jun 73		
	Avon	3 Jun 72			
1092	Thomas C. Hart	8 Oct 71	28 Jul 73		
	Avon	12 Aug 72			
1093	Capodanno	12 Oct 71	17 Nov 73		
	Avon	21 Oct 72			
1094	Pharris	11 Feb 72	26 Jan 74		
	Avon	16 Dec 72			
1095	Truett	27 Apr 72	1 Jun 74		
	Avon	3 Feb 73			
1096	Valdez	30 Jun 72	27 Jul 74		
	Avon	24 Mar 73			
1097	Moinester	25 Aug 72	2 Nov 74		
	Avon	12 May 73			
1098	Glover	29 Jul 63	13 Nov 65		Originally AGDE, then AGFF
	Bath	17 Apr 65			

DEG/FFG

		LD/Launch	Comm	Decomm	Fate
1	Brooke	10 Dec 62	12 Mar 66		
	Lock	19 Jul 63			
2	Ramsey	4 Feb 63	3 Jun 67		
	Lock	15 Oct 63			
3	Schofield	15 Apr 63	20 Apr 68		
	Lock	7 Dec 63			
4	Talbot	4 May 64	22 Apr 67		
	Bath	6 Jan 66			
5	Richard L. Page	4 Jan 65	5 Aug 67		
	Bath	4 Apr 66			
6	Julius A. Furer	12 Jul 65	11 Nov 67		
	Bath	22 Jul 66			
7	Oliver Hazard Perry	12 Jun 75	17 Dec 77		
	Bath	25 Sep 76			
8	McInerney	7 Nov 77	19 Nov 79		
	Bath	4 Nov 78			
9	Wadsworth	13 Jul 77	28 Feb 80		
	ToddSP	29 Jul 78			
10	Duncan	29 Apr 77	15 May 80		
	Todd	1 Mar 78			
11	Clark	17 Jul 78	9 May 80		
	Bath	24 Mar 79			
12	George Philip	14 Dec 77	18 Oct 80		
	ToddSP	16 Dec 78			
13	Samuel Eliot Morison	4 Dec 78	11 Oct 80		
	Bath	14 Jul 79			
14	Sides	7 Aug 78	11 Dec 80		
	ToddSP	19 May 79			
15	Estocin	2 Apr 79	10 Jan 81		
	Bath	3 Nov 79			
16	Clifton Sprague	30 Sep 79	21 Mar 81		
	Bath	16 Feb 80			
19	John A. Moore	19 Dec 78	14 Nov 81		
	ToddSP	20 Oct 79			
20	Antrim	21 Jun 78	26 Sep 81		
	Bath	27 Mar 79			
21	Flatley	13 Nov 79	20 Jun 81		
	Bath	15 May 80			
22	Fahrion	1 Dec 78	16 Jan 82		
	Todd	24 Aug 79			
23	Lewis B. Puller	23 May 79	17 Apr 82		
	ToddSP	29 Mar 80			

		LD/Launch	Comm	Decomm	Fate
24	*Jack Williams*	25 Feb 80	19 Sep 81		
	Bath	30 Aug 80			
25	*Copeland*	24 Oct 79	7 Aug 82		
	ToddSP	26 Jul 80			
26	*Gallery*	17 May 80	5 Dec 81		
	Bath	20 Dec 80			
27	*Mahlon S. Tisdale*	19 Mar 80	27 Nov 82		
	ToddSP	7 Feb 81			
28	*Boone*	27 Mar 79	29 May 82		
	Todd	16 Jan 80			
29	*Stephen W. Groves*	22 Sep 80			
	Bath	4 Apr 81			
30	*Reid*	30 Jul 80			
	ToddSP	27 Jun 81			
31	*Stark*	24 Aug 79			
	Todd	30 May 80			
32	*John L. Hall*	5 Jan 81			
	Bath	24 Jul 81			
33	*Jarrett*	11 Feb 81			
	ToddSP				
34	*Aubrey Fitch*	10 Apr 81			
	Bath	17 Oct 81			
36	*Underwood*	3 Aug 81			
	Bath	6 Feb 81			
37	*Crommelin*	30 May 80			
	Todd	1 Jul 81			
38	*Curts*	1 Jul 81			
	ToddSP				
39	*Doyle*	16 Nov 81			
	Bath				
40	*Halyburton*	26 Sep 80			
	Todd	13 Oct 81			
41	*McClusky*				
	ToddSP	1 Mar 82			
42	*Klakring*				
	Bath	10 Mar 82			
43	*Thach*				
	ToddSP	14 Jun 82			
45	*Derwert*				
	Bath	30 Jun 82			
46	*Rentz*				
	ToddSP	27 Sep 82			
47	*Nicholas*				
	Bath	31 Oct 81			
48	*Vandergrift*				
	Todd	10 Jan 83			
49	*Robert E. Bradley*				
	Bath				
50	—				
	Bath				
51	—				
	ToddSP				
52	*Carr*				
	Todd				
53	—				
	Bath				
54	—				
	ToddSP				
55	—				
	Bath				

Notes on Sources

This work is based largely on the *internal* papers of the U.S. Navy: records of the Bureaus of Construction and Repair (C&R) and Ships; of the Secretary of the Navy (SECNAV); of the General Board (GB); of the Ship Characteristics Board (SCB); and the Naval Ship Engineering Center (NAVSEC). In addition a variety of postwar reports, particularly those of the quasi-official Operational Evaluation Group (OEG), have been used; there are also official handbooks, especially the Bureau of Ordnance *Armament Summary*.

The papers of the pre-1939 bureau and the files of the Secretary of the Navy are held by the Navy and Army Branch (NNMO) of the National Archives. Wartime bureau *correspondence* files are held by the General Branch of the Archives (Suitland, Maryland: NNG). Other files, especially those of the Preliminary and Contract (Code 440) Design Divisions, are held at the Federal Record Center, Suitland (FRC) under Navy control; these latter include the postwar period. FRC also holds the records of the SCB. The General Board records (1900–1951), the wartime classified files of the Chief of Naval Operations and the Secretary of the Navy, and a variety of other naval documents including the Armament Summaries and the OEG reports, are held by the Naval Historical Center (NHC) at the Washington Navy Yard.

These files generally consist of masses of correspondence often duplicated in other files, so that a citation to one source does not indicate the absence of a document from others. Policy papers were generally found in SEC-NAV and GB files, which means that there is a paucity of general policy analysis available for the post-1950 period. To some extent the correspondence of the SCB reflects policy choices, but on a far narrower scale than the GB, which corresponds to the narrower purview of the SCB. To a limited extent reports such as those of the OEG and the LRO make up for this gap; no attempt has been made to obtain access to postwar SECNAV files.

For destroyers, the relevant GB files are 420 (construction program), 420-9 (destroyers and torpedo craft), 420-10 (navigation, including early sound gear), and 420-15 (undersea warfare, including ASW 1936–41). A useful file for extensive charts of current and "ultimate" fleet armament in early and mid-1941 is 420-11 (alterations).

The bureau files more frequently are purely technical. The principal C&R/BuShips correspondence series con-

sulted were (from 1926) DD/S1–1 (design), DD/L9–3 (modification), DE/S1–1, and DE/L9–3. Earlier files are not classified by subject. Particular use has been made of the extensive Design Books left by the Preliminary Design group. In many cases a summary Design History or (postwar) a Summary Report of Preliminary Design was written; in others, the appropriate correspondence was bound together and labeled "design history." For the period after 1970, NAVSEC Concept Design reports served much the same purpose. The 1915–20 designs were written up in books held by NNMO (Record Group 19, Entry 449; some material is also to be found in the accounts of Contract Design, Entry 448). Later files were held by the Navy. Unfortunately, many have been destroyed. Those consulted at FRC included Accessions 8995 (Leaders of 1928 and 1933, DD 364, DD 409, DD 421, the armored destroyer, the leader projects of 1939, the mass-production *Farragut* of 1940, the earliest escorts, and the *Fletcher* class), 10554 (Code 440 World War II destroyer files), 13754 (*Sumner/Gearing, Timmerman*, DE, DD 927), 63A3172 (DD 927, DDE, *Forrest Sherman*, postwar DEs, DLGs), 66A5033, 68A5879 (including FRAM, DDG 2), and 344-77-0515 (FRAM, DE 1052). Many of the files were very sketchy, but it was possible to supplement them with Letter Reports of designs (basically scaled-down Design Reports) produced by the designers for approval by SECNAV and the GB, and held in duplicate copies by NNMO and NHC.

The SCB was responsible, not merely for the initial specifications for ships but also for fairly detailed examination of the designs produced and for modifications to ships in service. Thus its files are quite useful for the postwar period; they include correspondence relative to Class Improvement Programs (CIPs). The relevant accessions at FRC are 62A2300 (Shipbuilding Program), 62A2329 (memoranda, including Approved Characteristics), 65A4538 (CIPs), and 65A5541 (miscellaneous material). To some extent the pre-1945 GB performed a function similar to that of the SCB, so that its records are somewhat similar in content. However, the attitude toward class improvement was not systematic until the fifties.

Special mention must be made of the series of GB hearings (1917–50) held by NHC, at which a variety of officers, including bureau chiefs, presented their views on new construction and on their aspects of naval policy. Much of the GB file material consists of supporting papers. Of great value has been a long series of hearings (1948) on the status and future of naval technology. The GB also collected a great mass of collateral documents, including the BuOrd *Armament Summaries* and many specialized classified reports. The latter included a series of four reports on material lessons of the Pacific War, compiled at the request of CincPac in the fall of 1945: Radar (Horne Board), Radio (Horne Board), Ordnance (Kraker Board), and Ship/Aircraft Types (Comstock Board). The radio report included an evaluation of sonar performance. No comparable series for the Atlantic has been found. Another valuable series in NHC is the proceedings of postwar ASW conferences (1946–52 and 1959 have been consulted). A formerly classified source of great value for wartime technology is the series of Summary Reports of the National Defense Research Committee (NDRC).

Korean War experience is summarized in an extensive series of Pacific Fleet Evaluation Reports, held by NHC and by CNA.

Armament data, especially details of changes, has been taken from official sources. The chief of these for 1912–42 was *Ships Data*, which appeared irregularly. Prior to 1912 the same tables were printed in the *Annual Report* of the Navy Department. The last prewar issue of *Ships Data* was published in 1938, but NHC holds the issue that was to have been published at the beginning of 1942, and GB records fill in the period 1938–41. From 1942 on, the NHC holds the BuOrd *Armament Summary*, which lists both current and "ultimately approved" batteries for all ships. For some time the *Summary* also listed a "temporarily approved" battery. NHC also has the weekly *changes* to the *Summary* for 1942–44, which permit the evolution of destroyer armament to be followed in a particularly detailed way.

There are several sources of technical data. For destroyers of the interwar period, the most complete hull and machinery specifications are to be found in the trials reports in RG80. For earlier ships, official trials reports were published in the Journal of the American Society of Naval Engineers, and considerable data is to be found in the Ship Information Books (SIB) published by C&R and held in RG19. Inclining Experiments (IX's; NHC 1036 for IX's through 1946) give loads, including ammunition capacities. When an experiment follows a refit, the IX booklet often summarizes the work done on refit. Turning data is taken largely from declassified David Taylor Model Basin (DTMB) reports, as is postwar trials data. Other postwar data is based on NAVSEC and Preliminary Design files.

In general, published accounts were used to organize the material taken from these primary sources. In a number of cases the major value of the published handbooks turned out to be the photographs they contained, which drew attention to the significance of items in official correspondence.

Chapter 1

The accounts of torpedo boat development are taken largely from the *Annual Reports* of the Secretary of the Navy from 1880 onward. The Bath story is based on Eskew. The report of the Army-Navy Board of 1885 was reproduced in the *Proceedings* of the U.S. Naval Institute (1889); that of the

1890 Policy Board was also printed in the same journal (January 1890). Roosevelt's and the C&R comments of 1898 are taken from the records of the Secretary of the Navy; the War Plans Board report, from the Navy records consolidated into the Office of Naval Records and Library and held as NNMO RG45. The bureau design of 1898 was described by Naval Constructor Hichborn in the SNAME paper of 1898. Notes on the progress of the builders are taken from a long report by Naval Constructor J. H. Linnad and Lt. L. H. Chandler in C&R 2403A. Maneuverability notes are taken from papers collected by Preliminary Design in connection with the Leader Design of 1919 (Research Data, RG19).

Chapter 2

The Winslow and Converse papers are in Bureau of Navigation files (NNMO); unfortunately, the copy in SECNAV files, which would have shown Bureau and General Board endorsements, has been mislaid. The GB building program, with C&R endorsements, is from C&R correspondence files (folded files, series 2182 A). Other GB and War College material is from GB files and letter books. The letter report on the *Smith* design, and the analysis of bids, are in the Letter Books of the Board on Construction (SECNAV file, NNMO); correspondence on the *Cassin* design is taken from C&R correspondence files (folded files, series 26160 E). Design Books and C&R files on the 1914–16 Programs (flat files, series 15272 A) have been used for the flush deckers, as well as for the big GB destroyer of 1912.

Chapter 3

Design books were available for both the flush-deck destroyers and for the special ASW type; in addition, there was extensive C&R, SECNAV, and GB correspondence on both. The copy of the *Wickes* report cited was found in a Foreign Destroyer Cover held by the British National Maritime Museum. It is a copy of a U.S. report. Other operator opinion is taken partly from C&R correspondence (File 22—D). Postwar alterations are based largely on GB papers, backed up by the Annual Reports of CinCUS Fleet (NHC) and Alden, *Flush Decks and Four Pipes*. World War II alterations are based on GB material, on the CNO/SECNAV file, on BuShips DD/L9–3, and on inclining experiment reports.

Chapter 4

Most of the material is taken from GB 420-9 and 420-15 (undersea warfare, which contains the November 1941 report). World War I ASW data (through 1922) is taken from C&R files and from *Naval Consulting Board of the United States*. The remarks of ComDesDiv 60 are from NDRC, *Subsurface Warfare*. Developments in ASW ordnance are described in the official BuOrd accounts of the two world wars. The level of sonar installation in 1934 is taken from a table in GB 420-10 (21 November 1933); accounts of ASW sensors in Hezlet and in Bowen have also proven useful.

Chapter 5

Design books were available for the leader projects and for destroyers from DD 364 on, although in many cases they were extremely fragmentary. C&R correspondence was also used for the 1927 destroyer project, and for some of the account of overweight in the late treaty ships. To some extent gaps were filled by SECNAV classified correspondence and by the GB hearings and 420-9 files, which also provided material for policy analysis, including the extensive papers of 1935–36. The GB hearings for this period were extremely useful. The account of machinery evolution is based largely on Bowen. The Atlantic Fleet alterations of 1941 have been taken from BuShips DD/L9-3 correspondence files. The account of armament alterations is based on GB 420-9, SECNAV/CNO, and the BuOrd *Armament Summaries*. Postwar material is taken from the SCB CIP files.

Chapter 6

The basis for this chapter was an extensive series of GB papers in 420-9, extending from the 1939 studies through 1942. The 1942 GB hearings were also useful for their commentary on the *Sumner* and post-*Sumner* concepts. Design books existed for all these classes with the exception of the experimental plants for *Fletcher*s (1940). However, only in the case of the DD 692/710 class was a detailed design history actually written. This provided material on light armament evolution and an attempt to analyze failings in speed. Notes on speed also came from documents written in connection with the DD 927/DL 2 class, e.g., in GB 420-9 and in the DD 927 design books. The account of the diesel and aircraft-carrying *Fletcher*s is largely based on GB 420-9; wartime SECNAV and BuShips files were also used to some extent. Postwar alterations are taken from BuOrd *Armament Summaries* and from the SCB CIP files; the account of the SCB 74/74A alterations is based partly on budget figures in Alden (1964), partly on FY 53 budget hearings, and partly on early versions of the FY 51 and later budgets in SCB and BuShips files. The habitability discussion is based on SCB material and on postwar BuShips correspondence.

Chapter 7

The GB file material has been supplemented by notes on DE evolution made by Samuel E. Morison in connection with his *History of U.S. Naval Operations* (NHC). Design books exist for all types except the APD and DER. Those for the two Gibbs & Cox designs, however, were fragmentary and included no drawings. FRC 13754 includes a very full DE design history with a chronology, as well as a reproduction of the Admiralty message of 11 February 1942. GB 420 included considerable material on the evolution of the war program. War alterations and proposed reconstructions were largely taken from BuShip (DE/L9-3) and SECNAV/CNO (NHC) files, supplemented by the BuOrd summaries. British comments were taken from the "Captain Class" (DE) Cover held by NMM. Postwar alterations are from SCB and BuShips (including 440) files.

Chapter 8

Organizational data is based largely on the Atlantic and Pacific Fleet organization tables held by NHC, as well as the administrative histories of both fleets. Most of the material on Pacific combat is from the COMINCH "Battle Experience" series. The 1943 and 1945 ASW engagements are based on material collected by the Atlantic Fleet in 1945 and microfilmed (as the "LANTFLT ASW PACKET") by NHC. Survivability notes are derived largely from BuShips *War Damage Reports* prepared by Preliminary Design, particularly the two major reports on destroyers. I have also relied on Morison's accounts, particularly of the great Typhoon; the *Warrington* data is from material held by the Ship's History Branch of NHC.

Chapter 9

Basic information of World War II ASW tactics was largely taken from NDRC reports on *ASW in World War Two* and on *Subsurface Warfare*. U.S. weapon development is based on the BuOrd official history; on *Subsurface Warfare* (homing torpedoes); on a wartime COMINCH magazine, the *U.S. Fleet Anti-Submarine Bulletin*, on a postwar ASW magazine, *FTP-221* (NHC), and on postwar General Board *Hearings*. The BuShips/BuOrd report of April 1945 was found in SECNAV papers in NHC. Limited use has also been made of descriptions of wartime sonars in the report of Project Hartwell, a 1950 evaluation of U.S. and Allied ASW forces. Grebe and postwar developments are taken from the ASW conferences and from the General Board *Hearings*, especially those for 1948.

Chapter 10

Wartime AAW weapons development is based largely on the BuOrd history; deployment is based on DD/L9-3; on the IX files; SECNAV/CNO files; GB files; and 1945 SCB files (NHC). Radar picket development is based largely on the University of Pittsburgh report and on SECNAV/CNO files. CIC and NTDS development is based on BuShips and SCB files as well as on Gebhardt. Missile development is based on Fahrney as well as on a variety of postwar BuOrd reports; Kelley was also useful. Primary OSD decisions were taken from DoD *Annual Reports* and from Draft Presidential Memoranda, now declassified. The postwar DER story was taken from General Board and BuShips (440) files. In the wartime DER, SECNAV/CNO material and the official report on combatant shipbuilding proved useful. DER refits are from SCB papers and the FRAM papers in 440 files.

Chapter 11

Design books remain for the various permutations of the big destroyers that became DD 927 and then DL 2; and also for DD 931. Papers filed with them include the SCB and design conferences cited. For DD 927/DL 2 wartime and postwar General Board *Hearings* and 420-9 files were also used. The postwar Destroyer Conference report is held by NHC. DD 931 papers include both a design report and an outline design history, the latter a chronology. Neither contains any direct references to the unusual gun arrangement of DD 931. Production planning is taken largely from budget figures in SCB Shipbuilding Program files. The Schindler Report was found in SCB files. Admiral Daniel's views are taken largely from BuShips (Preliminary Design) files.

Chapter 12

Design histories and extensive BuShips (particularly 440) and SCB files existed for DL 1, SCB 51, DE 1006, and for DE 1033. These files and the ASW conferences were used for the ASW destroyer and destroyer and destroyer escort conversions; so was the SIG book. DDC characteristics were from SCB files. ONI figures for the Soviet Fleet are taken from General Board *Hearings* (1948) and from the LOW Report (1950). The 1955 cost figures are taken from a BuShips presentation for the "Committee of Fifteen" (see below). Notes on ASW 1948–58 are taken from a variety of sources, including the Low Report, Project Hartwell, the ASW conferences (especially a long report on "Present Status of A/S Weapon Systems" for the 1952 conference). The 1950 VDS is taken from Project Hartwell. The genesis of RAT and ASROC is taken from OEG Study 561, "Evaluation of Proposed Long Range A/S Weapons" (June 1956); the fall of RAT is described by an SCB memo of 1957. Other OEG reports of 1956–59 were also useful for establishing the direction of U.S. ASW thinking—e.g., the rationale for DASH. However, the major source for DASH (and for Atlantic Fleet thinking) was a series of Atlantic Fleet papers in BuShips (Preliminary Design) files, supported by Admiral Daniel's personal recollections. Early DASH history has been taken from reports of the Operational Test and Evaluation Force: "Operational Evaluation of DASH aboard USS *Hazelwood*" (7 August 1961), "DASH Recovery Equipment and Techniques" (using an HTK drone) (21 November 1960), and the operation evaluation of the QH 50C (26 November 1963). Contemporary newspaper accounts, an unpublished letter by Gyrodyne defending DASH reliability (21 February 1967), and a draft statement by the Secretary of Defense for FY 66 were also consulted. The account of LAMPS is based entirely on published accounts, especially those appearing in *Aviation Week*. FRAM data is taken from 440 files; they include the original Blewett report and detailed design histories. The pre-FRAM *Sumner* conversion is from SCB CIP files.

Chapter 13

Preliminary design files were the basis for the accounts of DL 6/DLG 6, DLG 16, DLG 26, DDG FY 66/67, and DG/Aegis. The DDG 2 class and the improved DDGs for FY 60 are based on SCB and Code 440 files. Atlantic Fleet views were taken from NAVSEC (Preliminary Design) files and from Admiral Daniel himself. CIPs for DD 931 and the DLs are taken from a BuShips presentation (Project Poseidon) of 1960; and their implementation is based on the annual statements of the Secretary of Defense.

Chapter 14

Most of this material is based on NAVSEC design files. I have also benefited from Admiral Daniel's recollections of the origins of the DLGN program. *Bainbridge* power data is from a 1962 BuShips *Journal* article; SAR or S4G data is from Polmar, *Ships and Aircraft*, the standard unofficial handbook of U.S. warships. It has *not* been checked against any official source.

Chapter 15

Design reports and extensive NAVSEC files existed for SCB 199 and SCB 199A/B/C. NAVSEC files covered the abortive fast DEs of 1964–66. Seahawk is based on the BuShips Development Plan (1964) and on Gibbs & Cox and Bethlehem studies of 1963 and 1964 (see bibliography). The DX story is taken from a similar series of official reports, which include "DX/DXG Concept Formulation Plan" (1 February 1967); "DX/DXG Ship Development Plan" (30 July 1968), and the Major Fleet Escort studies. Approved characteristics for DD 963 were also consulted. PF (now FFG 7) development is largely based on the "Patrol Escort Concept Exploration Report" (July 1971). I also benefited greatly from the Leopold study of naval innovation, which included the pressure-firing issue and some elements of the origin of Seahawk. To some extent the DX/DXG story is based on the recollections of David Kassing of CNA, who participated in the original decisions.

Index

The Naval Institute Press is the book-publishing arm of the U.S. Naval Institute, a private, nonprofit professional society for members of the sea services and civilians who share an interest in naval and maritime affairs. Established in 1873 at the U.S. Naval Academy in Annapolis, Maryland, where its offices remain today, the Naval Institute has more than 100,000 members worldwide.

Members of the Naval Institute receive the influential monthly naval magazine *Proceedings* and substantial discounts on fine nautical prints, ship and aircraft photos, and subscriptions to the Institute's recently inaugurated quarterly, *Naval History*. They also have access to the transcripts of the Institute's Oral History Program and may attend any of the Institute-sponsored seminars regularly offered around the country.

The book-publishing program, begun in 1898 with basic guides to naval practices, has broadened its scope in recent years to include books of more general interest. Now the Naval Institute Press publishes more than forty new titles each year, ranging from how-to books on boating and navigation to battle histories, biographies, ship guides, and novels. Institute members receive discounts on the Press's more than 300 books.

For a free catalog describing books currently available and for further information about U.S. Naval Institute membership, please write to:

Membership Department
U.S. Naval Institute
Annapolis, Maryland 21402

or call, toll-free, 800-233-USNI.